EXAMPLES & EXPLANATIONS

Bankruptcy and Debtor/Creditor

EXAMPLES & EXPLANATIONS

Bankruptcy and Debtor/Creditor

Seventh Edition

Brian A. Blum
Professor of Law
Lewis & Clark Law School

Samir D. Parikh
Professor of Law
Lewis & Clark Law School

Wolters Kluwer

Published by Wolters Kluwer in New York.

Wolters Kluwer Legal & Regulatory U.S. serves customers worldwide with CCH, Aspen Publishers, and Kluwer Law International products. (www.WKLegaledu.com)

To contact Customer Service, e-mail customer.service@wolterskluwer.com, call 1-800-234-1660, fax 1-800-901-9075, or mail correspondence to:

Wolters Kluwer
Attn: Order Department
PO Box 990
Frederick, MD 21705

Printed in the United States of America.

1 2 3 4 5 6 7 8 9 0

ISBN: 978-1-4548-8320-3

Library of Congress Cataloging-in-Publication Data

Names: Blum, Brian A., author. | Parikh, Samir D., author.
Title: Bankruptcy and debtor/creditor / Brian A. Blum, Professor of Law, Lewis & Clark Law School; Samir D. Parikh, Professor of Law, Lewis & Clark Law School.
Description: Seventh edition. | New York : Wolters Kluwer, [2018] | Series: Examples & explanations | Includes bibliographical references and index.
Identifiers: LCCN 2018004029| ISBN 9781454883203 (alk. paper) | ISBN 1454883200 (alk. paper)
Subjects: LCSH: Bankruptcy–United States. | Debtor and creditor–United States. | LCGFT: Study guides.
Classification: LCC KF1524.85 .B58 2018 | DDC 346.7307/8–dc23 LC record available at https://lccn.loc.gov/2018004029

SUSTAINABLE FORESTRY INITIATIVE Certified Sourcing www.sfiprogram.org SFI-00756

About Wolters Kluwer Legal & Regulatory U.S.

Wolters Kluwer Legal & Regulatory U.S. delivers expert content and solutions in the areas of law, corporate compliance, health compliance, reimbursement, and legal education. Its practical solutions help customers successfully navigate the demands of a changing environment to drive their daily activities, enhance decision quality and inspire confident outcomes.

Serving customers worldwide, its legal and regulatory portfolio includes products under the Aspen Publishers, CCH Incorporated, Kluwer Law International, ftwilliam.com and MediRegs names. They are regarded as exceptional and trusted resources for general legal and practice-specific knowledge, compliance and risk management, dynamic workflow solutions, and expert commentary.

To Helen, Trevor, Nicole, Shelley, Matt, Bryce, Kylie, William, Lexie, and Katherine, with love
—B.A.B

To my family for their unwavering support
—S.D.P.

Summary of Contents

Contents

Preface

BANKRUPTCY AND DEBTOR/CREDITOR, SEVENTH EDITION

THE STYLE, APPROACH, AND PURPOSE OF THIS BOOK

This book combines expository text with examples and explanations. The textual portion provides a clear and readable exposition of the topic, beginning with the basics and moving to more intricate and advanced issues. It focuses on material that is likely to be covered in a bankruptcy course, treated in the depth that is appropriate to such a course. We have paid particular attention to writing the textual material clearly and accessibly. The examples and explanations follow the text in each chapter. The examples are factual problems that raise issues covered in the text, and the explanations offer an answer and analysis of the problems. They place doctrine and principles in a concrete context to illustrate the application of the law, and to allow students to test their knowledge and understanding of the topics covered in the text.

Bankruptcy and debtor/creditor law encompasses both state debt collection law and federal bankruptcy law. Bankruptcy law is the predominant component in most courses, and in this book. Chapters 3 through 21 are devoted to bankruptcy law, and Chapters 1 and 2 cover general principles of state debtor/creditor law. The treatment of state law in those chapters is broad and condensed. It emphasizes general themes and fundamental concepts that are crucial to an understanding of the treatment of debtor and creditor rights in the bankruptcy context.

CHANGES IN THE SEVENTH EDITION

The scope, approach, and style of this edition is the same as in previous editions, but we have made a number of changes. With regard to substantive coverage, we have consolidated the treatment of state debtor/creditor law, tightened the discussion of bankruptcy jurisdiction, and expanded the treatment of Chapter 11 reorganization. We have updated the material throughout the book, making numerous changes to textual discussion and adding many new cases.

THE GLOSSARY

Bankruptcy and debtor/creditor law contains many technical and jargon terms. These are explained in the text, but we also have included a lengthy glossary at the end of the book that provides easy access to definitions of the terms of art that are used in this area of the law.

Acknowledgments

We thank the many people who have helped over the years with successive editions of this book, including the Lewis & Clark law students who have done research for this and previous editions, and the editorial staff of Wolters Kluwer Law and Business. We also gratefully acknowledge the many students and professors who have used this book and who have offered comments and suggestions.

CHAPTER 1

The Debtor/Creditor Relationship, Unsecured Debt, Secured Debt, and Priorities

§1.1 DEBTORS AND CREDITORS

The first two chapters of this book provide an overview of the rules of state law governing the creation and collection of debt and introduce basic concepts about debt that are crucial to an understanding of both state debtor/creditor law and federal bankruptcy law. The remainder of the book focuses on bankruptcy law. Even if your bankruptcy course does not cover state debt collection law, these first two chapters provide some background information that is crucial to an understanding of bankruptcy law.

In the broadest terms, a debtor is a person who owes money, and a creditor is a person to whom money is owed. Of course, most people and corporate entities fill both roles in their financial relationships — they have debts due to them by some persons and owe debts to others. In most transactions, debtors pay their debts. However, where a debtor defaults on a debt, the law must provide mechanisms for the creditor to enforce the debtor's legal obligation to pay it. In establishing these mechanisms, the law must balance the creditor's right to enforce payment against the need to protect the debtor from unduly harsh or aggressive creditor conduct. Debtor/creditor law is essentially remedial in nature; it is concerned with the enforcement of debts rather than with their creation. However, the creditor's ability to enforce the debt and the debtor's power to resist payment are influenced by the circumstances and the terms under which the debt was created.

Where a debt is created contractually, the parties have the opportunity to think in advance about what might happen if the debtor fails to pay the debt when due, and to plan the transaction to ameliorate the problems that might result from the debtor's default.[1] As an initial matter, the careful prospective creditor will investigate the prospective debtor's creditworthiness to evaluate the risk of default. If the creditor does this and is satisfied with the debtor's creditworthiness, it can take the further precaution of including terms in the contract that put it in the best position to collect the debt if the debtor should default. There are many terms of this kind. For example, an acceleration clause enables the creditor to sue on the entire debt if the debtor fails to pay the installment currently due. Provisions entitling the creditor to receive financial statements and to conduct inspections at periodic intervals allow the creditor to monitor the debtor's business affairs and to anticipate unstable or deteriorating conditions. A clause that defines "default" broadly gives the creditor the power to commence collection activity in response to specified acts or circumstances, short of nonpayment of the debt. Provision for collection costs, late payment charges, and attorneys' fees gives the creditor the right to reimbursement for expenses that are normally unrecoverable. This is not an exhaustive list, but these examples show that the contract terms can be helpful to a creditor in policing the transaction or pursuing the debt. Of course, the debtor must agree to these provisions, recognizing that every right or power given to the creditor to facilitate the collection of the debt comes at some cost or detriment to the debtor. An informed and rational debtor must evaluate the risks and burdens imposed by such terms and decide whether the benefits of the transaction outweigh its burdens. Sometimes, the debtor's need for the credit might persuade it to agree to onerous collection provisions.

Contract rights against the debtor are helpful, but they are not an absolute protection against debtor default for two reasons. First, the law imposes limits on how far the creditor can go in imposing draconian debt collection measures on a debtor. Doctrines of contract law, such as unconscionability doctrine, the debtor's right to due process, rules of civil procedure, and other and state and federal[2] statutes circumscribe the extent to which a court will enforce harsh or one-sided contract terms. Second, contractual rights may not ultimately help the creditor if the debtor is in such

1. Where debts arise other than contractually—especially if they are created by an unexpected event, such as negligent injury giving rise to a tort claim—there may be no opportunity for planning. Even here, however, some general planning may have occurred. For example, one or both parties may have bought liability insurance.

2. For example, the Consumer Credit Protection Act (CCPA), Title XV of the U.S. Code, deals with such matters as discrimination in the grant of credit, credit reporting, disclosure of information in credit agreements, the issuance of credit cards, and the advertising of credit. The CCPA and other such statutes are not discussed in this book.

severe financial trouble that the debtor has no capacity to pay the debt. To gain fuller protection where the debtor cannot pay the debt, the creditor needs rights that are not totally dependent on the debtor's ability to pay. This protection takes the form of security. The two forms of contractual security in common use are suretyship or guarantee, and the security interest. Under a suretyship, a third party acceptable to the creditor undertakes to pay the debt if the debtor defaults. Obviously the security afforded by this arrangement is only as good as the financial health of the surety. A security interest is usually much more reliable and provides powerful rights to the creditor. Various forms of security interest and the rights that they provide are introduced and explained in sections 1.4 to 1.9. Thereafter they feature prominently in the discussion of bankruptcy in the rest of this book.

§1.2 STATE LAW AND FEDERAL LAW: AN INTRODUCTORY NOTE

The principal federal law in the area of debtor/creditor relations is the Bankruptcy Code.[3] However, the Bankruptcy Code is not applicable unless the debtor has become bankrupt. In the absence of bankruptcy, the rights of debtors and creditors are governed by the law prevailing in the state that has jurisdiction over the transaction. This law consists of state law and any federal statutes (other than the Bankruptcy Code) that are applicable to the enforcement of debt. (For example, federal statutes that apply generally to the collection of debt include provisions that restrict the garnishment of wages, regulate debt collection practices, protect entitlements under federal benefits programs, and confer special rights on the federal government to collect taxes or other revenues. These federal statutes regulating the enforcement of debt are not covered in this book.)

Discussion of bankruptcy law is deferred until Chapter 3. Chapters 1 and 2 condense and summarize generally accepted principles of state law governing the debtor/creditor relationship. This overview does not take into account variations in the laws of different states. Its purpose is to introduce and explain central principles and concepts of state law and to build a foundation for the later discussion of bankruptcy law.

3. *See* section 3.2.1 for an explanation of why bankruptcy law is federal and a discussion of the role of state law in a bankruptcy case.

§1.3 THE DISTINCTION BETWEEN SECURED AND UNSECURED DEBT AND AN OVERVIEW OF THE PROCESS OF COLLECTING UNSECURED DEBT

The difference between unsecured and secured debt is fundamental to debtor/creditor law. The following sections explain secured debt, and Chapter 2 presents an overview of the state law collection process. However, it is necessary to have some idea of the state law process for collecting unsecured debt to fully appreciate the secured creditors' powerful rights. Therefore, this section anticipates the discussion in Chapter 2 by providing a brief outline of the difficulties that an unsecured creditor could face in trying to collect an unpaid debt. Suppose Seller sold goods on credit to Buyer. The sales contract obliged Buyer to pay a specified price 30 days after delivery. The debt is a simple unsecured debt because Seller never took any steps to obtain security for the debt. Seller delivered the goods to Buyer, who accepted them without objection. Thirty days have passed and the debt is due, but Buyer has made no payment. Buyer has no complaint about the goods or grounds for withholding payment, but has simply defaulted. To be paid, Seller must take the initiative and pursue the debt.

Seller will probably begin by asking for payment. If this does not work, Seller may decide to hand the matter over to a collection agency or an attorney who will make further efforts at recovery by contacting Buyer. State and federal statutes and the common law of torts place limits on the tactics that may be used by a creditor or its collection agent or attorney in the collection of debt—particularly consumer debt.[4] As a general principle, collection efforts must be kept within reasonable bounds and may not harass, abuse, or coerce the debtor into paying the debt. Overzealous collection activity could give rise to liability for actual and punitive damages.

If approaches to Buyer do not result in payment of the debt, Seller may decide to resort to suit on the debt. Seller's attorney files and serves a complaint and, unless Buyer decides at this stage to dispute the debt, the case proceeds to judgment by default. Following judgment, Seller, the judgment creditor, is able to use the court's authority and public officers to enforce payment of the debt by the process of execution described in Chapter 2.

However, this enforcement procedure is subject to a significant practical limitation: Its success is dependent upon Seller being able to find executable assets of Buyer. If Buyer has no funds, income, or other assets to seize, there

4. Consumer debt is defined in section 5.3.2. In essence, it is debt incurred by an individual primarily for personal, family, or household purposes.

is no source from which to derive money to pay the debt. As discussed below and in Chapter 2, even if Buyer does have some property, Seller may not be able to seize it because it may be immune from execution or subject to the superior claims of others. In addition, a debtor who is trying to evade payment of debts may have concealed assets, so that they are hard to find or identify. Furthermore, a debtor who has failed to pay one creditor has possibly defaulted on other debts too. Several creditors may be involved in enforcement proceedings, and some may have begun the process of debt collection earlier or moved more quickly than Seller. As a result, Buyer's available property may have been seized before Seller has had the chance to execute. (Because Seller did not retain a security interest in the goods as explained in section 1.4, full unencumbered ownership of those goods passed to Buyer upon sale, and Seller has no special claim to them — they are fair game for any creditor who levies on them first.)

If Seller is unsuccessful in finding property upon which to execute, it has various investigatory procedures at its disposal to assist in trying to locate and execute upon property. (These are discussed in Chapter 2.) However, these procedures are only helpful if there are assets to uncover and if Buyer has not been dishonest and wily enough to secrete them thoroughly. If nothing is brought to light, Seller has to wait vigilantly in the hope that Buyer will eventually acquire property, whereupon further writs of execution can be issued. If not, the judgment eventually reaches the end of its term and expires unsatisfied.[5]

Seller's right to pursue collection efforts under state law could also come to an end if Buyer becomes bankrupt. Seller would become an unsecured creditor of the bankruptcy estate and typically would receive partial payment at best, or, in many cases, no payment at all. The unpaid balance of the debt would be discharged in the bankruptcy case and Seller would be barred from ever seeking payment of it.

In short, the unsecured creditor extends credit on the faith of the debtor's willingness and ability to pay. The creditor has legal means to extract payment from the debtor if that faith was misplaced, but employment of those means may not be successful because compulsion of payment is only possible to the extent that the debtor has economic resources. An unsuccessful judgment creditor is worse off at the end of the frustrated enforcement process because the size of the unpaid debt has been swollen by unrecovered collection expenses and legal fees.

5. *See* Chapter 2 for more detail. There is a possibility that a judgment creditor could obtain a judicial lien at some point in the suit, which may help the creditor to obtain some recovery. This is omitted here for simplicity but is discussed in section 1.6.2 and in Chapter 2.

§1.4 SECURED DEBT

§1.4.1 The Meaning of Security

A secured debt differs from an unsecured debt in one important respect: The personal obligation of the debtor to pay the debt is reinforced by the creditor's right *in rem* in certain property of the debtor. A right *in rem* is a right in the property itself, rather than just a personal right (*in personam*) against the debtor. This means that if the debtor fails to pay, the secured creditor may have recourse to the property to satisfy the debt. Most commonly, the debt is satisfied by the sale of the property and the application of its proceeds to the debt. In certain cases, however, the law permits the creditor to take over the property and to keep it in full settlement of the debt. A secured creditor is therefore in a much stronger position than an unsecured creditor: Not only does it have a right of action against the debtor on the debt, but it also has a claim to property of the debtor to back up that right.

This interest in property does not typically give the creditor title to the property but is characterized as a charge against it. In other words, the creditor does not acquire an ownership right in the property when the security interest is created. Rather, ownership remains with the debtor, encumbered by the creditor's interest. It is only when the debtor defaults on the debt that the creditor becomes entitled to take action to terminate the debtor's ownership and to sell the property or take transfer of it.

§1.4.2 Terminology

An interest in property to secure a debt is commonly called a lien, from the Latin verb *ligare* — to bind. Other common names are "security interest," "mortgage," and "encumbrance." In some contexts, these words are used more precisely — "lien" is sometimes used to describe nonconsensual security interests, created by law rather than by agreement, while "security interest" sometimes designates an interest created by contract under Uniform Commercial Code (UCC) Article 9, and "mortgage" is commonly associated with an interest created by contract in real property. The word describing the holders of security interests are "lienor" (or "lienholder"), "secured party," "mortgagee" (not to be confused with "mortgagor," the debtor whose property is mortgaged), and "encumbrancer." The property subject to the lien is usually called the collateral. The Latin roots of this name reflect the concept that it represents. It is a combination of *com* ("together with") and *latus* ("a side"), suggesting that the interest in property parallels the debt.

In addition to these general terms, different categories of lien have their own names. Liens created by contract are consensual liens, those arising from statute are statutory liens, those available under common law are common law liens, those awarded under principles of equity are equitable liens, and those that can be obtained in the course of court proceedings are judicial liens. Each of these categories of lien are explained and illustrated in section 1.6. As that section shows, each specific type of lien in those categories has its own label. For example, mechanic's liens and tax liens are both forms of statutory lien, and judgment liens and execution liens are both forms of judicial lien.

§1.4.3 The Relationship Between the Debt and the Collateral

a. The Link Between the Debt and the Collateral

For a lien or security interest to exist there must be both a debt and property of the debtor securing that debt. Without property, the debt cannot be secured. Most liens are created in a specific piece, class, or collection of the debtor's property.[6] Where the lien is created by contract, the parties agree on the collateral. Where a lien is created by operation of law or by judicial process, legal rules determine what property is subjected to the lien. As a general rule, lien rights can be created in almost every kind of property—real or personal, tangible or intangible. However, different types of liens may be confined to particular types of property. For example, a UCC Article 9 interest can relate only to personal property or intangibles, and in many states a judgment lien is confined to real property.

Although the lien and the debt are inextricably linked, they are distinguishable as two separate components of the creditor's parcel of rights: The debt is a personal claim against the debtor, while the lien is a right in the property. (As noted in section 1.4.1, the personal claim against the debtor is an *in personam* right, while the right in the property is *in rem*.) The relationship between these connected but distinct rights gives rise to the following consequences and attributes.

6. There are such things as general liens that encumber all the debtor's property. The federal tax lien is one example. However, general liens are not very common. Usually, the property to be subjected to the lien must be specifically described in the instrument that creates the lien or must be identified by a legal act, such as seizure.

b. The Distinction Between Personal Liability and the Charge on the Property

In many cases, the distinction between the debt as a personal obligation and the lien as a charge on the property is not practically significant. The debtor is usually the owner of the property, and a judgment foreclosing the lien is also a judgment on the debt. However, it sometimes happens that the right to foreclose the lien on the property is separated from the right to pursue the debtor for payment of the debt.

This occurs, for example, where state law requires the creditor to make an election of remedies (*i.e.*, to choose between suing on the lien or on the debt). It could also happen where the debtor has transferred the encumbered property, so that the creditor has to sue the new owner to foreclose the lien,[7] but must sue the debtor to recover on the debt. (Normally, the creditor would only be interested in suit on the debt if the property cannot be traced or its value is insufficient to satisfy the debt.) A third situation in which the debt and lien are separate occurs under certain statutes that allow a person to acquire a lien on property even without a contractual relationship between the lienholder and the owner. For example, if a subcontractor works on the improvement of real property under a contract with a prime contractor, the prime contractor is the person liable to the subcontractor on the debt. Unless the prime contractor is an actual agent of the owner, no contractual privity exists between the owner and the subcontractor. Nevertheless, if the subcontractor is not paid by the prime contractor, it is entitled by statute to file a construction lien (also called a mechanic's lien)[8] on the property. This lien can be foreclosed to satisfy the debt, even though the owner cannot be sued personally on the debt.

c. Noncontemporaneous Creation of the Debt and the Lien

Although the ultimate enforcement of the lien is predicated on the existence of a debt at the time of enforcement, it is possible that the lien and the debt could arise at different times and could be created by separate agreements or legal events. The fact that these rights can be created separately or successively can be very useful in some types of transactions. It can also present some interesting legal problems, which will be considered later. The present purpose is to introduce this concept and to describe situations to look out for.

(1) An unsecured debt can be subsequently secured. When it is originally created, a debt may be unsecured. At some later time, before the debt is paid, it could be changed into a secured debt. This could happen, for

7. As explained in sections 1.7 and 1.9, the transferee takes the property subject to the lien.
8. *See* section 1.6.3.

example, if the parties make a later contract under which the debtor grants a security interest to the creditor to secure the preexisting debt. It could also occur by nonconsensual means through the operation of a statute or the judicial process.

As long as the security is created before the time for enforcement has arrived, the debt will be enforceable as a secured debt. However, if some third party acquired rights in the property during the gap period between the creation and securing of the debt, those rights could be superior to the security interest. In addition, the delay in securing the debt could have consequences if the debtor later becomes bankrupt.

(2) A lien can be created in property in anticipation of future indebtedness. A prospective borrower and lender may plan a relationship under which funds or credit is to be provided by the lender in the future. Particularly when a long-term relationship is contemplated and a line of credit is to be advanced as the debtor needs it, it may be convenient for the parties to create a lien in property at the beginning of the transaction. Of course, the lien is not enforceable until advances are actually made by the creditor, but as soon as the debt arises, it will be secured by the preexisting lien. If a line of credit is provided, then each future advance will be secured by the lien. This arrangement protects the creditor to the fullest extent possible and avoids the inconvenience of creating a new security interest every time an advance is made. This type of transaction is illustrated in Example 3.

d. After-Acquired Collateral

As was stated in section 1.4.3a, a lien must attach to particular property; a lien in the abstract is meaningless. However, a lien can be created in a piece or class of property before that property has come into existence or before the debtor has acquired rights in it.

To create such a lien, the creditor completes the legal procedure to establish the lien before the debtor acquires the property, or all of the property, that will ultimately be subject to the lien. Prior to the debtor's acquisition of the property, the lien does not extend to it, of course, but as soon as it comes into the debtor's estate, the lien latches onto it. The property that will fall within the lien must be clearly identified when the lien is created. The utility of liens on after-acquired collateral is illustrated in Example 3.

e. Purchase Money Security Interests

It is common for people to borrow money or to obtain credit for the purpose of acquiring specific property. For example, the buyer of a home or a car usually pays only a portion of the price in cash and covers the balance by a bank loan or credit from the seller. When a loan or credit is given to the debtor for the express purpose of enabling the debtor to acquire particular property and the property is itself used as collateral to secure the debt, the lien is called a "purchase money security interest" (PMSI).

The link between collateral and debt is particularly striking when the debtor's acquisition of the collateral was made possible by the value given by the creditor. For this reason, strong equities favor the holder of a purchase money interest, who is sometimes given special concessions in law. For example, UCC Article 9 allows greater flexibility in the perfection of purchase money interests and enhances their priority under some circumstances. (For the most part, these rules are beyond the scope of this book.) In some situations the Bankruptcy Code treats a purchase money interest more generously. (*See, e.g.*, section 13.1.4(3).) Although it is important to recognize that purchase money interests sometimes receive more favorable treatment than other liens, this difference should not be exaggerated. For many purposes, they are merely one type of consensual lien, subject to the same rules that govern other liens of that kind.

§1.5 THE CREATION OF A LIEN

A lien must be created by following procedures prescribed by law. Different liens are established in different ways under a wide variety of statutes, common law rules, and equitable principles. These different types of lien are identified and explained in the next section. Although each has its own set of rules and precepts governing its creation, operation, and effect, some common principles can be stated in broad terms.

To be fully effectual, a lien must be valid not only against the debtor but against third parties as well. The process of creating a lien valid against the debtor is known as "attachment." Expansion of that interest to make the lien binding on third parties is called "perfection." Sometimes a single procedure is followed to achieve both attachment and perfection, but some liens require two separate legal acts to be accomplished.

The importance of a lien's validity against third parties cannot be too strongly emphasized. A creditor whose right to the property is enforceable only against the debtor has no protection against the claims of third parties who subsequently acquire rights in the property. Such a transferee of the property will be able to acquire it free of the lien, and the creditor will be left with a suit on the debt against the defaulting debtor. However, upon perfection of the creditor's right to the property, it is enforceable against most third parties who subsequently acquire the property or rights in it.

§1.5.1 Attachment

For a creditor to acquire a lien in the debtor's property, valid against the debtor, some transaction or relationship must exist from which such an interest arises. A creditor does not, merely by virtue of being owed money, receive rights in the debtor's property. The lien may attach because of the terms of a contract, because a statute or common law grants it to secure payment for services performed on the property, because equity recognizes the lien, or because the use of a particular judicial process gives rise to a lien. This is discussed more fully in section 1.6. For now, it may be observed that the law that provides for the creation of each type of lien will prescribe the requirements for attachment, such as the execution of a contract in proper form, the giving of a notice following the rendition of some service, or the completion of some other act or process.

§1.5.2 Perfection

The rules governing perfection vary depending upon the type of lien in question. For some liens, the very act of attachment required to create a lien valid against the debtor will simultaneously perfect the lien and make the interest effective against third parties, making any additional procedure unnecessary. However, many liens do not fall under this rule and do require some additional step to be taken before the lienholder's rights will avail against third parties. This usually involves either possession and control of the property by the lienholder or some form of recording designed to publicize the interest.

§1.5.3 Summary

The attachment date is the date on which the lien becomes enforceable against the debtor, but the perfection date is the date on which it becomes effective against third parties. This means that until the acts required for perfection have been completed, the lienholder is not fully protected. Although an enforceable lien exists against the debtor, it has not yet been turned into a right of universal effect. It could therefore be defeated if some third party acquires rights in the property, whether voluntarily or under compulsion of law. (This does not mean that every subsequent third party will necessarily take precedence over the unperfected lien. Some later transferees will not prevail over a prior unperfected lienholder. This is discussed in section 1.9.)

§1.6 THE DIFFERENT CATEGORIES OF LIEN

Lien classification is not simply a technical or formal exercise. It has significant substantive implications. The different categories of lien are each subject to distinct rules and produce different consequences for their holders, the debtor, and third parties. Each category of liens is made up of a number of specific liens. The liens in each category can be quite diverse in the needs they are designed to meet, the circumstances under which they arise, their procedural prerequisites, and the level of protection that they bestow on the lienholder.

What follows below is not a comprehensive treatment of all the liens that may be found in each category. However, some of the more common liens are described and used as illustrations.

§1.6.1 Consensual Liens

A consensual lien is created by contract between the debtor and the creditor. The two most common forms of consensual lien are a security interest in personal property, created under UCC Article 9, and a mortgage on real property. The contract must be valid and enforceable under the common law of contracts, and it must also comply with the specific rules of statute or common law that govern the creation of the particular security interest. At a minimum, the contract must describe the property and contain a grant of the interest to secure the debt. Other terms may be required for validity. Apart from that, the arrangement is consensual, so the parties have discretion in formulating the detailed terms and conditions under which the lien is granted and may be enforced.

The grant of the lien is usually part of the consideration demanded by the creditor for the extension of credit. It is often found in the contract that governs the underlying debt, or is executed simultaneously with it. However, as mentioned in section 1.4.3c, these two elements do not have to be contemporaneous. (Examples 1, 2, and 3 illustrate consensual liens.)

§1.6.2 Judicial Liens

Judicial liens arise out of the court proceedings initiated by the creditor for recovery of the debt. They are not dependent on a contract with the debtor but are imposed on the debtor's property as a consequence of a particular legal procedure followed in the suit. The distinction between attachment and perfection is not relevant to most judicial liens because a single act or event both creates and perfects the lien.

Some judicial liens may come into existence prior to judgment. For example, under some circumstances the plaintiff-creditor, through the process of prejudgment attachment,[9] may be entitled to seize property of the debtor and to have the property held as security for the prospective judgment. This seizure creates an attachment lien. Other judicial liens arise only upon or after judgment. For example, the judgment itself, when properly recorded or docketed in the prescribed recording office, creates a lien on real property in the county of recording or docketing.[10] The levy of execution on property following judgment gives rise to an execution lien on the property.[11]

Judicial liens are essentially last-ditch affairs. They are neither planned for nor obtained at the inception of the debt. A judicial lienholder is, in fact, nothing more than a formerly unsecured creditor who has been able to exercise the right to levy on property or to docket a judgment as part of the process of enforcing the debt by judicial action. As noted in section 1.3, there is an element of luck in acquiring the status of judicial lienholder. If the debtor is in some financial trouble, competition for assets may be fierce and a creditor may find that the debtor has no lienable property left. Even if a creditor is able to obtain a judicial lien, it may lose the advantage of gaining the lien if the debtor becomes bankrupt shortly after the lien is obtained, because the bankruptcy trustee may be able to avoid the lien as a preference. This is discussed in Chapter 12. Judicial liens are illustrated by Examples 5, 6, and 7.

§1.6.3 Statutory Liens

Many consensual and judicial liens are governed by statute. For example, UCC Article 9 applies to security interests in personal property, and the state's civil procedure code typically provides for judicial liens. However, even though these liens may be controlled or permitted by statute, they are not statutory liens. True statutory liens are not created by contract or judicial process but arise under the terms of a statute because the legislature has determined that a creditor of that class or a debt of that type is worthy of the protection of security, even in the absence of an agreement to create the lien. Some statutory liens have antecedents in common law and are merely legislative codifications or modifications of preexisting common law liens while others are legislative innovations.

There are many different types of statutory liens. Three of the most common are the landlord's lien, the repairer's lien (also known as the

9. *See* section 2.3.2.
10. *See* section 2.4.3.
11. *See* section 2.5.

artisan's lien), and the construction lien (also known as the mechanic's or materialman's lien.) These liens are described briefly as examples and are followed by a survey of some of the common features of statutory liens.

A landlord's lien is granted to a lessor of premises. Although this lien was originally a common law lien, it is now typically codified by statute. It was originally available to all landlords, but is now usually not permitted in residential leases and is confined to commercial premises. Because the lien arises by operation of law, the tenant need not agree to it. It comes into effect if the tenant defaults on rent payments. It extends to all the tenant's personal property brought onto the premises. The lien attaches at a specified date after the rent becomes due. To perfect the lien and maintain perfection, the landlord must take and retain physical possession of the tenant's personal property.

The repairer's lien was also created by common law but is now typically codified. It grants a lien to the repairer of personal property to secure the price or value of the repairs. Customarily, the lien is possessory — that is, possession is the act of publicity and control that creates and perfects the lien against the owner and third parties. Where possession is the required means of perfection, the repairer must keep the repaired property until he has been paid. The lien lapses if he relinquishes the property. Many contemporary statutes provide for filing as an alternative means of perfection. Where filing is a permitted means of perfection, a lienholder who complies with the filing requirements can return the property without losing the lien. (*See* Example 4.)

The construction lien is purely statutory in derivation and has no common law antecedent. It is available to any person who, at the request of the owner of real property or his actual or constructive agent, supplies labor, services, or material in connection with the repair or improvement of the real property. Because prime contractors on construction projects usually subcontract parts of the job, hire laborers, and buy materials to perform the construction, these subcontractors, laborers, and material suppliers are commonly protected by the construction lien statute, even though they never contracted directly with the owner of the property. The rules governing construction liens are particularly intricate, but their essential purpose and effect is quite straightforward: A contractor, subcontractor, or material supplier that is not paid for its work or services is entitled to assert a lien on the real property within a specific time after the completion of its performance. The right to the lien arises in inchoate form as soon as the value is furnished by the claimant and becomes enforceable if the person entitled to the lien is then not paid. The claimant must then take action to enforce the lien by perfecting it by notice, filing, and suit within the period prescribed by the statute. (*See* Example 4.)

Apart from these three, there are many other examples of statutory liens, such as the lien on crops or harvests in favor of agricultural workers to secure the value of their labor; the attorney's lien on a documentary work product, to secure professional fees; and liens in favor of the state and federal governments to secure unpaid assessed taxes. Some of these liens were originally recognized by common law, and others were created by statute.

While statutory liens all have particular features set out in the statute that creates the lien, they do typically have a number of features in common:

(1) A statutory basis. The lien is, of course, provided for by statute (either state or federal). The statutes are very specific about the type of debt and the class of creditor that may benefit from the lien and about the identity of the property that is subject to the lien. The transaction and the creditor must fall within the protected category for the lien to be claimed and the property must be lienable under the statute.

(2) Strict procedural requirements. Lien statutes prescribe the procedures that must be followed for creation of the lien and usually require the creditor to take certain steps to claim it. These requirements can be very exacting, and the courts normally demand careful compliance as a prerequisite to lien validity.

(3) Attachment and perfection. Most statutory liens are subject to the general principle that some form of notice or possession is required to effectuate the lien against the debtor, and some form of control or publicity is necessary to make the lien viable against third parties who claim rights in the property. Sometimes a single act will accomplish both ends.

(4) An underlying relationship. Even though statutory liens are not consensual, they are obviously founded in some underlying relationship between the lienholder and the person whose property is subject to the lien. In some cases this relationship may itself be contractual in nature, but contractual privity in the underlying relationship is not always a prerequisite. The lien may be based on other grounds, such as an implied agency, the breach of a statutory duty, or unjust enrichment. When conferring a statutory lien on a particular class of creditor, the legislature has made the determination that there is some equity in favor of the creditor or some special merit to its claim, so that the law should afford the protection of security, notwithstanding that such security was never bargained for with the debtor.

§1.6.4 Common Law Liens

Common law liens are quite similar to statutory liens in their underlying purpose and effect. The difference between common law liens and statutory liens is that common law liens have not been created or codified by statute but are recognized under principles of common law applied by the courts. Like statutory liens, common law liens arise by operation of law, without the agreement of the debtor, to secure an otherwise unsecured obligation incurred in a particular transaction recognized at common law as worthy of protection. The most familiar common law liens are very old. They apply only to personal property, and they require possession for their creation and continued validity. They arise only when possession of the personal property is obtained and expire as soon as it is lost.

As mentioned in section 1.6.3, many liens that originally arose from common law have been codified and have thereby been converted to statutory form.[12] In the process of codification, legislatures have often restricted or expanded the scope of the lien, imposed new regulations on it, or provided for perfection by filing as an alternative to the traditional possessory form. Because of this legislative activity, common law liens are less frequently encountered today than they used to be.

§1.6.5 Equitable Liens

Like judicial liens, equitable liens derive from the judicial process, though the circumstances and the purposes of their creation are quite different. Equitable liens do not arise as an incident of collection procedures at law, but are a remedy granted by the court in the exercise of its equitable jurisdiction.

The role of the equitable lien can be illustrated by an example: An employee embezzles money from an employer and uses it as part of the purchase price of a new car. The employer sues the employee for recovery of the embezzled funds. In awarding restitution, the court may impress an equitable lien on the car to ensure that the employer will be able to recover the stolen money by seizing and selling the very item that was bought with it.

The traditional role of equity is to provide relief where available legal remedies are inadequate. Therefore, a creditor who claims equitable relief must usually show that legal remedies cannot place it in its rightful position. However, the mere fact that legal remedies are inadequate or unavailable is not necessarily enough to make a case for equitable relief. The court will balance all the equities in exercising its discretion to grant a remedy in equity. For example, say that a subcontractor was hired by a prime

12. Several of the statutory liens used as examples in section 1.6.3, such as the artisan's lien, the landlord's lien, and the attorney's lien, originated at common law. In states that have not codified them, they are still based in common law.

contractor to perform work on a construction project. After it did the work, but before it was paid, both the prime contractor and the property owner became bankrupt, and the subcontractor had no prospect of recovering the price of its work from them as an unsecured creditor. The subcontractor would have been entitled to a construction lien on the owner's property to secure the value of the unpaid work, but the subcontractor failed to file the lien claim within the period required by statute. Because of this failure, the subcontractor has lost the legal protection of the statutory lien. Even though the subcontractor has no adequate legal remedy, the court would not be likely to award it an equitable lien on the property. To do so would undermine the procedural requirements of the statute and condone the subcontractor's negligent failure to protect its own interests.

§1.7 THE EFFECT OF A VALID LIEN

§1.7.1 The Lien's Effect Against the Debtor and Subsequent Transferees

A transfer of property conveys only those rights that the transferor has in the property. Therefore, a transferee acquires the debtor's property subject to any encumbrances on the debtor's ownership. This means that once the creditor has properly complied with the rules governing attachment and perfection of the lien, an interest is created in the property that is effective not only against the debtor but also against any third party who thereafter acquires an interest in the property, whether by voluntary transfer (*e.g.*, purchase) or involuntary transfer (*e.g.*, execution).

If the debtor defaults on the secured debt, the lienholder is entitled to foreclose on the lien, and the interest of any subsequent transferee is confined to whatever surplus may be left after the lien has been fully satisfied. There are exceptions to this general rule, which are dealt with in section 1.9. However, the rule is widely applicable, and in most cases the perfected lienholder is fully protected from the claims of persons whose interests arose after the lien.

§1.7.2 The Lien's Effect on Preexisting Third-Party Interests in the Property

The same rule that protects the lienholder against subsequent transferees makes the lien subservient to third-party interests in the property that were perfected before the lien. These preexisting interests may be earlier perfected liens or other recorded rights[13] that have been conveyed by the debtor or imposed on the property by law. (Section 1.9 has a more detailed discussion of the ranking of rights in property.)

Because the lien is subject to valid preexisting third-party rights in the property, a prospective lienholder should check filing records and make other appropriate inquiries before agreeing to give credit to the debtor on the strength of a security interest in property. If the lender does not investigate, it may later find that superior interests encumber all or a substantial portion of the property's value. (Of course, a nonconsensual lienholder, such as a judicial lienholder, does not have this opportunity for planning and must take the property as he finds it.)

§1.7.3 Oversecured and Undersecured Debt

The security afforded by collateral is only as valuable as the property itself. If the value of the property (or, the remaining value, if there are already senior claims of record) is less than the amount of the debt, a portion of the debt will be unsecured. When the property is liquidated, this unsecured balance — the deficiency — will be left unsatisfied. To collect it, the lienholder must undertake the uncertain collection process outlined in section 1.3.

To avoid or at least to minimize the risk of a deficiency, a prospective lienholder must satisfy itself that the debtor's equity (*i.e.*, the debtor's unencumbered economic interest) in the property is worth enough to cover the debt. If the value of the debtor's equity just barely covers the debt, the lienholder has no margin of safety to accommodate possible depreciation of the property or to cover accumulation of interest or any legal fees that may be incurred in trying to collect the debt. For this reason, a careful prospective lienholder tries to ensure that the value of the collateral exceeds the debt (as well as any senior claims) by a comfortable margin. This excess of collateral value over the debt is known as an "equity cushion": It is the debtor's surplus equity that can absorb any adverse change in the ratio of collateral to debt.

Thus, in addition to checking for preexisting interests in the proposed collateral, a careful prospective lienholder must also attempt to make a realistic appraisal of the property and an accurate prediction of likely decreases in its value. The lienholder should also take precautions to ensure that the property is protected from damage or destruction during the period of the lien. These precautions could include contract provisions that regulate the use of the property and require the debtor to keep it insured, as well as

13. In rare cases, certain unrecorded rights may be given precedence over a later lien, but the law usually protects only those prior rights that satisfy required recording or publicity.

periodic monitoring of the collateral. As stated before, these opportunities for planning are usually confined to consensual liens. A nonconsensual lienholder must usually settle for whatever property is available.

§1.8 ENFORCEMENT OF THE LIEN

The procedure for enforcing liens varies considerably depending on the type of lien involved. This description is therefore just a generalized overview of basic principles. A comparison between the lien enforcement process sketched here and the enforcement of unsecured debt, described in section 1.3, shows why security is such a potent right. (This comparison is also made in Examples 1 and 5.)

Liens are enforced by the process of foreclosure. Some liens require judicial foreclosure — the lienholder must obtain a judgment of foreclosure before proceeding with enforcement. Other liens can be enforced by creditor action immediately upon default, and the foreclosure does not come before a court unless it is challenged by the debtor or some other interested party. The realization of the collateral involves two steps. The first is the seizure of the property, and the second is its application to satisfaction of the debt.

§1.8.1 Seizure of the Property

As mentioned in sections 1.5.2 and 1.6, some liens are perfected by the creditor taking possession of the property. (For example, possession is the means of perfecting a possessory security interest under UCC Article 9 and some statutory or common law liens.) Because the lienholder is already in possession of the property at the time of default, no act of seizure is needed, although some form of notice may be required.

Where the lienholder does not already have possession at the time of default, it must seize the collateral as a prelude to foreclosure sale. With some liens, this seizure of the property can be accomplished by the lienholder on its own, without the assistance of the court. This is known as "self-help." In other cases (or if the debtor resists the lienholder's attempt at seizure), a court order and the employment of court officials is necessary. The lienholder may be able to replevy the collateral pending final determination of the suit if litigation concerning the foreclosure is likely to take some time.[14]

---

14. *See* section 2.3.4.

§1.8.2 Application of the Property in Satisfaction of the Debt

Once the property is placed under the lienholder's control, the process of realizing it takes place. There are two methods of applying the property to satisfaction of the debt: foreclosure by sale and strict foreclosure. Strict foreclosure is not universally available and can only be used with regard to certain types of liens, so foreclosure by sale is more typical.

a. Foreclosure by Sale

The most common method of applying the collateral to the payment of the debt is by foreclosure sale. In the case of some liens (a UCC Article 9 security interest, for example), the sale may be conducted by the lienholder itself, and in others the sale is handled by the sheriff or a similar court official. Normally, the sale is by public auction, but private sales by the lienholder are authorized for some liens (UCC Article 9, for example). Foreclosure sales are regulated by statute to ensure that they are honest, properly conducted, and offer the best chance possible of maximizing the proceeds of the sale. However, the reality is that these distress sales often do not realize as much value as the property would have attracted had it been sold in the normal course on the market. Therefore, unless the statute provides otherwise, foreclosure sales are not usually overturned merely because the price was not equivalent to the normal market value. There must be a showing that the lienholder failed to comply with proper foreclosure proceedings. With regard to some liens on some property, the debtor may have an equity of redemption, which allows the debtor to avert the foreclosure sale by paying the debt and costs in full before the sale.

Once the property has been sold in accordance with the prescribed procedure, the proceeds are applied to the payment of the debt, including the costs and charges of the sale. As a general rule, the creditor is entitled to claim the deficiency if the price realized is insufficient to cover the debt in full. The deficiency is an unsecured debt, so the creditor must follow the procedure outlined in section 1.3 and runs the usual risk of nonpayment described there. The general rule does not apply to all liens. In some cases, foreclosure operates as a waiver of the action on the debt, so that the deficiency cannot be recovered. If the price paid at the sale exceeds the amount of the debt and foreclosure costs, the surplus is applied to payment of the claims of any junior lienholders who are parties to the foreclosure.[15] If no such claimants exist, or if there is a surplus remaining after they have been paid, the balance is paid to the debtor.

---

15. *See* section 1.9.

The lienholder is usually allowed to bid and buy at its own public foreclosure sale. Where the distress price is lower than the market price, this enables the lienholder to buy the property at an advantageous price and to resell it at a profit, thereby reducing or even eliminating its loss. In cases where the lienholder is not barred from claiming the deficiency from the debtor and the debtor has executable assets, the lienholder gains an even greater advantage by buying the property at a distressed price because that price is credited against the debt and the lienholder can then recover the deficiency from the debtor.

b. Strict Foreclosure

For some liens, strict foreclosure is available to lienholders as an alternative to foreclosure by sale. In strict foreclosure, the lienholder does not sell the property but takes transfer of it from the debtor in full satisfaction of the debt. This means that the lienholder has no right to claim a deficiency and no obligation to pay any surplus to the debtor.

Although strict foreclosure may sometimes be the same in effect as the lienholder's purchase of the property at the foreclosure sale — especially where a deficiency action is barred after sale — the two remedies are distinct. At a foreclosure sale there is always a possibility of competing bids and a chance that a surplus may be realized. However, in strict foreclosure, no bidding takes place and there is no recoverable deficiency or accounting for surplus value. Therefore, a lienholder will only elect strict foreclosure if the value of the property equals or exceeds the debt. Because the debtor loses the surplus equity in strict foreclosure, this process is not allowed for many types of lien. Even where it is permitted (for example, in UCC Article 9), it is subject to limitations, controls, and a right of objection.

§1.9 PRIORITIES AMONG LIENS AND OTHER INTERESTS

§1.9.1 The Function of Priority Rules

It often happens that more than one lien is created in a single piece of property. For example, a homeowner whose home is already subject to a first mortgage may borrow money on the security of a second mortgage, or a car repairer may acquire a repairer's lien in a car that is already subject to a security interest, or a judgment creditor may acquire a judicial lien on property that is already encumbered by someone else.

When the property is valuable enough to accommodate all the liens against it as well as all legal costs and fees, ranking of the liens is not practically important. Foreclosure will generate enough proceeds to satisfy all the liens. However, when the property is worth less than the total amount of liens, there must be rules to determine how the fund should be distributed between them. The law does not usually treat all liens as equal so that they share in the proceeds of the collateral pro rata. Rather, it ranks the liens, and the proceeds are applied to the full satisfaction of each lien in order of priority until the fund is exhausted.

For example, suppose collateral worth $900 has three liens on it, each securing a debt of $500. The senior lien is paid in full. The second-ranking lien receives the remaining proceeds of $400, leaving an unsecured deficiency of $100. The junior lien receives nothing and becomes an unsecured claim.

This section introduces the concept of priority and surveys the general principles applicable to the ranking of liens and interests in property. Priority is a pervasive issue in debtor/creditor law, and the themes discussed here will be raised and built upon in Chapter 2 and in many later chapters on bankruptcy.

§1.9.2 The General Rule of Priority

The most common method of ranking is based on the chronological sequence in which the liens arose. That is, the earliest lien has first claim to the proceeds, followed by subsequent liens, in the order that they arose. The "first-in-time" rule derives from the general principle, introduced in section 1.7, that perfected rights in property are enforceable not only against the debtor, but also against third parties who subsequently acquire rights in the property. Therefore, if a debtor's property is already encumbered by a valid lien, a second and subsequent lien can only extend to the debtor's unencumbered equity in the property.

The effective date of a lien for priority purposes is usually its perfection date. This stands to reason, because it is perfection that makes the lien viable against persons other than the debtor.[16] Sometimes a statute or the common law recognizes an exception to this general rule and allows the lien's priority to date from attachment or to backdate to the date of attachment once it is perfected. (The effective date of liens is illustrated by Examples 6 and 7.)

§1.9.3 Departures from the First-in-Time Rule for the Protection of Certain Subsequent Lienholders

Although the earlier lien is generally given priority, in a number of situations a statute or a court decision creates an exception to this rule. Therefore,

16. *See* section 1.5.2.

while one can usually assume that liens rank in order of seniority, it is important to consult the law applicable to the competing interests to make sure that no exception applies. The repairer's (or artisan's) lien illustrates one situation in which the first-in-time rule does not apply. As noted in sections 1.6.3 and 1.6.4, a repairer of goods is entitled to a statutory or common law lien to secure the price or value of the repairs. This lien usually takes priority over an existing security interest in the goods because the repair has maintained or enhanced the value of the property. If the preexisting lien took priority over the repairer's lien, the senior lienholder would be unfairly benefited by the repair at the expense of the unpaid repairer.

§1.9.4 Priorities Between Liens and Other Interests in the Property

Priority disputes are not confined to competing lienholders. A co-owner or purchaser of the property, or some other person or entity that has legal or equitable rights in it, may be in competition with the holder of a lien. These priority disputes are governed by the same general rule that applies to competing liens: The interest that first took effect usually prevails. Therefore, a lien extends only to the debtor's own interest in property that is not fully owned by the debtor, for example because another person was a validly registered co-owner when the lien was perfected. Conversely, a transferee who acquires rights in the property after the effective date of the lien takes subject to the lien.

As in the case of competing liens, there are exceptions to this general rule, intended to protect certain parties who acquire rights in the property in good faith and in circumstances under which they are not expected to be concerned about other interests or to check public filing records. For example, a department store may have borrowed money to purchase inventory and may have secured the loan by giving the lender a security interest in the inventory. A rigid application of the first-in-time rule would mean that a customer who buys goods from the department store would take the goods subject to the lender's priority security interest in the inventory, and would be at risk of losing the goods if the store defaulted on its loan. Such a rule would make consumer transactions very risky and would inhibit retail trading, so the first-in-time rule is not applied in this case. Under UCC Article 9, title to the goods passes to the customer free of the lender's security interest in the store's inventory, provided that the purchase was an honest, routine transaction.

§1.9.5 A Summary of the Issues to Be Considered in Dealing with Priorities

The ranking of liens and interests becomes important when the property is not valuable enough to satisfy all the claims against it. Use a three-step process to determine priorities:

Step 1: Determine if all the competing liens and interests are valid and effective. An invalid or unenforceable claim to the property cannot have priority, even if it was purportedly created before its competitors. To decide this question, one must identify the liens or interests and the nature of the property in which they are asserted, and must then consult the applicable statute or common law rule to determine whether each lien or interest has been properly created and effected.

Step 2: Consult the applicable statute or common law rule to determine the effective date of each lien or interest. Usually, the effective date for priority purposes is the perfection date, but there are exceptions to this rule.

Step 3: Identify and apply the rules of ranking. The first-in-time rule commonly applies, but a statute or rule of common law may provide for a different treatment between these competing liens or interests.

EXAMPLES

Examples

1. Grim Repo, Inc. sold a video security system to Minnie Mart on credit for use in her convenience store. At the time of sale, Grim Repo had Minnie sign a security agreement that granted it a security interest in the security system to secure its purchase price. The security system qualifies as goods, and Grim Repo's interest is governed by UCC Article 9. The security agreement complies with Article 9 and is valid. Grim Repo immediately filed a copy of the agreement with the Secretary of State, which is the appropriate state recording office for Article 9 security interests.

   A few weeks later, Minnie failed to pay an installment due under the contract. She has persisted in her default despite a demand for payment by Grim Repo.

   What course of action can Grim Repo take? How do its rights differ from those of a seller who sold goods on unsecured credit?

2. How would you answer Example 1 if, just before Minnie stopped paying her installments, she sold the security system for cash to a used electronics store?

3. Pawnporker Industries, Inc. manufactures bacon and sausages, which it sells to grocery chains and wholesalers. It typically sells to its customers

on credit, and it always has a large volume of outstanding accounts receivable. Pawnporker's receipts from customers trickle in too slowly to meet its demands for cash. To ensure the liquidity needed to pay its expenses without having to wait for payments from its customers, Pawnporker entered into a loan agreement with Couchon Equity, Inc. The loan is secured by its customers' accounts. The security agreement provides that Couchon Equity will advance funds to Pawnporker in an amount equal to 75 percent of its current accounts receivable. As customers pay, Pawnporker is obliged to remit a percentage of its receipts to Couchon Equity to reduce the loan balance. All new accounts that are created by future sales will automatically be included in Couchon Equity's security interest. Provided that Pawnporker complies fully with the terms of the security agreement, Couchon Equity will make additional advances to Pawnporker in the future. These advances will fall within the existing security interest and will be secured by Pawnporker's accounts.

a. Can something as nebulous as accounts serve as collateral?
b. Is a transaction like this valid? More specifically, can parties create a security interest that covers not only existing collateral and advances, but also collateral that comes into being and advances that are made in the future?

4. One evening, as Alec Smart was returning home from work, he swung his car into his driveway. As was his habit, he jabbed at the button on his garage door opener as he entered the driveway at excessive speed, intending to zoom into the garage just under the rising door. Alec had executed this maneuver successfully in the past, and he enjoyed the sensation of split-second timing as the car barely cleared the moving door. On this occasion, he was not as agile as usual. His finger missed the button, and the door did not open.
   a. The next day he took his crumpled car to Arty Zan, a specialist in restoring auto bodies. Arty quoted a price of $6,000 to repair the damage, and Alec accepted. Arty set to work immediately and completed the repair two days later. When Alec arrived to collect his car, Arty presented his account. Alec told Arty that he had left his checkbook at home and promised to mail a check to Arty as soon as he returned home. Arty refused to release the car to Alec until he received payment of the repair charges. Is Arty justified in holding on to the car?
   b. On the same day that he took his car to Arty, Alec employed Mac & Nick's Construction Co. to remove his mangled garage door, repair the door frame, and install a new door. The contract price for this work was $5,000. Mac & Nick's completed the repair, and Alec gave it a check for $5,000. The check was subsequently dishonored. Does

Mac & Nick's have any security to protect it as it seeks to recover the money from Alec?

5. Buddy Beautiful bought a bodybuilding machine from Señor Lean Sweatshop on credit. He signed a contract that obliged him to pay the price of $3,000 in monthly installments over one year. This was a simple sale on credit. The contract did not grant a security interest to Señor Lean to secure the price. Two weeks after Buddy took delivery of the machine, one of his creditors obtained a judgment against him and obtained a writ of execution. The sheriff levied on the machine pursuant to the writ. Señor Lean found out about this before the sale in execution took place. Is Señor Lean entitled to demand release of the machine from the sheriff?

6. Crash Land Investments, Inc. owns a plot of land, which is its only asset. Although the land was worth about $500,000 a couple of years ago, there has been a downturn in the real estate market, and it is now reliably appraised at $250,000. Over the last five years, the following interests have been created in the property:
   a. Five years ago Crash Land borrowed money from Foremost Finance, Inc. and granted a mortgage in the property to Foremost to secure the loan. The mortgage was properly executed and recorded at the time that the loan was advanced. The current balance on the mortgage is $200,000.
   b. Two years ago, Crash Land borrowed money from Sequacious Security, Inc. and granted a second mortgage on the property to Sequacious to secure that loan. The mortgage was properly executed and recorded at the time that the loan was advanced. The current balance on the second mortgage is $80,000.
   c. Last year, Crash Land failed to pay taxes due on the property and the county recorded a tax lien on the property. The arrear taxes secured by the lien are $3,000.
   d. A few weeks before the county filed the tax lien, Sally Fourth obtained a judgment against Crash Land for $20,000. Sally docketed the judgment in the real property records of the county in which the property is situated a week after the tax lien was filed.

   Crash Land is insolvent and cannot pay its debts. If the property is foreclosed upon and realizes its value of $250,000, how should the proceeds be distributed? (Disregard foreclosure costs and assume that the full $250,000 is available to pay the claims against the property.)

7. Given your answer to Example 6, could any one of the parties have done anything earlier in its transaction to improve the priority of its claim to the proceeds of the property?

Explanations

1. Grim Repo has a consensual security interest in the security system, governed by UCC Article 9. The credit was given to Minnie to enable her to acquire the goods, so the security interest in the goods is a purchase money security interest. The security interest attached at the time of the properly executed security agreement. Upon recording the interest in compliance with Article 9, Grim Repo perfected it.

   Following Minnie's default, UCC Article 9 permits Grim Repo to repossess the goods. It may do so on its own, without a court order, provided that it can affect the repossession without a breach of the peace. After taking possession of the goods, Grim Repo has the right to sell them either at auction or by way of private sale. Article 9 also permits the alternative of strict foreclosure if specified conditions are satisfied. No court is involved in this stage of the procedure either, unless Minnie files a suit challenging some aspect of it. Even if Minnie is able to delay the sale by instituting court proceedings, Grim Repo will probably be able to obtain possession of the goods pending final determination of the action by applying for prejudgment replevin.

   If you compare Grim Repo's enforcement rights as described here with the enforcement rights of an unsecured seller, described in section 1.3, you will see that the secured creditor's priority right to seize and sell specified collateral gives it a significant advantage. It does not have to engage in the chancy and often futile and expensive process of trying to find assets to satisfy its judgment.

2. A third party has purchased the goods and taken transfer of them. As a general matter, Grim Repo, as a prior perfected secured party, will take precedence over the rights of a subsequent buyer of the goods under the first-in-time principle. There are some exceptions to this rule, but they do not apply in this case. (Note also that the cash received by Minnie from the sale qualifies as proceeds of Grim Repo's collateral and the security interest extends to the cash as well, provided that it can be identified as proceeds and Minnie still has it.)

3. a. Accounts can serve as collateral. Unlike the goods in Examples 1 and 2, the accounts have no physical existence. They are intangible claims that Pawnporker has against its customers. Nevertheless, they have economic value to the extent that they represent collectible funds due to the debtor in the future, and they are an asset that can be used as collateral to secure a loan to the debtor. Their intangible nature necessitates some variation in the rules governing the creation and enforcement of a consensual lien in them. These details are beyond our scope, but it is enough to note that as with goods, the interest must attach. This occurs when the agreement is executed, value is given by

the secured party, and the accounts come into existence. In addition, the interest must be perfected by filing. A security interest in accounts, as well as in many other intangible assets, is subject to UCC Article 9.

b. As stated in sections 1.4.3c and d, a security interest can be structured to cover after-acquired collateral and future advances. The interest is effective immediately with regard to the first advance and the current accounts. As new accounts arise, it will attach to them, and when further advances are made, they will be added to the debt secured by the collateral.

The facts of this Example illustrate why parties may wish to enter into a transaction of this type. They contemplate a continuing relationship that is much more complex than the single secured sale in Example 1. The collateral is not constant or fixed but will change over time as current accounts are paid by customers and new ones are generated by future sales. The debt will also fluctuate as payments are made, and new amounts are advanced.

Because it is inefficient for the parties to create a new security interest each time Pawnporker needs money and to file new financing statements each time new accounts are created, they have set up what is known as a floating lien at the beginning of the relationship. A security interest is created immediately in all the accounts of Pawnporker, both current and future, to secure both present and future advances. The description of the collateral in the agreement and the financing statement (*i.e.*, the document filed to record the interest) expressly covers after-acquired accounts.

A transaction of this kind requires careful monitoring by Couchon Equity. It must keep track of payments by Pawnporker's customers to make sure that the loan is being repaid as accounts are settled. It will not make new advances until a sufficient volume of new accounts have been generated to cover the existing loan balance plus the new advance. It will also ensure that the ratio of equity to debt stays within an acceptable margin of safety, so that there is an equity cushion to buffer its interest against reductions in collateral value resulting from uncollectable accounts or other contingencies.

This transaction is represented in Diagram 1a.

4. Arty and Mac & Nick's have both entered into contracts with Alec under which they have provided labor and materials for the repair of his property. However, neither of the repairers has been granted a consensual lien by Alec to secure the contract price.

It is common for states to afford such people special protection by granting them liens on the repaired property to secure the agreed price (or, in some cases, the reasonable value) of their services and supplies. The rationale for conferring lien rights on these claimants is that they

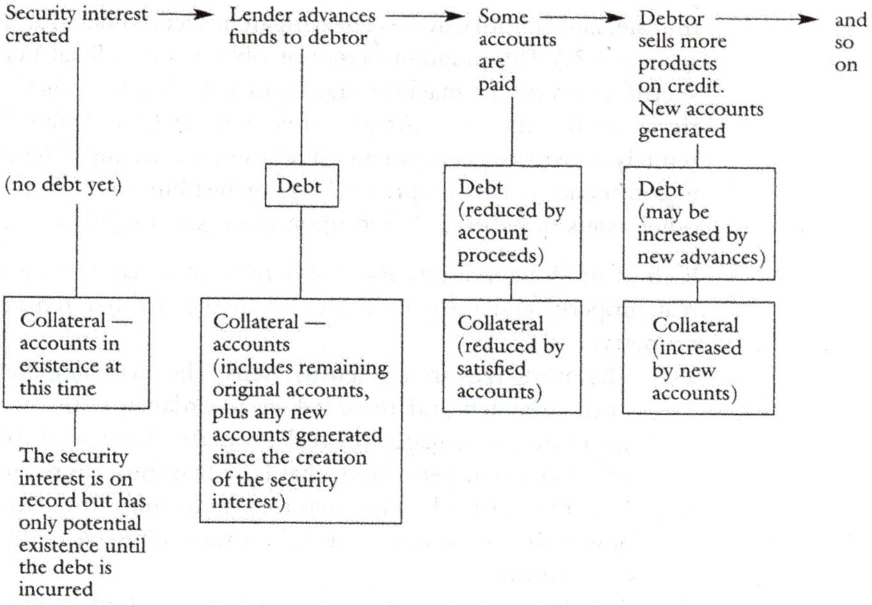

Diagram 1a

have furnished performance at the request of the debtor that has conserved or enhanced his property and that it would be unfair to allow the debtor to keep that benefit without paying for it.

a. Arty Zan is justified in holding on to the car. He has a repairer's lien (or artisan's lien), as described in section 1.6.3, which secures his claim for payment for the repairs to the car. Arty has retained possession of the car, so the lien is perfected. (Traditionally, possession is the only means of perfection, but some states now allow perfection by recording.) The lien is provided for by statute (or common law) so Arty acquires it by virtue of performing the repairs, and it is not necessary that Alec agree to grant the lien to Arty.

b. Mac & Nick's is entitled to a construction lien, as described in section 1.6.3. To acquire the lien, Mac & Nick's must follow the procedures set out in the statute to perfect it. Typically, the claimant is given a period of time after completion of the work to file a lien claim against the real estate records and must then commence suit on the claim within a specified time. The statute may contain additional procedures to give the owner notice of the lien, especially where the lien is asserted against residential property.

5. Señor Lean is an unsecured seller who retained no interest in or ownership of the machine sold to Buddy. Title to the machine passed upon

the sale, and Señor Lean was left with an unsecured debt for its price. (*See* section 1.3.) The judgment creditor obtained a judicial lien when the sheriff levied on the machine and Señor Lean has no basis to assert prior rights in the machine. As an unsecured creditor, Señor Lean's only remedy is to insist on payment under the contract and if Buddy defaults, to commence collection proceedings against him in the hope that he has other assets that can be levied upon to satisfy the judgment.

6. Each of the four interests asserted here must be capable of attaching to real property and must be perfected in the manner required for real property:

   a.-b. The mortgages are consensual liens. The facts state that both have been executed and recorded in accordance with the state's law governing mortgages on real property. Mortgages are normally effective upon perfection, that is, when they are recorded.

   c. The county's tax lien is a statutory lien. Unless the statute provides otherwise, it attaches and becomes effective only upon its recordation.

   d. The docketing of a judgment created a judgment lien (a judicial lien) that takes effect on recording in the county real estate records and extends to all real property that the debtor owns in the county. The recording of the judgment, rather than its grant by the court, is normally the effective date of the lien for priority purposes. (Judgment liens are discussed further in section 2.4.3.)

   Based on these principles, Foremost's mortgage was effective first, then Sequacious's mortgage, then the county's tax lien, and, finally, Sally's judgment. Having fixed the effective dates of the interests, we can determine the distribution of the proceeds of the property by applying the first-in-time rule. (This rule applies unless the governing statute or common law doctrine provides otherwise.) This means that Foremost's mortgage of $200,000 is fully satisfied out of the fund of $250,000, leaving a balance of $50,000. This balance is applied to the payment of the mortgage debt of Sequacious. That debt is $80,000, so it is not fully covered by the remaining value in the collateral, leaving a deficiency of $30,000. The county would have been third in line, and Sally would have been fourth, but the fund has run out, and they receive nothing.

7. Only Foremost, the senior secured party, recovered its claim in full. Sequacious received only partial satisfaction of its second mortgage, and the property did not have enough value to cover the two most junior liens. Sequacious, a consensual lienholder, must have known about Foremost's first mortgage when it agreed to lend money to Crash Land, secured by a second mortgage. Presumably, it realized that its interest would be junior to Foremost, but must have decided that the property

was valuable enough to cover both claims. It may have been at the time of the transaction, but the value of the property at the time of default is what counts. The downturn in the property market so significantly reduced the property's value that Sequacious was left only partially secured.

The county and Sally were both unsecured creditors who acquired their liens only after Crash Land defaulted in its payment of the unsecured debts. The county's ability to claim a lien is circumscribed by statute. Property tax liens can usually be filed only after the tax becomes delinquent. The statute could grant special priority to tax liens, but in the absence of a legislative decision to do that, they take effect only upon recording and do not supersede prior interests in the property. Sally extended unsecured credit to Crash Land. She did not protect herself by requiring security when entering the transaction. When she obtained and recorded her judgment, her judgment lien attached to whatever real property the debtor owned in the county. That property was already so heavily encumbered that it had no value left. This illustrates the point made in section 1.6.2 that judicial liens are essentially last-minute rights that may arise too late to be helpful.

CHAPTER 2

Debt Collection Under State Law

§2.1 PRELIMINARY OBSERVATIONS ON DEBT COLLECTION BY JUDICIAL PROCESS AT STATE LAW

Section 1.3 summarized briefly debt collection by court proceedings. This chapter overviews more fully state law procedures available to a creditor for the enforcement of a money obligation. Sections 2.2 through 2.8 cover state law judicial proceedings for the collection of debt. A creditor usually resorts to these collection procedures only after the debtor has not paid in response to requests or demands for payment. Section 2.9 introduces nonjudicial insolvency proceedings under state law.

This overview of state law judicial proceedings is generalized and does not take account of variations in the law of individual jurisdictions. It is chronological, moving from prejudgment process to the judgment itself and then to postjudgment enforcement methods. The focus here is on enforcement issues, both in the prejudgment stage of the case and after judgment. This activity takes place within a civil suit, which may or may not be defended. In some cases, the debtor may defend the suit and the creditor will not obtain judgment until it wins on the merits. However, where the debtor does not assert a defense on the merits, but simply will not or cannot pay, the creditor can obtain judgment by default. Whether or not the debtor contests liability, the creditor may be able to seek prejudgment remedies as the case proceeds. Once the creditor has obtained judgment, it must follow postjudgment collection procedures if the debtor fails to satisfy the debt voluntarily. At some point in the process of judicial enforcement, the creditor with a formerly unsecured claim may be able to obtain a judicial lien that secures the claim.

As mentioned in section 1.3, because the debtor's failure to pay may be symptomatic of more extensive financial difficulties, there is often some urgency in the pursuit of collection remedies. Other creditors may also be engaged in collection proceedings and competing for the debtor's assets. In addition, the collection efforts may be disrupted by a bankruptcy filing. The possibility of the debtor's bankruptcy is one of the hazards that creditors face in pursuing collection efforts at state law. There is always a danger that the debtor or a group of qualified creditors will file a petition for the debtor's bankruptcy while other creditors are in the process of attempting to enforce their claims through the state courts. If that should happen, the creditor is required by the bankruptcy stay to cease all debt collection efforts under state law. In addition, the trustee has the power to avoid certain prebankruptcy transfers, which may result in the overturning of any advantages that the creditor may have obtained through attachment, judgment, execution, or payment. The possibility of bankruptcy could influence decisions and strategies in the collection process: It may spur a creditor into speedy action, or it may have the opposite effect of encouraging a circumspect approach, so as not to precipitate a petition. Diagram 2a roughly traces the chronology of a debt collection case and identifies the principal issues that are discussed below.

§2.2 EXECUTABLE PROPERTY AND LEVY

Unlike a secured claim, which gives the creditor rights in the encumbered property,[1] an unsecured claim is not identified with any particular property. Therefore, unless the debtor pays the debt voluntarily, the creditor's ability to enforce payment is dependent on the creditor being able to seize executable property of the debtor and arrange for its sale in execution to generate funds to satisfy the judgment.[2] For this reason, the seizure and

---

1. *See* Section 1.4.3.

2. It used to be possible to compel payment of a debt by imprisoning the debtor until the debt was paid. Imprisonment for debt was recognized by the common law both in England and America until fairly recent times. The Romans were even nastier. They allowed execution on the person of the debtor, so that he could be seized and sold *trans tiberium* (across the Tiber) into slavery. Another possibility in Roman law was for creditors to divide up the body of the debtor and distribute it among themselves. The idea here was to terrorize the debtor's kin and friends into paying his debts. Although imprisonment for debt has generally been abolished in the United States, some states still allow a creditor to obtain a writ of *capias ad satisfaciendum* (body execution) under certain restricted circumstances. The right to body execution may, for example, be confined to cases where the debt arose out of willful or malicious conduct, or where the debtor is able to pay but deliberately evades payment of the judgment.

realization of the debtor's property is a recurring theme in debt collection by judicial process. Two concepts are central to this pervasive theme: executable property and levy.

§2.2.1 Executable Property

As noted in section 1.3, the debtor may have no property available for seizure because the debtor may already have disposed of it, or because it has already been seized by other creditors, or is encumbered by prior liens. In addition, even if the creditor owns unencumbered property, it may be fully or partially immune from the claims of creditors and nonexecutable.

In the absence of a specific rule to the contrary, one can generally assume that all the debtor's property, whether tangible or intangible, real or personal, is subject to the claims of creditors. However, some statutes and rules of common law provide exceptions to the general rule and make certain property nonexecutable. The reasons for protecting the property from creditors vary. They may arise from the identity and status of the debtor, the nature of the property, the nature of the claim, or some combination of these factors. The following are the most common bases for excluding property from execution. Although this is not an exhaustive list, these examples show that when property of the debtor is spoken of in the context of debt enforcement, there is always an implicit qualification that the property must be executable.

(1) Exemptions in favor of individual debtors. By statute, most states exempt certain property of an individual debtor from the claims of creditors. Broadly speaking, exemptions are intended to protect some of the debtor's property so that seizure by creditors does not leave the debtor destitute. (Chapter 10 discusses exemptions in detail in relation to bankruptcy, so they are just mentioned briefly here to emphasize that they are also available in collection proceedings under state law.)

State exemption statutes vary considerably. Some simply allow the debtor to select property up to a particular value; some specifically identify classes or items of property that are protected; some prescribe both categories of exempt property and value limitations. When the worth of the exemptible asset exceeds a value limitation, the asset is only partially exempt: It is subject to execution, but the debtor is entitled to be paid the amount of the exemption out of the proceeds. The surplus is then applied to the debt.

(2) Exemptions of statutory benefits. Apart from exemptions provided to individual debtors under the state's exemption law, other statutes may protect certain property from the claims of creditors. For example, a statute

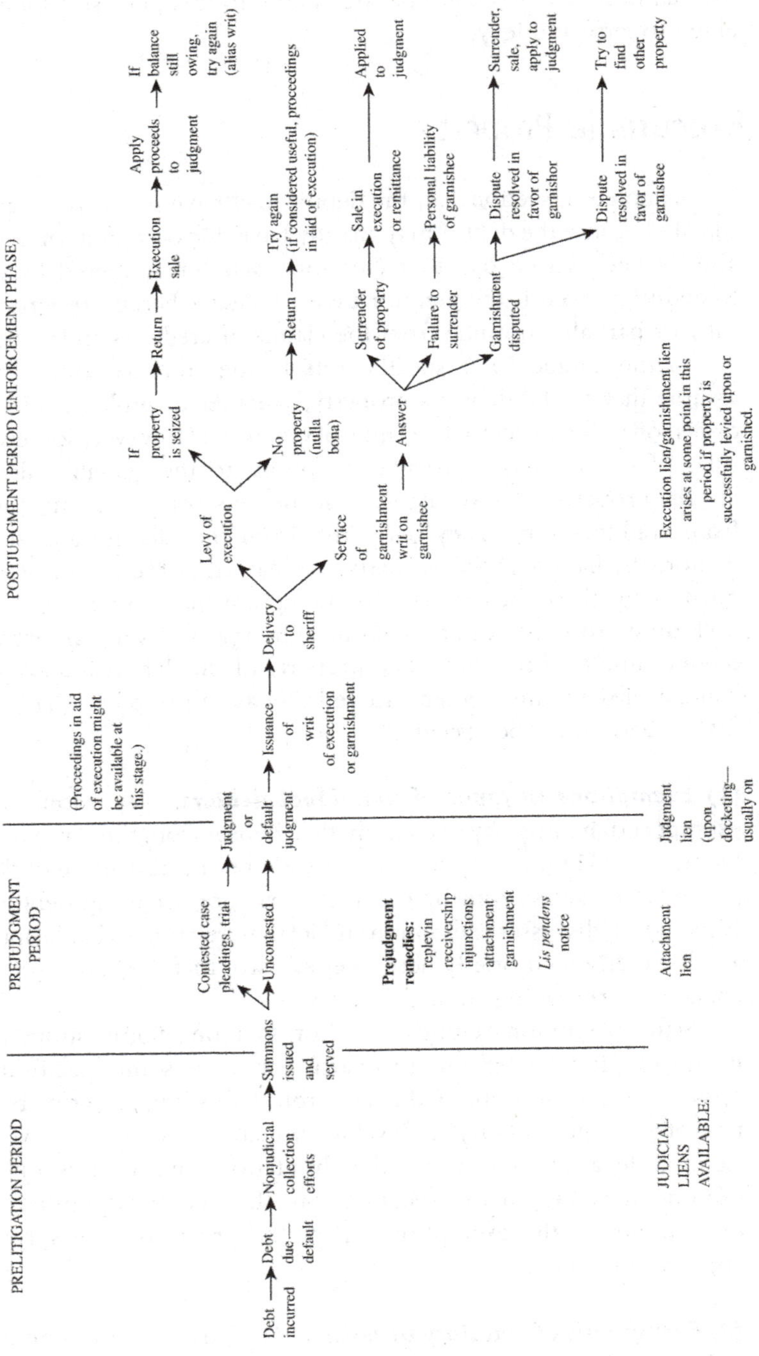
PRELITIGATION PERIOD
PREJUDGMENT PERIOD
POSTJUDGMENT PERIOD (ENFORCEMENT PHASE)
Debt incurred
Debt due— default
Nonjudicial collection efforts
Summons issued and served
Contested case pleadings, trial
Uncontested
Judgment or default judgment
(Proceedings in aid of execution might be available at this stage.)
Issuance of writ of execution or garnishment
Delivery to sheriff
Levy of execution
If property is seized
Return
Execution sale
Apply proceeds to judgment
If balance still owing, try again (alias writ)
No property (nulla bona)
Return
Try again (if considered useful, proceedings in aid of execution)
Service of garnishment writ on garnishee
Answer
Surrender of property
Sale in execution or remittance
Applied to judgment
Failure to surrender
Personal liability of garnishee
Garnishment disputed
Dispute resolved in favor of garnishor
Surrender, sale, apply to judgment
Dispute resolved in favor of garnishee
Try to find other property
Prejudgment remedies: replevin receivership injunctions attachment garnishment Lis pendens notice
JUDICIAL LIENS AVAILABLE:
Attachment lien
Judgment lien (upon docketing— usually on real property only)
Execution lien/garnishment lien arises at some point in this period if property is successfully levied upon or garnished.

Diagram 2a

conferring a benefit or entitlement, such as a pension or disability benefits, may provide that neither the right to receive the benefit nor the benefit itself may be seized by creditors of the beneficiary.

(3) Exclusions from execution based on public policy. Some assets are not executable because of various different public policies that are recognized by statute or common law. For example, a state may prohibit the assignment or transfer of liquor licenses whether by voluntary or involuntary means if it wishes to maintain control over the qualifications and character of those who are permitted to sell liquor. Another common exclusion from execution protects speculative claims in property. Uncertain interests such as equitable interests in property or contingent or unliquidated claims of the debtor are often not executable. The policy behind this is the protection of the debtor's rights in inherently valuable property that is probably of little worth to the creditor. Because the rights have an uncertain value, they are likely to realize very little in an execution sale in relation to their potential worth to the debtor. Publically owned property is a third example of nonexecutable property. Public property serves the interest of the community, so it is usually immune from execution by a creditor of the public authority, such as a municipality or state-owned entity.

§2.2.2 Levy

Levy is the act of a state official (typically the sheriff) asserting control over the debtor's property on the creditor's behalf. The procedures leading up to the act of levy are discussed in sections 2.3 to 2.6. The point to be made at this stage is that until the levy occurs, the debtor's property has not been subjected to the power of the law and the creditor acquires no rights in it by judicial process. The act of levy differs depending on the type of property involved. Levy on tangible personal property is usually the sheriff's act of physically seizing the property, removing it from the debtor, and taking it into custody. In some states, the sheriff may levy on tangible personal property (goods) by taking constructive possession of them by, for example, posting a notice on the goods. (In some states, constructive possession is permitted only where the goods are not readily removable.) The sheriff levies on real property, not by physical seizure, but by filing the writ in the real estate records. Intangible rights identified in an indispensable document (*e.g.*, a negotiable instrument or a share certificate) are levied on as if they were tangible goods — the sheriff takes custody of the document. Other intangible rights are levied upon by serving notice on the obligor through the process of garnishment.

Sometimes a writ will specify that the sheriff must levy on specific, identified property. It is quite usual, however, for the writ to simply indicate the amount of the debtor's claim and to call upon the sheriff to find and levy upon sufficient property of the debtor to satisfy it. After completion of the levy, the sheriff submits a return to the court, which reports the action taken and describes the property levied upon.

In summary, levy consists of the actual realization of the court's order or judgment by finding property, placing it *in custodia legis*, and removing it from the debtor's legal (and often physical) control. For many purposes, the act of levy is the legally and practically crucial event in the enforcement process, because it identifies and binds particular property of the debtor to the creditor's claim. In many instances, the levy is the act that gives rise to a judicial lien in the property, thereby affording the creditor some protection against subsequent third parties.

§2.3 JUDICIAL PREJUDGMENT REMEDIES

§2.3.1 General Principles Applicable to All Prejudgment Remedies

Prejudgment remedies (also known as provisional remedies or provisional process) are forms of relief available to an eligible litigant during the period between the commencement of suit and the final judgment in the case. Each prejudgment remedy has its particular purpose, but as a general matter they all serve the same basic goal: to permit the plaintiff to take steps early in the case to ensure that the ultimate judgment will not be a hollow victory. When a creditor initiates suit to recover an overdue debt, it may not know whether there will be any funds or assets to satisfy the debt by the time judgment is obtained. Prejudgment remedies take some of the risk out of the collection suit by allowing an eligible plaintiff[3] to secure executable property in anticipation of a successful judgment.

The most common of these remedies are outlined below. Each of the remedies has its own characteristics, purpose, and rules; each is available on specific grounds and may be sought only by a party who qualifies for it. The prejudgment seizure of some types of property is either forbidden or controlled very tightly. For example, the prejudgment garnishment of the wages of an individual debtor is heavily restricted or altogether prohibited.

---

3. Although under appropriate circumstances certain prejudgment remedies are available to defendants (*e.g.*, a defendant may seek an injunction to restrain some act of the plaintiff), these are primarily plaintiff's remedies. They are designed to enhance the plaintiff-creditor's chances of collecting on the ultimate judgment.

There are four characteristics common to all prejudgment remedies:

(1) Prejudgment remedies are ancillary in nature. They are related to and are inextricably tied to an underlying suit initiated by the plaintiff against the defendant. This means that the remedy cannot be sought or granted until the underlying suit has been commenced (or, in some states, is about to be commenced) and that the relief cannot survive if the underlying suit has been dismissed or terminated.

(2) Prejudgment remedies are necessarily provisional and temporary in nature. They are designed to last only until the disposition of the underlying case on its merits. Upon judgment, if the plaintiff succeeds in the action, the relief is incorporated into or superseded by the judgment and its enforcement remedies. If the plaintiff loses, the relief comes to an end. In addition, the defendant is likely to be entitled to an award of damages to compensate for loss caused by the provisional remedy, which, as it turned out, was not justified.

(3) Prejudgment remedies are awarded before the plaintiff has finally established its underlying case on the merits. The grant of the remedy deprives the defendant of property or restrains the defendant from acting before an adjudication of liability on the debt. Because the plaintiff has not yet obtained judgment on the debt when the prejudgment remedy is granted, the interim deprivation of property or the temporary restraint on the defendant's action could cause unjustified harm to the defendant if it later turns out that the plaintiff did not have a valid and enforceable claim against the defendant.

For this reason, prejudgment remedies are carefully controlled. The statutes under which they are granted usually reflect a cautious approach to provisional relief. They require the plaintiff to make a substantive application showing reasonable prospects of success on the merits, and they impose eligibility standards, procedural safeguards, bonding requirements, and plaintiff liability for misuse of the process. Courts typically construe these statutory controls strictly and do not grant relief unless there has been proper compliance with them.

(4) The defendant is entitled to due process in prejudgment proceedings. The federal constitution and state constitutions protect the defendant's due process rights in the context of prejudgment remedies. In particular, the Fourteenth Amendment requires[4] that the debtor be

---

4. The Fourteenth Amendment applies to state action. Although the creditor seeking the remedy may be a private person, state action lies in the judicial grant and enforcement of the remedy.

given adequate notice of the application for prejudgment relief and be afforded a meaningful opportunity to be heard by a judge before the relief is granted. A court can dispense with this notice and opportunity for a hearing and grant a prejudgment remedy ex parte only where the creditor can show, by nonconclusory factual allegations, that relief must be granted urgently and that there are compelling reasons for dispensing with prior notice and hearing. A common basis for granting the remedy ex parte is that the debtor is about to dispose of property and is likely to move more quickly in doing so or to take other evasive action if given notice of the application for the prejudgment remedy. Although the debtor may not be given advance notice of an ex parte application, due process requires that he must be given the opportunity for a prompt postseizure hearing and is entitled to compensation if the seizure turns out to have been wrongful.

§2.3.2 Attachment

The remedy of attachment allows the plaintiff who has an unsecured claim[5] to have the sheriff seize the defendant's property early in the case and keep it in legal custody so that when the plaintiff finally obtains judgment, the property is available to be executed upon. Like all prejudgment remedies, attachment is ancillary to a suit on a substantive claim, and only becomes available once the plaintiff has commenced suit on the claim. It is a drastic remedy in that it deprives the debtor of the possession and use of her property before the creditor has even obtained judgment, imposing potential hardship on the debtor. For this reason, the plaintiff must demonstrate eligibility for the remedy and comply exactly with its procedural requirements.

An eligible creditor applies for attachment by filing a notice of motion supported by an affidavit that establishes grounds for attachment and shows a prima facie underlying claim on the merits. To protect the debtor from unjustified attachment, the creditor must also post a bond guaranteeing the payment of compensation to the debtor if the debtor successfully challenges and overturns the attachment or the plaintiff fails to obtain judgment in the suit.

Attachment is not available to all plaintiffs nor in all types of cases, and is commonly confined to certain types of money claims, such as claims based on contract. It may not be allowed for consumer debts or unliquidated debts, and in some states, the plaintiff must show special circumstances, such as evasive behavior by the debtor. Traditionally, attachment is available

5. A secured creditor does not need the remedy of attachment because it already has a security interest in property of the debtor. A secured creditor may have the right to seize the collateral by self-help (*see* section 1.8.1), or if that is not permitted or possible, by using the judicial remedy of replevin, discussed in section 2.3.4.

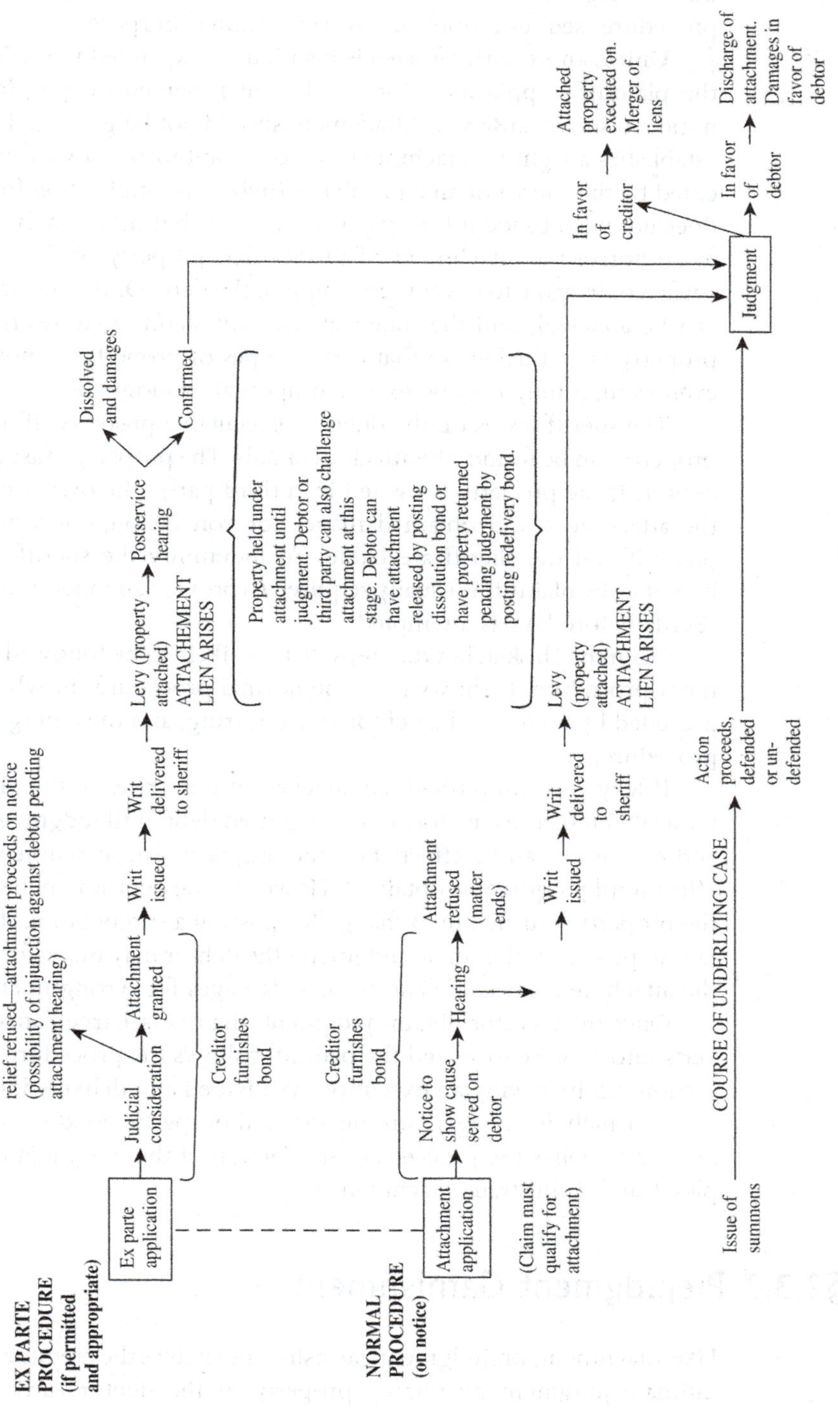
EX PARTE PROCEDURE (if permitted and appropriate)
Ex parte application
Judicial consideration
Attachment refused (matter ends) or ex parte relief refused—attachment proceeds on notice (possibility of injunction against debtor pending attachment hearing)
Attachment granted
Creditor furnishes bond
Writ issued
Writ delivered to sheriff
Levy (property attached) ATTACHEMENT LIEN ARISES
Postservice hearing
Dissolved and damages
Confirmed
Property held under attachment until judgment. Debtor or third party can also challenge attachment at this stage. Debtor can have attachment released by posting dissolution bond or have property returned pending judgment by posting redelivery bond.
NORMAL PROCEDURE (on notice)
Attachment application
(Claim must qualify for attachment)
Notice to show cause served on debtor
Creditor furnishes bond
Hearing
Attachment refused (matter ends)
Writ issued
Writ delivered to sheriff
Levy (property attached) ATTACHMENT LIEN ARISES
Issue of summons
COURSE OF UNDERLYING CASE
Action proceeds, defended or un-defended
Judgment
In favor of creditor
Attached property executed on. Merger of liens
In favor of debtor
Discharge of attachment. Damages in favor of debtor

Diagram 2b

only in legal actions and not in equitable suits. However, equity has a procedure, sequestration, that serves a similar purpose.

Unless an ex parte process is justified, as explained in section 2.3.1(4), the plaintiff's application for attachment is served on the debtor with a notice to show cause why attachment should not be granted. If the creditor establishes a right to attachment, the court authorizes a writ, which is executed by the sheriff or an equivalent official. The application for attachment does not need to identify any particular asset, but may simply ask the court to authorize the attachment of unspecified property of the debtor that is sufficient in value to cover the amount of the debt. Only executable property can be attached, and the state's attachment statute may restrict attachable property even further, so that certain types of property cannot be attached even though they may be executed upon after judgment.

The sheriff levies on the debtor's executable property. If no executable property can be found, the attachment fails. The property must belong to the debtor. If the property is owned by a third party, the owner can challenge the attachment and obtain damages for conversion, for which both the plaintiff and the sheriff are liable. To indemnify the sheriff for any such liability, the plaintiff is usually required to provide an indemnity bond to the sheriff before levy is attempted.

Diagram 2b sketches the steps that are likely to be followed in an attachment procedure. It shows both the normal procedure, in which seizure is preceded by notice to the debtor and a hearing, and the emergency ex parte procedure.

If levy is accomplished, an attachment lien arises in the property. This judicial lien secures the formerly unsecured debt until judgment is obtained and execution can be effected on the property. The attachment remains in effect until judgment is obtained. However, the debtor may be able to have the property returned in exchange for posting a surety bond. If the creditor fails to prosecute the suit to judgment, the debtor may move for discharge of the attachment for cause and to seek damages for wrongful attachment.

Once the creditor obtains judgment, the undischarged attachment converts into an execution and the plaintiff follows the procedure described in section 2.5 by having an execution writ issued and delivered to the sheriff, who formally levies again on the attached property, conducts an execution sale, and applies the proceeds to satisfaction of the judgment debt. (Examples 1 and 2 illustrate attachment.)

§2.3.3 Prejudgment Garnishment

Like attachment, prejudgment garnishment enables the creditor to secure the ultimate judgment by seizing property of the debtor early in the case. The fundamental difference between them is that attachment is used to seize property in the control of the debtor or to levy on real property by an act of recording, while garnishment is used to levy on the debtor's tangible personal property in the possession of a third party or to levy on an intangible obligation owed to the debtor. In other words, prejudgment garnishment is the proper remedy when levy involves a third party, either as possessor of the debtor's personal property or as obligor on an intangible right of the debtor's. Garnishment has procedures designed to protect the rights of this third party, to compel the third party's compliance with the writ, and to ensure that the debtor is given notice of the levy and an opportunity to oppose it.

In many states, prejudgment garnishment is just a variation of the attachment procedure, adjusted to accommodate the presence of the third party (the garnishee). Where this is so, the two remedies have the same rules and procedures except for those relating to the levy and response to the writ.[6] After the creditor (garnishor) has applied for the writ and the court has authorized it, the sheriff serves it on the garnishee and the debtor. The notice of garnishment to the debtor gives the debtor the opportunity to claim any available exemptions or make any appropriate challenges. As a general rule, all executable property is subject to garnishment as well. However, an individual debtor's salary, wages, or other earnings are so central to the debtor's survival that their garnishment is tightly restricted and is confined to a prescribed percentage of the wages. In the prejudgment period, garnishment of the individual debtor's wages and earnings may be completely barred.

The writ describes the garnishee's alleged obligation to the debtor or the debtor's property allegedly in the garnishee's possession. The garnishee must answer the writ, either acknowledging or denying that it owes the debt to the debtor or that it is in possession of the debtor's property. The garnishee must then turn over to the sheriff the money or property that the garnishee acknowledges to be owing and due to the debtor. The garnishee may acknowledge the debt or possession of the debtor's property but may assert that the debt is not yet mature or that the garnishee has the right to retain the property. If so, the garnishee is not obliged to pay or deliver the property to the sheriff immediately. Instead, it must undertake to pay the debt or surrender the property to the sheriff when the debt matures or the right to retain the property ends. The garnishee's answer may refuse payment or delivery by denying that it is indebted to the debtor or that it holds any of the debtor's property, or by asserting any rights or defenses that it may have against the debtor. The creditor may challenge this response, and the court will then make a summary adjudication of the garnishee's rights and order payment or surrender if it upholds the creditor's challenge.

---

6. In some states the remedies are more distinct. This discussion focuses on states in which prejudgment garnishment is just a variation of attachment.

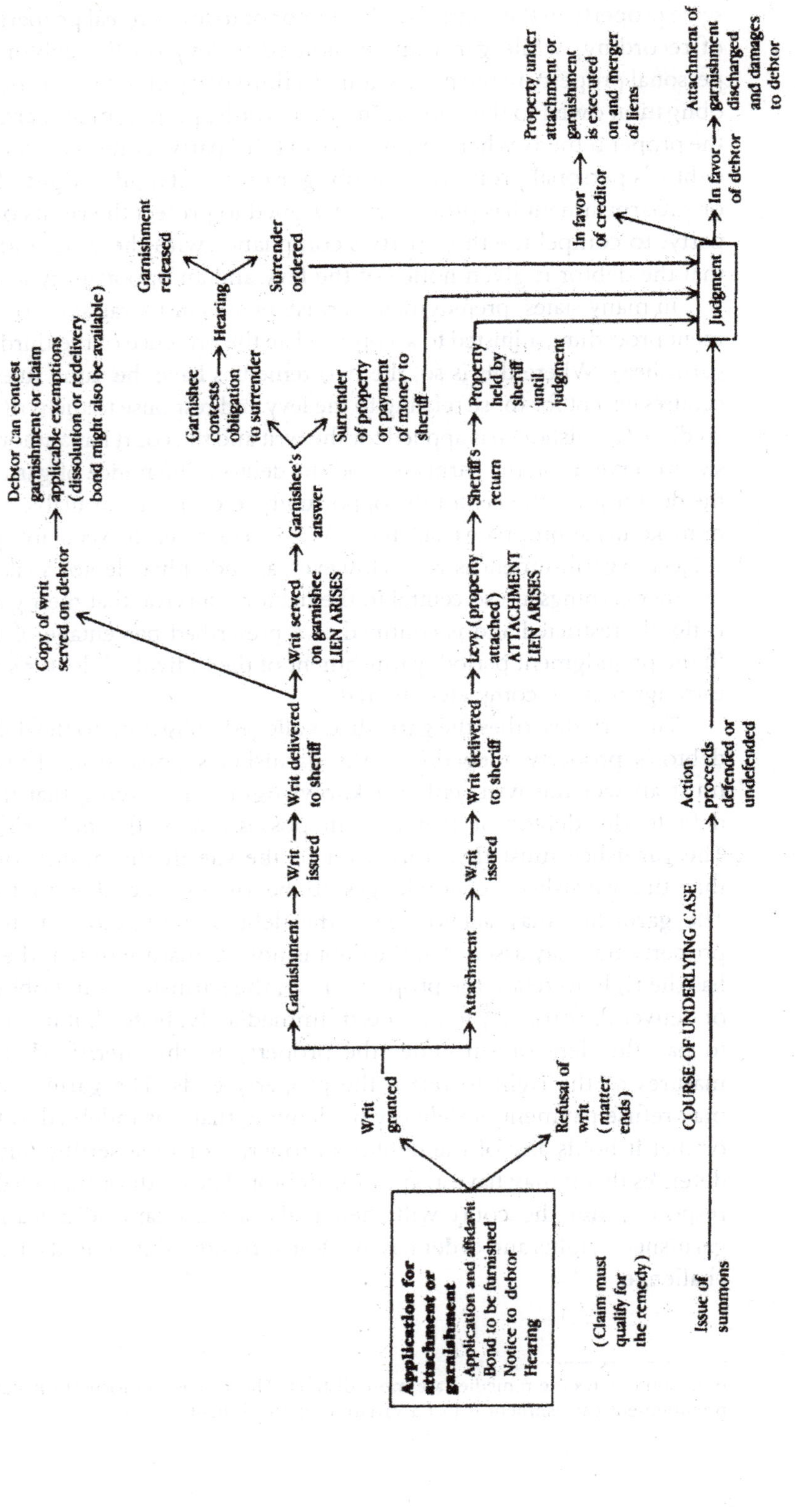
Application for attachment or garnishment
Application and affidavit
Bond to be furnished
Notice to debtor
Hearing
(Claim must qualify for the remedy)
Writ granted
Refusal of writ (matter ends)
Garnishment → Writ issued → Writ delivered to sheriff → Writ served on garnishee LIEN ARISES → Garnishee's answer
Copy of writ served on debtor → Debtor can contest garnishment or claim applicable exemptions (dissolution or redelivery bond might also be available)
Garnishee contests obligation to surrender → Hearing
Garnishment released
Surrender ordered
Surrender of property or payment of money to sheriff
Attachment → Writ issued → Writ delivered to sheriff → Levy (property attached) ATTACHMENT LIEN ARISES → Sheriff's return → Property held by sheriff until judgment
COURSE OF UNDERLYING CASE
Issue of summons → Action proceeds defended or undefended → Judgment
In favor of creditor → Property under attachment or garnishment is executed on and merger of liens
In favor of debtor → Attachment of garnishment discharged and damages to debtor

Diagram 2c

Whatever the basis of the answer, the garnishee is obliged to respond to the writ and answer it truthfully. Failure to do so or to surrender the garnishable asset to the sheriff renders the garnishee personally liable to the garnishor for any loss suffered. Furthermore, willful disregard of the writ may result in sanctions for contempt of court.

In most jurisdictions the levy of a writ of garnishment creates a lien in the garnished property equivalent to the attachment lien discussed in section 2.3.2. Once the property is taken into the custody of the law, it is retained, as in the case of attachment, until the final judgment in the underlying action. The rules governing the postseizure stage of the proceedings are usually the same as those for attachment. Diagram 2c sketches the sequence of prejudgment garnishment procedure and compares it to attachment.

§2.3.4 Other Prejudgment Remedies

(1) Prejudgment replevin. Prejudgment replevin (also called "claim and delivery") is a provisional remedy derived from the common law action of replevin. Replevin is a possessory action at law for the recovery of specific tangible personal property that has been wrongfully taken and detained or lawfully taken but thereafter wrongfully detained by the defendant. In its prejudgment version, it is only available to a plaintiff who has a right to immediate possession of specific property, and it can only be sought when the principal action includes a claim of possession of the property in question. The principal suit may be the action of replevin itself or some other possessory action. For example, a secured party under UCC Article 9 must sue to recover possession of the collateral if it cannot be obtained from the defaulting debtor by self-help. (*See* section 1.8.) Grant of the remedy entitles the secured party to immediate possession of the collateral pending the final determination of the case, thereby assuring that the debtor cannot harm or dispose of the collateral while the case is proceeding. The procedure for obtaining prejudgment replevin is similar to that for attachment, except that the creditor, not the sheriff, retains the property while the case is pending. As custodian of the property, the creditor is obliged to protect and preserve it. This duty is guaranteed by a surety bond. Like attachment, prejudgment replevin is provisional, so that the creditor must ultimately obtain judgment in the underlying possessory action. If the creditor fails to do so, the property is restored to the debtor who is entitled to damages for the wrongful seizure and retention of the property.

(2) Receivership. Although it has been codified in many states, receivership is an equitable remedy, available both prejudgment and postjudgment. A plaintiff who has some interest in an asset or estate may obtain a receivership in the prejudgment phase of a case by demonstrating a probability of success on the underlying action and that the property is in need of protection, preservation, or orderly liquidation by an impartial administrator. Like attachment, receivership removes property from the debtor, but it differs from attachment in that it allows the property to be actively administered or conserved to prevent its deterioration or to maintain its value. Receivership dispossesses the debtor of property pending resolution of the case on its merits, so it is subject to procedural rules and safeguards similar to those for attachment. Once the property has been seized, it is entrusted to the receiver, who is required to post a bond guaranteeing the proper administration of the property. The powers and duties of the receiver are defined in the court order. The receiver is an officer of the court and must report and account to it.

(3) Injunctions. Courts of equity have the discretion to issue injunctions to restrain or compel action that is likely to cause irreparable harm to the applicant. The injunction is a widely used remedy that is not confined to debt collection or to the prejudgment period. When used in a pending suit, the injunction's role is to forestall conduct of the debtor that threatens to undermine the creditor's ability to enforce the ultimate judgment. For example, a creditor who has reasonable grounds to believe that the debtor is about to conceal or dispose of executable assets can seek to enjoin that prejudicial activity. The debtor can be punished for contempt of court if the court issues the injunction and the debtor disobeys it. Therefore, unlike the remedies described above, the injunction does not result in removal of the property from the debtor, but relies on the sanction of contempt of court to persuade the debtor to obey the court's order.

As in the case of other prejudgment remedies, the application for an injunction must be supported by an affidavit that demonstrates grounds for relief. The affidavit must establish a probability of success in the underlying action and a likelihood of irreparable harm if the injunction is not granted. If the injunction is issued and later turns out to have been unjustified, the debtor has a claim for damages for wrongful enjoinder.

(4) Lis Pendens. When a suit is in progress in which title, possession, or other rights in real property are at issue, the creditor may file a notice of pendency (*lis pendens*) in the appropriate recording office, usually the deeds registry. The creditor does not need court authorization to file the notice. Once the notice is filed, any person who acquires rights in the property from the debtor is deemed to have constructive notice of the suit and takes transfer subject to the court's final disposition of the case. If the court ultimately grants judgment against the debtor, that judgment binds the transferee as well. The doctrine of *lis pendens* is not a prejudgment remedy, properly speaking, but it does provide some protection to a creditor in the prejudgment phase of litigation concerning rights to real property. *Lis pendens* differs from attachment in that the filing of the notice does not create a lien on the property. Rather, its effect is to warn third parties at large that the debtor's rights in the property are in dispute and that any interest transferred by the debtor is an uncertain one.

§2.4 THE JUDGMENT AND ITS ENFORCEMENT

§2.4.1 Judgment by Default or Consent (Confession)

(1) Default judgment. The judgment is the court's determination that the debt is due. In a case where the debtor contests liability, the court's judgment will follow a determination of the merits of the creditor's claim. However, if the debtor does not defend the suit, the creditor may obtain judgment by default. If the debt is a liquidated contract claim and personal service has been affected, some states follow the traditional practice of allowing the clerk of the court to grant the judgment. Otherwise, judgment must be granted by the court. Normally the procedure is summary. Provided that the uncontested allegations in the summons state a cause of action, the judgment is granted for the relief requested in the summons. Evidence is not normally required unless some matter has to be resolved by testimony, such as evidence to fix unliquidated damages. After the judgment has been granted, it is entered by the clerk of the court in the appropriate record. The judgment becomes effective upon entry. The debtor cannot normally appeal a default judgment, but may have grounds to apply for reversal of the judgment for excusable neglect or the creditor's fraud or misconduct.

(2) Consent or confession to judgment. A debtor who does not dispute the debt may not merely fail to defend the suit, but may explicitly admit liability for the debt and consent in writing to the entry of judgment. The formal waiver of the right to defend the suit is called a "consent" or "confession" to judgment. If made voluntarily and knowledgeably after default, courts usually accept it.

However, courts are less likely to accept a confession to judgment that is executed by the debtor at the time that the debt is incurred. This type of advance confession to judgment, included in the instrument of debt or contract, and before any default has occurred, is called a "cognovit" or a "warrant of attorney." It appoints the creditor as the debtor's agent so that the creditor can consent to judgment on the debtor's behalf if the debtor should later default on the debt. This type of advance waiver of the right to defend a debt collection suit abandons the debtor's due process rights and has a high potential for abuse, so it is heavily regulated by courts and legislatures. Federal Trade Commission rules make the confession to judgment an unfair trade practice in various kinds of consumer transactions, and many states forbid it entirely in consumer credit transactions. In other situations, even where a confession is permitted, it is valid only if fairly obtained in compliance with specific formal prerequisites.

§2.4.2 The Duration of the Judgment

After obtaining judgment, the creditor usually takes steps to enforce it as soon as possible. However, it sometimes happens that immediate execution is not possible or desirable: The debtor may have no executable assets or may persuade the creditor to defer execution pending promised voluntary payment of the judgment debt. Where enforcement of the judgment is delayed for any reason, the issue of its duration becomes relevant.

All judgments have a finite lifespan; they expire or become unenforceable after a period of years. The period varies from state to state and the rules concerning the continuing vitality of a judgment are not uniform. For example, the state's statute governing judgments may provide that a judgment lasts for a fixed period (say ten years) after which it expires and becomes unenforceable. The statute may allow an application to be made during the period for a renewal of the judgment to extend its effectiveness for a further span. Some statutes require periodic attempts at execution on the judgment during its lifetime, failing which the judgment becomes dormant and must be revived by motion before enforcement can be attempted. A creditor who does not obtain immediate satisfaction of the judgment must take care to follow whatever procedures are necessary to keep it alive and enforceable for its full term.

§2.4.3 The Judgment Lien

A creditor who obtains a final, liquidated money judgment in a court of general jurisdiction[7] is able to obtain a judgment lien, which is one of the judicial liens discussed in section 1.6.2. To create and perfect the lien, the creditor records the judgment in a docket maintained by the clerk of the court or in some other filing system (often, the county deeds registry) designated by state law.

Upon being docketed, the judgment creates a lien on all the real property in the county of which the debtor is the legal owner of record.[8]

---

7. The judgment of a court of limited jurisdiction may not be capable of creating a lien or may have to be recorded in a more senior court to establish a lien.
8. State law may or may not allow the lien to attach to interests less than full ownership, such as joint ownership rights.

The creditor can docket the lien in more than one county to cover property situated in different counties. In most states the lien is confined to real property.[9] It is not necessary that the property had any connection to the creditor's claim. It is subjected to the lien purely because it is owned by the debtor and located in the county in which the creditor docketed the judgment.

The lien is subject to any preexisting third-party interests recorded in the property, such as prior recorded mortgages and liens. The judgment lien may also be junior to an earlier, unrecorded interest in the property granted by the debtor to a good faith transferee for value. This is because the judgment lienholder is not a consensual lienholder who has extended credit to the debtor in reliance on real estate records and so the equities may dictate that the rights of the prior unrecorded interest-holder should be protected. As a general rule, the judgment lien is superior to any interest acquired in the property after the recording of the judgment lien. This rule is also subject to some exceptions where policy dictates that a subsequent bona fide transferee should be protected from the lien.

A judgment lien does not take precedence over any exemption to which the debtor is entitled. State statutes generally give an individual debtor an exemption in the home in which the debtor resides (called the homestead exemption). This exemption protects the debtor's homestead, fully or partially, from execution by a creditor, even where the creditor has obtained a judgment lien. If the property is fully exempt, the lien cannot affect it at all. Partially exempt property is lienable only to the extent of the debtor's nonexempt equity. Examples 3 and 4 deal with priority of judgment liens.

Once the judgment lien is recorded, it attaches not only to the real property held by the debtor at the time of filing but to any property in the county acquired by the debtor in the future, as long as the lien remains in effect. The lien will similarly encompass any improvements on the debtor's property and any increases in its value or augmentation of the debtor's rights in it. The judgment lien's attachment to after-acquired property rights of the debtor is an important advantage to the creditor. If the debtor owns no executable realty at the time of judgment or has only a small equity in existing property, the creditor can wait in the hope that new property will be acquired or the value of the debtor's interest will increase. Unless the statute provides a separate period of effectiveness for the lien, it lasts as long as the judgment. A judgment lienor therefore needs to be particularly sensitive to the question of duration of the judgment discussed in section 2.4.2. (Example 4 deals with the judgment lien on after-acquired property.)

9. In some states, a judgment lien can attach to personal property by filing in the registry where security interests in personal property are recorded. The discussion here focuses on judgment liens on real property.

When the lien is to be enforced, the lienholder follows a foreclosure procedure to sell the property and realize its proceeds. In some states the foreclosure of a judicial lien follows a public sale procedure such as that described in section 2.5. In others, special rules are prescribed for the foreclosure of a judgment lien.

§2.4.4 The Enforcement of Judgments in Other States

After a court has granted judgment, it is enforced by the means described in the following sections. However, enforcement activity is only permissible within the territorial boundaries of the court's state. To enforce a judgment in another state, the creditor must have the judgment recognized by a court in that state, whose own officials will enforce it. Under Article IV, section 1 of the Constitution, a state must give full faith and credit to a valid final judgment of another, provided that the judgment complies with the jurisdictional requirements of the Constitution and the law of the state in which it was granted.

State law prescribes the procedure to be followed by a creditor to have the judgment of another state recognized and enforced. There is some uniformity in this procedure because many states have adopted the Uniform Enforcement of Foreign Judgments Act (the Uniform Act). (The word "foreign" in the title of the Act refers to judgments of other states or to federal courts, not to judgments of the courts of foreign nations. A separate uniform act, mentioned briefly below, deals with judgments from other nations.)

The Uniform Act provides for a straightforward method of registering a foreign judgment by a clerical act, with recourse to the court of the recording state only if a dispute arises concerning the registration. This is a simpler process than the traditional means of enforcement, which requires the plaintiff to commence suit on the judgment in the second jurisdiction. This method remains an alternative even in states that have adopted the Uniform Act. (If the judgment is enforced by suit, the defendant is confined to defenses based on the validity of the judgment, and may not raise defenses on the merits.)

Judgments of the courts of foreign nations are not entitled to full faith and credit under the Constitution, and they are not subject to the same procedures or laws that govern the judgments of sister states. However, principles of international comity do favor the recognition of such judgments when the judicial process of the foreign nation satisfies standards of fairness and due process. At common law, courts in the United States have recognized and enforced the judgments of foreign courts where principles of comity and due process so dictate. This common law basis for recognition has been codified in the Uniform Foreign Money-Judgments Recognition Act. The courts of a state that has enacted it have discretion to recognize and enforce judgments of the courts of foreign nations if the judgment satisfies the standards mentioned above and recognition does not offend the state's public policy.

§2.5 EXECUTION

The creditor must resort to execution to enforce the judgment if the debtor does not pay it voluntarily. Execution is the process whereby the sheriff or an equivalent official is directed by a writ to find property of the debtor, seize it, and sell it to realize proceeds with which to pay the judgment debt. Execution is regulated by statute. Courts tend to insist upon strict compliance with the statutory requirements and to invalidate deficient executions.

(1) Writ of execution. After the creditor has obtained judgment, it begins the process of execution by having a writ issued by the clerk of the court, directing the sheriff to find and levy on property of the debtor and to report back to the clerk by a specific date (called the return date). The debtor can apply for a stay of execution pending appeal, but the stay is usually conditioned on the debtor furnishing a bond, which can be costly. The writ must usually be issued within a certain time of the judgment. If it is not, the judgment becomes dormant and has to be revived by motion or action.

(2) Levy. After issuance, the writ is delivered to the sheriff, who tries to levy on property of the debtor, often with the creditor's active guidance. The procedure for the levy of a writ of execution is basically the same as that for a writ of attachment. (*See* sections 2.2.2 and 2.3.2.) Personal property in the debtor's possession and documents that reify intangible rights are levied upon by seizure. The sheriff normally takes the property into custody pending the sale in execution, but some states permit cumbersome property to be left in the debtor's possession and posted with a notice of execution. Real property is levied upon by recording the writ in the real estate records. Other intangibles and personal property in the possession of a third party cannot be reached by a writ of execution but must be garnished.

After levy, the sheriff files a return reporting on the action taken and describing the property that has been levied upon. If the sheriff found no property, he so certifies by submitting a nulla bona ("no goods") return by the date specified in the writ.

As in the case of attachment, if the sheriff seizes property that belongs to a third party, the true owner is able to challenge the levy and claim damages for trespass or conversion. Some execution statutes provide an expedited procedure for adjudicating the adverse claim and having the property released from execution. The sheriff could be liable for any tort damages, so the plaintiff must provide an indemnity when delivering the writ.

Even though real and personal property are both subject to execution, the seizure and ultimate sale of real property is often subject to special restrictions, which have developed as a result of the historical importance of real property[10] and remain because real property is often the debtor's most valuable asset. For example, it is common for execution statutes to require the creditor to attempt levy on personal property first and to have recourse to real property only if insufficient personal property can be seized to satisfy the judgment. Also, the sale in execution of real property is usually subject to precautionary rules.

(3) Execution sale. As soon as possible after completion of the levy, the process of realization takes place. After advertising and notice to the debtor, the sheriff conducts a sale of the property by public auction. The sale procedures prescribed by execution statutes attempt to ensure that the fairest price possible will be obtained. Notwithstanding, it is generally accepted that the value of property is depressed at forced sales of this nature, and prices seldom approximate true market value.

The proceeds realized, less costs of execution, are remitted to the creditor in satisfaction of the judgment. If insufficient funds are generated to pay the judgment in full, the creditor may begin the process of execution again by issuing a further writ and attempting another levy and sale. If the sale proceeds exceed the debt and costs, the surplus goes in order of priority to any junior judgment creditors who participated in the sale. Any remaining surplus is paid to the debtor.

As mentioned earlier, the statute may afford special protection to the debtor where real property is sold in execution. These protective mechanisms may be available only when the debtor's residence is being sold and may not apply to other real property. For example, the statute may require an appraisal of the property before sale and will not permit the sale at a price that is less than a defined percentage of the appraised value. Some states provide for an automatic confirmation hearing at which the court must review and confirm the sale before it is final. If there has been some irregularity in the proceedings, or if the price is unconscionably low, the court can refuse confirmation.

---

10. In early common law the writ of execution, known as *fieri facias*, was confined to chattels. Real property could not be executed upon at all. If the debtor owned land, the creditor could obtain a writ of *elegit* that could reach a limited portion of the revenues from the land over a defined period of time.

(4) Redemption. Even after the sale, the property is not necessarily lost to the debtor. It is common for execution statutes to allow the debtor[11] to redeem real property sold in execution. The redemption must be effected within a fixed period after the sale by the payment of the redemption value of the property to the purchaser.[12] The redemption price is the price paid by the purchaser at the sale; it is adjusted upward to include interest and to reimburse the purchaser for any costs and expenditures on the property, and adjusted downward to give the debtor credit for the economic value of fruits and revenues received by the purchaser.

The right of redemption enables the debtor to reacquire the property at the approximate distress price, so it helps a debtor who is able to raise the necessary funds before the redemption period expires. Of course, it is not of great practical value to many debtors who have no hope of finding the cash needed for redemption. The disadvantage of statutory redemption is that the purchaser acquires uncertain title at the time of the sale. This makes purchase at execution unattractive to some potential buyers, and it further depresses the prices at such sales. As a result, some states have abolished or curtailed the right of postsale redemption.

(5) Execution lien. An execution lien attaches by operation of law to any property levied upon. Like the other liens discussed in this chapter, it falls within the general category of judicial liens. The effective date of the lien differs from one state to another. The date of levy seems to be the most prevalent alternative, but some states have selected the date of delivery of the writ to the sheriff or some other point in the process.

The purpose of the lien is to protect the creditor while the sale is pending. Because the sale is supposed to proceed expeditiously after levy, the lien is intended to be of fairly short duration and to last only as long as necessary to cover the property until realization by sale. It is not a long-term security interest, and it expires if the sale is not held within the period prescribed by the statute or, if no period is provided, within a reasonable time.

When several creditors have executed on the same property, or when there are competing interests in the property, the liens and interests must be

11. The right of statutory redemption may also be given to lienholders whose liens are junior to that of the execution creditor. It is therefore possible that there are two or more persons who are entitled to redeem. Multiple redemptions are not dealt with here. Even if a lienholder does redeem, the debtor has the ultimate redemption right and can redeem from the lienholder.

12. This statutory right to redeem property sold in execution should not be confused with the debtor's equity of redemption in the foreclosure of some security interests, alluded to in section 1.8.2. Where a security interest is foreclosed upon, the equity of redemption gives the debtor the right to avert the sale of the collateral by paying the debt before the sale takes place, but does not allow the debtor to redeem the property after sale.

ranked in accordance with rules of priority. The first-in-time rule applies unless there is specific provision to the contrary. If an execution creditor has a preexisting lien (*e.g.*, an attachment lien, judgment lien, or consensual lien), the execution lien merges with the earlier one and backdates for priority purposes.

§2.6 GARNISHMENT

Postjudgment garnishment is very much like the prejudgment remedy described in section 2.3.3. Where a writ of garnishment is issued after judgment it is usually just a variation of the execution procedure, with some differences to account for the protection of the garnishee's rights and to ensure that the debtor is notified of the garnishment.[13] The debtor's due process rights require that he receives a notice of garnishment—the fact that the debtor received notice of the suit itself does not satisfy this notice requirement. The notice to the debtor must set out his exemption rights and give him an opportunity to challenge the garnishment.

Upon delivery of the writ of garnishment to the sheriff, the levy follows the same course as the prejudgment procedure: In essence, the garnishee is obliged to answer the writ and must pay the debt due to the debtor or surrender the debtor's property or state grounds for not doing so. The garnishee may admit the obligation to the debtor, but assert the right to delay payment or turnover of the property if the debt is not due or the property is not returnable at the time of the writ. The debt or property must then be paid or surrendered to the appropriate court official on the date that it becomes due. The garnishee may deny owing a debt or holding property of the debtor, in which case the garnishee is not obliged to pay or turn over property unless the creditor successfully challenges that answer and the court orders payment or turnover. In many states a garnishment lien arises on levy. A garnishee who disposes of garnished property in violation of the writ becomes personally liable to the creditor for the loss suffered as a result of the disposition.

Upon payment of a garnished debt to the clerk of the court or the sheriff, the funds are remitted to the creditor to the extent necessary to satisfy the judgment. Property surrendered by the garnishee to the sheriff (whether voluntarily or after the court has conducted the hearing and ordered

13. In some states postjudgment garnishment is a separate suit against the garnishee, but it is more commonly just a variety of execution procedure.

surrender) is sold in execution in the same way as property levied on by a writ of execution.

§2.7 PROCEEDINGS IN AID OF EXECUTION

A creditor whose attempt at execution ended with a nulla bona return may suspect that the debtor has concealed executable property. Apart from any investigation a creditor may conduct on its own, there are two judicial procedures that the creditor may use to gain information from the debtor about the existence and whereabouts of executable assets.

(1) The creditors' bill in equity. This is a suit in equity that may be brought by a creditor after it has unsuccessfully attempted execution. It is a proceeding ancillary to the suit on the debt, and is commenced as a separate equitable action. As an equitable suit, it must be grounded on the creditor's showing that its remedies at law for the enforcement of the debt are exhausted or inadequate. This means that the creditor must either have received a nulla bona return or must be able to show that it would be fruitless to attempt levy.

The creditors' bill allows the creditor to obtain an order compelling the debtor or other persons with knowledge of the debtor's affairs to submit to an examination by the creditor in court. The bill can then be used to recover any assets that are revealed from a person who acquired them in fraud of creditors,[14] to enjoin their disposition, or to appoint a receiver to administer them pending execution. A creditors' bill can also be used to execute on equitable assets that cannot be reached by a writ of execution at law.

(2) Statutory proceedings in aid of execution. These are a less cumbersome alternative to the older creditors' bill. The process is part of the original suit, rather than a separate action. Statutory procedures provide at least for an examination or discovery, but some go beyond this and authorize the court to order payments by installments, to enjoin the disposition of property, to appoint a receiver, or to take other steps to apply the property to the satisfaction of the debt. In some jurisdictions the statutory inquiry proceedings, like the creditors' bill, can only be used after a nulla bona return unless execution is shown to be futile. In others, the examination can take place before any writ has been issued.

---

14. The creditors' bill is therefore available to recover fraudulently transferred property. However, as explained in section 2.8, there is an alternative, more streamlined, statutory process for avoiding a fraudulent transfer and recovering the transferred asset.

§2.8 FRAUDULENT TRANSFERS

Fraudulent transfers are covered fully in the context of bankruptcy in Chapter 14. It would therefore be repetitive to deal with them in any detail in this chapter. However, it is necessary to include here a brief survey of the creditor's right to avoid a fraudulent transfer by the debtor in the course of debt collection under state law. This power of avoidance is an important benefit to a creditor whose ability to execute has been subverted by the debtor's improper transfer of otherwise executable assets to a third party.

As explained in the overview of unsecured debt enforcement in section 1.3 and in section 2.1, after an unsecured creditor has obtained judgment against the debtor, it may discover that the sheriff cannot find any executable property on which to levy. There is nothing that the creditor can do to recover the judgment debt if the debtor truly has no executable assets. However, sometimes the lack of executable assets results from the debtor having disposed of property under circumstances that make the disposition avoidable. If so, state law provides a means for the creditor to avoid the transfer and recover the property or its value. Most states have one or another version of a uniform statute that allows a creditor to avoid a transfer made under stated circumstances. The *Uniform Fraudulent Transfer Act* (UFTA) is the most widely adopted model law.[15] Although the statute refers to "fraudulent" transfers, the creditor does not necessarily have to prove actual fraud. A transfer is avoidable under some circumstances even if there was no deliberate intent to defraud creditors.[16]

A perfected secured creditor does not need to use fraudulent transfer law to avoid the debtor's impermissible transfer of collateral because the perfected lien in the collateral is usually superior to any rights that the subsequent transferee of it may acquire. Therefore, fraudulent transfer law benefits an unsecured creditor who has no rights in the debtor's property and would otherwise be unable to execute on property that the debtor has disposed of before execution. The general principle of fraudulent transfer law is that the unsecured creditor can avoid a transfer of property by the debtor if that transfer was of the kind covered by the statute, and it has the

---

15. The UFTA was drafted in 1984 by the National Conference of Commissioners on Uniform State Laws. It is an update of an earlier uniform model law, the *Uniform Fraudulent Conveyance Act* (UFCA). In 2014, the National Conference updated the UFTA by promulgating the Uniform Voidable Transactions Act (UVTA), which has now been adopted by some states. Most of the substantive provisions of the UVTA are similar to those of the UFTA. The provisions of the UFTA are not cited or discussed in detail here, but are covered more fully in Chapter 14.

16. As stated in the previous footnote, the UVTA did not make significant substantive changes to the UFTA. However, the one significant change that it did make was to focus on "voidable" rather than "fraudulent" transfers to reflect the fact that the creditor does not actually have to show fraud to avoid some types of transfer.

effect of defeating the unsecured creditor's justifiable recourse to that property. Under the UFTA, the creditor's avoidance power extends back to transfers made within four years of the avoidance suit.

There are two alternative bases on which a creditor can avoid a transfer of property by the debtor. The one involves actual fraud by the debtor, and the other, commonly called "constructive fraud" does not require proof of actual fraud, but is avoidable on the basis of the debtor's financial condition at the time of transfer and the adequacy of consideration given by the transferee to the debtor. In both cases, the creditor sues the transferee of the property, either for return of the property itself, which the creditor then levies upon, or for a money judgment for the lesser of the value of the property at the time of transfer or the amount of the debt owing by the debtor. Even if the transfer otherwise qualifies for avoidance, the UFTA circumscribes the creditor's right of avoidance to protect a good faith transferee who gave value to the debtor in exchange for the transfer.

(1) Actual fraud. The ground of avoidance for actual fraud is available not only to a creditor whose claim existed at the time of the transfer, but also to a creditor whose claim arose after the transfer. In essence, a creditor can avoid a transfer of property made by the debtor with the deliberate motive of hindering, delaying, or defrauding debt collection by removing the property from the reach of creditors. Fraudulent intent is usually proven by circumstantial evidence of suspicious circumstances (known as "badges of fraud") from which dishonesty can be inferred. For example, shortly before the debtor defaulted on the debt, he transferred a valuable property to a family member, either as a gift or for a fraction of its value.[17]

(2) Constructive fraud. Even if the creditor cannot prove actual fraud, the UFTA recognizes that there are some transfers that have the effect of defeating the claims of creditors. These transfers are deemed to be constructively fraudulent—that is, deemed fraudulent as a matter of law, irrespective of the debtor's actual intent. Constructive fraud has two elements:

1. The debtor transferred the property for less than reasonably equivalent value. The determination of whether the debtor received reasonably equivalent value for the property transferred primarily involves a comparison between the value of the property transferred and the consideration that the debtor received for it. The lower the consideration in relation to the value, the higher the likelihood that this test is satisfied. However, although the disparity in exchange is

17. See section 14.2.2 for a detailed discussion of actual fraud.

highly important, it is not looked at in isolation, but is examined under the totality of the circumstances.[18]

2. The transfer occurred at a time when the debtor was in insolvent or financially precarious circumstances. There are three situations that constitute financial precariousness: First, the debtor was insolvent[19] at the time of the transfer or became insolvent as a result of the transfer; second, the debtor was undercapitalized for a business venture; or third, the debtor was about to incur debts that the debtor had no reasonable prospect of paying when they became due.[20] The ground of avoidance for insolvency is available only to a creditor whose claim existed at the time of the transfer, but the other two grounds are also available to a creditor whose claim arose after the transfer.

§2.9 STATE LAW INSOLVENCY PROCEEDINGS

§2.9.1 Introduction to State Law Insolvency Proceedings

The collection processes described in the preceding sections involve individual action by each creditor. Creditors act on their own and are concerned with the enforcement of their own claims. Although creditor activity may be individual, it is often not isolated — a debtor in financial difficulty is likely to have defaulted on several debts. When a number of creditors are attempting to enforce their claims, those furthest ahead in the collection process have the best chance of finding executable property. Competition for the debtor's resources can be handled more fairly and efficiently through an arrangement for the collective management of claims. By such a collective proceeding (so called to distinguish it from creditors' individual pursuits of their claims), the debtor may be able to deal with creditors in an orderly way and to preserve assets that would otherwise be seized and disposed of at distress prices in an execution sale.

Bankruptcy under federal law is the predominant and most powerful collective proceeding. However, state law does provide mechanisms that a debtor may use as an alternative to bankruptcy, to handle claims collectively

18. The test of reasonably equivalent value is explained more fully in section 14.2.3b.

19. Insolvency is determined by one of two well-established alternative tests. Under the balance sheet or bankruptcy test, insolvency is an excess of liabilities over assets. Under the equity test, insolvency is the inability to pay debts as they become due. Insolvency is discussed more fully in in section 14.2.3c.

20. These other forms of financial precariousness are discussed more fully in section 14.2.3c.

for the purpose of restructuring and compromising debts: compositions (including extensions) and assignments for the benefit of creditors. These procedures are sometimes called insolvency[21] proceedings. Although the debtor need not be insolvent to be eligible to use these proceedings, a solvent debtor is less likely to resort to them.

State law insolvency proceedings have one attribute in common with bankruptcy: They are designed to enable the debtor to deal with creditors as a group to achieve an overall settlement of their claims. However, bankruptcy is a much more powerful and pervasive remedy. Among other things, the Bankruptcy Code confers extraordinary rights on the trustee to collect and administer the estate, and it has unique provisions for the protection of creditor interests, the control of creditor activity, and the discharge of debts. State law proceedings do not have the same compulsive strength. They fall far short of being equivalents of bankruptcy and are constitutionally barred from providing equivalent relief.[22] As a result, the proceedings under state law are less formal, simpler, and more dependent on cooperation between the debtor and creditors.

State law insolvency is often a less desirable remedy than bankruptcy because it does not give the debtor the same protection as bankruptcy law. In some cases, however, bankruptcy is either not attractive to the debtor or is not feasible. There are many reasons why this may be. For example, the debtor may want to avoid the expense and formality of bankruptcy administration, or may not want the stigma of bankruptcy, or may not be eligible for bankruptcy relief.[23] Where bankruptcy is not a suitable option for the debtor, the state law procedures do at least provide some of the advantages that arise from the orderly management of debt. By surrendering assets for liquidation and distribution among creditors or by making a commitment to payment by future installments, the debtor may be able to persuade creditors that their interests are better served by cooperating in a collective proceeding rather than by attempting collection individually.

The two insolvency proceedings discussed here are voluntary: Only the debtor may bring them into effect. Although creditors may exert pressure on the debtor to make an assignment or a composition, they cannot initiate suit to force them on the debtor.

Under the common law, these insolvency proceedings are not judicial remedies. Unless a state has provided otherwise by statute, the debtor does not apply to court to sanction the proceeding, and the court does not supervise its performance. The court only becomes involved in the matter if a challenge or dispute arises.

---

21. Insolvency is defined briefly in footnote 19.
22. The federal bankruptcy power is discussed in section 3.2.
23. For a fuller discussion of eligibility for bankruptcy and some of the considerations that may motivate the filing of a bankruptcy petition, *see* Chapter 5.

§2.9.2 Compositions and Extensions

On hearing the word "composition," a normal person might think of Beethoven or Mozart scribbling down musical notes by the flickering light of a candle, or of Raphael or Tiepolo plotting out the spatial relationships between hordes of saints and seraphim. To a lawyer, the word simply means a contract. More specifically, in modern usage a composition is a contract between the debtor and two or more creditors under which a partial payment of claims is promised and accepted in full settlement.

An extension is a contract between the debtor and two or more creditors under which the debtor is allowed an extension of time within which to pay the debts. A single contract can include both a composition and an extension, providing for a reduction in the debt as well as an extension of the payment period.[24] From now on, the word "composition" is used to refer to a contract with both these elements.

Although compositions have been codified by some states (sometimes with additional statutory requirements), they are generally subject to the rules and principles of contract law. Thus, doctrines governing formation, performance, and breach all apply. Because compositions are contractual in nature, the specific structure of each one can be molded by the parties to meet the needs of their situation. As a contract, a composition needs consideration, which courts hold to be present by virtue of the creditors' mutual forbearance and the debtor's undertaking to procure assent from other creditors. It is not necessary that all participating creditors sign the same contract. They may each make a separate contract with the debtor, as long as the contracts are interdependent and entered into in reliance on others being executed.

As a contract, a composition binds only creditors who assent to it. They are not likely to agree to reduction or extension of their claims unless the debtor can persuade them that it serves their best interests to do so. This means, at a minimum, the debtor must demonstrate genuine financial distress and a good faith effort to deal with it. The distribution offered to creditors (which may be committed from future earnings or the liquidation of selected assets or both) must be enough to make it worthwhile for creditors to accept the settlement, rather than to press ahead with collection efforts. A debtor is held to a high standard of good faith in entering into a composition and must disclose financial information honestly and accurately. Creditors who are misled have grounds for avoiding the composition.

As long as two or more creditors accept the composition, consideration problems are overcome. A debtor is therefore able to make a legally valid

---

24. Because the purpose of a composition and extension is to resolve the debtor's financial problems by consent — by working out the debtor's financial problems — these agreements are sometimes called "workouts."

composition with fewer than all of the creditors. However, a composition cannot achieve its desired end if acceptance of the composition is not widespread because nonconsenting creditors will likely continue with individual collection activity, thereby preventing preservation of the debtor's estate and discouraging more cooperative creditors from exercising forbearance. A debtor may have some flexibility in offering preferred treatment to a creditor who holds out — as long as this is fully disclosed to other creditors. However, the other creditors may not be willing to enter the composition if one of them is treated more generously.

Once the composition is executed, its terms supersede the debtor's former obligations toward participating creditors. Consummation of the composition as promised satisfies the debtor's obligations under the composition as well as the debtor's original obligations that were subsumed in it. The consensual forgiveness of the unpaid balance of the original debt is an important advantage of a composition, because a state cannot grant a discharge to a debtor in the absence of creditor assent — the discharge is an incident of the bankruptcy power conferred on Congress by the Constitution. If the debtor breaches the composition, creditors are entitled to disregard it and to sue for the full outstanding balance of the original debt.

§2.9.3 Assignments for the Benefit of Creditors

An assignment for the benefit of creditors (sometimes abbreviated to ABC) is a voluntary transfer of property in trust by the debtor to another person (the assignee) with instructions to liquidate the property and to distribute its proceeds to those creditors who have elected to participate. The purpose of the assignment is to place the debtor's executable property in the hands of an impartial custodian so that individual creditors cannot levy on it, permitting its orderly liquidation and distribution for the benefit of the creditor body as a whole. The debtor transfers the property in trust to the custodian, specifying the terms on which it is to be realized and its proceeds distributed.

Each creditor may choose whether or not to participate in an ABC. However, unlike a composition, the ABC is not contractual in nature. The debtor's power to make the assignment is an incident of rights of ownership, deriving from the law of property. The ABC is a common law device, but it has been codified and regulated by statute in some states.

As you will see when liquidation bankruptcy (under Ch. 7 of the Code) is introduced in Chapters 3 and 5, the ABC has some similarity to liquidation in bankruptcy. However, the ABC is a weaker and less comprehensive remedy, and it affords considerably less protection to the debtor and creditors. For example, it does not stay the creditors' pursuit of any unassigned assets or shield the debtor from other collection pressure; and it does not confer on the assignee the extensive powers wielded by a bankruptcy trustee. Probably even more important, the ABC cannot, by statute, operate as a discharge because a state statute conferring a discharge of unpaid debt is an unconstitutional encroachment on the federal bankruptcy power. The constitutional problem does not arise if creditors themselves grant the discharge by agreement, but courts are wary of coerced consent. They generally demand that the assent be truly voluntary, and not simply imposed by a condition of participation in the ABC. In fact, many courts consider that the inclusion of such a condition is prima facie bad faith, and some states forbid it altogether.

An ABC is less formal than bankruptcy. In some states it requires no judicial approval or supervision at all and only comes before a court if someone challenges or disputes some aspect of it. In other states, judicial participation has been imposed by statute, but even there the procedure is much less involved than bankruptcy. Because an ABC lacks the force of bankruptcy, it is often not a workable alternative for the debtor. However, for the reasons mentioned in section 2.9.1, the ABC may suit some debtors more than bankruptcy.

An ABC is meant to benefit creditors, as its name suggests. If creditors derive no advantage from it, it is simply a conveyance of property by the debtor without return consideration, having the effect of removing the property from the reach of execution. As such, it is a fraud on creditors (a fraudulent transfer) and avoidable, as discussed in section 2.8. The debtor's discretion in deciding on the terms of the assignment is limited by this consideration and is subject to an overriding duty of good faith. An ABC that has the effect of frustrating and obstructing creditors rather than facilitating the evenhanded distribution of funds may be invalidated in its entirety or modified by the court.

There are a number of terms that are considered improper or, at best, questionable in an ABC. For example, ABCs usually cannot allow the debtor to retain the use or control of the property or to reserve some interest in it apart from the right to have any surplus proceeds returned; provide for the administration of the assets for an extended period; grant preferential treatment to a particular creditor;[25] stipulate that participating creditors must discharge the unpaid balance of their claims; or include less than all the debtor's executable property. In some states, these principles are based in common law. In others, statutes have been passed that codify them and may impose further restrictions.

After the instrument of assignment has been executed and the assignee has accepted the appointment, the debtor must deliver the property to the assignee. Ownership of the property passes to the assignee, who holds it in

25. Preferences are not generally forbidden under common law. Therefore, a fully disclosed preference may be permitted in some states. However, other states have changed this rule by judicial decision or statute and forbid preferences in ABCs.

trust for the benefit of the creditors. The assignee acquires no greater rights in the property than the debtor had. Therefore, the assignee's interest in the property is subject to any valid preexisting third-party rights.

On the effective date of the assignment, the property is treated as being *in custodia legis* and cannot be levied upon. The effective date of the assignment varies from one state to another: It may be the date of the instrument's delivery to the assignee, the date of the property's delivery, or the date the assignee accepted the transfer. In some states, the assignment must be recorded to become effective.

The assignee's essential task is to notify creditors, to call for claims, to realize the property, and to distribute the proceeds to those creditors who have proved claims. In addition to complying with the law governing the administration of assigned property, the assignee is bound by the terms of the assignment. The proper performance of the assignee's duties is secured by a surety bond. In some states the assignee is obliged to file an inventory, appraisals, and accounts.

On being notified of the assignment, a creditor may decide to participate in the ABC, file a claim, and receive whatever distribution is made. The creditor's participation is treated as tacit consent to any lawful conditions expressed in the deed of assignment. Alternatively, the creditor may refuse to participate. Unlike bankruptcy, an ABC does not stay collection activity, so the creditor is free to pursue efforts to recover the debt. As noted before, the creditor cannot execute on the property assigned under a valid ABC, so the creditor's prospects or immediate satisfaction of its claim outside of the ABC are poor. However, if there is some flaw or fraudulent design in the ABC, the creditor may be able to avoid it, unless the flaw is one that can be corrected.

Even if the ABC is valid, the creditor may be able to use it as the basis of an involuntary bankruptcy petition, provided that the requirements of §303(b)(2) of the Bankruptcy Code are satisfied. (*See* Chapter 6.) Stated broadly, the Code gives creditors the power, under some circumstances, to override the ABC and force the debtor into bankruptcy. If the petition is granted, the assignment is terminated and the assignee must surrender the property to the trustee.

Examples

EXAMPLES

1. About a year ago, Render Unto Seizure Bank (Bank) issued a credit card to Debtor with a $10,000 credit limit. For five months, Debtor used the credit card moderately, incurring relatively small monthly charges which he paid in full at the end of each month. However, six months ago, Debtor used the card to make purchases to the full $10,000 limit on the account. Debtor made the minimum required monthly payments for

two months, but then failed to make any monthly payments on the account. Bank wrote a demand letter to Debtor, but he failed to make any further payments. Bank has just commenced suit to recover the debt. It is concerned that Debtor is in financial difficulty and may also owe substantial amounts of money to other creditors. So far, there are no judgments recorded against Debtor, but Bank thinks that it is only a question of time before other creditors pursue collection proceedings. Bank would like to find and seize property of Debtor right away, before other creditors execute on it. Does Bank have any means of doing so?

2. Eartha Plott owns a piece of land. Two of Eartha's creditors claim interests in the land based on the following sequence of events:
   a. On January 15, Victor Pyrrhic, one of Eartha's creditors, commenced suit against her to recover a debt.
   b. On February 20, Lien & Hungry Loan Co., another of Eartha's creditors, commenced suit against her to recover a debt. Shortly after issuing summons, Lien & Hungry filed and served an application for attachment. Eartha failed to appear at the attachment hearing, and the court authorized a writ that was delivered to the sheriff. On March 10 the sheriff levied on Eartha's land by properly filing the writ in the real estate records.
   c. On March 20, Victor obtained default judgment in his suit against Eartha. On March 25, Victor docketed the judgment in the county in which the land is situated.
   d. On April 1, Lien & Hungry obtained default judgment in its action against Eartha. Its judgment was properly docketed on April 3.

   The land is worth $25,000. Victor's judgment is for $15,000, and Lien & Hungry's judgment is for $20,000.

   What are the creditors' interests in Eartha's land? How should they be ranked?

3. On January 15, Lienora obtained a money judgment against Homer LeBrave, which she properly docketed in the county on January 30.

   On January 20, Lienardo obtained a money judgment against Homer. He properly docketed the judgment in the county on January 25.

   At this time, Homer owned no real property in the county. However, on February 28 he acquired title to a piece of land that he inherited from his late father.

   Assume both judgments are still current and enforceable. How should they be ranked?

4. Homer owns a commercial building in another county. Lienardo discovered this property by searching the real estate records. He recorded his judgment in the second county on March 1. On April 30, Homer sold the property to Emptor B. Ware. Emptor did not check the real estate records

before he bought the property, and did not know about Lienardo's recording. He discovered it only when he attempted to take transfer of the title at the closing of the transaction. Is Lienardo's lien superior to Emptor's rights as purchaser of the property?

5. Penny Foolish owns and operates a small retail store from which she derives a modest but steady income. Although she runs her business carefully, she is undisciplined and irresponsible as a consumer. Through her abuse of credit cards she has accumulated an unmanageable amount of debt. She has tried to juggle her affairs and to make some payment to everyone, but she has fallen into arrears on most of her debts. Some creditors have threatened collection action. Because Penny's inventory and business assets are her only valuable executable property, she fears that she will lose her business if she cannot settle her debts.

   Penny has shredded her credit cards and wishes to try to make an arrangement with her creditors. What options are open to her?

6. Abraham ("Abie") Cede has made an ABC. Included in his assigned assets is a truck worth $10,000. The truck is subject to a valid, perfected security interest, securing a debt of $8,000.

   What happens to the rights of the secured party when Abie transfers the truck to his assignee?

Explanations

EXPLANATIONS

1. Bank is an unsecured creditor and has no rights in any property of Debtor. However, it may be able to find and seize some property of Debtor immediately through the process of attachment, under which it obtains a writ of attachment from the court and has the sheriff execute the writ by seizing some property of Debtor early in the case and keeping it in legal custody, so that when Bank finally obtains judgment, the property is available to be executed upon. Absent grounds for an ex parte process, Bank's application for attachment must be served on Debtor with a notice to show cause, calling on the debtor to state grounds for refusing the application. The debtor can challenge the application in response to the notice. The application for attachment need not identify any particular asset. If the court authorizes the attachment, the sheriff is called upon to levy on unspecified property of the debtor that is sufficient in value to cover the amount of the debt, and the sheriff then tries to find and levy on property of appropriate value. Upon the levy of attachment, Bank would acquire an attachment lien on the seized property that would have priority in the seized asset dating from the time of levy. Therefore, Bank's seizure of property by attachment now will create a lien in the attached property which will secure it until judgment and give Bank's

postjudgment execution on that property priority over any judicial lien that any other unsecured creditors might later obtain through levy on that property. When Bank ultimately obtains judgment, the attachment property will be executed upon and sold by the sheriff, with the sale proceeds applied to satisfaction of the judgment debt.

Bank may qualify for the attachment remedy provided that it complies exactly with the requirements for the remedy. It has already commenced suit, and the claim is a liquidated monetary claim based on contract, which is usually the type of claim that allows for attachment. (However, the law of the state may have other restrictions, such as a bar on attachment for consumer debts, or a requirement of special circumstances, such as a showing that the debtor is evading payment or is likely to abscond.) Bank must apply to court for attachment by filing a notice of motion supported by an affidavit that establishes grounds for attachment and shows a prima facie underlying claim on the merits. Bank must also post a bond which guarantees the payment of compensation to Debtor if Bank does not ultimately get judgment in the suit.

Of course, even if the court authorizes attachment, this does not guarantee that Bank will actually be able to levy on property. The attachment will fail unless Bank is able to find executable property. Even if Debtor has property, it may not be executable because Debtor is an individual and the property may be exemptable under state law.

2. This question involves a priority contest between two judicial liens on Eartha's land. The sequence of events is as follows:

Jan. 15	Feb. 20	Mar. 10	Mar. 20	Mar. 25	Apr. 1	Apr. 3
Victor commenced suit	Lien & Hungry commenced suit	Lien & Hungry levied attachment	Victor obtained judgment	Victor docketed judgment	Lien & Hungry obtained judgment	Lien & Hungry docketed judgment

Victor's judgment lien became effective when his judgment was docketed in the county on March 25. Lien & Hungry's judgment lien was docketed on April 3. However, Lien & Hungry had attached the land on March 10. An attachment lien was created upon levy, which was accomplished by recording the attachment in the real estate records. When Lien & Hungry obtained its judgment lien on April 3, that lien merged with the attachment lien, so that Lien & Hungry's priority backdated to March 10.

On the basis of the first-in-time rule, Lien & Hungry's lien has priority over Victor's lien. It is a first charge against the property for the full amount of $20,000 plus costs. Victor's lien extends only to the surplus of approximately $5,000. Victor will have to seek other assets to cover his deficiency.

This Example illustrates the value of attachment. By attaching the property at the commencement of its suit, Lien & Hungry was able to secure its ultimate judgment and to take priority over Victor. By failing to attach the property, Victor lost the advantage even though he commenced suit and obtained judgment first.

Eartha is an individual, so she is entitled to any exemptions provided by state law. Because the property is unimproved land rather than Eartha's home, it probably will not qualify as a homestead for purposes of a homestead exemption. However, the statute must be consulted to determine this and also to see whether Eartha might be able to claim a general exemption or some other category of exemption that could include the land. If it does, Eartha's exemption would protect her interest in the property to the extent of the dollar limit of the exemption.

3. The sequence of events is as follows:

Jan. 15	Jan. 20	Jan. 25	Jan. 30	Feb. 28
Lienora obtains judgment	Lienardo obtains judgment	Lienardo's judgment docketed	Lienora's judgment docketed	Homer acquires property

Although Homer is an individual, entitled to exemptions, the property is not his home, so as in the case of Eartha in Example 2, he probably has no homestead exemption in the property. Assume that is so and that the state exemption statute does not give him some other basis for asserting an exemption in the land. The question states that both judgment liens were properly recorded. Irrespective of when the judgment was obtained, a judgment lien becomes effective only upon docketing. It does not backdate to the time of judgment.

Had Homer owned real property in the county when the judgments were docketed, each would have attached to the property upon docketing. Because the first-in-time rule governs priority, Lienardo's lien, effective on January 25, would have had priority over Lienora's lien, which became effective on January 30. However, this property was only acquired by Homer on February 28. As explained in section 2.4.3, both liens automatically attached to the after-acquired property on February 28.

In some states, preexisting judgment liens are treated as effective on attachment to the after-acquired property. Even though they were docketed at different times, they attach simultaneously and rank equally. In other states, judgment liens or after-acquired property backdate to the time of docketing. Under such a rule, Lienardo's lien has priority.

4. Lienardo's judgment lien took effect before the property was sold to Emptor. Even if Emptor bought in good faith and without actual knowledge of the lien, the valid filing gave him constructive notice of the lien. The first-in-time rule applies and Emptor cannot acquire the property free of Lienardo's lien. (In some situations, the first-in-time rule is varied to protect a bona fide purchaser. However, Emptor's constructive notice disqualifies him from that status.)

5. Penny has a number of alternative means of trying to resolve her debt problems. She could select state law remedies such as those discussed in this chapter, or she could choose one of the forms of relief provided by the Bankruptcy Code. The advantages and drawbacks of bankruptcy will be discussed later. For the present, merely note that it is one of her options. Much more information is needed about Penny's affairs for a judgment to be made on her most appropriate course of action. The present facts do allow the following tentative observations to be made.

   First, an ABC will not fit Penny's needs. It requires the assignment and liquidation of all her executable property. Because she needs this property for her livelihood, an ABC defeats the purpose for which she seeks to approach creditors.

   Second, a composition may be possible provided that Penny's creditors are amenable to it and her financial affairs are such that she can make a proposal that will satisfy them. By negotiating a composition she will be able to avoid the loss of her business and will be able to settle her debts by proportional payment over time without the need for the expense and trauma of a bankruptcy case.

   Creditors of a business are often suppliers or others who have a stake in the survival of the business, so they may be amenable to a workout. However, Penny's creditors are not creditors of the business, so they may have less incentive to preserve it, especially if Penny's business assets are valuable enough to cover all her debts. However, creditors may be persuaded that acceptance of her offer is more advantageous than an uncertain race for her assets provided that Penny is insolvent and she proposes a reasonable plan of payment from future income. The percentage of payment on claims and the period of payment must be realistic and attractive in light of the creditors' prospects of immediate satisfaction. As noted before, the cooperation of creditors is essential to an effective composition.

Finally, Penny will have to consider filing a bankruptcy petition if significant creditors are hostile to the idea of a composition. Unlike a composition, bankruptcy compels creditors into a collective proceeding. The choice of bankruptcy relief is discussed further in Chapter 5.

6. Abie can transfer to the assignee only those rights that he himself has in the property. The truck therefore passes to the assignee subject to the security interest, which was properly perfected prior to the effective date of the assignment.[26] The secured party can assert its right to the collateral notwithstanding the assignment.

   The assignment of the collateral is likely to constitute a default under the security agreement, even if Abie is not behind in his payments on the truck. This entitles the secured party to foreclose on the truck. It may either recover the truck from the assignee or it may allow the assignee to sell the truck and to pay its secured claim as a priority charge on the proceeds. The assignee is entitled to any surplus that remains after the secured claim has been satisfied.

26. An assignee for the benefit of creditors is included in the definition of "lien creditor" in UCC 9-102(52). Under UCC 9-317(a)(2), a lien creditor takes priority over a secured party who has not perfected its security interest at the effective date of the assignment, but is junior to a secured party who has perfected by that date.

CHAPTER 3

The Nature, Source, and Policies of Bankruptcy Law

§3.1 WHAT IS BANKRUPTCY?

When a debtor becomes bankrupt, the debt collection procedures that are otherwise applicable in the jurisdiction are replaced by a powerful and wide-ranging system of laws and procedures. Bankruptcy has a profound impact on the debtor, creditors, and most other parties that have an interest in the debtor's affairs.

Bankruptcy takes different forms and is flexible enough to provide different goals. It is therefore difficult to devise a general definition of bankruptcy that is both precise and meaningful. However, one can begin to define bankruptcy by identifying some of the distinctive characteristics (expanded upon in the rest of this chapter) that make it so different from collection remedies under state law:

1. Bankruptcy is a remedial system provided for by federal law — more specifically, by Title 11 of the U.S. Code. (From now on, Title 11 is referred to as "the Code." When a Code section is cited, only the section symbol and number are used.)
2. It is a collective proceeding that draws in all the debtor's creditors and, with a few exceptions, encompasses all of the debtor's assets.
3. It is designed to fulfill two functions that are often in tension with each other: It affords relief to the debtor by resolving and settling current debts while at the same time protecting creditors and

guarding their interests. As part of this function, it is aimed at preserving and maximizing the value of the debtor's estate.

4. It is administered by a "system" consisting of specialized courts, government officials, and private persons.

§3.2 THE FEDERAL NATURE OF BANKRUPTCY LAW

§3.2.1 The Federal Power over Bankruptcy

Outside of bankruptcy, the creation, performance, and enforcement of obligations are governed by state law, or in the case of some obligations, by generally applicable federal nonbankruptcy law.[1] (For example, an obligation arising out of contract or tort is enforced in a state court under state law, while an obligation, say, to pay federal tax is enforced in a federal court under the Internal Revenue Code.). However, as soon as bankruptcy relief is sought, federal bankruptcy law is brought into effect. A new regime is established over the debtor's affairs that largely displaces the enforcement mechanisms that would normally be used outside of bankruptcy.

Bankruptcy law is federal because the Constitution grants to Congress the power "[t]o establish . . . uniform laws on the subject of bankruptcies throughout the United States." Art. I, §8. In addition, the supremacy clause states that the laws of the United States made pursuant to the Constitution shall be the supreme law of the land and take precedence over state laws. Art. VI, cl. 2.

Although the records of the Constitutional Convention say very little about the bankruptcy power, contemporaneous writings indicate that a centralized bankruptcy law was regarded as one of the economic reforms essential to a viable union. The frustrating diversity of the debtor/creditor laws of the Confederated States was a barrier to interstate commerce. By establishing a uniform bankruptcy law, the drafters hoped to promote commercial order and efficiency and to lessen the disruptive influence of local interests and rivalries. The need for uniformity and the nationwide enforcement of the bankruptcy remedy remain an important justification of federal bankruptcy power.

1. The term "nonbankruptcy law" is explained in section 3.2.2.

§3.2.2 Bankruptcy Law and Nonbankruptcy Law

The Code uses the rather inelegant term "nonbankruptcy law" to describe the generally prevailing law, both state and federal, that would be applicable to the debtor's property, rights, obligations, and transactions in the absence of bankruptcy. "Nonbankruptcy law" is therefore not a synonym for state law because it also includes federal law other than the Code. However, because state law governs most property, rights, obligations, and transactions that will be handled in the bankruptcy case, it is the predominant component of nonbankruptcy law.

In the absence of bankruptcy, nonbankruptcy law is the only law applicable to the debtor/creditor relationship. When bankruptcy occurs, bankruptcy law interacts with this body of prevailing nonbankruptcy law in a complex and multifaceted way. Under the Supremacy Clause, bankruptcy law preempts state law[2] to the extent that they are inconsistent. However, because bankruptcy law is primarily focused on the treatment of rights that arise under state law, the field of federal preemption is quite narrow: It relates to the way in which rights are handled and enforced, and is not usually concerned with their creation and validity. These questions are generally still resolved under state law, even in the context of bankruptcy. You will therefore see that many matters in a bankruptcy case are resolved by a complex interaction between bankruptcy and nonbankruptcy law. In the discussion of bankruptcy in the following chapters, there will be many examples of the interaction between nonbankruptcy and bankruptcy law. For the present, simply note that bankruptcy brings into effect a whole legal structure that may alter or affirm rights and procedures provided by the underlying network of state common and statute law and federal law. The extent to which nonbankruptcy law is overridden is usually expressed in the particular provisions of the Code. Sometimes, where congressional intent is less clear, questions of statutory interpretation may be presented.

§3.3 UNIFORMITY IN BANKRUPTCY LAW

As stated in section 3.2.1, national uniformity in bankruptcy law is mandated by the Constitution. However, this does not mean that the exact same body of law applies to every bankruptcy case across the nation. The reason for this, as stated above, is that rights in bankruptcy are frequently

2. In addition to preempting inconsistent state law, bankruptcy law may alter the effect of otherwise applicable federal nonbankruptcy law. This is not a matter of preemption. Rather, when provisions of bankruptcy law cannot be reconciled with other federal statutes, the court must interpret congressional intent to decide which is to prevail. *See* Example 2.

determined with reference to nonbankruptcy law, which consists predominantly of state law. Diversity in state law inevitably produces a different resolution of many identical issues in bankruptcy cases from state to state. However, over a century ago, the U.S. Supreme court made it clear that absolute and literal uniformity is not required. In *Hanover National Bank v. Moyses*, 186 U.S. 181 (1902), the Court established the fundamental principle governing uniformity: The requirement of uniformity is met when "the trustee takes in each state whatever would have been awardable to the creditors if the bankrupt law had not been passed." Therefore, while a uniform bankruptcy law is required, in the sense that the same rules and principles of bankruptcy law must apply nationwide, the impact of applicable local laws on that uniform bankruptcy law does not render the law nonuniform.

Quite apart from variations in nonbankruptcy law, the requirement of uniformity in bankruptcy law must be understood in light of the structure of the federal court system and the operation of judicial precedent. There are many diverse (and sometimes dramatically diverse) judicial interpretations of provisions of the Code. Because the decisions of bankruptcy and district courts do not create binding precedent, and because the courts of one circuit are not bound by decisions in another, it is common to find that sections of the Code are interpreted differently by different courts. The U.S. Supreme Court occasionally resolves divergent interpretations of bankruptcy law, but there are always numerous areas in which there is disagreement on bankruptcy law among the courts of different circuits.

§3.4 THE STATUTORY SOURCE OF BANKRUPTCY LAW

§3.4.1 Federal Bankruptcy Legislation

The current code, 11 U.S.C. §§101 *et seq.*, was enacted as the Bankruptcy Reform Act in 1978, and has been amended several times since then, as detailed below. It is the fifth bankruptcy statute enacted by Congress. The first three were passed at various times in the nineteenth century, but none of them lasted very long, and for much of that century there was no federal bankruptcy law, leaving debtor/creditor relations to be governed only by state law. In 1898, Congress passed the Bankruptcy Act, which turned out to be the first durable bankruptcy statute. It lasted, with much amendment and judicial embellishments, until it was replaced in 1978 by the current Code. By the end of the 1960s, it had become clear that the old Act was outdated and had been patched up too much by amendments, judicial decisions, and procedural rules promulgated by the courts. Congress therefore appointed a commission in 1970 to study the bankruptcy law and to recommend a new comprehensive statute. The commission's report and proposed statute, released in 1973, drew on the traditions established under the old Act, and preserved many of its rules and principles. However, it also made many significant changes to substantive law and procedure. The report was controversial, leading to much debate and the passage of different bills in each house of Congress. Ultimately, differences were resolved in compromise, and the 1978 Code was enacted. Some of the compromises were uneasy, and never finally settled the differences that underlay them. As a result, some of these questions continue to generate debate and calls for reform.

Since its enactment in 1978, the Code has been amended several times. In addition to occasional piecemeal changes to individual sections, it has been subjected to four wide-ranging amending statutes. The first, passed in 1984, was principally concerned with trying to overcome constitutional problems relating to bankruptcy court jurisdiction. (*See* section 4.2.1 for an overview of these constitutional problems.) The second, passed in 1986, made a number of small amendments, introduced a new form of debt adjustment for family farmers, and established a nationwide U.S. Trustee system.

The third, the Bankruptcy Reform Act of 1994, began its progress through Congress in 1992. It originated as a fairly comprehensive and extensive revision of the Code, but it was pared down to a less ambitious undertaking when it became apparent that its more controversial aspects would not pass. A compromise bill, with the controversial elements abandoned, was enacted in 1994 to deal with a variety of discrete problems that had arisen in the application and interpretation of the Code. These various changes affect both consumer and business bankruptcies, and they are noted in later chapters where pertinent to the topic under discussion.

The more complex and contentious issues were left for further consideration by a National Bankruptcy Review Commission established under the 1994 Act, whose charge was to evaluate and propose reforms to the Code. After extensive hearings and study, the Commission submitted its report in 1997. In some areas, the commissioners made unanimous recommendations for reform, but they disagreed on others, on which they submitted a majority and dissenting report. The most explosive issue that divided the commissioners was whether the bankruptcy system was too lenient on individual debtors. Some commissioners felt that it was, and that the Code should impose more rigorous payment requirements on individual debtors. Others concluded that the bankruptcy of most individual debtors resulted from economic factors beyond their control, such as job loss, the lack of medical insurance, and an inadequate social safety net. They therefore felt that more rigorous standards would simply increase the hardship of debtors without addressing the root problem of a high rate of individual bankruptcies.

The report engendered fierce reaction from the public and in Congress, and formed the backdrop to the fourth significant amendment to the Code, the Bankruptcy Abuse Prevention and Consumer Protection Act of 2005 (BAPCPA). Congress was very selective in picking which of the Commission's recommendations to adopt. It disregarded some of them and even passed some provisions that conflicted with what was recommended. Because some aspects of the statute were so controversial, it took Congress several attempts between 1998 and 2005 to pass it. The various amendments to the Code enacted in BAPCPA are discussed in the appropriate places throughout this book. For now it is enough to make two general observations about BAPCPA. First, it adopted a more rigorous approach to individual debtors, imposing tougher demands on debtors who are deemed to be capable of making greater payments to creditors in a bankruptcy case. Second, many provisions of BAPCPA were poorly drafted, leading to interpretational puzzles and divergent judicial resolutions of unclear language.

§3.4.2 The Structure and Organization of the Code and Ancillary Statutes

It is useful to take note of the structure of the Code and other laws pertaining to bankruptcy. An understanding of this structure can help you to find Code provisions and to recognize the scope of their application.

a. The Code Itself

In its current form (which has been somewhat changed since its original enactment in 1978) the Code consists of nine chapters: 1, 3, 5, 7, 9, 11, 12, 13, and 15. This book does not cover Ch. 9, which governs municipal bankruptcies; Ch. 12, which is available only to debtors who qualify as family farmers or family fishermen; or Ch. 15, which was enacted by BAPCPA to deal with cross-border (international) insolvency cases. The remaining six chapters fall into two broad categories. The first three (Chs. 1, 3, and 5) contain general provisions that are meant to apply to all bankruptcy cases under consideration unless they are irrelevant on the facts or some overriding provision in the specific governing chapter applies instead. The second three (Chs. 7, 11, and 13) are each devoted to a separate and different form of bankruptcy. When a bankruptcy petition is filed, one of these chapters must be selected, and the specific provisions of that chapter will govern the case, together with general Chs. 1, 3, and 5. The provisions of the other specific chapters are not of force unless they are expressly incorporated by the governing chapter. It is important to remember this because the temptation to generalize some of the sections in a specific chapter can be strong.

The three different types of bankruptcy covered by Chs. 7, 11, and 13 are explained more fully in Chapter 5. In short, Ch. 7 covers liquidation and may be used by both individuals and corporate entities where the goal is to liquidate the estate — that is, to realize its assets and distribute the proceeds to creditors. Chs. 11 and 13 allow a debtor to avoid liquidation by means of a plan of reorganization, under which the debtor devotes income or property to fund a distribution to creditors over time. Ch. 13 is the simpler of the two forms, and is confined to individual debtors with relatively small levels of debt. Ch. 11 is more complex and is more broadly applicable to both individual debtors and to corporate entities.

b. Other Statutes Related to Bankruptcy Cases

There are a number of federal statutes, in addition to the Code, that have a direct bearing[3] on bankruptcy. Title 28 of the U.S. Code has a number of important provisions relating to the bankruptcy system: Ch. 6 (§§151-158) deals with the appointment, duties, and functions of bankruptcy judges; Ch. 39 (§§581-589a) provides for the U.S. Trustee system; Ch. 85 (§1334) governs bankruptcy jurisdiction; and Ch. 87 (§§1408-1412) deals with matters of venue. These provisions of title 28 are covered in Chapters 4 and 6. Title 18 (not discussed further in this book) also has direct relevance to bankruptcy: 18 U.S.C. §§151-155 deals with crimes of dishonesty and embezzlement committed during the course of a bankruptcy case.

§3.4.3 Dollar Amounts in the Code

Many sections of the Code specify dollar amounts for a variety of different purposes, such as setting the debt limits for certain forms of relief, limiting the debtor's exemptions in property, limiting the amount of a qualifying claim that may be accorded priority status, or determining if a debtor's income is sufficient to support a payment plan. Until 1994, the Code had no mechanism for the adjustment of these dollar amounts for inflation, so they shrank in value as the years passed. The Bankruptcy Reform Act of 1994 brought the amounts up to date by increasing the dollar amounts to account for inflation over the preceding 16 years and provided for the administrative

3. These statutes must be distinguished from federal statutes, described in section 3.2.2, which are part of the nonbankruptcy law that is pertinent to transactions, rights, or obligations involved in the case. The statutes noted here deal directly with the operation of the bankruptcy system.

adjustment of dollar amounts every three years thereafter. The adjustments, based on changes in the Consumer Price Index, are made by the Judicial Conference of the United States at three-year intervals and apply to cases filed after the effective date of the adjustment, which is April 1.

The most recent adjustment took effect on April 1, 2016, and the next will be made on April 1, 2019. Because the 2016 dollar amounts are in effect at the time of writing this edition of the book, they are used in this edition. Note, however, that the adjusted dollar amounts apply only to cases commenced after their effective date. Therefore, a case commenced before April 1, 2016 or after April 1, 2019 will be subject to the dollar amounts in effect at that time. Although it is necessary to know the applicable amount in an actual bankruptcy case, for purposes of studying and understanding the law, you can simply rely on the amounts stated in this book and should not be confused if you see different amounts reflected in cases or in the version of the Code that you are using.

§3.4.4 The Bankruptcy Rules

The Code deals with the substantive law of bankruptcy. While it prescribes procedures in broad terms, it does not set out rules of procedure in detailed form. These rules have been promulgated by the Supreme Court in the exercise of its power under 28 U.S.C. §2075. They are intended to effectuate the provisions of the Code and are meant to supplement rather than contradict it. The rules may not alter substantive rights under the Code, and in the case of conflict the Code prevails. The Bankruptcy Rules incorporate some of the Federal Rules of Civil Procedure. Those that are not specifically included in the Bankruptcy Rules supplement them to the extent that they do not provide for a contrary procedure. In addition to the nationwide rules promulgated by the Supreme Court, each district court is empowered by Bankruptcy Rule 9029 to make its own local rules, provided that they are not inconsistent with the Bankruptcy Rules. This book does not focus on the Bankruptcy Rules, but does cite and mention them occasionally.

§3.5 THE POLICIES AND GOALS OF BANKRUPTCY LAW

§3.5.1 Introduction

The policies and goals of bankruptcy law are raised frequently in the discussion of the substantive rules and principles of bankruptcy law in the rest of this book. It is important to identify and understand the reasons for the substantive rules and the ends that they are intended to achieve. This section alerts you to the fundamental goals that underlie bankruptcy law. It is just an overview of the themes that will recur in the remainder of the book. As you read through this overview of bankruptcy policy, bear in mind:

1. Bankruptcy relief is usually sought only after the debtor's economic difficulties have become serious enough to merit the drastic step of a bankruptcy filing. Therefore, the principal goal of bankruptcy is to manage financial distress and to do the best job possible of preserving what can be saved for the benefit of the debtor, creditors, and others whose interests are impacted by the debtor's financial circumstances.
2. Bankruptcy law is sensitive to the rights that creditors and other parties have under nonbankruptcy law. Although bankruptcy will have an adverse effect on many of these rights, the goal is to affect them only to the extent necessary to further the aims of the Code.
3. Bankruptcy policy cannot be considered in a vacuum. There are many other public policies, reflected in other state and federal laws, which may be implicated in a bankruptcy case. Where other public policies have to be taken into account, these policies may not be congruent with policies of bankruptcy law, so it may be necessary to reconcile or prioritize countervailing policy goals. For example, the bankruptcy goal of providing relief to the debtor from prepetition obligations may not be in accord with the policies and the goals of criminal law, tort law, environmental law, or family law, which may be obstructed by releasing the debtor from those obligations. Sometimes the Code itself indicates how bankruptcy policy should be accommodated to other public policies, but in other cases courts are left with the task of deciding how to accommodate bankruptcy policy to other public interests.

§3.5.2 The Fundamental Goals and Policies of Bankruptcy

a. The Protection of Both Debtor and Creditor Interests

In its original conception, bankruptcy was purely a creditor's remedy. It allowed creditors to place a delinquent debtor in bankruptcy for the purpose of liquidating his assets for the payment of his debts. To the extent that the bankruptcy distribution was not enough to pay the debts in full, the debtor could be imprisoned until friends or family could raise the money to settle what he owed. As the law developed, it gradually became more sympathetic to the protection of an honest debtor who suffered financial adversity and could not pay his creditors in full. In modern law, it is well established that bankruptcy serves not only the interests of creditors, but also aims at providing relief from overwhelming debt to an honest debtor. It helps creditors by providing an evenhanded and controlled environment for the settlement of the debtor's affairs and the distribution of available assets. It helps the debtor by providing relief from the pressures of financial failure and making available the means of settling otherwise unmanageable debt.

Of course, the interests of the creditors and the debtor are often in conflict, so one of the difficult tasks of bankruptcy law is to strike an appropriate balance between them. The best way to balance these competing interests is subject to ongoing debate. Some commentators emphasize creditor protection and advocate for bankruptcy laws that will maximize creditor returns. Others take a broader view of the social costs and consequences of bankruptcy, and argue for rules that will best protect vulnerable debtors and place the least amount of stress on the social fabric. You will find the tension between these goals at the base of many discussions in later chapters of this book.

b. The Collective and Evenhanded Treatment of Creditors

The mandatory collective nature of the bankruptcy remedy is often identified as one of its most important hallmarks. Upon the filing of a bankruptcy petition, creditors are stayed from pursuing individual debt collection efforts and, whether they like it or not, are compelled to have their claims handled in the bankruptcy case. The debtor's assets at the time of the petition are placed under the control of the bankruptcy court and cannot be disposed of except in accordance with bankruptcy law. It is a fundamental principle of bankruptcy that creditors must be treated evenhandedly so that claims of equal legal rank must be treated the same. This does not mean that all creditors are paid the same. Secured claims are entitled to payment to the extent of their security interests, and the Code gives certain unsecured claims priority. However, differentiation between creditors is based on the strength of their legal rights, rather than on their speed in initiating collection procedures.

c. The Preservation of the Estate

One of the crucial goals of bankruptcy is the preservation of the debtor's assets. This both protects the debtor from creditor collection activity and protects creditors by preserving property so that it can ultimately be made available for distribution to pay their claims. Estate preservation is not simply a passive handover of the debtor's existing property. The Code provides several means by which the bankruptcy trustee can enhance the value of the estate, for example, by recovering dispositions, challenging claims to property, and dealing with unperformed contracts. In addition to protecting the debtor and creditors, the preservation of the estate of a business debtor can achieve wider social goals where the aim of bankruptcy is the debtor's rehabilitation. Successful rehabilitation can benefit employees of the debtor, the community in which the business operates, and customers or suppliers reliant on the business.

d. The Debtor's "Fresh Start"

Provided that the debtor has complied with the Code's requirements and has surrendered executable assets or sufficient property and future income for distribution to creditors, the debtor is entitled to a new financial beginning, unburdened by the unpaid balance of prebankruptcy debts. This is commonly referred to as the debtor's "fresh start," and it is a firmly established goal of modern bankruptcy law. There are several Code provisions that aim at the debtor's fresh start: for example, the individual debtor's exemptions, the limitations on property to be included in the estate, and the discharge. Of these, the discharge is the most central. It releases the debtor from the balance of prepetition debts that were not fully paid in the case. The fresh start has an obvious and important benefit to the debtor, but it is also intended to benefit society as a whole by giving the debtor the opportunity of becoming self-sufficient and productive. Of course, the discharge comes at the expense of creditors, who lose the unpaid balance of their claims. Therefore, the Code seeks to balance the debtor's fresh start against the protection of creditor rights, and has a number of provisions that allow courts to restrict or refuse the discharge where the debtor has engaged in dishonest, improper, or abusive conduct.

e. Efficient Administration

The Code and related statutes create a system to handle bankruptcy cases, so it is worth adding efficient administration to the goals of bankruptcy law, none of which could be properly achieved if the system for administering the law is inadequate. Many provisions of the Code and related statutes deal with the structure and operation of the bankruptcy system, the efficient implementation of the law, and the prevention of abuse. The question of whether current statutory provisions succeed in making the system as efficient as it could be is the subject of ongoing debate.

f. The Preference for Reorganization and Debt Adjustment

As introduced in section 3.4.2 and explained more fully in section 5.2, the Code provides for two forms of bankruptcy — liquidation and rehabilitation. In essence, in a liquidation (provided for in Ch. 7), all the debtor's prepetition property is taken over by the bankruptcy trustee who realizes it and uses the proceeds to pay creditors. Where the proceeds are insufficient to pay creditors in full, they receive payment only to the extent of available proceeds. Where the debtor is an individual, the balance of the debts is discharged provided that the debtor is in compliance with the requirements of the Code. In a rehabilitation case (provided for in Chs. 11 and 13),[4] the debtor is able to retain prepetition property and formulates a plan that provides for the settlement of debts from income and other sources over a period of time. As a general principle, the expectation in these chapters is that payments to creditors under the plan must at least equal but should ideally exceed what creditors would obtain in a liquidation. The Code has a preference for rehabilitation over liquidation. It could be argued that this is not really a goal in itself, but rather a mechanism through which bankruptcy may achieve its fundamental goals of creditor protection and the debtor's fresh start. Nevertheless, the Code's emphasis on rehabilitation as the preferred form of bankruptcy is strong, and therefore worth including in this overview of bankruptcy policies.

The benefits of rehabilitating a corporation are easy to see. If the corporation is liquidated, it dies. Its business comes to an end, its owners (shareholders) lose their investment, its employees lose their jobs, and its creditors recover no more than the liquidation value of its assets. Therefore, if it is possible to reorganize the corporation so that it emerges from bankruptcy as a viable business, creditors have a prospect of greater recovery and the enterprise can continue to provide jobs and to participate in the marketplace. (This does not mean that the corporation's employees and owners emerge unscathed. Reorganization often results in a reduction in the corporation's workforce and in employee benefits. Also, reorganization may wipe out the equity of prepetition shareholders and pass ownership to creditors or new investors.)

Where the debtor is an individual, liquidation under Ch. 7 is the debtor's only choice where he does not have enough income to support a payment plan that will give creditors at least as much as they would have gained from the liquidation. However, where a debtor does expect a good future income and has executable property of relatively low value, liquidation may be an attractive option to the debtor but a bad deal for creditors. By sacrificing his prepetition property to creditors, the debtor settles his debt at a fraction of its amount, obtains a discharge of the balance, and can keep his future income for himself. Although this promotes the fresh start policy, it has been a concern ever since the enactment of the Code in 1978 that liquidation can provide an easy way out for a debtor who has the financial ability to pay a greater percentage of his debts through rehabilitation under

4. As noted in section 3.4.2, Chs. 9 (municipal bankruptcy) and 12 (family farmer bankruptcy) also provide for rehabilitation, but those chapters are not covered in this book.

Ch. 13 or Ch. 11. Prior to the passage of BAPCPA, the Code provided some incentives to encourage an individual debtor to pursue rehabilitation rather than liquidation. However, the incentives were quite weak, which led to the argument that a firmer approach was needed to press individual debtors into making a greater effort to commit to a payment plan. Congress was persuaded by this argument, and it did include provisions in BAPCPA that make it more difficult for an individual debtor to seek liquidation bankruptcy under Ch. 7 where he has the apparent means to support a payment plan that would result in a greater return to creditors. Some believe that the BAPCPA amendments have achieved a better balance between debtor and creditor interests. Others criticize the amendments as creating undue complexity, causing hardship to many debtors, and hampering courts in the use of discretion to achieve fair and workable results in bankruptcy cases. (This is discussed in sections 5.4.3, 5.5, 5.7.2, and 6.8.)

Examples

EXAMPLES

1. Debtor sold a house to Buyer some years before Debtor filed a Ch. 7 petition. Although Buyer paid the full price of the house to Debtor, the parties never got around to executing and filing the documents that would transfer title to Buyer. Section 541(a) includes in property of the estate "all legal or equitable interests of the debtor in property as of the commencement of the case." Although the section does not state so expressly, it is well established that the question of whether a debtor has a legal or equitable interest in property must be determined under nonbankruptcy law.[5] Under the law of the state in which Debtor is domiciled, he is still owner of record and therefore continues to have a legal interest in the property. However, in the law of some other states, the sale of the house to a buyer and full payment of the price would extinguish the seller's rights in the property, so he would not be treated as having a legal interest in the house, despite the fact that the title is still registered in his name. The effect of this is that in Debtor's state, the house will be property of the estate, but in other states it would not be. Can an argument be made that different treatment of a debtor's interest in the house, dependent merely on the debtor's state of domicile, offends the constitutional requirement that Congress enacts a uniform law of bankruptcy?

2. A (hypothetical) federal statute enacted in 1975 provides for the issuance of a trading license to enable the license holder to import certain types of goods. The statute clearly states that the bankruptcy of the license holder

5. The issue of deciding what property of the debtor becomes property of the estate is discussed in sections 9.2 to 9.4.

results in automatic revocation of the license. As discussed more fully in Chapter 9, upon the filing of a bankruptcy petition, all the legal and equitable interests that a debtor holds as at the petition date become property of the bankruptcy estate under §541. The more inclusive the bankruptcy estate, the better creditors will fare in recovering their claims from the estate, so the policy of maximizing creditor returns is strongly implicated in ensuring that the estate does receive all the debtor's property. For this reason, §541(c) invalidates any provision in an agreement or applicable nonbankruptcy law that restricts the transfer of the debtor's property to the estate or that effects a forfeiture of it on bankruptcy. Does §541 preempt the provisions of the 1975 federal statute?

3. In college, Bratford Binge was described as a boy wonder. He was the youngest summa cum laude to graduate from a prestigious business school. As a result, he had no trouble landing a glorious job at an impressive salary. Although immensely talented at his work, Bratford was spoiled, and he denied himself nothing. As a result, he accumulated massive credit card debt by taking expensive vacations and eating at the finest restaurants. He now owes so much debt that, even on his generous salary, he cannot cope with the payments due his creditors. Because his expenditures are related to travel and entertainment, he has not acquired assets of any value. Bratford would like to eliminate this crushing debt and start over. Should he be able to file a bankruptcy petition so that he can enjoy the advantages of the Code's fresh start policy?

4. Precious Little, Inc. has filed a petition for liquidation under Ch. 7. It is badly insolvent. Its debts amount to $750,000 and the total value of its assets is $20,000. Its business has declined badly in the last couple of years, and its revenue is insufficient to cover its operating expenses. How does this significant disproportion between its assets and liabilities and its inadequate revenue affect the achievement of the goals of bankruptcy law in this case?

Explanations

1. As explained in section 3.3, this issue has been long settled. The constitutional requirement of uniformity means that the provisions of bankruptcy law enacted by Congress must apply nationwide. Congress cannot enact provisions that apply only to select states. Uniformity does not require that the rules in the Code apply with the same effect in each state. Section 541(a) does apply throughout the United States even though its interaction with the law of particular states may lead to different results. Section 541(a) is one of many provisions that require

recourse to nonbankruptcy law for the determination of rights that will be impacted by the bankruptcy case. This should not be surprising because it is one of the goals of bankruptcy law to try to mesh as closely as possible with rights held by parties under nonbankruptcy law.

2. Although federal bankruptcy law preempts conflicting state law, it is not appropriate to talk of preemption where the conflicting nonbankruptcy law is federal. Rather, the contradictory statutes must be reconciled by the process of statutory interpretation. The court must decide which provision was intended by Congress to be controlling. Congressional intent is clearest where one of the statutes expressly states that it overrides the other. In the absence of such a clear indication, a court will have to glean legislative intent by interpretation of the language of the statute, any legislative history, and enunciated or apparent policy goals. One of the canons of interpretation that may help in close cases is that Congress is supposed to remember what its earlier legislation said, so that a provision in a later statute is assumed to take precedence over an earlier conflicting statute. On the basis of this rule, the argument could be made that the Code, enacted three years after the other statute, was intended to override it. It must be stressed, however, that this canon of interpretation is just one factor to be considered, and it is not appropriately used where there are more reliable indications of congressional intent.

3. Bratford is a reckless spendthrift. He used credit irresponsibly and now wishes to discharge that debt and get a fresh start. Bankruptcy relief is intended to help the honest debtor who has encountered financial difficulty. A debtor whose financial troubles were caused by circumstances beyond his control, such as the loss of his job, unmanageable uninsured medical expenses, or the failure of his business, is a more sympathetic figure than a debtor who brought his problems upon himself by the irresponsible use of credit. Nevertheless, unless it can be shown that Bratford acted fraudulently or in bad faith in incurring the debt or in relation to the bankruptcy filing, his self-indulgent behavior is not likely to be grounds for refusing him bankruptcy relief. However, Bratford will be disappointed if he hopes to file a petition under Ch. 7 so that he can discharge most of his debt by sacrificing his few nonexempt assets. As explained in section 3.5.2 and discussed more fully in section 6.8, amendments to the Code by BAPCPA preclude Ch. 7 liquidation to an individual debtor like Bratford, who has a significant income, few assets, and owes primarily consumer debts. If Bratford seeks bankruptcy relief he will have to propose a plan under Ch. 11 or Ch. 13. To get the plan confirmed, he will have to commit his disposable income (his salary less his expenses as calculated under the Code) over some years to the payment of his debts. This is discussed in detail in Chapters 6 and 18. For now, this broad description of the obligation of higher payment,

imposed on an individual consumer debtor with a good income, is used merely to highlight the balance between the policies of debtor relief and creditor protection.

4. The goals and policies of bankruptcy law can only be fully satisfied where the estate is at least large enough to achieve all its purposes. Financial resources are needed to rehabilitate a business, and where, as here, the debtor has insufficient assets and no source of adequate future income, the Code's policy of providing a fresh start to the corporation and favoring its rehabilitation cannot be achieved. Where there is no means of funding a rehabilitation, it is simply not an option. This leaves the alternative of liquidation, but even here the paucity of assets means that the bankruptcy cannot fully satisfy all its desired ends. It can ensure that creditors are treated evenhandedly (so that the race for remaining assets can be stopped and any preferential payments made shortly before the filing can be recovered for the benefit of the estate as a whole), but the small pool of assets is likely to be expended fully or in substantial part on the costs of liquidating the bankrupt estate. This means that unsecured creditors will either receive no distribution at all or will receive a minimal payment on their claims.

   It is one of the sad realities of bankruptcy that many estates are just too poor to afford any significant distribution to unsecured creditors. The costs of administering an estate are paid as high priority before general unsecured creditors can receive anything, and these costs can be large. They include not only the trustee's compensation, but also any fees that must be paid to professionals (such as attorneys or accountants) engaged by the estate, and the costs of caring for and disposing of the estate's property. It does not take much to eat up a small estate, leaving it devoid of assets for funding a distribution. Of course, the policy of efficient and cost-effective administration dictates that the trustee's management of the estate should not be disproportionately expensive or wasteful, and the trustee has a duty to try to keep costs down as much as possible.

CHAPTER 4

The Bankruptcy Court, Officials, and Parties

§4.1 OVERVIEW

This chapter introduces and explains the role and duties of the many entities and persons who participate in a bankruptcy case.

Section 4.2 introduces the bankruptcy court, presided over by the bankruptcy judge. This is the central forum in which the bankruptcy case proceeds. The section outlines the jurisdiction and status of the bankruptcy court, which is established as a unit of the federal district court, through which it derives its jurisdiction under 28 U.S.C. §§1334 and 157.

Section 4.3 introduces and explains the role, duties, and compensation of the bankruptcy trustee, who administers the estate. The principal provisions governing the appointment and duties of the trustee in Chs. 7, 11, and 13 cases are §§701, 1104, and 1302 respectively, and the trustee's compensation is provided for in §§326 and 330. The section explains that in Ch. 11 cases, a trustee is not normally appointed and the functions of the trustee are commonly exercised by the debtor as a debtor in possession.

Section 4.4 explains the function of the U.S Trustee, a public official with wide responsibilities to oversee bankruptcy cases, whose powers and duties are provided for in 11 U.S.C. §§581-589a.

Section 4.5 identifies the debtor and explains the debtor's role in different forms of bankruptcy. Section 4.6 does the same with creditors of the estate. Section 4.7 discusses the role of attorneys and other professionals in a bankruptcy case. The appointment, duties, and compensation of attorneys and other professionals employed by the estate are governed by

§§327 to 330 and 503. Section 4.8 explains the Code's regulation of debt relief agencies, governed by §§526 to 528. Debt relief agencies include attorneys who provide bankruptcy assistance to the class of debtors protected by these sections. Section 4.9 briefly identifies other parties who may have an interest in bankruptcy cases.

§4.2 THE BANKRUPTCY COURT

§4.2.1 The Jurisdiction of the Bankruptcy Court

Section 3.2.1 explained that bankruptcy law is federal because the Constitution confers on Congress the power to establish uniform laws on bankruptcy. It follows that bankruptcy matters fall within the realm of the federal courts. Bankruptcy cases are handled by specialized bankruptcy courts. However, Congress has not conferred jurisdiction over bankruptcy cases directly on bankruptcy courts. Instead, 28 U.S.C. §1334 confers jurisdiction over bankruptcy on federal district courts. This jurisdiction covers not only the actual bankruptcy case itself, but also all matters that arise in or are related to the case. This means, in effect, that once bankruptcy is filed, all issues relating to the debtor's financial affairs fall within the jurisdiction of the federal courts. Under 28 U.S.C. §151, district courts then refer bankruptcy cases to bankruptcy courts, which are described as "units" of the district courts. The reason for this is that unlike district court judges, who are appointed with life tenure and protection from salary reduction under Article III of the Constitution, bankruptcy judges are appointed under Article 1 for fixed terms. The Constitution does not permit Congress to confer full jurisdictional power on Article I judges, so §§1334 and 157 grant this power to district courts, which then pass on to bankruptcy courts those adjudicative functions that may be exercised by them.

As a practical matter, bankruptcy courts, not district courts, are directly and intimately involved with the bankruptcy case from its inception to its final closing and deal, as courts of first instance, with all matters that require judicial supervision, determination, or approval during the course of the case. Where a bankruptcy court does not have the power to make a final disposition of a matter, it must make a recommendation to the district court, which ultimately enters the judgment.

This is not an ideal system. It would have been more efficient and less complicated for bankruptcy judges to be appointed under Article III with the full power to dispose of all matters arising in or related to the bankruptcy case. This was the recommendation made to Congress by the commission appointed at the time of the enactment of the Code in 1978, and again by the commission appointed in relation to the revision of the Code in

1994.[1] However, Congress did not follow this recommendation because of opposition to the creation of a new class of Article III judges.

A detailed discussion of the complexities of bankruptcy court jurisdiction is beyond our scope. In short, this is how the system operates.

As noted above, jurisdiction over the bankruptcy case and related matters is conferred on the district court by 28 U.S.C. §1334. The process of referral, the relationship between the district court and its bankruptcy "unit," and the exercise of power by the bankruptcy court is dealt with in 28 U.S.C. §157. Section 157(a) allows each district court to make a blanket referral of all bankruptcy matters to the bankruptcy court. Thus, the district court does not make case-by-case referrals; all bankruptcy litigation commences as a matter of course in the bankruptcy court. Under 28 U.S.C. §157(d), the district court retains ultimate control over all bankruptcy cases and it has the power, in exceptional cases, for good cause, to withdraw a case or portion of a case from the bankruptcy court.

The final disposition of bankruptcy litigation depends on the nature of the rights in issue. In simple terms, the bankruptcy judge's power to make a final judgment under the general referral from the district court extends to the bankruptcy case itself and to "core proceedings" arising in the case. To qualify as a core proceeding, the matter must concern a right that arises out of and owes its existence to the Code itself or is so inextricably linked to the administration of the bankruptcy case that the matter, by its nature, could arise only in a bankruptcy case. It is constitutionally permissible for the Article I bankruptcy judge to decide core matters because Congress itself created the rights adjudicated in these matters. However, the bankruptcy judge may not render a final judgment in matters that are noncore proceedings—matters related to the bankruptcy case but requiring the resolution of nonbankruptcy rights. Congress cannot entrust the disposition

---

1. Prior to the enactment of the Code in 1978, bankruptcy matters were handled by referees who were appointed by district courts. Because referees were not Article III federal judges, their power to dispose of cases was limited, and many issues arising in bankruptcy cases had to be finally decided by the federal district judge. The confusion and inefficiency generated by this system motivated the commission's recommendation to replace referees by Article III bankruptcy judges. Congress declined to do this and instead attempted to handle the jurisdictional problem by legislatively delegating the district court's bankruptcy jurisdiction to bankruptcy courts. In *Northern Pipeline Constr. Co. v. Marathon Pipe Line Co.*, 458 U.S. 50 (1982) the Supreme Court held that the legislative delegation was unconstitutional because Congress violated the separation of powers doctrine and the principle of judicial independence by granting full jurisdiction to Article I judges. Congress could have cured the constitutional flaw by appointing bankruptcy judges under Article III, but it chose instead to adopt the referral process, under which district courts refer bankruptcy matters to bankruptcy courts, which have limited power to dispose of matters. The ongoing complexity resulting from the failure to adopt the commission's recommendation in 1978 led the 1994 National Bankruptcy Review Commission to recommend again that bankruptcy judges be appointed under Article III, but Congress again declined to accept the recommendation, leaving this system in place today.

of these cases to a nontenured judge. Therefore, where a bankruptcy court deals with a related matter, it must submit its findings of fact and conclusion of law to the district court, which must review them de novo and make the final disposition.

As noted above, core proceedings involve rights created by or inextricably linked to the regulatory scheme set up by Congress. A nonexclusive list of core proceedings is set out in 28 U.S.C. §157(b)(2). However, this list is not entirely reliable because the Supreme Court made it clear in *Granfinanciera, S.A. v. Nordberg*, 492 U.S. 33 (1989) and in *Stern v. Marshall*, 561 U.S. 1058 (2011) that Congress cannot make something a core proceeding simply by declaring it to be one. The matter must qualify as a core proceeding under the test described above. In some situations, it is relatively easy to categorize a proceeding as core or noncore. For example, a decision to grant relief from the automatic stay,[2] which is purely an incident of the bankruptcy filing and would not exist outside of bankruptcy, is clearly a core proceeding. However, the resolution of the estate's claim against a party, arising out of an alleged breach of contract entered into between that party and the debtor prior to the bankruptcy, arises from rights under common law. It is not a core proceeding, but is merely related to the case. In other situations, the question of whether a matter is core or noncore is subtle and elusive and has generated much litigation. The mere fact that a matter requires resolution of nonbankruptcy law issues does not mean that it is noncore, because many such matters could be so linked to the administration of the estate that they fall within the core as matters that could arise only in the context of a bankruptcy case.

The bankruptcy court is permitted by 28 U.S.C. §157(c)(2) to make a final judgment in noncore proceedings with the parties' consent. In *Wellness International Network, Ltd. v. Sharif*, 135 S. Ct. 1932 (2015), the Supreme Court held that a bankruptcy court does have jurisdiction to decide a noncore matter if the parties knowingly and voluntarily consent to the bankruptcy court's adjudication of that matter. This consent need not be express, but could be implied provided that the parties, with awareness of the need for consent and the right to refuse it, voluntarily proceeded with the matter before the bankruptcy court.

The limited jurisdiction of the bankruptcy court has also led to other complications, involving such questions as the court's power to conduct jury trials and to penalize contempt of court. Notwithstanding the restriction on their power, bankruptcy courts do deal with most aspects of the bankruptcy case and do make final determinations on a wide range of issues that arise in the case. Even where the court cannot make a final determination of an issue, the findings of fact and conclusions of law by an expert specialist bankruptcy judge are given great weight by the district court.

2. The automatic stay and relief from stay are discussed in Chapters 7 and 8.

§4.2.2 Appeals from the Bankruptcy Court

In noncore proceedings, where the bankruptcy court's determination is merely a proposed finding of fact and conclusion of law, the district court makes the final order or judgment under 28 U.S.C. §157(c)(1). This is not an appeal from the bankruptcy court, of course, but just the district court's determination of the issue, which may or may not follow the bankruptcy court's recommendation. The decision of the district court is subject to appeal to the court of appeals and then to the Supreme Court in the usual way.

As explained in section 4.2.1, the bankruptcy court is empowered to render a decision in a core proceeding. Although the district court does not review this decision as a matter of course, the decision is appealable to the district court under 28 U.S.C. §158 or, if the circuit has established a bankruptcy appellate panel (BAP), to that panel, which substitutes for the district court as the court of first review. Following this initial appeal to the district court or the BAP, the judgment is appealable in the usual way.

Some circuits have exercised the power, conferred on them by 28 U.S.C. §158, to establish a bankruptcy appellate panel consisting of three bankruptcy judges,[3] to substitute for the district court as an appellate tribunal of first instance. The purpose of the BAP is to lift some of the workload from the district courts and to create a specialist appellate panel with great expertise in bankruptcy matters. There are restrictions on the power of a BAP to hear appeals. First, under §158(b)(1) and (c)(1) all the parties to the suit must consent to the submission of the appeal to the BAP. Second, under §158(b)(6) the majority of district judges in the district must have voted to authorize the BAP to hear appeals from that district. While the opinion of a BAP is likely to have strong persuasive weight, it is not clear that the decision binds bankruptcy courts in the circuit.

§4.3 THE TRUSTEE

§4.3.1 Appointment and Qualification, Generally

The trustee is a private person (not a public official) who represents and administers the bankruptcy estate. The trustee's duties vary, depending on the chapter under which the case is filed, as explained below. In broad terms, she is responsible for all aspects of estate administration, she litigates

3. Under §158(b)(5), members of the BAP panel must be from districts other than the district in which the case originated.

on behalf of the estate, processes and makes distributions on claims, controls estate property, investigates the debtor's affairs, and, in general, acts to further the interests of the estate and the collective interests of creditors. A trustee is required in cases under Chs. 7 and 13. A trustee is not usually appointed in a Ch. 11 case, in which the debtor assumes the trustee's functions as a debtor in possession, as explained in section 4.3.5. The Code authorizes the election of a trustee by creditors in cases under Chs. 7 and 11. In other cases, or where creditors do not exercise the right of election in a Ch. 7 or 11 case, the trustee is appointed by the U.S. Trustee (a public official) who is introduced in section 4.4. The trustee is appointed from a panel established by the U.S. Trustee, consisting of qualified persons who have applied to serve.

The Code does not have any detailed provisions relating to the qualifications of a trustee. Section 321 states general requirements of residency and competence. Sections 701, 1104(b), and 1302(a) require the trustee to be a "disinterested person," which is defined in §101(14) to exclude a wide variety of persons such as creditors, owners, insiders, officers, employees, and others whose interests are materially adverse to those of the estate. The Attorney General is required by 28 U.S.C. §586(d) to prescribe more detailed and specific qualifications for membership on the trustee panels. The qualifications so promulgated include honesty, impartiality, professional qualifications (such as a law degree or a CPA), and requirements of general competence and experience.

§4.3.2 The Trustee's Duty to Perform Duties Faithfully and Competently

The trustee has the duty to perform her duties faithfully and competently and is required by §322 to post a bond guaranteeing the proper performance of her duties. The trustee, and hence the issuer of the bond, is liable for any loss caused to an injured party if the trustee violates her fiduciary duty or is grossly negligent in administering the estate. The Code does not specify the standard of care to which the trustee must be held and courts disagree on that standard. Some courts hold that the trustee is liable only for willful and deliberate dereliction of duty, some hold the trustee liable for gross negligence, and some for ordinary negligence. In *In re Schooler*, 725 F.3d 498 (5th Cir. 2013) the court applied the gross negligence standard. Within 180 days of filing her Ch. 7 petition, the debtor inherited property from her father under a will that appointed her as executor of the estate. Property inherited by a debtor within 180 days of filing becomes property of the estate (*see* section 9.3.1c). Despite being asked repeatedly to do so by a creditor, the trustee failed to take timely action to remove the deceased estate from the debtor's control and to ensure that the inheritance was turned over to the estate. As a result, the debtor never surrendered the inherited property to the estate and eventually dissipated it. The creditor sued the issuer of the surety bond for loss caused by the trustee's failure to perform her duties satisfactorily. The court of appeals, defining gross negligence as an indifference to legal duty and an act or omission of a character more aggravated than mere failure to exercise ordinary care, upheld the judgments of both the bankruptcy court and the district court that the trustee had been grossly negligent: She delayed inordinately in pursuing the inheritance, despite the creditor's repeated urgings to take action, and even though it became clear that she had to move aggressively because the debtor would not turn over the assets voluntarily. As a result, by the time that she did take action, the debtor had disposed of the assets and dissipated the proceeds so that there was nothing left to surrender to the estate.

§4.3.3 The Removal of a Trustee

A trustee may be removed under §324(a) for cause, which includes incompetence, violation of fiduciary duty, misconduct, or conflict of interest. For example, in *In re IFS Financial Corp.*, 803 F.3d 195 (5th Cir. 2015) the bankruptcy court removed the trustee, an attorney, in a complex corporate liquidation under Ch. 7 and the court of appeals affirmed. The principal basis for his removal was that he incurred excessive expenses during a trip to New Orleans to argue the appeal of a matter in the case, and was not forthcoming with the court in itemizing the expenses accurately. The court of appeals noted that "cause" is not defined in the Code, but it includes conduct that justifies the court in losing faith in the trustee's commitment to honor his fiduciary duty and to put the estate's interests above his own.

§4.3.4 The Trustee's Role in Ch. 7 Cases

The duties of a trustee in a Ch. 7 case are set out in general terms in §704. In essence, the trustee's principal function is to liquidate and distribute the bankrupt estate. This primarily involves the collection of property of the estate, its realization, and its distribution to creditors. While this process may involve some interim administration of property to preserve its value, the trustee is not normally involved in the long-term management of the assets or operation of a business. The goal is to liquidate the estate as expeditiously as possible.

In pursuing this general goal, the trustee performs a number of specific duties discussed in succeeding chapters, such as investigating the debtor's affairs, employing professionals, recovering voidable dispositions, examining and contesting claims, litigating over estate interests, and making recommendations to the court on questions such as the debtor's discharge.

The permanent trustee only takes office at the meeting of creditors. Therefore, §701 provides for the appointment of an interim trustee by the U.S. Trustee. In voluntary cases, the interim trustee is appointed promptly after the filing of the petition, while in involuntary cases, the interim trustee is appointed only after the court has granted the involuntary petition. However, the court is empowered by §303(g) to order the earlier appointment if it is shown that the estate needs immediate protection. Unless creditors choose to elect a trustee at the creditors' meeting, the interim trustee becomes the permanent trustee.

§4.3.5 The Trustee's Role in Ch. 13 Cases

A trustee is also required in a Ch. 13 case. Her powers and duties are set out generally in §1302. As explained more fully in section 5.2, a Ch. 13 case differs from a liquidation case under Ch. 7 because its goal is not to liquidate the debtor's estate, but to revest all or part of the estate in the debtor upon confirmation of a plan of payment. Thus, the central role of the trustee is not the realization of property of the estate. The trustee is more concerned with other functions such as investigating the debtor's affairs, examining and contesting claims, recovering voidable dispositions, making recommendations on the debtor's plan, and ensuring its implementation. If the Ch. 13 debtor has a business at the time of bankruptcy, the debtor continues to operate it under the supervision of the trustee.

The process of trustee selection is also different in a Ch. 13 case. Unlike Ch. 7, Ch. 13 provides for the immediate appointment of a permanent trustee by the U.S. Trustee. There is no interim appointment and no provision for creditor election. In some regions, a trustee is appointed for each case, but in others, where the volume of cases warrants it, the U.S. Trustee is empowered by 28 U.S.C. §586(b) to appoint one or more standing trustees who serve as trustees for all Ch. 13 cases in the region. As in the case of persons appointed to the panel of trustees, the standing trustees must meet qualifications prescribed by the Attorney General.

§4.3.6 The Role of a Debtor in Possession, Trustee, and Examiner in Ch. 11 Cases

a. The Debtor in Possession

In a reorganization case under Ch. 11, the usual practice is not to appoint a trustee. Instead, the debtor exercises the trustee's function as debtor in possession, subject to the oversight of the court and creditors' committees. Unless the context indicates otherwise, the word "trustee" includes the debtor in possession whenever it is used in Code provisions relating to a Ch. 11 case. Because a reorganization, like a debt adjustment, is designed not to liquidate but to restructure and rehabilitate the debtor, the duties of the debtor in possession focus on the operation of the business of the estate and the creation and consummation of the Ch. 11 plan. In addition, the debtor in possession performs many other trustee functions, such as collecting estate property, challenging claims, and employing professionals. Some of the trustee's duties, such as investigation of the debtor's affairs and supervision of the debtor's activities, cannot be exercised by a debtor in possession. In a Ch. 11 case those functions are exercised by the creditors' committee.

b. The Appointment of a Trustee

Although the appointment of a trustee is not the norm in a Ch. 11 case, the court does have the authority to appoint a trustee for cause, or where necessary to protect the rights of creditors or other interest holders. This appointment is made under §1104 upon application of a party in interest or the U.S. Trustee, and follows notice and a hearing. Cause for the appointment includes dishonesty or incompetence by the debtor in possession. If the court orders the appointment of a trustee, §1104(b) permits a party in interest (which includes a creditor, equity interest holder, the debtor in possession, and the U.S. Trustee) to request the election of a trustee within 30 days of the court ordering the appointment of a trustee. If a timely request is made, the U.S. Trustee must convene a meeting of creditors at which the election takes place under the same procedure as in a Ch. 7 case. In the absence of a timely request, the U.S. Trustee makes the appointment in consultation with creditors and interest holders, and subject to the court's approval. Whether elected or appointed by the U.S. Trustee, the trustee must be a disinterested person and must be eligible under §321. The appointment can be terminated and the debtor returned to possession, on the application of a party in interest. §1105.

c. The Appointment of an Examiner

The appointment of a trustee displaces the debtor in possession as manager of the estate. If there are not grounds for such severe action, but some investigation of the debtor's management or conduct is appropriate, the court may appoint an examiner under §1104(b). This appointment also requires an application by the U.S. Trustee or a party in interest, followed by notice and a hearing. In estates of a specified size, the examiner must be appointed if the application is made. Otherwise, appointment is ordered only if the court finds this to be in the best interests of creditors and interest holders.

§4.3.7 Trustee's Fees

Trustee's fees are governed by §§326 and 330. The general rule is that a trustee is entitled to reasonable compensation for services, based on the nature of the services, the time spent, and the market rate for those services. The reasonable fee is determined by the court, and must fall within the range set by §§330 and 326. Section 330 provides for a minimum fee for trustees, and §326 prescribes maximum limits on the fee, based on the value of the distribution from the estate. The minimum payment to and limitations on the fees of standing trustees are set by 28 U.S.C. §586(e). The trustee's fee is an expense of administering the estate, which is given second priority for payment out of the funds of the estate. (Priorities are discussed in Chapter 17.)

§4.4 THE U.S. TRUSTEE

In addition to the judicial functions exercised by the bankruptcy court, there are many administrative and supervisory responsibilities relating to the case. These duties are performed by the U.S. Trustee.[4] The U.S. Trustee is a public official, and must not be confused with the bankruptcy trustee, the private person who administers the estate. U.S. Trustees are appointed by the Attorney General and each is responsible for a region of the country. The powers and duties of the U.S. Trustee are set out in 28 U.S.C. §§581-589a, as well as in various provisions of the Code itself.

The general responsibility of a U.S. Trustee is to ensure that the public interest is being properly served in the administration of bankruptcy cases. In addition to appointing trustees, the U.S. Trustee is responsible for supervising their work to ensure that estates are being competently and honestly administered. The U.S. Trustee also has extensive duties, enumerated in 28 U.S.C. §586, concerning other aspects of the bankruptcy case: monitoring plans under Chs. 11 and 13; ensuring that debtors are properly filing fees, schedules, and reports; watching for debtor abuse and other illicit behavior; and assisting the U.S. Attorney in prosecuting crimes committed in the course of a bankruptcy case. The U.S. Trustee is also empowered in a number of Code sections to participate in litigation and other proceedings arising in

4. Prior to the enactment of the Code in 1978, the bankruptcy judge exercised both judicial and administrative functions relating to the bankruptcy case. The court's administrative duties intruded on its judicial role, so the Code created the office of U.S. Trustee to take over these administrative functions. The office was initially tested as a pilot program in 1978 and made permanent in 1986.

the bankruptcy case, and may, for example, examine the debtor (§343), recommend dismissal of a case (§707), or object to a discharge (§727(c)). The Bankruptcy Abuse Prevention and Consumer Protection Act of 2005 (BAPCPA) expanded the statutory duties of the U.S. Trustee in evaluating whether an individual Ch. 7 debtor's filing is abusive under §707, and in arranging for and supervising credit counseling for the debtor. (This is discussed in sections 5.4.3 and 6.8.) BAPCPA also increased the U.S. Trustee's statutory supervisory responsibility in small business cases. (*See* section 20.3.1.)

While the bankruptcy court is responsible for the judicial supervision of the case, the U.S. Trustee's concern is administrative oversight. The U.S. Trustee is not an official of the bankruptcy court, but an independent officer who exercises those supervisory and administrative functions that cannot and should not be performed by the bankruptcy court itself. Also, as noted above, the U.S. Trustee can appear before the court as a party in various proceedings in the case.

§4.5 THE DEBTOR

§4.5.1 The Debtor's Role in the Case

The debtor is the person whose estate is administered in bankruptcy. With some restrictions discussed in Chapter 5, most persons, whether individuals or incorporated entities, are eligible to be debtors under one or more chapters of the Code. The debtor's role in the bankruptcy case is relatively passive in a Ch. 7 liquidation, where the trustee is responsible for administering the estate, liquidating assets, and making distributions to creditors. The debtor is typically more involved in the estate in rehabilitation cases. Where the debtor seeks to rehabilitate a business under Ch. 13, the debtor normally operates the business under the trustee's supervision. As explained in section 4.3.5, unless there are grounds to appoint a trustee in a Ch. 11 cases, the debtor becomes a debtor in possession who not only operates the business, but generally exercises the functions that a trustee would perform under other chapters.

§4.5.2 Equity Security Holders

A debtor that is a corporate entity has shareholders or other holders of ownership interests. The Code uses the term "equity security holder," defined in §101(16) to refer to persons who hold an ownership interest in a corporation or limited partnership. "Corporation" is defined in §101(9) to include a variety of incorporated entities. It is a fundamental principle that the interests of owners of a debtor are subservient to the claims of creditors. Therefore, the holders of ownership interests in an insolvent corporate debtor will not recover anything from the debtor on account of their interests in a Ch. 7 liquidation. However, in rehabilitation bankruptcy, there is a chance that the investment may be salvaged if a plan of reorganization can be devised under which the equity security holders are able to retain all or part of their interest in the corporation. They therefore have a stake in the debtor's reorganization effort under Ch. 11 and have the right to participate in the case. They may be represented by a committee similar in structure to a creditors' committee.

§4.6 CREDITORS AND CREDITORS' COMMITTEES

"Creditor" is defined in §101(10) to include any entity who has a provable claim against the estate. "Entity" is defined in §101(15) to include almost every kind of legal person, including both individuals and corporate entities. "Claim" is defined very broadly in §101(5) to cover all legal or equitable rights to payment, even if they are unliquidated, unmatured, contingent, or disputed. It is clear from these definitions that although creditors are brought together in bankruptcy's collective proceeding, they are a very diverse group with claims of different levels of certainty arising from a wide variety of transactions or relationships with the debtor or the estate. Furthermore, claims do not all have the same rank. With some exceptions, secured claims have the same status in bankruptcy as they have in nonbankruptcy law and are entitled to full payment from the proceeds of the collateral. In addition, the Code provides an order of priority for unsecured claims so that certain categories of claims are given preference over others.

As the representative of the estate, the trustee commonly acts in the collective interest of creditors through her efforts to enhance and preserve the value of the estate. However, although the trustee acts in the best interests of the creditor body as a whole, the trustee is not the representative of individual creditors. Frequently, the interests of the estate are opposed to those of an individual creditor or group of creditors, who are adversaries of the trustee. Litigation between the trustee and specific creditors is common.

When the debtor in possession acts as trustee in a Ch. 11 case, the debtor assumes fiduciary responsibilities. However, it requires an unusually charitable view of human nature to believe that a debtor in possession is likely to be as solicitous of creditor interests as an independent trustee would be. To ensure that creditor interests are properly safeguarded in a Ch. 11 case, the Code provides for the appointment of creditor committees.[5] Under §1102, the U.S. Trustee must appoint at least one committee of creditors holding unsecured claims. More than one committee can be appointed either if the U.S. Trustee deems it appropriate for the adequate representation of creditors or if a party in interest so requests.

The general duties of the committees are set out in §1103. They may employ legal counsel or other consultants, confer with the debtor in possession in the administration of the estate, conduct investigations into the debtor's financial affairs, participate in plan formation, and generally represent the interests of their constituent creditors. Ch. 11 usually involves negotiation between the debtor and creditors and between different creditor groups. The committees play a significant role in this respect as well. In short, the idea behind the creditors' committees is that they are representative bodies that safeguard the interests of the class of creditors they represent, not only in general oversight of the debtor but also in the negotiations that lead to the formulation of a plan.

The value of a creditors' committee is dependent on the committee taking an active role in the case. Studies have shown that in smaller Ch. 11 bankruptcies, creditors often do not have a large enough stake in the outcome of the case to participate vigorously or at all in the committee. As a result, creditors' committees often do not serve the vital monitoring and adversarial function they were intended to have. Therefore, if the debtor qualifies as a "small business debtor" (defined in §101(51D) to mean, essentially, a debtor in business with total debts of under \$2,566,050),[6] the court may dispense with a creditors' committee if a party in interest so requests. If no committee is appointed, the U.S. Trustee must fulfill the monitoring function that would have been exercised by the committee.

§4.7 ATTORNEYS AND OTHER PROFESSIONAL CONSULTANTS

§4.7.1 The Employment of Professionals by the Estate, the Debtor, and Creditors

The trustee, the debtor, and creditors are commonly represented by attorneys. In addition, they may require the services of other professionals (e.g., an accountant) for advice on the complexities of the case. These professional relationships are mostly governed by generally applicable rules of law and of

5. Creditor committees can also be appointed in Ch. 7 cases, but they are not very common.
6. This is the dollar amount as adjusted with effect from April 1, 2016. It will be adjusted again with effect from April 1, 2019. *See* section 3.4.3 for an explanation of the periodic adjustment of dollar amounts in the Code.

professional responsibility. However, some provisions in the Code affect attorneys for the debtor, creditor, and trustee. For example, §329 gives the court policing power over certain fees of the debtor's attorney, §327(c) allows the debtor's attorney to be appointed to represent the estate in certain matters, §503(b)(3) and (4) allow creditors to claim their legal fees for an involuntary petition and certain other matters from the estate as an administrative expense, and §1107(b) allows a creditor's attorney to act for the creditors' committee under certain circumstances.

If the estate requires the services of an attorney or other professionals, the trustee is authorized by §327(a) to engage such services with court approval. The reasonable fee due for the services rendered, if approved by the court, is treated as an administrative expense of the estate. Sections 327 to 330 and §503 govern the appointment and fees of attorneys and other professionals used by the estate. Trustees are often accountants or lawyers, and under §327(d) the court may authorize the trustee to perform professional services for the estate in that capacity. If the professional work is distinct from and in excess of the normal functions of a trustee, §328(b) allows the court to authorize additional compensation for it.

Under §330(a)(1), an attorney (or other professional) employed by the estate is entitled to be awarded "reasonable compensation for actual and necessary services rendered" and "reimbursement for actual, necessary expenses." Section 330(a)(3) sets out guidelines to be used by the court in determining the amount of reasonable compensation. They include the time spent, the customary rates charged, the necessity and benefit of the services, and whether the amount of time spent was reasonable. Under §503(b)(4) these fees are an administrative expense of the estate.

In a Ch. 11 case, where the debtor in possession acts for the estate, the attorney representing the debtor in possession is the attorney for the estate and her fees are covered by §303(a). However, in other cases, the debtor's attorney represents the interests of the debtor, while the trustee's attorney acts for the estate. It had not been clear whether the fees of the debtor's attorney were also covered by §330(a) in these cases. This doubt was resolved by the U.S. Supreme Court in *Lamie v. U.S. Trustee*, 540 U.S. 526 (2004), in which the Court held that the plain meaning of §330(a) does not authorize the payment of the debtor's attorney's fees as an administrative expense of the estate.

§4.7.2 Conflicts of Interest, Client Confidentiality, and Loyalty

a. Rules of Professional Responsibility

An attorney (or other professional) who is appointed trustee in a bankruptcy case, or one who represents the estate, the debtor, or some other party in interest, must be careful to comply with both the rules of professional responsibility and the provisions of the Code concerning the representation of parties. An ethical question that often arises in bankruptcy representation involves the avoidance of actual or apparent conflicts of interest. For example, Rule 1.7 of the ABA Model Rules of Professional Conduct prohibits an attorney from representing a client if the representation would cause a conflict of interest. Rule 1.6 forbids an attorney from revealing information relating to the representation of a client without the client's consent. Even after the representation ends, Rule 1.9 forbids the attorney from disclosing information relating to the representation of a former client or from using that information to the disadvantage of the former client. These rules of professional conduct require the attorney to make sure that her work in relation to the bankruptcy case is not affected by other relationships or interests, and that it does not compromise her duty to keep confidential information acquired in the representation of other clients.

b. Code Provisions Relating to an Interest Adverse to the Estate

In addition to these general rules of professional conduct, the Code itself addresses the question of conflicts of interest, confidentiality and the duty of loyalty to a client. Section 327(a) requires that an attorney (or other professional) employed by the estate does not hold or represent an interest adverse to the estate, and is a "disinterested person." An attorney holds an interest adverse to the estate if she has some personal interest (such as a prepetition claim against the debtor) that may undermine her duty of loyalty and independence. She represents an interest adverse to the estate if she acts for a client (such as a creditor of the estate or a stockholder of the debtor) whose interests actually or potentially conflict with those of the estate. "Disinterested person" is defined in §101(14) to exclude creditors, various persons with ownership interests in or close connections to the debtor, and persons who "have an interest materially adverse to the interests of the estate. . . ." A similar requirement of disinterest can be found in §327(e), governing the use by the estate of the debtor's attorney, and §1103(b), concerning representation of a creditors' committee. An attorney who acts as trustee is bound by fiduciary responsibilities to be impartial and independent (*see* section 4.3).

The degree to which an adverse interest disqualifies an attorney from representing the estate is not clear. The definition of "disinterested person" in §101(14) talks of an interest "materially adverse" to that of the estate, but §327(a) does not include a requirement of materiality. Some courts have allowed an attorney to represent the estate if she has a minor adverse interest that is not material (such as a small unsecured claim), but others have disqualified an attorney from representing the estate if she has any adverse interest, no matter how small.[7]

c. Disclosure to the Court

Since the court must approve the appointment of an attorney under §327(a), it is the court, not the attorney herself, who must make the ultimate decision on whether a disqualifying conflict of interest exists. To enable the court to make a proper determination, the attorney seeking appointment has the duty to disclose all relevant information. Failure to make disclosure of pertinent information is a serious breach of good faith that could subject the attorney to disciplinary proceedings and also result in forfeiture of fees under §328(c). The same is true of an attorney appointed to represent a creditors' committee under §1103. Rule 2014 requires the application for authorization to disclose all the attorney's connections with interested parties so that the court is informed at the time of application of any possible conflicts.

In re Hutch Holdings, Inc., 532 B.R. 866 (Bankr. S.D. Ga. 2015) illustrates the operation of the disclosure and disinterested requirements of §327. A law firm represented Hutch in its Ch.11 case and also represented Hutch's sole shareholder in his individual Ch. 11 case, filed a few days later. Attorneys in the firm filed applications for appointment as attorneys for the debtors in possession in both cases. In their application to represent the corporation, the attorneys did not disclose that they represented its owner in the other case, and likewise did not disclose their representation of the corporation in the owner's case. Following the U.S. Trustee's objections to the attorneys' applications, the attorneys withdrew their application for employment in the individual case and the court considered whether they qualified as disinterested persons in their representation of the corporation. The court noted that there is no per se rule forbidding an attorney from representing the estates of both a corporation and its owner, and each case must be evaluated on its facts. The court found that while there was a potential for a conflict of interest in such a situation, no actual conflict or significant risk of conflict arose on the facts of this case. As a result, the attorneys were not disqualified from representing the corporate debtor. Nevertheless, the court sanctioned the attorneys' violation of their disclosure obligations by disallowing them any fees or expenses associated with their failure to comply with the disclosure requirements.

---

7. The 1994 National Bankruptcy Review Commission recommended that §327(a) be amended to clarify that an insubstantial adverse claim should not disqualify an attorney, but BAPCPA did not make this change. This question therefore remains unresolved.

d. Conflict of Interest Arising Out of an Installment Arrangement for the Payment of Fees

An awkward conflict of interest situation can arise where an attorney agrees to take on the bankruptcy representation of a client who does not have the means to pay the attorney in full in advance of the filing of the petition. For example, an individual debtor who seeks Ch. 7 bankruptcy relief engages an attorney to file the petition and represent him during the case. Ideally, the attorney should determine a flat fee (a retainer) to cover both the prepetition and postpetition representation of the debtor, and should ensure that the fee is paid in full in advance of the petition. Provided that the fee is fair and legitimate, it will not be overturned in the bankruptcy case, and because the debtor has paid in full, the attorney will not be a creditor in the bankruptcy. However, if the debtor cannot afford to pay the full fee in advance, the attorney must make other arrangements. The obvious solution may seem to be to allow the debtor to pay the fee in installments. However, it is not usually practical to delay filing the petition while the debtor pays the fee, and if the petition is filed immediately so that the installments extend into the period after the petition, the unpaid balance of the fee will be classified as a general unsecured debt. This is because the contract under which the debtor agreed to pay the retainer was entered into before the petition was filed.[8] As a result, the attorney will be stayed from taking any action to collect the debt, which will eventually be paid only to the extent of the Ch. 7 distribution and discharged.

In addition to the problem of collecting the fee, the attorney's status as an unsecured creditor creates a conflict of interest that could result in the attorney's disqualification from representing the debtor. For example, in *In re Waldo*, 417 B.R. 854 (Bankr. E.D. Tenn. 2009), the court held that by taking postdated checks in payment of the fee and not informing the debtor that they would likely not be payable, the attorney created a conflict of interest. In *In re Martin*, 197 B.R. 120 (Bankr. D. Colo. 1996), the court upheld the trustee's objection to such a fee arrangement on the grounds that the attorney had a conflict of interest because his self-interest created a disincentive to advise the debtor that his own fee was unsecured, dischargeable, and unenforceable. Some courts, recognizing the need to make it easier for indigent debtors to secure representation, have been less inclined to disqualify an attorney on grounds of conflict where installments were still due on the fee after the petition was filed. See *In re Hines*, 147 F.3d 1185 (9th Cir. 1998).

---

8. It becomes a general unsecured claim because, as noted in section 4.7.1, the U.S. Supreme Court made it clear in *Lamie v. U.S. Trustee*, 540 U.S. 526 (2004), that the debtor's attorney's fee is not covered by §330(a)(1). It therefore cannot be approved as an expense of the estate and does not qualify for priority as an administrative expense.

One way to avoid this problem is to structure the representation arrangement differently: Instead of entering into a contract for a flat fee in advance of filing, the attorney should segregate the fees for prepetition and postpetition services. The fee for prepetition services must be paid before the filing, and the fee arrangement should specify that the fees for postpetition services only become due and payable once the services are performed. Because fees for postpetition services are not prepetition debts, they are not subject to the stay or the discharge, and there is no unsecured debt that could create a conflict of interest. See *In re Mansfield*, 394 B.R. 783 (Bankr. E.D. Pa. 2008).

§4.8 DEBT RELIEF AGENCIES

§4.8.1 The Meaning of "Debt Relief Agency": Persons, Including Attorneys, Who Provide Assistance or Representation in Connection with a Modest-Value Consumer Bankruptcy Case

BAPCPA added §§526 through 528 to the Code with the goal of strengthening the professional standards applicable to a "debt relief agency" that assists or represents a person in connection with a consumer bankruptcy case involving nonexempt assets of relatively small value. "Debt relief agency" is defined in §101(12A) to include "any person who provides any bankruptcy assistance to an assisted person in return for the payment of money or other valuable consideration . . ." as well as petition preparers. The definition excludes various persons such as nonprofit organizations, creditors of the debtor who assist in debt restructuring, and authors of books. "Bankruptcy assistance" is broadly defined in §101(4A) to cover a variety of goods and services provided to an "assisted person," such as advice, document preparation, or representation in connection with a bankruptcy case. "Assisted person" is defined in §101(3) to mean any person whose debts consist primarily of consumer debts and whose nonexempt property has a value of less than $192,450.[9]

Although these provisions do not expressly mention attorneys, the definitions are broad enough to include an attorney who represents a debtor with regard to any aspect of the bankruptcy case. The question of whether attorneys are debt relief agencies had engendered much uncertainty. Most bankruptcy courts held that they were included, but some held otherwise.

9. This is the amount as adjusted under §104 with effect from April 1, 2016. *See* section 3.4.3.

This question was settled by the U.S. Supreme Court in *Milavetz, Gallop & Milavetz, P.A. v. U.S.*, 559 U.S. 229 (2010). The court held that the plain language of §101(12A), bolstered by its legislative history, makes it clear that Congress did intend to include attorneys in the definition. Although attorneys do fall within the definition of "debt relief agency," that definition is qualified by the requirement that the person must provide the bankruptcy assistance "in return for the payment of money or other valuable consideration." Therefore, an attorney who acts for an assisted person pro bono should not be classified as a debt relief agency. See *In re Reyes*, 361 B.R. 276 (Bankr. D. Fla. 2007) *aff'd* 2007 WL 6082567 (S.D. Fla 2007).

An "assisted person" is commonly a debtor. However, the language of §101(3) uses the word "person" rather than "debtor," and "bankruptcy assistance" is therefore not clearly confined to services provided to the debtor. An attorney who provides assistance in a bankruptcy case to a creditor or other party in interest may fit the definition of a debt relief agency if that client's debts consist primarily of consumer debts and his nonexempt property is worth less than $192,450. An attorney's representation of a person other than the debtor does not constitute services relating to the relief of that person's client. Therefore, it may be that Congress did not actually intend the definition to apply to nondebtors even though the plain language appears to include them. In any event, the practical effect of including nondebtors in the definition of "assisted person" may not be significant because a debt relief agency that represents someone other than the debtor does not appear to be subject to the regulation and restrictions set out in §§526 to 528. In *Milavetz*, the U.S. Supreme Court read those sections as governing only those who offer bankruptcy-related services to consumer debtors.

§4.8.2 The Regulation of Debt Relief Agencies

Sections 526 to 528 set out the rules that apply to debt relief agencies. Section 526 imposes restrictions on their conduct, §527 sets out the disclosures that they are required to make to an assisted person, and §528 specifies the content of the agency's required written contract with an assisted person and prescribes required content in advertisements. These sections are quite detailed and are full of vague, ambiguous, and obscure language. Their gist is as follows.

Section 526(a) contains prohibitions on deceptive or improper conduct. Section 526(a)(1) prohibits a debt relief agency from failing to perform a service that was undertaken. Sections 526(a)(2) and (3) forbid the agency from making misleading statements or misrepresentations itself and from advising an assisted person to do so. Section 526(a)(4) forbids the agency from advising an assisted person to incur more debt "in contemplation of" filing a bankruptcy case. Section 526(b) makes any waiver of protections or rights under the section unenforceable against the assisted person. Section 526(c) provides for remedies and penalties against a debt relief agency that violates §§526 to 528, in addition to any remedies that are otherwise available under state law. The section states that a contract in material violation of the provisions is void and cannot be enforced by any person other than the assisted person. The debt relief agency is liable to the assisted person for actual damages, reimbursement of fees, and attorney's fees and costs for any intentional or negligent failure to comply with these provisions or with other material requirements of the Code, or where the case is dismissed for failure to file documents. In addition to suit by the assisted person, an action to enjoin a violation or for damages may be brought by the state in either state or federal court. Finally, the district court, either on its own motion or on motion of the U.S. Trustee or the assisted person, may enjoin intentional or persistent violations of the provisions or impose civil penalties on the agency. Section 526(d) makes it clear that §§526 to 528 do not curtail the ability of the state to regulate the practice of law. Nor do they affect or exempt compliance with any state law, except to the extent that the state law is inconsistent with the provisions of those sections.

Section 527 requires debt relief agencies to make extensive written disclosures to an assisted person, to explain the need for accurate information in the petition and supporting documents, to alert the assisted person to the availability of legal assistance, and to caution the assisted person about various aspects of bankruptcy, including eligibility for and choice of relief. The agency must also provide the assisted person with necessary information on how to assemble the content of and complete the lists of creditors, the schedule of assets and liabilities, and other documentation required to be filed by the assisted person under §521.

Section 528(a) requires the agency to enter into a written contract with the assisted person before the bankruptcy petition is filed, conspicuously setting out the services to be provided and the fees to be charged. An executed copy of the contract must be given to the assisted person. Section 528(b) requires specific disclosures in advertising that identify the advertiser as a debt relief agency and clearly describe the nature of the bankruptcy assistance being offered.

§4.8.3 The Constitutionality of §§526 and 528 as Applied to Attorneys

In *Milavetz*, the U.S. Supreme Court considered the constitutionality of §§526 and 528, as applied to attorneys, and concluded that the provisions did not violate the U.S. Constitution. The court of appeals had held that the prohibition in §526(a)(4) on advising an assisted person to incur more debt in contemplation of filing bankruptcy violated the attorney's First Amendment rights. The court of appeals found this prohibition to be overbroad because it covered not only improper advice, but also appropriate and lawful advice that constitutes prudent bankruptcy planning. It thereby chilled speech that is fundamental to the attorney-client relationship. The Supreme Court[10] held that the court of appeals had interpreted the words "in contemplation of" bankruptcy too broadly to refer to all advice to incur any additional debt when contemplating bankruptcy. However, on a proper and commonsense reading of the phrase, taken in the context of the section and in light of the use of that phrase in bankruptcy law generally, the prohibition focuses on advice to engage in abusive or manipulative conduct such as the loading up on debt with the expectation of discharging it. Section 526(a)(4) does not preclude an attorney from counseling the client about incurring new debt in contemplation of filing a bankruptcy case or in recommending that the debtor take on new debt for legitimate, nonabusive purposes.

The disclosure requirements relating to advertising, prescribed by §528, were also challenged in *Milavetz* as a violation of the First Amendment. The Court rejected this argument, holding that the disclosure requirement is not an impermissible limitation on commercial speech, but merely a requirement to provide information, which is constitutionally permissible provided that it is rationally related to the government's interest in safeguarding consumer debtors from deceptive advertising. The court found that the section's disclosure requirements satisfy this standard: They are intended to combat the problem of misleading advertisements, and they require only the divulgence of the advertiser's legal status as a debt relief agency and the type of assistance to be provided.

§4.9 OTHER PARTICIPANTS

In the preceding sections, the principal participants in a bankruptcy case have been introduced. However, every debtor is different; depending on the debtor's activities, interests, and affairs, there may be a variety of other persons who are not necessarily creditors, but whose rights are at stake in the case. For example, the debtor may be a party to unperformed (i.e., executory) contracts that may be assumed or rejected by the estate; most debtors have debtors of their own who become debtors of the estate; some

10. The court's judgment was unanimous. However, Justices Scalia and Thomas delivered concurring opinions in which they concurred in the judgment and in most of the majority's reasoning, but disagreed with the majority on narrow questions that are not detailed here.

debtors have dependents; some have sureties or other co-obligors. Also, bankruptcy may attract the interest of a public agency. For example, the Securities and Exchange Commission may be concerned with, and is entitled to be heard in, a Ch. 11 case.

Examples

1. Luce Canons, an attorney, performed some legal work for Down & Out Enterprises, Inc., for which he charged a fee of $5,000. Down & Out has not paid the fee, and it has now filed a Ch. 11 petition. Down & Out, as debtor in possession, has asked Luce Canons to represent it in a lawsuit to recover a debt due to the estate. Should Luce Canons accept the case?

2. Lex Lawman used to be the attorney for Erstwhile Enterprises, Inc. Lex represented Erstwhile for many years and had handled all its legal work, becoming thoroughly familiar with its affairs. A year ago, Erstwhile terminated its relationship with Lex and hired another lawyer to represent it. Lex has not done any legal work for Erstwhile since then. Erstwhile has now filed a Ch. 11 petition. May Lex represent a creditors' committee in the bankruptcy case?

3. Bill A. Billhours had long been the attorney for Adverse Investments, Inc., a corporation of which his friend Able Skimmer was president and principal stockholder. When Adverse Investments filed a Ch. 11 petition, it applied under §327(a) for the court to approve Bill as its attorney. Bill disclosed that he had been Adverse Investments' legal advisor prior to its bankruptcy, but failed to mention that he had also legally represented Able in his personal affairs for many years. The court approved Bill's appointment, and he set to work conscientiously and vigorously representing the estate in negotiations aimed at developing a plan of reorganization. The negotiations broke down when creditors discovered that Able had made several transfers of funds from Adverse Investments to himself and his family members shortly before the petition was filed. The creditors' committee successfully applied to oust the debtor in possession from control of the estate and to replace it with a trustee. The trustee terminated Bill's employment and hired her own counsel. She is now investigating whether Able's transfers of corporate assets were fraudulent.
   a. Bill has applied to court for compensation for the services that he rendered to the estate from the time of his appointment until his dismissal. It is conceded that he performed good-quality legal work for the estate during his tenure as its counsel, and no one contends that he participated in or even knew about Able's transfers of corporate property. Notwithstanding, the trustee objects to Bill receiving any payment of his fees. Is this a sound objection?

b. Quite apart from the issue of whether Bill is entitled to his fees, consider his responsibilities with regard to the trustee's investigation of the improper conduct of Able and Adverse Investments. Is the information obtained by Bill during his representation of Adverse protected by the attorney-client privilege?

4. The law firm of Filenow & Palater handles a large volume of consumer bankruptcies. When it is engaged by a prospective debtor, the firm charges a flat fee to cover the fees for the prepetition work, the filing of the petition, and basic postpetition representation. Where a client cannot afford to pay the flat fee in advance of the bankruptcy, the firm accepts a down payment on its fee and permits its client to pay the balance in monthly installments in the period following the petition. The firm has the client sign postdated checks, which are then banked as they become due. Is this a good practice?

5. Fido Fidelio is an attorney and a member of the panel of trustees established by the U.S. Trustee. He was appointed as the trustee of a corporation in liquidation under Ch. 7. At the time of his appointment he filed the required declaration of disinterestedness, but did not mention in the declaration that he had represented a former employee of the debtor some time ago. During the course of that representation, Fido learned of financial improprieties committed by the debtor. Should Fido have disclosed the former relationship with the debtor's ex-employee? Does this representation render Fido unqualified to act as trustee for the debtor?

EXPLANATIONS

Explanations

1. Luce Canons must obtain court approval of his appointment as attorney for the estate under §327(a). In the application for approval, he must disclose to the court the fact that he is an unsecured creditor of the estate. The court will not approve his appointment unless he qualifies as a disinterested person who does not hold an interest adverse to the estate. One of the requirements to qualify as a disinterested person, as defined in §101(14), is that the person is not a creditor. (*See* §101(14)(A).) This would seem to settle the matter, because Luce is owed $5,000 by the estate for unpaid prepetition services. Several courts have disposed of this issue in those simple terms. However, other courts have been less wedded to the literal language of §101(14)(A), and have held that the mere fact that the attorney has a claim against the estate should not automatically disqualify him. The case must be examined to decide if there is an actual conflict between the attorney's interest as a creditor and the estate's interests that he will represent in the task to be accomplished

on behalf of the estate. For example, if the attorney is retained to represent the estate in recovering a voidable preference paid to another creditor, it would seem that the attorney's interest is congruent with rather than opposed to that of the estate. By contrast, the potential for adverse interests is strong if the attorney's role is to represent the estate in negotiating a plan of reorganization with creditors.

Note that this is a Ch. 11 case, so the estate is administered by the debtor in possession. The basis for disqualifying Luce is that he is a creditor, and not because he represented the debtor prior to bankruptcy. In a Ch. 11 case, §1107(b) makes it clear that an attorney is not disqualified merely because he represented the debtor before bankruptcy. However, the circumstances of that prior representation could give rise to an actual or potential conflict, so it must be disclosed to the court and evaluated. Some courts have held that in a Ch. 11 case, the fact that fees are still owed from that prior representation of the debtor is not in itself enough to preclude representation of the estate. See, for example, *In re Talsma*, 436 B.R. 908 (Bankr. N.D. Tex. 2010), which concerned the estate's employment of the debtor's pre-petition accountant who was still owed fees for the prepetition work.

2. The ethical barrier to Lex's representation of the creditors' committee is not a concurrent conflict of interest (a conflict of interest between two current clients) because Lex is no longer Erstwhile's lawyer. However, Rule 1.6 of the ABA Model Rules of Professional Conduct forbids an attorney from divulging the information relating to the representation of a client. This duty of confidentiality continues even after the attorney-client relationship ends, as reflected in Rule 1.9(c), which states that a lawyer who has formerly represented a client may not reveal information relating to the representation of the former client or use that information to the former client's disadvantage.

   During the course of their attorney-client relationship, Lex was privy to details of Erstwhile's affairs. He gained this information relatively recently, so it is most likely still relevant and could be used against Erstwhile on behalf of the creditors' committee. In fact, Lex's duty of competent representation of his new client would compel him to divulge or use any knowledge of Erstwhile's affairs that would advance its interest against Erstwhile. Lex therefore cannot adequately represent Erstwhile's creditors without violating the trust and confidence inherent in his former relationship with Erstwhile. *In re Kujawa*, 112 B.R. 968 (Bankr. E.D. Mo. 1990), is a particularly startling example of an attorney's violation of confidence. The law firm represented the debtor for about two years. It represented him in several lawsuits, counseled him on bankruptcy issues, and had intimate knowledge of his affairs. A few months after doing legal work for the debtor, the law firm represented some of his creditors in a petition to place him into involuntary bankruptcy. When those creditors retained other counsel, the firm represented another group of creditors who sought to intervene in the case. The firm also filed as an intervening creditor on its own behalf for unpaid fees owed by the debtor. The court granted the debtor's motion to disqualify the firm and ordered the firm to pay the debtor's costs and attorney's fees relating to the motion. The bankruptcy court's disposition was upheld on appeal, subject to a reduction in the amount of the award (see *In re Kujawa*, 270 F.3d 578 (8th Cir. 2001)).

Even in the absence of any actual detrimental information that Lex may have about Erstwhile's affairs, his switching of sides would still be wrong because it would create the appearance of impropriety and would justify Erstwhile in feeling betrayed. See, for example, *In re Global Video Communications Corp.*, 19 Bankr. Ct. Dec. (CCR) 1311 (Bankr. M.D. Fla. 1989); *In re Davenport Communications Ltd.*, 19 Bankr. Ct. Dec. (CCR) 1980 (Bankr. S.D. Iowa 1990).

3. a. The facts of this example are loosely based on *Rome v. Braunstein*, 19 F.3d 54 (1st Cir. 1994), in which the court refused to award the attorney compensation for his services even though he performed valuable work, he did not act contrary to the interests of the estate, and there was no indication that he had collaborated in or knew of the owner's dishonesty. The court said it is not necessary to identify a negative impact on the estate. It is enough that the attorney put himself in the position in which his loyalty was weakened and he might be tempted to give tainted advice. It is the court's role, not the attorney's, to decide if the attorney is disqualified from representing the estate. The attorney's failure to make immediate and candid disclosure to the court precluded the court from exercising this function. (Quite apart from the sanction under §328, an attorney who fails to avoid a conflict of interest is subject to disciplinary action by the bar.) The objection in Bill's case is therefore sound and the court may deny all compensation to him under §328(c).

   b. This question raises an ancillary issue: When a trustee is appointed and proceeds to investigate possible improprieties by the debtor's management, is the debtor's attorney precluded by attorney-client privilege from furnishing information that he obtained during the course of representing the debtor? In *In re Blinder, Robinson & Co., Inc.*, 123 B.R. 900 (Bankr. D. Colo. 1991), the court resolved this question by finding that the trustee succeeded to the debtor's right to waive the attorney-client privilege. The court reasoned that if this were not so, the management of the debtor would control the privilege and could frustrate the trustee's investigation and shield itself from the trustee's efforts to find misappropriated assets.

4. The safest practice would be to require payment of the full fee before the petition is filed. However, because the debtor does not have the means to pay the full retainer in advance, Filenow & Palater has entered into an installment plan with him. There are two problems with the installment plan. First, because the contract under which payments are to be made was entered into before the petition was filed, the balance due on the fee will be classified as a general unsecured claim, and most, if not all of it, will be unpaid and discharged. Second, because it has made itself a creditor of the debtor, the firm has created a conflict of interest that may preclude it from representing the debtor. Where a debtor cannot afford to pay the retainer in advance, it would be better to structure the representation arrangement by separating the fees for prepetition and postpetition services. The fee for prepetition services must be paid before the filing, and the fees for postpetition services should be made due and payable only upon performance of the postpetition services. Because these fee claims will now arise only after the petition, they will be post-petition debts of the debtor, rather than claims against the estate.

5. A trustee must qualify as a "disinterested person" as defined in §101(14). In *In re AFI Holdings, Inc.*, 530 F.3d 832 (9th Cir. 2008), the court found, using a "totality of the circumstances" test, that a similar former relationship precluded the trustee from qualifying as a disinterested person. His knowledge of prior improprieties committed by the debtor could affect the independence and impartiality required of a trustee. In his declaration of disinterestedness filed with the court, a trustee must fully set out all interactions and past connections with the debtor, a creditor, or any other party in interest so that the court has full information on which to make its decision on disinterestedness. The trustee's failure to disclose the relationship to the court constituted cause for his removal under §324.

CHAPTER 5

Debtor Eligibility and the Different Forms of Bankruptcy Relief

§5.1 OVERVIEW

The distinction between liquidation under Ch. 7 and rehabilitation under Chs. 11 or 13[1] was introduced in section 3.5.2(f) and is taken up again here and examined from the perspective of a debtor who is about to file a bankruptcy petition. This chapter is concerned with the eligibility of different debtors for the alternative forms of bankruptcy relief provided in Chs. 7, 11, and 13, the factors that may influence a debtor in selecting between those alternatives, and the possibility of postpetition conversion from one form of relief to another.

Section 5.2 is a general overview of the distinction between liquidation and rehabilitation bankruptcy. Section 5.3 identifies different types of debtor — corporations, individuals, consumers, and businesses. In some circumstances different Code sections apply to different types of debtors, but in many situations the distinctions between them are fact-based and arise from the different nature of their financial and economic dealings and circumstances.

Section 5.4 deals with general eligibility for bankruptcy relief under §109(a). It also discusses a temporary barrier to the eligibility of a debtor who has made successive bankruptcy filings (§109(g)) and the requirement

1. Chs. 9 (municipal bankruptcy) and 12 (family farmer bankruptcy) are also concerned with rehabilitation, but are not discussed in this book.

of credit counseling that must be satisfied for the eligibility of an individual debtor (§109(h)). Section 5.5 details the specific eligibility requirements for Chs. 7, 11, and 13, provided, respectively, in §§109(b), §109(d), and §109(e). Section 5.6 discusses the conversion of a case from one chapter to another under §§706, 1112, and 1307. Section 5.7 identifies factors that are relevant to a debtor's choice of relief, and section 5.8 outlines the principal differences between Chs. 7, 11, and 13 that may be relevant to a debtor's choice of relief.

§5.2 THE DISTINCTION BETWEEN LIQUIDATION AND REHABILITATION

§5.2.1 Liquidation

Liquidation under Ch. 7 aims at the surrender and dissolution of the debtor's executable estate for the purpose of generating a fund to be applied to the payment of creditors. After the filing of the Ch. 7 bankruptcy petition, a trustee is appointed who has responsibility for collecting the debtor's nonexempt unencumbered assets, turning them into liquid form by converting them to cash, and making a distribution to creditors who have proved claims in the estate. The fund is paid out to creditors in the Code's order of priority. Because it is common for Ch. 7 debtors to be insolvent, most creditors, particularly those who hold nonpriority unsecured claims, receive only a pro rata payment of their claims. Often, the pro rata distribution is no more than a small fraction of the claim, and in quite a high percentage of cases, the estate has so few assets that after the costs of administration are paid, there are no funds left to pay unsecured creditors any distribution at all. The unpaid balance is usually discharged when the debtor is an individual. A corporate debtor does not receive a discharge under Ch. 7. As a result, it becomes a shell with no assets, no business, and an accumulated unpaid debt. The defunct corporation is usually deregistered under state corporation law. If not, the existence of the undischarged debt creates a strong disincentive to anyone who might wish to revitalize the shell.

§5.2.2 Rehabilitation Bankruptcy

Chs. 11 and 13 each have their own rules and principles, which are discussed more fully in Chapters 18, 19, and 20. However, they share a common purpose that distinguishes them from Ch. 7. Their general goal is not to liquidate the debtor's assets[2] but to provide the debtor the opportunity of preserving all or part of the prepetition estate in return for a commitment (formulated in a plan of rehabilitation) to make specified payments or other distributions of value to creditors over a period of time. The level of payment required by the Code is too complex for discussion at this point and is left for Chapters 18 to 21. As a general yardstick, one can say that the premise of the Code is that the value received by creditors under the plan must at least be equal to the present value of what creditors would have received if the debtor had been liquidated under Ch. 7. Of course, this is regarded as the minimum. The goal is that creditors will, in fact, do better than they would have in a liquidation. The Bankruptcy Abuse Prevention and Consumer Protection Act of 2005 (BAPCPA) added provisions to the Code that emphasize this goal. Prior to BAPCPA, the Code largely used incentives to encourage individual debtors to choose rehabilitation over liquidation. BAPCPA amended Ch. 7 to make it much more difficult for an individual consumer debtor to choose liquidation over rehabilitation where the debtor has the means, calculated under a complex formula, to make payments under a plan of rehabilitation. This is discussed generally in section 5.5 and in Example 2, and in more depth in section 6.8. In addition BAPCPA amended Ch. 13 (and Ch. 11 in relation to individual debtors) to impose a more stringent standard on the debtor in determining how much the debtor can afford to pay in the Ch. 13 or Ch. 11 case. (*See* sections 18.8.3 and 19.3.2.)

Rehabilitation under Chs. 11 or 13 is only a viable alternative to liquidation if the debtor has some reasonable prospect of honoring the commitments made in the plan. As a requirement of having the plan confirmed by the court, the debtor must be able to show that it is feasible and that there is likely to be a stream of income or other sources of funding or property to support the plan. Once the plan has been confirmed by the court, it becomes the blueprint for the debtor's rehabilitation. During the period that the debtor is in bankruptcy, that is, from the filing of the petition until the ultimate consummation of the plan, creditors are not permitted to pursue any collection activity outside the bankruptcy process, and the debtor has the opportunity to restructure business operations or to reorder financial affairs with the goal of achieving financial health. If the debtor fails to consummate the plan, the debtor might end up in liquidation. Alternatively, the case might be dismissed so that the creditors' collection rights under state law are restored.

---

2. Some or all of the debtor's assets might be liquidated as part of a rehabilitation plan, and Ch. 11 recognizes the possibility of a liquidation plan that fully liquidates a corporate debtor. Nevertheless, the principal goal of rehabilitation bankruptcy is to preserve the assets of the estate.

The discharge of prepetition debts is an important element of bankruptcy. Both individuals and corporations can receive a discharge in rehabilitation bankruptcy. The discharge rules vary. *See* Chapter 21.

§5.2.3 A Practical Perspective on the Distinction Between Liquidation and Rehabilitation

Although it is possible to draw a fairly clear line between liquidation and rehabilitation based on the premises and the provisions of the Code, it is important to remember that matters become much muddier as the Code is applied in actual cases. Some of this lack of precision will become apparent later, as we take a closer look at the various specific aspects of the different types of bankruptcy, but a general observation may be helpful at the start. Although some cases do proceed exactly along the lines of a pure liquidation (that is, all the estate's assets are realized and the proceeds distributed) or a full rehabilitation (that is, the plan is completely and successfully consummated, leaving the debtor rehabilitated and creditors better off than they would have been had liquidation occurred), things are often not that tidy. For example, an individual Ch. 7 debtor has various means of avoiding the liquidation of all her property, primarily because of exemptions, but also because when the property is subject to a security interest, it may be possible for the debtor to make an arrangement with the secured creditor to keep the property in exchange for a commitment to keep paying installments due on the contract. Likewise, a rehabilitation plan under Ch. 11 or Ch. 13 may provide for the partial liquidation of assets as a means of deriving the resources needed to fund the plan. Furthermore, rehabilitation is usually a long-term process, dependent on predictions of future economic conditions, the debtor's abilities, and the cooperation of creditors or other persons (such as an employer, a lender, or investor) whose help is needed in the debtor's revival. Even if the plan is not unrealistically optimistic to begin with, economic conditions may be less than desired, the debtor may just not have the ability to do what is needed, or the anticipated cooperation may not be forthcoming. This may lead to the failure of the rehabilitation attempt and ultimate liquidation. In the end, creditors may be worse off than they would have been had liquidation taken place immediately.

§5.3 DIFFERENT TYPES OF DEBTOR

Before discussing eligibility for relief, it is useful to identify the different types of natural or legal persons that may become debtors under the Code and to draw some distinctions between them. A debtor is a "person or municipality concerning which a case under this title has been commenced." §101(13). "Person" includes an individual, partnership, and corporation, but not a governmental unit. §101(41). The Code therefore identifies four categories of debtor: individuals, partnerships, corporations, and municipalities. This book does not deal with municipal or partnership bankruptcy, so the important distinction for our purposes is between individuals and corporations.

§5.3.1 Individuals and Corporations

"Individual" is not statutorily defined. It means a real, honest to goodness, living, breathing, warm-blooded mammal of the species *homo sapiens*. Section 101(9) defines "corporation" to include a variety of juristic persons, both incorporated and unincorporated. Most commonly, it includes limited liability entities of different kinds. It also includes some partnerships in which the partners have limited liability equivalent to that of corporate shareholders. However, it does not include other forms of partnership. For example, in *In re Dewey & LeBoeuf LLP*, 518 B.R. 766 (Bankr. S.D.N.Y. 2014) the court determined that a limited liability partnership (LLP) was a corporation because state law conferred limited liability protection equivalent to that of corporate shareholders. The classification of an entity as a corporation, rather than a partnership, could have significant consequences because the Code treats partnerships differently from corporations and individuals.

The distinction between corporate and individual debtors is pervasive, because the impact of bankruptcy on a corporation is bound to differ in many respects from that on an individual. Sometimes these differences are purely factual, reflecting the different scope and nature of corporate and individual economic operations. However, they sometimes arise from Code provisions that reflect a policy of conferring rights or imposing duties on one type of debtor but not on the other. For example, exemptions are intended to save the individual debtor from penury, so they are made available to individuals but not corporations. It is therefore important to pay attention to whether a particular Code section speaks generally of "the debtor" or is restricted to the narrower category of "individual debtor."

§5.3.2 Consumer and Business Debtors

It is easy to draw the distinction between individual and corporate debtors, because corporations are distinct legal entities in nonbankruptcy law and the Code itself recognizes this. It expressly provides for different treatment of individuals and corporations in several respects. By contrast, the Code itself does not as clearly articulate the difference between consumer and business debtors. The only definition pertinent to the distinction is §101(8), which describes a "consumer debt" as one "incurred by an individual primarily for a personal, family or household purpose." From this it is clear that one should not simply equate individual and consumer debtors: An individual is not a consumer debtor unless the bulk of his or her debt is incurred in the course of domestic consumption. Where an individual debtor owns a business as a sole proprietorship or otherwise incurs debts in the course of commercial or other activity unrelated to household or personal purposes, some of his debts are likely to be consumer debts and some business debts.

For many purposes, it is not legally significant to differentiate between consumer or business debtors because most provisions of the Code apply equally in the bankruptcy of each. When the Code intends to provide a special rule for one or the other, it does so expressly. An important example is §707(b), which provides for the dismissal of a Ch. 7 case on grounds of abuse where the debtor is an individual whose debts are primarily consumer debts. (*See* section 6.8.)

Notwithstanding, the distinction between consumer and business debtors is functionally significant and pervasive because the property, obligations, and affairs of a consumer are likely to be quite different from those of a business. This creates factual differences between these two types of bankruptcy so that provisions of the Code relevant to the one often just do not come into issue in the other. The importance of this factual difference is accentuated by the distinct policy concerns that dominate each type. Business bankruptcies tend to implicate larger concerns of economic welfare, such as productivity, market stability, and employee protection. Consumer bankruptcies often highlight social policies such as the prevention of homelessness and the protection of the common person and her dependents, the social ills of the abuse of credit, and shortcomings in the social safety net. It should be stressed, however, that this distinction is likely to be more obvious where the business is a legal entity distinct from its owners (such as a corporation), and has operations of some size. At the margins, the difference between business and consumer bankruptcies is less functionally significant. For example, the stereotypical consumer debtor is a person who earns his income from employment and spends most of it on living expenses or on buying goods and services for personal use. However, if the same debtor is self-employed or engages in business activity, his purchases, loans, and credit card debt may commingle household and business transactions.

Because of these very different factual contexts and policy concerns, it is common for consumer and business bankruptcy to be seen as quite distinct legal regimes. This dichotomy is reflected not only in specialization by practitioners, but also in the way that some books, articles, and law school courses are organized. Although it is important to keep this in mind, it is also necessary to recognize that many provisions of the Code do not differentiate between consumers and businesses, and are potentially applicable to both.

Within the field of business bankruptcy, there is a practical distinction between small and large businesses. As noted already, different practical considerations and some different legal rules apply to those businesses that are incorporated and those that are conducted by the individual owner in unincorporated form. Even among incorporated businesses, there are significant distinctions between the scope of operations and needs of small and large enterprises. In particular, many complex procedures in Ch. 11 were drafted with large corporations in mind, and they have proved to be cumbersome and unduly burdensome and complicated in the rehabilitation of smaller businesses. There has been growing recognition of this since the Code was enacted in 1978. Congress began to make changes to the Code to simplify the rules relating to small businesses when it enacted a special chapter (Ch. 12) in 1986 to provide a simplified version of Ch. 11 for family farming businesses. However, Congress has never extended this to other small businesses.[3] It has, however, enacted some provisions in Ch. 11 that allow for an expedited procedure for debtors that fall within the statutory definition of "small business debtor." These expedited procedures are discussed in section 20.3.1.

While this book often points to the difference between consumers, small businesses, and large corporations, it is not so organized as to treat each category as a self-contained subject. Rather, because they do have so many rules and principles in common, the preferred approach here is to focus on substantive topics, and to point out, where appropriate, that certain rules and procedures are applicable to or are likely to be more relevant to some types of debtors than to others.

§5.4 DEBTOR ELIGIBILITY

§5.4.1 General Qualifications Under §109(a)

Section 109 states who may be a debtor under the Code. Section 109(a) sets out the general qualification for bankruptcy relief. It is broad, and covers most persons (including individuals and corporations) that are resident or domiciled in or conduct business, or own property in the United States. This general qualification is narrowed by the more specific eligibility requirements for each chapter. A debtor must meet both the general requirement

3. Some years ago, a bill was proposed to create a new Ch. 10 for small businesses other than family farms, but it was never enacted.

under §109(a) and the requirements for the specific chapter under which relief is sought. Section 109 is sometimes described as providing threshold qualifications: Qualification under §109 is necessary for the debtor to be entitled to relief. However, even if the debtor is eligible, other provisions in the Code may preclude relief. For example, a debtor may be eligible for Ch. 13 but may not be able to satisfy the further requirements for plan confirmation, or the debtor may be eligible for some forms of relief under a voluntary petition but may not be compelled into that chapter by an involuntary petition.

§5.4.2 Limitation on Successive Filings Under §109(g)

Section 109(g) imposes a temporary (180 day) limitation on general eligibility to prevent abusive successive filings by individuals.[4] Section 109(g)(1) precludes an individual from becoming a debtor if, within the preceding 180 days, he was a debtor in a case that was dismissed because of willful uncooperative or disobedient behavior. Willfulness requires more than inadvertence. The party moving to dismiss the case must show deliberate conduct.

Section 109(g)(2) precludes eligibility if, within the preceding 180 days, the debtor requested and obtained the voluntary dismissal of a prior case following a creditor's application for relief from stay. Section 109(g)(2) is intended to make it difficult for a debtor to file consecutive petitions for the purpose of obstructing creditors' collection efforts at state law by interrupting them with the automatic stay. Courts differ on the exact scope of this subsection, and three different approaches have emerged.

Some courts take the §109(g)(2) at its face meaning, interpret the word "following" to mean "after," and apply it mechanically, so that the debtor is barred from filing for bankruptcy simply if voluntary dismissal occurred subsequent to the filing of a motion for relief from stay. For example, in *In re Richardson*, 217 B.R. 479 (Bankr. M.D. La. 1998), the court concluded that the clear language of §109(g) indicates that Congress intended to impose a simple standard for barring serial filings, and that the test is simply one of sequence—the section comes into effect whenever a motion for voluntary dismissal is made after a motion for relief from stay. The court

4. Apart from §109(g), which makes a debtor ineligible for relief for the 180-day period, §§727(a)(8) and (9) (discussed in section 21.5.2) place a restriction on the debtor's ability to get a discharge in a Ch. 7 case for a number of years after obtaining a discharge in an earlier case. Although both §109(g) and §727 aim at the problem of successive bankruptcies, they are distinct and should not be confused.

declined to adopt a more flexible reading of the section because it felt that this would weaken its effectiveness in curbing abusive serial filings.

Some courts have adopted a causal approach, interpreting the word "following" to mean "as a result of" so that there must be some causal link between the request for relief from stay and the voluntary dismissal. These courts consider that such an interpretation is more in accord with the purpose of §109(g)(2), which is aimed at curbing abuse and therefore should only apply where the voluntary dismissal was in response to the request for relief from stay. See, for example, *In re Payton*, 481 B.R. 460 (Bankr. N.D. Ill. 2012).

Some courts have adopted a discretionary approach, recognizing that, notwithstanding the literal language of §109(g)(2), courts have the discretion to permit the debtor to file for relief where a strict application of the section would lead to an absurd or unjust result. The discretionary approach takes into account factors such as the good faith of the creditor seeking dismissal and whether creditors would be unfairly prejudiced by failure to dismiss. See, for example, in *In re Beal*, 347 B.R. 87 (E.D. Wis. 2006). In *In re Covelli*, 550 B.R. 256 (Bankr. S.D.N.Y. 2016) the court adopted the approach that the debtor is not automatically ineligible under §109(g)(2), so that the clerk of the court must accept the petition and the court must thereafter rule on whether the debtor's case should be dismissed on the grounds of the debtor's voluntary dismissal of the prior case within the preceding 180 days.

In many cases, there may not be a significant difference between the causal approach and discretionary approach because they are likely to lead to the same result. For example, in *In re Riviera*, 494 B.R. 101 (BAP 1st Cir. 2013) the debtor filed a Ch. 13 petition on the eve of foreclosure of a mortgage on his property. He failed to make postpetition mortgage payments and the mortgagee obtained relief from stay. The debtor dismissed the case and immediately filed a second Ch. 13 petition to stay the mortgage foreclosure. The court said that it did not have to decide which approach to use because the case should be dismissed under any approach—there clearly was a causal connection between the relief from stay and the voluntary dismissal, this prejudiced the creditor by delaying the scheduled foreclosure sale, and this was exactly the kind of practice that the section was intended to defeat.

In addition to the question of the proper meaning of §109(g) in relation to the debtor's successive filings, there is an apparent absurdity that arises out of the literal language of the section. By providing that no individual "may be a debtor" under the Code, §109(g) suggests that the debtor is impervious to an involuntary petition during that 180-day period as well. This cannot be the intended result, considering that the rule is aimed at debtor abuse and should not deprive creditors of their involuntary bankruptcy remedy.

§5.4.3 Limitation Requiring Credit Counseling Under §109(h)

a. The Purpose of §109(h)

When Congress enacted BAPCPA, it had been persuaded that many individual bankruptcies result from financial incompetence, ignorance, and mismanagement, as well as the abuse of credit. In an attempt to address this problem, and to ensure that individual debtors understand the impact of a bankruptcy filing, BAPCPA added subsection (h) to §109. Section 109(h) requires individual debtors to receive credit counseling as a prerequisite to eligibility for bankruptcy relief. The principal purpose of prepetition counseling is to give the debtor the opportunity, before filing the petition, to have assistance in evaluating her financial position and to become informed about the consequences of bankruptcy, the different choices of bankruptcy relief, and alternatives to filing for bankruptcy. Although §109(h) seeks to further the laudable goal of educating debtors in financial management, it was controversial when enacted and it has proved to be troublesome. It is criticized as not being particularly effective in achieving its goal, while creating a procedural and administrative barrier to prompt debtor relief. In *In re Elmendorf*, 345 B.R. 486 (Bankr. S.D.N.Y. 2006), the court summed up the section's shortcomings by noting that this "facially well-intentioned" provision "has evolved into an expensive, draconian gatekeeping requirement" that has not achieved its purpose, while making it more difficult for deserving debtors to obtain timely relief. In *In re Enloe*, 373 B.R. 123 (Bankr. D. Colo. 2007), the court noted that there is a "developing consensus . . . that the credit counseling requirement is largely a procedural hurdle without value or consequence." Not surprisingly, courts have struggled to develop a rational and coherent application of §109(h), given its dubious value, its negative impact on debtors, and its poor drafting.

b. The Requirement of Counseling Under §109(h)(1)

Subsection 109(h)(1) provides that an individual may not be a debtor under any chapter of the Code unless he has received a briefing from an approved nonprofit budget and credit counseling agency during the 180 days preceding the date of filing the petition. The briefing may be given to the debtor individually or in a group, and it may be in person, by phone, or via the Internet. The provision gives rise to administrative and practical questions, such as the determination of reliable standards for approving an agency and the development of Internet- or phone-based programs that provide meaningful education. It has also raised a number of interpretational issues. One of these is whether the debtor may receive the counseling on the same day that she files the petition. Section 109(h)(1) requires the debtor to have received the counseling "during the 180-day period preceding the date of filing of the petition." Some courts have interpreted this language literally to mean that the counseling must have been completed by not later than the day before the petition is filed, while others have held that because the filing of the petition is generally the legally significant point for many purposes in bankruptcy, counseling may occur on the same day as the petition, as long as it precedes the petition. *In re Francisco*, 390 B.R. 700 (B.A.P. 10th Cir. 2008), discussed this debate and sided with the courts that have taken the latter approach. Another interpretational issue is whether §109(h) applies to involuntary petitions. Taken literally, the language "an individual may not be a debtor" suggests that §109(h) applies whether the petition is voluntary or involuntary. However, the court pointed out the absurdity of such an interpretation in *In re Oberle*, 2006 WL 3949174 (Bankr. N.D. Cal. 2006), and refused to allow a debtor to dismiss an involuntary petition on the grounds that he had not received the mandatory credit counseling under §109(h). The court pointed out that such a literal reading of §109(h) would obliterate creditors' ability to seek involuntary relief.

The most profound interpretational difficulty relates to the impact on the court's discretion of the language in §109(g) that "an individual may not be a debtor" under the Code if he has not received the required counseling. Some courts have concluded that the section is jurisdictional in nature so that if the debtor has not complied with or demonstrated statutory grounds for dispensing with credit counseling, the petition must be stricken and the court may not entertain it. Other courts, such as *In re Baruch*, 564 B.R. 424 (M.D. Fla. 2016) and *In re Zarnel*, 619 F.3d 156 (2d Cir. 2010), have held that the section is not jurisdictional, but rather sets forth elements that must be established to sustain the voluntary bankruptcy proceeding. On this interpretation, the petition brings a bankruptcy case into existence, even if the failure to comply with §109(h) may ultimately lead to dismissal of the case for cause under §707(a).[5] The practical significance of this conclusion is that some of the incidents of filing the petition, such as the automatic stay, will come into effect immediately. The question of whether §109(h) is jurisdictional and mandatory also affects the court's discretion to waive or loosen the counseling requirement where the debtor has not complied with it at all or has not fully complied with it. If §109(h) is mandatory, a court has no equitable power to waive its requirements, which are prerequisites to filing. See *In re Giles*, 361 B.R. 212 (Bankr. D. Ut. 2007)

5. Section §707(a) gives the judge discretion to decide whether to dismiss a case for cause. It is discussed in section 6.7.

and *In re Gee*, 332 B.R. 602 (Bankr. W.D. Mo. 2005).[6] However, if §109(h) is not jurisdictional and mandatory, a court does have the discretion to provide relief from its provisions where requiring strict compliance would cause manifest injustice to the debtor. For example, in *In re Hess*, 347 B.R. 489 (Bankr. D. Vt. 2006), debtors in two separate cases had failed to obtain counseling before filing the petition. Although neither debtor qualified under any of the exceptions in §109(h) (discussed in section 5.4.3c), the court allowed them to obtain the counseling after filing. The court reasoned that although §109(h) did not itself give the court discretion to forgive noncompliance and allow postpetition counseling, that discretion can be found in §707(a), under which the court has the power to dismiss a case for cause. In deciding to exercise its discretion, the court examined all the equities of the case, including the debtors' good faith and reasonable efforts to comply with §109(h) and the lack of prejudice to other parties.

Although the question of whether §109(h) is jurisdictional and mandatory usually arises where the debtor is seeking to avoid dismissal of the case, it has sometimes arisen where the debtor has sought to dismiss the case voluntarily. This has happened, for example, where the debtor filed a voluntary petition without undergoing the required counseling. Thereafter, the debtor had second thoughts about being in bankruptcy and sought to dismiss the case on the grounds that he never received the required counseling. (Under §707(a) even a voluntary dismissal by the debtor requires court approval for cause.) Courts have generally not allowed a debtor to rely on his own failure to follow the requirements of §109(h) as a basis for voluntary dismissal. See, for example, *In re Mendez*, 367 B.R. 109 (B.A.P. 9th Cir. 2007) and *In re Timmerman*, 379 B.R. 838 (Bankr. N.D. Iowa 2007). Both courts rejected the argument that §109(h) was jurisdictional. *Timmerman* noted that although lack of eligibility is cause for dismissal under §707(a), the court has the discretion under that section to refuse to dismiss a case on motion of the debtor where the debtor had not acted in good faith.

c. Circumstances under Which Prepetition Counseling May Be Excused: §109(h)(2), (3), and (4)

To provide some flexibility to debtors who cannot comply with the credit counseling requirement before filing the petition, Congress made provision in §109(h)(2), (3), and (4) for a softening of the requirement in limited, narrow circumstances. In some situations, the court may dispense with the counseling. In others, the court may merely allow it to be deferred for a

6. *Giles* based its conclusion not only on the clear language of §109(h) that requires absolute compliance, but also on the principle that courts should not develop new exceptions because Congress has already provided specific, narrow exceptions in subsections 109(h)(2), (3), and (4), discussed later in this section.

short period after the petition. These subsections are clearly intended to be limited in scope, and courts have generally interpreted them in that spirit.

Section 109(h)(2): Lack of Available Counseling Services Section 109(h)(2) dispenses with the counseling if the U.S. Trustee for the debtor's district of residence determines that the approved nonprofit counseling agencies in the debtor's place of residence are not able to cope with the demand for services created by §109(h)(1) and cannot reasonably provide the additional services. The U.S. Trustee must reassess this situation at least annually.

Section 109(h)(3): Exigent Circumstances Section 109(h)(3) permits the court to grant the debtor a temporary "exemption" from counseling under "exigent circumstances" so that the debtor may file the petition before receiving the counseling and obtain the counseling shortly afterward. (Therefore, although §109(h)(3) uses the words "exemption" and "waiver," it does not forgive compliance completely, but just allows for an extension of time.) This subsection is designed to deal with situations in which the debtor has an urgent need to file and cannot obtain the counseling expeditiously enough. The requirements of §109(h)(3) are strict, and the grounds for getting an extension are limited. To obtain the extension, the debtor must submit a satisfactory certification to the court describing exigent circumstances that justify the filing of the petition despite the absence of prepetition counseling, and establishing that the debtor sought but could not obtain requested counseling during the seven-day period[7] beginning on the date the debtor made the request.

"Exigent circumstances" are not defined in the Code. Courts have held that circumstances are exigent where the immediate need for action renders counseling infeasible. The question of what constitute "exigent circumstances" can be difficult. In *In re Romero*, 349 B.R. 616 (Bankr. N.D. Cal. 2006), the court described exigent circumstances as a threat of serious and immediate creditor action that would render it infeasible to obtain counseling before filing the petition. In *Romero* the creditor action in question was the impending garnishment of the debtor's wages. In *In re Cleaver*, 333 B.R. 430 (Bankr. S.D. Ohio 2005), the court found that the impending loss of the debtor's home through a sheriff's sale was an exigent circumstance. In *In re Henderson*, 364 B.R. 906 (Bankr. N.D. Tex. 2007), the court found that the debtor had demonstrated exigent circumstances because he urgently needed to file the petition to stay foreclosure on his home. Many courts have addressed the question of whether a debtor can claim exigent circumstances where the urgency has come about because he failed to take timely

7. The section originally provided for a five-day period, which was increased to seven days in 2009.

action to avert the crisis. Both *Romero* and *Cleaver* did not find that the debtor's delay in dealing with the foreseeable creditor action precluded relief. By contrast, in *In re Dixon*, 338 B.R. 383 (B.A.P. 8th Cir. 2006), the court refused to find impending foreclosure to be an exigent circumstance where the urgency was self-inflicted by the debtor through failure to act promptly on receiving the notice of foreclosure. (*See also* Example 4.)

In addition to showing exigent circumstances, the debtor must satisfy the court that he requested but was unable to obtain credit counseling services from an approved agency during the seven-day period beginning on the date that he made the request. It is not clear if the statute means that the debtor cannot file at all until the expiry of the seven-day period or if the debtor can file immediately, provided that he can show that the counseling services will not be available for seven days after they were requested. In *In re Otero*, 2010 WL 580033 (2010) (not reported in B.R.), the court held that the request must be made at least five days[8] before the bankruptcy filing. The debtor had filed his bankruptcy petition on the day that the foreclosure sale of his home was to take place. He contacted the credit counseling agency on the same day but was not able to get the counseling before the time scheduled for the sale, so he filed the petition with a request for temporary waiver under §109(h)(3). The court found that the debtor had demonstrated exigent circumstances but did not qualify for the waiver because the agency would have been able to provide the counseling within five days of the request, even if it could not have done so before the foreclosure sale. In *Romero* and *Henderson*, the courts read the section more sympathetically and held that the debtor could file before the expiry of the five-day period, provided that he could show that the agency's services would not be available within that period. (In *Henderson* the debtor had consulted with his attorney on a Saturday and the attorney determined that the petition must be filed by the following Tuesday to forestall the foreclosure sale. On the advice of his attorney, the debtor tried many times on the weekend and Monday to obtain Internet counseling, but he could not get a connection to the site until the day after the petition was filed.) (*See also* Example 4.)

If the court is satisfied with the debtor's certification of exigent circumstances, it may authorize the deferral of the counseling for a period of up to 30 days after the petition. The court can extend this period to a maximum of 45 days for cause. Many courts have indicated that all the requirements of §109(h)(3)—the debtor's certification of exigent circumstances, the showing of an unsatisfied request for counseling, and the court's finding that the certification is satisfactory—must be strictly complied with before the court can permit the debtor to file a petition in advance of obtaining the counseling. For example, in *In re Hubbard*, 332 B.R. 285 (Bankr. S.D. Tex.

8. As indicated in footnote 7, the period has now been increased from five to seven days.

2005), the court refused a Ch. 13 debtor's motion to extend the time for credit counseling for 45 days because the debtor's unverified motion contained no affidavit or other declaration as to its accuracy and therefore did not qualify as a certification. In addition, the debtor had not demonstrated exigent circumstances and did not show that she had requested but could not obtain counseling within five days of the request. The court also noted that if the debtor wanted an extension beyond the 30-day period to 45 days, she must separately show cause and explain why she needs the extra time. In *In re Cleaver* the court found exigent circumstances, but nevertheless refused to find that §109(h)(3) was satisfied. The court dismissed the case because the debtor's motion did not contain a written affirmation of the truth of its contents, so it did not constitute a certification, and the debtor made no attempt to obtain counseling. In *In re Mingueta*, 338 B.R. 833 (Bankr. C.D. Cal. 2006), the court, while noting that the requirements of §109(h) were among the most absurd provisions of BAPCPA, held that the mandate of §109(h)(3) is unambiguous and must be strictly enforced. It therefore refused to accept an unsubstantiated request to extend the time for filing the certification and dismissed the case.

Most courts require that the certification be an attestation, sworn to by the debtor under penalty of perjury. See *In re Cobb*, 343 B.R. 204 (Bankr. C.D. Ark. 2006). However, some courts have been less exacting, and have allowed the debtor to make an unsworn written and signed certification that the facts asserted are true.

Section 109(h)(4): Incapacity Section 109(h)(4) authorizes the court, after notice and a hearing, to dispense with counseling if the debtor establishes an inability to comply because of incapacity, disability, or active military duty in a combat zone. This is sometimes called the "permanent exemption" from credit counseling because it completely excuses compliance, rather than just allowing an extension of time to comply. Section 109(h)(4) makes it clear that these excuses are confined to narrow and severe circumstances. The military duty must be in a combat zone; the subsection defines incapacity narrowly to mean mental impairment of such severity that the debtor is incapable of making rational decisions about his financial responsibilities; and disability is defined to mean that the debtor is so physically impaired as to be unable, after reasonable effort, to participate in the briefing. In *In re Ramey*, 558 B.R. 160 (BAP 6th Cir. 2016) the court rejected the debtor's claim of disability under §109(h)(4) because, even though she had suffered from health problems, she was not so physically impaired as to be unable to participate in counseling. The court said that because Congress has specifically defined incapacity and disability, the court cannot use any other definition. In *In re Anderson*, 397 B.R. 363 (B.A.P. 6th Cir. 2008), the debtor, incarcerated in state prison, filed a motion to be excused from counseling on grounds of disability.

The court dismissed the case, holding that incarceration was not a disability as contemplated by §109(h)(4), and that the debtor could have received phone counseling.

§5.5 ELIGIBILITY FOR RELIEF UNDER EACH OF THE SEPARATE CHAPTERS

In addition to the general qualifications, each chapter has its own eligibility requirements. Eligibility for Ch. 7 is set out in §109(b), for Ch. 11 in §109(d), and for Ch. 13 in §109(e).[9] These qualifications are summarized here, and some of them are considered in Examples 1 and 2.

§5.5.1 Ch. 7 (§109(b))

Ch. 7 relief is widely available. Anyone who may be a debtor under the Code may be a debtor under Ch. 7 except for railroads, insurance companies, and various kinds of banking and investment institutions. (The financial failure of these types of businesses is dealt with by other statutes.) A debtor may be placed in Ch. 7 bankruptcy voluntarily or involuntarily.

Although §109(b) provides for wide Ch. 7 eligibility, it is subject to an important qualification under §707(b). Where the debtor is an individual whose debts are primarily consumer debts, §707(b), as amended by BAPCPA, requires the court to dismiss the Ch. 7 case if it finds that the granting of relief would be an abuse of Ch. 7. Abuse is presumed under §707(b) if an individual consumer debtor has disposable income deemed sufficient to make payments under a Ch. 13 plan. (This is known as the "means test" and is fully discussed in section 6.8.) Section 707(b) does not, strictly speaking, impose an eligibility requirement. Grounds for dismissing a case must be distinguished from threshold eligibility requirements of the kind set out in §109. However, the effect of §707(b) is to create a significant barrier to Ch. 7 relief for individual consumer debtors whose disposable income is not low enough or whose circumstances are not desperate enough to allow them to pursue Ch. 7 relief.

9. This book does not cover eligibility for relief under Ch. 9 (municipal bankruptcy), set out in §109(c), and Ch. 12 relief (family farmers), set out in §109(f).

§5.5.2 Ch. 11 (§109(d))

In essence, §109(d) makes Ch. 11 relief available to any person who is eligible to be a debtor under Ch. 7. (Section 109(d) sets out some specified exceptions to this general rule for various kinds of brokers and financial institutions, which need not concern us.) A debtor may be placed in Ch. 11 voluntarily or involuntarily.

Because the means test in §707(b) applies only in a Ch. 7 case, it presents no barrier to an individual consumer debtor's filing under Ch. 11. However, a debtor may not avoid the means test by filing under (or converting the case to) Ch. 11 and then proposing a plan that is equivalent to liquidation under Ch. 7. Although Ch. 11 does contemplate the possibility of a liquidating plan for other debtors, an individual consumer debtor is required to propose a rehabilitation plan in Ch. 11, under which the debtor commits future earnings or income to the payment of creditors. BAPCPA added subsection (8) to the mandatory plan requirements in §1123(a), which makes it clear that the plan proposed by an individual consumer debtor must provide for payments to creditors from the debtor's future earnings or income.

§5.5.3 Ch. 13 (§109(e))

Only an individual with regular income whose debt falls within the limits of §109(e) may be a debtor under Ch. 13. A debtor may not be placed in Ch. 13 involuntarily. Section 109(e) sets out three distinct requirements for eligibility. First, the debtor must be an individual; second, he must have regular income; and third, his total debt at the time of filing must not exceed the prescribed limit.

An "individual with regular income" is defined in §101(30) to mean an "individual whose income is sufficiently stable and regular to enable such individual to make payments under a plan under chapter 13. . . ." Section 109(e) does not state the date on which the regular income requirement must be measured. The date of filing is pertinent, but the court may consider this issue prospectively, so that even if the debtor does not have regular income at the time of filing, he will be eligible if he has a good prospect of regular income when the time for payments under the plan arrives. If the debtor has a job and earns a periodic wage or salary, there is little difficulty in establishing that he has a stable and regular income. This is true even if he is an at-will employee who could be fired at any time. However, where the debtor's earnings come from a less conventional or predictable source, there could be a dispute over his eligibility for Ch. 13. For example, in *In re Baird*, 228 B.R. 324 (Bankr. M.D. Fla. 1999), the debtor lost his job and suffered a stroke after filing the Ch. 13 petition but before the plan was confirmed.

The court found that regular voluntary payments under the plan[10] by the debtor's son qualified as regular income. The court noted that it did not matter that the payments were voluntary and that the debtor's son could cease making them at any time, because the same might be said of a debtor's salary under an at-will employment contract.

Section 109(e) imposes debt limits that confine Ch. 13 to debtors with relatively small estates, as measured by the extent of indebtedness. Under the dollar amounts currently in effect, a debtor is not eligible for Ch. 13 relief unless her noncontingent, liquidated[11] unsecured debts are less than $394,725, and her noncontingent, liquidated secured debts are less than $1,184,200. (As with other dollar amounts, these debt limits will be next adjusted under §104 with effect from April 1, 2019.) If the debtor's secured or unsecured debts exceed the limit, she may not obtain Ch. 13 relief; she must file for rehabilitation under Ch. 11. (Liquidation under Ch. 7 may also be an alternative for some debtors but will not be available to a consumer debtor whose income exceeds the means test discussed in section 6.8.)

A debtor and spouse may file a joint Ch. 13 petition, but their combined debts must be within the limits set for an individual. An individual who is otherwise qualified for Ch. 13 but is a stockbroker or commodity broker cannot file under Ch. 13.

§5.6 CONVERSION FROM ONE CHAPTER TO ANOTHER

§5.6.1 General Principles

The selection of relief under a particular chapter is not irreversible. The debtor and other parties in interest are able, subject to certain restrictions, to apply to court to convert a case under one chapter into a case under another. Each chapter of the Code has its own rules and limitations relating to conversion. Sections 706, 1112, and 1307 govern conversion from Chs. 7, 11, and 13, respectively. A case cannot be converted to a particular chapter unless the debtor is eligible for relief under that chapter. Therefore,

10. The challenge to the debtor's eligibility was made some time after the petition had been filed but before plan confirmation. Under §1326 a debtor is required to begin making payments under the proposed plan 30 days after filing the petition. Therefore, payments under the proposed plan must begin before confirmation.

11. A debt is contingent if the debt has been created (for example, by contract or tort) but the debtor's obligation to pay it will only arise upon the occurrence of an uncertain future event. A debt is therefore noncontingent if the debtor's payment obligation is not subject to any such future contingency. A liquidated debt is one that is capable of being calculated by arithmetical means from established information. The meaning of contingent and liquidated debts is discussed more fully in section 17.2.2.

the eligibility requirements (discussed in section 5.5) apply to conversions as they do to the original petition. With some limitations, a case can be converted from one chapter to another at any time during the course of the bankruptcy proceeding. Conversion is not confined to the initial stages of the case.

There are various reasons why a party may seek to convert a case. For example, a debtor may have filed a petition for relief under Ch. 13. During the course of the case, it may become apparent to the debtor that this was not the best choice, or circumstances may have changed to alter the prospects of successful debt adjustment. The debtor is able to convert the case into a case under another chapter, such as a liquidation under Ch. 7. Creditors and other parties in interest may also seek conversion of a case. For example, if creditors can show that the debtor's Ch. 13 case is abusive or has little chance of successful consummation, they can apply for conversion of the case to Ch. 7 as an alternative to applying for dismissal of the case. Both voluntary and involuntary cases can be converted. For example, after creditors have filed a petition for involuntary relief under Ch. 7, the debtor may convert the case to Ch. 11 or 13, thereby avoiding liquidation in favor of debt adjustment.

§5.6.2 Conversion by the Debtor

The debtor is treated more liberally than other parties in converting from one chapter to another. Section 706(a) allows the debtor to convert the case from Ch. 7 to a case under Ch. 11, or 13, §1112(a) allows the debtor to convert a Ch. 11 case to Ch. 7, and §1307 allows the debtor to convert the case to Ch. 7. These sections contain few restrictions on the debtor's discretion to convert the case. Notice and a hearing are not needed and the debtor is not generally required to show cause for the conversion. Although the right to convert under these sections is broad, it is not absolute. In *In re Marrama*, 549 U.S. 365 (U.S. 2007), the U.S. Supreme Court held that although §706(a) is written in permissive terms, the bankruptcy court has the discretion to forbid the conversion if it is motivated by bad faith or is an abuse or manipulation of the Code. In *Marrama* the debtor filed misleading schedules and made a transfer of valuable property for the purpose of insulating it from creditors' claims. When the trustee sought to recover and liquidate the property, the debtor moved to convert the case to Ch.13. The majority of the Supreme Court affirmed all the lower courts in holding that the debtor had forfeited the right to convert. The court found the basis for the bankruptcy court's discretion to refuse conversion in §706(d), which allows conversion only if a debtor "may be a debtor under such chapter," read with §1307(c), which allows a case to be dismissed for cause. The court reasoned that because there was cause to dismiss the Ch. 13 case for bad faith, it cannot be said that the debtor may be a debtor under that chapter. The court also found that the bankruptcy court had discretion to refuse conversion under the general power conferred in §105(a) to issue orders to accomplish the aims of the Code. *Marrama* was concerned with a motion to convert a Ch. 7 case to Ch. 13. It is not clear what impact the decision has on conversions to other Chapters. In *In re Euro-American Lodging*, 365 B.R. 421 (Bankr. S.D. N.Y. 2007), the court held that the decision did apply to a conversion to Ch. 11. However, in *In re DeFrantz*, 454 B.R. 108 (B.A.P. 9th Cir. 2011), the court held that differences in procedural rules justified not applying *Marrama* to a conversion from Ch. 13 to Ch. 7, which the debtor could accomplish as a matter of right.

§5.6.3 The Impact of §707(b) on the Debtor's Ability to Convert from Ch. 13 to Ch. 7

As noted in section 5.5.1, the grounds for dismissal of a Ch. 7 case for abuse in §707(b) must be distinguished from threshold eligibility for Ch. 7. Nevertheless, some courts have interpreted §707(b) as creating a barrier to an individual debtor converting a Ch. 13 case to Ch. 7. Section 707(b) requires the dismissal of a Ch. 7 case filed by an individual debtor whose debts are primarily consumer debts if the granting of relief would be an abuse of Ch. 7. Abuse is presumed if the debtor's income exceeds the means test set out in the section.[12] By its terms, §707(b) applies to a case "filed" by a debtor under Ch. 7. It is not clear if the subsection is applicable where a debtor first files under Ch. 13 and then converts the case to Ch. 7. Courts have differed in answering this question. Some courts adopt a plain meaning approach and hold that the use of the word "filed" and the omission of any reference to conversion in §707(b) makes the means test inapplicable where the original case is filed under Ch. 13 and later converted to Ch.7. See, for example, *In re Layton*, 480 B.R. 392 (Bankr. M.D. Fla. 2012) and *In re Fox*, 370 B.R. 639 (Bankr. N.J. 2007). Other courts have rejected the plain meaning approach on the grounds that the purpose of §707(b) is to preclude Ch. 7 relief to a debtor who does not qualify for it under the means test. To allow a debtor to evade the means test by first filing under Ch. 13 and then converting to Ch. 7 undermines the intent of the section. See, for example, *In re Kellett*, 379 B.R. 332 (Bankr. D. Or. 2007). The court in *Layton* responded to this concern by observing that if a debtor deliberately uses this strategy to evade §707(b), the court has the means, either under §707(a) (dismissal for

12. *See* section 6.8 for a full discussion of §707(b).

cause) or §105 (the court's general power to issue appropriate orders), to dismiss the case.

§5.6.4 Conversion by Parties Other Than the Debtor

Chs. 7, 11, and 13 all provide for the conversion of a case at the instance of a party other than the debtor, but the wording of the provisions differ: Section 706(b) allows the court to convert a Ch. 7 case to Ch. 11 "at any time" on request of a party in interest, and after notice and a hearing. Section 1112(b) allows the court to convert a Ch. 11 case to Ch. 7 on request of a party in interest, after notice and a hearing, for cause, and upon determining that conversion is in the best interests of creditors and the estate. Section 1307(c) similarly allows the court to convert a Ch. 13 case to Ch. 7 on request of a party in interest, after notice and a hearing, for cause, if this serves the best interests of creditors. Note that none of these provisions allow for the conversion to Ch. 13 at the instance of a party other than the debtor. The restrictions applicable to an involuntary petition, discussed in Chapter 6, apply to conversion as well. Creditors cannot place the debtor into Ch. 13 by an involuntary petition, so the case cannot be converted to that chapter without the debtor's consent.

Section 706(b) does not contain language, as found in §§1112(b) and 1307(c), requiring a showing of cause and the best interests of parties. Nevertheless, the decision to grant a motion to convert from Ch. 7 to Ch. 11 is within the court's discretion, and courts do evaluate cause and the best interests of all parties in exercising this discretion. For example, in *In re Parvin*, 549 B.R. 268 (W.D. Wash. 2016) the district court upheld the bankruptcy court's conversion of a Ch. 7 case to Ch. 11 at the behest of the U. S. Trustee where creditors would receive no more than 20 percent of their claims in Ch. 7 and the debtor, an orthopedic surgeon, would earn a high enough salary to pay creditors in full over three years under a Ch. 11 plan.

§5.6.5 The Impact of Conversion on the Commencement Date of the Case

As explained in sections 6.4 and 6.6, the dates of the filing of the petition and the order for relief are significant for many purposes. When a case is converted, the date of conversion is treated like the filing of a new case for some purposes but not for others. Section 348 sets out the rules concerning the impact of conversion and indicates which incidents of bankruptcy are treated as arising on the conversion date and which of them continue to be measured from the original petition or order for relief.

As noted in section 5.8, in a Ch. 7 case, the individual debtor's postpetition income is not included in estate, but in a Ch. 13 case §1306 includes the debtor's postpetition earnings in the estate, and portion of those earning are applied under §1322 to the payment of creditors under the plan. If the debtor converts a case from Ch. 13 to Ch. 7, §348(f) provides that unless the debtor has made the conversion in bad faith, property of the Ch. 7 estate consists of property of the estate as at the date of the original petition which remains in the possession or control of the debtor at the date of conversion. (If the conversion is in bad faith, the date for determining property of the estate is the date of conversion.)

As regards the debtor's postpetition earnings, the effect of §348(f) is that the debtor's future income no longer enters the estate, but belongs to the debtor. During the course of the Ch. 13 case, prior to its conversion to Ch. 7, the debtor would have been paying to the trustee that portion of the debtor's postpetition income allocated to the payment of creditors under the plan. All such payments received by the trustee and distributed to creditors are not refundable to the debtor. However, in some cases, at the time of conversion the Ch. 13 trustee may be holding accumulated funds from the debtor's postpetition earnings that have not yet been paid out to creditors. Courts had disagreed about whether those funds should be distributed to creditors or returned to the debtor. The Supreme Court resolved this issue in *Harris v. Viegelahn*, 135 S.Ct. 1829 (U.S. 2015). It held that it would be inconsistent with the purpose of §348(f) to pay out any accumulated and undistributed funds to creditors after the debtor has converted the case. Upon conversion, the case is governed by Ch. 7, under which the debtor's postpetition earnings are part of his fresh start estate. The funds must therefore be returned to the debtor.

§5.7 THE DEBTOR'S CHOICE OF RELIEF

When a debtor is eligible for relief under more than one chapter of the Code, the debtor must decide which form of relief is most appropriate. In most cases, the choice is between liquidation or some form of rehabilitation. However, some debtors may qualify for more than one of the rehabilitation chapters and must decide not only between liquidation or rehabilitation but also between the advantages and drawbacks of the different applicable types of rehabilitation. A full understanding of the factors that influence choice of relief can only come after a thorough study of bankruptcy law, so a detailed discussion of this issue is premature at this stage. However, section 5.8 provides some guidance on these factors by summarizing the significant differences between the different forms of bankruptcy relief. Some of the issues that influence the choice of relief are introduced in Examples 1, 2, and 3.

§5.7.1 Corporate Debtors

For a corporate debtor in financial difficulty, the choice between liquidation (whether under Ch. 7 or Ch. 11) and rehabilitation under Ch. 11[13] is stark. Liquidation means the end of the debtor. Its business closes down, its assets are sold off, its employees lose their jobs, and the ownership interests of its stockholders are wiped out. It is only by seeking reorganization that the corporation has any prospect of overcoming its financial problems and surviving as a viable business.

§5.7.2 Individual Debtors

The individual debtor's choice between liquidation under Ch.7 or rehabilitation under Ch. 13 or Ch. 11 is not as dramatic. In either event, the individual will be able to handle her financial difficulties, and may hope to emerge from bankruptcy with a discharge and a fresh start. Therefore, the debtor's choice of relief will be heavily influenced by the determination of which form of bankruptcy best serves her interests. However, the debtor is not given untrammeled discretion in making this decision.

Ever since the enactment of the Code in 1978, Congress has assumed that the amount of disposable income that a debtor could commit to payments under a Ch. 13 plan, and hence the extent of creditor recovery under that chapter, would likely be higher than the liquidation value of the debtor's nonexempt assets. For this reason, the Code, as originally enacted, tried to encourage debtors to choose Ch. 13 over Ch. 7 by providing incentives, such as a broader Ch. 13 discharge. By the time that it enacted BAPCPA in 2005, Congress had been persuaded that the incentives were not effective and that many debtors who could afford to pay more under a Ch. 13 plan were choosing Ch. 7 liquidation as an easy way out: a debtor with relatively low-value nonexempt assets and a comfortable future income could shield that income by giving up the assets. This conclusion was controversial. The opposing view was that the perceived abuse of Ch. 7 was greatly exaggerated and that many Ch. 7 consumer debtors were in genuine financial distress and in need of Ch. 7 relief. Nevertheless, Congress decided that there was a problem with consumer abuse of liquidation bankruptcy, and enacted the means test, discussed in section 6.8, which creates a presumption of abuse where an individual Ch. 7 debtor has the apparent means to support a payment plan under Ch. 13.

---

13. As explained in section 5.5.3, a corporation is not eligible for Ch. 13 relief, so it can reorganize only under Ch. 11.

§5.8 A SUMMARY OF THE SIGNIFICANT DIFFERENCES AMONG CHS. 7, 11, AND 13 THAT MAY INFLUENCE THE CHOICE OF RELIEF

As noted in section 5.2, the principal choice to be made in selecting bankruptcy relief is that between liquidation and rehabilitation. However, even if rehabilitation is selected, there are differences among the rehabilitation chapters that will make one of them more appropriate than the others. This is a brief overview of the significant differences among the forms of bankruptcy relief under Chs. 7, 11, and 13 that may have a bearing decision of which form of bankruptcy should be selected. Of course, as explained in section 5.5, the debtor's choice between chapters is confined to those chapters for which the debtor is eligible. This summary of the important differences in the various forms of bankruptcy is intended to give you a broad perspective. It is necessarily simplified and lacks the detail and qualifications that will become apparent in the treatment of these topics in the following chapters of the book. (Examples 1, 2, and 3 illustrate how some of these differences among the Code chapters may be relevant to a debtor's choice of relief.)

(1) Involuntary petition. An involuntary petition can be filed only in a Ch. 7 or 11 case.

(2) The automatic stay. The stay applies under all chapters, but it protects certain co-debtors only in Ch. 13 (§1301). However, in Chs. 7 and 11, the court has the discretion within its general equitable powers under §105 to enjoin action against a co-debtor where appropriate.

(3) Property of the estate. In a Ch. 7 case and a Ch. 11 case involving a corporation, property of the estate consists of the debtor's property at the time of the petition. Postpetition property is generally not part of the estate. In a Ch. 13 case, or a Ch. 11 case involving an individual debtor, the estate consists of both property of the debtor at the time of the petition and postpetition property (§§541, 1115, and 1306).

(4) The disposition of estate property. In a Ch. 7 case, estate property is liquidated and the proceeds distributed to creditors. An individual debtor is entitled to claim exemptions in some property under §522. It may be possible for the debtor to reacquire estate property by redemption under §722 or reaffirmation under §524. In cases under Chs. 11 and 13, estate property is revested in the debtor upon confirmation of the plan, except to the extent that the plan allocates it to the payment of claims (§1141 and 1327). An individual debtor is entitled to exemptions under these chapters too, but because estate property revests in the debtor, exemptions play a different role here — they factor into the analysis of the debtor's minimum required payments under the plan.

(5) The debtor's postpetition income. A Ch. 7 case does not affect the debtor's postpetition income, which is part of his fresh start estate. In cases under Ch. 13, the debtor's disposable postpetition income must be applied to payments under the plan (§§1322(a) and 1325(b)). There is no set rule on postpetition income in a corporate Ch. 11 case. Its allocation to the plan depends on the terms of the plan. However, an individual Ch. 11 debtor must commit disposable postpetition income to the plan (§§1123 and 1129).

(6) Sources of funding payments to creditors. In a Ch. 7 case, the funding of payments comes primarily from the proceeds of nonexempt estate property (§§704 and 726). In a Ch. 11 case, the debtor has flexibility in devising sources of funding, such as the sale of assets, future income, investments, or loans. Payment may be in money, property, or securities (§1123). In a Ch. 13 case, plan payments are funded by disposable future income, but property of the estate may be sold to generate funds, or may be surrendered to satisfy creditor claims (§1322).

(7) The administrator of the estate and operator of the debtor's business. In a Ch. 7 case, the trustee administers the estate and, if the debtor has a business, conducts short-term business operations. The business is liquidated as soon as possible (§§701 to 703 and 721). In a Ch. 11 case, the debtor in possession assumes the functions of the trustee and operates the business, unless there is cause to appoint a trustee (§§1104 and 1108). In a Ch. 13 case, a trustee is appointed and performs investigative and supervisory functions. If the debtor has a business, he continues to operate it under the trustee's supervision but does not have the status of a debtor in possession (§§1302 and 1304).

(8) Conversion of the case to another chapter. In cases under Chs. 7 and 13, the debtor has a broad but not absolute right to convert the case to another chapter for which the debtor is eligible (§§707 and 1307). A creditor can convert a Ch. 7 case to Ch. 11 for cause (§706). A creditor can convert a Ch.13 case to Ch. 7 for cause (§1307). In a Ch. 11 case, the debtor has a right to convert with some limitations (§1112). A creditor can convert the case to Ch. 7 for cause (§1112).

(9) Dismissal of the case. A Ch. 7 case may be dismissed by the debtor or other party in interest only for cause. In the case of an individual consumer debtor, abuse of the Code is cause for dismissal by a creditor or other party in interest (§707). A Ch. 11 case may be dismissed by the debtor or another party in interest for cause (§1112). In a Ch. 13 case, the debtor has a broad but not absolute right to dismiss. Other parties in interest can dismiss for cause (§1307).

(10) The duration of the case. In a Ch. 7 case, property is realized and the proceeds distributed as expeditiously as possible (§704). There is no statutory limit to the duration of a Ch. 11 plan, but an individual Ch. 11 debtor must commit disposable income to the plan for five years (§1129(a)(15)). In a Ch. 13 case, the maximum payment period for a debtor who earns below the median family income is three years or, with court approval, five years. The maximum (and possibly also the minimum) payment period for an above-median debtor is five years (§1322).

(11) Standards fixing the minimum level of payment to creditors. There is no minimum level of payment prescribed in a Ch. 7 case because creditors cannot get more than the proceeds of the liquidation of the estate. These proceeds are distributed in the order of priority prescribed by the Code. Secured claims are paid to the full value of their collateral. Unsecured claims are ranked in priority order. Where the estate is badly insolvent, claims with lower priority (in particular, general unsecured claims) may get no payment at all (§§506, 507, and 726). The standards for minimum payment in a Ch. 11 case are complex. Their applicability is dependent on whether the debtor has been able to negotiate creditor assent to the plan, or must force it on unwilling classes of creditor in a cramdown. The complexity of these rules defies encapsulation here. They are governed by §1129 and are explained in section 20.4. In cases under Ch. 13, secured claims are entitled to payment in full to the value of the collateral. The debtor may surrender the property to the creditor. However, if the debtor chooses to keep the collateral, the creditor retains its lien, and the payments made on the secured claim under the plan must equal the present value of the claim — that is, its face value plus interest. Priority claims must be paid in full, and payments to general unsecured claims must at least equal the present value of what they would have received in a liquidation. In addition, the debtor is required to commit all disposable income to the plan for a prescribed period (§§1322 and 1325).

(12) Claim classification. Apart from the statutory classifications of claims into secured, priority, and general claims, alluded to in item (11), there is no claim classification in a Ch. 7 case. However, in Chs. 11 and 13, the debtor does have some ability to designate classes of creditor in the plan and to treat those classes differently, provided that there is a rational basis for the classification and the discrimination is fair (§§1122, 1123, 1129, and 1322).

(13) The cure of default and restructuring or modification of secured obligations. In a Ch. 7 case, the debtor cannot usually keep encumbered property by restructuring the obligation, unless the debtor enters into a reaffirmation agreement with the creditor under §524. One of the benefits of rehabilitation under Ch. 11 or Ch. 13 is that the debtor is able (with some limitations) to cure default and restructure secured obligations (§§1123 and 1322).

(14) Creditor participation in formulating and voting on a plan. There is no plan in a Ch. 7 case, so this is inapplicable. Creditor consent does not feature in a Ch. 7 distribution. In a Ch. 11 case, creditors are involved in plan formulation and under some circumstances may even propose a plan in competition with the debtor's plan. Creditors vote on the plan, and the debtor needs a prescribed level of creditor approval to get the plan confirmed (§§1103, 1121, 1125, 1126, and 1129). In a Ch. 13 case, only the debtor may propose a plan, and creditors do not vote on it. The plan is confirmed if it complies with the Code requirements (§§1321, 1325, and 1327).

(15) Discharge. A corporation cannot receive a discharge under Ch. 7 (§727) but can receive a discharge under Ch. 11 (§1141). An individual may receive a discharge under all chapters of the code. There are differences in the debts encompassed by the discharge under the different Code chapters, and there is also some variation among chapters on the time that the discharge is granted and the basis for denying the discharge or excluding debts from it (§§523, 727, 1141, and 1328).

Examples

1. Virtuous Victual Company, L.L.C. makes organic microwaveable meals that it sells at wholesale to supermarkets. Virtuous Victual Company had done well until it suffered a series of calamities last year. Expensive equipment broke down and had to be replaced; its workers went on strike, shutting down its operations for three months; and bacteria in its packaged food made consumers seriously ill, resulting in lawsuits claiming millions of dollars in damages.

   These crises have drained Virtuous Victual Company's resources and have left it exposed to extensive potential liability to its poisoned customers. In addition, adverse publicity has badly damaged sales of its products. Virtuous Victual Company has not been able to keep current on repayment of its debts, and many of its loans are in default.

Virtuous Victual Company has decided to seek bankruptcy relief. Under which chapters is it eligible for relief? What factors should it take into account in choosing between the chapters for which it is eligible?

2. What impact would it have on your answers to Example 1 if the debtor was not Virtuous Victual Company, L.L.C., but rather Ms. Virtue Victual, doing business as a sole proprietor under the trade name "Virtue's Victual Company"? Virtue owes $15,000 on credit cards for consumer purchases, and her unsecured business debts for rent, supplies, and operating expenses are $250,000. In addition, she has a mortgage of $300,000 on her home, and a mortgage of $500,000 on her business premises.

3. Viva Voce is a singer of modest talent. She ekes out a living by performing at weddings, minor clubs, and similar venues. In a typical year, she manages to find between ten and twenty jobs, and her income varies from one year to the next, depending on the nature and quality of the engagements. This year, her earnings were $55,000. Last year she earned $40,000, and the year before, $52,000.

   Viva's earnings are not enough to cover her living expenses, so she has relied on several credit cards to buy the goods and services that she needs. As a result, she has accumulated $100,000 in debt. She has used all her cards to the full extent of her credit limit, so she cannot use them anymore. She can barely afford to make the minimum required monthly payments on the cards. Viva has no nonexempt assets, and she understands that she would probably be able to discharge all her debt with no payment by filing a petition under Ch. 7. However, she feels that this would be morally wrong, and she would like to make an effort to pay off at least some of her debt under a payment plan. Is she eligible to file a petition under either Ch. 11 or Ch. 13?

4. Bud Getary has been in financial difficulty for some time. On February 1, he consulted with a nonprofit credit counseling agency approved by the U.S. Trustee and received advice on how to manage his debt and negotiate with creditors for payment extensions. He followed the advice and managed to make agreements with his creditors for the time extensions. However, he could not cope with the payment schedule and soon fell behind. Several creditors initiated collection proceedings. On August 5 the finance company that held a security interest in his car repossessed it. On August 6, he received notice that his bank account had been garnished by another creditor. On August 7, he consulted an attorney, who recommended immediate bankruptcy filing to stay the foreclosure on the

car and the garnishment. The Ch. 13 petition was filed on August 7. On August 8, Bud's attorney realized that Bud's consultation with the credit counseling agency had occurred more than 180 days prior to the petition. He therefore advised Bud to call the same nonprofit agency again to receive further counseling by phone. Bud did this on August 9. Bud satisfies the eligibility requirements for Ch. 13 as set out in §109(e).

Is there any other barrier to his eligibility for relief? If so, is there anything that he can do to overcome that barrier?

Explanations

EXPLANATIONS

1. Virtuous Victual Company, L.L.C., a limited liability company, falls within the broad definition of "corporation" in §101(9). It is clearly eligible for relief under Chs. 7 and 11 because none of the exclusions in §109(b) or (d) are applicable. As noted before, these two chapters of the Code are the most universally available. As a corporation, Virtuous Victual Company may not be a debtor under Ch. 13, which is confined to individuals. §109(e). In deciding whether to liquidate its business or attempt to rehabilitate it, a corporate debtor must determine, in essence, whether its financial difficulties are such that it is feasible to restructure the business operation and deal with its liabilities. If there is no prospect of reorganization, liquidation is the appropriate choice, which can be accomplished either under Ch. 7 or Ch. 11.[14] It will result in cessation of the corporation's business, the realization of its assets, and the distribution of the proceeds to creditors. The corporation will not be rehabilitated and it will become defunct, and the shareholders will lose their equity in the corporation.

   On the other hand, if there is a prospect that the corporation's business can become viable again after reorganization, Ch. 11 is an attractive alternative. It gives the debtor a great deal of flexibility in reordering its affairs. The filing of the Ch. 11 petition gives the debtor the ability to negotiate with creditors under the protection of the Code in an attempt to formulate a plan of reorganization that will allow it to continue in business while compromising its debts and restructuring its operations. Among other things, it may sell off unprofitable or unwanted assets or operations; reject or restructure its contractual relationships; resolve unliquidated, contingent, and disputed claims; and alter the terms of its secured obligations. The debtor usually remains in control of its business as a debtor in

14. As mentioned in footnote 2, it is possible to liquidate a corporation under Ch. 11. The ultimate impact of liquidation will be the same as in Ch. 7, but the debtor retains greater control of the liquidation process.

possession and is entrusted with administration of the estate. If the debtor is able to have a plan confirmed and can consummate it, it will ultimately emerge from bankruptcy in a more efficient and viable form. Although existing shareholders are not assured of retaining any equity in the reorganized corporation, they do at least have a shot at doing so.

The facts of this question are not detailed enough for a full analysis of Virtuous Victual Company's prospects of effective reorganization. However, there are some hints that Ch. 11 may be feasible. The corporation's financial problems have been caused by a series of setbacks, rather than by marketing or management difficulties (although the calamities may, of course, be attributable to lapses in management). Some ugly product liability claims have to be disposed of, but if the corporation is able to deal with this issue and restore consumer trust, its business could revive and become profitable again.

2. On this variation of the facts, the business is not a corporation, legally distinct from its owners (shareholders), but simply the individual debtor herself, Virtue Victual, doing business in her individual capacity under a trade name. The fact that the trade name includes the word "Company" does not change this. Therefore, if the debtor elects to rehabilitate instead of liquidate, she may not be confined to a choice between Chs. 7 and 11, but may be able to choose Ch. 13 instead of Ch. 11. The fact that Virtue's debts are mostly business debts, not consumer debts, does not disqualify her from Ch. 13 bankruptcy. Although Ch. 13 is commonly associated with consumer bankruptcies, it is not confined to consumer cases and is available to any individual debtor who satisfies its other eligibility requirements. In fact, many small businesses are conducted as sole proprietorships, and it is quite common to find Ch. 13 debtors who aim not only to deal with household and personal debt, but also handle business debt and attempt to save a business.

   To qualify for Ch. 13 relief under §109(e), the individual debtor must have regular income and must fit within the debt limits of noncontingent, liquidated, unsecured debts of less than $394,725 and noncontingent, liquidated, secured debts of less than $1,184,200. The question does not give us enough information to determine if Virtue has regular income. (This issue is covered in Example 3.) The question does tell us that she is within the debt limits for her noncontingent, liquidated unsecured and secured debts ($265,000 unsecured and $800,000 secured). In addition, she apparently has great potential tort liability to her poisoned customers. This would put her over the unsecured debt limit, but if her tort liability is not yet liquidated at the time that she files her petition, it is not included in the debt calculation under §109(e) for eligibility purposes. These debts are unliquidated because their amount cannot be computed arithmetically from settled facts, such as a contract term or other known figures, but can only be determined following a trial and judgment or a settlement agreement.[15] If Virtue elects to file under Ch.13, she has an incentive to file as soon as possible, before the tort claims become liquidated and push her over the debt limits.

If Virtue does not qualify for Ch. 13 relief, either because she cannot show stable and regular income or because her debt is too high, she would be confined to Ch. 11 for rehabilitation relief. If she is eligible for Ch. 13 relief, she would have to decide whether Ch. 13 or 11 is more suitable to her circumstances. Section 5.8 gives you some broad idea of the differences between Chs. 11 and 13 that may influence a debtor in choosing between those chapters. As a general matter, Ch. 13 is much simpler and more streamlined, so it is often the best choice for a small business debtor who is eligible for it. However, Ch. 11 gives the debtor more control over the estate and allows greater flexibility.

As regards the choice between rehabilitation (under either Ch. 11 or Ch. 13) and Ch. 7 liquidation, many of the same considerations apply as those outlined in Explanation 1. An individual debtor also has to be concerned about the potential that she will not be allowed to obtain Ch. 7 relief under §707(b), but this section will not apply to an individual in business whose debts are not primarily consumer debts. Unlike a corporation, Virtue will survive Ch. 7. (As regards an individual debtor, "liquidation" is not really used in the same sense as, say, Joseph Stalin may have used it.) Nevertheless, Ch. 7 will result in the liquidation of Virtue's nonexempt assets (both business and personal) and the termination of her business, so if she believes that there is a chance of rehabilitating the business, Ch. 13 is the better alternative.

3. Ch. 11 is widely available to both individual and corporate debtors, so Viva would be eligible to file a petition under Ch. 11. However, she has an estate of modest proportions and her financial affairs are not complex, so Ch. 13 would be more appropriate for her than Ch. 11. Ch. 13 is simpler and has fewer procedures and safeguards that have to be complied with. A trustee is appointed, so the debtor plays a less active role in administering the estate. Creditors, too, have lesser rights of involvement. The only reason a debtor like Viva would choose Ch. 11 over Ch. 13 would be ineligibility for Ch. 13.

---

15. Do not confuse the issue of excluding a debt for eligibility purposes from the issue of allowing the debt as a claim against the estate. If Virtue decided to pursue Ch. 13 relief, the tort claimants will prove claims in the estate which will be admitted or rejected and resolved by negotiation or litigation. Also, do not confuse unliquidated and contingent debts. Although Virtue's liability to the poisoned customers is dependent on a jury finding that Virtue is liable for their injuries, that does not make the debt contingent. A contingent debt is one that is conditional upon a future uncertain event occurring. The tortious conduct creating the debt has already occurred. The jury determination is a process of fact finding, not a legal contingency in the sense that the term is used in law. (Some courts have taken a different view and have treated disputed debts as unliquidated or contingent.)

As an individual debtor, Viva is eligible for relief under Ch. 13 if she satisfies the prerequisites of §109(e). That section has three prerequisites: She must be an individual, she must have regular income, and her noncontingent liquidated unsecured and secured debts must not exceed the maximum amount allowed. Two of these requirements are clearly satisfied: she is an individual and her debts are not even close to the maximum allowed. The only doubt is whether she has regular income.

Section 101(30) defines an "individual with regular income" as one whose income is sufficiently stable and regular to enable payments to be made under the Ch. 13 plan. Over the last three years, Viva's income ranged from a low of $40,000 to a high of $55,000. She does not have a steady job, but enters into short-term contracts for various performances each year. Although the Code does not require a person to be a regular wage earner to qualify for Ch. 13, it does require some predictability in income so that performance under the plan is reasonably assured. When a debtor is in Viva's position, the court must assess the likelihood of a reliable source of income, based on all of her circumstances: for example, her ability to budget irregular earnings, the likelihood of her being able to secure future performance engagements, and the amount she needs to maintain herself. In short, while the stability of Viva's income is an issue, she is not necessarily disqualified because of its irregularity as long as the facts show sufficient reliability to support a plan.

Viva may therefore satisfy the threshold requirement of eligibility for Ch. 13 relief. This means only that she can file for relief under that chapter, but does not ensure that she will be successful in formulating and ultimately consummating a Ch. 13 plan. Discussion of Ch. 13 requirements for the contents of the plan and the debtor's duties and obligations in the Ch. 13 case is deferred to Chapter 18.

4. Bud was not eligible for relief at the time that he filed the petition because he did not satisfy the requirements of §109(h)(1). Although he did receive credit counseling from an approved credit counseling agency before the petition, the counseling occurred about 188 days before he filed his petition, which is more than the allowed statutory period of 180 days. Some (but not all) courts are willing to exercise discretion in allowing something short of strict compliance with the requirements of §109(h). However, it is likely a rare case in which the court would consider the requirements of §109(h) to have been satisfied by counseling received prior to the statutory 180-day period. This did happen in *In re Enloe* (cited in Section 5.4.3(a)). The court found that it had discretion to depart from the strict language of §109(h)(3). It held, under all the circumstances of the case, that counseling received by the debtor 189 days before the petition was sufficient to satisfy §109(h)(3). The court felt that this was justified because the debtors delayed filing while they attempted to sell

their home to avoid foreclosure and bankruptcy; the debtors' failure to receive counseling again before they filed was due to their attorney's oversight; the debtors' financial circumstances had not changed since the counseling; and the debtors did undergo further counseling after filing the petition. Bud's counseling was about the same distance away from the petition as *Enloe's*, but there is no indication of the special circumstances that motivated the court's flexibility in that case. In any event, many courts would disagree with the *Enloe* court's exercise of discretion in light of the plain language of §109(h)(3).

Bud could try to invoke one of the three exemptions from prepetition counseling set out in §109(h)(2), (3), and (4). He clearly does not qualify for the exemptions in subsections (2) and (4), so his only chance to avoid dismissal of his case is to ask the court to validate his postpetition counseling under subsection (3). The requirements for the court's approval of postpetition counseling under §109(h)(3) are stringent.

§109(h)(3)(B). The counseling must occur within the short time limit specified—30 days from the petition, or for cause, not more than 45 days. Bud's counseling did occur within this period—he received it the day after filing the petition.

§109(h)(3)(A). The debtor must file a motion with the court to approve the postpetition counseling. The motion must include a certification, satisfactory to the court, asserting specific facts that describe and explain the exigent circumstances that merit deferral. The certification must state that the debtor requested the services of an approved agency, but was unable to obtain them during the seven-day period after he requested them. Many (but not all) courts require the certification to be attested to under oath. Bud cannot satisfy the certification requirement because of his complete failure to seek counseling immediately before filing the petition. He cannot certify that he requested and was unable to obtain the services during the seven-day period after requesting them, even on a sympathetic reading of §109(h)(3), such as that adopted by *In re Henderson* and *In re Romero*, cited in section 5.4.3(c).§109(h)(3)(A)(i). The circumstances must be exigent. "Exigent circumstances" are not defined in the Code, but, as noted in section 5.4.3, impending creditor action, such as foreclosure on or seizure of important property, could qualify as exigent circumstances. However, some courts are less sympathetic to a claim of urgency where the debtor has failed to take earlier steps that may have prevented matters reaching a crisis point. Bud is confronted with a crisis that could qualify as exigent circumstances, and some courts may so find. However, a court that adopts a more rigorous standard for exigent circumstances may regard him as the author of his own misfortune because he stopped paying creditors and then waited for the inevitable creditor response before consulting an attorney.

CHAPTER 6

The Commencement and Dismissal of the Bankruptcy Case

§6.1 OVERVIEW

This chapter covers the commencement of voluntary and involuntary bankruptcy cases and the dismissal of a bankruptcy case by the debtor (voluntary dismissal) or by the court or a party in interest other than the debtor (involuntary dismissal).

Section 6.2 briefly explains the venue of a bankruptcy case, governed by 28 U.S.C. §§1408, 1409, and 1412. Sections 6.3 to 6.5 deal with the voluntary bankruptcy petition, filed by the debtor under §301 (or by joint debtors under §302) and the supporting documents that the debtor must file under §521. Voluntary petitions constitute the great majority of bankruptcy filings. Section 6.6 deals with less common involuntary petitions, filed by creditors under §303. It covers the qualifications for filing an involuntary petition under §§303(a), (b), and (c), the grounds for relief under §303(h), and petitioner liability for dismissal of the petition under §303(i). For the sake of simplicity, the Ch. 7 case involving an individual debtor is used as the model for this discussion. With some variations, bankruptcy under the other chapters follows a similar path in the initial stages. Diagram 6a traces the sequence of routine core proceedings in a Ch. 7 case. The time periods are as stated in the Rules, but most can be extended by the court.

Sections 6.7 and 6.8 cover dismissal of the case. Although dismissal is not confined to the early stages of the case, motions to dismiss the case are often filed soon after the case is filed, so this is a convenient place to discuss

Rough Skeleton Showing the Sequence of a Ch. 7 Case

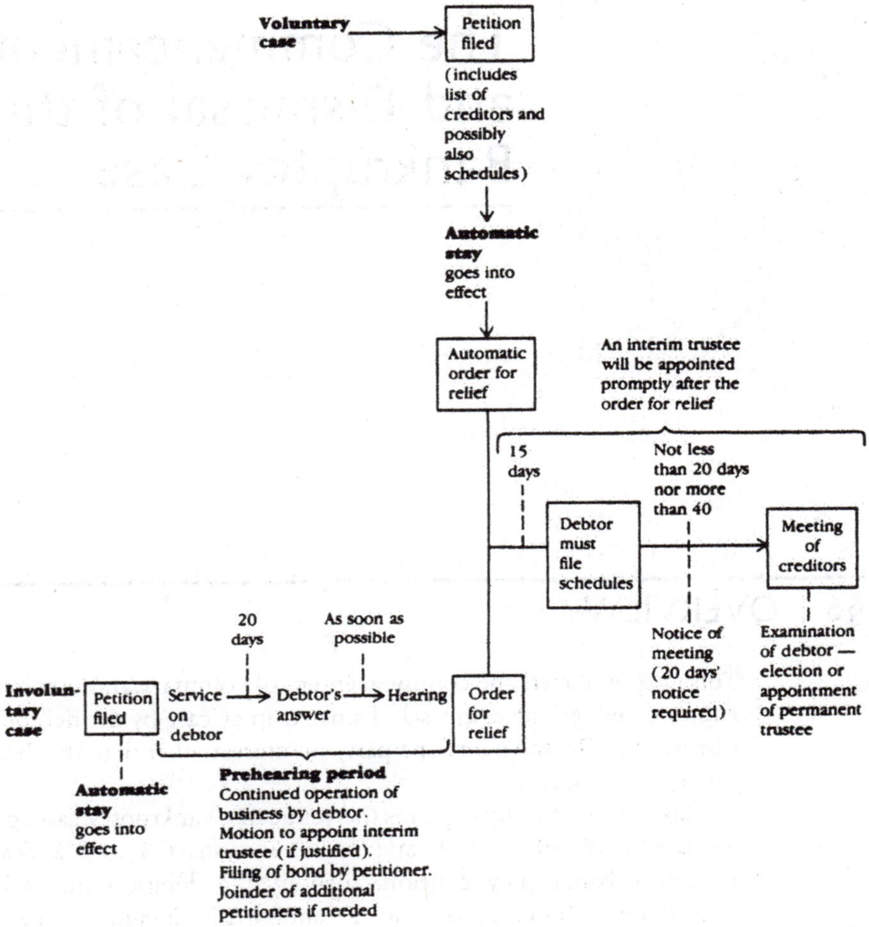

Diagram 6a

them. Section 6.7 covers the provisions for voluntary and involuntary dismissal in Chs. 7 (§707), 11 (§1112), and 13 (§1307), and the effect of dismissal under §349. Section 6.8 deals with dismissal of a Ch. 7 case on the grounds of abuse under §707(b).

§6.2 VENUE

As noted in section 4.2.1, 28 U.S.C. §1334 grants jurisdiction over bankruptcy to district courts generally. 28 U.S.C. §§1408, 1409, and 1412 deal with the question of which federal district is the most appropriate geographical locale for the disposition of the proceedings. As with other sections of title 28, these provisions refer only to the district court. Once venue is determined, the bankruptcy courts in that federal district deal with the proceedings under the general referral from the district court. Venue rules curtail the petitioner's or plaintiff's freedom to choose a geographic location for the bankruptcy case or other proceedings. They are intended to prevent forum shopping and to make it difficult for a person to initiate proceedings in an unsuitable place that is awkward or inconvenient for other parties in interest. This does not mean that the correct venue is always convenient for everyone. The appropriate location could be distant from the situs of a transaction or property or from the home base of a party. However, restrictions on venue give the courts some control over the choice of federal district by the debtor, petitioning creditors in an involuntary case, or plaintiffs in related cases.

The venue rules are not discussed here in detail. As a general matter, the proper venue of the bankruptcy case is determined by the debtor's location (defined in §1408 by alternative tests) for the 180 days before the petition.[1] Under §1409, the venue of the case itself is also usually the proper venue for proceedings ancillary to the case, but the section recognizes exceptions to this rule in defined circumstances under which another venue is more appropriate. Section 1412 empowers a court to transfer of a case to another district in the interest of justice or for the convenience of the parties.

§6.3 THE VOLUNTARY CASE

As mentioned above, for the sake of simplicity this discussion of the voluntary petition is based on a Ch. 7 filing by an individual debtor. When an attorney is consulted by a client who needs bankruptcy relief, the first task is to obtain information about the client's affairs. Detailed knowledge is required for the accurate completion of the schedules that must be filed with, or shortly after, the petition. In addition, the attorney needs a comprehensive understanding of the debtor's economic history and current financial position to fulfill the role of counseling the debtor on choice of relief, identifying potential problems, and planning the appropriate course of action to be taken in the case. For example (without attempting

1. A corporate debtor filing under Chs. 7 or 11 has far more flexibility in choosing venue. Pursuant to §1408, a corporate debtor may file its petition in any district where: 1) the debtor's principal place of business is located; 2) the debtor's principal assets are located; 3) the debtor is incorporated; or 4) a case concerning an affiliate of the debtor is pending. This flexibility has led to blatant forum shopping in corporate bankruptcy cases. *See* Samir D. Parikh, *Modern Forum Shopping in Bankruptcy*, 46 Conn. L. Rev. 159 (2013).

to be definitive), the attorney needs to have information about the debtor's location to determine venue, and to have full details about the debtor's financial history, assets and liabilities, business affairs, pending lawsuits, disposition of assets, income, and future plans and desires.

Once all this information is gathered, the case is commenced by filing a petition. (Ideally, an attorney should not file a petition until she has all the pertinent information and can assess the impact of filing and anticipate potential problems. However, reliable information is not always available. In addition, sometimes the need to file immediately means having to proceed without complete information.) In a voluntary case, the filing of the petition operates automatically as an order for relief—that is, as an order placing the debtor in bankruptcy. The form of the petition set out in the Bankruptcy Rules (Form B101) is simple. It does not even look like a pleading, because it has been designed so it can easily be completed by checking boxes, and can be computer-generated. In essence, it provides information about the debtor, contains minimal assertions establishing venue and eligibility for relief, and identifies the chapter under which relief is sought. A consumer debtor must acknowledge understanding the choice of relief, and this acknowledgment must be certified by the debtor's attorney. The debtor's signature of the petition certifies the accuracy of the allegations in the petition and constitutes an assertion, under Rule 9011, that the petition is filed in good faith and not for abusive purposes.

The supporting documents required by §521 and the Bankruptcy Rules are filed with, or shortly after, the petition. They include a list or schedule of liabilities, with the identity of creditors so that the clerk can notify them of the filing; a schedule of property; a schedule of claims, properly categorized into secured and unsecured classes, and identified as to whether they are contingent, liquidated, or disputed; a claim of exemptions; a schedule of income and expenses; a schedule of executory contracts; a summary of the debtor's financial history and current financial position; and a statement of intent by the debtor with regard to the proposed surrender of encumbered property, or its retention by reaffirmation or redemption, or the avoidance of any liens on it. The Bankruptcy Abuse Prevention and Consumer Protection Act of 2005 (BAPCPA) significantly increased the debtor's duty to provide information and disclosures under §521. Section 521(a) requires the debtor to file copies of payment advices and other evidence of payments received from an employer in the 60 days before the petition, an itemized calculation of net monthly income, and a statement of reasonably anticipated increases in income or expenses over the next 12 months. Section 521(e) requires the debtor to file a copy of the debtor's federal income tax return for the most recent tax year prior to the petition. Section 521(b) requires the debtor to file a certificate from the nonprofit credit counseling agency consulted by the debtor under §109(h) (*see* section 5.4.3), showing what services were rendered to the debtor.

§6.4 THE VOLUNTARY PETITION AS AN ORDER FOR RELIEF

In an involuntary case, the debtor does not become bankrupt until a hearing is held and the court gives judgment granting the creditors' petition. *See* section 6.6. This judgment is referred to in the Code as the order for relief. In a voluntary case, there is no formal adjudication of bankruptcy. In terms of §301(b), the filing of the petition automatically places the debtor in bankruptcy. In other words, in a voluntary case, the filing of the petition itself constitutes the order for relief.

Many provisions in the Code specify that certain consequences come into effect on the filing of the petition. Others specify that the date of the order for relief is the relevant date for particular purposes. It is important to remember that in voluntary cases, the filing and the order for relief are the same date, while in involuntary cases they are different. For example, §701 requires an interim trustee to be appointed after the order for relief. This means that the trustee is appointed immediately after the petition in a voluntary case but is only appointed after the hearing and adjudication of bankruptcy in an involuntary case. (Even in an involuntary case, a creditor can apply to court for the appointment of a trustee before the order for relief. The creditor must show cause, such as grounds to believe that the debtor will mismanage the estate in the interim period.) By contrast, §362 provides that the automatic stay comes into effect upon filing of the petition. Therefore, in both voluntary and involuntary cases, the stay takes effect at the commencement of the case.

§6.5 JOINT CASES, JOINTLY ADMINISTERED CASES, AND CONSOLIDATION

§6.5.1 Joint Cases

If spouses own assets and owe obligations jointly, the bankruptcy of only one of the spouses does not provide full relief to the family as an economic unit: The nonbankrupt spouse remains liable on joint debts. Therefore, both spouses may need to file for bankruptcy. They may file separate petitions but are permitted by §302 to file a joint case. This saves costs, because the joint debtors pay a single filing fee and a single set of administrative costs. Joint filing does not mean that the estates of the spouses are combined. The court has the discretion under §302 to allow them to be consolidated or to require them to be kept separate. The considerations that affect the decision to consolidate or separate the estates are noted below. A joint petition can only be filed voluntarily. Creditors cannot file an involuntary petition against spouses jointly. In an involuntary case, the creditors of each spouse must file a petition against the spouse that is their debtor. Often spouses are joint debtors, so the separate petitions could be filed by the same creditors.

Section 302 is applicable only to spouses. The Code does not define "spouses," but the plain meaning of §302 is to confine the availability of joint petitions to those who are legally married under state law. The Defense of Marriage Act (DOMA) used to define marriage for all federal law purposes as confined to heterosexual marriage, but the Supreme Court invalidated DOMA as a violation of the Fifth Amendment in *United States v. Windsor*, 133 S. Ct. 2675 (2013). Since then, same-sex spouses qualify as spouses for purposes of the Code, provided that they are married under state law. In *in re Villaverde*, 540 B.R. 431 (Bankr. C.D. Cal. 2015) the court held that a couple who had chosen not to marry, but instead to register as domestic partners, did not qualify as spouses for the purpose of filing a joint petition.

There is no provision in the Code for a joint case to be filed by debtors other than spouses (for example, affiliated corporations or a corporation and its owner), no matter how closely connected or related they may be. (A partnership is treated as a separate entity under the Code, so a partnership petition is not a joint petition.) Although the bankruptcy of a corporation may result in its owner's bankruptcy as well, these two separate legal entities must file separate petitions.

§6.5.2 Joint Administration

Even though closely related debtors other than spouses cannot file a joint petition, the court is able to order the joint administration of their cases. Joint administration keeps the estates separate so that each has its own assets and liabilities but places the estates under the administration of the same trustee, thereby cutting down administrative costs and allowing for the more convenient disposition of the cases. Joint administration is therefore an administrative device to save costs and allow for the more efficient handling of the separate estates. It is provided for in Rule 1015(b).

§6.5.3 Consolidation of Cases

a. Procedural Consolidation

Rule 1015(a) provides for the procedural consolidation of cases where two petitions have been filed in the same court involving the same debtor. This might occur, for example, where two sets of creditors have both filed involuntary petitions against the same debtor. The rule permits the court to combine the cases. As only one debtor is involved, procedural consolidation is distinct from the other situations described here.

b. Substantive Consolidation

In addition to the above type of procedural consolidation, the court also has the power as a court of equity to order the substantive consolidation of cases against separate debtors. Substantive consolidation is not provided for in the Code, but is a judicially devised remedy based on the court's equitable discretion. Where spouses (whether they have filed jointly or separately) or other closely related debtors, such as an individual and his corporation or a parent corporation and its subsidiaries, are in bankruptcy, the court can combine their estates so that assets are pooled and creditors of each become creditors in the consolidated estate.

Substantive consolidation is different from joint administration because it combines the two separate estates into a single bankruptcy estate. This could prejudice creditors of the debtor with the higher asset-to-debt ratio. Substantive consolidation is therefore not routinely permitted even if the debtors are closely affiliated, and a court will not likely use its equitable consolidation power unless the party seeking consolidation can prove that the overall equities favor consolidation. This may happen where creditors have dealt with the debtors as a single economic unit, without relying on their separate identities, or where it is apparent that the affairs of the debtors are so entangled that it is very difficult to separate their assets and liabilities. For example, in *In re Owens Corning*, 419 F.3d 195 (3d Cir. 2005), the court refused to permit the consolidation of the estates of the parent corporation and its 17 subsidiaries because it would have had a negative impact on the rights of creditors of the parent by eliminating guarantees from the subsidiaries, the affairs of the debtors were not so entangled that they could not be separated, and consolidating the estate would not result in significant cost savings to the benefit of all creditors. In *In re Amco Insurance*, 444 F.3d 690 (5th Cir. 2006), the court held that the bankruptcy court had abused its discretion in allowing the substantive consolidation of the estates of a corporation and its principal shareholder where the equities did not favor it. In addition, the bankruptcy court had ordered the consolidation *nunc pro tunc*, so that it took effect at a time before the shareholder had filed his bankruptcy petition. The court held that it is not permissible to consolidate estates with effect from a date prior to the bankruptcy of both debtors.

There is a link between substantive consolidation and the equitable remedy of piercing the corporate veil, in which a court disregards the separate identity of the corporate entity and its shareholder. While the doctrines are conceptually related, they are distinct. *In re Petters Co., Inc*, 506 B.R. 784 (Bankr. D. Minn. 2013) contains a full discussion of the factors to be taken into account and the considerations to be weighed in deciding whether the estates of debtors should be substantively consolidated.

§6.6 INVOLUNTARY CASES

§6.6.1 Introduction

Involuntary cases make up quite a small percentage of the bankruptcy filings each year. Section 303, which governs involuntary cases, has many restrictions and limitations, making involuntary relief available only in a narrow range of circumstances. To obtain an involuntary order for relief, petitioners must satisfy two distinct sets of requirements. First, the qualifications for filing prescribed by §§303(a), (b), and (c) must be met. Thereafter, if the debtor opposes the involuntary petition, there must be a hearing of the controverted involuntary case, at which the petitioners must establish grounds for relief under §303(h). Congress deliberately set these exacting requirements for an involuntary petition to deter a creditor from using the remedy of involuntary bankruptcy as a tool for collecting an isolated debt and to ensure that placing the debtor into involuntary bankruptcy serves the interests of the creditor body as a whole.[2] As an additional disincentive to inappropriate use of an involuntary petition, if the petition is not successful, the petitioners could be liable to the debtor for attorney's fees, costs, and damages. This is discussed in section 6.6.3.

§6.6.2 Qualifications for Filing Under §§303(a), (b), and (c)

An involuntary petition is permitted only if all the qualifications set out in §§303(a), (b), and (c) are satisfied.

a. §303(a): The Nature of the Debtor and the Relief

The debtor must be subject to involuntary bankruptcy. Most debtors can be subjected to an involuntary petition, with a few exclusions set out in §303(a). An involuntary case may not be filed against a noncommercial (essentially, charitable) corporation or a farmer (as defined in §101(20)). Section 303(a) confines involuntary petitions to cases under Chs. 7 and 11. A debtor cannot be placed involuntarily into bankruptcy under Ch. 13.

---

2. See *In re Murrin*, 477 B.R. 99 (D. Minn. 2012).

b. §303(b): The Number and Qualification of Creditors

Section 303(b)(1) requires that the aggregate amount of claims held by all the petitioners be at least $15,775,[3] excluding claims that are contingent as to liability, the subject of a bona fide dispute as to liability or amount, or secured by a lien. (As discussed below, there must be at least three petitioning creditors unless §303(b)(2) applies.) That is, to determine if the monetary qualification for the petition is satisfied, any contingent claim, bona fide disputed claim, or secured claim held by the petitioners is excluded. Having excluded these claims, the total balance of the amounts due to the petitioners must be at least $15,775.

(1) Secured claims. Section 303(b)(1) does not completely exclude secured creditors from participating in the petition. Section 303(b)(1) uses the language "more than the value of any lien on property of the debtor securing such claims. . . ." If a creditor is fully secured (that is, the collateral is worth at least as much as the debt), none of its claim can be counted. However, if a creditor is only partially secured, the debt can be counted to the extent that it exceeds the value of the collateral.

Section 303(b) relates only to whether the claim qualifies the creditor to be a petitioner in an involuntary case. The subsection has no impact on the manner in which the claim will be treated in the estate if the court grants the petition and places the debtor in bankruptcy.

(2) Contingent claims. The meaning of contingent is discussed in section 17.2.2. A broad definition is enough for present purposes: A contingent claim is one that is conditional on a future uncertain event. The debtor's potential liability has already been created by contract or by wrongful act (so the legal basis for the debt has already been created), but the debtor will only become liable to pay the debt if a future uncertain event occurs.

(3) Claims subject to bona fide dispute. Subsection §303(b)(1) states that a debt cannot be counted for purposes of qualifying the petition if it is "the subject of a bona fide dispute as to liability or amount." The words "as to liability or amount" were added to §303(b)(1) by BAPCPA. Prior to the amendment, some courts had held that a dispute that related only to the amount of the claim did not render the whole claim subject to a dispute, so the undisputed portion could be counted for qualification purposes. Courts are divided on the question of whether the language added by BAPCPA overturned cases decided prior to its enactment, holding that a

---

3. This is the current amount under the 2016 administrative adjustment to dollar amounts under §104. The amount will be adjusted again with effect from April 1, 2019. *See* section 3.4.3 for an explanation of these dollar adjustments.

creditor was qualified to petition based on the undisputed portion of the claim. Some courts continued to adopt that approach, while others held that a bona fide dispute as to any portion of the claim would disqualify the claim under §303(b)(1), even if some part of the claim was not disputed. See, for example, *In re Regional Anesthesia Associates*, 360 B.R. 466 (Bankr. W.D. Pa. 2007), in which the court held that provided that the dispute arises out of the same transaction as the claim and is directly related to the claim, the dispute disqualifies the entire claim for purposes of §303(b)(1). The same approach was adopted in *Fustolo v. 50 Thomas Patton Drive, LLC.*, 816 F.3d 1 (1st Cir. 2016) on the grounds that this interpretation is a straightforward reading of the language of the section and better serves the section's purpose of protecting a debtor from coercive tactics.

Although "bona fide" may suggest a subjective test of honest belief in the merits of the claim, courts generally adopt a stricter objective standard and require that there is either a genuine dispute of material fact or a meritorious legal argument against the claim.[4] The dispute must be specific and articulated, not merely a general denial or challenge. In *In re Dilley*, 339 B.R. 1 (B.A.P. 1st Cir. 2006), the court said that once the petitioner establishes the existence of a claim, it creates a prima facie case that it is undisputed, and the debtor must then show that there is a bona fide dispute. To do this, the debtor cannot simply deny the claim, but must present facts that demonstrate, by a preponderance of the evidence, the existence of a bona fide dispute.[5] As noted in *In re TPG Troy, LLC*, 793 F.3d 228 (2d Cir. 2015) the court does not adjudicate the dispute at this stage, but merely determines if there is a genuine dispute. The dispute must relate to the debt itself, so the debtor cannot claim that a debt is disputed merely because she has a counterclaim against the creditor arising out of a different transaction or event.

A court judgment upholding a creditor's claim resolves the dispute, ending the debtor's ability to assert that the claim is subject to a bona fide dispute. However, this conclusion is less certain if an appeal of the judgment is pending at the time of the petition. Some courts have held

---

4. See *In re TGP Troy, LLC*, 793 F.3d 228 (2d Cir, 2015); *In re Byrd*, 357 F.3d 433 (4th Cir. 2004); and *In re Dilley*, 339 B.R. 1 (B.A.P. 1st Cir. 2006).

5. In *In re Dilley* the debtor had been indicted for killing his estranged wife and his mother. His two children witnessed the alleged murders. The debtor had pleaded not guilty to the charges, and the criminal case was pending when the estate of the debtor's deceased ex-wife and the guardians of his two children filed an involuntary petition against him. The claim of the ex-wife's estate was for wrongful death and for maintenance, and the children's claims were for the intentional infliction of emotional distress and for support. Although the debtor had not presented any facts to demonstrate a bona fide dispute, the bankruptcy court held that the debtor's not-guilty plea in the criminal case was sufficient to establish a bona fide dispute as to liability. The B.A.P. reversed, holding that a not-guilty plea was no better than a bare denial of liability. It did not demonstrate a bona fide dispute because it did not present substantial factual or legal questions bearing on liability.

that merits of the appeal must be evaluated to decide whether the debtor's appeal continues the bona fide dispute. Other courts have held that this question is appropriate only if the judgment has been stayed pending the appeal. However, if the judgment is not stayed, it terminates any bona fide dispute on the claim, notwithstanding the appeal. In *Fustolo*,[6] the bankruptcy court adopted the first approach, but the court of appeals adopted the second. Because the judgment had been stayed, the court evaluated the merits of the appeal and found that the debtor's arguments on appeal had sufficient merit to constitute a continuation of the bona fide defense.

(4) The number of creditors. The number of petitioners required for an involuntary petition depends on the size of the creditor body. In simple terms, if the debtor has 12 or more creditors, at least 3 must join in the petition. If the debtor has 11 or fewer creditors, only 1 petitioner is needed. The petitioners must, of course, satisfy the claim requirements described in section 6.6.2 b paragraph (3). The qualification of a party as a creditor is measured as at the date of the petition. In *In re Faberge Restaurant of Florida*, 222 B.R. 385 (Bankr. E.D. Fla. 1997), the court held that a debtor could not defeat an involuntary petition by paying a petitioner after the petition had been filed.

(i) *The three-creditor rule where the debtor has 12 or more creditors.* The purpose of the three-creditor rule is to protect a debtor from an involuntary petition by a single creditor who cannot muster support for the petition from any other creditors. To prevent evasion of the rule, courts require the petitioning creditors to be separate legal entities independent of each other. The creditors may be related (such as a parent corporation and its subsidiary or a shareholder and his corporation) provided that they each have genuinely separate claims against the debtor, and neither controls the other. Therefore, a creditor cannot artificially create another creditor by, say, assigning part of its claim to the other entity.

Courts look at all the circumstances of the relationship between related petitioners to decide if each of them has independent decision-making capacity. For example, in *In re Sims*, 994 F.2d 210 (5th Cir. 1993), the three petitioners were affiliated corporations that had the same officers. Notwithstanding that relationship, the court found them to be separate entities for purposes of §303(b). Each petitioner's claim arose out of a different transaction entered into by the debtor and that petitioner. The petitioners operated in different regions as distinct businesses, had separate bank accounts, and had strictly honored corporate formalities in

6. *Fustolo v. 50 Thomas Patton Drive, LLC.*, 816 F.3d 1 (1st Cir. 2016).

their ownership of assets, the payment of taxes, and their dealings with each other. (The analysis used to decide if a corporate entity is a truly independent petitioner is analogous to that conducted by courts under the equitable doctrine of piercing the corporate veil, which is used to hold a shareholder liable for corporate debts where he has employed the corporation manipulatively and inequitably.)

(ii) *Filing by a single creditor where the debtor has fewer than 12 creditors.* Not all creditors are counted in deciding if the debtor has fewer than 12 creditors. Section 303(b)(2) sets out a formula that excludes five categories of creditors from the count. The subsection expressly excludes employees of the debtor, insiders of the debtor, and recipients of avoidable transfers. In addition, the subsection, by using the language "12 *such* holders" refers back to the "holders" described in §303(b)(1), which excludes another two classes — holders of contingent claims and holders of claims subject to a bona fide dispute.

The reason for requiring only one petitioner where the debtor has fewer than 12 creditors is that it would be very difficult to find three petitioners in such a small creditor pool. Holders of contingent and disputed claims are excluded from the count because they are not qualified to be petitioners. Employees, insiders, and recipients of avoidable transfers are excluded because they have a stake in preventing the debtor's involuntary bankruptcy and are not likely to join an involuntary petition.

A couple of cases illustrate how creditors are counted for the purpose of §303(b)(2). In *In re Skye Marketing Corp.*, 11 B.R. 891 (Bankr. E.D.N.Y. 1981), the court reduced the debtor's list of 24 creditors to fewer than 12 by excluding an insider, voidable claims, and contingent claims. By contrast, in *Atlas Machine and Iron Works v. Bethlehem Steel Corp.*, 986 F.2d 709 (4th Cir. 1993), the petitioning creditor argued that about 60 of the debtor's 66 creditors should be excluded from the count because the debts owing to them were not overdue and should therefore be regarded as disputed. The argument was that because the debts were not due yet, the debtor would have disputed the obligation to pay if the creditors sued on them at the time of the petition. The court rejected this argument on the basis that a debt is not to be treated as disputed unless it involves a meritorious existing conflict.

(5) The nature of §303(b): jurisdictional or substantive. Where a requirement is jurisdictional, it must be satisfied as prerequisite for filing a case. If the requirement is not satisfied, the court has no subject matter jurisdiction to entertain the petition. However, if a requirement is not jurisdictional, but merely a substantive element to be established for relief, the petition is effective to commence the case, and the court can grant relief if the debtor waives objection by failure to challenge the petition. There had been some question over whether the requirements of §303(b) are jurisdictional. However, this no longer seems to be the correct view. In *Arbaugh v. Y&H Corp.*, 546 U.S. 500 (2006), the Supreme Court articulated the general principle that a court should not interpret statutory requirements as being jurisdictional unless Congress has made it clear in the language of the statute that it intends them to be. The court again enunciated this principle in *Stern v. Marshall*, 564 U.S. 462 (2011) in relation to consent to bankruptcy court jurisdiction. On the basis of this general principle, §303 should not be treated as jurisdictional because there is no language in §303 to suggest Congressional intent to make it jurisdictional. Subject matter jurisdiction over claims arising under the Code is conferred by 28 U.S.C. §1334, and the requirements of §303 are more properly treated as elements to be proved to obtain relief.[7]

c. §303(c): Subsequent Joinder of a Petitioner

If a single creditor files the petition genuinely believing that the debtor has fewer than 12 creditors, and it later appears that there are more, the petitioner may solicit additional petitioners. Section 303(c) permits a qualified creditor to join the petition at any time before the case is dismissed or relief is ordered. Although §303(c) does not expressly allow the court to cut short the period in which additional petitioners must be found, *In re DSC, Ltd.*, 486 F.3d 940 (6th Cir. 2007), held that the court has the discretion to curtail the time for joinder by setting a bar date. In *In re Bock Transportation, Inc.*, 327 B.R. 378 (B.A.P. 8th Cir. 2005), the court stressed that a single petitioner must have a genuine and reasonable belief that the debtor has fewer than 12 creditors. If the petitioner does not have this reasonable belief but files in the hope that she will later find two more creditors to join the petition, the court may refuse to allow the joinder and dismiss the case. See also *In re Luxeyard*, 556 B.R. 627 (Bankr. D. Del. 2016) in which the court observed that if the single petitioning creditor filed the petition in bad faith, the court may prohibit it from later joining other creditors. The petitioner acts in bad faith if, at the time of filing the petition, it knows that a single-creditor petition does not satisfy §303(b). However, bad faith is not confined to that situation. Even where a single creditor is sufficient under §303(b), the petition can be dismissed on grounds of bad faith if the creditor filed the petition for an improper purpose. This ground of bad faith is discussed in section 6.6.5.

---

7. See *In re Trusted Net Media Holdings, LLC*, 550 F.3d 1035 (11th Cir. 2008) and *In re Zarnel*, 619 F.3d 156 (2d Cir. 2010). Section 4.2.1 explains bankruptcy jurisdiction and discusses *Stern v. Marshall*. *See also* section 5.4.3 for a discussion of a similar issue relating to the requirement of credit counseling.

§6.6.3 Procedures from the Filing of the Petition to the Order for Relief

An involuntary petition is served on the debtor. If the debtor does not controvert the petition, §303(h) requires the court to order relief by granting the petition. To controvert the petition, the debtor must file an answer within the period prescribed by the rules. The answer may raise defenses available to the debtor under nonbankruptcy law (a substantive defense to the claim of a petitioner) or under the Code (such as failure to satisfy §303), or may move to dismiss the case on grounds such as improper venue. A trial follows on the issues raised by the pleadings, and the petitioners must establish one of the two grounds for relief set out in §303(h). (The petitioners are only required to establish grounds for relief under §303(h) if the debtor controverts the involuntary case.) In challenging the petition, the debtor may demand a bond under §303(e) to secure any costs or damages that may be awarded if the petition is dismissed.

During the period of delay between the filing of the petition and the grant of the order for relief, §303(f) permits the debtor to continue the operation of a business and to deal with property. However, following notice and a hearing, §303(g) allows the court to order the appointment of an interim trustee to take over the debtor's affairs upon a party in interest showing that the debtor is likely to mismanage property or harm the estate by this activity.

§6.6.4 The Grounds for Relief

Section 303(h) permits the court to grant an order for relief in a contested involuntary petition only if the petitioners are able to establish one of two alternative grounds for relief:

1. The debtor is generally not paying debts as they become due, unless such debts are the subject of a bona fide dispute as to liability or amount; or
2. Within 120 days before the filing of the petition, a custodian was appointed or took possession of the debtor's property. This requirement is not satisfied if the custodian was appointed to take possession of less than substantially all the debtor's property for the purpose of lien enforcement.

The grounds for relief serve an important function in contested involuntary cases: They constitute a justification for forcing an unwilling debtor into bankruptcy and limit the power of creditors to obtain bankruptcy relief.

It is not enough for creditors to show merely that the debtor owes them money and has not paid. By demonstrating one of the two grounds of relief, they also show that the debtor's financial problems are more general. The two situations that constitute grounds of relief are indicative of broad financial instability in the debtor's affairs.

The requirement that creditors establish grounds for relief has a long tradition in bankruptcy law. Prior to 1978, the petitioners had to establish that the debtor had committed one of several "acts of bankruptcy" that included making fraudulent or preferential transfers, admitting inability to pay, or making an assignment for the benefit of creditors. The grounds in §303(h) replace these acts of bankruptcy by substituting circumstances regarded as directly relevant to the debtor's financial condition. The two grounds are alternative. Only one need be established by the petitioners.

a. General Nonpayment of Due Debts (§303(h)(1))

Section 303(h)(1) requires a general pattern of nonpayment of undisputed mature debts during the period immediately preceding the petition. The general failure to pay due debts is known as equity insolvency. Insolvency on the equity test is a good barometer of the debtor's financial difficulty because wide default on debts is a manifestation of financial distress. Congress used the equity test in §303(h) instead of the alternative test for insolvency, called the "balance sheet" test, based on an excess of liabilities over assets. The theory is that it is likely to be easier for petitioning creditors to gather information on the debtor's nonpayment of debts than to access the debtor's financial information required to show insolvency on the balance sheet test.

In deciding whether a debtor is generally not paying due debts, courts are obviously influenced by the percentage of debts in default, both in number and value. The more widespread the default and the larger the proportionate value of overdue debt, the more likely that general nonpayment will be found. However, courts also look beyond the bare figures and take into account such factors as the relative importance of the unpaid debts, the length of time that they are overdue, the extent to which the size of overdue payments has increased over a period of time, the degree of irresponsibility shown by the debtor, and other factors that tend to demonstrate that the debtor's position is precarious enough to justify involuntary relief.[8]

The requirement that unpaid debts not be subject to a bona fide dispute means that if the debtor's reason for not paying the debt is a legitimate

8. See *In re Westside Community Hospital Inc.*, 112 B.R. 243 (Bankr. N.D. Ill. 1990) and *In re Murrin*, 477 B.R. 99 (D. Minn. 2012). Example 3 deals with the test of general nonpayment of debts.

factual or legal dispute with the creditor, the debt may not be taken into account in deciding whether the debtor is generally not paying debts when due. Courts generally apply the same objective test here as they do when considering whether a petitioner's claim is the subject of a bona fide dispute for purposes of qualifying the petitioners: There must be a prima facie meritorious defense. Thus, "bona fide" is not wide enough to cover an honest but misguided dispute by the debtor. See, for example, *In re Rimell*, 946 F.2d 1363 (8th Cir. 1991).

Where a debtor has only one creditor, default on that debt inevitably constitutes universal default. Nevertheless, some courts have refused to grant involuntary relief where the debtor has only one creditor on the basis that the nonpayment of a single debt is contrary to the concept of general nonpayment. An exception is made to this rule where there is evidence of fraud by the debtor. In *In re Concrete Pumping Service, Inc.*, 943 F.2d 627 (6th Cir. 1991), the court questioned the propriety of precluding the use of §303(h)(1) in a single-creditor case. It considered that general nonpayment should be found where there is default on the debtor's only debt, and the totality of the circumstances justifies relief.

b. The Appointment of a Custodian Within 120 Days Prior to the Petition (§303(h)(2))

Section 101(11) defines "custodian" to mean a receiver or trustee appointed under nonbankruptcy law or an assignee for the benefit of creditors. The appointment could result from a voluntary arrangement initiated by the debtor or from a court order in a nonbankruptcy case. Custodial proceedings are usually used by or against insolvent debtors. Therefore this ground, like the first one, is premised on a manifestation of the debtor's insolvency. By filing an involuntary petition, concerned creditors are able to take the debtor's estate out of the state law trusteeship and bring it under the aegis of the Code. However, they must act within 120 days of the appointment or taking of possession. Section 303(h)(2) is expressly not available when the appointment of the custodian is for the purpose of enforcing a lien against less than substantially all of the debtor's property.

§6.6.5 Creditor Good Faith in the Filing of the Petition

Section 303(b) sets out the statutory requirements to be satisfied by the petition and §303(h) articulates the grounds for relief to be established by the petitioners if the debtor controverts the petition. Section 303 states no other requirements, so it is arguable that provided petitioning creditors satisfy the requirements articulated in the section, the court should grant the petition. However, debtors have sometimes made the argument that even though the petition satisfies the statutory requirements, the court has the discretion to deny the petition if it has been filed in bad faith. The debtor made such an argument in *In re Forever Green Athletic Fields, Inc.*, 804 F.3d 328 (3rd Cir. 2015). It was undisputed that the petitioners satisfied the requirements of §303(b) and that the debtor was not generally paying its debts as they became due under §303(h). Nevertheless, the debtor sought dismissal of the petition on the grounds that the creditors' motivation in filing the petition was to gain advantage over other creditors by coercing the debtor to pay them ahead of its other creditors. The court acknowledged that §303 articulates no good faith requirement,[9] and that some courts have adopted the position that the motivations of the petitioners are irrelevant, as long as they satisfy the statutory criteria. Nevertheless, the court held that as a court of equity, the bankruptcy court has the discretion to deny a petition where, under the totality of the circumstances, the petitioners have filed it, not with the goal of advancing the collective interests of creditors, but for improper purposes, contrary to the spirit and goals of the Code, such as to obtain a tactical advantage or to serve only the petitioners' own self-interest. The totality of the circumstances standard was expounded on in *In re Luxeyard*:[10] The basic inquiry is whether the creditor had filed the petition for an improper purpose—that is, for a purpose for which it was not appropriate to seek bankruptcy relief. A wide range of purposes would fall into this category, including malice, harassment, seeking an advantage inconsistent with the goals and purposes of bankruptcy, or attempting to advance the petitioner's interests over those of other creditors. Although "bad faith" may suggest a subjective test, the test here is objective—it is not based on the petitioner's actual motivations, but on whether a reasonable creditor would have considered it appropriate to file the petition under the circumstances.

§6.6.6 The Effect and Consequences of the Order for Relief in an Involuntary Case

The order for relief is the judgment placing the debtor in bankruptcy. As noted before, in an uncontroverted case, the court grants the order for relief under Ch. 7 or Ch. 11 if the petition satisfies §303(b) and in a controverted case, where the petition satisfies both §303(b) and satisfies §303(h). The effect of the order for relief is explained in section 6.4. Following

9. The court noted that the statutory requirements of §303 do not include good faith, and that the only allusion to good faith in §303 is in §303(i). That subsection (explained in section 6.6.7) is not pertinent to this question, but provides for damages to be awarded against a creditor after the dismissal of a petition filed in bad faith.
10. 556 B.R. 627 (Bankr. D. Del. 2016).

the order for relief, the debtor must file the schedules discussed in section 6.3. The time period for filing them is the same as in a voluntary case but is measured from the order for relief rather than the petition date. Unless an interim trustee was appointed for cause earlier in the proceedings, the interim trustee is appointed after the order for relief.

§6.6.7 Petitioner Liability for Dismissal of the Petition

Creditors who petition for involuntary bankruptcy take a risk. Section 303(i)(1) authorizes the court to award costs and a reasonable attorney's fee to the debtor if the petition is dismissed, unless the dismissal is by consent of all parties and the debtor waives the right to the award. Section 303(i)(2) authorizes the court to award compensatory or punitive damages against a petitioner that filed the petition in bad faith. Section 303(i) states that the court "may" grant judgment for costs, attorney's fees, or damages, so the decision to make any such award is within the discretion of the court.

(1) Attorney's fees and costs under §303(i)(1). To obtain an award of attorney's fees and costs, the debtor need not show that the petition was filed vexatiously or in bad faith. Bad faith is a requirement for an award of damages under §301(i)(2), but it is absent from §301(i)(1). This does not mean that bad faith is irrelevant to a determination to award costs and attorney's fees because the presence or absence of bad faith is one of the factors the court takes into account in exercising its discretion.[11] Some courts adopt a very loose standard for awarding costs and attorney's fees and make the award as a matter of course where the petition fails. Others hold that the dismissal of the petition creates a presumption in favor of the award unless the creditor can show circumstances that overcome the presumption.[12] Still others adopt an even more stringent standard for making an award. For example, in *In re Starlite Houseboats, Inc.*, 470 B.R. 191 (Bankr. D. Kan. 2012), the court found that a true exercise of discretion based on the totality of the circumstances is most consistent with the plain language of the section and with the usual rule that each party bears its own litigation expenses. In evaluating the totality of the circumstances, the court takes into account factors such as the merits of the petition, the motivations and reasonableness of the creditors in filing it, and any improper conduct on the part of the debtor. (In *In re Starlite Houseboats* the petition was dismissed because the claim of one of the three creditors was disqualified as being subject to a bona fide dispute. The court refused to award costs and

---

11. See *In re Hentges*, 351 B.R. 758 (Bankr. N.D. Okla. 2006).
12. See *In re Maple-Whitworth, Inc.*, 556 F.3d 742 (9th Cir. 2009) and *Higgins v. Vortex Fishing Systems, Inc.*, 379 F.3d 701 (9th Cir. 2004).

attorney's fees to the debtor because the petitioners had legitimate motives for seeking bankruptcy protection and reasonably believed that the claim was valid and undisputable.)

Where three creditors have joined to file the petition, each of the petitioners is liable for costs and fees. *Maple-Whitworth* held that the debtor may proceed against all of the petitioners, or against only some of them. It is within the bankruptcy court's discretion to determine how the liability for the fees and costs should be apportioned. It could hold the petitioners jointly and severally liable, or it could hold only some of them liable and may apportion liability among them depending on their culpability.

(2) Damages for bad faith filing. In addition to an award of fees and costs, the court is authorized under §303(i)(2) to award the debtor compensatory or punitive damages against a petitioner who filed the petition in bad faith. Damages are awarded only against a bad faith petitioner and not against any of the other petitioners who did not act in bad faith. Courts have used various tests in deciding whether a petitioner has filed in bad faith. Generally, they include the use of the petition vexatiously, frivolously, or for an ulterior motive or improper purpose. For example, a creditor acts in bad faith where it files to obtain a disproportionate advantage, or it uses bankruptcy where state collection remedies are more appropriate, or it is motivated by spite, ill will, or malice. See, for example, *In re John Richards Home Building Co., LLC*, 312 B.R. 849 (E.D. Mich. 2004), in which a homeowner who had a dispute with the builder of his $3 million home filed an involuntary petition against the builder on the basis of that disputed claim. The bankruptcy court found that the petition was a vindictive attempt to intimidate the builder and harm his business reputation. The district court affirmed the bankruptcy court's award to the builder of $4.1 million in compensatory damages, $2 million in punitive damages, and costs and attorney's fees.

In *In re Miles*, 430 F.3d 1083 (9th Cir. 2005), the court held that by vesting exclusive bankruptcy jurisdiction in federal district courts and providing a comprehensive remedial scheme in §301(i), Congress intended the remedies provided for in §301(i) to be the exclusive remedies available for the improper filing of a bankruptcy petition. They completely preempt state law causes of action such as malicious prosecution, abuse of process, defamation, and intentional infliction of emotional distress. The court reasoned that it would undermine the uniformity of bankruptcy law and federal control of the bankruptcy system to permit state law or state courts to decide on the propriety of a petition and the consequences of wrongful filing. The court also held that the remedies under §301(i) are available only to the debtor and may not be sought by third parties, such as the debtor's spouse or other entities related to the debtor.

§6.7 GENERAL GROUNDS FOR DISMISSAL OF A BANKRUPTCY CASE — VOLUNTARY DISMISSAL, CAUSE, AND IMPROPER DEBTOR CONDUCT

This section deals with general grounds of dismissal by the debtor, a creditor, or another party in interest. The more specific form of dismissal for abuse in a Ch. 7 consumer case is discussed separately in section 6.8.

Each chapter of the Code has its own section governing dismissal: §§707, 1112, and 1307. These are the same sections that provide for conversion from one chapter to another, which indicates that conversion and dismissal are alternative remedies. Conversion is appropriate if the applicant (either the debtor or a party in interest) wishes the case to continue under a different chapter of the Code, while dismissal is the better remedy if the applicant wishes the case to be terminated.

The issues involved in dismissal can be intricate. This survey deals only with a broad description of its scope and purpose. Dismissal ends the bankruptcy case: The debtor and the estate are released from bankruptcy and the creditors' collection rights at state law are no longer stayed. Section 349 lists the effects of dismissal. There are myriad reasons why a debtor, creditor, or other party in interest may seek dismissal of a case, and depending on the circumstances, dismissal may serve or run counter to the interests of different parties. There are four different situations in which the case may be dismissed:

(1) Voluntary dismissal by the debtor in a voluntary case. A debtor who has filed a voluntary case may, in effect, seek to "withdraw" the petition by requesting dismissal. In a Ch. 7 or Ch. 11 case the debtor must show cause for dismissal, and the case can be dismissed only after notice and a hearing. *See* §§707(a) and 1112(b). In Ch. 13, the debtor has a broad right to dismiss unless the case has previously been converted to Ch. 13 from another chapter. Section 1307(b) states that the court "shall" dismiss the case on request of the debtor unless it had been converted to Ch. 13 from another chapter. The clear statutory language indicates that the debtor's right to dismiss an unconverted Ch. 13 case is absolute, and many courts have so interpreted it.[13] However, other courts have read into these sections a discretion to deny the debtor's motion to dismiss if the debtor has acted in bad faith or has abused the bankruptcy process. This qualification of the debtor's absolute right to dismiss is based on the U.S. Supreme Court's

13. See *In re Williams*, 435 B.R. 552 (Bankr. N.D. Ill. 2010).

opinion in *Marrama v. Citizen's Bank of Massachusetts*, 549 U.S. 365 (U.S. 2007). *Marrama* did not involve a debtor's motion to dismiss but was concerned with the debtor's attempt to convert a Ch. 7 case to Ch. 13. The court held that the debtor could not convert the case to Ch. 13 because he had forfeited the right to proceed under Ch. 13 as a result of his bad faith conduct. (*Marrama* is discussed in section 5.6.2.) Although voluntary dismissal was not involved in the case, some courts have read the opinion as indicating that the same principle would apply to dismissal. For example, in *In re Rosson*, 545 F.3d 764 (9th Cir. 2008), the court rejected the debtor's argument that he had an absolute right to dismiss his Ch. 13 case, and upheld the bankruptcy court's discretion to deny his motion to dismiss on grounds of bad faith. However, this approach was criticized in *In re Williams* on the basis that the debtor's absolute right to dismiss is unequivocally provided for in §1307(b), and *Marrama* was concerned with the different statutory provisions governing conversion from Ch. 7 to Ch. 13.

(2) Voluntary dismissal by the petitioners in an involuntary case. Petitioners in an involuntary case may also decide to withdraw their case. Section 303(j) requires that such a voluntary dismissal be preceded by notice to all creditors and a hearing. If the debtor does not consent to the dismissal, the petitioners could be liable for costs or damages under §303(i). As noted in section 6.6.1, costs and fees may be awarded even if the petition was filed in good faith. If the petition was filed in bad faith, the court may also award compensatory, and even punitive, damages to the debtor against any petitioner that was guilty of bad faith.

(3) Dismissal for cause by a party other than the petitioner. Dismissal for cause is available under all chapters of the Code. The motion to dismiss must be heard by the court after notice. As discussed in section 6.6.3, the debtor may move to dismiss an involuntary petition on the grounds that there is a defect in the case or that it has not been properly prosecuted. Also, a creditor or other party in interest may move to dismiss the debtor's voluntary case for cause. Cause may consist of any one of a variety of reasons. Each of the sections dealing with dismissal sets out a nonexclusive list of some of these reasons, which, in the case of a voluntary petition, include various types of dilatory or uncooperative behavior by the debtor.

(4) Dismissal by the court on grounds of lack of cooperation, abuse of process, or bad faith. Various provisions of the Code empower the court to dismiss the case on specific or general grounds of improper conduct by the debtor. For example, §§707(a)(3), 1112(e), and 1307(c)(9) allow the U.S. Trustee to move for dismissal if the debtor in a voluntary case fails timely to file the information and schedules required under §521.

In addition to these specific provisions, the court's equitable power under §105(a) allows it, on the motion of a party in interest or *sua sponte*, to dismiss a case in appropriate circumstances.

A common basis for dismissing a case on the motion of a party in interest or by the court is that the debtor filed the petition in bad faith. Bad faith is well established as cause for dismissal under Chs. 11 and 13 because each of those chapters requires the debtor's plan to be proposed in good faith. As discussed in section 6.8.4, bad faith is also a cause for the dismissal of a consumer debtor's Ch. 7 case under the express terms of §707(b). However, the general grounds of dismissal in §707(a) make no express reference to bad faith as a cause for dismissal, and there is no provision in Ch. 7 that expressly imposes an obligation of good faith on a Ch. 7 debtor. The nonexclusive list of grounds for dismissal set out in §707(a) includes only various forms of procedural noncompliance such as unreasonable delay by the debtor and failure to pay fees or to file required schedules. Although the list in §707(a) is nonexclusive and can therefore include cause beyond that specified, courts are divided on whether bad faith may be one of those causes. Some courts have concluded that §707(a) does not allow for dismissal on grounds of bad faith. They reason that the non-exclusive list of grounds for dismissal includes only forms of procedural noncompliance and that any additional unspecified basis for dismissal must likewise be based on technical or procedural violations of the Code. In addition, had Congress intended to include bad faith as a ground of dismissal under §707(a), it would have included it, as it did in §707(b), when it extensively amended §707 in BAPCPA.[14] Other courts have disagreed with this approach and have held that there is nothing in §707(a) that indicates congressional intent to restrict courts to dismissal for procedural noncompliance. Good faith and candor are prerequisites to the bankruptcy relief of a deserving debtor, and the court always has the discretion to dismiss a case on grounds of the debtor's lack of honesty or abusive motives.[15] In *In re Schwartz*, an arbitrator had awarded about $560,000 against the debtor, in favor of his principal creditor. Between the time of the award and the filing of a Ch. 7 petition, the debtor engaged in lavish consumer spending. The court said that the debtor's depletion of his assets for luxury consumption and his failure to make any effort to pay

---

14. See *In re Adolph*, 441 B.R. 909 (Bankr. N.D. Ill. 2011) and *In re Padilla*, 222 F.3d 1184 (9th Cir. 2000).

15. See *In re Krueger*, 812 F.3d 365 (5th Cir. 2016); *In re Schwartz*, 799 F.3d 760 (7th Cir 2015); *Perlin v. Hitachi Capital America Corp.*, 497 F.3d 364 (3d Cir. 2007); and *In re Lombardo*, 370 B.R. 506 (Bankr. E.D.N.Y. 2007).

down the amount owing to the creditor was cause for dismissal of the Ch. 7 case.[16] Quite apart from the basis of dismissal under 707(a), some courts have found the authority to dismiss a Ch. 7 case for bad faith in §105(a), which grants courts the general power to make orders necessary or appropriate to carry out the provisions of the Code.[17]

Courts that treat bad faith as grounds for dismissal evaluate many factors and look at all the circumstances of the case in deciding whether a debtor has filed a petition in bad faith. The factors that may indicate bad faith include the absence of attempts to pay creditors, the failure to reduce living expenses to a reasonable level, manipulation of assets and finances, a lack of candor in dealing with creditors or the court, and the ability to make substantial payments to creditors under a Ch. 11 or Ch. 13 plan. There is some controversy over the appropriateness of considering the debtor's ability to pay creditors under a plan. Some courts consider that any such means test should be confined to §707(b), and is not authorized in §707(a). Others, such as *Perrin*, hold that the fact that §707(b) specifically requires the court to consider the consumer debtor's ability to support a Ch. 13 plan does not lead to the negative implication that consideration of the debtor's ability to pay is excluded from the general grounds of dismissal in §707(a).

§6.8 DISMISSAL OF A CH. 7 CONSUMER CASE ON GROUNDS OF ABUSE

§6.8.1 The Basic Purpose of §707(b)

Section 707(b) applies only to consumer debtors—that is, "individuals whose debts are primarily consumer debts." The meaning of this is explained in section 6.8.2. There has been a longstanding debate over the question of whether access to Ch. 7 liquidation should be easily available to all consumer debtors, or tightly restricted, so that it is reserved for those consumer debtors who really cannot afford to support a Ch. 13 plan. In passing the original version of §707(b) in 1984, Congress aimed at a perceived abuse of the Code by some consumer debtors in selecting liquidation under Ch. 7 when they could pay off significantly more debt under Ch. 11 or Ch. 13. Congress felt that the Code made it too easy for consumer

16. Although the debtor's conduct could be characterized as bad faith, the court deliberately did not use bad faith as a basis for dismissal. It said that it is not necessary to show bad faith for dismissal if the debtor's conduct justifies refusing Ch. 7 relief.
17. See *In re Kestell*, 99 F.3d 146 (4th Cir. 1996).

debtors with few or no executable assets, but adequate incomes, to take the easy way out by liquidating their low-value estates under Ch. 7 instead of making the effort to pay a greater portion of their debt from future earnings. As enacted in 1984, §707(b) left it to the discretion of bankruptcy courts to determine, case-by-case, whether a consumer debtor's Ch. 7 filing was a "substantial abuse" of Ch. 7. The debtor's ability to support a Ch. 13 plan was a strong indication that the Ch. 7 filing was a substantial abuse. The 1984 version of §707(b) was quite restricted. It could be invoked only by the court on its own motion or by the U.S. Trustee, and contained a presumption in favor of granting Ch. 7 relief.

Following the passage of §707(b), there was ongoing debate over whether it was good policy and whether it was achieving its purpose. Some argued that the section was necessary to curb abuse, but that it was too weak and had not been effective in curbing abuse. Others contended that claims of abuse were exaggerated and that most Ch. 7 debtors had genuine financial distress that called for Ch. 7 relief. The question of whether §707(b) should be amended to make it more restrictive divided the 1994 National Bankruptcy Review Commission. The majority did not recommend imposing any further restrictions on Ch. 7 relief, while dissenting commissioners recommended that Congress impose a means test that would exclude consumer debtors from Ch. 7 if they had sufficient future income to pay more of their debt under a Ch. 13 plan. The Congressional majority agreed with the dissenting commissioners. After several attempts to pass a reform bill, Congress did eventually enact BAPCPA in 2005, amending §707(b) to include the means test described in section 6.8.3. The amendment of §707(b) is probably the most controversial change that was made by BAPCPA. Its critics have questioned its premise and have argued that it causes hardship to debtors who are not trying to abuse the Code and really cannot afford to make payments under a Ch. 13 plan. In addition to this policy concern, the BAPCPA amendment to §707(b) is badly drafted and written in convoluted language that is difficult to read. Courts have had to unravel this poor drafting in applying the section.

The purpose of §707(b) is to prevent an individual consumer debtor from pursuing liquidation under Ch. 7 if he can afford a payment plan under Ch. 13 or Ch. 11. A debtor's Ch. 7 filing is presumed to be abusive if the debtor's financial resources exceed the means test prescribed by §707(b). The debtor may be able to rebut the presumption of abuse and remain in Ch. 7, but the section makes it clear that the debtor will only overcome the presumption by making a compelling case, showing special circumstances. If the debtor's financial resources are small enough to be below the level prescribed by the means test, the presumption does not arise. The case will only be dismissed if the party seeking dismissal can establish grounds based on the debtor's bad faith or the totality of the circumstances.

§6.8.2 §707(b) Applies Only to an Individual Debtor Whose Debts Are Primarily Consumer Debts (§§707(b)(1) and 101(8))

The first determination to be made is whether §707(b) applies to the debtor in question. The section applies only if the debtor is an "individual debtor . . . whose debts are primarily consumer debts." The Code does not define "individual," but it means a human, as opposed to an incorporated entity. The term "consumer debt" is defined in §101(8) to mean "debt incurred by an individual primarily for a personal, family, or household purpose." Although consumer debts are often thought of as being incurred in relation to consumable goods and services, courts generally read the definition in §101(8) more broadly to include debt used to acquire or maintain capital assets, provided that these assets are used for personal or household purposes. In *In re Price*, 280 B.R. 499 (B.A.P. 9th Cir. 2002), the court, following *In re Kelley*, 841 F.2d 908 (9th Cir. 1988), held that a debt incurred to buy a home and secured by a home mortgage is a consumer debt.

As a general guideline, a debt arising from a transaction motivated by the generation of income is not a consumer debt. Courts evaluate the nature, source, and purpose of the debt in deciding whether an individual's debt should be classified as a consumer debt. Debts related to the operation of a debtor's business are clearly not consumer debts, but even where a debtor does not have a business, some of her debts do not qualify as consumer debts. For example, courts have held that a debt for income tax is not a consumer debt, even if the debtor uses all her income for personal, household, or domestic purposes. Tax liability arises from the production of income, not its expenditure, and action to generate income is commercial in character. In addition, courts have observed that because tax liability is imposed by law and is not assumed voluntarily, the debt does not fit comfortably into the definition's requirement that it is incurred with a consumption "purpose."[18] A debt for unpaid property or sales taxes is likewise generally not treated as a consumer debt. At first sight, a property tax on a debtor's home or a sales tax on consumer goods or services seems to be incurred for domestic and household purposes and seems, like a mortgage or car loan, to be a debt relating to the acquisition or upkeep of the debtor's household or personal property. However, courts apply the reasoning that the debt is involuntary and incurred for public purposes, rather than for household or personal purposes. Therefore, even if the debt is not a business debt, this does not mean that it is a consumer debt. This was the reasoning

18. See *In re Rucker*, 454 B.R. 554 (Bankr. M.D. Ga. 2011) and *In re Brashers*, 216 B.R. 59 (Bankr. N.D. Okla. 1998).

applied in relation to a debt for personal property taxes (a sales tax on a car that the debtor had bought) in *In re Stovall*, 209 B.R. 849 (Bankr. E.D. Va. 1997).[19]

Courts have had difficulty in characterizing student loan debts. Some courts have held that education is an inherently personal benefit because knowledge is instilled in the student's mind. On this theory, it is a consumer debt. Other courts have held that education enhances a student's ability to earn, so educational debt is better characterized as incurred for a profit motive, and hence not a consumer debt. The situation is complicated further by the fact that many students use a portion of their loans for tuition and a portion for living expenses. In *In Re Rucker*, 454 B.R. 554 (Bankr. M.D. Ga. 2011) the court grappled with these questions and concluded that it is not possible to apply a *per se* rule to categorize a student loan debt. Instead, the court must examine the debt to determine whether and to what extent it was incurred for personal or profit purposes. In *Palmer v. Laying*, 559 B.R. 746 (D. Colo. 2016), the debtor incurred the student debt in relation to a doctorate in business administration. The entire debt was used to pay for tuition and books, and none of it was used for living expenses. The debtor testified that his motive in pursuing the doctorate was to improve his business knowledge so that he could ultimately open his own business. The court held that these factors led to the conclusion that the debtor had a profit motive in incurring the educational debt, so it should be characterized as a business debt, not a consumer debt.

Note that both §707(b) and §101(8) use the word "primarily." Both sections contemplate that the individual may have some debt that is not consumer debt but that when the debtor's total indebtedness is analyzed, consumer debt predominates. In deciding whether an individual's debts are primarily consumer debts, courts tend to focus on the value but also take number into account.[20] Where a debtor has both consumer and nonconsumer debts and the consumer debts are significantly greater in both number and amount, it is relatively easy to conclude that the debtor primarily owes consumer debts. However, this question is harder where there is a close equivalence between the consumer and nonconsumer debts, or where one category predominates in amount and the other in number. Courts tend to avoid any mechanical formula and try to glean the underlying nature and pattern of the debtor's affairs by looking at a combination of factors, including the number, amount, and nature of the debts as well as any other relevant circumstances. (*See* Examples 4 and 5.)

---

19. See also *In re Westberry*, 215 F.3d 589 (6th Cir. 2000).
20. See *In re Booth*, 858 F.2d 1051 (5th Cir. 1988) and *In re Kelley*, 841 F.2d 908 (9th Cir. 1988).

§6.8.3 Determining Whether the Consumer Debtor's Current Monthly Income Is Above or Below the Median Family Income for the Debtor's State (§§707(b)(6) and (7))

a. The Relationship between the Debtor's Income and the Median Family Income

Once it has been established that the individual debtor's debts are primarily consumer debts, the next inquiry must be conducted under §707(b)(6) and (7) to determine if the debtor's income exceeds or is below the "median family income of the applicable state," that is, the debtor's state of residence.[21] Under §101(39A) "median family income" for the debtor's state is based calculations of annual income for families of various sizes, reported by Bureau of the Census.

In this inquiry, the comparison of the debtor's income with the median family income serves the purpose of deciding whether the debtor is subject to the presumption of abuse. No presumption of abuse applies to a debtor whose income is below the median, and his case will not be dismissed unless actual abuse is established. A debtor whose income is above the median is subjected to the means test, and if he does not qualify under it, a presumption of abuse arises.

b. Determining the Debtor's "Current Monthly Income"

The debtor's "current monthly income" is defined in §101(10A) to mean the average monthly income from all sources that the debtor receives during the six-month period ending on the last day of the calendar month preceding the filing. (The definition has some qualifications about the ending date of the time period, which are not discussed here.) The definition specifies that it does not matter whether or not the income is taxable, and it includes regular payments made by another entity to the debtor for

---

21. By using the median income of the debtor's state as a yardstick, §707(b) inevitably treats debtors from different states differently because median state incomes vary. It is therefore possible that a debtor's income may exceed the median in one state but fall below it in another. In *Schulte v. United States*, 529 F.3d 343 (6th Cir. 2008), the debtor challenged the constitutionality of §707(b) on the grounds that its use of the median state income violated the constitutional requirement that Congress enact a uniform law of bankruptcy. The debtor's income exceeded the median for his home state but would have been below the median in several other states. The court, applying the test of uniformity enunciated by the U.S. Supreme Court in *Hanover National Bank v. Moyses*, 186 U.S. 181 (1902) (discussed in section 3.3), rejected the debtor's argument. As long as the law is uniform in its general operation, the constitutional requirement of uniformity is not violated merely because the law operates differently as a result of the laws or circumstances applicable in different states.

household expenses. These regular payments could be contributions to living expenses made by a spouse, other relative or friend, or from any other source.[22] For example, in *Blausey v. U.S. Trustee*, 552 F.3d 1124 (9th Cir. 2009), the court held that disability insurance benefits received regularly by the debtor should be included in the debtor's current monthly income.

The essential point about this definition is that it requires the debtor's income for a very short period — six months before the petition — to be averaged. It makes no allowance for longer-term income patterns, future changes in income, or temporary increases or decreases in income within the six-month period (such as the debtor being unemployed during any period, or working unusual amounts of overtime). *In re Littman*, 370 B.R. 820 (Bankr. D. Idaho 2007), described the income calculation as a snapshot of the debtor's income at the time of filing, intended as an immediate screening device. It is a bright-line cutoff that does not take into account whether the prefiling income is an accurate reflection of the debtor's actual prospective income during the course of the bankruptcy.[23] *In re Norenberg*, 554 B.R. 480 (Bankr. D. Mont. 2016), illustrates the rigidity of the formula for calculating the debtor's current monthly income. The debtor filed his Ch. 7 petition on December 21, 2015. Therefore, the six-month period for determining the debtor's current monthly income ended on November 30, 2015. The debtor's wife received a royalty check on December 2. Although the debtor's wife apparently used this money to pay for household expenses, the court held that the debtor was correct in not including it in his income calculation because his wife received it within the short gap between the ending of the statutory six-month period and the debtor's Ch. 7 filing. The court observed that the definition of current monthly income in §101(10A) is plain, and it is not up to the court to deviate from it. In this case, the rigidity of the formula favored the debtor by omitting actual income from the calculation. In another case, it might have the opposite effect. This does not mean that the court has no discretion to take reality into account. Where the debtor's prefiling income is unusually inflated in the six-month period, this could form the basis of a showing of special circumstances to rebut the presumption of abuse. (*See* section 6.8.6.) Conversely, if

---

22. However, the definition expressly excludes Social Security benefits and certain payments made to victims of war crimes and terrorism.

23. As discussed in section 18.8.3.b, if the debtor files under Ch. 13 (either because his Ch. 7 case is dismissed for abuse under §707(b) or because he chooses to file under Ch. 13) the debtor's current monthly income features in the calculation of the debtor's projected disposable income for purposes of determining the minimum amount that the debtor must pay to general unsecured creditors under the plan. In calculating projected disposable income, the court will take into account whether the debtor's current monthly income, as calculated under the statutory formula, is a reasonable representation of the income that the debtor will be likely to earn over the period of the plan.

the six-month income is unusually deflated, the debtor's actual prospective income could be the basis of dismissal for actual abuse. (*See* section 6.8.4.)

Because the median family income is an annual average, the debtor's current monthly income must be multiplied by 12 to get the debtor's annual income for comparison purposes. (Example 6 contains an exercise in comparing the debtor's current monthly income with the median family income.)

c. The Different Treatment of Above- and Below-Median Debtors

If the debtor's income is greater than the median, any party in interest can move for dismissal of the case, and the formula set out in subsection (b)(2) must be used to decide if the presumption applies. However, the presumption does not apply to a below-median debtor. (*See* Example 6 for an illustration of this point.) This is because Congress accepted that debtors who earn less than the median family income do not earn enough to make any appreciable payment to creditors under a Ch. 13 plan and that such debtors should be allowed to obtain Ch. 7 relief unless abuse is clearly apparent as a ground for dismissal. Subsections (b)(6) and (7) therefore place two restrictions on the dismissal of a below-median debtor's Ch. 7 case for abuse. First, under subsection (b)(6), only the court on its own motion or the U.S. Trustee can initiate a dismissal under §707(b). The motion to dismiss may not be made by the other parties in interest who would otherwise have standing to move for dismissal. Second, subsection (b)(7) creates what is called a "safe harbor." It precludes application of the presumption of abuse where the debtor's current monthly income (for this purpose, combined with that of his spouse, even if the petition is not a joint petition) is less than the applicable median family income. (Note that the calculation of the debtor's current monthly income is different for purposes of subsections (b)(6) and (7).)

§6.8.4 The Finding of Abuse Where the Presumption of Abuse Does Not Apply

In cases where the presumption of abuse does not arise or is rebutted, the court may nevertheless dismiss the Ch. 7 case for abuse under §707(b)(1) if the applicant for dismissal establishes, or the court on its own motion determines, that the filing is abusive. BAPCPA added subsection (b)(3) to provide guidelines on what the court should consider in deciding if there has been abuse in the absence of the presumption: Whether the debtor has filed the petition in bad faith or the totality of the circumstances of the debtor's financial situation demonstrates abuse. The grounds of bad faith and totality of the circumstances are derived from pre-BAPCPA case law and are separate and distinct grounds for dismissal. The ground of bad faith covers situations in which the debtor's conduct shows improper motives for filing the petition.[24] The totality of the circumstances test allows the court to consider a variety of factors to decide if, on balance, the filing constitutes an abuse of the Code. Courts take a number of considerations into account, including, for example, whether the petition was a response to sudden illness or calamity, whether the debtor had made excessive consumer purchases or racked up debt before filing, whether the debtor's budget is reasonable, whether the debtor had made attempts to deal with his creditors through negotiation or state law remedies, and whether the debtor's schedules are accurate. Courts are divided on the question of whether the debtor's ability to support a Ch. 13 plan should be taken into account in deciding abuse under the totality of the circumstances. Some courts consider this a proper consideration, while others hold that the means test calculation covers this issue, which should not be raised again in determining abuse on the totality of the circumstances.[25]

In its reference to the totality of the circumstances test, subsection (b)(3) refers specifically to the filing of a Ch. 7 petition for the purposes of rejecting a personal services contract. This is a response to a number of cases where a well-paid debtor — typically a recording artist — sought to use bankruptcy as a means of getting out of a contract so that she could make a more lucrative contract with someone else. That motivation would be taken into account in determining abuse based on the totality of the circumstances.

§6.8.5 The Formula in §707(b)(2) to Determine If the Presumption of Abuse Applies

As noted before, §707(b)(1) contains the basic rule that the court, on its own motion or on the motion of the U.S. Trustee, the trustee, or any party in interest, may dismiss a case filed by an individual whose debts are primarily consumer debts if the court finds that the granting of relief would be an abuse of Ch. 7. Section 707(b)(2) makes it easier to establish abuse by creating a presumption of abuse under prescribed circumstances. The presumption arises if, based on the formula set out in §707(b)(2), the debtor's disposable income would be sufficient to support a payment plan under Ch. 13. This is the means test that has often been mentioned

24. As discussed in section 6.7, the grounds for dismissal for bad faith are expressly mentioned only in §707(b), so there is some difference of opinion on whether they might also be a basis for dismissal under §707(a). This is also discussed in Example 5.

25. For examples of cases that deal with this issue and the other considerations to be taken into account in deciding abuse on the totality of the circumstances, see *In re Kulakowski*, 735 F.3d 1296 (11th Cir. 2013) and *In re Walker*, 381 B.R. 620 (Bankr. M.D. Pa. 2008).

previously in this book and has been the subject of so much debate and disagreement. It is important to understand the mechanics of the means test: If the debtor is shown to have disposable income in excess of that prescribed by the formula, a presumption arises that the debtor is abusing the provisions of Ch. 7. Unless the debtor can rebut this presumption, grounds for dismissal under §707(b)(1) are established. Section 707(b)(2)(C) requires the debtor's schedule of income and expenditures, filed under §521, to provide information on current monthly income as well as a calculation showing whether the presumption applies. Under the former version of §707(b), courts had considerable discretion in deciding whether substantial abuse existed. Section 707(b)(2) is deliberately intended to reduce that discretion and to impose a less flexible test under which the court "shall" presume abuse if the calculation of the debtor's income and expenses under the prescribed formula shows that the debtor will have disposable income deemed sufficient to support a five-year Ch. 13 plan.

The formula for determining the presumption of abuse is set out in §707(b)(2)(A)(i) and is incorporated into Official Bankruptcy Forms 122A1 and A2. Diagram 6b sets out this formula.

1. Calculate the debtor's **current monthly income** as defined in §101(10)(A).
2. *Deduct from this monthly income* **the debtor's monthly expenses**, which are determined by adding together the amounts allowed under subsections (b)(2)(A)(ii), (iii), and (iv).
3. This will provide a figure for the debtor's **net monthly income** (that is, his disposable income).
4. This disposable income is then *multiplied by 60* to provide a **five-year total figure** for the debtor's **net disposable income.**
5. This 60-month disposable income figure is then *compared to the prescribed standards*. Abuse is presumed if the figure is **not less than the lesser of:**
   a. the greater of 25% of the debtor's nonpriority unsecured claims in the case, or $7,700,

   or

   b. $12,850.[26]

Diagram 6b

26. The dollar amounts in §707(b)(2)(A)(i) are adjusted every three years under §104. The amounts here are those in effect from April 1, 2016. They will be adjusted again with effect from April 1, 2019.

That is, if the debtor's disposable income in item 4 of the formula equals or exceeds the amount calculated under item 5, the debtor fails the means test and the presumption of abuse arises. The debtor must then try to rebut the presumption to avoid dismissal of the Ch. 7 case. The components of this formula need further explanation:[27]

(1) The debtor's current monthly income. The meaning of "current monthly income" has already been explained in section 6.8.3. It is essentially the average of the monthly income that the debtor derived from all sources within the six months before filing the petition. As noted before, this six-month snapshot of the debtor's earnings may or may not accurately represent his real historic earnings over a longer term or his likely prospective earnings.

(2) The debtor's monthly expenses. Subsections (b)(2)(A)(ii), (iii), and (iv) set out the permissible monthly expenses that the debtor may deduct from her current monthly income to arrive at the net disposable income. These provisions are very restrictive: Their purpose is to control very tightly what a debtor may claim as living expenses. The expense allowances are complex and raise many interpretational questions. They fall into three broad categories: living expenses, secured debt payments, and priority debt payments.

With a few adjustments, mentioned below, the maximum living expenses that the debtor may claim are fixed by the National Standards and Local Standards issued by the I.R.S. and in effect for the debtor's place of residence at the time of the order for relief. (These standards may be found on the websites of the I.R.S. and the U.S. Trustee.) Some of the standardized expenses are applicable nationwide, and some take local conditions into account. The I.R.S. promulgated these standardized expense allowances for its own purposes. They are guidelines to provide a consistent approach in determining how much a delinquent taxpayer should be required to pay each month under a payment plan to satisfy a tax debt. Congress decided to use these same standards for the purpose of controlling a debtor's claim of living expenses for purposes of §707(b). The standards include amounts for housing, utilities, transport, food, clothing, and other necessary expenses for the support and welfare of the debtor. In calculating expenses for the purposes of the formula, the debtor may use the amounts specified in the standards even if they are higher than the debtor's actual expenses. However, the debtor is confined to the amount specified in the standards, even if his own actual expenses are higher.

---

27. *See* Example 6 for an exercise in applying the formula.

Courts had been split on whether a debtor was allowed to claim a listed expense irrespective of whether he actually incurred any expense in that category. For example, the standards allow the debtor to include a set amount for vehicle ownership expenses. Some courts only permitted a debtor to include this amount in his expenses if he actually had payments on a car loan or lease. Other courts held that because the expenses were standard, the debtor could deduct an expense item irrespective of his personal circumstances. This question was settled by the U.S. Supreme Court in *Ransom v. FIA Card Services, N.A.*, 131 S. Ct. 716 (2011),[28] which held that a debtor who owns his car free of debt and has no actual loan or lease expenses cannot claim the car ownership expense. The court reached this conclusion on a plain meaning interpretation of §707(b)(2)(A)(ii)(1), which allows the debtor to claim "applicable" expense amounts under the National and Local Standards. In its ordinary meaning, "applicable" connotes appropriate and relevant expenses that correspond to the debtor's actual financial circumstances. The court found this reading of the section to be reinforced by the Code's purpose of maximizing payment to creditors. (Although the debtor could not claim car ownership expenses, he was entitled to claim the allowance for car operating costs, which is included as a separate item in the Standards.) The Supreme Court focused only on the question of whether a debtor who had no expenses in the category could claim the standard expense. It expressly did not decide whether the debtor with lower actual expenses could claim the standard expense. In *Lynch v. Jackson*, 853 F.3d 116 (4th Cir. 2017) the court held that under the plain language of §707(b)(2)(A)(ii)(1), if a debtor has some expenses in a standard category, he is entitled to use the full higher amount specified in the standards. The court emphasized that the section used the words "shall" and "applicable" with reference to the standards, as opposed to the word "actual" used in the same sentence to refer to other monthly expenses.

In addition to the expenses allowed by the I.R.S. standards, §707(b)(2) recognizes a limited and carefully circumscribed group of additional expenses that a debtor can include as expenses in his budget. Some are generally available, and some apply only to debtors in special circumstances. For example, all debtors may claim reasonably necessary health and disability insurance; a debtor can claim an increase of up to 5 percent in the I.R.S. standards for food and clothing if the debtor demonstrates this as reasonable and necessary; a debtor may claim a housing and utility allowance above the

---

28. *Ransom* involved a Ch. 13 case, so the calculation of the debtor's disposable income was for the purpose of determining the amount the debtor was required by §1325(b)(2) to pay under the plan, not for the purpose of deciding if a Ch. 7 petition should be dismissed. However, §1325(b)(2) uses the Local and National Standards adopted by §707(b)(2) in calculating disposable income for Ch. 13 purposes.

I.R.S. standards if these are his actual costs and if he can demonstrate why the expense is reasonable and necessary; a debtor who has been supporting an elderly, chronically ill, or disabled household member or family member may include those payments provided that they are a continuation of payments made before bankruptcy, they are actual, reasonable, and necessary expenses, and the dependent is not able to pay these expenses himself; some allowance is made for additional educational expenses for a dependent child, subject to a maximum amount and to proper explanation and justification.

Because the goal of the budget is to determine how much disposable income a debtor would have in a Ch. 13 case, the debtor's monthly expenses also take into account some of the payments and expenses that the debtor would incur in a Ch. 13 case in relation to secured and priority debts. Therefore, a debtor who is eligible for Ch. 13 may include in her monthly expenses the actual expenses of administering a Ch. 13 plan in the district in which the debtor resides, up to 10 percent of projected plan payments. The debtor may also include as expenses her average monthly payments on secured debts. These payments are calculated by using the total of all amounts due on secured debt in each month over the 60-month postpetition period, plus any additional amounts that the debtor would have to pay a secured claimant to keep possession of her primary residence, motor vehicle, or other property reasonably necessary for the support of the debtor or her dependents. The debtor's allowable expenses also include the amount that would be payable on priority claims in a Ch. 13 case, calculated by adding all the priority claims in the estate and dividing them by 60 to get the monthly payment amount. Although a debtor can include secured and priority claims in her budget, the subsection makes it clear that payments due on unsecured debt are not to be included. The obvious reason for this is that the formula seeks to establish the debtor's disposable income available to pay these very claims.

The provision for including secured and priority debts in the expense calculation is expressed here in simplified terms that mask its many interpretational difficulties. One of these is whether some degree of double-counting results from allowing the debtor both a standard I.R.S. living expense deduction and a secured claim deduction for an automobile and a home.

(3) The final calculation. After the debtor's current monthly income and allowable monthly expenses have been determined, the expenses are deducted from income to give a net monthly surplus, which is the amount that the debtor is deemed to have available to pay to the trustee each month under a Ch. 13 plan. The final calculation (in point 5 of the formula set out in the box above) is intended to determine if this disposable income is sufficient to support a viable Ch. 13 plan. The calculation sounds really confusing because of its horrible combination of "less," "lesser," and "greater." It boils down to this: If, after the debtor's allowable monthly expenses are deducted from her current monthly income:

1. There is $128.33 or less left over per month as disposable income, the debtor's 60-month disposable income is $7,700 or less. The debtor therefore satisfies the means test (more accurately described as a "lack of means" test), and the presumption of abuse does not apply.
2. There is $214.16 or more left over per month as disposable income, the debtor's 60-month disposable income exceeds $12,850. The debtor therefore fails the means test, and the presumption of abuse applies.
3. There is between $128.33 and $214.16 left over per month as disposable income, the presumption applies if the debtor's 60-month disposable income exceeds 25 percent of her nonpriority unsecured debt.

Stated slightly differently, if the debtor's monthly repayment capacity under the formula is less than $128.33, no presumption arises. If it is more than $214.91, the presumption takes effect. If it is between these two amounts, the presumption only arises if the debtor's 60-month payment capacity exceeds 25 percent of her nonpriority unsecured debt. Say, for example, that the debtor's monthly repayment capacity is $150, making a 60-month capacity $9,000. His nonpriority unsecured debt is $34,000, 25 percent of which is $8,500. Abuse is presumed. However, if his nonpriority unsecured debt is $37,000, no presumption arises because 25 percent of the debt is $9,250, which exceeds his 60-month capacity.

§6.8.6 Rebuttal of the Presumption of Abuse

Although the presumption of abuse arises because the debtor's 60-month disposable income exceeds the limits set by §707(b)(2), the debtor has an opportunity to rebut the presumption. (As mentioned in section 6.8.4 above, if the presumption is rebutted, the court must decide whether or not to dismiss the case under the considerations set out in subsection (b)(3).)

Subsection (b)(2)(B) sets out what a debtor must show to rebut the presumption. The basis for rebuttal is written in narrow and stringent terms. Subsection (b)(2)(B)(i) provides that the presumption of abuse may only be rebutted by demonstrating special circumstances, such as a serious medical condition or a call to active military duty, and only to the extent that the special circumstances justify an increase in expenses or an adjustment to current monthly income for which there is no reasonable alternative.

The two examples of special circumstances set out in the subsection suggest that Congress has quite desperate circumstances in mind to justify a departure from the standardized expenses or the statutorily determined current monthly income. Therefore, although courts are given some flexibility in subsection (b)(2)(B) to take the debtor's personal circumstances into account and to mitigate any harsh or unrealistic results of the standardized means test, this discretion seems quite circumscribed. Courts have differed on how stringent a test to employ in deciding whether the debtor has shown circumstances sufficiently exigent to rebut the presumption. Some courts have refused to find the debtor's circumstances compelling enough to overcome the presumption unless they are equivalent in severity to the two examples set out in the section, and are beyond the debtor's control. Others have adopted a more flexible approach and have been willing to overturn the presumption on a showing by the debtor of a reasonable basis for finding that the disposable income projected by the formula is unrealistic. For an example of a case that adopts the more flexible approach, see *In re Littman*, 370 B.R. 820 (Bankr. D. Idaho 2007).

Subsection (b)(2)(B)(ii) places the burden on the debtor to provide full itemization, documentation, and an explanation of any claim of adjustment. Subsection (b)(2)(B)(iii) requires the debtor to attest under oath to the accuracy of the information. Subsection (b)(2)(B)(iv) provides that the presumption of abuse may only be rebutted if the adjustments established by the debtor have the effect of reducing the debtor's disposable income to a level below that which gave rise to the presumption in the first place. That is, if the court accepts the debtor's claim of special circumstances, the adjustments to expenses or income are made, and the end result of the formula (the final step of item 5 of the formula in section 6.8.5) must be recalculated. The presumption is only rebutted if the ultimate figure, as adjusted, shows a low enough 60-month disposable income to pass the means test.

§6.8.7 Sanctions

Subsections 707(b)(4) and (5) are intended to sanction improper or vexatious conduct, either by the attorney representing a debtor or by a party in interest who files a motion to dismiss. Subsection (b)(4)(C) provides that an attorney's signature on a petition or other pleading or motion constitutes a certification that the attorney has reasonably investigated the circumstances; has determined that the petition, pleading, or motion is well grounded in fact and warranted in law; and has no knowledge, after inquiry, that any information in the document is incorrect. Subsection (b)(4)(B) authorizes the court, on its own motion or on motion of a party in interest, to award the trustee's costs and attorney's fees against the debtor's attorney where the court grants the trustee's motion to dismiss for abuse and the court finds that the debtor's attorney has acted wrongfully in filing the case by violating the provisions of Bankruptcy Rule 9011. Subsection (b)(4)(C) also allows for the award of a civil penalty against a debtor's attorney for a violation of Rule 9011.

Subsection (b)(5) allows for an award of attorney's fees and costs to the debtor where the debtor successfully contests a motion to dismiss and the party in interest (other than the trustee or the U.S. Trustee) acted unjustifiably in moving to dismiss the Ch. 7 case.

§6.9 THE CREDITORS' MEETING

After the order for relief, the U.S. Trustee must convene a meeting of creditors under §341. The meeting is held in all cases, whether under Ch. 7, 11, or 13. Rule 2003 requires the meeting to take place between 21 and 40 days after the order for relief in a Ch. 7 or 11 case (the periods are slightly different in a Ch.13 case), subject to some leeway for the court to set a different time. Under Rule 2002, the clerk of the court must give creditors at least 21 days' notice of the meeting.

Section 341 requires the U.S. Trustee to preside at the creditors' meeting. The bankruptcy judge is not involved and is in fact barred from attending by §341(c). The principal purpose of the meeting is the examination of the debtor under §343 by creditors, the trustee, or the U.S. Trustee. A debtor who fails to appear or to answer truthfully can be penalized by dismissal of the voluntary petition, denial of the discharge, or even criminal charges if perjury or fraud are involved. Rule 2004 governs the content and scope of the examination, which may range over the debtor's financial affairs, conduct, and other matters relevant to the administration of the estate or the discharge. In addition to examining the debtor, creditors in a Ch. 7 case may elect a trustee or a creditors' committee at the meeting. As noted in sections 4.3.1 and 4.6, this power is not frequently exercised.

EXAMPLES

Examples

1. Cookie Crumbles owns and operates a bakery. She has the following creditors:
   - i. Seven trade creditors to which she owes a total of $100,000 for goods supplied on unsecured credit.
   - ii. Her dough supplier, U.O. Dough Co., to which she owes $20,000 for goods supplied. This debt is secured by a perfected security interest in accounts receivable valued at $3,000.

iii. A finance company, to which she owes $15,000 on a loan, secured by a perfected security interest in equipment worth $20,000.
iv. A bank, to which Cookie is obligated under a suretyship agreement. She executed the suretyship to guarantee a loan of $50,000 made by the bank to her son. The bank's loan to Cookie's son is not yet payable, and therefore not in default.
v. Two employees, to whom she owes $5,000 in arrear wages.
vi. An advertising agency, which claims $8,000 for advertising services. Cookie has refused to pay the agency because she says it failed to properly perform services under their contract.
vii. Cookie's mother, who lent her $12,000 to pay operating expenses.

Cookie's bakery business has been struggling over the last several months, and she has had trouble paying her debts. She has missed payments to five of her seven trade creditors, as well as to U.O. Dough Co., the finance company, and her employees. She has managed to make arrangements for extensions with two trade creditors, the finance company, and her employees, but the other three trade creditors have commenced collection proceedings against her. Cookie's mother has not yet asked for payment of her loan. Cookie is litigating with the advertising agency over its claim. U.O. Dough Co. has just filed an involuntary Ch. 7 petition against her. Is U.O. Dough Co. qualified to file the petition?

2. Assuming that U.O. Dough Co. is qualified, may it file the petition on its own, or must it find two other creditors to join as petitioners?

3. Irrespective of your answers to Examples 1 and 2, assume that U.O. Dough Co. is qualified and may file the petition on its own. Cookie controverts the petition. Does it seem, on the facts given, that U.O. Dough Co. will be able to establish grounds for relief?

4. An individual debtor has just filed a Ch. 7 petition. Her schedule of assets and liabilities shows that she has three secured debts totaling $300,000 and 15 unsecured debts totaling $90,000. Her largest secured debt, constituting 60 percent of her total secured indebtedness, is a loan for the purchase of investment property, secured by the property itself. The other two secured debts, making up the remaining 40 percent, are a home mortgage and a purchase money interest on an expensive luxury car. Of her unsecured debts, 14 are for credit purchases of consumer goods and services. These make up 50 percent of her total unsecured debt. The other half of her unsecured debt consists of a single debt for attorney's fees incurred in litigation concerning her investment activities. Is the debtor's case subject to dismissal under §707(b)?

5. Tex E. Vader has just filed a Ch. 7 petition. His largest debts are owed to the federal and state governments for arrear income taxes and overdue property taxes on his home. Although part of this indebtedness is a

nondischargeable priority claim (as will be discussed in sections 17.5.4 and 21.5.4), the greater portion of it does not qualify for priority treatment and will be discharged in the Ch. 7 case. These tax debts constitute about 70 percent of the claims against the estate. The rest are for consumer loans and credit cards. Tex earns a good income and could afford to pay a significant part of his dischargeable debt under a Ch. 13 plan. He has filed a Ch. 7 petition because, as he has told many people, "I worked hard for that money and need it more than the government does."

Should Tex's petition be dismissed for abuse?

6. Lo Wages is unmarried and lives alone in a rented apartment. She is employed as a bartender. Her gross monthly salary before taxes is $2,000, and she also receives income from tips that varies from month to month. Her total tip income for the last six months was $3,000. Her kindly grandmother sends her a check of $100 every month "to help her out," and has been doing so regularly for some years. Three months ago, Lo took unpaid leave for two months to travel.

   Lo has been living above her means and has accumulated debt of $75,000, all incurred in purchases of consumer goods and services. Lo finds it impossible to pay off this indebtedness, and her creditors are losing patience. Lo's only assets are a retirement account, an old car, a small bank account, and miscellaneous clothing, furniture, and household goods.

   Lo wishes to file a Ch. 7 petition because she does not like the idea of committing herself to sacrificing any of her future income to the payment of her creditors under a Ch. 13 plan. It is clear that if Lo enters Ch. 7 bankruptcy, her creditors will receive little or no payment because her assets are either exempt or of low value.

   Assume that the median family income for a single person in Lo's state of residence is $40,000 per annum and that Lo's allowable monthly expenses, based on the I.R.S. National and Local Standards plus the additional expenses permitted by §707(b)(2), amount to $4,000 per month.

   a. If Lo files a Ch. 7 petition, is it likely that her case will be dismissed for abuse?
   b. Change the above facts as follows: In addition to her salary, tips, and the payment from her grandmother, Lo receives $2,500 a month from a trust fund established by her father for her benefit. Does this additional fact make it likely that her case will be dismissed for abuse?
   c. How does the answer to question (b) change if Lo's allowable expenses under §707(b)(2) are $4,400 per month?
   d. How does the answer to question (b) change if Lo's allowable expenses under §707(b)(2) are $4,300 per month?

EXPLANATIONS

Explanations

1. U.O. Dough Co. is qualified to be a petitioner. Although it has some security for its claim, the value of the collateral is only $3,000. U.O. Dough Co. therefore has an unsecured deficiency of $17,000. Its unsecured claim exceeds the $15,775 required by §303(b)(1). (As noted in section 6.6.2, the qualifying amounts in §303(b) are adjusted periodically under §104.) The facts do not suggest that there is any problem in satisfying the other qualifying requirements of §303(b): The claim is not contingent or subject to a bona fide dispute.

2. Even though U.O. Dough Co. qualifies as a petitioner, it cannot proceed on its own unless Cookie has 11 or fewer creditors. Section 303(b) requires 3 creditors to file the petition if the debtor has 12 or more creditors. Cookie has 14 creditors—7 unsecured trade creditors, U.O. Dough Co., the finance company, the bank, 2 employees, her mother, and the advertising agency. However, not all of these creditors are counted for the purpose of §303(b). In counting the number of claim holders for the purpose of determining whether there are fewer than 12, employees, insiders, and transferees of avoidable transfers are excluded by the express terms of §303(b)(2). In addition, §303(b)(2) says that there must be fewer than 12 "such holders." The "such" refers to the claimants described in §303(b)(1), whose claims must be noncontingent and undisputed. Thus, in addition to the three express exclusions, §303(b)(2) also excludes from the count all holders of contingent or bona fide disputed claims. The bank's claim on the suretyship is contingent because a surety's obligation is contingent on a future uncertain event—the default of the principal debtor. Cookie's son has not yet defaulted on the debt. The advertising agency's claim is subject to a dispute that is apparently bona fide—there seems to be a legitimate dispute that is currently under litigation. In addition, the claims of the two employees and Cookie's mother are excluded because they are insiders as defined in §101(31). Although a secured claim cannot be counted for the purpose of determining the aggregate amount of debt for the creditor qualifications under §303(b)(1), secured creditors are not excluded from the creditor count under §303(b)(2). The reference to "such holders" in §303(b)(2) relates only to the requirements of noncontingency and lack of bona fide dispute in §303(b)(1). Therefore, neither U.O. Dough Co. nor the finance company is excluded from the creditor count.

   Once the five creditors listed above are excluded, Cookie is left with nine creditors for the purpose of §303(b), and U.O. Dough Co. may petition on its own.

3. If the debtor controverts the petition, §303(h) requires the petitioner to establish one of two grounds for relief. The second ground in §303(h) does not apply. No custodian had been appointed or took possession of Cookie's property. Relief must therefore be based on the fact that Cookie is not paying her debts as they become due. The express language of §303(h)(1) excludes bona fide disputed debts from the determination of general nonpayment. Therefore, provided that Cookie's dispute over the advertising agency's debt has genuine merit, it must not be treated as an unpaid debt. If that debt is excluded, Cookie is in default on 8 of her 14 debts. However, she has made extension agreements with all but 3 of these creditors. In determining whether a debtor is generally not paying debts as they become due, the court takes into account not only the number, value, and importance of overdue debts but also the debtor's overall financial situation, including the period and circumstances of default, arrangements made with creditors to cure defaults, and the debtor's general financial viability. A court will not likely place a debtor in involuntary liquidation if it appears that the debtor may overcome her financial adversity and that the overall interests of the debtor and her creditors are best served by allowing the debtor to try to cope with her financial difficulties under state law. Although we do not have enough facts for a final determination, it appears that U.O. Dough Co. will not likely be able to establish grounds for relief.

4. Section 707(b) is only applicable to an individual whose debts are primarily consumer debts. Section 101(8) defines "consumer debts" as those incurred primarily for personal, family, or household purposes. A debt incurred to acquire a capital asset (such as a home or a car) is properly characterized as a consumer debt if the asset is to be used for personal or household purposes. Conversely, if the motive of a transaction was the generation of income, the indebtedness arising from it is not a consumer debt. Only two of the debtor's debts have a business purpose — the secured claim for the purchase of the investment property and the attorney's fee. This means that two out of three secured debts, constituting 40 percent in value of total secured debt, and 14 out of 15 unsecured debts, constituting 50 percent in value of the total unsecured debt, are consumer debts. If the secured and unsecured debts are looked at in combination, 16 of 18 of her debts, constituting 42 percent of her total debt in value are consumer debts: They are a majority of her debts in number, but a minority in amount.

   In deciding whether an individual's debts are primarily consumer debts, courts tend to look at both the number and value of the debts. In this case, these factors pull in opposite directions. The relative amounts of consumer and nonconsumer debt may be decisive, but it is difficult to predict this with certainty. If the court finds that the nonconsumer debt predominates, the only basis for dismissal is for cause under §707(a). If it finds that the debts are primarily consumer debts, the debtor will be subject to dismissal for abuse under §707(b).

5. If the tax debts are consumer debts, Tex's debts would clearly be primarily consumer debts, and the issue would be whether the petition should be dismissed for abuse under §707(b). However, as explained in section 6.8.2, tax debts (whether for income tax or property tax) are generally held not to be consumer debts. Income tax liability is incurred in the production of income—an economic pursuit, and liability for both income and property taxes is imposed by law and therefore cannot be said to be incurred by the debtor for personal, family, or household purposes.

   Although Tex's filing seems to be abusive—he is trying to use Ch. 7 to discharge debt that he could afford to pay under a Ch. 13 plan—Tex's debts are not primarily consumer debts in nature, so the case cannot be dismissed for abuse under §707(b). Therefore, if the court considers it proper to dismiss Tex's case, it has to do so on grounds other than abuse under §707(b). There are two other possible bases of dismissal.

   The court has the power to dismiss a case on the general ground of cause under §707(a). As discussed in section 6.7, it is not clear if "cause" under §707(a) includes bad faith or abuse of the provisions of Ch. 7. Some courts have confined §707(a) to procedural noncompliance and have declined to extend it to bad faith and abuse. Other courts have disagreed, and have held that the court does have discretion to dismiss for bad faith under §707(a). Given the Code's goal of affording relief to an honest and deserving debtor, the latter approach seems more appropriate. Apart from dismissal under §707(a), the court should be able to order dismissal of the case by using its general power under §105(a) to make any order necessary or appropriate to carry out the provisions of the Code.

6. a. Lo is an individual, and the facts state that her debt is all consumer debt, so §707(b) is clearly applicable. To determine how it will operate in Lois's situation, we divide the inquiry into logically successive steps.

   Step 1. Determine Lo's current monthly income as defined by §101(10A). This includes all the actual income that Lo receives from all sources over the six-month period ending on the calendar month prior to filing the petition, added up and divided by six to get a monthly average. (Section 101(10A) does not expressly say whether or not this is pretax income, but Official Bankruptcy Form 122A1 uses gross income.) The definition makes it clear that income includes income from all sources, not just salary, irrespective of whether the income is taxable, and including regular contributions to the debtor's living expenses from other people. (The definition excludes Social Security payments or payments to the debtor on account of her status as a war or terrorist victim.)

Therefore, the fact that Lo only earned a salary for four of the last six months reduces her current monthly income for the purpose of §707(b), even though the trip may be a one-time event, and Lo normally works full-time and plans to continue to do so. Her total income from all sources in the last six months is $11,600 ($8,000 in salary, $3,000 in tips, and $600 from her grandmother). By dividing this figure by six, we get a current monthly income of $1,933.

Step 2. Compare the debtor's income to the median income for the debtor's state. The presumption of abuse does not apply if the debtor's current monthly income multiplied by 12 (to get the debtor's annual income) is less than the median annual income for a household of the debtor's size in the debtor's state of residence. If the presumption does not apply, only the court on its own motion or the U.S. Trustee may raise the issue of abuse and the petition can be dismissed only if abuse is established on other grounds. Lo's annual income is $23,196 ($1,933 multiplied by 12). Because Lo lives alone, this must be compared to the median family income for a single-person household in Lo's state, as published by the Census Bureau. The facts state that this is $40,000. Lo's annual income is lower than the median, so the presumption is inapplicable. Lo's Ch. 7 case can only be dismissed on other grounds, at the instance of the court or the U.S. Trustee. We do not get beyond step 2 on these facts, but question (b) allows us to proceed to step 3.

b. The additional income changes matters considerably.

Steps 1 and 2. Lo's current monthly income is now increased by the trust fund payments, which come to $15,000 for the six months prior to the petition. Her total income for the six-month period is therefore $26,600 ($11,600 plus $15,000). By dividing this figure by six, we arrive at a current monthly income of $4,433. This figure multiplied by 12 gives us an annual income of $53,196, which exceeds the applicable median family income. Because Lo's income is higher than the median, the formula in §707(b)(2) must be applied to decide if there is a presumption of abuse.

Step 3. Apply the formula to determine Lo's disposable monthly income. To perform this step, we must deduct Lo's monthly expenses from her current monthly income to determine if the income she has available each month after paying her expenses is deemed enough to support a Ch. 13 plan. For the income figure, we use her current monthly income of $4,433, as calculated in step 1. For her expenses, we do not use her own budget and are not concerned with what she actually spends or what she says she needs. Rather, we use the standardized expenses promulgated by the I.R.S. in its National Standards and Local Standards, together with those additional expenses authorized by §707(b)(2). The nature of these expenses is explained in section 6.8.5. The facts state that her allowable monthly expenses are $4,000. After her allowable expenses are deducted from her current monthly income, she is left with a surplus of $433 per month, which is the disposable income that she is deemed to have each month after paying her necessary living expenses.

Step 4. Determine if Lo's disposable income is high enough to trigger the presumption of abuse. Lo's monthly disposable income must be multiplied by 60 to give her total expected disposable income over the period of a five-year repayment plan. If this figure is under $7,700, the presumption does not apply. If it is over $12,850, the presumption does apply. If it is between these two figures, the presumption applies if the five-year disposable income exceeds 25 percent of Lo's general unsecured debt. Lo's five-year disposable income is $25,980 ($433 multiplied by 60), so she is well over the $12,850 ceiling and her filing is presumed abusive. Her Ch. 7 petition will be dismissed unless she can rebut the presumption by showing special circumstances as explained in section 6.8.6.

c. Steps 3 and 4 need to be recalculated if we increase Lo's allowed monthly expenses to $4,400. She now has monthly disposable income of $33 ($4,433 minus $4,400). Her five-year disposable income ($33 multiplied by 60) is $1,980, which is below the $7,700 minimum. Although Lo's income is high enough to call for application of the formula, once her expenses are taken into account, her five-year disposable income turns out to be too low to give rise to the presumption of abuse.

d. Again, we must recalculate steps 3 and 4. Lo's monthly expenses are now $4,300, which, deducted from her income of $4,433, leaves her with a monthly disposable income of $133. Multiply this by 60 to get a five-year disposable income of $7,980. This is between the minimum cutoff of $7,700 and the maximum of $12,850, so the presumption only applies if $7,980 exceeds 25 percent of Lo's general unsecured debt. Twenty five percent of $75,000 is $18,750, which is more than Lo's 60-month disposable income. The presumption does not arise.

CHAPTER 7

The Automatic Stay (§§362(a), (b), (c), and (k))

§7.1 OVERVIEW OF THE AUTOMATIC STAY[1]

In simple terms, the automatic stay is an injunction that arises by operation of law immediately upon the commencement of the bankruptcy case. The act of filing the bankruptcy petition is all that is required to bring it into effect. No application for the injunction is made, and no court order is needed.

Section 362(a) imposes a wide-ranging prohibition on all activity outside the bankruptcy forum to collect prepetition debts from the debtor or to assert or enforce claims against the debtor's prepetition property or estate property. Section 362(b) delineates a list of activities that are exempt from the stay. Section 362(c) provides when the stay terminates — the timing of which varies based on the disposition of a case and the chapter under which the petition was filed. Section 362(d) offers parties the ability to petition the bankruptcy court to lift the stay as to certain activities. The section delineates the necessary showing. Section 362(d) is one of the most important Code sections and is addressed separately in Chapter 10. Section 362(k) lists damages an individual may seek for violations of the automatic stay, including attorneys' fees and punitive damages.

Before studying the details of these provisions, it is helpful to outline the purpose, nature, and scope of the stay.

1. Some subsections of §362 address extremely specialized bankruptcy issues that have little practical relevance. Discussion of these sections has been omitted.

§7.2 THE PURPOSE OF THE AUTOMATIC STAY

The automatic stay is arguably the most fundamental protection offered to debtors by federal bankruptcy law. It is essential to the accomplishment of two central goals: the debtor's fresh start and the evenhanded treatment of creditors. By halting individual creditor action to enforce or collect debts owed by the debtor, the stay prevents depletion of the debtor's assets and preserves them for surrender to the trustee or retention by the debtor in possession. Creditors can no longer seek advantage by pressing on with nonbankruptcy enforcement measures. They are compelled to channel their claims through the bankruptcy process. In addition to preserving the estate, the stay gives the debtor sanctuary from creditor pressure so that orderly liquidation can be arranged or a plan formulated for the debtor's rehabilitation.

The stay is also vital to the bankruptcy court's power to deal effectively with the case and related litigation. By stopping enforcement proceedings in other courts, it allows the bankruptcy court to exercise its jurisdiction and to assume a central role in a case it is overseeing. Henceforth, all litigation relating to the case must be brought before the bankruptcy court and will be resolved there, unless the court itself permits continuation of the proceedings elsewhere by abstaining or granting relief from the stay.

§7.3 BASIC TENETS OF THE STAY

As stated before, the stay is an automatic injunction that bars a broad range of action against the debtor, the property of the debtor, and property of the estate. The nature and scope of the stay can be best understood if the following general principles are kept in mind.

(1) The stay comes into effect upon the filing of the petition. This holds true for both voluntary and involuntary cases. In an involuntary case, therefore, the stay precedes the order for relief and operates much like a preliminary injunction prior to the adjudication of bankruptcy.

(2) The stay is binding on all entities. "Entities" is defined in §101(15) to include individuals, corporate entities of all kinds, and governmental units. Consequently, the stay applies to state and federal courts. For example, imagine that in a contract dispute involving the sale of real property, a state court judge has already held a trial, ruled, and approved a written order adverse to Debtor. Debtor files for bankruptcy. The automatic stay would prevent the judge from entering her order, even though the entry is merely an administrative act.

The stay also applies to bankruptcy courts that are not adjudicating estate assets in a particular case. For example, imagine that Debtor files for bankruptcy in California. Debtor's former business partner files for bankruptcy in Texas and alleges that Debtor engaged in fraudulent conduct. The Texas bankruptcy court would not be allowed to oversee a fraudulent transfer proceeding against Debtor. The automatic stay would apply and prevent the bankruptcy court from moving forward with any proceeding against Debtor. As described in more detail in Chapter 8, the Texas bankruptcy court would have to seek relief from stay in order to hold any proceedings against Debtor.

(3) The effectiveness of the stay does not depend on creditors' notice of the filing. The stay binds an array of parties as soon as the petition is filed, even if these parties only find out about it later. Therefore, a creditor cannot seek to retain an advantage gained by violating the stay on the grounds that it had no knowledge of the bankruptcy when it took the action barred by the stay. Some courts have characterized acts in violation of the stay as voidable, so that the trustee or the debtor must apply to court to have the act set aside. The majority of courts, however, holds that actions taken in violation of the automatic stay are void and have no effect as a matter of law; no affirmative steps need be taken to avoid them.[2] *See* section 7.7 and Example 1.

Although innocent violations of the stay are ineffective, deliberate violations can have even more serious consequences. In addition to losing any advantage gained by the violation, a willful transgressor is liable to the debtor for any actual damages suffered and, if the transgression is egregious, for punitive damages. The violator may also be held in contempt of court. *See* section 7.7 and Example [1].

(4) The debtor cannot waive the stay. Imagine that Company, Inc. is experiencing financial difficulties. Company's primary lender offers Company access to a new line of financing but requires that the Company waive the automatic stay as to any of the lender's collection efforts in the event Company files for bankruptcy. Company believes that this new financing will allow it to avoid bankruptcy entirely. Would such a provision be enforceable in bankruptcy? Could you argue that the automatic stay is in place to protect the debtor; therefore, the debtor should be allowed to waive it? The answer is that this provision would not be enforceable. The stay is designed to protect the debtor, but it also protects the creditor body and

---

2. See, for example, *Church Mut. Ins. Co. v. American Home Assurance Co.*, 422 F. App'x 15, 18 (2d Cir. 2011).

myriad other stakeholders. Consequently, any provision attempting to waive the stay is unenforceable.

(5) The stay generally remains in effect until the case is closed or dismissed. (*See* section 7.5 for details.) Section 362(c) governs the duration of the automatic stay. It provides that the stay terminates with respect to property of the estate when the property ceases to be property of the estate and — with respect to the debtor and property of the debtor — the earliest of when the case is closed or dismissed or when the court grants or denies a discharge. Section 362(c) also limits or eliminates the applicability of the stay if one or more prior cases were dismissed in the one-year period preceding the petition date. Subject to certain qualifications, if the debtor has had one prior case dismissed within the preceding year, the stay terminates on the 30th day after the later petition is filed. In the event the debtor has had two or more cases dismissed in the preceding year, §362(c) prevents the stay from taking effect. The bankruptcy court may extend the stay or allow it to take effect upon a showing that the later case was filed in good faith as to the creditors to be stayed.

Further, the stay ends in the event that an involuntary petition is denied. However, the stay is effective pending the order for relief, so any act in violation of the stay prior to dismissal of the case is ineffective and could result in sanctions. The same is generally true in a voluntary case: Although dismissal ends the stay, the termination of the stay is prospective, not retrospective, so the dismissal does not validate or excuse violations that occurred before dismissal. Courts are not in agreement on the effect of the stay where a voluntary case is dismissed because the debtor is ineligible for relief under §109. Some courts have interpreted the requirements of §109 as jurisdictional because the section talks of who may or may not be a debtor under the Code. On this view, the filing is a nullity where the debtor is ineligible for relief, so that no stay arises at all. The more prevalent view, however, is that §109 is not jurisdictional, but merely sets out qualifications to be satisfied to avoid dismissal of the case. On this approach, even if the case is dismissed, the stay was effective between the time of filing and dismissal, and creditor action in violation of the stay can be sanctioned. See, for example, *In re Brown*, 342 B.R. 248 (Bankr. D. Md. 2006); *In re Zarnel*, 619 F.3d 156 (2d Cir. 2010), in which the courts held that the stay was effective until dismissal, even though the debtor was ineligible for relief for failure to undergo the credit counseling required by §109(h). (*See also* section 5.4.3.)

(6) Upon the debtor's discharge, the stay is succeeded by a discharge injunction. Pursuant to §524(a), if a discharge is granted in a case, a discharge injunction permanently enjoins efforts to collect discharged debt. Therefore, for many creditors the advent of the stay forever ends collection efforts under nonbankruptcy law. (Qualifications to this broad observation are discussed in section 7.5 and Chapter 8.)

(7) The stay applies in all forms of bankruptcy. There are significant differences between liquidation and the different forms of rehabilitation. Therefore, the impact of the stay is likely to vary depending on the type of relief sought. For example, because Ch. 7 is intended to provide for the expeditious liquidation of the estate, the stay is likely to focus on preservation of property and the protection of the debtor for the relatively short period during which the estate is collected, realized, and distributed. By contrast, a debtor under Ch. 11 is engaged in plan formulation, negotiations, the operation of a business, and the use of estate assets. The debtor's ability to restrain creditor action during this process of restructuring is vital to the success of the rehabilitation effort, but creditors assume a greater risk of loss while the debtor uses estate property and works on reorganization. If the attempt at rehabilitation fails, the delay in enforcement of rights caused by the stay could have resulted in irreparable damage to a creditor. The means of ameliorating this problem is discussed in Chapter 10.

(8) The stay does not preclude action in the bankruptcy court. Creditors and other parties in interest may institute proceedings in the bankruptcy court itself concerning matters that are otherwise subject to the stay.

(9) The stay is not an end in itself. It does not determine the validity of claims or dispose of them. The stay simply suspends action on the claim outside of the bankruptcy process. In due course the claim will be asserted against the estate and will be dealt with in the claim process. Any issues concerning the claim will be adjudicated by the bankruptcy court itself or will be resolved in another forum following relief from stay.

(10) Although the stay is comprehensive, it does not cover every conceivable activity. When the stay does not apply to a particular action but it is in the best interests of the estate to restrain that action, §105 gives the court the power to issue an injunction. The injunction under §105 is not automatic and must be issued by the court following an application on notice and a hearing. The applicant for the injunction must demonstrate good cause for the grant of relief.

§7.4 THE SCOPE OF THE STAY: §§362(a) AND (b)

Section 362(a) delineates the activities prohibited by the automatic stay. The section prescribes eight different categories of activity that must stop when the petition is filed.[3] Section 362(b) delineates specific activities that are not subject to the stay.

§7.4.1 Acts Precluded by the Stay — §362(a)

Acts stayed by §362(a) can be classified into three broad categories:

(1) Acts against the debtor. Sections 362(a)(1), (2), (6), (7), and (8) prohibit all acts against the debtor relating to the collection of claims that arose before the commencement of the bankruptcy case. This includes the commencement or continuation of judicial or administrative proceedings to adjudicate or enforce the claim as well as private nonjudicial action (such as correspondence, personal contact, or exercise of a right of setoff) aimed at recovering the debt. In most cases, a creditor's attempt to collect a debt by nonjudicial means takes the form of an oral or written communication to the debtor seeking payment or threatening consequences of nonpayment. These acts primarily implicate §362(a)(6). This section does not insulate debtors from all communication from creditors. Rather, the section prohibits creditor communication that threatens immediate action by a creditor, such as foreclosure or a lawsuit. Creditors who engage in non-coercive, non-harassing communications with debtors do not violate the stay as long as the communication does not represent an attempt to collect on a prepetition debt.[4]

Some collection activity can be surprisingly innovative. For example, in *In re Hampton*, 319 B.R. 163 (Bankr. E.D. Ark. 2005), a car dealer installed a "PayTek" device on cars sold on credit to debtors with poor credit ratings. The device disabled the car unless the driver entered a valid code number before starting the car. The code was valid for only one month, so that each month the buyer had to get a new code from the dealer, which she received only upon making her monthly payment. After the buyer filed for bankruptcy, the dealer became very uncooperative about giving her new monthly codes. The court held that this was a violation of the stay.

---

3. If a particular act is not mentioned in §362(a) and the subsection cannot be interpreted to encompass it, the act is not subject to the stay. To prevent it from occurring, the debtor or trustee must convince the court to use its injunctive powers under §105.

4. See, e.g., *In re Duke*, 79 F.3d 43 (7th Cir. 1996) (court found that creditor had not violated the stay by sending debtor's counsel a letter postpetition that read: "There is a balance of $317.10 on this account. Should your client elect to reaffirm the Sears account upon liquidation of the outstanding balance in accordance with the Reaffirmation Agreement, charge privileges will be reinstated with a line of credit in the amount of $500.00. Enclosed are copies of the proposed Reaffirmation Agreement. Your courtesy and cooperation in this matter are greatly appreciated. Please let me know if we may be of further assistance.").

Most of the provisions in §362(a) are aimed at staying action relating to the enforcement of prepetition debts due by the debtor or actions relating to property of the estate. However, §362(a)(1) is broad enough to extend beyond attempts to pursue debts. It states, in general terms, that the filing of the petition stays "the commencement or continuation . . . of a judicial, administrative, or other action or proceeding against the debtor that was or could have been commenced before the commencement of the case. . . ." This broad language could include a suit for an injunction and other similar actions, even though the actions may not be for the purpose of debt collection and merely seek to restrain the debtor from acting in a way that harms the plaintiff's rights. For example, imagine that Debtor signed an employment contract with her company that contained an enforceable covenant not to compete. Debtor leaves her job and then files for bankruptcy. Her company's attempt to enforce the covenant not to compete would be subject to the stay.[5]

However, a court may recognize a "judicial exception" to the stay where the injunction aims to restrain the debtor's tortious or illegal conduct. For example, in *Dominic's Restaurant of Dayton, Inc. v. Mantia*, 683 F.3d 757 (6th Cir. 2012), the court found that the stay did not apply to contempt proceedings in state court to enforce an injunction against the debtor's infringement of the plaintiffs' trademark. The court reasoned that if the stay was to be applied to these proceedings, the debtor would be able to continue to violate the plaintiff's rights with impunity. Notwithstanding cases like this, a party who continues any kind of proceeding against the debtor after the petition is filed takes the risk that the action will violate the stay. The safest course of action is to seek relief from stay before continuing the proceedings.

The stay of actions against the debtor applies only to prepetition claims. Postpetition transactions by the debtor do not give rise to claims against the estate but are the debtor's own responsibility. They can be enforced against the debtor through the normal collection methods of nonbankruptcy law.

(2) Acts against property of the debtor. Section 362(a)(5) prohibits any steps to create, perfect, or enforce a lien against property of the debtor to secure a prepetition claim. As explained in Chapter 11, the debtor's prepetition property becomes property of the estate. However, it commonly happens that while the bankruptcy case is pending the debtor begins to acquire a new estate, which consists of prepetition property that may have been returned to the debtor and postpetition property acquired by the debtor. Section 362(a)(5) protects the debtor's postpetition property by forbidding prepetition creditors from seeking to satisfy their claims by attempting to establish or enforce liens against the debtor's postfiling

5. See generally *Udell v. Standard Carpetland USA, Inc.*, 18 F.3d 403 (7th Cir. 1994).

property. The stay covers only prepetition debts. A postpetition creditor has full rights of enforcement against the debtor's property.

(3) Acts against property of the estate. A bankruptcy estate is created upon the filing of the petition. (*See* Chapter 11.) The preservation of estate property and the evenhanded treatment of creditors call for a wide-ranging stay on all postpetition activity that seeks to remove property from the estate or establish or enforce an interest in it. The stay of action against estate property is wider than the stay protecting the debtor and property of the debtor because it applies to both prepetition and postpetition claims. A postpetition creditor of the debtor has no claim to property of the estate and has no right to try to reach estate property. However, the estate itself may incur obligations. The stay prevents creditors of the estate from taking action to assert their claims against estate property outside of the normal claim procedures.

The stay of activity against property of the estate is provided for in §362(a)(2), (3), and (4). Section 362(a)(2) prohibits attempts to enforce prepetition judgments against estate property and is most frequently invoked when a creditor seeks to enforce a prepetition foreclosure judgment. Section 362(a)(3) prohibits the physical taking of estate property and refusals to turnover estate property within a creditor's possession. Recently, courts have held that §362(a)(3) also prohibits intangible acts to exercise control over estate property.[6] With certain limited exceptions,[7] §362(a)(4) precludes an act to perfect a security interest after the filing of a bankruptcy petition.

§7.4.2 The Impact of the Stay on Setoff Rights

Under nonbankruptcy law, where two persons are mutually indebted, the debts may be set off against each other. That is, either party may deduct the amount due to him from what he owes the other. An account in a bank or other depository institution is a debt due by the bank to its customer. Therefore, if the customer also owes money to the bank, it can refuse to permit withdrawal from the customer's account, and can set off the monies in the account against what the customer owes. Section 553 gives full effect to nonbankruptcy setoff rights in bankruptcy and treats the creditor with a right of setoff as a secured claimant to the extent of the setoff. For example, if

---

6. See, e.g., *In re Johnson*, 548 B.R. 770, 790 (Bankr. S.D. Ohio 2016) ("[I]t is well recognized that actions against nondebtors that would have an 'adverse impact' upon the property of the estate are subject to the automatic stay under §362(a)(3).").

7. Section 362(a)(4) is subject to §§546(e) and 547(e)(2)(A), which allow for postpetition perfection in limited instances.

the debtor has borrowed $10,000 from a bank and has $4,000 in an account at the bank, upon the debtor's bankruptcy the bank has a secured claim of $4,000 and an unsecured claim of $6,000. (Setoff is discussed in Chapter 13.)

However, §362(a)(7) would prohibit the bank from actually exercising its right of setoff. That is, although it will ultimately have the right to claim the setoff, the bank cannot simply effect the right of setoff upon the filing of the petition by taking the funds in the account. It must seek the permission of the court to do so by applying for relief from stay. This creates a problem for the bank because the customer can destroy the bank's setoff right by withdrawing the funds from the account before the bank is able to get relief from stay. In *Citizens Bank of Maryland v. Strumpf*, 516 U.S. 16 (1995), the U.S. Supreme Court protected creditors from this vulnerability by allowing the creditor to freeze the account pending relief from stay. It held that the placing of a temporary administrative hold on a bank account while the bank applies for relief from stay is not, in itself, a violation of §362(a)(7). The court reasoned that a temporary freeze merely suspends payment from the account and does not constitute an exercise of the right of setoff by permanently removing the funds from the account. To refuse to recognize the creditor's power to do this would eviscerate its right to claim a setoff, which is preserved in bankruptcy by §553. It is also inconsistent with §542(b), which requires a party to pay a debt due to the estate only when it is due and payable. The court also rejected the debtor's argument that the hold violated two other provisions of §362(a). It did not violate §362(a)(3) because the hold was not an act to obtain possession of or control over estate property. From the bank's perspective, the account was not property, but merely a debt to the estate. Nor did it violate §362(a)(6), which precludes the creditor from attempting to recover a claim from the debtor.

Strumpf makes it clear that it applies only where the hold is temporary, so the creditor must move diligently to obtain relief from stay. *In re Wicks*, 215 B.R. 316 (E.D.N.Y. 1997), demonstrates the consequence of delay. In that case, the debtor's credit union placed a hold on the account upon learning of the bankruptcy and did nothing about applying for relief from stay until the debtor initiated proceedings, four months later, to obtain damages for violation of the stay. The court said that because the credit union had shown no intent to move diligently for relief from stay, the hold could not be regarded as temporary, within the contemplation of *Strumpf*, and it must therefore be taken to be an actual attempt to exercise the right of setoff in violation of §362(a)(7).[8]

---

8. See also *In re Schafer*, 315 B.R. 765 (Bankr. D. Colo. 2004).

§7.4.3 Activity Excluded from the Stay — §362(b)

Section 362(b) sets out a long list of actions that are excluded from the stay (several of which were added by the Bankruptcy Abuse Prevention and Consumer Protection Act of 2005 [BAPCPA]). Many of the acts represent specialized bankruptcy issues with little practical relevance. Consequently, this section addresses only the four most widely applicable exclusions to §362(a). As a general matter, the exclusions from the stay reflect a decision by Congress that in some situations the interests of the debtor and the estate would not be harmed by permitting the identified action to continue without leave of the court, or that the rights being enforced are important enough to permit continued enforcement without interruption from the stay.

(1) Criminal actions and enforcement: §362(b)(1). Criminal prosecution is conducted by the government for the protection of its citizens, and there is a strong policy that bankruptcy should not interfere with the government's power to enforce criminal law. A debtor may not evade or forestall criminal proceedings by filing bankruptcy. Indeed, bankruptcy court should not become a haven for criminals.

The exclusion of criminal enforcement from the stay is usually uncontroversial. However, a distinct minority of courts inquire into the purpose behind prosecuting the debtor, applying what is commonly referred to as the "motivation test." Under this approach, courts will not exempt prosecution actions that are principally designed to force the debtor to make payment to a creditor under the threat of criminal prosecution. For example, imagine that Debtor writes a check to a local business for services rendered, but there are insufficient funds in Debtor's bank account, and the check is returned. Debtor files for bankruptcy. The local district attorney contacts Debtor and indicates that Debtor will face criminal prosecution unless the local business is repaid promptly. Debtor is unable to pay and a criminal action is brought. Should §362(b)(1) exempt the action? The vast majority of courts hold that §362(b)(1) creates an absolute rule that exempts criminal prosecutions from the automatic stay.[9] These courts do not inquire into the motivation of the prosecution. However, some courts invoke the motivation test and attempt to determine if a prosecutor is initiating criminal proceedings in the hope that the debtor will be pressured to pay a prepetition debt. Consequently, where debt collection motives are intertwined in the criminal case, a few courts will examine the motive of the prosecution and will stay the criminal proceedings if

9. See, e.g., *In re Gruntz*, 202 F.3d 1074 (9th Cir. 2000) and *In re Bartel*, 404 B.R. 584 (B.A.P. 1st Cir. 2009).

the debtor can prove that the true motivation of the proceedings is to coerce payment of the debt rather than to punish a violation of the law.[10]

(2) Family support obligations: §362(b)(2). The impact of bankruptcy on a debtor's dependents is a matter of ongoing concern. This is particularly so where the dependents are also creditors because the debtor has support obligations to them under a prior agreement or court order. To prevent a debtor from using bankruptcy to evade these support obligations, the Bankruptcy Reform Act of 1994 enacted a number of provisions giving these debts special treatment, including higher priority, exclusion from the operation of the exemptions, nonavoidability of a lien securing them, and nondischargeability. BAPCPA continued the trend started in 1994 by further strengthening support obligations in various ways.

The exception to the stay in §362(b)(2) is one of the provisions designed to protect a debtor's dependents from the consequences of the debtor's bankruptcy filing. Under §362(b)(2)(A) the stay does not bar the commencement or continuation of a civil action or proceeding to establish paternity or to establish or modify a domestic support obligation.[11] BAPCPA expanded §362(b)(2)(A) to include proceedings concerning child custody or visitation, to dissolve a marriage, and regarding family violence. Section 362(b)(2)(B) also excludes from the stay the collection of a domestic support obligation from property that is not property of the estate—that is, from the debtor's own property.

(3) Specified creditor action to consolidate nonbankruptcy rights: §362(b)(3). The stay does not affect certain specified actions taken by a creditor under nonbankruptcy law to perfect or consolidate rights against the debtor or the estate. The rationale for these exceptions is that they are merely legal procedures that the creditor is entitled to take under nonbankruptcy law to validate a legitimate claim. For example, under §362(b)(3) a creditor may perform acts to perfect or to maintain or continue perfection if that action is recognized by §546 or 547 as binding on the estate. Example 4 illustrates this permissible conduct.

---

10. See *In re Perrin*, 233 B.R. 71, 78 (Bankr. D. N.J. 1999) (concluding that if state's motive is collection of prepetition debt then prosecution is subject to the automatic stay).

11. The term "domestic support obligation" was substituted by BAPCPA for the phrase "alimony, maintenance, and support." Although the terms mean roughly the same thing, "domestic support obligation" is more comprehensive. It is defined in §101(14A) to include debts in the nature of alimony, maintenance, or support, established by a separation agreement, divorce decree, property settlement agreement, court order, or determination of a governmental unit. The debt must be owed to or recoverable by a spouse, a former spouse, a child, a party responsible for the child, or a governmental unit.

(4) Proceedings by governmental units to enforce police or regulatory powers: §362(b)(4). The stay does not apply to the commencement or continuation of an action or proceeding by a governmental unit to enforce its police and regulatory power. This includes the enforcement of a judgment other than a money judgment. More specifically, §362(b)(4) provides that the automatic stay does not prevent a governmental unit from suing a debtor or continuing suit postpetition to prevent fraud, or ensure adherence to environmental protection, consumer protection, safety, or similar police or regulatory laws.

When §362(b)(4) is applicable, the government may pursue any enforcement up to the stage of judgment. If the judgment is not monetary in nature, the government may continue beyond the stage of judgment. However, if the judgment is for money, the proceedings must end at the point of judgment and the further enforcement is stayed. The government will then file their claim in the bankruptcy case for the monetary debt. For example, in *In re Mystic Tank Lines Corp.*, 544 F.3d 524 (3d Cir. 2008), the state was held not to have violated the stay by obtaining a postpetition judgment against the debtor in state court for the cost of cleaning up petroleum contamination for which the debtor was responsible. The stay would apply to the collection of the judgment debt, but the state had not attempted to collect it, and had proved a claim in the estate based on the judgment.

Not every kind of action or proceeding by a governmental unit is an exercise of police or regulatory power. Governments often engage in commercial transactions. In this role their claims are no different from those of private creditors and are subject to the stay. It is a question of fact whether the government is acting as a regulator in the public interest or is just in the position of a creditor, pursuing only its own interest. This factual question is determined by examining the nature of the transaction or relationship, its purpose, and its underlying policy motivation. The interrelated tests used by courts to determine if governmental action falls within or is outside the exception are the "pecuniary purpose" and "public policy" tests. The essential question is whether the government's action is aimed at protecting public safety or welfare or is merely taken for the pecuniary purpose of gaining advantage over other creditors in the collection of a debt. Naturally, a law can have dual purposes of promoting public welfare and protecting a government's pecuniary interest. Courts have ruled that even where one purpose of a law at issue is to protect the pecuniary interest, the exception may still apply if the *primary* purpose of the law is to promote the public welfare. For example, in *Lockyer v. Mirant Corp.* 398 F.3d 1098 (9th Cir. 2005), the court held that action to overturn an antitrust violation by compelling the divestiture of electrical plants was a matter of public welfare and fell within the exception. In *N.L.R.B. v. P.I.E. Nationwide, Inc.*, 923 F.2d 506, 511-512 (7th Cir. 1991) the court found the exception to apply to proceedings before the National Labor Relations Board to prevent an unfair labor practice. In *Safety-Kleen, Inc. v. Wyche*, 274 F.3d 846, 866 (4th Cir. 2001), the court held that the primary purpose of financial assurance regulation "is to deter environmental misconduct and encourage the safe design and operation of hazardous waste facilities," which clearly promotes the public welfare. In *U.S. v. Coulton*, 594 Fed. Appx. 563 (11th Cir. 2014), an attorney filed a bankruptcy petition prior to a final hearing on the contempt charges that had been filed against him. Notwithstanding the bankruptcy filing, the court continued with the contempt hearing, finding that the attorney was in contempt and imposing a monetary sanction. The debtor appealed, arguing that the court's actions violated the automatic stay. On appeal, the circuit court upheld the lower court's decision, ruling that the action represented a vindication of the regulatory power of the judiciary and was exempted by §362(b)(4). However, enforcement of the monetary sanction was stayed pending further action by the bankruptcy court.[12] The fact that proceedings may ultimately result in a money judgment does not necessarily disqualify the proceedings as regulatory. Often, a monetary assessment is needed to penalize violations of policy or to effect a regulatory purpose. For example, in *In re Commonwealth Companies, Inc.*, 913 F.2d 518 (8th Cir. 1990), a civil fraud action brought by the United States under the False Claims Act was held to be regulatory and excluded from the stay up to the point of enforcement under §362(b)(4). The court found that the goal of the suit was not merely to recover compensation for fraud, but also to penalize it and to deter such conduct by others. The court made it clear that once a money judgment was obtained, the enforcement of that judgment is stayed. The exception to the stay in §362(b)(4) only permits enforcement of nonmonetary judgments.[13]

By contrast, in *In re Corporation de Servicios Medicos Hospitalarios de Fajardo*, 805 F.2d 440 (1st Cir. 1986), the Puerto Rican Department of Health was held not to be entitled to rely on §362(b)(4) to continue with an action arising out of a contract with the debtor to operate hospital services. In *In re FV Steel Wire Co.*, 324 B.R. 701 (Bankr. E.D. Wis. 2005), the court found that enforcement of a consent decree to clean up hazardous waste involved nothing more than payment into a fund and was outside of the exception. In *In re Nortel Networks, Inc.*, 669 F.3d 128 (3rd Cir. 2011), the court found the exception did not apply because the action to enforce a government-created scheme to protect pension funds was purely pecuniary. In addition, the government-created entity that sought to enforce the scheme did not qualify as a governmental unit because it was not set up as a government entity.

12. See also *Marshall v. Washington State Bar Ass'n*, 448 F. App'x 661 (9th Cir. 2011).

13. See also *California ex rel Brown v. Villalobos*, 453 B.R. 404 (D. Nev. 2011) (ruling that fines and penalties for improperly influencing state pension fund officials served a public purpose and were regulatory, not pecuniary).

§7.5 TERMINATION OF THE STAY

The stay of a particular activity may be lifted by the court following an application for relief from stay under §362(d). This is discussed in Chapter 8. Apart from that, §362(c)(1) and (2) provide for termination of the stay in the normal course of the bankruptcy proceedings. The subsections treat the stay of acts against estate property differently from the stay of other acts. BAPCPA added §§362(c)(3) and (4) to grounds for terminating the stay. These subsections deal with abusive serial filings by providing for termination of the stay where the debtor has engaged in this improper strategy.

§7.5.1 Termination of the Stay of Acts Against Estate Property

Under §362(c)(1), the stay of acts against estate property continues until the property is no longer property of the estate. Property may be released by the estate for different reasons. For example, the trustee may sell it in the course of liquidation; it may be abandoned to a claimant because neither the debtor nor the estate has any equity in it; or it may be abandoned to the debtor as exempt. Section 362(c)(1) is of limited effect. It does not authorize proceedings against the property following release by the estate, but merely makes the stay inapplicable to the extent that it was grounded on the fact that the estate had an interest in the property. Although it is no longer property of the estate, it may still be protected from the stay on some other ground. For example, if property is abandoned to the debtor as exempt, it still cannot be subjected to the claims of prepetition creditors, who remain bound by the stay of actions against the debtor and the debtor's property (*see* Example 2). However, a postpetition creditor of the debtor could perfect a security interest in it or seize it in execution, because postpetition claims are not affected by the stay of acts against the debtor or the debtor's property.

§7.5.2 Termination of the Stay of Other Acts

The stay of all acts other than acts against property of the estate continues in effect under §362(c)(2) until the case is closed or dismissed or a discharge is granted or denied, whichever occurs first. If the reason for termination of the stay is the dismissal of the case, creditors can take action to enforce their claims under nonbankruptcy law following the dismissal. If the reason for termination of the stay is the grant of a discharge, the stay is immediately succeeded by the discharge injunction under §524(a)(2), which permanently enjoins the creditor from collecting whatever portion of the debt was not paid from the estate. The discharge may not extend to all debts. As discussed in Chapter 21, some debts may be excluded from the discharge and therefore are not covered by the discharge injunction. The creditor may proceed to recover an undischarged debt after the stay terminates. If the debtor is denied a discharge altogether (*see* Chapter 21), all creditors may proceed with enforcement actions under nonbankruptcy law.

§7.5.3 Termination of the Stay Following Serial Filings

BAPCPA added §362(c)(3) and (4) in an attempt to address the problem of abusive serial filings by an individual debtor. As many courts have noted, the language that appears in these sections is dense and almost incomprehensible. In broad terms, the sections intend to make it much more difficult for an individual debtor to file successive petitions for the purpose of using the stay to frustrate creditor collection actions. Because §707(b) contemplates that a debtor whose Ch. 7 case is dismissed for abuse should have the opportunity to refile under Chs. 11 or 13, §362(c)(3) and (4) do not apply where the case had been dismissed under §707(b).[14]

Section 362(c)(3) limits the duration of the automatic stay where the debtor had filed a prior case that was pending within the year preceding the petition and that case was dismissed. In that case, the automatic stay expires automatically on the 30th day after the latter case is filed, unless extended by the bankruptcy court. The debtor has the option of attempting to extend the stay past 30 days but must demonstrate by clear and convincing evidence that the second bankruptcy filing was made in good faith.

However, the precise effect of the section's language is difficult to determine. The section states that the stay "with respect to any action taken with respect to a debt or property securing such debt or with respect to any lease shall terminate with respect to the debtor on the 30th day after the filing of the later case." Section 362(c)(3) applies whether the current case is voluntary or involuntary. Because §362(c)(3) refers to "any action taken" it is unclear if it applies only to creditors who have actually taken action to enforce the debt prior to the filing of the second petition. Some courts have held that the use of this language indicates that the stay does not terminate in its entirety but only terminates with regard to those creditors who had "taken action"—that is, instituted judicial or other formal collection proceedings prior to the filing of the current petition.[15] Other

---

14. *See* Section 6.8 for an explanation of the operation of §707(b).
15. See, e.g., *In re Stanford*, 373 B.R. 890 (Bankr. E.D. Ark. 2007).

courts disagree, and hold that the section terminates the stay entirely after the 30-day period with regard to all creditors, whether or not they have taken any action to enforce the debt.[16]

The words "with respect to the debtor" have also created interpretational difficulties. It is unclear whether §362(c)(3) terminates the stay only against the debtor and property of the debtor, or if it also applies to the property of the estate. Most courts have held that the reference to the debtor and the absence of any reference to estate property means that the stay terminates only as against the debtor and the debtor's property.[17] Other courts have interpreted the words "with respect to the debtor" as having nothing to do with distinguishing estate property from the debtor and his property. Rather, they interpret these words as relating back to the beginning of §362(c)(3), which refer to both single and joint cases. In other words, these courts argue that the reference to the debtor merely makes it clear that in a joint case, the termination of the stay only effects the debtor who runs afoul of §362(c)(3). The courts who favor this interpretation argue that it is reinforced by the legislative history and the section's purpose because it gives creditors the greatest degree of protection against bad faith serial filings.[18]

To prevent expiration of the stay after 30 days, the debtor must apply to the court before the end of the 30-day period. If, after notice and a hearing, the court finds that the new filing is in good faith, the court may continue the stay, with or without conditions, against all or particular creditors. If the stay is to continue against a particular creditor, §362(c)(3)(ii) creates a presumption that the petition was not filed in good faith if that creditor had moved for relief in the prior case and the application for relief was still pending at the time of dismissal of the case, or the creditor had received relief from stay. Where the debtor seeks continuation of the stay as against all creditors, §362(c)(3)(C)(i) creates a presumption that the petition was not filed in good faith where 1) the debtor filed more than one previous case in the preceding year, 2) the debtor has failed to perform properly in the prior case, 3) the debtor has not had a substantial change in his financial affairs since the prior dismissal, or 4) there is no basis for believing that the current case will result in a discharge or a fully performed plan.[19] The presumption can be rebutted only by clear and convincing evidence of good faith. Good faith is determined on the totality of the circumstances, including such factors as the timing of the filing of the later petition, how the debts arose, the reason for the dismissal

16. See *In re James*, 358 B.R. 816 (Bankr. S.D. Ga. 2007).
17. See, e.g., *In re Jump*, 356 B.R. 789 (B.A.P. 1st Cir. 2006).
18. See *In re Reswick*, 446 B.R. 362 (B.A.P. 9th Cir. 2011).
19. Pursuant to §362(i), the presumption does not apply if the prior case terminated because the debtor entered into a debt repayment plan.

of the prior case, any change in the debtor's circumstances, and the debtor's conduct and apparent motivation. In essence, the debtor has the onerous burden of convincing the court that the debtor's honesty and the equities justify allowing the stay to remain in effect.[20]

Section 362(c)(4) governs situations in which the debtor had filed two or more prior cases that were pending within the preceding year and were dismissed. The multiple prior filings more strongly suggest abuse, so the debtor does not get the 30-day grace period, and the stay does not go into effect at all. The court can order the stay to take effect with regard to all or some creditors if, within 30 days of the petition, the debtor is able to show that the filing was not in bad faith. Section §362(c)(4)(D) contains a presumption of bad faith similar to that in §362(c)(3) that can only be rebutted by clear and convincing evidence to the contrary.

§7.6 THE EFFECT OF THE STAY ON LIMITATION PERIODS — §108

Under nonbankruptcy law, creditors' claims are subject to statutes of limitation. Because the stay halts lawsuits and collection efforts, a creditor may be prevented from initiating suit within the time required by nonbankruptcy law. If the bankruptcy case is not dismissed and the claim is settled and discharged in the course of bankruptcy, the postpetition expiry of the limitation period is irrelevant. The discharge injunction under §524 precludes any further enforcement action and the creditor cannot commence proceedings in another court.

However, a creditor's right to continue nonbankruptcy enforcement proceedings revives if 1) the bankruptcy case is dismissed, 2) relief from stay is granted, or 3) the debt is excluded from the discharge. The stay does not toll the limitation period entirely. Section 108(c) gives the creditor an opportunity to commence suit after termination of the stay. It provides, in essence, that if the claim is subject to a limitation period[21] and that period had not expired before the petition was filed, it will not expire until the time fixed by nonbankruptcy law or 30 days after notice of the termination or expiry of the stay, whichever is later. In other words, if the nonbankruptcy limitation period had not expired and has more than 30 days to run when the creditor is notified of termination of the stay, suit must be commenced

20. See *In re Baldesssaro*, 338 B.R. 178 (Bankr. D.N.H. 2006) and *In re Charles*, 332 B.R. 538 (Bankr. S.D. Tex. 2005).

21. Including not only a statute of limitations but also a period fixed by court order or contract.

in the remaining limitation period. But the creditor has 30 days following notice to commence suit if the period expired during the stay or will expire within 30 days of notice of termination.

§7.7 THE CONSEQUENCES OF VIOLATING THE STAY

§7.7.1 The Nullification of Advantages Gained by the Violation

The stay binds creditors as soon as the petition is filed, whether or not they have knowledge of it, and any act in violation of the stay, whether innocent or deliberate, is ineffective to give the actor any advantage. Apparent legal rights acquired in violation of the stay are a nullity, and the creditor is obliged to restore any money or property (or its value). There are differences on how courts view the legal effect of an act that violates the stay.[22] Some courts regard an act in violation of the stay as voidable; the act remains effective unless the debtor or trustee moves in bankruptcy court to have it set aside.[23] However, the majority view is to treat the act as void. The actor gains no legal advantage from it, even if no motion for avoidance is made.[24] These courts argue that actions taken in violation of the stay are void because the purpose of the provision is to offer debtors broad protection from creditors. This purpose is best furthered if all violations are rendered void, not merely voidable.[25]

§7.7.2 Willful Violations: Compensatory Damages, Including Costs and Attorneys' Fees

Although an innocent violation of the stay renders the act ineffective, a deliberate violation has further consequences. It could result in an award of costs, attorney's fees, and compensatory and punitive damages under §362(k)[26] or a sanction for contempt of court. Section 362(k)(1) provides that an individual injured by a willful violation of the stay "shall recover actual damages, including costs and attorneys' fees and, in appropriate

22. See *Kimbrell v. Brown*, 651 F.3d 752 (7th Cir. 2011) (noting debate among federal courts over whether actions filed in violation of the automatic stay are void or merely voidable).
23. See, e.g., *Barnes v. Barnes*, 279 F. App'x 318, 320 (5th Cir. 2008).
24. See, e.g., *Church Mut. Ins. Co. v. American Home Assurance Co.*, 422 F. App'x 15, 18 (2d Cir. 2011).
25. See *Burkart v. Coleman (In re Tippett)*, 542 F.3d 684, 690–91 (9th Cir. 2008).
26. Section 362(k) was formerly numbered (h). The numbering was changed by BAPCPA.

circumstances, may recover punitive damages." Section 362(k) uses the word "individual" rather than "debtor" or "entity," which, in its plain meaning, confines the remedy to natural persons. Some courts have interpreted it this way and have held that an artificial person, such as a corporation, has no remedy under §362(k). For example, in *In re Just Brakes Corporate Systems, Inc.*, 108 F.3d 881 (8th Cir. 1997), the court emphasized not only that "individual" is consistently used in the Code to refer to a natural person but also pointed out that the subsection was originally enacted in 1984 as part of a package of amendments relating to consumers. Nevertheless, other courts have extended the remedy to corporations.[27] Even if §362(k) does not provide a remedy to debtors other than individuals, a court has the power under §105 to award compensatory damages, as discussed below. However, it is unclear if the court's general powers under §105 extend to an award of punitive damages.

To receive damages for a willful violation of the stay under §362(k)(1), the individual[28] need only show that the creditor knew of the stay and intended the action that violated it. No specific intent to cause injury is required. A violation is not excused because the creditor had a good faith belief that it was entitled to take the action at issue. See, for example, *In re Johnson*, 501 F.3d 1163 (10th Cir. 2007) (the creditor disbelieved information that the debtor had filed a petition, and thought it was a ruse to delay enforcement) and *In re Kaneb*, 196 F.3d 265 (1st Cir. 1999) (the creditor was liable for damages even though it erroneously believed that it had obtained relief from stay). Further, a violative act taken without knowledge of the stay can become willful if the violator fails to remedy the violation after receiving notice of the stay.

Upon a showing of willful violation of the stay, the individual is entitled to receive compensatory damages for any economic loss that resulted from the violation. To recover compensatory damages, the individual must provide concrete evidence of loss that can be ascertained with reasonable certainty. For example, in *In re Frankel*, 391 B.R. 266 (Bankr. M.D. Pa. 2008), the

---

27. See *Cuffee v. Atlantic Bus. & Cmty. Dev. Corp.*, 901 F.2d 325, 329 (3d Cir. 1990) and *Budget Serv. Co. v. Better Homes of Virginia, Inc.*, 804 F.2d 289, 292 (4th Cir. 1986).

28. Section 362(k)(1) is most commonly used by individuals who are debtors. However, the plain meaning of the section's language does not confine the remedy to debtors. An individual other than the debtor may have standing to claim damages if she can show that 1) the violation caused her loss, 2) she has a personal stake in the outcome of the case, and 3) she is in the class of person intended to benefit from the statute. See *St. Paul Fire & Marine Ins. Co. v. Labuzan*, 579 F.3d 533 (5th Cir. 2009) (ruling that individual creditors of the debtor could claim damages under §362(k) if they could establish injury distinct from the injury to the estate itself); *In re MD Promenade, Inc.*, 51 BCD 22 (Bankr. N.D. Tex. 2009) (debtor's landlord awarded damages as a result of creditor's improper removal of property from the debtor's premises); but see *In re Newcomer*, 416 B.R. 166 (Bankr. D. Md. 2009) (holding that the debtor's wife was neither a debtor nor a creditor, and thus was not in the class of persons intended to benefit from the automatic stay).

court refused to award compensatory damages to the debtor where both the fact and extent of loss was conjectural.

As part of those compensatory damages, the debtor is entitled to costs and attorneys' fees. Courts had been divided on the scope of the costs and attorneys' fees. In *Sternberg v. Johnston*, 582 F.3d 1114 (9th Cir. 2009), the court read the words "actual damages" to cover only fees and costs incurred in challenging the stay violation but not to include those incurred in seeking a damages award. Other courts criticized this ruling.[29] In 2015, the Ninth Circuit acknowledged that it had erroneously interpreted subsection (k), joining the vast majority of courts in holding that §362(k) does in fact authorize an award of attorneys' fees incurred prosecuting an action for damages.[30]

§7.7.3 Emotional Distress Damages

Some courts have allowed emotional distress damages as part of the compensation for injury where the debtor can 1) demonstrate she has suffered significant harm, 2) clearly establish the significant harm, and 3) establish a causal connection between that significant harm and the violation of the automatic stay—as distinct, for instance, from the anxiety and pressures inherent in the bankruptcy process.[31] For example, in *In re Kaneb*, 196 F.3d 265 (1st Cir. 1999), the circuit court recognized the availability of emotional distress damages under §362(k) and awarded the debtor damages. In that case, the debtor was able to provide specific information about how he was socially ostracized after one of his creditors improperly publicized his bankruptcy filing. The circuit court upheld the bankruptcy court's award of emotional distress damages. However, other courts have refused to award emotional distress damages unless there is an actual financial loss. For example, in *Aiello v. Providian Financial Corp.*, 239 F.3d 876 (7th Cir. 2001), the circuit court refused to allow emotional distress damages in the absence of a recognized tort, even though the creditor's attempts at collection were quite aggressive. The court reasoned that the stay's purpose does not extend to protecting a debtor's emotional peace of mind.

---

29. See, e.g., *Duby v. United States*, 451 B.R. 664, 676–77 (B.A.P. 1st Cir. 2011) ("What good is it to be entitled to damages and attorneys' fees for a violation of the automatic stay if it costs a debtor much more in unrecoverable fees to recover such damages and recoverable attorneys fees?") (citation omitted).

30. See *Schwartz-Tallard v. America's Servicing Co.*, 803 F.3d 1095 (9th Cir. 2015) (en banc).

31. See *Dawson v. Washington Mut. Bank*, 390 F.3d 1139, 1149-51 (9th Cir. 2004) (denying the debtor's damage request because the debtor had failed to establish that he had suffered significant emotional harm caused directly by the stay violation).

§7.7.4 Punitive Damages

Punitive damages are not appropriate in all cases of willful violation and are generally awarded only where the violation is malicious or particularly egregious. Courts have considered the following five factors in determining whether to award punitive damages: 1) the nature of the creditor's conduct (which takes into account the knowledge of the creditor); 2) the creditor's ability to pay damages; 3) the creditor's level of sophistication; 4) the creditor's motives; and 5) any provocation by the debtor.[32] Punitive damages are not always proportional to actual damages.

Examples

1. DeLay & Co., Inc. defaulted on a loan from Blitzkrieg Bank. The bank commenced a collection suit, obtained default judgment, and issued a writ of execution. On June 1, the sheriff levied on office equipment owned by DeLay & Co. Under state law, a lien arose in the property upon levy. An execution sale is scheduled for June 15. On June 14, Blitzkrieg received notice from the clerk of the bankruptcy court informing it that DeLay & Co. had filed a voluntary Ch. 7 petition on May 31. Because the collection suit was so close to its conclusion, the bank decided that it made sense to proceed with the sale, thereby avoiding the need to become involved in the bankruptcy proceedings. Was that a good decision?

2. Last year, Debtor borrowed money from his bank. When he failed to repay the loan on its due date in February, the bank commenced suit to recover the amount of the loan. The bank obtained judgment at the end of June. Debtor filed a Ch. 7 petition on July 1. After the petition had been filed, the bank wished to execute on its judgment. There are two vehicles parked outside Debtor's home. One is an old car, abandoned to Debtor by the trustee because it is exempt, and the other is a motorbike purchased by Debtor from his postpetition income. Can the bank execute on either of these assets?

3. Debtor became involved in a dispute with his neighbor over a new fence erected by the neighbor. Debtor believed that the fence encroached on his property. During the dispute, Debtor became so enraged that he assaulted the neighbor and caused him serious personal injury. Debtor also threatened to destroy the fence. Shortly after the attack, the state initiated a criminal prosecution against Debtor for assault. In addition, the neighbor commenced proceedings in state court to recover damages

32. See *Weary v. Poteat*, 627 Fed.Appx. 475 (6th Cir. 2015).

for his injury and to enjoin Debtor from damaging or removing the fence. After these actions were commenced, Debtor filed a bankruptcy petition. At that time, both of the proceedings were pending. How will the stay affect them?

4. Two months prior to Debtor's bankruptcy, a contractor completed an alteration to his home. The contractor has not been paid. Under the state's mechanic's lien law, the contractor is entitled to a lien on the property to secure the price of the work. Under the statute, the lien attaches to the property with priority effective from the date of commencement of the work, provided that the claimant files a lien claim in the deeds registry within three months of completion. The claimant is required to commence action to foreclose the lien within six months of filing the claim. The contractor had not filed a lien claim by the petition date. Does the stay prevent the contractor from filing the lien and commencing suit in the periods prescribed by the state statute?

5. For several months before his bankruptcy, Debtor neglected to have his garbage hauled away. It has accumulated in piles in the front yard of his house. In June, the city health department warned Debtor that if he did not have the garbage removed, action would be taken against him. Debtor ignored the warning. Not only has he failed to clean up the existing garbage, but he continues to add new refuse to the heap.

   On July 1, Debtor filed a bankruptcy petition. On July 5, the city initiated suit in municipal court to enjoin further dumping and to compel Debtor to remove the existing garbage. In the event that Debtor fails to obey the cleanup order, the city asks the court for authority to clean up Debtor's yard itself and to charge him for the cleanup costs. Was the city allowed to commence this proceeding? If the municipal court grants the order, can the city enforce it without leave of the bankruptcy court?

6. Debtor failed to pay tuition due to the university she attends. She subsequently filed a bankruptcy petition. While her case was pending, she asked the university for a transcript. It refused to provide the transcript because Debtor had not paid her tuition. Is this a violation of the stay?

7. Percy Verence operates a debt collection agency. When he receives notice of a bankruptcy filing, his usual practice is to enter that information on his computer system so that his staff knows not to send dunning letters to the debtor. Tess De Stress is one of the debtors from whom Percy has been trying to collect money. Percy received notice that Tess had filed a petition and he entered the information in his system. However, because of a glitch in the system, the information did not show up in Tess's records. As a result, a staff member sent a dunning letter to Tess after the petition had been filed. Tess is emotionally fragile as a result of her financial difficulties and bankruptcy. She was terribly upset to receive the

dunning letter. Has Percy willfully violated the say? If so, can Tess recover damages for emotional distress?

EXPLANATIONS

Explanations

1. No. Blitzkrieg's correct response would have been to surrender the property to the trustee and to prove a claim in the estate for its unpaid debt, which would ultimately be paid at the rate payable to other general unsecured claims. The stay took effect on May 31 upon the filing of the petition. Any action taken subsequent to that is a violation of the stay. As noted in section 7.7, the majority view is that an act in violation of the stay is void, so any advantage obtained by the creditor is a nullity.

   The levy on June 1 violated §362(a)(2), which forbids enforcement of a prepetition judgment against the debtor or property of the estate. The levy also violates §362(a)(1), which bars the continuation of judicial proceedings against the debtor, and §362(a)(4), which prohibits any act to create, perfect, or enforce a lien against property of the estate. (The levy creates a judicial lien and DeLay & Co.'s property became property of the estate under §541 on the date of the petition.) The fact that Blitzkrieg did not know of the bankruptcy filing when it levied on June 1 does not validate the levy. The stay takes effect whether or not the creditor knew of it, so Blitzkrieg's execution lien is a nullity and the property or its proceeds must be returned to the estate.

   By continuing with the sale in execution after acquiring knowledge of the bankruptcy, Blitzkrieg compounded its violation of the stay and became a willful transgressor. As discussed in section 7.7, this could lead to liability beyond the restoration of the property or its value to the estate. Damages and fees are not recoverable by the debtor under §362(k) because the debtor is a corporation, not an individual. However, Blitzkrieg could be subject to sanctions for contempt of court or could be held liable for compensatory damages under §105(a).

2. The bank is an unsecured judgment creditor. It may not move unilaterally to satisfy its claim but must wait for a pro rata distribution from the estate. The car has been abandoned to Debtor, so it is no longer property of the estate and is not subject to the stay on actions against estate property under §362(a)(2), (3), and (4). However, the car is now Debtor's property, and levy is stayed by §362(a)(1), which forbids the continuation of process to recover a prepetition claim against the debtor. The bike was never estate property, but levy against it is likewise stayed by §362(a)(1). Alternatively, §362(a)(5) applies: As the levy would create a judicial lien on the bike and car, it violates the bar on action to create a lien on the debtor's property to secure a prepetition claim.

3. The criminal case against Debtor is not stayed. Section 362(b)(1) excludes from the stay the commencement or continuation of a criminal action or proceeding against the debtor. The reason for this exclusion is that bankruptcy should not intrude upon the operation of the state's criminal law system.

   The suit for personal injury damages is clearly stayed by §362(a)(1). The claim for the injunction does not aim to recover money or property from Debtor or the estate. Nevertheless, it is covered by the plain language of §362(a)(1), which does not confine actions or proceedings to suits for the payment of money but extends to the commencement or continuation of a proceeding that was or could have been commenced against the debtor before the petition, as well as to a proceeding to recover a prepetition claim. There is no statutory exclusion relating to injunctions in §362(b). A court adopting a plain-meaning approach to §362(a) would likely hold that the proceedings for the injunction are stayed, so that the neighbor must apply for relief from stay if he wishes to continue with his suit. However, a court that adopts a purpose-based approach may hold that the stay does not apply to the suit for an injunction, the aim of which is not to enforce a debt but to restrain postpetition tortious conduct by the debtor.

4. Debtor's home became the property of the estate upon the filing of the petition. In the absence of an exception in §362(b), any attempt to perfect the lien by filing offends both §362(a)(4) and §362(a)(6). Commencement of the foreclosure suit is barred by §362(a)(1).

   However, §362(b)(3) does provide an exception to the stay for perfection of the lien. It provides that the stay does not apply to any act to perfect or to maintain or continue perfection of an interest in property to the extent that the trustee's rights and powers are subject to such perfection under §546(b). (Section 546(b) is explained more fully in Chapter 14.) In simple terms, it recognizes the effectiveness against the estate of a provision of nonbankruptcy law that permits perfection of an interest to backdate upon completion of the act of perfection. In the context of this case, §546(b)(1)(A) upholds the rule of state law that allows the builder to perfect the mechanic's lien by filing within three months of completion, thereby acquiring a lien effective as from the date of commencement of the work. Section 362(b)(3) excludes the act of perfection from the stay, so that it can be accomplished within the portion of the statutory period that remains unexpired after the petition has been filed. Perfection by filing is affected by the normal procedure prescribed by state law. However, if seizure of the property or commencement of suit is required to complete perfection, §546(b)(2)(A) requires that this act is substituted for by giving notice to the trustee.

Although the builder is able to proceed with the lien filing as if no bankruptcy has occurred, he cannot commence suit within the subsequent six-month statutory period. Instead, he must give notice to the trustee under §546(b) within that period, which will give him a valid lien and a secured claim. The purpose of these provisions is to protect statutory liens by deferring to extended perfection periods conferred under state law.[33]

5. The stay under §362(a) applies to all entities, including governmental units. However, §362(b)(4) excludes from the stay the commencement or continuation of an action or proceeding by a governmental unit, defined in §101(27) to include a municipality, to enforce its police or regulatory power. The collection and disposal of waste is surely within the city's regulatory power. Section 362(b)(4) further permits the enforcement of a judgment other than a money judgment obtained for the purpose of exercising that power.

   The city's suit aims to enjoin Debtor's violation of the law and to compel him to cure his prior noncompliance, or to pay the city for doing so. The judgment is both a prohibitory injunction forbidding future violations of the law and a mandatory injunction compelling rectification of a prior breach of the law. The bar on future violations is not a money judgment and is excluded from the stay under §362(b)(4). However, the cleanup order is a money judgment that requires the estate to spend money in doing the work itself or to pay the city to do it. The cleanup order is therefore not excluded from the stay under §362(b)(4), and the city cannot proceed beyond the judgment to enforce it unless it applies for and receives relief from stay.

6. If the refusal of a transcript is used as a means to persuade or coerce a debtor into paying a prepetition tuition debt, it is a violation of the stay—an act to recover a claim against the debtor barred by §362(a)(6). It should be noted, however, that qualifying debts for educational loans or benefits are nondischargeable under §523(a)(8) (discussed in Chapter 21). If the debt for tuition qualifies for exclusion from the discharge, action to recover it will cease to be stayed once the stay terminates upon the court's grant of the discharge to the debtor. However, until that happens, the university is bound by the stay, and any attempt to collect the debt will violate the stay. *In re Parker*, 334 B.R. 529 (Bankr. D. Mass 2005) and *In re Kuehn*, 563 F.3d 289 (7th Cir. 2009).

7. Courts are generally not sympathetic to a defense that "the computer did it" and hold creditors accountable for properly functioning office

---

33. Note that any valid lien that the builder asserts may be subject to avoidance under §545(2). See section 12.3.

systems. The simple fact that Percy had knowledge of the filing and deliberately sent out the dunning letter is enough to make the violation willful. No ill motive or specific intent to violate the stay need be shown. This was the approach taken in *In re Wingard*, 382 B.R. 892 (Bankr. W.D. Pa. 2008). Like Tess, the debtor in *Wingard* suffered no economic harm as a result of receiving the dunning letter, but sought emotional distress damages because he claimed that the letter aggravated the distress that he experienced as a result of the bankruptcy. The court recognized that emotional distress damages are recoverable under §362(k)(1), but to receive them the debtor must clearly establish significant psychological or emotional injury and must show a causal connection between the harm and the violation of the stay. Where the creditor's action is not egregious and aggressive, the debtor must produce corroborating evidence to prove the harm and cannot rely only on self-serving testimony.

CHAPTER 8

Relief from Stay and Adequate Protection (§362(d))

§8.1 OVERVIEW OF THE RELIEF FROM STAY PROCESS

Chapter 7 described the automatic stay's breadth and impact and how it prevents acts to collect prepetition debts or assert an interest in estate property. Sometimes the claimant's right to continue the stayed activity outweighs the interest of the estate or the debtor in suspending it. To enable the court to safeguard the rights of claimants in such circumstances, §362(d)-(g) provide a procedure under which the court can grant relief from stay if the claimant establishes grounds for it.

Section 362(d) is the central provision for seeking relief. Section 362(d)(1) provides that relief from stay may be granted for "cause." Cause can exist in a variety of circumstances, including 1) where a secured creditor's interest in estate property is not adequately protected, 2) to permit litigation to continue in a different, more appropriate forum, 3) where a creditor is pursuing a claim against the debtor merely to seek payment from insurance proceeds, and 4) where the debtor has acted in bad faith.

Section 362(d)(2) directs a court to lift the stay where 1) the debtor has no equity in the property against which the creditor wishes to act, and 2) the property is unnecessary to the debtor's effective reorganization — oftentimes because an effective reorganization is highly unlikely.

Section 362(d)(3) offers a special basis for relief applicable only in "single asset real estate" cases. Abusive filings often occur in this context, and §362(d)(3) offers creditors additional protections as a result.

Section 362(d)(4) was added by the Bankruptcy Abuse Prevention and Consumer Protection Act of 2005 (BAPCPA) and applies in certain instances where the stay relates to real property subject to a secured claim and the court finds that the filing was part of a scheme to delay, hinder, or defraud creditors.

Section 362(e) (f), and (g) deal with ancillary procedural and evidentiary matters. Section 362(e) is intended to encourage speedy disposition of relief from stay motions. Section 362(e)(1) covers only motions that involve acts against property of the estate. In essence, it provides for an automatic grant of the application for relief unless the court acts on the application and orders a continuation of the stay within 30 days of the motion's filing date. The court has some flexibility in postponing the final determination of the motion by making a preliminary order in the 30-day period, but the application must be resolved finally within 30 days of the preliminary order unless the parties otherwise consent or there are compelling circumstances. Section 362(e)(2), added by BAPCPA, applies to relief from stay motions that involve consumer debtors and when any provision of §362(a) is implicated—not just acts against property. The section provides that the stay terminates 60 days after a request for relief from stay unless the court makes a final determination within that 60-day period. The period can be extended only by consent of all parties in interest or by the court for compelling reasons.

Section 362(f) permits the court to grant emergency relief following an ex parte application where 1) the interest of the party seeking relief will be irreparably harmed if relief is not given immediately, and 2) there is no time for notice and a hearing. Section 362(g) addresses the applicable burden of proof. The section provides that a creditor seeking relief from stay has the burden on the issue of the debtor's equity in property—customarily invoked by §362(d)(2)—and the party opposing relief has the burden of proof as to all other issues. Section 362(g) apportions the ultimate burden of proof under §362(d). Notwithstanding the section's language, the party seeking relief must still make a prima facie case that relief is appropriate or the motion will be dismissed.

Applications for relief from stay are common because the stay affects a wide range of conduct and assets. Although they are often made almost immediately after the petition has been filed, motions for relief from stay could arise at any time during the case. A party who wishes to obtain relief from stay must file the appropriate motion, and courts are directed to grant relief after notice and a hearing if grounds for relief are shown. Under §102(1), the phrase "after notice and a hearing" means that appropriate notice must be given, but that a hearing need only be held if a party in interest requests it. The motion is a "contested matter"—a proceeding on motion rather than a trial—and is governed by Rules 4001 and 9014.

If the court grants relief from stay, the order benefits only the party who applied for it and covers only the activity in issue in the application. The stay remains in effect as to all other persons and all other matters.

§8.2 FORMS OF RELIEF

Section 362(d) sets out four alternative forms of relief from stay: termination, annulment, modification, or conditioning. This allows the court flexibility in providing relief that is most appropriate to the circumstances.

Termination of the stay is the lifting of the stay so that the applicant can commence or resume the suspended activity. Termination ends the stay only from the time of the order, so it does not validate prior acts in violation of the stay.

Annulment terminates the stay retroactively, so that the stay is treated as if it was never in effect; prior acts in violation of the stay become valid. Annulment is therefore regarded as an extraordinary remedy and is usually used only in exceptional circumstances (e.g., when the debtor has abused the system and the applicant's actions were in good faith and not in willful violation of the stay).

Modification of the stay is appropriate when the court decides to permit some activity but not to allow the applicant full rights to proceed with the enforcement of the claim. For example, the court may modify the stay by allowing the applicant to continue with litigation to the point of judgment, but not to proceed with enforcement of the judgment. Modification is a form of partial or limited relief.

If the court conditions the stay, it leaves the stay in effect, subject to the debtor or trustee satisfying some condition. If the relief from stay motion is based upon the grounds that the claimant's interest in property is deteriorating, the court could allow the stay to continue in effect on condition that the trustee takes steps to halt the deterioration or to compensate for it. For example, in *In re FRE Real Estate*, 450 B.R. 619 (Bankr. N.D. Tex. 2011), the court was not willing to lift the stay entirely to allow a secured creditor to foreclose on property necessary for the debtor's reorganization. At the same time, the court did not believe that it was appropriate to force the secured creditor to essentially finance the debtor's bankruptcy case. Consequently, the court ordered that continuation of the stay be conditioned on the debtor's parent company making certain monetary deposits with the court during the case and the debtor confirming a plan of reorganization by a specific date.

Diagram 8a summarizes the different dispositions of an application for relief from stay.

Relief from Stay — Alternative Dispositions

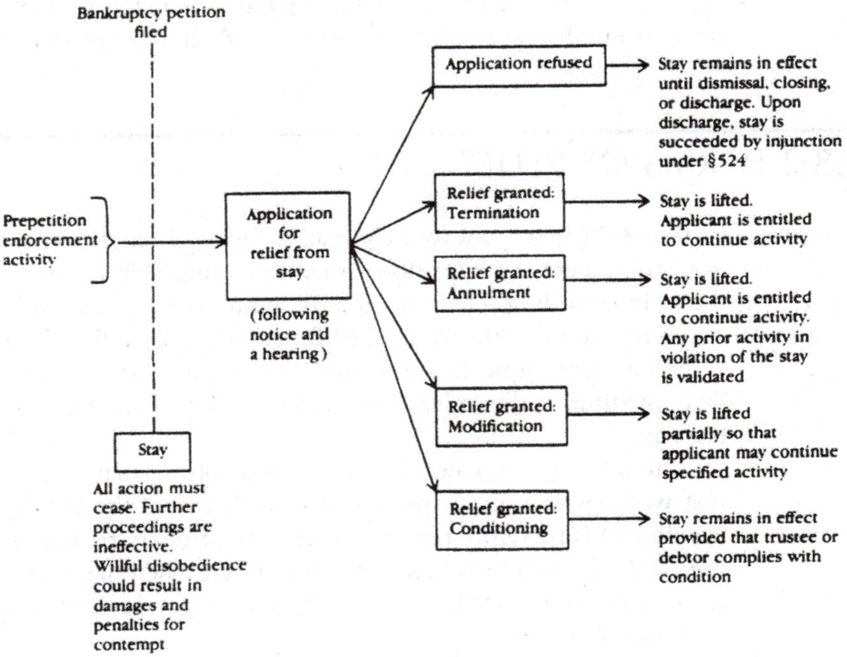

Diagram 8a

§8.3 GROUNDS FOR RELIEF

Section 362(d) sets out four separate grounds for relief from stay. Section 362(d)(1) is the broadest in scope and offers relief if a creditor can establish "cause." This section is available as a basis for relief from the stay for any act described in §362(a) against the debtor, or against property of the debtor or the estate. Section 362(d)(2)'s scope is far more narrow and applies only to the stay of acts against property. The two grounds are independent of each other. Only one of them need be satisfied for relief to be granted. Section 362(d)(3) is a special basis for relief applicable only in "single asset real estate" cases. Section 362(d)(4) applies in certain instances where the stay relates to real property subject to a secured claim and the court finds that the filing was part of a scheme to delay, hinder, or defraud creditors. Each of these bases for relief is explained below.

§8.3.1 Relief from Stay for Cause (§362(d)(1))

Section 362(d)(1) directs the court to grant relief from stay if the applicant has cause for relief, including lack of adequate protection of the applicant's interest in property. The one and only example of "cause" provided by the section is where a creditor's interest is not adequately protected. Section 8.4 offers a comprehensive exploration of adequate protection. Unfortunately, aside from that one example, §362(d)(1) does not specify what constitutes cause for relief.

Courts have been afforded discretion in evaluating motions seeking relief under §362(d)(1). A variety of reoccurring circumstances have been identified as constituting "cause" for relief. For example, cause may exist 1) to permit litigation—including arbitration proceedings—to continue in a different, more appropriate forum,[1] 2) where a creditor is pursuing a claim against the debtor merely to seek payment from insurance proceeds,[2] and 3) where the debtor has acted in bad faith.[3] In deciding whether cause exists, courts weigh the harm that will be suffered by the applicant if the stay is continued against the interests of the estate or the debtor protected by the stay. For cases that discuss the various factors that may be relevant to a showing of cause for relief, see *In re Mazzeo*, 167 F.3d 139 (2d Cir. 1999); *In re Mendoza*, 111 F.3d 1264 (5th Cir. 1997); and *In re Robbins*, 964 F.2d 342 (4th Cir. 1992).

In most motion proceedings, the applicant for relief bears the burden of proving cause. However, as to motions for relief from stay, §362(g) places the ultimate burden of proof on the party opposing relief (i.e., the debtor or trustee). Thus, the applicant has the initial burden of going forward. It must allege cause and establish a prima facie case that cause exists; failure to do so will cause the court to dismiss the motion. However, if the applicant can fulfill this initial burden, the ultimate burden of proof falls on the party opposing the motion. The burden is allocated in this way because the stay is a form of injunction. Since the stay is automatic, the trustee or the debtor do not have to apply for it and are initially relieved of the burden of establishing grounds for it. This places them in a better position than the normal applicant for an injunction, who must show grounds for relief. Therefore, once the continuation of the stay is challenged, the debtor or trustee must take up the burden of justifying its continued applicability.

---

1. See *In re Scarborough-St. James Corp.*, 535 B.R. 60, 67–68 (Bankr. D. Del. 2015).
2. See *In re Fernstrom Storage & Van Co.*, 938 F.2d 731 (7th Cir. 1991).
3. See *In re Merchant*, 256 B.R. 572 (Bankr. W.D. Pa. 2000) (holding that debtor had acted in bad faith; debtor had filed a petition in order to delay or hinder its creditors and had no intention of effectuating a realistic plan of reorganization).

§8.3.2 Relief from Stay of Acts Against Property on the Grounds That the Debtor Has No Equity in the Property, and the Property Is Not Necessary to an Effective Reorganization (§362(d)(2))

Section 362(d)(2) applies only to the stay of acts against property and cannot be used to obtain relief from stay of acts against the debtor. Where acts against property are in issue, this ground is an alternative to relief for cause under §362(d)(1). Section 362(d)(2) has two conditions that must both be satisfied for relief to be granted: 1) the debtor has no equity in the property, and 2) it is not necessary for an effective reorganization. In essence, the applicant's right to enforce its claim against the property should not be further suspended because neither the debtor nor the estate will obtain an economic advantage by keeping the property.

Under §362(g), the applicant for relief bears the burden of proving that the debtor has no equity in the property, and the party opposing relief bears the ultimate burden of proof on all other issues. This means that the applicant must establish that the value of the property does not exceed existing valid encumbrances. The applicant must allege and make a prima facie showing of the other elements of §362(d)(2), but the burden of nonpersuasion falls on the party opposing relief.

a. The Debtor's Lack of Equity in the Property (§362(d)(2)(A))

The debtor's equity is the value in the property in excess of all encumbrances on it. If there is an exemption in the property or it has revested in the debtor under a plan, this equity is wholly or partially owned by the debtor. Otherwise, it is property of the estate. Thus, reference to the debtor's equity in property in §362(d)(2) includes both the debtor's and the estate's interests in the property.

The existence and extent of the debtor's equity is determined by valuation of the property. The Code's general policy on valuation is expressed in §506, which concerns the valuation of secured claims and instructs courts to place a realistic value on the property in light of the purpose of the valuation and the property's proposed use or disposition. For example, if the property will be disposed of on the market by a private sale, market value should be used rather than foreclosure value. Valuation is usually established by expert testimony. When the parties' witnesses disagree, the court must resolve the conflict by assessing the reliability, credibility, and relevance of their valuations. The court may accept one of the appraisals or make a determination of value based on the evidence taken as a whole. For examples of actual cases involving valuation issues in an application for relief from stay, see In re Sutton, 904 F.2d 327 (5th Cir. 1990); In re FRE Real Estate, 450 B.R. 619

(Bankr. N.D. Tex. 2011); and *In re Castle Ranch of Ramona*, 3 B.R. 45 (Bankr. S.D. Cal. 1980). *See also* Examples 1 and 2.

If the debtor is found to have equity in the property, relief from stay cannot be granted under §362(d)(2) because one of its two elements is not satisfied. Further inquiry into the role of the property in an effective reorganization is not necessary. However, §362(d)(2)'s second element becomes relevant if no equity exists.

b. The Property Is Not Necessary to an Effective Reorganization (§362(d)(2)(B))

Section 362(d)(2)(B) has two dimensions for courts to consider. Courts must evaluate the debtor's prospects of an *effective* reorganization and to what extent the property at issue is *necessary* for that endeavor.

Reorganization is the principal goal of Ch. 11, and §362(d)(2)(B) was drafted with Ch. 11 cases in mind.[4] In a Ch. 11 case, the debtor usually attempts to operate its business while formulating and effectuating a plan to restructure its debts and reorganize its operations. Therefore, if property is a necessary component of the debtor's business operations, depriving the debtor of the ability to use the property will damage its chances of overcoming its financial difficulties. For this reason, the mere fact that the debtor has no equity in the property is not enough to warrant relief from stay; the property also must not advance the debtor's attempt at successful reorganization. Because §362(d)(2)(B) requires that the property be necessary to an "effective" reorganization, it is not enough for the debtor to show that the property will be used in its reorganization. The debtor must also establish that the proposed reorganization is feasible. This prediction can be difficult to make. While not addressing the issue in depth, the Supreme Court indicated a broad guideline by dictum in *United Savings Association of Texas v. Timbers of Inwood Forest Associates*, 484 U.S. 365 (1988): The debtor must show that there is a reasonable prospect of successful reorganization within a reasonable time.[5]

---

4. Because §362(d)(2)(B) uses the word "reorganization," there has been some question about whether it applies only in Ch. 11 cases or also in cases under Ch. 12 or 13. This is because Ch. 11 is officially entitled "reorganization," while Chs. 12 and 13 are headed "debt adjustment." Nevertheless, the majority of courts read "reorganization" broadly to include rehabilitation under Chs. 12 and 13. Thus, one should treat §362(d)(2)(B) as requiring that the property is not necessary to the debtor's fresh start, whether the debtor is in business or is a consumer who may need the property for personal rehabilitation, and irrespective of whether the case has been filed under Chs. 11, 12, or 13. (*See* Example 2.) In a Ch. 7 case, no reorganization is contemplated so the property cannot be necessary to an effective reorganization. Therefore, in a Ch. 7 case the second test is satisfied as a matter of course: if the debtor has no equity in the property, relief from stay should be granted.

5. See also *In re Mercado*, 523 B.R. 755, 762–63 (B.A.P. 10th Cir. 2015) and *In re SW Boston Hotel Venture, LLC*, 449 B.R. 156, 179 (Bankr. D. Mass. 2011).

Courts have exhibited a proclivity to deny motions for relief from stay at the outset of a case. The rationale is that the debtor's prospects for a successful reorganization are difficult to assess at that stage. However, courts may be more receptive to a relief motion if the reorganization has been limping along for some time and no longer looks promising. For example, in *In re Sun Valley Ranches*, 823 F.2d 1373 (9th Cir. 1987), the application for relief was made after the debtor had been in Ch. 11 bankruptcy for three years, during which time it had suffered losses and the property had declined in value. It also had become clear that the debtor could not pay the amount proposed in the plan. The court lifted the stay.[6] For further illustrations of the application of §362(d)(2)(B), *see* Examples 1 and 2.

§8.3.3 Single Asset Real Estate Cases (§362(d)(3))

Section 362(d)(3) was added in 1994 and was amended by BAPCPA. The section attempts to address complaints by mortgage holders that the stay was being abused in "single asset real estate" (SARE) cases. Section 362(d)(3) applies only to a SARE case, which is defined in §101(51B) to be a case in which the debtor (other than a family farmer) derives substantially all of its gross income from the rental of a single piece of real property that is, essentially, either used as commercial premises or as an apartment complex larger than four units. Prior to 2005, the definition had a debt ceiling that confined it to smaller cases. However, BAPCPA eliminated the debt ceiling. In short, a case satisfies the definition of a SARE case if the debtor's only significant business is the ownership of a single piece of income-producing real estate, and the debtor is engaged only in the passive activity of collecting rent and conducting maintenance of the property and other activity incidental to business of renting the property. If the debtor conducts some other substantial income-producing business activity in addition to the rental business, the case does not qualify as a SARE case.[7]

The type of problem that §362(d)(3) is designed to deal with arises where the SARE debtor defaults on its mortgage and files a Ch. 11 petition to forestall foreclosure, without a realistic immediate prospect of successful reorganization. Although cases of this kind could be disposed of on the basis of relief from stay under §362(d)(1) or (2), Congress decided to address the problem more directly by enacting subsection (d)(3). Section 362(d)(3) is therefore a ground for relief completely separate from and alternative to the grounds in §362(d)(1) and (2). In essence, its purpose is to prevent dilatory

6. See also *In re Bowman*, 253 B.R. 233 (B.A.P. 9th Cir. 2000).
7. See *In re Scotia Pacific Co., LLC*, 508 F.3d 214 (5th Cir. 2007).

behavior by putting pressure on the debtor to devise a workable plan within a relatively short period after the order for relief—usually 90 days. If this task proves to be impossible, the section requires the debtor to make payments equal to interest to the mortgage holder. The mortgagee may obtain relief from stay if the debtor does neither of these things.

§8.3.4 *In Rem* Relief Relating to Real Property Collateral (§362(d)(4))

BAPCPA added subsection (4) to §362(d) to counter a form of debtor abuse in which the debtor—sometimes with the collusion of related entities—files successive bankruptcy petitions to frustrate the foreclosure of a security interest in real property. The section imposes two requirements for lifting the stay: 1) the moving creditor's claim must be secured by the real property in question; and 2) the court must find that the petition was filed as part of a scheme to delay, hinder, or defraud[8] creditors that involved either a) the transfer of all or part ownership of, or other interest in, the real property without the consent of the secured creditor or court approval or b) multiple bankruptcy filings affecting the real property.[9]

To establish fraud, the applicant must prove that the debtor made fraudulent misrepresentations, knowing they were false, with intent to deceive, inducing reliance by the creditor to its detriment. See, for example, *In re Smith*, 395 B.R. 711 (Bankr. D. Kan. 2008) and *In re Muhaimin*, 343 B.R. 159 (Bankr. D. Md. 2006). In *Muhaimin* the court addressed the burden of proving the debtor's fraud under §362(d)(4). Although the debtor bears the burden of persuasion under §362(g), the applicant has the initial burden of going forward to establish prima facie grounds for relief for fraud.

If the creditor obtains relief from stay under §362(d)(4), it may file the order for relief in the appropriate real estate records under state law. The order will then be binding in any other bankruptcy case (whether filed by the debtor or someone else) that would affect the property for a period of two years after entry of the order. Because this order for relief from stay binds the real property upon being filed, it is referred to as an *in rem*

---

8. Section 362(4)(d) refers to a "scheme," which denotes that the debtor's abusive conduct must be part of a deliberate overall plot or plan to hinder, delay, or defraud creditors. As originally enacted, the section used the language "delay, hinder, and defraud," which led courts to conclude that it was not enough for the applicant to show hindrance and delay. It must also show fraudulent intent. The word "and" was replaced by "or" by an amendment in 2010, making it clear that Congress intended delay, hindrance, and fraud to be alternative bases for relief.

9. Courts have held that the timing and filing of several bankruptcy cases forms an adequate basis to infer a scheme to hinder, delay, or defraud creditors. See *In re Blair*, 2009 BL 274111, at *4 (Bankr. E.D.N.Y. Dec. 21, 2009).

order. An order of this kind can be extremely valuable. For example, imagine that Company X files a bankruptcy petition, and Creditor gets relief from stay pursuant to §362(d)(4). However, before the foreclosure process can proceed, Company Y—an entity related to the debtor—files a bankruptcy petition and claims an interest in the property. Section 362(d)(4) prevents Company Y from arguing that the automatic stay automatically precludes Creditor's collection efforts against the property. The *in rem* nature of relief under §362(d)(4) makes it binding on any party that has an interest in the property. Any due process concerns in this circumstance are alleviated by §362(d)(4) itself, which provides a means for courts to grant relief from a prior *in rem* order.[10]

§8.4 LACK OF ADEQUATE PROTECTION AS CAUSE FOR RELIEF FROM STAY UNDER §362(d)(1)

§8.4.1 The Interests Entitled to Adequate Protection

As stated earlier, the lack of adequate protection is the only cause for relief from stay that is expressly mentioned in §362(d)(1). The concept of adequate protection plays a significant role in applications for relief from stay and also arises in connection with the trustee's dealings with encumbered estate property.[11]

Section 362(d)(1) permits relief from stay when the applicant's interest in property is not adequately protected. Adequate protection is only available to holders of interests in property of the estate or the debtor and cannot be sought by unsecured creditors. Section 362(d)(1) is thus confined to claimants such as secured creditors, lessors who have leased property to the debtor, co-owners of the debtor's property, and others with a valid interest in property. The existence of such a valid interest in property is determined with reference to nonbankruptcy law. In the remainder of the discussion, the secured claim is used to exemplify an interest for which adequate protection is sought.

§8.4.2 The Circumstances Under Which the Need for Adequate Protection Arises

When the petition is filed, the debtor's property becomes property of the estate under §541. Property of the estate includes property that is subject to

10. See *In re Montalvo*, 416 B.R. 381, 387-88 (Bankr. E.D.N.Y. 2009).
11. Adequate protection is raised again in Chapter 16.

liens or security interests because all the debtor's legal and equitable interests in property fall within the estate. These encumbrances remain effective against the estate provided that they are valid under nonbankruptcy law and do not have qualities that make them avoidable in bankruptcy (discussed in Chapters 12 and 13). At the appropriate time, the secured creditor is entitled to be paid out the full value of the secured claim (whether in a lump sum or by installments under a plan) or to have the property abandoned so that it can be foreclosed upon. In the interim, the stay prevents the secured creditor from taking any action to enforce the interest.

The stay creates a risk for the secured creditor. In the absence of the stay it could have foreclosed on the property immediately upon the debtor's default and applied the proceeds to satisfaction of its claim. But the stay prevents immediate foreclosure. Consequently, the creditor faces the risk that its collateral may decline in value while the stay is in effect; if the property eventually has to be realized, it may generate diminished proceeds. If the collateral value drops below the amount of the debt, the reduction in value eats away the security, reducing the secured portion of the claim and increasing the deficiency. This risk of delay in realization may sometimes be a problem in a Ch. 7 liquidation, but the nature of a Ch. 7 case usually makes adequate protection less of an issue because collateral is normally liquidated or abandoned quite promptly, and is not usually used extensively by the estate. The situation is different in cases under Chs. 11 and 13, where the debtor or the estate usually proposes to keep and use the property while the claim is paid off under the plan. As plan payments can extend over some time, the secured creditor is exposed to a much more substantial risk of devaluation. The risk of loss does not materialize if the debtor's rehabilitation is successful. In that case, the plan is consummated, and the secured claim is eventually paid in full. However, if the debtor's attempt at rehabilitation fails, the estate ends up in liquidation and the secured creditor is left to its recourse against the property for the unpaid balance of the debt. If the relationship between the debt and the value of the property has changed adversely during the period of the stay, the creditor has been prejudiced by having to wait. Adequate protection is intended to reduce the secured creditor's risk of loss from the stay by requiring the trustee to take action to protect the collateral's value. If realization becomes necessary in the future, the creditor will not suffer a loss that would have been avoided by immediate foreclosure.

Consequently, property is often times found to be inadequately protected where the property's value is depreciating steadily. For an oversecured creditor, a finding of inadequate protection requires that any decline in collateral value must be projected to completely erode the creditor's equity cushion during the course of the bankruptcy case. In these instances, the debtor must either demonstrate that it has or will provide some means of adequately protecting such value or relief from stay may be granted.

Note that the interest to be protected is the present value of the collateral. Section 362(d)(1) is not intended to allow the claimant to improve its position by making up a deficiency that previously existed. In addition, in *United Savings Association of Texas v. Timbers of Inwood Forest Associates, Ltd.*, 484 U.S. 365 (1988), the U.S. Supreme Court held that adequate protection does not cover any loss that the creditor may suffer as a result of not having the ability to reinvest the proceeds of the property on immediate foreclosure. The Court said that the interest in property to be protected is the value of the property itself, not the right to take possession of the property and realize it. (*See* Example 4.)

§8.4.3 Factors to Be Considered in Determining the Need for Adequate Protection

To decide whether the security interest is adequately protected, a comparison must be made between the present ratio of property value to debt and the predicted future ratio if the property is to be kept and used or disposed of as proposed by the estate. Three questions must be asked:

(1) If the stay is lifted and foreclosure proceeds, what is the claimant likely to receive? This requires a factual determination of the present value of the property in relation to the debt.

(2) If the stay is left in effect and the estate deals with the property as proposed, what is likely to happen to the value of the property in relation to the debt? This inquiry involves a calculation of the rate of increase or decrease of the debt and a comparison to the future value of the collateral. To predict future value, account must be taken of such factors as appreciation or depreciation of market value, deterioration of the property through use, hazards to the property, and insurance coverage.

(3) What is the likelihood of successful rehabilitation? In a Ch. 7 case, the first two inquiries are sufficient to determine the need for adequate protection because the only issue is whether delay in liquidation will prejudice the secured claim. In rehabilitation cases, this third inquiry must be pursued. The risk of eventual liquidation of the property under adverse circumstances is diminished when there is a good chance that the debtor's plan will be consummated. Therefore, if the debtor's prospects of recovery seem good, the lower probability of liquidation may offset some uncertainty about the future debt-collateral ratio.

As these factors indicate, the need for adequate protection is a factual issue that calls for an overall assessment of the vulnerability of the collateral.

To make this assessment, the court must determine the present and predicted future value of the collateral (usually proven by expert testimony), must take into account any potential hazards to the property, and must evaluate the efficacy of the debtor's rehabilitation efforts. This factual determination can be difficult, particularly where conflicting testimony is offered by the parties. For example, imagine that a Ch. 11 debtor owes $100,000 to a secured creditor. That debt is secured by a lien on a piece of machinery with a present value of $100,000. If foreclosure took place immediately, the secured claim would be paid in full (less the foreclosure costs, which are ignored here for the sake of simplicity). If the stay remains in effect and the estate uses the machine during the course of its rehabilitation efforts, the machine will depreciate by 20 percent per annum. If the rehabilitation fails in a year's time and the machine is then realized, the secured claim will be worth only $80,000. Unless the plan provides for reduction of the debt by at least $20,000 during this period or for some other means of offsetting the depreciation, the interest is not adequately protected and relief from stay should be granted.

By contrast, say that the present value of the machine is $150,000 and the debt is $100,000. The claim is oversecured. This surplus of debtor equity in the property over the secured claim is called an "equity cushion."[12] The existence of the equity cushion means that the value of the property will exceed the debt even if the property depreciates at 20 percent over the course of the next year . . . If the rehabilitation fails after one year, the secured creditor will still receive full payment of the secured claim. Therefore, at this stage[13] the interest is adequately protected, and there is no cause to grant relief from stay.[14] An equity cushion is often important in adequate protection cases. A secured claim is invariably protected if the property is valuable enough to provide a buffer of unencumbered equity to accommodate likely depreciation. Of course, courts have difficulty resolving the question of whether such an equity cushion exists and how large it should be to ensure protection. For a useful example of a case concerning this issue, see *In re Alyucan Interstate Corp.*, 12 B.R. 803 (Bankr. D. Vt. 1981). *See also* Example 2.

As noted in section 8.4.2, the secured creditor is only entitled to protection of the present value of its interest and cannot demand an improvement in its position. For example, imagine that the debtor's outstanding obligation is $100,000, the present value of the collateral is $90,000, and

12. *See* Section 1.7.3 for a further explanation of this term.

13. Although the equity cushion may adequately protect the claimant at this stage, that protection will diminish as the cushion shrinks unless the estate makes payments to reduce the debt. Therefore, even if the claimant is not entitled to relief from stay at present, it may seek relief later.

14. Once again, complicating factors such as the accrual of interest and foreclosure costs are disregarded here.

depreciation is predicted to be 20 percent per annum. Adequate protection requires maintenance of the $90,000 value or, in other words, nine-tenths of the secured claim; it does not require that the debtor rectify the under-secured creditor's $10,000 deficiency. Assuming there are no changes in these circumstances, the creditor will have a $10,000 general unsecured claim in the case to go along with its $90,000 secured claim.

§8.4.4 The Means and Method of Furnishing Adequate Protection

The Bankruptcy Code does not define "adequate protection" but §361 provides three examples of how adequate protection may be furnished. Section 361's enumerated forms of adequate protection are not mutually exclusive. Courts have discretion to combine any or all of them to fashion adequate protection.

The three methods of providing adequate protection suggested by §361 are the following:

(1) Cash payments (§361(1)). If the estate has sufficient income, it can make cash payments to the claimant to reduce the debt and maintain the ratio between the claim and the property value.

(2) Additional collateral (§361(2)). If there is unencumbered property in the estate, the trustee can provide adequate protection by granting a lien on additional property or replacing the existing lien with a lien on property of greater value.

(3) The grant of an "indubitable equivalent" (§361(3)). The third suggested form of adequate protection is the most general. Section 361(3) authorizes the trustee to propose adequate protection by giving the claimant any form of relief that will result in realization of the "indubitable equivalent" of the claimant's interest in property. This quaint term, standing in sharp contrast to the otherwise pedestrian statutory prose, was lifted from an opinion by Learned Hand, who knew how to turn a phrase. The formulation sets a standard for measuring the protection, rather than suggesting a means of providing it. It requires the court to decide whether a means of protection proposed by the trustee ensures that the claimant will certainly receive no less than the value of its property interest.

The most common form of creditor protection under the "indubitable equivalent" provision is where a creditor has a significant equity cushion in the property at issue. Courts have ruled that a significant equity cushion by itself can establish that a creditor is adequately protected.

Aside from a significant equity cushion, courts have refused to recognize the vast majority of debtor attempts to offer the indubitable equivalent of a creditor's interest. Section 361(3) expressly excludes the grant of an administrative expense priority as a means of providing adequate protection. Congress felt that such a grant is too uncertain a means of protection, because the estate may not have sufficient assets to pay administrative expenses in full.[15] Further, the hope to be compensated as a result of a legal judgment is generally too speculative to represent an indubitable equivalent. In *In re Rocco,* 255 F. App'x 638 (3d. Cir. 2007), the debtor claimed that the secured creditor would receive the indubitable equivalent of its interest because the debtor believed it would secure a favorable outcome to pending litigation. The court deemed this potential outcome too speculative.

As stated in section 8.3.1, the trustee, frequently the party opposing relief from stay, bears the burden of proving that an interest is adequately protected. If the trustee believes that the interest is not at risk, he or she will seek to prove that nothing need be done to bolster it. If it seems that adequate protection is lacking, the trustee has the initiative of offering corrective measures of the kind suggested in §361. The court then determines whether the interest is adequately protected and grants relief from stay if it is not. See, for example, *In re Blehm Land & Cattle Co.,* 859 F.2d 137 (10th Cir. 1988). Relief need not take the form of an immediate lifting of the stay. If the court determines that adequate protection is lacking and that the proposed measures are insufficient to cure the problem, it can condition the stay on the trustee taking specified action to protect the interest. It is also possible for the trustee and claimant to settle the adequate protection issue by agreeing to the form of protection to be provided. Such an agreement can be made an order of the court.

§8.4.5 The Failure of Adequate Protection: Superpriority Under §507(b)

As stated in section 8.4.3, the determination that the interest is adequately protected is based on evidence of present value and predicted future value. This evidence is speculative and could be wrong. If realization of the property eventually becomes necessary, it may turn out that deterioration of the property-debt ratio was worse than anticipated, so that the interest was not adequately protected.

15. Administrative expenses are a second priority unsecured claim and are paid before most other unsecured creditors. Nevertheless, they still face the risk of nonpayment. Priorities are discussed in section 17.5.

Section 507(b) is intended to provide relief to the secured creditor under these circumstances. It states that if the trustee provided adequate protection to a claimant, and the protection turns out to be inadequate, the shortfall is treated as a priority claim that ranks at the top of the administrative expense priority category. As described in section 17.6.4, administrative expenses are paid as a second priority under §507(a)(2), just below qualifying first-priority domestic support obligations. The superpriority granted to the shortfall resulting from the misjudgment of adequate protection therefore places the claim for the shortfall in a position senior to administrative expenses and all other priority claims in §507 except for first-priority domestic support claims. As long as the estate has sufficient funds after settling secured claims and paying any first-priority claims, the superpriority assures payment of the shortfall.

Section 507(b) is not clearly drafted. Not only does it send the reader on a wild goose chase by a cryptic reference to §507(a)(2), but it also has some restrictive language that appears to confine superpriority relief to cases in which the trustee has actually furnished adequate protection. The section begins with the words, "If the trustee . . . provides adequate protection. . . . " Literally interpreted, it therefore appears to apply only if the trustee takes action to provide adequate protection, which may occur by consent, or may follow the court's determination that adequate protection must be furnished. It does not appear to apply when the court has refused relief from stay on the basis that adequate protection already exists without further bolstering by the trustee. In *LNC Investments v. First Fidelity Bank*, 247 B.R. 38 (S.D.N.Y. 2000), the court concluded that although a different interpretation of the labyrinthine and ambiguous language of §507(b) is plausible, the better approach is to give literal effect to the word "provides" and to exclude from the section situations in which the court found that the creditor was already adequately protected, and that no further steps were required to protect its interest. Notwithstanding that the plain meaning of the language points to this result, it seems unfair in principle to distinguish cases in which protection was provided from those in which the court found it to be unnecessary. In both cases, the miscalculation left the claimant with a deficiency. (*See* Example 3.)

EXAMPLES

Examples

1. Maladroit Manufacturing Co., Inc. has filed a bankruptcy petition under Ch. 7. Among the debtor's assets is a large piece of machinery that forms an integral part of its manufacturing plant. The machine was purchased on credit from Lien Machine, Inc. for $500,000 about two years prior to bankruptcy. At the time of sale, Lien Machine perfected a security interest in the machine to secure the price. The current balance on the debt is

$200,000. Maladroit had defaulted in its payments prior to filing the petition, and Lien Machine had been about to foreclose on the machine when the petition was filed.

Almost immediately after the petition was filed, Lien Machine applied for relief from stay under §362(d)(2) so that it could continue its foreclosure. At the hearing on the relief motion, an appraiser hired by the estate testified that the market value of the machine is $250,000. Lien Machine offered evidence by two appraisers. The first one testified that the market value of the machine is $195,000. The other testified that the value of the machine, if sold by auction in a foreclosure sale, is not more than $150,000.

a. Is Lien Machine likely to obtain relief from stay under §362(d)(2) in this Ch. 7 case?
b. Would the answer be different if Maladroit had filed a petition under Ch. 11?

Note: Lien Machine seeks relief under §362(d)(2). This question is confined to grounds for relief under that provision and does not address the alternative ground for relief for cause under §362(d)(1).

2. Rocky Shoal filed a Ch. 13 petition last month. His prize possession, and his only asset of economic value, is a sailboat that he uses for recreation. He bought the boat on credit from High Seize Boating Co. two years ago. Under the sales contract, he undertook to repay the loan in monthly installments over five years and granted High Seize a security interest in the boat to secure the balance of the price. The security interest is validly perfected under state law and unavoidable.

Rocky defaulted in his payments two months before filing the petition. High Seize had initiated foreclosure proceedings that have been suspended by the automatic stay. At the time of the filing of the petition, the balance due on the loan was $30,000.

High Seize has applied for relief from stay under §362(d)(2) on the ground that Rocky has no equity in the property, and it is not necessary for an effective reorganization. As an alternative, High Seize also argues that it has cause for relief under §362(d)(1) because its interest in the boat is not adequately protected.

There is conflicting evidence on the value of the boat. The appraiser testifying on behalf of High Seize places a present market value of $30,000 on the boat and predicts that it will depreciate 10 percent during the next year. The appraiser estimates that the boat would realize only $20,000 in a distress foreclosure sale. The trustee's appraiser estimates the market value of the boat to be $50,000 and its distress sale value to be $35,000. She disagrees that the boat will depreciate over the next year:

Rocky has taken meticulous care of it, and the market for good used boats is vigorous.

a. Does High Seize have grounds for relief from stay under §362(d)(2)?
b. Does High Seize have grounds for relief under §362(d)(1) as a result of lack of adequate protection?

3. Assume that the court, in evaluating the evidence in High Seize's application for relief from stay, finds that the boat is indeed worth $50,000, leaving an equity cushion of $20,000. The court also determines that the value of the boat is likely to remain stable, that the boat is fully insured, and that Rocky has a good prospect of successful rehabilitation. Because the equity cushion is sufficient to accommodate interest that accrues on the claim and will also act as a buffer for any unexpected drop in market value, the court finds the interest to be adequately protected and refuses relief from stay under §362(d)(1). Because the debtor has equity in the property, relief is also refused under §362(d)(2).

   Rocky's Ch. 13 plan is confirmed. Under the plan he proposes to pay High Seize its full $30,000 plus interest over a three-year period and to retain the boat, which remains subject to the lien until the plan is consummated. About a year after the plan confirmation, Rocky loses his job. He can no longer afford payments under the plan and converts the case to Ch. 7. At this time, the balance of the debt to High Seize is $22,000. The trustee attempts to liquidate the boat so that High Seize can be paid and any surplus can be placed in the estate's general fund. However, because of an economic recession, the used boat market has collapsed. The best offer received for the boat is $20,000. Because High Seize realizes that it will do no better itself, it does not object to the trustee's sale. The proceeds of the sale are paid out to High Seize. What can be done about the shortfall?

4. Asset Indigestion, Inc. recently filed a Ch. 11 petition. Its principal asset is a piece of real property subject to a mortgage held by Linger Longingly Loan Co. At the time of the petition, the debt secured by the mortgage was $450,000. The value of the property has declined over the last few years as a result of an economic slump in the region. The experts agree that its value at the time of the petition is $425,000 and that the property market has stabilized. Although there is little prospect of prices rising in the near future, they are not likely to decline either.

   Linger Longingly has applied for relief from stay on the ground that its interest lacks adequate protection. It argues that if the property were sold immediately, the proceeds of $425,000 would be realized and could be invested elsewhere to generate income. If the estate is allowed to keep the property, Linger Longingly will be delayed in realizing it and therefore loses the opportunity of reinvestment. Should relief from stay be granted?

5. Multilien Investments, Inc., a debtor in Ch. 11, owns a piece of real property worth $5 million. It owes $4.7 million to Premier Mortgage Co. on a first mortgage, $600,000 to Secundo Security Co. on a second mortgage, and $400,000 to Trinity Finance Co. on a third mortgage. Premier has moved for relief from stay under §362(d)(2) on the ground that the debtor does not have an equity in the property and that it is not needed for an effective reorganization. The debtor opposes the motion. It is joined in its opposition by the two junior lienholders, who realize that if Premier is allowed to foreclose now, Secundo will recover only a fraction of its debt from the proceeds, and Trinity's lien will be wiped out. They feel that if the debtor is allowed to keep the property, a predicted upward trend in the market may benefit their interests. They argue that if one just takes into account the mortgage of Premier, the party seeking relief, the debtor does have an equity of $300,000 in the property, and this should preclude Premier from getting relief under §362(d)(2). Is this a good argument?

Explanations

1. a. Is Lien Machine likely to obtain relief from stay in this Ch. 7 case? Two elements must be satisfied for relief to be granted under §362(d)(2). First, the debtor must have no equity in the property. (Because the debtor's prepetition property becomes property of the estate, the debtor's equity is in fact the estate's equity in the property.) The equity is measured by the excess in the property's value over the amount of the debt secured by the property. There is no dispute that the debt is $200,000. The question in issue, to determine the debtor's equity in the property, is the value of the property. Under §362(g), Lien Machine bears the burden of proving that the debtor has no equity in the property.

   Valuation is a factual question that is often based on conflicting opinion evidence. If the evidence of the estate's appraiser is accepted, the debtor does have equity in the property; the creditor's evidence contradicts this. The court must attempt to determine a realistic valuation based on the credibility of the witnesses, the proposed use and disposition of the property, and any other relevant factors. One of the issues suggested by the question is whether market value or distress sale proceeds is a more realistic figure. The machine is to be liquidated, but there may be an opportunity to sell it on the market by private sale, rather than by auction.

   If the court finds that the property is worth more than $200,000, the debtor has equity in the property, and relief from stay cannot be granted under §362(d)(2). If the property is found to be worth

$200,000 or less, the first element is satisfied, and the second must be determined: Because this is a Ch. 7 case, the property cannot be necessary for an effective reorganization, and this element is inevitably satisfied. Therefore, unless the debtor has equity in the property, the grounds for relief under §362(d)(2) are satisfied and the stay will be lifted.

b. Is the answer different if Maladroit had filed under Ch. 11? The first part of the test remains the same, but the question of whether the property is necessary to an effective reorganization is now relevant. To decide this, two factors must be considered: (1) the debtor must need the property for its reorganization efforts, and (2) the debtor must have a prospect of successful reorganization. Section 362(g) places the burden on the debtor (as the party opposing the relief) to prove these matters. As this is a Ch. 11 case, the debtor in possession represents the estate.

The question indicates that the machine is an integral part of the plant, thereby suggesting that the debtor may be able to satisfy this aspect of the test. No information is given on the prospects of Maladroit's success in its effort to reorganize. However, because the application is made very early in the Ch. 11 case, the court is likely to lean in favor of giving the debtor a chance and will be less exacting in the level of proof required to show the likelihood of rehabilitation.

Even if relief from stay is refused at this stage, Lien Machine will be able to make a new application if circumstances change. Also, even though consideration of §362(d)(1) has been excluded by this question, it should be noted that any possible deterioration in the debt-collateral ratio could serve as grounds for relief under that section.

2. a. Relief under §362(d)(2). Rocky may or may not have equity in the property, depending on the valuation fixed by the court. As in Example 1, the experts clash on the valuation issue: On High Seize's evidence, Rocky has no equity in the property, but the trustee's figures show otherwise. Also, the choice between distress liquidation value and market value has to be made based on the likely disposition of the boat. Thus, the court must not only resolve the conflict on value, but must also decide what standard of valuation is most realistic. High Seize bears the risk of nonpersuasion under §362(g).

If the debtor has no equity in the property, one of the two requirements for relief under §362(d)(2) is satisfied, and the question of whether the property is needed for an effective reorganization must be considered. Although there is some dissent on the question, §362(d)(2)(B) is generally regarded as being applicable in Ch. 13 cases, in spite of the use of the word "reorganization." In Ch. 13, the question is whether the asset is necessary for the debtor's rehabilitation — that is, whether it is needed to affect a fresh start. This is apparently purely recreational property that is not used to support or shelter Rocky or to enable him to earn income. It is therefore very likely that the court will find that the property is not necessary to the debtor's "effective reorganization."

In summary, if the court determines that Rocky has no equity in the property, and also finds the property not to be necessary for an effective reorganization, relief from stay will be granted under §362(d)(2). However, even if these grounds for relief are not satisfied, High Seize may still have cause for relief under §362(d)(1) if its interest is not adequately protected.

b. Relief for lack of adequate protection. The property interest to be protected here is High Seize's valid, perfected security interest in the boat. (Remember that it is the interest in property, not the debt, that requires protection.) If the property is worth as much or more than the debt, the interest in the property is the full amount of the debt. If the property is worth less than the debt, part of the debt is unsecured, and the right to adequate protection relates only to the portion secured by the property. Once again, the valuation of the property is an important factual issue.

To decide whether High Seize's interest is adequately protected, the present and predicted future relationship between the debt and collateral value must be compared. The process of determining current value for the purpose of §362(d)(1) is the same as it is for §362(d)(2). It must be decided whether market or liquidation value is the proper measure, and the evidence must be weighed to decide what that value is. Also, the probability and extent of future change in that value in relation to the debt must be determined.

Assume that the testimony of the trustee's appraiser is accepted, and that High Seize usually resells repossessed property on the retail market, making market value the proper measure. The market value of the boat is $50,000 and the debt is $30,000. An immediate foreclosure would yield enough to pay the secured claim in full with costs and interest, and a surplus would remain for the estate. As the trustee's appraiser predicts a stable or rising value for the boat, this position will not deteriorate. An oversecured creditor is entitled to receive interest on its claim and costs until the surplus equity is exhausted, but there is a large enough equity cushion to accommodate increase in the debt by the addition of interest and costs. In short, on the trustee's evidence, the interest is adequately protected.

High Seize's appraiser fixes the current market value at the same level as the debt — $30,000. An immediate sale would give High Seize almost full payment of its claim after deducting sale costs. However, as there is no equity cushion and the appraiser predicts a decline in the value of the boat, a delay in foreclosure will prejudice High Seize. Even though Rocky will pay off the debt over time under his plan, it is not clear that those payments will be high enough or will begin soon enough to offset the decline in collateral value. If not, relief from stay must be granted unless the trustee is able to offer additional protection under §361. This could take the form of an immediate cash payment to reduce the debt, the provision of additional collateral, or any other means of ensuring that High Seize will receive the indubitable equivalent of its interest. The facts indicate that Rocky has no other valuable property, so augmentation of the collateral may not be possible. It is not clear whether the other means are open to him.

Of course, the court is not obliged to accept either of the two conflicting appraisals. It could decide a figure and rate of depreciation somewhere between those offered by the parties. The court would then decide, based on its factual finding, whether there is a sufficient equity cushion to protect the interest from deterioration. Although present and future value are very important considerations in deciding adequate protection, they are not the only factors to be taken into account. The debtor's prospects of rehabilitation are also relevant, and a strong likelihood of success may counteract some doubt in valuation. Also, because Rocky will retain and use the boat while the Ch. 13 plan is being consummated, adequate protection also requires that High Seize's interest is protected by insurance from loss or destruction of the collateral.

3. Assuming that the court's estimate of value at the time of the application was correct (it may not have been, but this will never be known), there has been a gross miscalculation of market trends. As a result, the protection of the interest was not adequate. Section 507(b) states that if the trustee "provides" adequate protection but that protection ultimately turns out to have been inadequate, the shortfall is to be given priority over all administrative expenses. (Section 507(b) is obscurely drafted, but this is its basic meaning.) Therefore, if §507(b) applies, its effect would be to elevate the unsecured claim for the shortfall to rank at the top of administrative expenses, which are a second priority claim. That is, the deficiency would be paid immediately after any qualifying first-priority domestic support obligations and before any other unsecured claims, including other second-priority administrative expenses. Unless Rocky owes qualifying first-priority domestic support obligations that are large enough to eat up the entire value of the estate, there is a good prospect that the deficiency would be paid. High Seize's problem is that the language of §507(b) may not cover its situation. While some courts read the

subsection to cover situations in which the court finds no need to provide adequate protection, others emphasize the word "provides" and hold that the subsection covers only situations in which the trustee has actually provided adequate protection. In the present case, the trustee was not called on to provide any protection because the court concluded that the interest was already adequately protected.

4. Linger Longingly's argument sounds plausible because it will not be paid interest on its undersecured claim by the estate pending confirmation of the plan,[16] so estate retention of the property deprives it of the immediate opportunity to invest the property proceeds gainfully. However, as noted in section 8.4.2, the U.S. Supreme Court held in *United Savings Association of Texas* that the interest in property to be protected is the value of the property itself, not the economic benefit of realizing it and using the proceeds gainfully. The court reasoned that undersecured creditors are not entitled to receive interest on their claims under §506, so §362(d) should not be available to allow an undersecured creditor to circumvent §506. If the loss of interest was to be a ground for adequate protection, undersecured creditors could obtain relief from stay as a matter of course under §362(d)(1).

   The inability to get pendency interest places undersecured creditors in a difficult position and causes them losses where the prospects for successful reorganization are uncertain and the debtor is struggling (with attendant delay) to devise a confirmable plan. This may motivate them to look more carefully at the possibility of seeking relief either for cause (such as that the poor prospects of reorganization call into question the debtor's good faith in filing the Ch. 11 case), or on the basis of §362(d)(2). By definition, the debtor has no equity in the property where the mortgage is undersecured, and the poor prospects of success may establish that the property is not needed for an effective reorganization.

   The ground for relief in §362(d)(3) may be available because this is a single asset real estate case as defined in §101(51B). Linger Longingly will be able to obtain relief from stay if Asset Indigestion cannot devise a feasible plan of reorganization within the prescribed period after the order for relief (which is 90 days, subject to some qualifications), or if that cannot be done, if Asset Indigestion fails to make interest payments to Linger Longingly from the end of that period.

---

16. Section 506(b) is discussed in section 17.6.3. In a Ch. 11 case, prior to confirmation of a plan, an unsecured or undersecured creditor is not entitled to receive interest on its claim. These creditors can demand that they are paid interest after confirmation so that they receive the present value of their claims. Present value is calculated by adding interest to the face amount of the debt. This is explained in Chapters 18, 19, and 20.

5. All circuit courts that have addressed this issue have rejected the argument made by Secundo and Trinity.[17] Indeed, in evaluating a motion under §362(d)(2), courts must consider *all* liens against the subject property and not just the lien of the creditor moving for relief from stay. A debtor's "equity" equals the difference between the value of the property and that of all the liens against it, regardless of whether the liens belong to the movant or to other creditors. This approach is easy to reconcile with §362(d)(2)'s plain language. Although the Code does not itself define what is meant by debtor's "equity," it is generally understood to mean the debtor's (or estate's) remaining economic interest in property—the surplus owned by the debtor (or estate)—after all liens on the property have been satisfied. If there is more than one lien on the property, the debtor is entitled only to what is left after all have been satisfied. It therefore goes against common usage, and is not supported by any statutory language, to define "equity" for purposes of §362(d)(2) as meaning whatever is left after the senior lien is satisfied. This was the view taken in *In re Indian Palms Associates, Ltd.*, 61 F.3d. 197 (3d Cir. 1995), which insisted on using the plain and accepted meaning of "equity." The court noted that it is appropriate to disregard junior liens for the purposes of deciding whether the senior lienholder has an equity cushion that will adequately protect its interest. The reason for this is that from the perspective of the senior lienor, it does not matter if the debtor himself, or other junior interests, are entitled to the value in the property in excess of the lien. In either event, the excess value is available to act as a cushion to the senior lien. However, just because "equity cushion" is used to describe value in the property that may not actually qualify as debtor's equity in the usual sense does not mean that a similar meaning is appropriate in §362(d)(2). The role that debtor's equity plays in that section is quite different. There, the fact that the debtor (or estate) has an economic interest in the property is one of the justifications for allowing the estate to keep it.

Of course, the finding that the debtor has no equity in the property does not end the inquiry. The next question to be decided is whether the property is necessary for an effective reorganization. The example does not provide facts to decide this.

---

17. See *In re Gindi*, 642 F.3d 865, 875 (10th Cir. 2011); *In re Nichols*, 440 F.3d 850, 855–56 (6th Cir. 2006); *In re Indian Palms Assocs., Ltd.*, 61 F.3d 197, 206 (3rd Cir. 1995); *In re Sutton*, 904 F.2d 327, 329 (5th Cir. 1990); *In re Boomgarden*, 780 F.2d 657, 664 n.7 (7th Cir. 1985); *Stewart v. Gurley*, 745 F.2d 1194, 1195 (9th Cir. 1984); but see *In re Cote*, 27 B.R. 510, 513 (Bankr. D. Ore. 1983); *In re Palmer River Realty, Inc.*, 26 B.R. 138, 140 (Bankr. D.R.I. 1983); and *In re Certified Mortgage Corp.*, 25 B.R. 662, 663 (Bankr. M.D. Fla. 1982).

CHAPTER 9

Property of the Estate (§541)

§9.1 OVERVIEW OF THE BANKRUPTCY ESTATE

The filing of a bankruptcy petition creates a fictional estate into which a diverse group of assets is transferred. The estate is a new legal entity, separate from the debtor. Bankruptcy courts may only administer assets that are part of this estate. This limitation is significant because it affects the assets a debtor may use postpetition and those that may be utilized for the benefit of creditors. But what assets constitute estate property?

Section 541 delineates the assets that are included in the bankruptcy estate and the ones that are excluded. As noted in the legislative history, the section's purpose is to "bring anything of value that the debtors have into the estate."[1]

Section 541(a) and its seven subsections list different types of estate property. Section 541(a)(1) captures all property in which the debtor has a legal or equitable interest at the commencement of the case. Section 541(a)(2) applies to community property states and captures certain interests of the debtor and the debtor's spouse in community property. Section 541(a)(3) recognizes that certain sections of the Bankruptcy Code allow the trustee to recover property based on wrongful conduct and brings this property into the estate. Section 541(a)(4) captures any interest in property

1. Some subsections of §541 address extremely specialized bankruptcy issues of little or no practical relevance. Apart from a brief mention in this overview, these subsections are not discussed.

preserved for the benefit of the estate or ordered transferred to the estate due to subordination, pursuant to §510(c), or an automatic preservation of an avoided transfer under §551. Section 541(a)(5) addresses certain property received by the debtor within 180 days after the filing of the bankruptcy petition if the property would have been property of the estate had the debtor possessed it at the time the petition was filed. This subsection addresses 1) bequests, devises, or inheritances of which the debtor is the recipient; 2) property settlements with the debtor's ex-spouse; and 2) life insurance policies or death benefit plans. Section 541(a)(6) clarifies that certain property derived from property of the estate is property of the estate. Finally, §541(a)(7) provides that any interest in property that the bankruptcy estate acquires after the commencement of the case belongs to the estate.

Section 541(b) provides a nonexhaustive list of excluded property. Section 541(b)(1) excludes any power that the debtor could exercise solely for the benefit of another party. Section 541(b)(2) addresses nonresidential real property and provides that a lease of this nature is not property of the estate to the extent that 1) it had terminated prior to the commencement of a lessee-debtor's bankruptcy case, and 2) the lessee-debtor does not have any interest in the lease. Section 541(b)(3) provides that a debtor's accreditation status as an educational institution is not property of the estate. Section 541(b)(4) excludes from the estate farmout agreements pursuant to which the debtor had assigned oil or gas rights to a third party. In 1994, the exclusion for proceeds from money orders sold by the debtor — current §541(b)(9) — was added.

The Bankruptcy Abuse Prevention and Consumer Protection Act of 2005 (BAPCPA) added four subsections to §541(b). Section 541(b)(5) excludes from the estate funds placed in an education individual retirement account for the benefit of the debtor's child, stepchild, grandchild, or stepgrandchild. Section 541(b)(6) provides a similar exclusion for funds contributed to a trust pursuant to a state tuition program for the benefit of the debtor's child, stepchild, grandchild, or stepgrandchild. Section 541(b)(7) excludes funds withheld or received by an employer for payment as contribution to an employee-benefit plan. Finally, §541(b)(8) excludes personal property held by certain possessory pledgees.[2]

Section 541(c) attempts to negate certain contractual and statutory provisions that undermine federal bankruptcy law. The section targets provisions that 1) restrict the transfer of a debtor's interest in property to the bankruptcy estate, or 2) alter the rights or obligations of a debtor due to some adverse financial event. Subsection (c)(1) invalidates transfer

2. This subsection was intended to protect pawnbrokers and similar parties by allowing these parties to retain forfeited collateral if the debtor failed to timely redeem the property prior to the petition date.

restrictions on estate property. Subsection (c)(2), however, provides an exception for a restriction on a transfer of the debtor's beneficial interest in a trust that is enforceable under applicable nonbankruptcy law, which is customarily state law.

Section 541(d) offers an exception to §541(a)'s reach. The subsection excludes from the estate assets in which the debtor holds a legal interest but not an equitable one. For example, assume that prior to the commencement of a bankruptcy case, **the debtor** is the trustee for a real property trust and manages rental property for the benefit of an underage child. **Section 541(d) clarifies that when the debtor files for bankruptcy** her legal interest in managing the trust becomes part of the bankruptcy estate but the equity interest in the rental property—the *res* of the trust and any income generated from that *res*—would not.

Finally, BAPCPA also enacted §541(f). The section subjects certain Code provisions to the power of state regulators to restrict property transfers by nonprofit corporate debtors. The section was enacted in response to a number of high-profile bankruptcy cases that undermined the power of state regulatory agencies to restrict bankruptcy asset sales of nonprofit hospitals to for-profit entities.

§9.2 DISPARATE TREATMENT OF PROPERTY ACQUIRED POSTPETITION

Section 541 applies to cases filed under Code Chs. 7, 11, and 13.[3] The section focuses primarily on the property interests held by the debtor at the time of the petition. In most cases, the debtor continues to acquire property after the petition has been filed, such as new income from employment or business, or returns from prepetition transactions, investments, or assets. It is necessary to decide whether this new property falls into the estate or is retained by the debtor as part of the new fresh start estate. The chapter under which relief is sought affects this question.

a. Individual Debtor Ch. 7

In an individual debtor Ch. 7 liquidation there is a clear line of demarcation between the debtor and the estate. This line coincides with the petition date. On the petition date, all estate property—as defined by §541—passes to the estate, and the debtor loses her legal interest. In due course, all this

3. Ch. 12 addresses the bankruptcy of a family farmer or fisherman. This Code chapter is not addressed in this book.

Flow of Property in a Ch. 7 Case

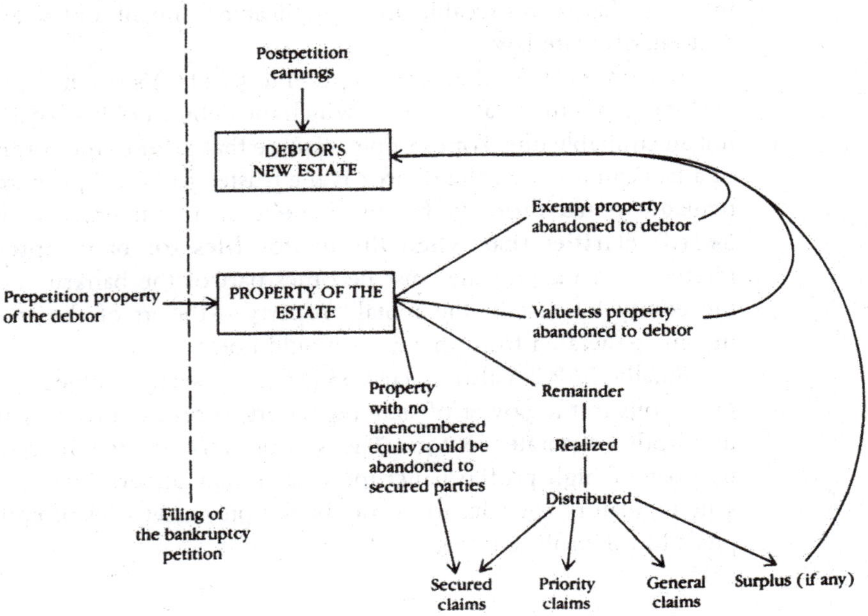

Diagram 9a

property (with the exception of property that is abandoned by the trustee as discussed in section 9.6) is liquidated and its proceeds distributed to creditors. At the same time as the petition is filed and the bankruptcy estate is created, the individual Ch. 7 debtor[4] is creating a new estate that is not subject to the bankruptcy process. This new estate consists of earnings and property acquired by the debtor after the filing as well as property that has been released to the debtor from the estate as exempt or abandoned by the trustee as having no economic value. For example, a debtor may continue working postpetition. Earned income related to postpetition services would not be estate property. Indeed, these postpetition assets of the debtor are the basis of her fresh start. As mentioned in sections 7.4.1 and 7.6, prepetition creditors cannot reach them because they are stayed from doing so pending

4. A corporation in liquidation cannot be rehabilitated. (*See* sections 5.2.1 and 21.1.) It therefore does not acquire a new estate. When the corporation's bankrupt estate has been liquidated, the corporation ceases to operate and is ultimately de-registered.

Flow of Property in a Ch. 13 Case

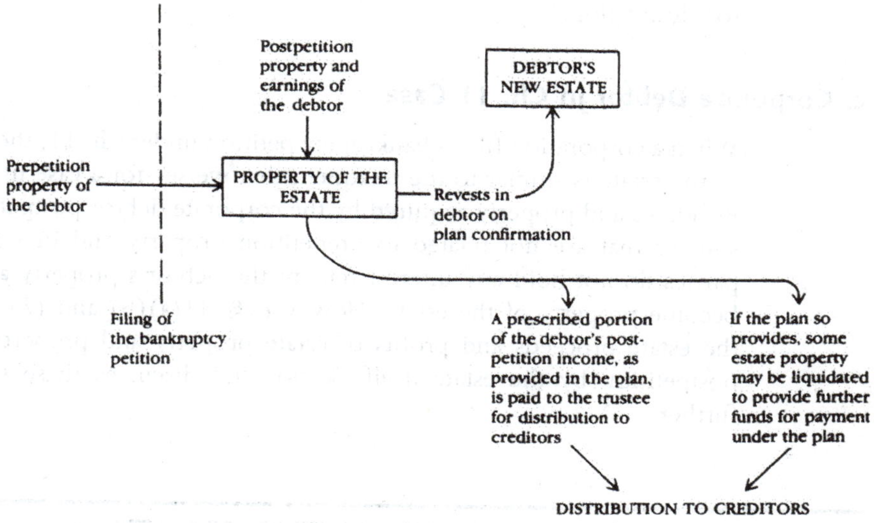

Diagram 9b

the debtor's discharge. Upon discharge of a prepetition debt, the creditor is permanently enjoined from collecting that debt.

Diagram 9a shows the flow of property into and out of the Ch. 7 estate of an individual debtor, and the birth of the debtor's postbankruptcy estate.

Diagram 9b shows the flow of property into and out of the Ch. 13 estate.

b. Ch. 13 and Individual Debtors in Ch. 11 Cases

Cases involving individual debtors under Chs. 11 and 13 present a treatment different than Ch. 7. In Ch. 13, §1306 provides that property of the estate includes property qualifying under §541 at the time of petition *and* all property (as defined in §541) acquired and all remuneration for services earned by the debtor up to the time that the case is closed, dismissed, or converted. In other words, §1306 provides for property and income of the debtor to continue entering the estate until the case comes to an end, either because the plan is consummated or because the debtor's plan of rehabilitation fails. Section 1115, added by BAPCPA, extended this rule to an individual Ch. 11 case. In the event of confirmation, all property in the estate that is not otherwise disposed of under the plan revests in the debtor. However, if the debtor's attempt at rehabilitation fails and the case is converted to Ch. 7, the debtor's right to keep estate property ends, and the property is surrendered to the trustee for liquidation.[5]

c. Corporate Debtor in Ch. 11 Case

When a corporation files a bankruptcy petition under Ch. 11, the treatment of the estate is similar to the treatment that we see for a case under Ch. 7. Revenues and property acquired by the corporate debtor postpetition from sources that are not related to prepetition property and in which other parties do not hold any interest remain the debtor's property and do not become property of the estate. However, §541(a)(6) and (7) include in the estate proceeds and profits of estate property and property acquired postpetition by the estate itself. Section 9.3 discusses these subsections further.

---

§9.3 PROPERTY INCLUDED IN THE ESTATE

§9.3.1 Legal and Equitable Interests of the Debtor at the Time of the Petition (§541(a))

Section 541(a) and its seven subsections list different types of estate property. Not surprisingly, this section addresses a dizzying array of assets and issues. Luckily, only a small subset of these issues is discussed frequently in bankruptcy cases. The following sections address this subset.

a. Causes of Action (§§541(a)(1) and (a)(7))

Section 541(a)(1)'s language is the broadest in scope, capturing all of the debtor's legal and equitable interests in property as of the commencement of the case. Section 541(a)(7) captures any interest in property that the estate acquires after the commencement of the case. Consequently these two subsections bring into the bankruptcy estate causes of action belonging to the

5. Postpetition property and earnings are included in cases under Chs. 11 and 13 to enable the trustee to supervise these assets while the debtor is performing under the plan. Because the property vests in the debtor upon confirmation of the plan, and the debtor retains possession of it, the trustee's control of the property is legal rather than physical. See §§1306(b), and 1327. The trustee does handle property that is to be distributed under the plan so that installments due by the debtor under the plan are paid to the trustee for distribution. Because there is usually no trustee in a Ch. 11 case, the debtor in possession contracts the property.

debtor or arising from property of the estate. A cause of action does not need to be filed prior to the petition date in order to become estate property.[6] Causes of action can represent estate property even if contingent, unliquidated, or derivative. The key inquiry is whether the cause of action was sufficiently matured as of the commencement of the bankruptcy case to constitute "an interest of the debtor in property." For example, imagine that Lessor owns rental property in New York. Unbeknownst to Lessor, one of his tenants has moved out of his rental apartment and appropriated all of the new appliances Lessor installed just last year. Lessor files a bankruptcy petition under Ch. 7 and learns of the theft three weeks later. Lessor's cause of action against his tenant is property of his bankruptcy estate because all facts supporting the claim occurred prepetition. The claim was mature on the petition date. This result is unaffected by the fact that Lessor had not brought suit before the petition date or that Lessor did not know that he held this cause of action when he filed for bankruptcy.

Furthermore, a line of cases holds that certain causes of action that accrue *after* the petition date can be property of the estate. Indeed, a claim that is immature on the petition date can be estate property if it has sufficient roots in the debtor's prebankruptcy activities and is not entangled with the debtor's fresh start. For example, imagine that Debtor hired an accountant to prepare her taxes. After filing her tax return, Debtor discovers significant problems with the filing. Before she can take any action, her deteriorating financial position forced her to file a bankruptcy petition under Ch. 7. In bankruptcy, Debtor retains an attorney and files a malpractice action against the accountant. At Debtor's request, the bankruptcy court allows her to prosecute the action with the recovery going to the bankruptcy estate. After reaching a settlement, Debtor discovers that her attorney failed to assert a number of claims against the accountant, and the claims are now time-barred. Can Debtor sue her attorney once her bankruptcy case is closed or does the claim belong to her bankruptcy estate? A number of courts have held that a debtor's cause of action against her attorney is estate property because it was rooted in the debtor's prepetition activities. The malpractice affected the value of the original malpractice action against Debtor's accountant, which was a prepetition cause of action that represented property of the estate. In other words, because the original cause of action against the accountant belonged to the estate—including the claims that could have been but were not asserted—a malpractice suit

6. In fact, a cause of action can become estate property even if the debtor failed to include it in the bankruptcy schedules. Judicial estoppel does not bar the bankruptcy trustee from pursuing claims that the debtor failed to disclose. However, judicial estoppel can bar a debtor who fails to disclose a cause of action from pursuing that action after the bankruptcy case is closed. See, e.g., *Marable v. Marion Military Inst.*, 595 F. App'x 921, 923-24 (11th Cir. 2014).

against Debtor's attorney in connection with those omitted claims is also estate property.[7]

b. Wages and Commissions (§541(a)(6))

The treatment of wages and commissions is a particularly important issue for individual debtors. Section 541(a)(6) provides that earnings from services performed by an individual debtor postpetition are excluded from estate property. However, courts have construed this exception narrowly. Consequently, courts have struggled to classify wages and commissions that are premised on both pre- and postpetition services of the debtor. For example, imagine that prior to filing a Ch. 7 petition, Debtor worked for a company that routinely paid him a year-end bonus, as well as commissions based on the clients that he convinced to purchase the company's widgets. The bonuses were distributed in March and were only paid if Debtor was still employed in good standing at the time of distribution. Further, the bonuses were solely at the employer's discretion. The commissions were paid five months after a client made its purchase. If Debtor filed a bankruptcy in November and then received a bonus in the following March and a commission payment in April, does either payment become property of the estate?

Courts have split on this issue. Under the majority view, courts initially inquire whether any postpetition services are necessary to obtain the payment at issue. If none are necessary, then the payment will be part of the bankruptcy estate. However, if postpetition services are necessary, then the court determines the extent to which the payments are attributable to prepetition services. The portion of the payment allocable to prepetition services will be property of the estate. To the extent that bonuses and other similar payments received by a debtor postpetition are sufficiently rooted in a debtor's prepetition past, the payment can be included as property of the estate. In these cases, courts have prorated the payment so only that portion of the payment that relates to the debtor's prepetition labor becomes property of the estate.

The minority view is that if the debtor must perform any postpetition services, regardless of how trivial, the entire payment is captured by §541(a)(6)'s earnings exception and cannot be property of the estate. These courts reason that in instances when postpetition income is dependent upon the debtor's postpetition services, the amounts do not constitute property of the estate because the debtor had no legally enforceable interest in the payment on the petition date.

---

7. See, e.g., *O'Dowd v. Trueger*, 233 F.3d 197 (3d Cir. 2000). However, a number of courts disagree with this approach, arguing that a cause of action can represent estate property only if the debtor or the bankruptcy trustee could have brought the claim at the commencement of the bankruptcy case. See, e.g., *Burgess v. Sikes*, 438 F.3d 493, 498 (5th Cir. 2006).

c. Inheritances and Property Settlements (§541(a)(5))

Except for cases filed under Ch. 13, property that a debtor receives post-petition does not generally become estate property. Section 541(a)(5) creates a notable exception. Under this exception, certain property received by the debtor within 180 days after petition date becomes estate property. The property subject to this exception includes two primary classes: 1) bequests, devises, and inheritances, and 2) property settlements with the debtor's spouse.

The first class involves property received pursuant to a will triggered by the death of testator. For example, during the 180-day period after Debtor files bankruptcy, her father passes away. Her father's will provides that Debtor inherits a boat and a car. Pursuant to §541(a)(5), these assets would become property of Debtor's bankruptcy estate. But what if the will is not admitted to probate until after the 180-day period has expired? Is section 541(a)(5)'s 180-day window activated by the death of Debtor's father or the admission of the will to probate? Courts have uniformly agreed that §541(a)(5) merely requires a vested entitlement in order to bring property into the estate. The entitlement was created by the father's will and became vested in Debtor when her father passed away. Consequently, the dispositive event is the death of the testator, not the date the will is admitted to probate.

The second class involves property—not including alimony[8]—received by a debtor pursuant to a divorce decree or other similar marital dissolution agreement. For example, two weeks after Debtor files a bankruptcy petition, he and his spouse file a divorce petition. Shortly after the filing of the divorce petition, a divorce decree is entered that awards Debtor real property that he did not originally own. Section 541(a)(5)(B) clarifies that this property is property of the bankruptcy estate. The fact the debtor may receive the real property more than 180 days after the filing of the bankruptcy petition is not dispositive. The operative date for purposes of the 180-day period in §541(a)(5) is the date that Debtor became entitled to acquire the real property under state law. However, due to variations in state law, bankruptcy courts have reached different conclusions in assessing when exactly a debtor becomes "entitled to acquire" property. Some courts have held that a debtor does not become entitled to acquire real property in this context until entry of the final divorce decree. Other courts have held that the debtor's entitlement can arise when the divorce action has been initiated coupled with a request for an equitable distribution.

---

8. Courts agree that section 541(a)(5) does not cover alimony payments. Alimony payments are a personal right, not the type of property right that is customarily captured in a debtor's bankruptcy estate.

d. Cyberproperty (§541(a)(1))

A new issue that has emerged under §541(a)(1) is whether a debtor's cyberproperty becomes estate property. Treatment of internet domain names is the biggest issue. There are few opinions addressing this issue but courts that have ruled on this matter have found that domain names are estate property. Ownership of an internet domain name is a defined interest because the owner has the right to sell the name and exclude others from its use.[9] Further, a Facebook page[10] and social media accounts[11] for a business debtor have also been found to be estate property.

§9.3.2 Invalidating Restrictions on the Transfer of Property to the Bankruptcy Estate (§541(c))

Although the debtor's interest in property is determined by nonbankruptcy law, the deference to nonbankruptcy law is not absolute. Section 541(c) invalidates any provision of nonbankruptcy law as well as any condition created by contract or transfer instrument that restricts the transfer of property rights so that they do not pass to the estate on bankruptcy. Therefore, if the debtor has a property right under nonbankruptcy law but a contract or state law declares that right nontransferable to the estate or forfeited upon the debtor's bankruptcy, the restriction is ineffective. Section 541(c) is intended to prevent a state or a private party from circumventing §541(a).

An important exception to this rule is set out in §541(c)(2), which validates in bankruptcy a "restriction on the transfer of a beneficial interest of the debtor in a trust that is enforceable under applicable bankruptcy law." The plain meaning of this provision makes it applicable to a retirement fund that is subject to an anti-alienation provision under nonbankruptcy law. However, some courts of appeal refused to apply it to such funds on the basis that the legislative history of §541(c)(2) indicates that Congress intended this exception to apply only to spendthrift trusts recognized as nonexecutable under applicable state law. The U.S. Supreme Court rejected this approach in *Patterson v. Shumate*, 504 U.S. 753 (1992). The Supreme Court held that because the meaning of §541(c)(2) was clear, there was no occasion to resort to legislative history. In its plain meaning, §541(c)(2) covers all trusts, including retirement funds, that are subject to restrictions on alienation enforceable under nonbankruptcy law. The Court therefore held that a retirement plan that qualified as tax exempt under the Employee Retirement Income Security Act (ERISA) did not enter the estate because

9. See *Kremen v. Cohen*, 337 F.3d 1024 (9th Cir. 2003).
10. *In re CTLI*, 528 B.R. 359 (Bankr. S.D. Tex. 2015).
11. *In re Borders Grp.*, 453 B.R. 459 (Bankr. S.D.N.Y. 2011).

ERISA requires a qualifying plan to preclude assignment or alienation of benefits under the plan. The Court considered that this plain-meaning approach was also consistent with ERISA's policy of protecting pension benefits, which outweighed the bankruptcy policy of broad inclusion in the estate.

Lower courts have applied *Patterson* to include retirement plans that are not ERISA-qualified, provided that the plan satisfies the applicable requirements of §541(c)(2): 1) the debtor must have a beneficial interest in the trust; 2) there is a valid anti-alienation provision restricting the transfer of the debtor's interest; and 3) the restriction is enforceable under applicable nonbankruptcy law on the petition date.

§9.4 PROPERTY EXCLUDED FROM THE ESTATE

§9.4.1 Property Explicitly Excluded from the Estate (§541(b))

Section 541(b) explicitly excludes certain property from the bankruptcy estate. Many of the subsections were enacted long ago at the behest of influential businesses but have little practical relevant today.[12] The most prominent issues that arise under §541(b) are addressed below.

a. Education Trusts (§541(b)(5))

Section 541(b)(5) allows an individual debtor to exempt from creditors certain education individual retirement account (IRA) and state tuition plans for her child's postsecondary education. The section generally excludes from estate property any funds[13] that the debtor 1) placed in an educational IRA and 2) deposited at least 365 days prior to filing bankruptcy. The funds must be for the benefit of the debtor's child, stepchild, grandchild, or stepgrandchild.

12. For example, Section 541(b)(9) offers protection for companies specializing in money orders.

13. The section places a monetary limit on the exclusion for funds deposited in the account between one and two years before bankruptcy. This limit is adjusted every three years by the Judicial Conference of the United States

b. Tuition Programs (§541(b)(6))

Section 529 of the Internal Revenue Code exempts certain qualified state tuition programs (referred to as "529 plans") from taxation. All 50 states and the District of Columbia have passed legislation authorizing college savings accounts, but state treatment of these accounts varies. Prior to October 17, 2005, the date BAPCPA took effect, 529 plans were considered to be property of the estate and generally nonexempt property. Section 541(b)(6), enacted by BAPCPA, explicitly excludes certain tuition program funds from property of the estate. More specifically, funds[14] are excluded if 1) they are contributed to a state-sponsored 529 plan not later than 365 days before the petition filing date, 2) the designated beneficiary of the account was a child, stepchild, grandchild, or stepgrandchild of the debtor for the taxable year for which funds were paid or contributed, and 3) for aggregate amounts paid to 529 plans for the same beneficiary, the contributed funds do not exceed the total contributions permitted under the Internal Revenue Code.

c. Retirement Accounts (§541(b)(7))

Section 541(b)(7) addresses contributions made to only those specific plans listed in the subsection. The delineated plans are 1) ERISA plans; 2) employee benefit plans that are governmental plans under 26 U.S.C. §414(d); 3) deferred compensation plans; 4) tax-deferred annuities; and 5) health insurance plans pursuant to state law (collectively, the "Qualifying Plans").

Section 541(b)(7) excludes from the estate two types of contributions made to Qualifying Plans. Primarily, amounts withheld by an employer from the wages of employees for payment as contributions to a qualifying plan are excluded. Income is typically "withheld" when an employee has a present entitlement to the income, but the employer does not transfer the income to the employee, usually with the intention of contributing the funds to one of the qualifying plans. Second, amounts received by an employer from an employee as contributions to a qualifying plan are also excluded. This second category includes funds that the employee possessed at some point in time and transferred to an employer with the intention of having the funds contributed to one of the Qualifying Plans.

14. The section places a monetary limit on the exclusion for funds deposited in the account between one and two years before bankruptcy. This limit is adjusted every three years by the Judicial Conference of the United States

d. Possessory Security Interests (§541(b)(8))

Section 541(b)(8) was enacted to protect pawnbrokers and similar parties by allowing these parties to retain forfeited collateral if the debtor failed to timely redeem the property prior to the petition date. The provision has also been relied upon by companies that provide short-term loans in exchange for liens on borrowers' personal property, typically motor vehicles.

Section 541(b)(8) recognizes that the pawnbrokers' rights in pawned, pledged, or transferred property are invariably different from the rights that a holder of a security interest or other lien has in encumbered property to secure a debt. More specifically, a pawnbroker generally enjoys the automatic right of full ownership of pawned property in the event that the borrower does not timely redeem the property.

Pursuant to §541(b)(8), a debtor's interest in pledged or sold tangible personal property is generally excluded from property of the estate if 1) the property is in the possession of the pledgee or transferee; 2) the debtor has no obligation to repay the money, redeem the collateral, or buy back the property; and 3) the debtor has not exercised any applicable right to redeem the property in a timely manner.

§9.4.2 Trusts and Trust Property (§541(d))

In some cases, a debtor is in possession of property on the petition date, but that property is being held in trust for another. In that instance, the Code acknowledges the crucial distinction between a legal interest and an equitable interest in property. Property of the bankruptcy estate does not include any interest in which the debtor holds only bare legal title. Indeed, §541(d) provides that debtors do not own an equitable interest in property that they hold in trust for another. Property subject to §541(d) will be excluded from property of the estate and cannot be distributed to creditors.

For example, imagine that a general contractor is hired to build a structure on a vacant lot. The general contractor hires a subcontractor to pour the foundation. The contract between the parties provides that the general contractor must create and control a bank account for the sole purpose of paying the subcontractor (the "Bank Account"). Unfortunately, the general contractor experiences distress and files a Ch. 7 bankruptcy petition. Both the subcontractor and the bankruptcy trustee claim an interest in the money in the Bank Account. Section 541(d) provides that, although an express trust was not created, the general contractor held these funds in constructive trust for the subcontractor. Therefore, the funds are not part of the bankruptcy estate.

§9.5 THE EFFECT OF CONVERSION FROM CH. 13

Because property of the Ch. 7 estate is fixed at the date of the petition while property and earnings continue to enter the Ch. 13 estate after the petition, conversion from Ch. 13 to Ch. 7 gives rise to the question of whether the converted Ch. 7 estate includes property acquired by the debtor after the petition but before the conversion.

Section 348 deals with the effect of conversion. Its general rule, in §348(a), is that although the conversion constitutes the order for relief under the chapter to which the case is converted, the original petition date remains the effective date of commencement of the case for all purposes except those specified in the section. Section 348(f) was added to the Code in 1994 to resolve a split among courts over the question of whether property of the Ch. 7 estate, in a case converted from Ch. 13, was to be determined at the time of conversion or at the time of the original Ch. 13 filing. Section 348(f) governs conversions from Ch. 13 to Ch. 7. Section 348(f) provides that if the debtor's conversion is in good faith, the property of the Ch. 7 estate includes only the property of the original Ch. 13 estate that is still in the debtor's control or possession at the time of conversion. If the conversion is in bad faith, the Ch. 7 estate expands to include all the property acquired by the debtor (and hence by the Ch. 13 estate) up to the time of conversion.

§9.6 THE TRUSTEE'S POWER TO COMPEL DELIVERY OF PROPERTY OF THE ESTATE ("TURNOVER" UNDER §542)

Section 521(a)(4) obliges the debtor to surrender all property to the trustee when the petition is filed. Under §542, any property of the debtor in the possession of other persons must be delivered to the trustee or its value accounted for; likewise, a debt due to the debtor must be paid to the trustee. The duty to deliver property to the estate ("turnover") under §542 applies even if the estate's equity in the property is small. Section 542(a) expressly applies to all property that may be used, sold, or leased by the trustee, or that may be exempted by the debtor. The link between this turnover requirement and the automatic stay is apparent. Even a creditor with an interest in property is obliged to relinquish possession to the trustee. If the creditor wishes to recover the property so that the interest can be enforced, application must be made for relief from stay. Section 542(a) makes an exception to the duty of delivery to the trustee for property that is of inconsequential value or benefit to the estate.

If the property is in the hands of a custodian, including an assignee for the benefit of creditors or a receiver or trustee who was appointed in nonbankruptcy law to administer any property of the debtor, then §543 applies rather than §542. Section 543 requires the turnover of and accounting for all the debtor's property or its proceeds in the control of the custodian. As soon as the custodian receives knowledge of the bankruptcy, the administration of the nonbankruptcy insolvency proceedings end and no further distributions may be made. The purpose of §543 is to ensure that upon bankruptcy, the trustee supersedes any nonbankruptcy trustee of the debtor's property. The section protects certain parties to whom the custodian has incurred obligations in the course of administering the property, and it provides for compensation to be made to the custodian for services rendered.

Provisions in both §§542 and 543 protect persons who have transferred property or made payments to third parties or to the debtor in good faith and without knowledge of the bankruptcy filing. Unless those exceptions apply, if a person fails to deliver estate property voluntarily the trustee is able to compel delivery by court order. In addition, §502(d) provides for the disallowance of the entire claim of a creditor who has failed to turn over property recoverable by the trustee.

§9.7 ABANDONMENT OF PROPERTY BY THE TRUSTEE (§554)

Some property that enters the estate is of no value or benefit to the estate. This may be because it 1) is fully encumbered and is not needed for the debtor's rehabilitation, 2) is fully exempt and cannot be liquidated for the benefit of creditors, 3) costs more to maintain than it is worth, or 4) has no economic value. The efficient administration of the estate and fairness to the debtor (and any other holder of an interest in the property) dictate that such property should be given up by the estate. Section 554 permits the court to authorize or order its abandonment. The initiative to abandon property may be taken by the trustee under §554(a) or applied for by a party in interest under §554(b). In either event, notice and a hearing are required. Under §102, this means that notice must be given to parties in interest, but a hearing is only held if objection is made. Section 554 does not indicate to whom the property is abandoned. However, abandonment divests the estate of all interest in the property, and it reverts to the debtor, whose rights in the property are restored as if no bankruptcy had occurred. Upon abandonment, the property remains subject to the automatic stay as property of the debtor. If someone other than the debtor has a possessory interest in the property (for example, a secured creditor who had lawfully seized the property prior to the filing) the court may abandon the property to that party. However, because the debtor still has a legal or equitable interest in the property, the party with the possessory interest must seek relief from the stay to foreclose on it.

Section 554(c) provides that at the close of the case, property that was included in the debtor's schedule but was not administered in the estate will be abandoned to the debtor. If it happens that any property is left in the estate at the end of the case, it is returned to the debtor. This situation is only likely to occur if the estate was not insolvent, so that all the property was not needed to pay claims, or if a particular item of property was worthless and unrealizable but was not abandoned to the debtor earlier in the case.

Examples

1. At the time of filing a petition for Ch. 7 relief, an individual debtor has the various interests described below. Which of these interests become property of the estate under §541?
   a. **Tort claim.** A year before the petition, the debtor was injured by a negligently driven automobile. At the time of the petition, the debtor's claim against the driver had not yet been litigated. Is the tort claim property of the estate?
   b. **Refrigerator.** About five months before bankruptcy, the debtor borrowed money from Newgate Loan Co. to finance the purchase of a refrigerator. When the funds were advanced, Newgate properly perfected a security interest in the refrigerator in accordance with state law. One month before bankruptcy, the debtor defaulted on the loan payments, and Newgate took possession of the refrigerator for the purpose of foreclosing on its security interest. By the time the petition was filed, Newgate had not yet held its foreclosure sale. Is the refrigerator property of the estate?
   c. **Furniture.** Two weeks before bankruptcy, the debtor held a garage sale at which she sold a well-worn dining room suite to Reese Cycle. Reese could not take delivery of it immediately because he needed to borrow a truck from a friend to haul it away. Nevertheless, he paid for it in cash at the time of the sale.

      Before Reese managed to arrange for the truck, the debtor filed the bankruptcy petition. Is the dining room suite, which is still in the debtor's possession, property of the estate?

d. **Retirement plan.** Some years prior to filing, the debtor began to participate in a tax-exempt retirement plan under the ERISA. For the purpose of meeting the statute's requirements for tax-exempt status, the plan contained an anti-alienation provision that precluded the assignment or alienation of benefits under the plan. The benefits under the plan have not matured. Is the debtor's retirement nest egg property of the estate?

e. **Season tickets.** Prior to filing, the debtor subscribed to baseball season tickets. The contract under which she bought the tickets clearly states that the subscription is not transferrable. However, season subscriptions are often sold by holders, and the team does not usually challenge the sales. On this occasion, it does claim that the tickets are not property of the estate. Is it correct in its assertion?

f. **Website.** Prior to filing, the debtor properly registered the Internet domain name www.comingtoamerica30.com. Paramount Studios intends to remake the 1988 comedy *Coming to America* and have the new film coincide with the 30th anniversary of the original film's release. After the petition date, the studio contacts the debtor about purchasing the domain name she registered. May the debtor sell the domain name?

2. Although property acquired by a Ch. 7 debtor after the petition is generally part of the debtor's new estate, §541(a) includes certain postpetition receipts in the estate if they have an appropriate connection with prepetition property. Consider whether the following postpetition acquisitions are property of the estate:

a. **Kittens.** At the time of the petition, the debtor owned a highly pedigreed pregnant cat. The cat produced a litter three weeks after the filing. Who owns the kittens?

b. **Postpetition income.** The debtor sold her business about 11 months before filing the petition. At the time of sale, the debtor entered into a noncompetition agreement with the purchaser under which the debtor agreed, for an additional consideration of $100,000 per year (separate from the consideration paid for the business), not to compete with the business in a specified area for a period of five years. The annual payments were to be made at the end of each of the five years. About a month after the petition, the debtor received the first payment. Is it property of the estate?

c. **Inheritance.** Three weeks after the petition the debtor's Uncle Lucrum died, leaving her a generous bequest. What happens to the debtor's inheritance?

EXPLANATIONS

Explanations

1. Sections 541 and 542 should be applied as follows:
   a. **Tort claim.** Do not forget that state law determines if and when a property right arises. As a general rule of state law, tort liability is created as soon as the tort is committed, so the debtor had a property right in his claim for damages when he filed the petition. It does not matter that the debtor had not yet sued on it and it is unliquidated. The inclusive language of §541 is broad enough to include unliquidated claims for damages. The claim is therefore property of the estate.
   b. **Refrigerator.** The foreclosure sale has not yet taken place, and it is stayed upon the advent of bankruptcy. Even though the debtor defaulted on the loan, and foreclosure proceedings had begun prior to the petition, the debtor still owned the fridge under state law, and this ownership interest passed to the estate under §541(a)(1). (Of course, the debtor's ownership interest may not be very valuable if the secured debt is close to or equal to the value of the collateral. Nevertheless, it exists, and had the sale occurred prior to bankruptcy the debtor would have been entitled to any surplus sale proceeds or to a redemption right under state law.) Newgate may apply for relief from stay so that foreclosure can proceed. Until such relief is granted, the estate is entitled to the refrigerator and the trustee can demand turnover under §542.

      Again, it must be stressed that the existence and extent of the debtor's property interest is a matter of state law. In *In re Kalter*, 292 F.3d 1350 (11th Cir. 2002), the secured party had repossessed vehicles prepetition but had not yet sold them at the time of the debtor's bankruptcy. The court determined that under state law, ownership of the collateral passed to the secured party on repossession, so the debtor had no property interest in the vehicles at the time of the petition. By contrast, in *In re Moffett*, 356 F.3d 518 (4th Cir. 2004), the court found on similar facts, under a different state's law, that the debtor's right of redemption and to any surplus that might exist after the sale only expires upon the sale of the vehicle. The debtor therefore had a property interest that passed to the estate.
   c. **Furniture.** Although §541 affects transfer of the debtor's property to the estate, nonbankruptcy law—in this case UCC Article 2—determines the nature and extent of the debtor's rights in property. Article 2 provides for the passage of title when the goods were identified to the contract, so the sale passed title to Reese and the suite does not become property of the estate.
   d. **Retirement plan.** The fund in the retirement plan is prepetition property of the debtor that would enter the estate under §541(a)(1) unless the prohibition on transfer is effective in bankruptcy. Section

541(c)(1) generally overrides restrictions on the transfer of property under contract or nonbankruptcy law, so that such property passes to the estate in spite of the restriction. However, §541(c)(2) provides an exception to §541(c)(1) where the restriction on transfer relates to the debtor's beneficial interest in a trust and the restriction is enforceable under nonbankruptcy law. As discussed in section 9.3.3, a retirement plan with valid restrictions on transfer under nonbankruptcy law, such as those imposed by ERISA, is covered by §541(c)(2) and does not enter the estate.

e. **Season tickets.** The facts of this example are based on *In re Platt*, 292 B.R. 12 (Bankr. D. Mass. 2003), in which the trustee claimed that the debtor's Boston Red Sox season tickets were property of the estate. The trustee ultimately lost on an issue of proof—he could not show that the debtor actually owned the tickets in his personal capacity. However, the court said that had the trustee been able to prove this, the tickets would have become property of the estate. The nontransferability clause in the season ticket subscription contract would not have been upheld under §541(c)(1) because the team's practice was to permit transfers.

f. **Website.** Though there are limited opinions addressing this type of issue, courts that have addressed it have held uniformly that a domain name is property. Indeed, a domain name can be sold. In 2010, Facebook acquired the domain name "www.fb.com" from The American Farm Bureau for approximately $8.5 million. Further, a registrant who owns a domain name can exclude others from using that address. Consequently, the domain name is brought into the bankruptcy estate pursuant to §541(a)(1). It can be sold by the bankruptcy trustee, and the funds can be distributed to creditors.

2. The postpetition acquisitions are dealt with in the following way:

   a. **Kittens.** The cat became property of the estate upon the debtor's bankruptcy. Although the litter was born after the petition, it is property of the estate under §541(a)(6), which includes in the estate all proceeds, product, offspring, rents or profits of or derived from estate property.

   b. **Postpetition income.** Although the earnings from the noncompetition agreement accrue postpetition, the agreement creating the right to the earnings was entered into prepetition. In *In re Andrews*, 80 F.3d 906 (4th Cir. 1996), the debtor argued that the payments due after bankruptcy under such an agreement are not property of the estate, but are earnings from services performed by the debtor after the commencement of the case, excluded from the estate under §541(a)(6). The debtor's reasoning was that he became entitled to the payments by refraining from competing, and this forbearance did constitute an ongoing service that he performed for the purchaser after the petition. The court disagreed, observing that it was too much of a stretch to include inaction in the concept of performance of services under §541(a)(6). Furthermore, the court reasoned that the purpose of the exclusion in §541(a)(6) was to facilitate the debtor's fresh start by separating from the estate whatever new income he may earn by postfiling endeavors. The proceeds from the noncompetition agreement were not of this nature, but arose out of and were ancillary to the sale of an asset before bankruptcy. As such, the earnings derived from the debtor's prepetition activities, and were more properly viewed as proceeds of estate property. (A dissent in the case agreed with the debtor's argument that the payments should be treated as earnings from the postpetition service of forbearing from competition.)

c. **Inheritance.** Section 541(a)(5) includes in the estate any property that the debtor acquires or becomes entitled to by bequest, devise, or inheritance within 180 days after the petition, if such property would have qualified as property of the estate had the debtor an interest in it at the time of the petition. The inheritance would have been property of the estate had Uncle Lucrum died before the debtor filed the petition, so it satisfies §541(a)(5) and is estate property.

CHAPTER 10

Exemptions, Redemption, and Reaffirmation

§10.1 OVERVIEW

This chapter is concerned with ways in which a debtor may recover property that has entered the estate. The provisions discussed here are largely applicable to individual debtors and are most directly relevant in Ch. 7 cases. Sections 10.2 through 10.8 cover the exemptions claimable by an individual debtor under §522. While exemptions are claimable by individual debtors in all forms of bankruptcy, they have the most direct application in a Ch. 7 case because the debtor may claim the release of fully exempt property from the estate, or cash payment of the amount of the exemption in partially exempt property. In Chs. 11 and 13, where the debtor may obtain release of estate property under the plan, exemptions are relevant to the determination of the minimum payment required of the debtor under the plan.

Section 10.2 explains the concept and purpose of exemptions. Section 10.3 discusses the manner in which exemptions are determined under §522 (b) and (d). Section 10.4 describes the nature of exempt property under §522(d). Section 10.5 describes the procedure for claiming exemptions and objections to the claim of exemptions under §522 (l). Section 10.6 discusses the extent to which a debtor may legitimately enter into transactions before filing the bankruptcy petition for the purpose of maximizing exemptions. Section 10.7 explains the provisions of §522(o), (p), and (q), designed to curb prepetition manipulations by a debtor to enhance her homestead exemption claim. Section 10.8 covers the debtor's power under §522(f) to avoid certain liens that impair exemptions.

Section 10.9 discusses the individual debtor's limited right to redeem tangible personal property in a Ch. 7 case. Section 722 provides for the right of redemption, and §521 sets out the procedure the debtor must follow to effect it.

Section 10.10 explains the process under which a debtor may enter into a contract with a creditor to reaffirm a dischargeable debt under §524. Section 524 is part of Ch. 5, which is applicable in all forms of bankruptcy. However, it is most commonly used in a Ch. 7 liquidation where a debtor seeks to use reaffirmation to save the collateral from liquidation. Reaffirmation is not confined to this use, and a debtor may be persuaded to reaffirm a dischargeable unsecured debt. Reaffirmation, especially of an unsecured debt, is often not in the interests of a debtor and undermines the debtor's fresh start, so §524 has a number of provisions designed to caution and protect the debtor from ill-advised, misinformed, or coerced reaffirmation agreements.

Section 10.11 explains the "ride through" that is permitted by some courts. Where allowed, this is an alternative means that a debtor may use to retain property subject to a security interest by maintaining contractual payments to the lienholder. The "ride-through" is not expressly authorized by the Code, but is dealt with in part by §521(a).

§10.2 THE CONCEPT OF EXEMPTIONS

Exemptions are discussed here in connection with bankruptcy. Recall, however, that they are also available in collection proceedings under state law. As explained in section 2.2.1, state exemption statutes designate specific property or types of property that cannot be levied upon by creditors in state debt collection proceedings.

Exemptions are only available to individual debtors and, as explained in sections 10.3 and 10.5, they cannot be claimed in property to the extent that it is subject to a valid and unavoidable consensual or statutory lien on property. Whether under state law or in bankruptcy, the goal of exemptions is to insulate certain of the debtor's property from the claims of creditors so that the debtor does not lose all his property by seizure or liquidation. In bankruptcy, property released to the debtor as exempt forms part of the debtor's new estate, thereby helping the debtor to gain a fresh start. As the following sections explain, the amount and value of property that a debtor can exempt varies greatly depending on which exemption regime applies. In some cases, the value of exemptions available to a debtor could be significant, and in other cases it could be modest.

Exemptions are provided for in §522. They are claimable by individual debtors in all cases, whether under Chs. 7, 11, or 13. Exemptions are used most directly in Ch. 7 cases, where fully exempt property is released and the cash value of partial exemptions is paid out from the estate to the debtor. In cases under Chs. 11 and 13, estate property vests in the debtor upon confirmation of the plan, except as otherwise provided for in the plan. (*See* section 9.2.) Therefore, the debtor does not directly use exemptions to reacquire estate property; instead, exemptions help the debtor because they are deducted from the liquidation value of the estate. This liquidation value is one of the factors taken into account in determining the minimum level of payment required for plan confirmation. (Standards for plan confirmation are explained in Chapters 18 and 20.) Exemptions are also relevant in all cases for the purpose of lien avoidance under §522(f), which is discussed in section 10.8.

§10.3 EXEMPTIONS APPLICABLE IN BANKRUPTCY CASES

§10.3.1 The State's Power to Substitute Its Own Exemptions for Federal Exemptions

The Bankruptcy Act of 1898 provided for exemptions to individual debtors in bankruptcy, but it did not designate which property of the debtor would be exempt. Instead, it deferred to state exemption laws so that the exemptions available to the debtor in the bankruptcy case would be whatever exemptions were allowed to the debtor under the law of the debtor's state. When the Code was enacted in 1978, there was disagreement over whether the Code should continue the old approach of using state exemptions in bankruptcy or should instead provide a uniform set of federal exemptions applicable to all individual debtors, irrespective of their state of domicile. Section 522 was a compromise between these opposing views. Section 522(d) provides a set of uniform bankruptcy exemptions, but §522(b) allows a state to elect to substitute its own exemptions for those listed in §522(d).[1] This has come to be known as the "opt-out."

1. Soon after the enactment of the Bankruptcy Act, the constitutionality of its deference to state exemption laws was challenged on the grounds that this violated the requirement of Art. VI, cl. 2 that Congress establish a uniform law of bankruptcy throughout the United States. The Supreme Court upheld the Act's incorporation of state exemption law in *Hanover National Bank v. Moyses*, 186 U.S. 181 (1902). The Court set out the fundamental principle (introduced in section 3.3) that absolute and literal uniformity is not required. Although the provisions of federal bankruptcy law must themselves be uniform throughout the United

There are two important limitations on the states' power to opt-out of §522(d). First, a state cannot provide for different sets of exemptions applicable in bankruptcy and in collection cases under state law. If the state opts out, the same exemptions available under state law become the bankruptcy exemptions for debtors domiciled in that state.[2] Second, the opt-out relates only to §522(d), which lists the property that the debtor may exempt. It does not apply to other provisions of §522, which cannot be varied by the states.

The state opts out of §522(d) by enacting a statute that specifically does not authorize debtors domiciled within its jurisdiction to use the exemptions listed in §522(d). Those debtors are confined to exemptions provided by state law, together with any applicable federal nonbankruptcy exemptions (such as exemptions provided for Social Security benefits or other protected benefits conferred by federal statutes other than the Code). If a state has not opted out, a debtor domiciled in that state may choose to claim either the exemptions provided in §522(d) or the applicable nonbankruptcy exemptions, and will claim whichever set of exemptions gives him the greatest benefit. (The debtor must choose either the state exemptions or the §522(d) exemptions. He cannot pick some exemptions from the state set and others from the federal set.)

The majority of states have opted out, so debtors are commonly not entitled to claim the exemptions set out in §522(d); they are confined to the same exemptions in bankruptcy as are available in collection proceedings in nonbankruptcy law. Many states have exemption laws that are roughly similar to the exemptions in §522(d), so it sometimes does not make a dramatic difference if state exemptions apply rather than the exemptions listed in §522(d). However, some state exemption laws are very different from the set of exemptions provided for in §522(d). Therefore, if the state has opted out, a debtor domiciled in that state may have exemptions that are dramatically better or worse than those listed in §522(d) or claimable by a debtor domiciled in another state.

The issue of uniform exemptions was revisited by the 1994 National Bankruptcy Review Commission. In its 1997 report, the majority of the Commission criticized the widely divergent treatment of debtors that resulted from deference to state law, and recommended that Congress

---

States, they can take into account variations in state law. The test is not whether bankruptcy law will lead to the same outcome in every state, but whether the superstructure of bankruptcy law is evenly imposed. A few years after the Code was enacted, its continued deference to state law exemptions was again challenged on the grounds that Congress had failed to comply with the constitutional requirement of uniformity in bankruptcy law. *In re Sullivan*, 680 F.2d 1131 (7th Cir. 1982), *cert. denied*, 459 U.S. 992 (1983) rejected this argument on the precedent of *Hanover National Bank*, and it now seems settled that there is no constitutional bar to adopting state exemptions in bankruptcy.

2. See *In re Wallace*, 347 B.R. 626 (Bankr. W.D. Mich. 2006).

eliminate the states' right to opt out of the standard exemptions in §522(d). Congress declined to follow this recommendation in enacting the Bankruptcy Abuse Prevention and Consumer Protection Act of 2005 (BAPCPA), so the Code continues to allow states to opt out.

§10.3.2 Determining Which State's Law Governs Exemptions — the Debtor's Domicile

The law of the state of the debtor's domicile determines which set of exemptions applies in the bankruptcy case. Domicile requires both actual residence and a present intent to remain. (Temporary removal to another jurisdiction does not defeat domicile if the debtor intends to return.)

Because the debtor's domicile at the time of the petition can have a significant impact on what property the debtor can claim as exempt, a debtor may make the strategic decision to move to and establish domicile in a state with favorable exemptions in anticipation of the filing. Section 522(b)(3)[3] provides that the law that governs the debtor's exemption rights is the law of the state in which the debtor was domiciled for the 730 days (two years) immediately preceding the petition. If the debtor has not been domiciled in any single state for that 730-day period, the applicable exemption law is that of the state in which the debtor was domiciled in the 180 days immediately preceding the 730-day period, or for a longer portion of that 180 days than any other place. That is, if the debtor has been domiciled in a state for the two years immediately before the petition, that state's exemption law applies. If the debtor has not been domiciled in the same state for the two years immediately before the petition, we must then look back to the six-month period immediately before those two years to determine domicile. Section 522(b)(3)(C) contains a safety net for a debtor who cannot establish the requisite domicile in any state under the section — in that case federal exemptions in §522(d) apply.

Section 522(b)(3) makes it very difficult for a debtor to move to a hospitable state for the purpose of enhancing her exemptions. In close cases, the determination of the proper domicile can be tricky. For example, in *In re Dufva*, 388 B.R. 911 (Bankr. W.D. Mo. 2008), the debtors were domiciled in Missouri. However, before moving to Missouri, they had been domiciled in Nevada, which had more generous exemptions. The debtors claimed Nevada

3. Section 522(b)(3) was amended by BAPCPA in 2005 to make it harder for a debtor to engage in strategic planning to establish a favorable domicile. Before the amendment, the rule in §522(b) for determining domicile for exemption purposes was quite lenient. The section applied the exemption law of the state in which the debtor was domiciled for the 180 days (about six months) prior to the petition. If the debtor had not been domiciled in a single state during the period, the law of the place of longest domicile in the 180-day period was used.

exemptions on the grounds that they had established domicile in Missouri only 729 days before filing, and had been domiciled in Nevada during the 180-day period before that. To resolve the issue, the court had to go through a tortuously finicky counting and interpretational exercise, which led it to conclude that the debtors were in fact domiciled in Missouri for the 730 days before filing.

§10.4 THE NATURE OF EXEMPT PROPERTY

Exemptions are granted at the expense of creditors, whose recourse is limited to nonexempt assets. Because exemptions detract from creditor interests, they are limited and controlled to confine them to a level regarded as appropriate by the legislature to accomplish the goal of preventing the debtor's impoverishment. As explained in section 10.2, the list of exemptions claimable by an individual debtor in bankruptcy is set out in §522(d). However, because most states have opted out of that section and substituted their own exemptions, the actual exemptions allowed by §522(d) are commonly inapplicable. This variation of exemptions, based on the state of the debtor's domicile, could be quite dramatic. However, many state statutes provide for exemptions that are not significantly different from those provided for in §522(d).

Section 522(d) and many state exemption statutes list specific types of property that may be exempted, with a dollar limit on most categories. The problem with this method of granting exemptions is that a debtor's ability to take advantage of exemptions is dependent on the extent to which her property coincides with the exemptions provided for in §522(d) or the applicable state statute. (For example, §522(d) grants exemptions for a car and tools of trade. A debtor who owns a car or tools of trade can claim exemptions for those items, but a debtor who does not own property of that kind cannot substitute other property and so loses those exemptions.) In addition to recommending that Congress establish a uniform set of bankruptcy exemptions by eliminating the states' right to opt out of §522(d), the majority of the 1994 National Bankruptcy Review Commission recommended that the list of exempt property in §522(d) be replaced with a lump sum dollar limit, so that a debtor could pick whatever property she wanted to exempt up to that limit. This change would have eliminated the problem of disparate treatment of debtors with different types of property and would have allowed all debtors the same total exemption amount, irrespective of the type of property they own. Congress did not follow this recommendation.

Although §522(d) is not applicable in most bankruptcy cases because of the opt-out, it serves as a model of what a common set of exemptions looks like. It specifies the types or classes of property that may be claimed as exempt and imposes a value limit on most categories of exempt property. Almost every category of exemption listed in §522(d) has a value limitation. Some have a specified dollar limitation[4] that is quite modest, and some require the court to make a determination of the amount reasonably necessary for the support of the debtor and dependents. To be exempt, an asset must fit within one of the specified categories. To the extent that the asset is worth more than the exemption limit (or to the extent that the debtor has more assets in that category than may be claimed as exempt) the exemption is only partial, and the value over the exempt amount falls into the estate. The only category of exemption in §522(d) that allows the debtor the ability to select an asset to exempt (that is, provides for a general exemption in an asset of the debtor's choice) is the so-called "wildcard exemption" explained later in this section.

For debtors who own a home, the homestead exemption provided in §522(d)(1) is usually the most important and valuable. It covers $23,675 of the value of real or personal property that the debtor or a dependent uses as a residence. Other exemptions include a motor vehicle (§522(d)(2)), household furnishings and goods (§522(d)(3)), a modest amount of personal jewelry (§522(d)(4)), tools of trade on which the debtor depends for a livelihood, (§522(d)(6)), certain interests in life insurance policies, (§522(d)(7) and (8)), professionally prescribed health aids (§522(d)(9)), and various pension, disability, or alimony payments (§522(d)(10), (11) and (12)). One exemption category, the "wildcard exemption" under §522(d)(5), differs from the others in that it does not apply to any specific category or type of property, but can be used to exempt any property that the debtor chooses. It has a relatively small dollar limit that can be increased to if the debtor does not claim the homestead exemption. (Example 4 provides an exercise in determining how the exemption categories would be applied to a debtor's assets.)

§10.5 THE PROCEDURE FOR CLAIMING EXEMPTIONS

Under §522(l) the debtor must claim exemptions by filing a list of exempt property (Official Form 106C). If the debtor fails to file the list, a dependent

4. The dollar limits in §522(d) stayed constant for almost 20 years from the enactment of the Code in 1978 to 1994. The Bankruptcy Reform Act of 1994 updated the amounts and provided in §104 for their administrative adjustment every three years based on increases in the Consumer Price Index. (*See* section 3.4.3.) The last adjustment took effect on April 1, 2016, and the next will be on April 1, 2019. The figures used in this chapter are those promulgated in 2016.

of the debtor may do so, thereby safeguarding the exemptions. Rules 1007 and 4003(a) require the list of exemptions to be included with the schedule of assets, which must be filed with the petition or within 14 days after the order for relief. Under Rule 1009, the debtor is able to amend the claim of exemptions at any time up to the closing of the case.

A party in interest has the right to challenge the debtor's claim of exemptions. Rule 4003(b) requires objection to be filed within 30 days of the creditors' meeting. Rule 4003(c) places the burden on the objector to prove that the exemption is improperly claimed. Section 522(l) states that unless such an objection is made, the property is exempted as claimed. Therefore, if the trustee, U.S. Trustee, and creditors are not vigilant, the debtor could get away with an excessive exemption claim. In *Taylor v. Freeland & Kronz*, 503 U.S. 638 (1992), the Supreme Court held that if the trustee or a party in interest fails to file the objection within the 30-day period (or within such extended period as the court allows), the right to object is barred and the exemption stands, even if the debtor had no colorable basis for claiming it. In *Schwab v. Reilly*, 560 U.S. 770 (2010) the court clarified that its decision in *Taylor* applied only where, on the face of the claim of exemptions, the property does not qualify as exempt, either because there is no exemption for that type of property, the cited Code section does not support the exemption, or the debtor's statement of the value of the property exceeds the statutory limit. However, provided that on the face of the schedule, the property claimed as exempt and the asserted value of that property fall within a statutory exemption category, failure to object to the value assigned by the debtor to that property within the time set out in Rule 4003 does not bar a later challenge to its claimed value. The Court noted that an exemption covers only the debtor's interest in the property, not the property itself, so the trustee is not bound by the debtor's valuation if it turns out that the property is worth more than the debtor asserted.

It is unclear if a second 30-day objection period is created if the debtor converts the case from one chapter to another. Some courts have held that a second 30-day objection period arises after the creditors' meeting following conversion, while others hold that conversion does not create a second objection period.[5]

5. See, e.g., *In re Brown*, 375 B.R. 362 (Bankr. W.D. Mich. 2007), which discusses the conflicting case law and chooses the former approach.

§10.6 EXEMPTION PLANNING

§10.6.1 Prepetition Arrangements to Maximize Exemptions

The legislative history of §522 indicates that a debtor should be able to plan for bankruptcy and take advantage of available exemptions by selling nonexempt property and using the proceeds to buy exempt property before filing the petition. In light of this, courts have recognized that the prepetition conversion of nonexempt assets into exempt property is not per se wrongful. However, it can become wrongful if the debtor engages in fraudulent or dishonest conduct in the process of organizing his estate before filing to maximize exemptions. The line between permissible bankruptcy planning and dishonest behavior is not always easy to draw. This creates a hazard for the debtor's attorney, who must be careful about how she advises the debtor before the petition is filed. The attorney must inform the debtor of the permissible scope of prepetition planning while not encouraging or collaborating in dishonest dealings.

Courts take several factors into account to decide if prepetition planning has been legitimate. Some of the indicia of dishonesty and manipulation include the use of credit to acquire or enhance an interest in exempt property, the concealment of the activity, and other conduct designed to mislead creditors. In *In re McCabe*, 280 B.R. 841 (Bankr. N.D. Iowa 2002), the court found that in the absence of any of these indications of dishonesty, the debtor's prepetition acquisition of exempt property was permissible. (The debtor bought a valuable gun prior to filing his petition because he knew that Iowa exemption law provided for an unlimited firearm exemption, and he wished to take advantage of it.)

§10.6.2 The Sanctions for Fraudulent Prepetition Manipulation

Where a debtor has behaved dishonestly or fraudulently in the prebankruptcy period in manipulating his estate to maximize exemptions, the court has the power to sanction this conduct by dismissing or converting the case or denying the debtor a discharge. In addition, fraudulent conduct could result in the criminal prosecution of the debtor.

Courts had also assumed that they had the inherent power under §105(a) to deny the exemption on grounds of the debtor's bad faith conduct. However, in *Law v. Siegel*, 134 S.Ct. 1188 (2014) the Supreme Court indicated that courts do not have this power. The case did not involve exemption planning, but concerned a debtor who had created a sham mortgage on his house. The debtor's house, worth about $360,000 was subject to a genuine mortgage of about $150,000 and an exemption (under state law) of $75,000. The debtor had created this fictitious mortgage of about $150,000 to make it appear that the mortgages and his exemption covered the entire value of the house, so that there was no remaining equity in the house for the estate. When the trustee discovered that the mortgage was false, he sued the debtor to recover the unencumbered equity in the house and eventually obtained that judgment. In the process, the trustee had incurred legal costs of over $500,000 and the bankruptcy court granted the trustee's motion to surcharge the debtor's exemption to defray these costs. The Supreme Court held that the bankruptcy court had exceeded its powers in surcharging the exemption because the fees were administrative expenses which could not be charged against the exemption under §522(k). The Court stated that a bankruptcy court may only deny an exemption if there is a statutory basis for doing so, and that it has no general equitable power to refuse to honor an exemption on a ground not specified in the Code. Although *Law* involved the question of surcharging an exemption as a sanction for fraud in claiming the exemption, its pronouncement that a court may not deny an exemption on grounds other than those stated in the Code is much broader, and has been understood by lower courts to deprive them of the basis to sanction bad faith conduct (including improper conduct in the prepetition planning context) by disallowing an exemption.[6]

§10.7 THE IMPACT OF IMPROPER EXEMPTION PLANNING AND OTHER PREPETITION MISCONDUCT ON THE HOMESTEAD EXEMPTION

One of the most glaring abuses of prepetition exemption planning and manipulation of the nonuniform exemption system has related to the homestead exemption. Although BAPCPA did not go as far as the Commission recommended in tackling this problem by standardizing exemptions, it did enact new provisions in §522 designed to restrain the abuse. Section 522(d) and most state exemption statutes give the debtor a limited and often modest exemption in the value of her residence. For example, the homestead exemption in §522(d)(1) is in the amount of $23,675.[7] Many state

6. See, e.g., *In re Elliot*, 544 B.R. 421 (BAP 9th Cir. 2016) and *In re Baker*, 791 F.3d 677 (6th Cir. 2015).

7. This amount is subject to periodic adjustment under §104. This is the amount promulgated with effect from April 1, 2016. The amount will be adjusted again with effect from April 1, 2019. *See* section 3.4.3.

homestead exemptions are similarly of small amount in relation to the value of the home. This means that a debtor cannot claim the home as exempt in full; he is limited to a relatively small portion of his equity in the home. A few states have considerably larger homestead exemptions, and a handful provide for an unlimited homestead exemption—that is, the complete exemption of the debtor's equity in the home. This means that debtors in some states are treated far more generously than in others. It has also given some debtors the means to manipulate the system by shifting wealth into a homestead before they file bankruptcy. There have been cases in which a debtor who was domiciled in a state with a generous homestead exemption greatly enlarged his homestead exemption prior to filing by realizing all his nonexempt property and using the proceeds to buy a homestead or to pay down the mortgage on his existing homestead. This manipulation has not been confined to debtors who already live in a state with a generous or unlimited homestead exemption. There have been cases in which a debtor who lived in a state with a small or limited homestead exemption realized nonexempt assets, moved to a state with a generous or unlimited homestead exemption, and invested those proceeds in a home. Where the debtor was wealthy and the state had an unlimited homestead exemption, the homestead exemption created by this process could shelter millions of dollars from creditors.

Section 522(o), (p), and (q) create controls to curb these abuses of the homestead exemption. (In *Law*, the Supreme Court cited these provisions as examples of statutory limitations on exemptions arising from debtor misconduct.) These subsections are written in the mind-boggling form common to so many of the provisions in BAPCPA. In essence, they do not cap overly generous state homestead exemptions in most cases. However, they do provide for controls on high homestead exemptions in certain circumstances in which the debtor has behaved dishonestly or manipulatively. Remember, as discussed in section 10.3.2, that in addition to the controls in §522(o), (p), and (q), the domicile provisions of §522(b)(3) prevent the debtor from moving to a state on the eve of bankruptcy to take advantage of desirable exemptions (including a generous homestead exemption). The controls that are imposed on the homestead exemption under §522(o), (p), and (q) boil down to this:

Section 522(o) reduces the debtor's homestead exemption under state law to the extent that the value of the debtor's interest in the homestead is attributable to the disposition of nonexempt property in the ten years before the petition, with intent to hinder, delay, or defraud creditors. The basic idea is that if the debtor had sold nonexempt property in the ten years before bankruptcy and had invested the proceeds in exempt homestead property, the exemption will be reduced by the amount of that investment if intent to hinder, delay, or defraud creditors can be shown. It is not itself fraud for the debtor to realize nonexempt property and to use the proceeds to enlarge his exemptable equity in the homestead. For §522(o) to apply, the party challenging the debtor's exemption claim must show that this activity was for the purpose of hindering, delaying, or defrauding creditors. That is, that the debtor engaged in this activity with the intent to evade the payment of debt or to deceive and defraud creditors. Deception may be present, for example, where the debtor seeks to conceal transactions, makes misrepresentations to creditors, or realizes the nonexempt property well below its value. Because the language in §522(o) is the same as that used in §548 in relation to fraudulent transfers and in §727 in relation to denial of the discharge, the tests of fraudulent intent developed by the courts under those sections, including the use of badges of fraud, are applicable here.[8]

Section 522(p) limits the debtor's interest in a homestead exempted under state law to an amount of $160,375[9] if the debtor acquired the homestead within 1,215 days (about three years and four months) of the petition. The purpose of the section is to place a restriction on the kind of exemption planning in which a debtor buys an expensive home in a state with a high or unlimited homestead exemption. The application of the section is relatively clear where the debtor buys new property. However, it is less clear where the debtor newly establishes a homestead on property that he already owns. Section 522(p) applies to an "interest" that the debtor "acquired" during the 1,215-day period. In *In re Greene*, 583 F.3d 614 (9th Cir. 2009), the debtor had owned a parcel of undeveloped land for about ten years. About a year before he filed a Ch. 7 petition, he brought a trailer onto the property, began to live in it, and recorded a declaration of homestead with the county. In his Ch. 7 case, he claimed the full value of the land ($240,000) as exempt under the state homestead exemption. A creditor challenged the exemption and argued that even if the property was a homestead, the debtor had acquired the homestead within the 1,215-day period and should be confined to the limit in §522(p). The court conceded that §522(p) is ambiguous on the question of when the debtor acquires an exemptible interest, but it concluded that the acquisition of interest means when the debtor acquired ownership of the property, not when he began to use it as a homestead. The court distinguished a homestead claim, which is a personal right granted by statute, from an interest in property on which the exemption is dependent.

There are some exceptions to the limitation imposed by §522(p), the most notable of which is that it does not apply to the extent that proceeds of a prior home acquired before the 1,215-day period are transferred into the

8. See *In re Roberts*, 527 B.R. 461 (Bankr. N.D. Fla. 2015); *In re Anderson*, 386 B.R. 315 (Bankr. D. Kan. 2008), *aff'd* 406 B.R. 79 (D. Kan. 2009); and *In re Maronde*, 332 B.R. 593 (Bankr. D. Minn. 2005).

9. This is the amount in effect with effect from April 1, 2016. The amount will be adjusted again under §104 in 2019.

new home. *In re Summers*, 344 B.R. 108 (Bankr. N.D. Ariz. 2006), illustrates how §522(p) operates: The debtors were domiciled in Arizona, which has opted out of §522(d). The Arizona homestead exemption was $150,000. The debtors had bought a home worth $465,000 in the 1,215-day period. After deducting the amount owing on the home mortgage, the debtors had an equity of $210,000 in the home. Although Arizona law would have allowed an exemption of $150,000, the debtors would normally have been confined to an exemption of $125,000[10] under the limit imposed by §522(p). However, $54,000 of the purchase price of the house was proceeds from the sale of the debtor's previous homestead, so this amount could be added to the $125,000 limit under §522(p). This did not mean, however, that the debtors would have been entitled to an exemption of $179,000, because the state exemption of $150,000 was the upper limit of the amount of the exemption.

Section 522(q) caps the homestead exemption at $160,375[11] where the debtor has been guilty of certain kinds of misconduct. Section 522(q)(1)(A) confines the debtor's homestead exemption to $160,375 if the debtor has been convicted of a felony that, under the circumstances, demonstrates that the filing of the bankruptcy case was an abuse of the Code. Section 522(q)(1)(B) imposes that cap if the debtor owes a debt that arises from specified kinds of wrongful act, including fraud or deceit in a fiduciary capacity or any criminal act, intentional tort, or willful or reckless misconduct that caused serious physical injury or death. In *In re Larson*, 513 F.3d 325 (1st Cir. 2008), the court held that negligent vehicular homicide qualified as a criminal act that caps the homestead exemption under §522(q)(1)(B). The section does not require mens rea, nor does it have the prerequisite (as does §522(q)(1)(A) that the debtor has been convicted of the crime.

Subsections (p) and (q) begin with unfortunately chosen language. They are stated to apply where the debtor "as a result of electing under subsection (b)(3)(A)" exempts property under state or local law. The word "electing" suggests that the subsections only apply where the state has not opted out, because if the state has opted out, the debtor is bound by state exemptions and has no right to make any election. At least one court has given the language this literal interpretation.[12] The problem with this literal interpretation is that it renders §522(p) and (q) virtually useless because so few states allow for the election. Other courts have rejected this approach. They have found the language of the subsections to be ambiguous and have consulted legislative history, which indicates congressional intent to cap the

10. $125,000 was the dollar amount of the cap under §522(p) at the time of the case. (As indicated in the text, it is now higher.)

11. Again, as adjusted with effect from April 1, 2016.

12. See *In re McNabb*, 326 B.R. 785 (Bankr. D. Ariz. 2005).

exemption in all states in which state law has an exemption in excess of $160,375.[13]

§10.8 THE DEBTOR'S POWER TO AVOID CERTAIN INTERESTS THAT IMPAIR EXEMPTIONS

§10.8.1 General Scope and Purpose of the Debtor's Avoidance Power

As a general rule, a debtor's exemption in property does not avail against the holder of a valid consensual security interest in that property. By granting the interest, a debtor has effectively waived the right to assert the exemption against the consensual lienholder. Statutory liens, conferred by the legislature to protect persons who have enhanced or preserved the value of the property, are also usually immune from exemption claims. By contrast, an exemption normally does take precedence over a judicial lien that attaches to the property. Judicial liens are acquired by the very process of seizure or judgment against which exemptions are meant to protect the property.

The purpose of §522(f)(1)(A) is to give effect to the primacy of the debtor's exemptions over judicial liens, by empowering the debtor to avoid them to the extent that they impair her exemptions. Section 522(f)(1)(B) creates a limited exception to the general rule that exemptions cannot be used to avoid consensual security interests. It extends the debtor's avoidance power to nonpossessory, nonpurchase-money security interests in specific classes of exempt property. This exception reflects Congress's determination that these types of security interest are predatory and should not be permitted to undermine the debtor's exemptions.

§10.8.2 Judicial Liens

Section 522(f)(1)(A) allows the debtor to avoid a judicial lien in exempt property to the extent that the lien impairs an exemption to which the debtor would have been entitled in the absence of the lien. With an exception relating to domestic support obligations, §522(f)(1)(A) applies to all judicial liens, whether created by prejudgment proceedings, by recording of the judgment, or by postjudgment proceedings such as execution. Also, unlike §522(f)(1)(B), it applies to all types of exempt property.

---

13. See, e.g., *In re Kaplan*, 331 B.R. 483 (Bankr. S.D. Fla. 2005) and *In re Summers*, 344 B.R. 108 (Bankr. N.D. Ariz. 2006).

The exclusion of domestic support obligations (as defined in §101(14A)) from the debtor's avoidance power reflects a strong policy, manifested in a number of provisions enacted by the Bankruptcy Reform Act of 1994 and reinforced by BAPCPA, that a debtor should not be able to use bankruptcy to evade domestic support obligations. The protection of domestic support recipients is provided for in several provisions of the Code. For example, the enforcement of domestic support obligations is not subject to the automatic stay (see section 7.4.3), and these obligations are also given top priority over other unsecured claims and are nondischargeable (see sections 17.5.4 and 21.5.4). In the present context, §522(f)(1)(A) does not permit the debtor to avoid a judicial lien that enforces a domestic support obligation, even if that lien impairs an exemption to which the debtor would otherwise be entitled.

§10.8.3 Avoidable Nonpossessory, Nonpurchase-Money Security Interests

Section 522(f)(1)(B) creates a narrow exception to the general rule that consensual liens take priority over an exemption in the collateral: The debtor may avoid a nonpossessory, nonpurchase-money security interest in specified household or consumer goods, tools of trade, or professionally prescribed health aids to the extent that the security interest impairs an exemption in such property.[14] The scope of §522(f)(1)(B) is very limited. The security interest can be avoided only if all three requirements of the section are satisfied: The secured party must not have perfected the interest by taking possession of the collateral, the loan or credit must not have been provided to enable the debtor to acquire the collateral, and the impaired exemption must relate to one of the three types of property specified. Section 522(f)(1)(B) is aimed at a particular type of transaction under which a creditor secures the debt by filing a security interest in household goods or other necessities already owned by the debtor. In many cases, the property is likely to be worth more to the debtor than its realization value, so that the threat of foreclosure gives the creditor great power over the debtor. Congress was concerned about abuses in transactions of this type, which it

14. Section 522(f)(4) defines "household goods" for the purpose of §522(f)(1)(B). It contains a long list of what does and does not qualify as household goods. The definition is expressly for the purpose of §522(f)(1)(B), so its restrictions should not be applicable to the term as it is used in §522(d)(3). That is, although a particular item may be omitted from the list of household goods in §522(f)(1)(B), this does not necessarily mean that it does not qualify as a household good for the purpose of claiming an exemption for it under §522(d)(3).

regarded as manipulative and unethical. It therefore subordinated them to the debtor's exemption.

The Bankruptcy Reform Act of 1994 added §522(f)(3), a limited qualification to the debtor's power to avoid a nonpossessory, nonpurchase-money lien in tools of trade where state law exemptions apply and the state either has no monetary limit on the exemption or prohibits the avoidance of consensual liens on exempt property. The subsection is obscurely drafted and its purpose unclear. It imposes a dollar limit on the extent to which the debtor may avoid the lien, so its apparent effect is to limit the amount of the debtor's avoidance under these circumstances.

§10.8.4 Avoidance "to the Extent" of Impairment

Section 522(f) does not necessarily result in the total avoidance of the judicial liens and security interests covered by the subsection. It permits avoidance only to the extent necessary to preserve the exemption. Therefore, if the debtor's equity in the property exceeds the exemption, the lien or security interest remains a valid charge on the nonexempt portion of the equity. For example, assume that the debtor owns a piece of equipment used as a tool of trade. The value of the equipment is $3,000. The debtor's exemption under §522(d)(6) is $2,375.[15] If a judicial lien attached to the property securing a judgment of $1,000, it would impair the debtor's exemption to the extent of $375. (That is, if the judicial lien was allowed in full, the debtor's equity in the property would be reduced from $3,000 to $2,000, but the debtor's exemptible interest in the property is $2,375.) The lien can therefore be avoided to the extent of $375, so it becomes a secured claim for $625 and an unsecured claim of $375. Had the value of the collateral been $2,375 or less, the lien would have been avoided entirely, and had the collateral been worth $3,375 or more, it would not have been avoidable at all. *See* Example 1.

§10.8.5 A State Cannot Override the Avoidance Power in Its Opt-Out Statute

As explained in section 10.3, states have the power under §522(b) to enact legislation substituting nonbankruptcy exemptions for those provided in §522(d). In conferring this power on the states, §522(b) refers only to the substitution for exemptions listed in §522(d). It does not authorize states to override any other provisions of §522. In *Owen v. Owen*, 500 U.S.

15. This is the amount with effect from April 1, 2016. The amount will be adjusted again under §104 in 2019.

305 (1991) the Supreme Court held that the states' power to opt-out pertains only to the selection of exemptions under §522(d), and not to the federal remedy of lien avoidance provided in §522(f). Therefore, a state statute that gives a lien precedence over exemptions is ineffective to override the debtor's avoidance power under §522(f). The Court focused on the language of §522(f), which allows avoidance of the lien to the extent that it "impairs an exemption to which the debtor would have been entitled" under §522(b). The Court reasoned that the inquiry called for by this language is not whether the lien impairs an exemption to which the debtor is actually entitled under the state statute, but whether it impairs one to which the debtor would have been entitled if no lien existed. In *In re Cleaver*, 407 B.R. 354 (B.A.P. 8th Cir. 2009), the court, applying *Owen*, held that a lien on a tool of trade (a truck) could be avoided under §522(f) even though the state had opted out of the federal exemptions and had no tool of trade exemption. The court reasoned that avoidance of a lien on a tool of trade was permitted by the federal remedy of lien avoidance under §522(f), even if tools of trade were not included in the state's list of exemptions.

§10.8.6 How Impairment Is Measured

Although *Owen* set the basic meaning of "impairment," it did not resolve the question of how that impairment is measured. Congress attempted to provide some guidance on this issue in the Bankruptcy Reform Act of 1994 by adding §522(f)(2). Section 522(f)(2)(A) defines "impairment" by setting out an arithmetical formula. To find the amount of impairment:

1. Determine what the value of the debtor's interest in the property would be — that is, the full interest or equity that the debtor would have in the property — in the absence of liens. (When the debtor is the sole and absolute owner of the property, this is equivalent to the full value of the property.)
2. Add together:
   a. the lien to be avoided plus
   b. other liens on the property plus
   c. the amount of the debtor's exemption.
3. Compare 1 and 2. The exemption is impaired to the extent that 2 is greater than 1.

   Where there is more than one lien on the property, §522(f)(2)(B) makes it clear that once any lien is avoided, the avoided lien is not taken into account in calculating the total of "other liens" for the purpose of avoiding any remaining lien.

   The formula seems quite easy to work with in an uncomplicated case. However, it does raise some questions and present interpretational difficulties, under some circumstances. The following three examples show the basic operation of the formula in two easy cases and then in one more difficult one.

Example 1: One judicial lien

Say that a homestead worth $200,000 is subject to an exemption of $50,000. There is only one judicial lien of $180,000 on the property. The lien can be avoided to the extent that:

> *The total of*
> the amount of the lien itself ($180,000) plus
> other liens ($0) plus
> the exemption ($50,000)
> = $230,000
> *exceeds*
> the value that the debtor's interest would have in the property in the absence of liens ($200,000).

Therefore, the lien is avoided by $230,000 − $200,000 = $30,000. As a result, it remains a lien on the property to the extent of $150,000.

Example 2: Two judicial liens

Say that the same property is subject to two judgment liens, the senior is for $100,000 and the junior is for $80,000. Although §522(f)(2)(A) does not say so, the avoidance must be directed at the junior avoidable lien first. (If this were not so, the avoidance of the senior lien first would elevate the junior lien in priority, because under §522(f)(2)(B), the avoided senior lien would not be taken into account in that second avoidance action.) The calculation is therefore:

> *First, apply the calculation to the junior lien.*
> The total of
> the junior lien ($80,000) plus
> "all other liens"—the senior lien ($100,000)—plus
> the exemption ($50,000)
> = $230,000
> *exceeds*
> the debtor's equity interest ($200,000).

Therefore, the junior lien is avoided, by $230,000 − $200,000 = $30,000. As a result, it survives only to the extent of $50,000.

> *Next, apply the calculation to the senior lien.*
> The total of
> the senior lien ($100,000) plus

"all other liens"—the remaining unavoided portion of the junior lien ($50,000)—plus
the exemption ($50,000)
= $200,000.

This is exactly equal to the debtor's unencumbered equity, and it, therefore, does not impair the exemption at all and is unavoidable.

Example 3: A first mortgage, a judicial lien, and a second mortgage

Say that the homestead, worth $200,000 and subject to an exemption of $50,000, has three liens on it. The first is a consensual first mortgage of $70,000, perfected a year before bankruptcy. The second is a judgment lien of $80,000, recorded eight months before bankruptcy. The third is consensual second mortgage of $60,000, perfected six months before bankruptcy. If this was nonexempt property, the priority of the three interests would simply be based on the first-in-time rule. This would mean that the first mortgage would be entitled to full payment of $70,000, then the judgment lien would be entitled to full payment of $80,000. Finally, the second mortgage would be third in line. It would only be paid what is left of the value of the property, $50,000, and would have an unsecured deficiency of $10,000.

As the property is exempt, the debtor is able to use §522(f)(1)(A) to avoid the judicial lien, but not the consensual liens. (The consensual liens cannot be avoided under §522(f)(1)(B) because the homestead is not one of the exemptions protected by that subsection.) Therefore, the assumption that we made in the prior illustration, that the junior lien must be avoided first, cannot apply to the second mortgage. The avoidance is directed at the judgment lien only. The calculation is as follows:

The total of
the amount of the judgment lien ($80,000) plus
all other liens ($130,000) plus
the exemption ($50,000)
= $260,000
exceeds
the value that the debtor's interest would have in the property in the absence of liens ($200,000).

Therefore, the judicial lien is avoided to the extent of $60,000. It becomes a secured claim of $20,000 and an unsecured claim of $60,000. The twist here is that this does not mean merely that the debtor's exemption is preserved. It also has the effect of elevating the second mortgage above the judicial lien. That is, avoidance under §522(f)(1)(A) benefits not only the debtor, but also the unavoidable consensual lien that would otherwise be junior to the judicial lien. This can be seen if we set out the distribution of the proceeds of the property: first mortgage, $70,000; second mortgage, $60,000; exemption $50,000; unavoided portion of judgment lien, $20,000. On similar facts, the court in *In re Kolich*, 328 F.3d 406 (8th Cir. 2003), found this apparent anomaly to be a little unsettling, but nevertheless consistent with the intent of Congress in enacting the formula in §522(f)(2). The bankruptcy court had excluded the junior mortgage from the calculation, thereby holding that the judgment lien did not impair the exemption. The bankruptcy appellate panel (BAP) reversed, and the court of appeals affirmed the BAP. The court of appeals reasoned that Congress deliberately included "all other liens" in the impairment formula, so there was no justification, on the plain wording of the subsection, to disregard the junior mortgage. The holder of the judgment lien argued that the literal application of the formula gave a windfall to the junior mortgagee, but the court was not persuaded. It said that Congress could have drafted the formula to exclude junior consensual lines from the calculation, but did not. This demonstrates congressional intent to treat consensual liens more favorably, even if it means that avoidance of the judicial lien would have the effect of elevating their priority. Similarly, in *In re Brinley*, 403 F.3d 415 (6th Cir. 2005) *cert. denied*, 126 S. Ct. 1164 (2006), the court likewise avoided the second-priority judgment lien to the extent of its impairment of the exemption, even though this benefited a third-priority second mortgage.

§10.9 THE INDIVIDUAL DEBTOR'S REDEMPTION RIGHT IN CH. 7 CASES

Under §722, when property is subject to a lien that secures a dischargeable consumer debt, an individual debtor in a Ch. 7 liquidation may redeem the property from the lienholder. The property must be tangible personal property intended primarily for personal, family, or household use and it must have been either exempted or abandoned. As the above restrictions show, redemption is available only in narrow circumstances. Under §521(a)(2) the debtor must file a statement of intention within 30 days of the petition indicating whether or not the property will be redeemed. (This is one of the supporting documents filed with the petition, as described in section 6.3.) Section 521(a)(3) requires the redemption to be affected within 30 days of the first date set for the meeting of creditors unless the court grants additional time for cause.

By redeeming the collateral, the debtor in effect buys it from the secured creditor for the amount of the allowed secured claim. If the value of the collateral is equal to or exceeds the debt, the debt will be fully allowed as a secured claim provided that is valid and unavoidable. To redeem, the debtor must pay the claim in full. However, if the collateral is worth less than the debt (so that the creditor is undersecured), the allowed secured claim, and hence the redemption price, is limited to the value of the collateral.

Section 722 requires the property to be abandoned or exempt. Unless the lien is avoidable under §522(f), the existence of an exemption does not reduce the redemption price to be paid to the lienholder. As noted in section 10.8, exemptions do not avail against liens except to the extent provided in §522(f). The requirement of abandonment or exemption relates to the existence or extent of the estate's interest in the unencumbered equity in the property. If the collateral value is exactly equal to or less than the secured debt, the estate has no interest in the property, so it is likely to be abandoned, thereby allowing the debtor to redeem it by settling the secured claim. Similarly, if the property is worth more than the debt but the equity is fully exempt, the estate has no interest in it and redemption can be affected by paying the secured claim. However, if the equity exceeds the debtor's exemption, the estate does have an interest in the property, and redemption is not possible unless the debtor first pays out the estate's interest so that the trustee will abandon the property. Following abandonment, the debtor may redeem by paying the redemption price to the secured claimant. (Example 5 illustrates this point.)

Section 722 states that the debtor must pay the lienholder the amount of the allowed secured claim "in full at the time of redemption." This language was added to the section by BAPCPA to make it clear that the debtor must redeem in cash, and may not redeem by installments (as some courts had permitted prior to the amendment). This means that redemption is not practical for a debtor who has no means to raise the necessary cash after having filed bankruptcy. A debtor in that position cannot salvage encumbered property in a Ch. 7 case unless a reaffirmation agreement can be negotiated with the secured creditor.

The debtor's right to redeem is provided for only in Ch. 7 cases because redemption is not needed in Chs. 11 and 13. Under those chapters, the debtor is able to retain desired property upon confirmation of a plan providing for protection of the security interest and periodic payments on the debt. The rehabilitation process under Chs. 11 and 13 in fact permits the debtor to "redeem" collateral by installments under the plan. Therefore, a debtor who wishes to keep property, but cannot afford to redeem it for cash, has an incentive to choose rehabilitation rather than liquidation under Ch. 7. However, even in a Ch. 7 case, the debtor may have alternatives to redemption, as discussed in the next two sections.

§10.10 REAFFIRMATION

§10.10.1 The General Principles of Reaffirmation

A reaffirmation agreement is a contract between the debtor and a creditor under which the debtor agrees to pay a debt that would otherwise be discharged. Reaffirmation therefore diminishes the debtor's discharge, which is one of the important benefits of bankruptcy. For this reason, the Code adopts a cautious approach to the validation of reaffirmation agreements to ensure that the debtor understands the impact of the agreement, that it is in the debtor's interests, and has not been coerced or unfairly imposed by the creditor.

Reaffirmation agreements are included in §524, which deals generally with the effect of the debtor's discharge, and are governed by subsections (c), (d), (k), (l), and (m). These long and detailed subsections are intended to ensure that the debtor is fully informed about the effect of a reaffirmation agreement and to protect the debtor from an inappropriate reaffirmation. They include a lengthy standard disclosure that must be provided to the debtor by the creditor at or before the time of signing the agreement.[16]

§10.10.2 Why Would a Debtor Give Up the Right to Discharge the Debt by Reaffirming It?

Section 524 makes no express distinction between secured and unsecured debts, and both are capable of being reaffirmed if the requirements of the section are satisfied. However, as explained below, there is a very important practical difference between the reaffirmation of these two classes of debt which makes courts much more wary of approving the reaffirmation of unsecured debt.

(a) The Reaffirmation of Secured Debt as an Alternative to Redemption

Reaffirmation of secured debt is commonly used by a debtor to save the collateral from liquidation. As stated in section 10.9, redemption under §722 is available only in very narrow circumstances. If the property does not qualify for redemption or the debtor cannot find the cash to redeem, reaffirmation could be an alternative means of keeping collateral that would otherwise be liquidated in a Ch. 7 case. Because reaffirmation is consensual,

16. The length of these provisions was greatly increased by amendments enacted by BAPCPA, which expanded the disclosure and added other debtor protections.

the debtor cannot force the secured creditor to reaffirm. The debtor must negotiate with the secured creditor and must usually provide an incentive—some benefit beyond that expected from liquidation of the property—to persuade the creditor to assent. (*See* Example 7.) If the debtor intends to reaffirm a secured debt, the statement of intent under §521(a)(2) must so indicate, and the debtor must perform that intent within 30 days after the first date set for the meeting of creditors, unless the court has extended that period for cause.

Unlike redemption, reaffirmation is not confined to Ch. 7 cases. However, because Chs. 11 and 13 allow the debtor to retain property by providing for payments under a plan, the debtor does not need to use reaffirmation to keep property. In fact, if the debtor's primary goal is to prevent the liquidation of encumbered property, bankruptcy under Ch. 11 or 13 may be easier and less expensive than attempting to negotiate reaffirmation agreements in a Ch. 7 case.

(b) The Reaffirmation of Unsecured Debt

Where reaffirmation is used by a debtor as a means of keeping property that would otherwise be liquidated, the rationale for the reaffirmation is clear. However, there is less obvious advantage to a debtor who reaffirms an unsecured debt. There are various reasons why a debtor may wish to pay an unenforceable unsecured debt: for example, creditor pressure, the desire not to damage a relationship, the hope of future credit, or guilt. Where the reaffirmation does not give the debtor a clear economic benefit, the court should look even more carefully at the transaction to ensure that the requirements of §524 have been satisfied.

Reacting to abuse by large providers of consumer credit, which were found to have routinely bullied bankrupt customers into entering reaffirmation agreements, the majority report of the 1994 National Bankruptcy Review Commission recommended that reaffirmation should be confined to secured debt, and no longer permitted to the extent that a debt is unsecured. Congress did not adopt this recommendation in BAPCPA and decided, instead, to strengthen the creditor's disclosure requirements relating to reaffirmation and to provide for more rigorous enforcement to ensure that creditors follow them.

§10.10.3 The Creditor's Risk of Violating the Automatic Stay or the Discharge Injunction

Under §524(c)(1) a reaffirmation must be made before the debtor has been granted the discharge. During the time leading up to the discharge, all creditor action to collect the debt is stayed under §362 (discussed in Chapter 7). Therefore, a creditor that approaches the debtor before the grant of the discharge to propose a reaffirmation agreement runs a risk of violating the automatic stay. A creditor who seeks or executes a reaffirmation agreement after the debtor's discharge is not in compliance with the reaffirmation requirements of §524 and could incur sanctions for the violation of the discharge injunction (discussed in Chapter 21).

(a) The Automatic Stay

Sometimes the debtor may initiate negotiations for a reaffirmation agreement, and sometimes the creditor may be the party that first proposes reaffirmation to the debtor. A creditor who approaches the debtor to suggest reaffirmation takes the risk that the debtor will object to the overture and claim that the creditor has violated the stay. Courts generally do not consider a mere suggestion of reaffirmation to be a per se violation of the stay, and recognize that by providing for a reaffirmation process in §524, the Code must be somewhat tolerant of creditor-initiated proposals for a reaffirmation agreement. But if the creditor's conduct is overbearing, coercive, deceptive, or harassing, a court may well find that the creditor has overstepped the mark and is using §524 as a pretext for trying to evade the strictures of the stay. As discussed in section 7.7, this could render the creditor liable for costs, fees, and damages under §362(k) (formerly (h)) or for sanctions for contempt of court under §105(a). This distinction between legitimate negotiation and disregard for the stay is illustrated by *In re Estrada*, 439 B.R. 227 (Bankr. S.D. Fla. 2010); the court held that the creditor had violated the stay by intimating in a standard reaffirmation letter that the debtor could avoid the consequence of negative credit reporting by reaffirming. (The creditor escaped sanctions because the court was persuaded that the creditor had not intended to threaten the debtor and had since changed the wording of its standard reaffirmation letter.)

Where the debtor approaches the creditor to discuss reaffirmation, the creditor is not as much at risk of violating the stay. For example, in *In re Jamo*, 283 F.3d 392 (1st Cir. 2002), the debtor, not the creditor, initiated contact, offering to reaffirm a debt secured by a home mortgage. The creditor refused to enter a reaffirmation agreement for the mortgage debt unless the debtor also agreed to reaffirm some unsecured debts that the debtor owed to the creditor. The debtor claimed that this was a violation of the stay, but the court disagreed. It noted that reaffirmation is a contract, and the creditor can take advantage of its bargaining leverage and refuse to make the contract unless the debtor agrees to its terms. This is not a violation of the stay as long as the creditor does not engage in coercive or harassing conduct. Nevertheless, even where a debtor approaches the creditor to suggest a reaffirmation agreement, the creditor must be cautious not to overstep the border between reasonable negotiation and conduct that could be interpreted as an improper effort to collect debt in contravention of the stay.

b. The Discharge Injunction

Section 524(c)(1) confines reaffirmation to the predischarge period. Therefore, a creditor cannot execute a valid reaffirmation agreement after the debtor has been granted a discharge, and the agreement violates the discharge injunction provided for in §524(a). This is illustrated by *In re Sandburg Financial Corp.*, 446 B.R. 793 (S.D. Tex. 2011). The creditor had entered into a reaffirmation agreement with the Ch. 11 debtor. However, the agreement did not comply with §524 in that it was made after the discharge, did not contain the required disclosures, and was not filed with the court. The court found the reaffirmation agreement invalid and held that the creditor's attempt to enforce it was a willful violation of the discharge injunction. The court found the creditor in contempt and imposed a compensatory contempt sanction, awarding the debtor damages. The creditor had argued that it should not have had to comply with §524 because it had given the debtor new and independent consideration for entering into the agreement. Like other courts, the court held that the furnishing of new consideration does not excuse the creditor from complying with §524 where the agreement reaffirms a dischargeable debt.

§10.10.4 The Restrictions on Reaffirmation Agreements

Because the debtor's discharge is such an important consequence of bankruptcy, the Code places a number of restrictions on reaffirmation agreements. To be enforceable, the agreement must comply with the following conditions set out in §524(c) and (d). (Note that the restrictions in §524(c) and (d) apply only to reaffirmation agreements, that is, to contracts under which debtors undertake the obligation to pay the debts. Under §524(f), they do not apply when, instead of promising payment, the debtor actually makes a voluntary payment of the debt.)

1. The agreement is valid only to the extent that it is enforceable in nonbankruptcy law. At common law, the debtor's promise to pay a discharged debt does not require consideration because the original consideration given by the creditor creates a "moral obligation" sufficient to support the new promise. However, statutory or common law policing doctrines such as unconscionability, fraud, and duress may make the agreement avoidable under nonbankruptcy law.

2. The agreement must have been made before the discharge is granted and it must be filed with the court.
3. The debtor may rescind the agreement at any time before the discharge is granted, or within 60 days of the agreement having been filed in the court, whichever is the later. The agreement must conspicuously express this rescission right.
4. The creditor must provide the debtor with a disclosure statement containing the information set out in §524(k) at or before the time of signing the agreement.
5. If the debtor was represented by an attorney when the agreement was negotiated, the attorney must file a declaration with the agreement stating that the debtor's consent was informed and voluntary, that the agreement does not impose an undue hardship on the debtor or a dependent, and that the attorney fully advised the debtor of the legal effect and consequences of an agreement of that kind, and of default under it. Where a debtor is legally represented, her attorney may be in the awkward position of having to go against her wishes. The debtor may want to reaffirm, but the attorney cannot certify that the reaffirmation will not impose an undue hardship on the debtor. The attorney cannot simply give in to the debtor's wishes; she must conduct a proper assessment of her financial situation. If the attorney signs the certificate without justification, she could be sanctioned. For example, in *In re Vargas*, 257 B.R. 157 (Bankr. D.N.J. 2001), an attorney who failed to conduct a proper hardship evaluation was required to disgorge his fees. (Some courts may allow the attorney to withdraw where she feels that she cannot give the certificate, so the duty of vetting the agreement falls to the court.)[17]

   Section 524(m) creates a presumption of undue hardship where the scheduled payments on the debt exceed the debtor's disposable monthly income, as reflected in the debtor's financial data submitted in support of the reaffirmation. The debtor can rebut the presumption by showing additional sources of income. If the presumption does not apply and the other requirements of §524 are met, the agreement becomes effective as soon as it is filed with the court. However, if the presumption applies, the court must conduct a hearing on notice to determine the question of undue hardship.
6. If the debtor was unrepresented at the time of negotiating the agreement and is an individual, the agreement needs court approval that is granted only if the agreement does not impose undue hardship on the debtor or a dependent and is in the debtor's best interests. (This requirement of court approval does not apply to a "consumer debt

17. See, e.g., *In re Brown*, 95 B.R. 35 (Bankr. E.D. Va. 1989).

secured by real property" — that is, a mortgage reaffirmation on the debtor's home.) The court evaluates undue hardship and the best interests of the debtor only where the debtor is unrepresented or the presumption of undue hardship applies. Otherwise the attorney's declaration is sufficient.[18]

7. At the time for the individual debtor's discharge, the court may hold a discharge hearing at which the debtor must be present in person. If the debtor had not been represented by an attorney at the time of negotiating the agreement, the court must use the occasion of the discharge hearing to tell the debtor that the agreement is not required by law. The court must explain its effect and must determine whether or not the agreement satisfies all the requirements described above. Section 524(d) makes it clear that this procedure is not to be followed if the debtor was legally represented in entering the agreement.

§10.11 THE CH. 7 DEBTOR'S RETENTION OF THE COLLATERAL UNDER THE ORIGINAL CONTRACT — THE "RIDE-THROUGH"

As noted earlier, §521(a)(2) requires the debtor to file a statement of intention concerning the retention or surrender of property securing a consumer debt, and to state whether redemption or reaffirmation will be sought. Section 521(a)(2) expressly provides only for surrender, redemption, or reaffirmation. However, some (but not all) courts have recognized an additional way for a debtor to keep property subject to a security interest. If the debtor has not defaulted on payments on the secured debt, some courts have allowed the debtor to retain the collateral while continuing to pay installments to the secured party as required by the contract. This is known as a "ride-through" because the secured transaction rides through the bankruptcy without being formally administered and dealt with as part of the estate. Where a court permits the ride-through the creditor must allow the debtor to keep the collateral as long as she remains current on the payments required by the contract. If the debtor later defaults, the creditor can foreclose on the collateral, but any deficiency would be discharged. (That is, although the creditor can enforce the security interest by foreclosing on the debt upon default, the debtor is not be liable to the creditor for any deficiency.)

Section 521(a)(6), enacted by BAPCPA, prohibits the ride-through under certain circumstances. The section states that in a Ch. 7 case, an individual debtor shall not retain personal property as to which a creditor

18. See *In re Morton*, 410 B.R. 556 (B.A.P. 9th Cir. 2009).

has a secured claim for its purchase price unless the debtor has entered into a reaffirmation agreement or has redeemed the property. Section 521(a)(6) therefore makes it clear that redemption for cash or reaffirmation are the only courses available to an individual debtor, and the ride-through is not a permissible alternative in situations covered by the section: the case must be under Ch. 7, the debtor must be an individual, the property securing the debt must be personal property, and the creditor's interest must secure the purchase price of the collateral (that is, it must be a purchase money interest). Because the section focuses only on situations in which all those elements are satisfied, some courts have held that the ride-through is still allowed in other cases. For example, in *In re Hart*, 402 B.R. 78 (Bankr. D. Del. 2009), the court allowed a ride-through in relation to real property.

Where §521(a)(6) applies and the ride-through is not permitted, the debtor can retain the collateral only by making a timely election under §521(a) to redeem or reaffirm and following through with a timely exercise of that intention. If he does not, §362(h) terminates the automatic stay with regard to the property that secures the claim and removes it from the estate so that the creditor can proceed to foreclose on it.[19] In one specific situation—where the debtor had entered into a reaffirmation agreement, but the court refused to approve it—some courts have made an exception to this result and have allowed the debtor to use the ride-through even though the elements of §521(a)(6) are satisfied.[20]

Examples

EXAMPLES

The Examples involving exemptions are based on the list of exempt property in §522(d). The federal exemptions provided in §522(d) are used for convenience and illustrative purposes even though, in most cases, state law exemptions substitute for those in §522(d), either because the state has opted out under §522(b) or the debtor elects state law exemptions. This does not matter for present purposes because the Examples based on that section raise principles applicable to exemption issues generally. The Examples use the exemption amounts in §522(d), as adjusted under §104 with effect from April 1, 2016. The amounts will be adjusted again with effect from April 1, 2019.

1. Melody is a composer by profession. She has managed to sell some of her musical compositions, but she has struggled for recognition in the world

19. Section 362(h) permits the trustee to retain the property in the estate and to forestall foreclosure by showing that the property is of consequential benefit or value to the estate. If this is established, the court must order the debtor to deliver the property to the trustee, and the creditor is entitled to adequate protection.

20. See, e.g., *In re Dumont*, 581 F.3d 1104 (9th Cir. 2009); *In re Baker*, 400 B.R. 136 (D. Del. 2009); and *In re Moustafi*, 371 B.R. 434 (Bankr. D. Ariz. 2007).

of music. She lives in a cold rented garret and owns no property of value except for a concert grand piano on which she composes. Despite her poor credit rating, Melody was able to procure a loan of $5,000 from Fleshpound Finance Co., secured by a security interest in the piano. The security interest was properly perfected under state law.

About a year later, Melody filed a Ch. 7 petition. At the time of the filing, the balance of the loan is $3,500. The piano is worth $6,000. Can Melody avoid the security interest under §522(f)?

2. An individual Ch. 7 debtor owns a small house valued at $250,000, subject to a security interest of $240,000. She earns her living by housesitting for people when they travel. She usually has about ten housesitting jobs a year, which means that she lives in other people's homes for a total of about 30 weeks in a year. When she is not housesitting, she lives in her own house. Is the debtor entitled to an exemption in the house? If so, how much can she exempt? What would her exemption be if the house was not subject to a mortgage?

3. The value of the house was given in Example 2. It is the prerogative of law professors to fabricate convenient facts. Courts are not supposed to exercise the same creativity with regard to fact-finding. How would the value of the debtor's home be decided in a bankruptcy case?

4. The property in the Ch. 7 estate of Earnest Everyman is valued at $52,000. It consists of the following assets: Earnest's equity of $30,000 in his home; furniture, appliances, household goods, and personal effects, with a total value of $16,000 (none of these items is worth over $600); a car worth $4,000; and carpentry tools worth $2,000, used by Earnest in his job.

   Aston Martin, another Ch. 7 debtor, loves old cars. Instead of buying a house, furniture, and other items of ordinary personal property, he has chosen to live modestly in a cheap furnished apartment. He has used all his savings to buy a vintage sports car worth $48,000. As a result, his Ch. 7 estate consists of household and personal effects worth $4,000 (none of these items is worth over $600) and the car.

   What is the maximum that each of these debtors can exempt under §522(d)? What does the comparison of their exemptions say about the emphasis, underlying policy, and possible inequity of the Code's exemption scheme?

5. Given the answer to Example 4, should Aston have sold his sports car before filing his bankruptcy petition and used the proceeds to buy property that qualifies as exempt?

6. One of the assets in the Ch. 7 estate of Eva Porate is a diamond ring. About a year before bankruptcy, Eva had obtained a loan from Unrequited Loan

Co. to buy the ring and had granted Unrequited Loan Co. a valid security interest in the diamond ring to secure the loan.

At the time of bankruptcy, the balance of the loan is $5,000. The ring is valued at $6,500. Eva would like to redeem the ring. Can she do so? How does the answer change if the ring is valued at $4,500 or $7,000?

7. As in Example 6, the ring is worth $6,500 and the balance of the debt, secured by Unrequited's valid and unavoidable security interest, is $5,000. Assume that Eva would be entitled to redeem the ring, but cannot raise the cash needed to do so. Eva wishes to enter into a reaffirmation agreement with Unrequited Loan Co. under which she will repay the debt in installments and keep the ring.

   Eva's salary is just sufficient to support herself and a minor child. If she scrimps very hard and forgoes a few meals a week, she can put aside $200 per month to pay Unrequited Loan Co. This is $75 less per month than she was obliged to pay under the original security agreement, so she needs an extension of time to pay off the debt. Eva is willing to pay interest at the rate fixed in the original contract, and Unrequited would retain its security interest. Is Eva able to use the reaffirmation process to keep the ring?

8. Another of Eva Porate's debts was an amount of $5,000 owed on a credit card. After the issuer of the card received notice of Eva's bankruptcy filing, it wrote a letter to her in which it noted the outstanding balance on the card and stated, "We realize that you have the right to discharge this debt in your bankruptcy case. However, before you do this, we urge you to bear in mind that bankruptcy can have a serious impact on your ability to obtain credit in the future. We therefore invite you to consider entering into the attached reaffirmation agreement. If you elect to make this agreement and you repay the outstanding balance due to us in installments as reflected therein, we will reinstate your credit card with your former credit limit. Please discuss this with your attorney, who will explain the procedure you must follow to reaffirm this debt." Has the credit card issuer done anything wrong in sending this letter?

Explanations

1. The piano should qualify as a tool of trade in which Melody may claim an exemption of $2,375 under §522(d)(6). Property qualifies as a tool of trade if it is used by the debtor to earn her livelihood. Although Melody uses the piano to compose, and not to perform, she is a composer by profession and needs the piano to do her work, from which she is trying to earn a living. Compare *In re Gregory*, 245 B.R. 171 (B.A.P. 10th Cir. 2000), in which the court refused to allow the debtor, a security guard, to claim a pistol as a tool of trade. The debtor argued that he used the

pistol for practice, but the debtor's employer supplied a pistol that the debtor used on the job, and the employer did not require him to have another pistol for practice. Although some courts have questioned whether expensive equipment should qualify as a tool or implement of trade and have interpreted the exemption to apply only to small hand implements or devices of modest value, most courts do not adopt such a restrictive approach.

Fleshpound's security interest in the piano is a nonpossessory, nonpurchase-money interest, and tools of trade are one of the three categories of property covered by the avoidance provisions of §522(f)(1)(B). Melody can avoid the security interest to the extent that it impairs her exemption. If only the tools of trade exemption in §522(d)(6) is used, the lien cannot be avoided. That exemption is limited to $2,375, and she has a $2,500 equity in the piano beyond the amount of the security interest. Thus, the interest does not impair the exemption, which can be fully paid out of the equity with a surplus over for the estate.

However, §522(f) states that the security interest can be avoided to the extent that it "impairs an exemption to which the debtor would have been entitled" in a tool of trade. It does not say that the exemption is confined to the amount allowed for a tool of trade under §522(a)(6). A debtor is able to apply the general exemption in §522(a)(5) to property that is otherwise nonexempt, or to augment an existing exemption. If Melody applies the general exemption to the piano, she will be able to exempt its full value, because the general exemption is $1,250, plus up to $11,850 of the unused homestead exemption, which is available to Melody because she does not own a home. In *In re McNutt*, 87 B.R. 84 (B.A.P. 9th Cir. 1988), the court allowed the debtor to apply the general exemption to a tool of trade to increase the extent of avoidance under §522(f). If Melody is able to avoid the security interest in its entirety, she will be able to keep the piano, and Fleshpound will be left with a general unsecured claim.

2. The debtor may claim the homestead exemption under §522(d)(1), provided that the debtor or a dependent uses the property as a residence. The value of the exemption is $23,675. (A debtor is able to increase it to $24,925 by adding the $1,250 general exemption provided for in §522(d)(5). Assume for the sake of this question that the debtor has used the general exemption for another asset, so the amount of the homestead exemption is $23,675.)

   The general rule is that the debtor's temporary absence from the homestead, with a specific intent to return, does not prevent the debtor from claiming the exemption. Although the debtor's absences do add up to more than half a year, they are temporary and the debtor does always return to her home, which is her permanent abode.

This property, worth $250,000, is subject to a mortgage of $240,000, so the debtor's equity in the home is worth only $10,000. The debtor's exemption is subordinate to a valid consensual security interest in the property.[21] By granting the mortgage, the debtor is taken to have waived the exemption as against the mortgagee. This is recognized by §522(c)(2).

Therefore, the debtor may claim an exemption in the house to the extent of the equity of $10,000. However, the debtor does not necessarily lose the full unused balance of the homestead exemption. The unused portion of her homestead exemption is $13,675. Section 522(d)(5) allows her to add to the general exemption up to $11,850 of this amount to her general exemption, which can be applied to exempt any other property.

The trustee will abandon the house because the mortgage and the exemption consume the entire value of the house, leaving no value in it for the estate. (Had the mortgage on the house been, say, $200,000, the debtor would have had a $50,000 equity in the house. After the mortgage debt had been paid, the debtor would have been entitled to claim the full amount of the $23,675 exemption, and the balance of $26,325 would be paid to the estate.)

3. Section 522(a)(2) defines value for the purposes of §522 as the fair market value of the property at the date of the petition, or when property enters the estate after the petition, at the date that the estate acquires the property. The determination of fair market value is a factual issue to be decided on all the available evidence. This can in itself be a difficult question to resolve. (Some of the difficulties in valuing property are discussed in relation to relief from stay in section 8.4.2 and in Examples 1 and 2 of Chapter 8.)

   In addition, courts have had difficulty in interpreting what is meant by fair market value in the bankruptcy context. If the facts suggest that the property will not be sold on the open market but will be liquidated, the use of market value results in artificially high appraisal. The impact of an unrealistic appraisal could be to the advantage or disadvantage of the debtor, depending on the facts. For example, in some cases a high valuation could harm the debtor by leading to the conclusion that the equity in the property exceeds the debtor's exemption. In other cases, a low valuation could make it appear that the debtor has no equity over a security interest, so that the property is abandoned to the secured

21. Section 522(f) clearly does not apply to this mortgage, so there is no basis for the debtor to use that section to avoid it.

claimant, or an application for relief from stay is granted. For this reason, some courts have been influenced by liquidation value where this has seemed more realistic, in spite of the reference to market value in §522(a)(2).

4. Each of the estates is worth $52,000, yet Earnest's exemptions are greater than Aston's. Earnest can claim exemptions in a total amount of $43,325, made up as follows:
   a. Homestead under §522(d)(1), limited to $23,675.
   b. Household goods and personal effects under §522(d)(3) to a maximum aggregate value of $12,625. (Because no item is worth more than §600, this amount is not reduced by the cap on individual item value in §522(d)(3).)
   c. Motor vehicle under §522(d)(2), limited to $3,775.
   d. Tools of trade under §522(d)(6). He can claim the full $2,000 value because it is under the cap of $2,375.
   e. General exemption of $1,250 under §522(d)(5), to be applied to nonexempt property or to enhance an existing exemption category.

   Aston's total exemptions are $20,875. He can exempt all his personal and household goods. Their total value is $4,000, which is under the $12,625 cap, and no item is worth more than $600. He can partially exempt the sports car to the extent of $16,875 by adding together his motor vehicle exemption of $3,775 under §522(d)(2) and his wildcard exemption under §522(d)(5). Because Aston does not claim a homestead exemption, the wildcard is $13,100 ($1,250 plus $11,850 not used for the homestead exemption).

   The advantage of specifying exemption categories with dollar limits is that the legislature can control exemptions and confine them to property and amounts that the legislature deems essential to the debtor's reasonable needs. The drawback of this approach is that it can result in groundless discrimination between debtors whose needs and interests vary from the generalized preconception of the legislature. The problem of unequal treatment can be avoided by allowing debtors to choose any property to exempt, up to a maximum lump sum amount. Congress declined to follow the recommendation of the 1994 National Bankruptcy Review Commission to make this change.

5. As noted in section 10.6, courts, relying on the legislative history of §522, have been willing to countenance the prepetition conversion of nonexempt assets into exempt property provided that the conversion does not constitute bad faith. A debtor's ability to engage in prepetition exemption planning mitigates the concern about the unequal treatment of debtors raised in Explanation 4. Provided that Aston simply makes the conversion by selling the car at market value and reinvesting the proceeds

in exempt property, his conversion is likely to be permissible. However, if he goes beyond that and engages is deceptive or manipulative transactions (for example, if he uses credit to buy or increase the value of exempt property) he could be sanctioned, such as by denial of a discharge.[22]

6. The ring can be redeemed only if all the requirements of §722 are satisfied: Eva must be an individual (she is), the ring must be tangible personal property (it is), the ring must be intended primarily for personal use (it is), the debt must be a consumer debt, incurred to buy the ring (it is), the debt must be dischargeable (it is),[23] and the property must be exempt or abandoned. The satisfaction of this last requirement varies depending on the value of the ring.

   The ring is worth $6,500: Unrequited's claim of $5,000 is fully secured with a surplus of $1,500 (less any costs and additional interest) that constitutes the debtor's equity in the property. The equity is exemptable by Eva under §522(d)(4), which provides for a $1,600 exemption in jewelry held for personal, family, or household use. Provided that Eva has claimed the ring as exempt, she may redeem the ring by paying Unrequited the amount of its secured claim of $5,000. The redemption price must be paid in cash. Eva may not redeem by installments. (She also cannot reduce the secured claim below $5,000 by avoiding it under §522(f) because it is a purchase money interest.)

   The ring is worth $4,500: The ring is worth $500 less than the loan, Unrequited is undersecured. Eva has no exemption in the ring because Unrequited's unavoidable security interest takes priority over her exemption. However, even though the ring is not exempt, the trustee will abandon it because there is no value in it for the estate. As a result, the last requirement is satisfied in this situation too. Section 722 permits redemption by payment of the secured claim, the value of the collateral sets the upper limit on the redemption price. Eva can therefore redeem by paying Unrequited $4,500. She does not need to pay it the full amount of the $5,000 debt.

22. Had the exempt property been a homestead, the basis for policing the conversion for impropriety would have been governed by §522(o). It reduces the amount of the debtor's homestead exemption to the extent that, with intent to hinder, delay, or defraud creditors, the debtor acquired or increased an exempt homestead interest in the ten years before the petition by converting nonexempt property.

23. Discharge is discussed in Chapter 21. Under certain circumstances, detailed in that chapter, a debt may be excluded from the discharge. Assume that none of those circumstances are applicable on the facts of this case.

The ring is worth $7,000: The redemption price is set at the amount of the debt ($5,000) as in the first example. However, unlike in the first example, the debtor's equity of $2,000 exceeds the $1,600 exemption. The estate has a $400 interest in the property, so that it is not fully exempt and will not be abandoned by the trustee. To satisfy the requirements of §722 and effect redemption, Eva must pay the estate $400 so that the trustee will abandon the property. This means that Eva must be able to raise $5,400 in cash to redeem the property.

7. Reaffirmation is a consensual arrangement, and Unrequited will likely not have much incentive to agree to enter a reaffirmation agreement if immediate liquidation would fully settle its claim. Because the collateral is worth $6,500, Unrequited's secured claim will be settled in full upon impending liquidation of the property with a surplus of $1,500 (less costs and any additional interest). For this reason, Eva may not be able to persuade Unrequited to forgo immediate liquidation in exchange for a promise of extended payments from a debtor who will struggle to make payments.

   Had the value of the ring been less than the debt, Eva would have been in a better bargaining position because she could have offered to reaffirm the debt in full. The creditor would have an incentive to agree because in the absence of reaffirmation, the deficiency is an unsecured claim that would most likely receive partial payment, at best, from the estate, with the balance being discharged. This, combined with other factors (such as an attractive interest rate and a likelihood that the ring would not depreciate in value over the term of payment so that later foreclosure will not result in loss), could outweigh the risk of default under the reaffirmation agreement.

   Even if Unrequited could be persuaded to enter into a reaffirmation agreement, the provisions of §524(c) and (d) must be satisfied. These restrictions are intended to protect the debtor from the coerced or uninformed assumption of liability for a discharged debt. In addition to imposing requirements to ensure that the debtor acted voluntarily and was fully informed in entering into the reaffirmation, §524 requires an impartial review of the agreement. If Eva was represented by an attorney when negotiating the reaffirmation, the attorney must certify that the agreement is informed and voluntary and that it does not impose an undue hardship on her or her dependent. If Eva was not legally represented when negotiating the reaffirmation, the court cannot approve the agreement unless it is satisfied that it is in the debtor's best interests and does not impose an undue hardship on her or her dependent.

   Reaffirmation agreements under which the debtor receives some advantage, such as the right to retain property that would otherwise be liquidated, are generally regarded as more justifiable than those that merely reaffirm unsecured debts. However, the facts indicate that Eva cannot afford the reaffirmation and that the proposed payments will impose a strain on her household budget. The ring is not a necessity, and Eva's efforts to keep it seem irresponsible. If Eva is legally represented, her attorney would be hard-pressed to certify the reaffirmation as not imposing an undue hardship on her and her child. If she is not legally represented, the court would have similar difficulty and would in addition be likely to find that the agreement does not serve her best interests.

Where a debtor cannot use redemption or reaffirmation to keep property in a Ch. 7 case, Ch. 13 may be an alternative if the debtor can afford to pay under a Ch. 13 plan. Ch. 13 enables a debtor to force creditors to allow her to retain property and to accept payment of the debt by installments.

8. As discussed in section 10.10, a creditor who approaches the debtor to propose reaffirmation takes the risk that its action may be construed as an attempt to recover a claim against the debtor in willful violation of the automatic stay. (§362(a)(6).)

   Most courts will not find a violation of the stay if the creditor's proposal for reaffirmation is not aggressive, coercive, or harassing. Also, it is wiser for the creditor to make the approach through the debtor's attorney, and to make sure that the debtor is fully informed about the nature and effect of the reaffirmation. Any deception or nondisclosure could cause problems for the creditor. Although the distinction between an incentive and a threat can be quite subtle, the letter in Eva's case may not overstep the mark and violate the stay. The warning of a bad credit rating could be construed as vaguely threatening, but it does not seem strong enough to be coercive. It does not really indicate that this creditor would take any action adverse to the debtor if the offer is refused. Further, as the creditor would have no obligation to extend credit to the debtor in the future, the hint that it may not do so unless the debtor reaffirms is not properly regarded as a threat.

CHAPTER 11

The Trustee's Avoidance Powers: General Principles and Policies

§11.1 OVERVIEW

The Bankruptcy Code's avoidance powers enable the trustee to set aside certain transactions entered into by the debtor prior to the filing of the bankruptcy petition. The avoidance powers are aimed primarily at transfers of property by the debtor, but some are also applicable to obligations assumed by the debtor.[1] Section 101(54) defines "transfer" to include every mode of disposing of property or an interest in it. A transfer may be voluntary or involuntary, direct or indirect, or absolute or conditional. It may be an outright disposition of property, such as a sale or a gift, or the grant of a lien or security interest, or other interest in it. The term is intended to be defined expansively.[2]

The avoidance of prepetition transfers and obligations is part of the trustee's function of collecting estate property and maximizing the estate's value. The discussion of property of the estate in Chapter 9 expresses the general rule that property enters the estate only to the extent that the debtor has an interest in it, as determined under nonbankruptcy law. The trustee's avoidance rights qualify that general rule by enabling the trustee to avoid

1. All of the Code's avoidance provisions relate to the prepetition period except for §549, which is concerned with postpetition transactions.
2. See *Barnhill v. Johnson*, 503 U.S. 393, 400 (1992) and *In re Whitley*, 848 F.3d 205, 208 (4th Cir. 2017).

transactions and recover property that the debtor had no right to reverse or recover under nonbankruptcy law.

Some of the trustee's avoidance rights are unique to bankruptcy law while others have counterparts that may be used by a creditor outside of a bankruptcy proceeding. The trustee's array of avoidance rights, both created by the Code and derived from principles of nonbankruptcy law, place the trustee in a much stronger position than any creditor could occupy outside of bankruptcy.

This chapter 1) offers a general introduction to the bankruptcy trustees' avoidance powers, 2) outlines some procedural issues and common themes, and 3) explains the rationale supporting each power. Chapters 12, 13, and 14 present a more thorough exploration of the avoidance powers.

§11.2 THE STRUCTURE OF THE AVOIDANCE PROVISIONS

Before discussing the trustee's avoidance powers, it is helpful to identify the Code sections that delineate these powers and describe their functions.

1. Sections 544, 545, 547, 548, and 553 allow a trustee to avoid a variety of prepetition transactions. These sections prescribe the specific transactions that are avoidable and prerequisites for avoidance.
    a. Section 544 allows the trustee to avoid transfers and obligations that could have been avoided under nonbankruptcy law by an actual unsecured creditor or by specified hypothetical claimants. For example, imagine that Company, Inc. gave its local bank a security interest in its manufacturing equipment in exchange for a $100,000 loan. Unfortunately, the bank's counsel forgot to perfect the security interest. Company, Inc. is forced to file a Chapter 11 petition two months later and manages its case as the debtor in possession. In bankruptcy, Company, Inc. could rely on §544 and avoid the bank's security interest in the manufacturing equipment. This is a devastating result for the bank. Company, Inc. would still owe the bank any unpaid portion of its loan, but the bank would be a general unsecured creditor facing a fractional payment.
    b. Section 545 gives the trustee limited power to avoid certain kinds of statutory liens. For example, state laws provide repairers of goods and various other service providers statutory liens upon the items they repair in the event of nonpayment. In most cases,

these liens are not effective against third parties unless the service provider takes the additional step of filing a lien notice or otherwise perfecting the lien. Section 545 allows a trustee to avoid such a lien if—under applicable state law—the lien would not be enforceable against a bona fide purchaser, regardless of whether such a purchaser exists.

c. Section 547 allows the trustee to avoid preferential transfers that occurred within 90 days (or in the case of insiders, within one year) before the petition. For example, imagine that Company, Inc. has $10,000 in available cash but owes $10,000 to each of five unsecured suppliers. Company, Inc. has no other creditors. Company Inc.'s president decides to pay $10,000 to the supplier owned by his brother, and Company, Inc. files a Ch. 7 petition the next month. In bankruptcy, the other four suppliers expect to receive a fraction of what they are owed. Section 547 allows the trustee of Company, Inc.'s bankruptcy case to avoid the $10,000 prepetition payment as a preference. The funds would become part of the bankruptcy estate, and all five suppliers could share equally in that recovery.

d. Section 548 gives the trustee the power, similar to that available to creditors under state fraudulent transfer law, to avoid fraudulent transfers and obligations that occurred within a year before the petition. For example, imagine that Debtor is financially insolvent. He senses that his creditors are going to attempt to seize the valuable assets he owns. He decides to sell his car to his best friend for $20,000, even though he bought the car just last year for $100,000. A trustee in Debtor's subsequent bankruptcy case could rely on §548 and attempt to avoid the sale, recovering the car for the benefit of the estate.

e. Section 553 allows the trustee to avoid setoffs to the extent they involve disallowed claims or arise out of certain transactions within 90 days prior to the petition. For example, imagine that two months ago Company, Inc. owed its primary supplier $10,000 for supplies. At that time, the supplier owed Company, Inc. $2,500 for some consulting services. Sixty days later, Company, Inc. still owed its supplier $10,000, but the supplier had received additional services and owed Company, Inc. $7,500. The supplier effectuated a setoff and reduced the amount Company, Inc. owed to $2,500. Company, Inc. filed a Ch. 7 petition the next month. Section 553 would allow the bankruptcy trustee in Company, Inc.'s case to avoid the setoff and recover $5,000 from the supplier because, during the 90-day period prior to the bankruptcy filing, the supplier improved its position by $5,000.

2. Section 552 is not technically an avoidance provision, but it does have the effect of partially avoiding floating liens[3] that attempt to cover collateral acquired postpetition. Under §552, a security interest in after-acquired property is confined to such collateral acquired up to the time of bankruptcy and proceeds of that collateral. The interest does not attach to property acquired by the estate or the debtor after the petition is filed. For example, imagine that Company, Inc. secures a loan from its local bank and gives the bank a floating lien on all of Company, Inc.'s inventory of stuffed animals. The lending agreement has an after-acquired property clause that extends the bank's floating lien to future inventory that Company, Inc. acquires. Company, Inc. encounters some financial distress and files a Ch. 11 petition. After filing, the bankruptcy court allows Company, Inc. to use some of the unencumbered funds in its bank account to purchase additional inventory for the upcoming holiday season. Section 552 would negate any attempt by the bank to assert that its lien extends to this new inventory.
3. Although it is also not an avoidance power in the same sense as the others, §558 should be included in this list. It allows the trustee to succeed to any defense that the debtor may have against any entity. Hence, if the debtor has an avoidance right under nonbankruptcy law (e.g., the right to rescind a transfer on grounds of the transferee's fraud), the trustee may exercise that right for the benefit of the estate.
4. Section 549 permits the trustee to avoid unauthorized postpetition transfers. For example, imagine that Debtor transferred all of her membership interest in a limited liability company to her mother shortly after filing a Ch. 7 petition. Section 549 would permit the trustee in bankruptcy to avoid this transfer and recover the interest for the estate's benefit.
5. Section 546 imposes limitations on the avoidance powers. It contains a statute of limitations and also subjects the trustee's avoidance rights to provisions of nonbankruptcy law that confer protection on certain transferees in specified transactions.
6. Sections 550 and 551 govern the effect of avoidance. Section 551 allows the estate to take over the rights the defeated transferee had in estate property to ensure that the avoidance benefits the estate rather than the holders of junior interests in the property. Section 550 provides for the recovery of property by the estate following avoidance of the transfer. Section 502(d) adds further force to the obligation to surrender property by providing for the disallowance of the claim of a transferee who fails to turn over property to the estate.

---

3. This type of transaction is explained in section 1.4.3 and Example 3 of Chapter 1.

The provisions discussed in this section are concerned with the trustee's avoidance power. Remember, however, that the debtor has the right under §522(f) to avoid certain liens that impair exemptions. (*See* section 10.8.) Further, this list of relevant statutory provisions would be incomplete without a reminder that §101 must be consulted for the definition of many terms used in the avoidance sections.

§11.3 APPLICABILITY OF THE AVOIDANCE POWERS IN LIQUIDATION AND REHABILITATION CASES

The avoidance powers are applicable in all cases under the Code, whether filed under Chs. 7, 11, or 13. However, they have a somewhat different effect in rehabilitation and liquidation cases. In a case under Ch. 7 the trustee's exercise of the avoidance powers directly benefits the creditor body. Recovered property swells the value of the fund to be distributed, and the avoidance of encumbrances and obligations adjusts the share in the fund by eliminating claims against the estate or demoting claims from secured to unsecured status.

In cases under Chs. 11 and 13, the link between the creditors' interest and the avoidance power is not as direct, because much (if not all) of the estate property ultimately reverts to the debtor. Therefore, the debtor may be the principal beneficiary of avoidance actions. The advantage to creditors from avoidance derives from the fact that the liquidation value of the estate sets a minimum level of payment under the plan. The recovery of property enlarges that liquidation value and thereby raises the minimum standards for confirmation of the plan. Also, as in liquidation cases, the avoidance of encumbrances or obligations expands the value of the estate to the benefit of creditors generally.

§11.4 EXERCISE OF THE AVOIDANCE POWER BY A DEBTOR IN POSSESSION OR OTHER PARTIES

All the avoidance provisions specifically confer the avoidance power on the trustee. As noted in section 4.3, in Ch. 11 cases the debtor in possession normally exercises all the powers of a trustee. It is therefore common for the debtor in possession to represent the estate in avoidance litigation. From the creditors' perspective, this leads to a paradoxical result where the entity who made the transfer or incurred the obligation is seeking to avoid it. However, the debtor in possession is not exactly the same entity that existed prepetition. In bankruptcy, the debtor in possession operates in a new capacity with new powers and fiduciary obligations.

Avoidance rights cannot normally be exercised by anyone other than the trustee or debtor in possession. There are some narrow exceptions to this. In a Ch. 11 case, the court might authorize a creditors' committee to avoid a transfer if the debtor in possession unjustifiably fails to do so. Although the creditor's committee cannot simply take the initiative and sue, the court has the discretion to authorize suit.[4] Also, §522(h) provides for another limited exception for individual debtors. If a transfer of exempt property is avoidable and the trustee does not attempt to avoid it, the debtor may do so provided that the transfer was involuntary and the debtor did not conceal the property.

§11.5 THE AVOIDANCE SUIT AND THE ENFORCEMENT OF A JUDGMENT OF AVOIDANCE (§550)

The trustee must commence suit in the bankruptcy court to avoid a transfer or obligation. The suit takes the form of an adversary proceeding—essentially, a civil lawsuit within the bankruptcy case. Avoidance suits are included in the list of core proceedings in 28 U.S.C. §157(b)(2)(F), (H), and (K). This indicates that Congress considered them to be centrally related to the bankruptcy process and fully within the jurisdiction of the bankruptcy courts. However, as discussed in section 4.2.1, Congress's determination of whether a matter is a core proceeding is not dispositive; the Supreme Court has cast doubt on the characterization of avoidance actions as core proceedings because they involve the adjudication of rights under nonbankruptcy law.

If the avoidance action concerns an obligation incurred by, or an interest in property granted by, the debtor, the court's determination of avoidability results either in disallowance of the claim against the estate or in invalidation of the claim to the property. If the action is aimed at the avoidance of a transfer of property by the debtor, judgment in favor of the trustee obliges the transferee to return the property or its value to the estate. Section 550 governs the enforcement of this obligation. Section 550(a) allows the trustee to recover the property (or its value, if the court so orders) from the initial transferee who received or benefited from the transfer and from any subsequent transferee. Although this means that there may be more than

4. See *Official Committee of Unsecured Creditors of Cybergenics Corp. v. Chinery*, 330 F.3d 548 (3d Cir. 2003) and *In re The V Companies*, 292 B.R. 290 (B.A.P. 6th Circ. 2003).

one person liable for the property or its value, §550(d) makes it clear that the estate can only obtain a single satisfaction.

Section 550(b) limits the trustee's right to recover from a subsequent transferee who takes the property for value, in good faith, and without knowledge of the voidability of the transfer (i.e., a bona fide purchaser). A bona fide purchaser is not liable to return the property or its value; any later transferee who takes in good faith is also protected from avoidance. Section 550(b) applies only to subsequent transferees and cannot be used as a defense by the person who acquired the property from the debtor. Once grounds for recovery are established, the trustee's power to recover from the initial transferee is absolute.

Under §550(e), any transferee who acquired the property in good faith but who is not entitled to protection under §550(b) is given a lien on the property to secure the lesser of the net cost of any improvement made to the property after transfer (offset by profits from the property) or the increase in value resulting from the improvement. This lien is available to both the initial transferee and to any subsequent transferee who does not satisfy the requirements of §550(b), provided that the transferee acted in good faith in acquiring the property.

In many cases, the initial transferee of property is a creditor who acquired the property in satisfaction of a debt. When the transfer is avoided, the previously settled indebtedness becomes an unpaid claim once again. To encourage such transferees to surrender property to the estate following avoidance of the transfer, §502(d) provides for the disallowance of the transferee's claim against the estate unless the property is returned. In *In re PRS Ins. Grp., Inc.*, 331 B.R. 580, 587 (Bankr. D. Del. 2005), the court observed that this provision is intended to be coercive rather than punitive. The section is designed to put pressure on the creditor to turn over the property to the estate within a reasonable time after having been ordered to do so.

§11.6 PRESERVATION OF THE TRANSFER FOR THE BENEFIT OF THE ESTATE (§551)

Section 551 states that any avoided transfer is preserved for the benefit of the estate with respect to property of the estate. This means that when the trustee avoids an interest in estate property, the estate automatically succeeds to the avoided rights in the property. This allows the trustee to assert those rights against any other interest in the property that is junior to the avoided interest. Say, for example, that there are two security interests in a piece of estate property. Both are valid under state law, and the first security interest has priority over the second. If the senior interest is avoidable in bankruptcy[5] but the junior interest is not, the trustee avoids the senior interest and is then able to assert its priority over the junior one. Were it not for §551, the avoidance of the superior interest would simply promote the junior lien, which would then enjoy the senior position and become the first-in-line claimant to the proceeds of the property. Section 551 ensures that when the trustee exercises the avoidance power, it is the estate, rather than the holder of the junior interest, that benefits from the avoidance.

However, §551 does not cure defects in the avoided interest. For example, imagine that a bank had an unperfected lien in Debtor's car. Debtor filed a Ch. 7 petition and claimed an exemption in her car. The trustee relied on §544 to avoid the bank's unperfected lien and then argued that §551 affords the estate a lien on the car. The court would not accept this argument because the bank did not have an enforceable lien against the car. By invoking §551, the trustee merely stepped into the bank's shoes and holds the bank's defective and unenforceable lien.

§11.7 THE STATUTE OF LIMITATIONS AND "REACH-BACK" PROVISIONS

Two statutes of limitation pertain to the period within which the trustee must act to assert the avoidance powers.

First, §546(a) requires that actions or proceedings for avoidance be commenced at the latest before the case is closed. However, the closing of the case is the outside limit for the commencement of avoidance proceedings. Even if the case has not yet closed, the limitation period ends on the later of two years from the order of relief, or (provided that the first trustee is appointed or elected within that two-year period) one year from the first trustee's appointment or election. There is a split of authority over whether the section is a waivable statute of limitations. The majority view is that the provisions are waivable, meaning that a party may waive the limitations period under §546(a) by, among other things, executing a tolling agreement or failing to assert a statute of limitations defense in its answer.[6]

Second, §550(f) requires that actions or proceedings to recover property following avoidance be commenced within the earlier of one year after

5. Section 13.1 explains how an interest could be avoidable in bankruptcy notwithstanding its validity under state law.

6. See, e.g., *In re Raynor*, 617 F.3d 1065 (8th Cir. 2010); *In re Pugh*, 158 F.3d 530 (11th Cir. 1998); *In re Texas Gen. Petroleum Corp.*, 52 F.3d 1330 (5th Cir. 1995); *In re Rodriguez*, 283 B.R. 112 (Bankr. E.D.N.Y. 2001); but see *In re Frascatore*, 98 B.R. 710 (Bankr. E.D. Pa. 1989) (ruling that §546(a) is a statute of repose and precludes suits after the limitations period has run).

the transfer has been avoided or by the time that the case is closed or dismissed.

These provisions recognize that avoidance proceedings consist of two distinct stages: the action of avoidance itself and the enforcement of the judgment of avoidance by proceedings to compel turnover of the property under §550. Of course, the trustee is able to make the avoidance and turnover claims in the same suit and judgment on these issues can be granted simultaneously.

These limitation periods must be distinguished from so-called "reach-back" provisions contained in the avoidance sections themselves. Some powers of avoidance apply only to transfers that occurred within a specific period before the petition. That is, the trustee can "reach back" only so far into the prebankruptcy period to avoid certain transfers. These periods are noted in the discussion of the different avoidance powers in Chapters 12 to 14. While the reach-back provisions prescribe the retrospective temporal range of the avoidance power, limitation periods require the trustee to initiate avoidance proceedings within a specific period during the bankruptcy case. (*See* sections 13.1.2 and 14.3.4 for further discussion of this distinction.)

§11.8 THE GENERAL PURPOSE AND GOALS OF THE AVOIDANCE POWERS

Before becoming involved in the intricacies of the avoidance powers, it is useful to identify the principal policies that motivated their enactment and that continue to influence courts in their interpretation. These broad policy themes are not served equally by all the avoidance provisions. Each section is designed to achieve specific ends with regard to particular types of transactions. However, there are common threads, and a survey of them at the outset helps create a perspective from which the detailed rules may be viewed. The themes raised here will arise again in a more concrete context in Chapters 12 to 14.

(1) Most avoidance powers are intended to facilitate the bankruptcy goals of preservation of the estate and collective treatment of claims. Two of the fundamental bankruptcy policies identified in section 3.5.2 are the preservation of the estate and collective treatment of claims, leading to the optimum distribution to creditors in the order of priority prescribed by law. These policies could not be effectively realized if the trustee was able to look no further than the remnants of the debtor's estate at the time of the filing of the petition. In many cases, the debtor's bankruptcy is preceded by a period of financial crisis in which creditors jostle for advantage by collection activity, and the debtor responds to pressure by making payments to particular creditors or by disposing of property. Much activity in this period could be abnormal or contrary to regular business practices; some of it could be dishonest or manipulative.

By permitting the trustee to go back into the prebankruptcy period and to avoid dispositions made and obligations incurred irregularly or illegitimately, the Code gives the trustee's power of preservation some retrospective effect. The trustee is able, to some extent at least, to ameliorate the harm caused by disruptions prior to the filing of the petition. The avoidance enhances the value to the estate by restoring property to the estate or reducing claims against it. In addition, the avoidance of a transfer to a creditor deprives that creditor of the inappropriate advantage obtained in the period preceding bankruptcy and brings the creditor into bankruptcy's collective process. Some commentators argue that the avoidance powers have a preventative function that goes beyond the case at hand: discouraging creditors from seeking advantages because gains will be undone in bankruptcy. In reality, the possibility of avoidance offers no disincentive at all, because the risk of having to return an avoided transfer will be far outweighed by the prospect of benefit if bankruptcy does not occur in the near future.

(2) The avoidance provisions attempt to differentiate between legitimate and illegitimate transactions. It will become clear when the prerequisites for avoidance are discussed in Chapters 12 to 14 that the avoidance powers do not extend to every prepetition transfer or obligation. They are aimed at transactions that are perceived by Congress to be irregular or illegitimate, in that they unfairly or unjustifiably diminish the estate or undermine the proper order of distribution in bankruptcy. This limitation on the avoidance powers is important. If every prepetition transfer or obligation could be overturned, the risk of a debtor becoming bankrupt would make all credit transactions hazardous and unappealing. Furthermore, it is one of bankruptcy's fundamental policies that rights under nonbankruptcy law should be interfered with only to the extent necessary to achieve essential restructuring goals, including estate preservation and uniform treatment of similarly situated creditors. In creating the avoidance provisions, Congress was sensitive to the tension between effecting the goals of bankruptcy and protecting legitimate rights under nonbankruptcy law. Accordingly, the avoidance provisions constantly call for the distinction to be drawn between legitimate and illegitimate transactions.

(3) The avoidance powers are frequently used to invalidate unpublicized rights. This point is really a subcategory of the previous one, but the issue of unpublicized rights is important enough to be highlighted as a distinct policy concern. The law requires that certain rights must be publically recorded so that their existence can be ascertained by any person who searches the public records. For example, title to real property and some personal property (such as motor vehicles) must be recorded in the appropriate public repository. Similarly, as we saw in section 1.5, most liens and encumbrances must be recorded or otherwise publicized to be perfected—that is, effective against parties other than the debtor. The public record protects those persons who deal with the debtor by informing them of the debtor's ownership in the property and of any limitations on it. A "secret lien"—that is, an unpublicized encumbrance in the debtor's property—creates a potential for abuse by the debtor and a danger of misplaced reliance by third parties. For this reason, where an interest in property is not properly publicized by recording or otherwise, the unpublicized right will not avail against a creditor who was unaware of it when extending credit, and it will not avail against the trustee if the debtor files for bankruptcy.

The failure to publicize a lien or other interest may be the result of deliberate collusion between a debtor and the creditor where the parties do not want it to be known that the interest has been granted. However, more commonly the failure to publicize is the result of inadvertence, error, or delay. Whether or not the lack of publicity is deliberate, the law does not generally protect unpublicized interests.[7] Therefore, as a general rule, when nonbankruptcy law requires an act of publicity to perfect a lien or right in property, failure to complete the act makes the lien or right avoidable unless particularly strong equities favor the holder.

7. In some narrow circumstances, equity may recognize an interest that is not properly recorded, giving rise to an equitable lien or interest. (*See* section 1.6.5.) However, even an equitable lien or interest is based on some form of publicity that substitutes for proper recording. (*See* section 1.6.5.)

CHAPTER 12

The Trustee's Avoidance Powers: Unperfected Interests (§544) and Statutory Liens (§545)

§12.1 OVERVIEW

Section 544 is designed to grant the trustee the same avoidance rights that would be available to certain creditors and bona fide purchasers under nonbankruptcy law. Section 544 does not create rights of avoidance, but rather confers a status on the trustee under which avoidance rights under nonbankruptcy law may be exercised. However, the concentration of these nonbankruptcy rights in the hands of the trustee, combined with the operation of the legal fictions described below, gives the trustee a collection of powers that could not be held by an actual creditor under nonbankruptcy law. Section 544 affects only prepetition liens and conveyances.[1] Section 544 deals only with avoidance. A trustee must rely on §550 to recover avoided transfers for the benefit of the estate.

The two subsections of §544 are distinct and provide different avoidance powers. Subsection (a) is referred to as the "strong-arm clause" because it allows the trustee to avoid certain prepetition liens and conveyances. More specifically, the subsection allows the trustee to avoid an unrecorded lien or conveyance if applicable nonbankruptcy law would prevent the lienholder from asserting its interest against a party without knowledge of the unrecorded lien or conveyance. Subsections (a)(1), (2), and (3) offer the trustee different rights based on the property involved. Under subsection (a)(1), the trustee may exercise the rights of a judicial lien

1. The trustee's power to avoid postpetition transfers is governed by §549, which is discussed in Chapter 14.

creditor as to property that does not constitute real property. Under subsection (a)(2), the trustee is granted the rights of an unsatisfied execution creditor. And under subsection (a)(3), the trustee may exercise, with respect to real estate, the rights of a bona fide purchaser. It is important to note that these powers are hypothetical. The trustee may rely on these powers to avoid unrecorded transfers regardless of whether an actual lien creditor, unsatisfied execution creditor, or bona fide purchaser exists. The trustee's actual knowledge is irrelevant for avoidance. The trustee is presumed to have no prior knowledge of the unrecorded transfer.

Subsection (b)(1) allows the trustee to rely on applicable nonbankruptcy law and step into the shoes of an unsecured creditor who may avoid a prepetition transfer. The most common use of the avoidance power under §544(b)(1) is to allow the trustee to exercise a creditor's avoidance rights under state fraudulent transfer law. Unlike subsection (a), the trustee may not rely on a hypothetical creditor to avoid a transfer under subsection (b). Rather, the trustee bears the burden of demonstrating the existence of an actual unsecured creditor with avoidance rights under applicable nonbankruptcy law.

Subsection (b)(2) restricts a trustee's ability to avoid certain charitable contributions to charities and nonprofit organizations.

Section 545 is designed to address the situation where state legislatures attempt to circumvent the Code's priority scheme. The section allows the trustee to avoid statutory liens 1) that arise due to the debtor's precarious financial condition, 2) that are not enforceable against a bona fide purchaser, or 3) for rent or liens of distress for rent that upset the priority scheme established under federal bankruptcy law. The section does not apply to liens that arise by agreement.[2] Lienholders affected by avoidance are relegated to general unsecured creditors.

§12.2 THE AVOIDANCE OF UNPERFECTED INTERESTS UNDER §544

§12.2.1 §544(a) and the Trustee's Status as a Hypothetical Lien Creditor, Execution Creditor, or Bona Fide Purchaser of Real Property

Section 544(a) is known as the "strong arm" clause — a nickname inherited from its predecessor in the Bankruptcy Act. It confers three hypothetical

2. See *In re Buckskin Realty Inc.*, No. Chapter 11, 2016 BL 314659, at *8 (Bankr. E.D.N.Y. Sept. 23, 2016).

roles on the trustee: that of judicial lienholder, unsatisfied execution creditor, or bona fide purchaser of real property depending on the property involved and the circumstances surrounding avoidance.

Section 544(a) expressly declares that the trustee's assumption of any of these hypothetical positions is not dependent on the existence of an actual creditor or purchaser. The trustee is not a successor to the existing rights of any person, but obtains the status as a matter of law. This means that even though there was no actual creditor or purchaser in existence who could have exercised these rights prior to the petition, the bankruptcy filing brings the avoidance rights into effect. Section 544(a) also states expressly that the trustee's rights of avoidance are not affected by any knowledge that the trustee or any creditor may have. This is because the trustee acts in an official capacity and occupies the applicable status hypothetically. Any knowledge that would affect the equities against a real purchaser or lien creditor should therefore not be applicable to the trustee. (*See* Example 3.)

a. The Trustee as Judicial Lienholder Under §544(a)(1)

Section 544(a)(1) gives the trustee the power to avoid any transfer of property or any obligation incurred by the debtor that would be avoidable under nonbankruptcy law by a creditor who has a judicial lien on all the debtor's property as at the date of the petition.[3] "Judicial lien" is defined in §101(36) to mean a lien arising out of judgment, levy, or some other judicial process. Section 544(a)(1) places the trustee in the position of a hypothetical lien creditor as at the date of the petition, but it actually gives the trustee greater powers than an actual lien creditor would have. Despite the use of the term "voidable" in §544, a lien creditor who has priority over a claimant under state law does not in fact avoid a junior claim. It just takes priority over that claim to the extent of the lien. The claim remains valid and can still be asserted in the proceeds of the property that are left after the senior lien creditor is paid. For example, imagine that on January 5 a secured party lends $100,000 to the debtor and enters into a security agreement with the debtor under UCC Article 9. The security agreement gives the secured party a security interest in the debtor's equipment, which is valued at $100,000. The secured party fails to file a financing statement as required by Article 9 and never perfects the interest. On February 1, a lien creditor—who obtained judgment against the debtor for $60,000—levies execution

3. The actual language of §544(a)(1) is rather more convoluted. It refers to a creditor who extends credit and gets a lien at the time of the commencement of the case. This language was intended to make it clear that the Code meant to overturn some pre-Code case law that is no longer of concern to us. The reference to "simple contract" merely signifies that the judicial lien to be used in the hypothesis must be an ordinary one and not one that is given special priority under nonbankruptcy law.

on the equipment and thereby acquires a judicial lien. Under state law, the lien creditor takes priority over the secured party's unperfected security interest. This means that the lien creditor is paid first out of the proceeds of the equipment and receives $60,000. However, the secured party's security interest does not disappear. The interest remains valid to the extent of the surplus value of the collateral and gives the secured party the right to recover the $40,000 balance of the proceeds. By contrast, imagine that there is no judicial lienholder. Instead, the debtor files for bankruptcy on February 1. If the trustee avoids the security interest entirely under §544(a)(1), the full value of the property belongs to the estate. The secured party loses its security interest and becomes a general unsecured claimant. (This is further illustrated by Example 1.)

Section 544(a)(1) can be used to avoid different types of unrecorded property interests—including consignments or quitclaim deeds—but it is most often used to address unperfected security interests in personal property under UCC Article 9. The trustee's status as judicial lienholder will trump the vast majority of parties holding unrecorded liens but not all. Indeed, imagine that a restaurant bought a $10,000 walk-in cooler from Big Bo's Appliance Depot. The restaurant paid a $2,000 down payment and borrowed the balance from Big Bo's. Big Bo's attorney filed a financing statement in the secretary of state's office, but the walk-in cooler is a fixture under applicable state law and a local fixture filing was necessary. The restaurant subsequently files for bankruptcy, and the trustee attempts to avoid Big Bo's interest. The trustee is forced to rely on §544(a)(1) since the lien at issue does not affect real property.[4] Section 544(a)(1) confers upon the trustee the status of judicial lien holder. However, under state law (UCC 9-334(e)(3)) any Article 9 filing is good perfection against a lien creditor. The trustee would not be able to avoid Big Bo's security interest under §544.

b. The Trustee as a Creditor with a Nulla Bona Return Under §544(a)(2)

Section 544(a)(2) gives the trustee the avoidance power that would be available in nonbankruptcy law to a creditor who obtains a nulla bona return on an execution as at the date of the petition. This provision is not much used because it only applies where state law gives a creditor special avoidance rights after a nulla bona return. Few states have such a law, and this subsection is seldom used.

4. A fixture could qualify as real property for other purposes, but not for the purpose of §544(a)(3), which expressly applies only to real property other than fixtures. Note that to the extent the trustee wishes to avoid a security interest in real property, §544(a)(3)—explored in 12.2.1c—allows the trustee to assume the status of a bona fide purchaser.

c. The Trustee as a Hypothetical Bona Fide Purchaser of Real Property Under §544(a)(3)

Bona Fide Purchaser

Section 544(a)(3) gives the trustee the avoidance power that would be available in nonbankruptcy law to a bona fide purchaser of real property from the debtor who obtained and perfected that status on the date of the petition. Federal law determines whether a trustee qualifies under §544(a)(3), but "state law determines if the trustee's status as a bona fide purchaser will defeat the rights of a person against whom the trustee seeks to assert those powers."[5] Under state law a bona fide purchaser often has more powerful rights than a judicial lienholder. This is because some unperfected interests in real property are given priority over a subsequent judicial lien in the property, but not over a later bona fide purchaser. Where interests in real property are vulnerable to avoidance, the hypothetical bona fide purchaser status therefore augments the trustee's power beyond that of a hypothetical lien creditor. (The value of this hypothetical status of the trustee is illustrated by Example 3.)

Like the other provisions of §544(a), this subsection is expressly not dependent upon the existence of an actual bona fide purchaser. Simply stated, §544(a)(3) employs the fiction that the trustee is a perfected bona fide purchaser of real property as of the date of the petition. If, under nonbankruptcy law, such a bona fide purchaser of real property would take precedence over the preexisting interest in it, the trustee can avoid the debtor's transfer of that interest.

Actual and Constructive Knowledge

To qualify as a bona fide purchaser under state law, a person must purchase the property in good faith, for value, and without knowledge or constructive notice of the prior rights in the property. Of course, as a hypothetical bona fide purchaser, the trustee is legally presumed to satisfy these requirements, and §544(a) expressly states that the avoidance rights under the section are not affected by any actual knowledge that the trustee or a creditor may have. Although actual knowledge of interest is not legally relevant, constructive notice is. The rights of the estate should not be affected by what the trustee or a creditor might know because the trustee is merely an official representing the estate, not an actual participant in a purchase transaction whose knowledge may affect the equities of the case. However, constructive notice is a legal fiction imputed to a person irrespective of what he actually knows for the purpose of protecting an earlier equitable interest that has achieved a level of publicity sufficient to be treated as quasi-perfection. For this reason, it should bind the trustee as hypothetical occupant of the status, in the same way as it would bind an actual party.[6]

---

5. In *re Zubenko*, 528 B.R. 784, 788 (Bankr. E.D. Cal. 2015).
6. See *McCannon v. Marston*, 679 F.2d 13 (3d Cir. 1982).

Constructive notice is most obviously present where the interest has been properly recorded (called "record notice"). However, it may also be furnished by some form of publicity that falls short of proper recording, but that would give notice of the interest to a reasonable purchaser (called "inquiry notice"). In *In re Polo Builders*, 433 B.R. 700 (Bankr. N.D. Ill. 2010), the deed conveying the property to a buyer was not recorded at the time of the petition, so there was no record notice of the buyer's interest. However, inquiry notice could be attributed to the trustee because the buyer had moved into the property and was in possession of it. Further, in many states where an awareness of certain facts would prompt a reasonably prudent purchaser to make an inquiry into those facts, the purchaser — and by extension the trustee — cannot subsequently seek to avoid an encumbrance that an inquiry would have revealed.[7]

By contrast, the court did not attribute notice of the rights of an unrecorded mortgagee in *In re Deuel*, 594 F.3d 1073 (9th Cir. 2010). The holder of the unrecorded mortgage argued that the trustee had constructive notice of it and therefore could not avoid it under §544(a)(3) because the debtor had disclosed the mortgage in her schedule which was filed with the petition. The court rejected this argument. The trustee's status as a bona fide purchaser arises on commencement of the case, and even if the schedules are filed simultaneously with the petition, the moment of commencing the case must be distinguished from the filing of the schedules, which cannot be taken as filed until after there is a case to file them in. Therefore, notice of matter in the schedule cannot be attributed to the trustee as of the commencement of the case.

§12.2.2 The Trustee's Status as Successor to an Actual Unsecured Creditor Under §544(b)

a. §544(b)(1)

i. Existence of Actual Unsecured Creditor

Section 544(b)(1) states that the trustee may avoid any transfer made or obligation incurred by the debtor that is avoidable under prevailing nonbankruptcy law by a creditor holding an allowable unsecured claim. Unlike §544(a), this subsection does not create a hypothetical status. Rather, it provides for the trustee's succession to the avoidance rights of an actual

7. See *In re Etienne Estates at Wash. LLC*, 2016 BL 99367, at *9 (Bankr. E.D.N.Y. Mar. 30, 2016) ("[T]he recorded assignment of mortgage . . . explicitly references the [unrecorded encumbrance]. . . . Moreover, the Forbearance Agreement . . . references the [unrecorded encumbrance]. . . .").

unsecured creditor. Note that the rights conferred on the trustee are those of an unsecured creditor. The trustee cannot use this provision to acquire the more powerful rights of a lienholder. Although an actual unsecured creditor must be in existence, the creditor need not have proved a claim in the estate. The subsection merely requires that there be an actual creditor who holds a claim that would be allowable if proved. The power of avoidance under §544(b)(1) is not deemed to arise on the date of the petition. Although the trustee succeeds to the avoidance right on the petition date, the effectiveness of the right against the transferee is determined as of the actual date the claim arose; that is, the date that the real-life creditor became entitled to exercise it.

ii. Reliance on State Law

The scope of the trustee's rights under section 544(b)(1) is determined by nonbankruptcy law, invariably state law. Quite simply, subsection (b)(1) allows a trustee to rely on state law to avoid a prepetition transfer by the debtor. The subsection is most frequently invoked to avoid a prepetition fraudulent transfer. In those instances, a trustee will rely on either the Uniform Fraudulent Transfer Act (UFTA) or its successor, the Uniform Voidable Transactions Act (UVTA).[8] But why would a trustee rely on subsection (b)(1) when §548 gives the trustee the nonderivative power to avoid fraudulent transfers? (*See* section 14.3.) Section 544(b)(1) is helpful in many cases because §548 allows the trustee to avoid fraudulent transfers made within two years before the petition.[9] However, the statute of limitations under the UFTA and the UVTA is four years. Therefore, if a transfer occurred three years before the petition date, the trustee would not be able to avoid the transfer under §548. But if there is an actual creditor who has the right to avoid the transfer under applicable state law—either the UFTA or the UVTA—the trustee can use §544(b) to take over that creditor's avoidance rights on which the statute of limitation period has not yet run. (*See* Example 2.) Further, some state's fraudulent transfer laws provide broader powers of avoidance than §548.

Where the trustee uses §544(b), the state law statute of limitations therefore operates as an alternative reach-back period. This must be distinguished from the statute of limitations under the Code, which limits the period during which the trustee must bring an avoidance suit after the bankruptcy case has been filed. For example, in *In re American Energy Trading, Inc.*, 291 B.R. 159 (Bankr. W.D. Mo. 2003), the fraudulent transfers

8. Most all states have adopted the UFTA, though a growing number have replaced the UFTA with the UVTA. Despite a few significant differences, the bases for avoiding a transfer are substantially the same under the UFTA and the UVTA.

9. The period used to be one year, but was extended to two years by the Bankruptcy Abuse Prevention and Consumer Protection Act of 2005 (BAPCPA).

occurred in August 1999. The Ch. 11 case was filed in September 1999, and the trustee brought the suit to avoid the transfer under §544(b) in July 2002. Under state law there was a four-year statute of limitations, which would have allowed the trustee to reach back to avoid the transfer. However, the trustee failed to bring the avoidance suit within two years of the commencement of the case, as required by §546(a), so the court dismissed the trustee's suit as time-barred.

Although the trustee's avoidance right under §544(b) is based on the right of an actual creditor, there is one respect in which the trustee's avoidance power is more extensive than that of the creditor. Where a creditor has the right to avoid a fraudulent transfer under state law, the creditor can avoid it only to the extent of the debt due to that creditor. For example, if the debtor fraudulently transferred property worth $10,000, and the debt due to the creditor is $2,000, the creditor can avoid the transfer only to the extent of $2,000. This means that the creditor would either get a money judgment of $2,000 against the transferee, or if the property is returned, the creditor would execute upon it and would get only $2,000 of its proceeds (and costs) and the rest would go to the debtor. However, if the trustee uses §544(b) to succeed to the rights of the creditor, an old doctrine, derived from *Moore v. Bay*, 284 U.S. 4 (1931), extends the trustee's avoidance power to the entire transfer. The legislative history of §544(b) indicates that Congress intended the *Moore v. Bay* doctrine to continue to apply under the Code.[10]

The fact that the trustee has used the rights of an actual creditor to avoid a transfer and recover property for the estate does not mean that the creditor who had the avoidance rights under nonbankruptcy law is entitled to special treatment. *Moore v. Bay* held that if the trustee recovers a transfer by using the rights of an actual creditor under §544(b), the transferred property is returned for the benefit of the estate and distribution to all creditors. The creditor whose rights were used continues to have merely a nonpriority unsecured claim against the estate.

b. §544(b)(2): The Charitable Exception

Section 544(b)(2), added to the Code by an amendment enacted in 1998, restricts a trustee's ability to avoid certain contributions to charitable and nonprofit organizations. If a transfer satisfies the definition of a "charitable contribution" that is used in §548[11] and cannot be avoided under that section, a trustee cannot attempt to avoid the transfer under §544. As

---

10. See *In re DLC, Ltd.*, 295 B.R. 593 (B.A.P. 8th Cir. 2003) and *In re JTS Corp.*, 617 F.3d 1102 (9th Cir. 2010).

11. *See* section 14.3.6. The term is defined in the Internal Revenue Code and captures a contribution that is made by a natural person and consists of a financial instrument or cash.

more fully explained in section 14.3.6, this safe harbor protects aggregate contributions of up to 15 percent of a debtor's gross yearly income, though some courts have ruled that the safe harbor may also protect amounts in excess of 15 percent in cases where the debtor can establish a pattern of giving more than 15 percent of her gross yearly income.[12] The subsection is intended to protect charitable organizations, particularly churches, from having to return to the estate tithes and contributions of limited amount. The safe harbor is limited to cases involving constructive fraud; transfers made with actual fraudulent intent are not protected.

§12.2.3 Exceptions to Avoidance Under §546

a. The §546(b) Exception to §544

Section 546(b) creates an exception to §544. Under UCC Article 9, the holder of a purchase money security interest has a grace period of 20 days from the date the debtor receives possession of the collateral to perfect that interest. The Code recognizes this state law privilege. Consequently, if a bankruptcy case commences during this 20-day period, §546(b) precludes the trustee from attempting to avoid such a lien until the 20-day perfection period expires. Section 362(b)(3) allows for postpetition perfection in this instance, notwithstanding the automatic stay. If the interest holder perfects its interest during the 20-day period, the interest holder is afforded retroactive perfection to the date the collateral was received by the debtor. *See* Example 5 for a further illustration of §546(b).

b. §546(c) and Preservation of Seller's Reclamation Rights

As stated in section 1.3, an unsecured seller of goods has no special interest in the goods once title has passed to the buyer. If the buyer fails to pay, the seller is in the position of a general unsecured creditor. A limited exception to this rule, derived from common law, is provided for in UCC §2.702. Under common law, a buyer is deemed to make an implied representation of solvency when purchasing goods; if the buyer was insolvent upon receiving the goods, and the seller was unaware of this, the seller may rescind the contract and reclaim the goods on grounds of fraud. UCC §2.702 codifies this right, although in qualified form: If a buyer receives goods on credit while insolvent, and the seller did not know of the insolvency at the time, the seller may demand return of the goods within ten days of receipt unless the buyer has made a written misrepresentation of solvency within three months of delivery.

---

12. See *In re Witt*, 231 B.R. 92 (Bankr. N.D. Okla. 1999).

Section 546(c) subjects the trustee's right of avoidance to any right of reclamation available to a seller under statute or common law, provided that the seller is able to demonstrate that 1) the goods were delivered to the debtor no earlier than 45 days before the petition, 2) the debtor was insolvent at the time of delivery, and 3) the seller sold the goods to the debtor in the ordinary course of the seller's business. If these requirements are satisfied, the seller may reclaim the goods by a demand in writing made no later than 45 days after the date of the debtor's receipt of the goods. If the 45-day period expires after the commencement of the bankruptcy case, the written demand must be made within 20 days of the commencement of the case.[13]

Example 6 illustrates §546(c)'s operation.

As delineated by §§546(c) and 503(b)(9), a seller that fails to give notice to the buyer is able to claim the price of the goods as a priority administrative expense if the goods were delivered to the buyer within 20 days of bankruptcy.

§12.3 THE AVOIDANCE OF STATUTORY LIENS UNDER §545

The nature and purpose of statutory liens was discussed in section 1.6.3. Section 101(53) defines them as liens "arising solely by force of a statute on specified circumstances or conditions. . . ." The definition includes common law liens of distress for rent, and it expressly excludes consensual security interests and judicial liens even if they are provided for by statute. The bankruptcy definition comports with the general meaning of the term under nonbankruptcy law.

The trustee's power to avoid statutory liens is provided for and delimited by §545, which is narrow in its scope. As a general rule, a statutory lien that is validly obtained and perfected under nonbankruptcy law is fully effective upon the bankruptcy of the debtor and cannot be avoided unless it fits into one of three categories specified by §545.[14]

---

13. The time periods in §546(c) were amended by BAPCPA.

14. Courts have held that §545 is the only method by which the trustee can avoid a statutory lien. See *Saslow v. Andrew*, (In re Loretto Winery, Ltd.), 898 F.2d 715, 717–18 (9th Cir.1990) and *In re Sullivan*, 254 B.R. 661, 667 (Bankr. D. N.J. 2000). For these courts, a statutory lien may not be avoided using another of the trustee's avoiding powers. For example, the trustee may seek to avoid a statutory lien perfected during the preference period. But if the lien cannot be avoided under §545, the trustee may be precluded from attempting to avoid the lien under §547. See *In re Aquatic Pools, Inc.*, No. 15-11406 t11, 2017 BL 38700, at *4 (Bankr. D.N.M. Feb. 08, 2017) ("The Court will assume for the purposes of this opinion that Debtor is proceeding under both §§544 and 545, and has the right under one or both of those sections to avoid unperfected federal tax liens on personal property.").

Under §545(1), a statutory lien is avoidable if it is specially created to take effect only upon the debtor's insolvency, bankruptcy, or financial distress. By providing for a lien that arises upon the debtor's financial distress, the state turns a formerly unsecured claim into a secured one; thereby tampering with the order of priority in bankruptcy and infringing upon the federal bankruptcy power.

Under §545(2), a statutory lien is avoidable if it is not perfected or enforceable against a hypothetical bona fide purchaser who is deemed to have purchased the property on the date of commencement of the case. This subsection is similar to §544(a)(3), in that it gives the trustee the hypothetical status of a bona fide purchaser as at the petition date so that the trustee can avoid the lien if it could have been avoided under nonbankruptcy law by a bona fide purchaser of the property. Unlike §544(a)(3), it is not confined to real property.

Under §§545(3) and (4), statutory liens for rent or of distress for rent are avoidable in bankruptcy.[15] This subsection invalidates landlord's liens in bankruptcy, whether created by statute or common law. The discrimination against liens for rent or distress of rent predates §545 and stems from the policy decision made some time ago that lessors should be treated as unsecured creditors and not be given any special rights in bankruptcy unless they have obtained a consensual security interest in the lessee's property. The traditional landlord's lien is not protected in bankruptcy, even though it is generally still available in state law to a landlord of nonresidential property.

The trustee's limited power to avoid statutory liens reflects the policy goals outlined in section 11.8. Most statutory liens are conferred on particular classes of creditor by state law or federal nonbankruptcy law because the legislature has determined that these claimants have a special need for protection. If the Code allowed the trustee to overturn statutory liens that were validly obtained under nonbankruptcy law, it would undermine this protection. Hence, apart from landlord's liens, statutory liens are avoidable only where they are an usurpation of the bankruptcy power or are insufficiently perfected for protection under nonbankruptcy law. Example 5 offers an illustration of §545.

EXAMPLES

Examples

1. Rock Bottom, Inc. has just filed a voluntary petition under Ch. 7. About a year ago the company borrowed money from Confidential Credit Corp. and secured the loan by granting Confidential a security interest in equipment used in its business. A security agreement and financing statement

15. "Distress" in this context stems from the word "distraint," which means the seizure or detention of a chattel.

were properly executed by the parties, but Confidential neglected to record the interest because of a clerical oversight. This error was only discovered after the company had filed its bankruptcy petition. Rock Bottom still owes a substantial balance on its loan.

Can the trustee in Rock Bottom's estate use §544 to avoid Confidential's security interest?

2. Dell Inquent had been in financial difficulty for many years before his bankruptcy. Two years and three months before his petition, when threatened by impending judgments in collection suits, Dell transferred a valuable antique desk to a friend. Although the desk was worth $15,000, Dell gave it to his friend as a gift, subject to the understanding that the friend would donate it back when Dell's financial position became less hazardous.

   One of Dell's creditors, who has an unsecured claim of $1,000 allowable against Dell's estate, had the right to avoid the disposition of the desk under the state's fraudulent transfer law but never exercised that right.

   a. Can the trustee take over the creditor's avoidance right under §544?
   b. If so, to what extent can the transfer of the desk be avoided?
   c. If the trustee avoids the transfer and recovers the desk, is the creditor whose rights were assumed entitled to any priority in the proceeds of the desk?

3. a. Manny Fest bought a condominium from No Con Do, Inc., a property developer. The parties executed a contract of sale in terms of which Manny paid a down payment and obliged himself to pay the balance of the price in monthly installments. The sale should have been recorded, but it was not, so the real estate records reflected No Con Do, Inc. as the owner of the condominium.

   Manny moved into the condominium immediately after the contract was signed. He remained in possession of the property, and continued to pay his monthly installments. About a year after he bought the condominium, No Con Do, Inc. filed a voluntary Ch. 7 petition.

   Under state law, a written but unrecorded purchase of real property makes the purchaser an equitable owner of the property. Equitable ownership is superior to all interests except for those of a bona fide purchaser of the property from the owner of record. To qualify as a bona fide purchaser, a person must purchase the property in good faith, for value, and without knowledge or constructive notice of the prior rights to the property. Clear and open possession of the property serves as constructive notice of the equitable owner's interest. Can the trustee avoid Manny's equitable ownership of the condominium under §544?

b. Change the facts in (a) as follows: Manny Fest paid the down payment but never occupied the condominium. He had purchased it as an investment and left its management as a rental unit in the hands of No Con Do, Inc. No Con Do, Inc. subsequently filed a Ch. 11 petition and, acting in its capacity as debtor in possession, seeks to avoid Manny's interest under §544(a)(3).

   Should it succeed?

4. Charlene Woodson has been donating $80,000 to her church every year for the last ten years. As a senior executive at BlueBit, Charlene's gross yearly income has been approximately $400,000 during this time. Unfortunately, the company's business took a turn for the worse three years ago. That year, Charlene's bonus was slashed, and her gross income for the year was only $200,000. Nevertheless, Charlene still electronically transferred $40,000 into the church's bank account. Charlene was insolvent at the time of the transfer.

   The next year, Charlene realized that she could not donate any more money to her church, and she stopped contributing. Surprisingly, she was able to avoid bankruptcy for three years but filed a petition last month. In bankruptcy, the trustee intends to rely on applicable state law pursuant to §544(b)(1) and avoid the $40,000 donation to the church Charlene made three years ago. Assume applicable state law provides for a four-year statute of limitations and the trustee is able to produce an actual creditor harmed by the transfer.

   a. What is the church's best defense to keep the entire $40,000 donation?
   b. Assume that the trustee has an e-mail Charlene sent to the church right before the last donation in which she states, "My situation is really bad right now. I'm probably going to file for bankruptcy soon. But I don't want my creditors to get all of my money so I'm going to donate $40,000 to the church tomorrow. It just feels like the right thing to do." Could this e-mail affect the church's defense?

5. Ownerous Investments, Inc. filed a Ch. 7 petition on July 1. During the previous May it had entered into a contract with Jerry Bilt, a building contractor, to execute an alteration to a building that it owned. Jerry began work in early May and completed the job near the end of June. Although Jerry was to be paid in full on completion of the work, Ownerous failed to pay him. Jerry had taken no action to enforce his claim by the time Ownerous filed its petition.

   Under the state's construction lien statute, Jerry is entitled to a lien to secure his claim. He is not obliged to take any action to create the lien at the time of commencing work. The statute gives him three months following completion of the work in which to file a claim of lien. He must then institute action to foreclose the lien within six months of filing the claim. Provided that the claim is filed and suit is commenced within the prescribed periods, the lien is effective from the date on which construction commenced. What is the status of Jerry's claim against the estate?

6. On June 25, Red Alert sold his expensive propane barbecue and meat smoker to Pearl Loin, a coworker. Pearl took delivery of the barbecue on that day. The parties agreed that she would pay for it at the end of the month. On June 28, Pearl filed a bankruptcy petition. On June 30, Pearl told Red of this, and informed him that she could not pay for the barbecue. Red immediately demanded its return, and Pearl referred him to her trustee. Should the trustee accede to Red's demand?

EXPLANATIONS

Explanations

1. Quite inadvertently, Confidential's loan to Rock Bottom, Inc. was much more confidential than anticipated. It failed to publicize its interest by filing, and thereby became the holder of a "secret lien." There is a general policy against the enforcement of unrecorded interests in bankruptcy as well as under nonbankruptcy law because unrecorded interests are potentially prejudicial to third parties who may deal with the debtor in reliance on the appearance that no encumbrance exists. With some exceptions, this policy precludes enforcement of the unpublicized interest, even if the failure to record was not deliberate against a third party.

   The unperfected interest is avoidable under §544(a)(1), which gives the trustee the hypothetical status of an ordinary judicial lienholder who acquired a lien on all Rock Bottom, Inc.'s lienable property (including the business equipment) on the date of the petition. This status enables the trustee to avoid Confidential's unperfected interest, because applicable nonbankruptcy law—in this case, UCC §9.317(2)—gives a judicial lien priority over a security interest that was unperfected at the time that the lien arose. The effect of avoidance is to leave Confidential with a general unsecured claim against the estate.

   Section 544(a)(1) can only be used when the interest remains unperfected at the time of the petition. Had Confidential realized its error and perfected the interest before the petition was filed, the interest could not have been avoided under §544(a). (However, if the last-minute filing had occurred within 90 days of the bankruptcy, the perfected security interest would have been avoidable as a preference under §547, discussed in Chapter 13.)

2. The facts in this Example illustrate the trustee's succession to the rights of an actual creditor under §544(b).
   a. Although §548 also empowers the trustee to avoid fraudulent transfers, it cannot be used in this case because it reaches back only two years before the petition date. By taking over the creditor's avoidance power under nonbankruptcy law, the trustee is subject to the statute of limitations applicable to the creditor's suit, which may extend back further in time. For example, it is four years under the UFTA and the UVTA. This allows the trustee to reach back four years to avoid transfers in that time. (Note, however, as explained in section 12.2.2, the trustee must bring the suit within two years of the order for relief as required by §546(a).) It is not necessary that the creditor has proved a claim in the estate, provided that the claim is an allowable unsecured claim. The facts indicate that it is. The actual creditor could have avoided the transfer, and the trustee can therefore do likewise.
   b. It is clear that if the creditor had exercised the avoidance rights under state law, the transfer could have been avoided only to the extent necessary to satisfy the claim, that is, $1,000. However, if the trustee uses §544(b) to succeed to the rights of the creditor, the *Moore v. Bay* doctrine (explained in section 12.2.2) extends the trustee's avoidance power to the entire transfer.
   c. Under the *Moore v. Bay* doctrine, the trustee's recovery of property under §544(b) is for the benefit of the estate as a whole. The creditor whose rights were used remains a general unsecured creditor.
3. a. Under the rules of state law outlined in the Example, the trustee cannot avoid Manny's interest by assuming any of the roles provided in §544. State law does not give priority to a hypothetical lien creditor or a creditor with a nulla bona return, so the trustee has no right to avoid under §544(a)(1) or (2). No actual creditor has avoidance rights to which the trustee could succeed under §544(b). The trustee would have been able to avoid the interest as a hypothetical bona fide purchaser of real property under §544(a)(3) but for the fact that Manny's open possession constitutes constructive notice of his rights. It may seem at first glance that the constructive notice should not affect the trustee's avoidance power because §544(a) states that the avoidance power may be exercised regardless of any knowledge of the trustee or of any creditor. However, this applies only to any actual knowledge, not to constructive knowledge of the trustee, which is merely a legal fiction based on a finding that an equitable interest is sufficiently publicized to be protected.
   b. Under the changed facts, there is no constructive notice of Manny's interest. The trustee can avoid the interest under §544(a)(3) as a

hypothetical bona fide purchaser of real property. In a Ch.11 case, the debtor in possession exercises the trustee's powers, including the power to avoid transfers and obligations under §544. This creates an anomaly where the debtor, the very corporation that sold the interest and has full knowledge of it, now seeks to avoid it as a debtor in possession. Some courts have refused to allow a debtor in possession to use §544(a)(3) to avoid an unrecorded interest arising out of a transaction in which it participated prior to the time that it became bankrupt. However, most courts permit a debtor in possession to use §544(a)(3) on the reasoning that when a debtor becomes a debtor in possession, it acts in a new capacity as representative of the estate. The avoidance of the transfer does not merely further its own interests, but the interests of creditors as well. See *In re Eads*, 69 B.R. 730 (Bank. 9th Cir. 1986), *aff'd in part sub nom In re Probasco*, 839 F.2d 1352 (9th Cir. 1988) and *In re Sandy Ridge Oil Co.*, 807 F.2d 1332 (7th Cir. 1986).

4. a. This type of fact pattern normally ends with an avoidance action under §548. But in this case, the trustee is relying on state law pursuant to §544(b)(1) to take advantage of the longer statute of limitations. Section 548 offers a two-year look back period while state law generally offers a four-year period.

   The church must first establish that the $40,000 donation was a "charitable contribution" as defined by §548(d)(3) (which refers to the Internal Revenue Code). This should not be difficult because Charlene is a "natural person" and the donation consisted of a cash transfer. However, §548 provides that the safe harbor only applies to aggregate contributions up to 15 percent of a debtor's gross yearly income. The donation at issue occurred during a year when Charlene's gross income was $200,000. 15 percent of $200,000 is $30,000. The church will most likely not be able to keep the entire donation. However, some courts have allowed charitable organizations to keep in excess of this 15 percent cap where it can demonstrate a pattern of giving in excess of the cap. Charlene has regularly given in excess of the 15 percent cap. The Example states that over a ten-year period, she normally gave approximately 20 percent of her gross yearly income. During the year in question, Charlene once again gave 20 percent of her gross income for that year ($40,000 is 20 percent of $200,000). The court may allow the church to keep the entire amount based on Charlene's pattern of giving.

   b. The charitable exception under §544(b)(2) applies to constructively fraudulent transfers, but it does not affect a transfer the debtor made with actual intent to defraud creditors. The trustee will bear the burden of proving intentional fraud under the UFTA or the UVTA, depending on which is incorporated into applicable state law. If the trustee can establish that Charlene made the donation with intent to defraud her creditors, §544(b)(2) will not protect the donation from avoidance.

5. Statutory liens are generally upheld in bankruptcy provided that they are valid and perfected under nonbankruptcy law. This principle is reflected in §545(2), which allows the trustee to avoid a statutory lien only if it would be avoidable by a bona fide purchaser of the property at the time of bankruptcy. As in §544(a), the hypothetical status in §545(2) requires reference to the nonbankruptcy law governing the lien. The construction lien statute protects Jerry from a bona fide purchaser of the property provided that he complies with the requirements for perfection within the statutory time limits. The statute backdates Jerry's lien, so that if someone had purchased the property from Ownerous on the petition date, the purchaser's interest would have been junior to the inchoate construction lien, provided that Jerry thereafter made the lien filing in the prescribed three-month period and commenced suit to foreclose the lien within six months from the recording date.

   The advent of bankruptcy before the end of the statutory perfection period does not detract from Jerry's right to complete the perfection requirements. Section 546(b) preserves the backdating rules of nonbankruptcy law as long as they are generally applicable and are not created to take effect only upon the debtor's insolvency or bankruptcy. However, §546(b) changes the procedure to be followed to complete perfection. The filing of the claim of lien takes place as normal under state law and is excluded from the stay by §362(b)(3). (*See* Example 4 in Chapter 7.) However, instead of commencing the foreclosure suit thereafter, Jerry must give notice to the trustee within the period prescribed by the state statute for the commencement of suit.

   This example shows that the policy against unrecorded interests is not absolute because the construction lien statute, in effect, allows Jerry to have an unrecorded lien on the property for some months. This reflects a legislative policy that the protection of the lienholder outweighs the need to protect persons who subsequently deal with the debtor. In fact, some statutory liens do not require recording at all, but arise automatically and avail against all subsequent purchasers of the property. Such liens are protected in bankruptcy under §545. This is illustrated by *In re Loretto Winery Ltd.*, 898 F.2d 715 (9th Cir. 1990) (an automatically perfected, unpublicized statutory lien in favor of grape growers was effective against a bona fide purchaser under §545(2) and therefore unavoidable in bankruptcy).

6. Outside of bankruptcy, Red is entitled to reclaim the goods under UCC §2.702 if he can show that Pearl was insolvent when she received the

barbecue and he only discovered this afterward. Red made a reclamation demand for the barbecue within about five days after it was received by Pearl, which is well within the 10-day period under UCC §2.702. Section 546(c) gives effect to the seller's reclamation right in bankruptcy if the additional requirements of that section are satisfied. In this case two conditions are satisfied, but two are not. Pearl received the goods in the 45-day period before the petition, and Red reclaimed them within 20 days of the petition. However, the demand was not in writing, and Red, being a consumer, did not sell the goods in the ordinary course of his business.

CHAPTER 13

The Avoidance of Preferences and Debt Setoff

§13.1 PREFERENTIAL TRANSFERS UNDER §547

§13.1.1 Overview

Section 547 allows for avoidance of a preferential transfer. A "preference" is a debtor's prepetition transfer that allows one creditor to receive more money or value through the bankruptcy proceedings than another creditor who is similarly situated. The ability to avoid such a transfer is a unique feature of federal bankruptcy law. Indeed, under state law, a debtor invariably enjoys the freedom to pay some creditors in full while ignoring others.[1] For example, imagine that Company, Inc. has $60,000 in available cash, but owes $60,000 to each of three unsecured creditors. Company, Inc. decides to pay Creditor 1 in full and default on its obligations to Creditor 2 and Creditor 3. Under state law, Creditor 1 cannot be forced to share the payment it received with the other creditors.

However, the Bankruptcy Code is premised on a distinct set of principles. One such principle is that of equality and the notion that similarly situated creditors should be treated alike. To effectuate this policy, it is not enough that creditors are treated evenhandedly after the petition has been

1. As noted in section 2.9.3, there is one area of nonbankruptcy law in which a debtor is not permitted to treat a creditor preferentially. Where the debtor makes an assignment for the benefit of creditors, the preferential treatment of a creditor could make the assignment invalid.

filed; the trustee must have the power to avoid preferential transfers by the debtor in the period immediately preceding the bankruptcy filing. In returning to our example, imagine that Company, Inc. filed for bankruptcy one week after its $60,000 payment to the first creditor. The payment could be identified as a preference payment and avoided under section 547. If the payment is avoided, Creditor 1 would have to return the $60,000 payment to the bankruptcy estate[2] and all of Company, Inc.'s creditors—including Creditor 1—could share in these funds. Imagine that after the preference payment is recovered for the estate and all administrative fees have been paid, there is $60,000 in the bankruptcy estate, and the only parties with recognized claims against the estate are Creditor 1, Creditor 2, and Creditor 3. Each would receive $20,000 in satisfaction of Company, Inc.'s obligation. The preference action has disadvantaged Creditor 1 but benefited the creditor body as a whole.

Section 547 is aimed at creditors to whom the debtor owed an obligation prior to the transfer at issue. Therefore, unlike §548 and state fraudulent transfer law—which are covered in Chapter 14—§547 is not concerned with the recovery of dispositions that were made with fraudulent intent or for inadequate value. Under §547, there is no requirement that the court take into account the state of mind of the debtor or transferee, and there is no requirement of bad faith, knowledge, or deliberate advantage-taking. The fact that the debtor did not intend to make a preferential payment is irrelevant. Section 547's assessment is entirely objective: a transfer is avoidable if it has the external attributes delineated in §547.[3]

Section 547 has two operative subsections: §547(b) confers the power of avoidance on the trustee, listing five elements that must be satisfied for the transfer to be avoidable. Every one of these elements must be satisfied. Section 547(c) contains exceptions to the trustee's avoidance power. Even if a transfer meets all the requirements of §547(b), it cannot be avoided to the extent that it fits within one of the exceptions in §547(c). Section 547(c) only becomes relevant if all the elements of §547(b) are satisfied. If they are not, the transfer is unavoidable, and recourse to §547(c) is not necessary.

In addition to §547(b) and (c), there are a number of other subsections of §547 that are discussed in this chapter:

1. Section 547(a) supplements the definitions in §101 by defining some terms that are not included in the general definition section.

---

2. Creditor 1 would have a $60,000 claim against the estate after the avoidance.

3. Preference rules have not always been as objective as they are under §547. Under the Bankruptcy Act, the trustee had to show that the transferee had reasonable cause to believe that the debtor was insolvent at the time of transfer. This standard survived partially in the 1978 Bankruptcy Reform Act, but was eliminated entirely in 1984.

2. Section 547(e) sets out a formula for determining when a transfer takes place. This determination can be crucial in avoidance suits, and it is explained in section 13.1.3.
3. Sections 547(f) and (g) are concerned with the burden of proof in avoidance suits. Section 547(g) requires the trustee to prove all the elements of avoidance under §547(b), but this burden is alleviated in part by §547(f), which rebuttably presumes the debtor's insolvency in the 90 days preceding the petition. Under §547(g), the transferee must prove the grounds for nonavoidability if it invokes one of the exceptions in §547(c).

§13.1.2 The Elements of §547(b)

To be avoidable under §547(b), the transfer must satisfy every one of the following requirements.

(1) There must have been a transfer of an interest in property of the debtor to or for the benefit of a creditor (§547(b)(1)). The transfer is the transmission of value from the debtor to the creditor, either directly or in an indirect way, so as to confer a benefit on the creditor. "Transfer" is defined in §101(54) in very broad terms to cover a wide variety of dispositions. It includes all dispositions of property, whether direct or indirect, absolute or conditional, voluntary or involuntary. It also includes the creation of liens on property. "Creditor" is defined in §101(10) to mean, essentially, the holder of a claim against the debtor that arose at the time of or before the order for relief. "Claim," in turn, is given a wide-ranging definition in §101(5). In short, it includes all rights to payment in law or equity.

The property interest transferred must have been property of the debtor. In most cases where a debtor makes a transfer, it is clear that the debtor transferred her own property. However, where a third party provides funds to the debtor for the purpose of paying a specific debt, the debtor's use of those funds to pay the designated debt may not constitute a transfer of the debtor's property. For example, the debtor owes $100,000 to Creditor 1. The debtor borrows $100,000 from Creditor 2 for the expressly agreed purpose of using that money to settle the debt to Creditor 1 and uses the money for that purpose. Under the judicially created "earmarking" doctrine, a court may find that this transaction is simply a substitution of creditors so that the payment of $100,000 to Creditor 1 was, in effect, made with property of Creditor 2 rather than the debtor's property. Courts use somewhat different tests to decide if it is appropriate to find earmarking. For some courts, the determinative question is whether the debtor had dispositive control over the funds used to pay Creditor 1. If the debtor acquires control and actual ownership of the funds, so that the debtor has the power to use them for other purposes, the funds do not qualify as earmarked and there has been a transfer of the debtor's property. Other courts treat the payment as earmarked if there is a clear and express agreement between the new lender and the debtor that the funds will be used only to pay the specific debt, the debtor does perform the agreement in accordance with its terms, and the transaction as a whole did not result in any diminution of the debtor's estate. See, for example, *In re Wells*, 561 F.3d 633 (6th Cir. 2009) (an advance to the debtor by one credit card issuer was not earmarked to pay down the balance on another credit card because the debtor had complete control of the funds and the discretion to use them for purposes other than paying down the other credit card); *In re Entringer Bakeries, Inc.*, 548 F.3d 344 (5th Cir. 2008) (no earmarking because the funds were deposited in the debtor's general bank account, giving it legal title, all indicia of ownership, and control of the funds); and *In re Adbox, Inc.*, 488 F.3d 836 (9th Cir. 2007) (earmarking could not be used because there was no proof of an agreement under which the debtor clearly committed to use the funds to pay the designated debt).

Section 547(b)(1) requires that the creditor benefit from the transfer, but the benefit may be direct or indirect. Most cases involve a payment to a creditor or some other obvious benefit, but in some cases the benefit is obscure. For example, imagine that a corporate debtor has a prepetition obligation to Creditor 1 that is supported by a guarantee from an affiliate of the debtor. In other words, the guarantor promises to pay the debt in the event the debtor defaults. Though it may seem odd, the guarantor is actually one of the debtor's creditors because the guarantor holds a contingent claim against the debtor. Imagine that the debtor pays the primary obligation two weeks before filing for bankruptcy. The payment to Creditor 1 may be a preference, and Creditor 1 could be forced to disgorge the funds. At the same time, the payment also constitutes a transfer "for the benefit of" the guarantor—an indirect benefit to that creditor—because the payment eliminated the guarantor's contingent liability. Thus, if the payment was in fact a preference, the trustee could recover from either Creditor 1 or the guarantor.[4]

(2) The transfer must have been for or on account of an antecedent debt (§547(b)(2)). "Debt" is defined in §101(12) to mean liability on a claim. (As mentioned in section 13.1.2.1, "claim" is comprehensively defined in §101(5).) Although the Code defines debt, it offers little guidance on the meaning of "antecedent," except for the language in subsection (b)(2): "owed by the debtor before such transfer was made." Apparently, the debt

4. Section 550 addresses a trustee's ability to compel a disgorgement after a transfer has been ruled to violate §547.

is "antecedent" if it arose before the transfer was made. This is true even if the period of time between the two sides of the exchange is very short.[5]

The Code does not provide rules for determining when the debt came into being. The question of when the debt arose — that is, when the debtor became legally obligated to the creditor — must be determined under non-bankruptcy law. The creation of the debt must not be confused with the due date for payment of the debt. It is common for a debt to arise (that is, for liability to be created) some time before the time that this liability is fixed, mature, and unconditionally payable. (For example, in a loan transaction, the debt arises as soon as the money is advanced, but the debt does not become payable until the due date for the loan to be repaid.)

(3) The debtor must have been insolvent at the time of the transfer (§547(b)(3)). "Insolvent" is defined in §101(32), which uses the balance sheet test (liabilities exceed assets at fair valuation) rather than the equity test (not generally paying debts as they fall due) to determine insolvency. Valuation assessments can be complicated because the value of both assets and liabilities must be determined. Prior to 1978, the Code required the trustee to establish that the creditor receiving the transfer at issue had reasonable cause to believe that the debtor was insolvent. Congress eventually recognized the difficulty in making such a showing and, in 1978, the requirement was replaced by §547(f)'s presumption of insolvency. Section 547(f) presumes the debtor was insolvent during the duration of the 90-day period prior to the petition date. The presumption is not conclusive, but the creditor bears the burden of proof in attempting to rebut the presumption.[6] Section 547(f)'s presumption applies only to the 90-day period prior to the petition date. Consequently, in preference actions brought against insiders, the insolvency issue remains a contentious matter.[7]

(4) The transfer must have occurred within the prepetition avoidance period (§547(b)(4)). The avoidance period is 90 days before the filing of the petition, unless the transferee is an insider (the meaning of which is explained in section 13.1.2.4a), in which case it is one year before the

5. If there is only a short delay between the creation of the debt and the transfer, one of the exceptions in §547(c) will probably apply, as discussed in section 13.1.4. However, for the purposes of satisfying §547(b), all the trustee needs to establish is that the debt arose at some time before the transfer was made.

6. See *In re Int'l Polymers, Inc.*, 359 B.R. 868 (Bankr. E.D. Tenn. 2005).

7. Some courts have adopted the retrojection theory, which eases the trustee's burden in these cases. Under the retrojection theory, the court will presume that a debtor was insolvent for purposes of section 547 if 1) the debtor was insolvent before or on the date of the first preferential transfer, 2) the debtor was insolvent on or after the date of the last preferential transfer; and 3) there was no significant change in the debtor's assets or liabilities in the interim period. See *In re Cox Motor Express of Greensboro, Inc.*, No. 14-10468, 2017 BL 25152, at *8 (Bankr. M.D.N.C. Jan. 27, 2017).

petition. There is some controversy regarding whether the court should count the avoidance period backward from the bankruptcy date or count forward from the transfer date. The majority of courts have adopted the former approach. In most cases, this would not be a crucial issue, but it could be determinative where the last day of the count falls on a nonbusiness day or a holiday. We believe that the best approach is to count backward from the petition date and to not extend the period further backward when the day 90 falls on a nonbusiness day or a holiday.

Insiders

Where the transfer was made more than 90 days before the petition but within a year of it, the transfer is avoidable against an insider. "Insider" is defined in §101(31) to include a variety of persons with a close relationship to the debtor, such as relatives of an individual debtor and officers of a corporate debtor. The word "includes" in the definition indicates that the list of insiders expressly identified in the definition is not exclusive. Any other person who had a close and influential relationship with the debtor — referred to as "nonstatutory insiders" — could qualify. Nonstatutory insiders are those who "fall beyond the literal letter of the law, but are captured within the spirit of the law. . . ."[8]

To decide if a person should be found to be a nonstatutory insider, courts take all the circumstances of the relationship into account, including the intimacy of the relationship, knowledge of the debtor's affairs, access to inside information, and the degree to which the person could control or influence the debtor.[9] For example, in *In re McIver*, 177 B.R. 366 (Bankr. N.D. Fla. 1995), the debtor's live-in companion was held to be a nonstatutory insider. Even a creditor could be a nonstatutory insider if it had a sufficiently close connection to the debtor. However, courts will not generally find a creditor to be an insider unless the relationship was unusually close and it allowed the creditor to exercise control over the debtor, to influence the debtor's decision making, and gave it access to inside information. For example, in *In re U.S. Medical, Inc.*, 531 F.3d 1272 (10th Cir. 2008), the creditor was held not to be a nonstatutory insider, even though it had an exclusive distributorship agreement with the debtor, was the sole supplier of the debtor's product, could designate a director on the debtor's board, and held 10 percent of the debtor's stock. The court found that the creditor did not use its position to exercise control over or unduly influence the debtor.[10]

---

8. See *In re Top Hat 430, Inc.*, 557 B.R. 744, 748 (Bankr. D. Minn. 2016).
9. See, e.g., *Farrar v. Warda & Yonano, LLP* (In re Bella Vista by Paramont, LLC), 549 F. App'x 648, 649 (9th Cir. 2013).
10. But see *Shubert v. Lucent Techs. Inc.* (In re Winstar Comm'cns, Inc.), 554 F.3d 382, 398 (3d Cir. 2009) (transferee's ability to coerce debtor into transactions not in debtor's interest "amply demonstrate" creditor's status as insider).

In *In re QuVis*, 446 B.R. 490 (Bankr. D. Kan. 2011) a creditor was held not to be a nonstatutory insider by virtue of its power to appoint a director and to inspect the debtor's books where the creditor was one of several similarly situated lenders, and its rights gave it no unique insider information.

The "Deprizio Rule"

Section 550(c), added to the Code in 1994, and §547(i), added by the Bankruptcy Abuse Prevention and Consumer Protection Act of 2005 (BAPCPA), make it clear that the one-year reach-back period applies only to an insider; it cannot be used against a noninsider even if the transfer to the noninsider indirectly benefited an insider. These provisions overturn prior caselaw (named the "Deprizio rule" after the case that created the troublesome rule),[11] which permitted a transfer to be avoided against a creditor who was not an insider if the transfer to that creditor conferred an incidental benefit on someone else who was an insider. For example, if the debtor pays a debt to a noninsider that is guaranteed by an insider, the payment of the debt confers an indirect benefit on the insider by eliminating the insider's liability under the guarantee. The one-year reach-back does not apply to the payment merely because the insider was indirectly benefited.

(5) The transfer must have improved the creditor's position (§547(b)(5)). The transfer must have enabled the transferee to receive more than it would have received if the transfer had not been made and the debt had been paid at the appropriate rate under a Ch. 7 distribution. This element, called the improvement-in-position test, is the heart of §547(b). The test's basic purpose is to determine whether the prebankruptcy transfer gave the creditor a higher level of payment on its claim than it has the right to receive. It is this attribute of the transfer that makes the creditor's advantage illegitimate and undermines bankruptcy's collective process.

Irrespective of whether the case had been filed under Chs. 7, 11, or 13, the test requires a hypothetical Ch. 7 liquidation to be calculated. A comparison must then be made between the total payment that the transferee would receive if the transfer is left intact and the total payment that it would receive if the transfer was restored to the estate and the transferee proved a claim in the estate for the debt that had been reduced or eliminated by the transfer. If the first figure is higher than the second, the improvement-in-position test is satisfied. For example, imagine that the debtor owed $52,000 to Creditor 1 and paid that creditor $2,000 a few weeks prior to filing for bankruptcy. Creditor 1 filed a general unsecured claim for $50,000 in the bankruptcy case. General unsecured creditors in the case

11. See *Levit v. Ingersoll Rand Financial Corp.* (In re V.N. Deprizio Construction Co.), 874 F.2d 1186 (7th Cir. 1989).

were entitled to a 90 percent distribution in the case. Creditor 1 recovered $47,000 on its claim.[12] However, if the debtor had not made the $2,000 prepetition payment, Creditor 1 would not have received such a large recovery. Indeed, without the prepetition payment, Creditor 1 would have recovered only $46,800.[13] The prepetition payment allowed Creditor 1 to receive a larger recovery on its claim, satisfying §547(b)(5).

The hypothetical liquidation is calculated as of the petition date, and the trustee must establish the hypothetical liquidation distribution by a reliable, rationally based analysis of the financial situation as at that date. This may require the testimony of an accountant or other qualified expert. See *In re Falcon Products*, 381 B.R. 543 (B.A.P. 8th Cir. 2008); *In re Connolly North America LLC*, 398 B.R. 564 (Bankr. E.D. Mich. 2008).

In most cases involving a transfer to an unsecured creditor, it does not take complex calculations to determine that the improvement-in-position test is satisfied. Unless the estate is solvent enough to pay unsecured creditors in full, a transfer to the creditor that eliminates or reduces its unsecured claim will easily be established as preferential. For example, in *In re Polo Builders*, 433 B.R. 700 (Bankr. N.D. Ill. 2010), the debtor settled the unsecured creditor's debt in full within 90 days of the petition. Just a rough tally of the debtor's debts and assets made it clear that unsecured creditors would not receive any more than 22 percent of their claims. The 100 percent received by the transferee clearly improved its position.

In many cases, a creditor is able to seek recovery from entities aside from the debtor. For example, there may be a guarantor of the debt at issue. In such cases, a creditor could argue that section 547(b)(5) is not satisfied because the creditor would have been paid in full by the guarantor. Hence, the payment did not improve the creditor's position. Courts have rejected this argument. *United Rentals v. Angell*, 592 F.3d 525 (4th Cir. 2010) is the leading case. In that case, the debtor had entered into a subcontract with the creditor for the supply of equipment on a construction project and had executed a payment and performance bond under which a surety undertook to pay the creditor if the debtor defaulted. The debtor made payments to the creditor during the 90-day prepetition period, which clearly satisfied the other elements of §547(b). The question in issue was whether the payments satisfied the improvement-in-position test of §547(b)(5). The creditor argued that the payments did not improve its position because, upon default, the creditor would have been able to enforce its rights under the bond and claim full payment from the surety. The court rejected this argument, holding that the critical question was not whether the creditor would have been able to receive payment from another source had the transfer not

12. $2,000 + ((.90)($50,000)) = $47,000.
13. (.90)($52,000) = $46,800.

been made, but rather, would the creditor have been entitled to the same level of distribution from the estate. This approach aligns with underlying preference policies by focusing on a transfer's impact on the bankruptcy estate and whether the transfer depleted estate assets that would have otherwise been available to creditors.

The operation of the improvement-in-position test is illustrated in Examples 1, 2, and 4.

§13.1.3 The Timing of the Transfer

(1) The general rule governing timing of the transfer under §547(e). The timing of the transfer is crucially important for a number of purposes. For example, the date of the transfer must be known to decide if it falls within the avoidance period, if it was for an antecedent debt, or if the debtor was insolvent when it was made. Section 547(e) provides the formula for determining the date of the transfer. In broad terms, §547(e) treats the transfer as having occurred on the date on which it became effective between the parties under nonbankruptcy law. However, if, under nonbankruptcy law, some act is required to perfect the transfer (e.g., the filing of a financing statement to perfect the transfer of a security interest in the debtor's property), the transfer will occur only on the date of perfection, unless the act of perfection is completed within 30 days of the transfer taking effect.[14] (Examples 1, 3, and 4 address timing issues.)

(2) Under §547(e)(3) the transfer does not occur until the debtor acquires rights in the property. Section 547(e)(3) provides a further qualification. It states that for the purposes of the section, a transfer is not made until the debtor has acquired rights in the property transferred. This means that even if the act of perfection (such as the public filing) occurs within 30 days of the transfer taking effect, the timing of the transfer is delayed if the debtor has not yet acquired an interest in the property. In other words, the 30-day rule does not apply to property that the debtor does not own at the time of perfection, even though she may anticipate acquiring it in the future. The date of transfer is delayed until she actually acquires the property. *In re Morehead*, 249 F.3d 445 (6th Cir. 2001) illustrates the significance of this rule. In that case, the creditor obtained judgment against the debtor in 1995 and served a continuing wage garnishment on the debtor's employer in 1997, under which the employer automatically deducted the garnished amount from the debtor's wages in each future month. The debtor filed his Ch. 7 petition in November 1997. The issue was

---

14. Prior to 2005, the period was ten days. BAPCPA increased the period to 30 days.

whether the wage garnishments during the 90 days before bankruptcy were avoidable preferences. The bankruptcy court held that they were. The court reached this conclusion because, under state law, the creditor obtained a perfected garnishment lien on all the garnished wages when it served the garnishment order on the employer in 1997. The court of appeals reversed on the basis of §547(e)(3), holding that even though the transfer was perfected outside the 90-day period, the debtor did not acquire rights to the wages until he earned them. Further, the court rejected the theory, adopted by other courts, that once garnishment occurs, the debtor loses the right to the portion of his wages that have been garnished.[15]

(3) The definition of "perfection" in §547(e)(1). Because the timing of the transfer is often dependent on the date it was perfected, the meaning of "perfection" is important. Section 547(e)(1) defines perfection for the purposes of §547 with reference to nonbankruptcy law. In the case of real property, perfection is complete as soon as a subsequent bona fide purchaser "cannot" acquire a superior interest in the property, and perfection of all other property is complete as soon as an ordinary judicial lienor "cannot" acquire superior rights. Under most nonbankruptcy law, perfection will occur only from the time that the act required for perfection is accomplished.[16]

However, with regard to certain types of interest, nonbankruptcy law permits the effective date of the interest to backdate to some specified earlier time. Section 546 generally recognizes and preserves these backdating rules in bankruptcy. However, in *Fidelity Financial Services v. Fink*, 522 U.S. 211 (1998), the Supreme Court held that the same rule does not apply in §547(e), because the language of that section indicates that "perfection" is used there in a different sense. In §546, "perfection" is used to mean the legal conclusion that the interest is perfected, but in §547(e) it is used to mean the act necessary to effect that perfection. The court found this meaning to be apparent from the fact that §547(e) says that perfection occurs when a creditor on a simple contract "cannot acquire" a superior judicial lien. The court reasoned that a creditor *can* acquire a superior judicial lien at any time during that gap period, even though that lien would lose priority to the transferee if the transferee thereafter performed the act of perfection that would give it retrospective effect. Unless and until that act is performed, the judicial lienholder "can" acquire a superior lien, and it is only when the act of perfection is complete that it "cannot" any longer achieve priority. For this reason, §547(e)(1) must be interpreted to date

---

15. See also *Matter of Jackson*, 850 F.3d 816, 820 (5th Cir. 2017) (adopting the majority approach espoused by the *Morehead* court); but see *In re Coppie*, 728 F.2d 951, 953 (7th Cir. 1984).

16. For example, filing the proper document in the correct records office.

perfection only from the time that the final act of perfection, and not from any earlier date to which it would relate back under state law.

In *In re Taylor*, 599 F.3d 880 (9th Cir. 2010), the court held that under *Fidelity Financial Services* the grace period allowed by state law for perfection of a security interest in a vehicle did not apply. As a result, the transfer of the security interest occurred on the date of actual filing of the interest with the state, not on its backdated effective date under state law. In *In re Johnson*, 611 F.3d 313 (6th Cir. 2010), the court affirmed the B.A.P.'s application of *Fidelity Financial Services* where the final act of perfection was out of the hands of the creditor and had to be accomplished by a state official. The security interest was in a motor vehicle and had to be perfected by notation on the certificate of title. Even though state law treated the perfection as taking effect when the creditor filed the proper documentation with the Department of Motor Vehicles, the court held that perfection for purposes of §547(e) was a matter of federal law, and that the final act of perfection under §547(e) occurred only when the state actually made the notation. (The timing of perfection is discussed further in Example 4.)

§13.1.4 Exceptions to Avoidance Under §547(c)

Section 547(c) provides nine exceptions to the trustee's avoidance power under §547(b). As stated before, the most efficient sequence of analysis is to determine first if the transfer is avoidable under §547(b). If it is not, there is no occasion to use §547(c); if it is, §547(c) should be consulted to determine if any of the exceptions apply. Once the trustee has established that the transfer is avoidable, the burden shifts to the transferee under §547(g) to prove that an exception is applicable.

The exceptions in §547(c) refine and qualify the avoidance power to distinguish legitimate ordinary-course business dealings from last-minute preferences. In this way, the Code preserves transactions that are technically preferential because they satisfy all the elements of §547(b) but do not truly confer an inappropriate advantage on the recipient. This abstract observation is more clearly demonstrated in the discussion of the specific exceptions.

All the exceptions apart from §547(c)(6), (8), and (9) preclude avoidance of the transfer only "to the extent that" it is covered by the exception. It is therefore possible for a transfer to be partially avoidable. The nine exceptions are as follows:

(1) A substantially contemporaneous exchange for new value (§547(c)(1)). Although it satisfies all the requirements for avoidance under §547(b), a transfer may not be avoided to the extent that it represents a substantially contemporaneous exchange for new value. The protection of exchanges of this kind is consistent with the policies underlying the avoidance of preferences. The transaction is a regular commercial exchange that is reasonably thought of as concurrent, not a last-minute attempt by the creditor to thwart the order of distribution in bankruptcy.

Substantially Contemporaneous Exchange

For a transfer to qualify for the §547(c)(1) defense, the transfer 1) must have been intended by the creditor and the debtor to be a substantially contemporaneous exchange for new value given to the debtor, and 2) was *in fact* a substantially contemporaneous exchange of new value. As to the first requirement, a determination of the parties' intent is a question of fact and must be based on some clear manifestation. Courts will not infer intent based on ambiguous actions or words.[17]

The second requirement is that the transfer must be in fact substantially contemporaneous. Unfortunately, §547(c)(1) provides no guidance on what constitutes substantial contemporaneity. Creditors concerned about the second requirement's ambiguity often structure transactions so that there is no doubt about the transfer's satisfaction of §547(c)(1). For example, imagine that a creditor agrees to continue delivering raw materials to a financially distressed customer, but on the condition that a full cash payment coincides with each delivery. This arrangement would clearly satisfy §547(c)(1). But transactions where payment is not immediate could still qualify. For example, imagine that a distressed debtor pays for its raw materials by check. The parties could consider this transaction to be substantially contemporaneous. However, payment occurs only when the check is cleared by the bank — customarily a few days after the sale. The majority position is that this transaction could qualify under §547(c)(1) because the phrase "substantially contemporaneous" is flexible and adjusts to the facts of each particular case.[18] Immediate payment is not necessary. This conclusion is based in part on §547's legislative history, which provided that a payment by check could be a contemporaneous exchange. The same approach has been applied to credit sales. For example, in *In re Hechinger Investment Co. of Delaware, Inc.*, 489 F.3d 568 (3d Cir. 2007), the court found that short-term credit was substantially contemporaneous where the parties understood that the price of goods shipped would be paid on or before they arrived at the buyer's premises.

---

17. See *In re Genmar Holdings, Inc.*, 776 F.3d 961, 964 (8th Cir. 2015) (ruling that a settlement agreement between the creditor and the debtor failed to explain certain provisions and, consequently, court could not assess the parties' intent for a contemporaneous exchange from the document).

18. See, e.g., *In re Sierra Concrete Design, Inc.*, 2015 BL 228068, at *12 (Bankr. D. Del. July 16, 2015); see also *Pine Top Insurance Co. v. Bank of America National Trust & Savings Ass'n*, 969 F.2d 321 (7th Cir. 1992).

New Value

"New value" is defined in §547(a)(2) to mean money, goods, services, or new credit, and can also include the release of property previously transferred by the debtor, provided that the original transaction is unavoidable. A party claiming a Section 547(c)(1) defense "must prove with specificity the new value given to the debtor" and that the new value "had a value at least as great as the amount of the alleged preferential transfer."[19] New value does not always come in the form of money. The term includes money, or money's worth in new credit, goods, services, or property.

(2) Ordinary-course payments (§547(c)(2)). Section 547(c)(2) excepts a transfer from avoidance to the extent that both the creation of the debt and its payment qualify as ordinary-course transactions. That is, two distinct requirements must be satisfied:

1. The debt itself must have been created by a transaction that was in the ordinary course of business or financial affairs of both the debtor and the transferee.

2. The payment of the debt was made either 1) in the ordinary course of business or financial affairs of the debtor and transferee, **or** 2) according to ordinary business terms.

Prior to 2005, this second requirement read differently. To satisfy it, the transferee had to show both that the payment was in the ordinary course of the parties' business or financial affairs (a more subjective test based on the attributes of the parties' own commercial practices) and that it was in accord with ordinary business terms (a more objective test based on practices in the market). BAPCPA, following the recommendation of the 1994 National Bankruptcy Review Commission, amended §547(c)(2) to make these requirements alternative rather than conjunctive. The reason for the change is that it is unnecessary to subject the payment to both a subjective and an objective test because a transfer that satisfies either is the kind of routine transaction to be protected.

Section 547(c)(2) is meant to prevent the avoidance of normal pre-bankruptcy transfers that conform to the debtor's pattern of dealing and can fairly be regarded as usual and routine. These are not the kinds of transfers intended to give the creditor an unfair advantage on the eve of bankruptcy, and they create a legitimate expectation that the transfer will not be disturbed if the debtor becomes bankrupt. It is a question of fact, to be determined under all the circumstances of the transaction, as to whether the debt was incurred and paid in the ordinary course. Many different types of transactions are protected from avoidance by the exception. For example,

---

19. *Campbell v. The Hanover Ins. Co.* (In re ESA Envtl. Specialists, Inc.), 709 F.3d 388, 398–99 (4th Cir.2013).

it covers regular trade purchases by a business debtor on short-term credit, payments made by a consumer for regular monthly expenses such as utilities or services, and regular monthly payments on long-term debt[20] incurred in the ordinary course of the debtor's affairs.

A. First Requirement: Debt Incurred in the Ordinary Course of Business or Financial Affairs

The first requirement is that the debt was incurred in the ordinary course for both parties. Courts evaluate whether the incurrence of the debt in question is consistent with the parties' custom prior to the preference period. The focus is on identifying anomalies and irregularities that would indicate an attempt by a creditor to secure an advantage over other similarly situated creditors in bankruptcy. In many cases, a lender may issue a loan in the ordinary course of its business, but incurrence of the debt is not ordinary from the debtor's perspective and the creditor will not be able to invoke §547(c)(2).[21]

B. Second Requirement: Payment Made Either 1) in the Ordinary Course of Business or Financial Affairs of the Debtor and Transferee (§547(c)(2)(A)), <u>**or**</u> (b) According to Ordinary Business Terms (§547(c)(2)(B))

1. In the Ordinary Course of Business of Financial Affairs of the Debtor and Transferee (§547(c)(2)(A))

A creditor may be able to invoke §547(c)(2)'s defense if it can establish that the preference payment at issue was made in the ordinary course of business or financial affairs of the debtor and the transferee. This requirement demands an inquiry into the relationship between the debtor and creditor. Courts generally assess the entire documented history between the parties[22] and consider the following factors:

a. the length of time the parties were engaged in the transactions at issue;
b. whether the amount or form of tender differed from past practices;
c. whether the debtor or the creditor engaged in any unusual collection or payment activity; and

---

20. Since the decision of the U.S. Supreme Court in *Union Bank v. Wolas*, 502 U.S. 151 (1991), it is clear that ordinary-course payments on long-term debt can qualify for the exception under §547(c)(2).

21. See *Harrah's Tunica Corp. v. Meeks (In re Armstrong)*, 291 F.3d 517 (8th Cir. 2002) (ruling that the casino could not avail itself of the §547(c)(2) defense because—though extension of credit to the gambler was within the ordinary course of the casino's business—the borrowing was not ordinary to the debtor, who sought the credit in a failed attempt to secure enough winnings to cover huge losses arising from his financial embezzlement).

22. See *In re Newpage Corp.*, 555 B.R. 444, 452 (Bankr. D. Del. 2016).

d. whether the creditor took advantage of the debtor's deteriorating financial condition.[23]

Where the parties have had an ongoing relationship, the creditor must establish a baseline period for comparison, which could be as long as three years. Substantial deviations from this baseline are generally not protected. However, recent case law has demonstrated that payments received weeks or even months after the contractual due date may still be ordinary for §547(c)(2)'s purposes if they align with the established baseline practice between the parties. For example, in *In re Quebecor World (USA), Inc.*, 491 B.R. 363 (Bankr. S.D.N.Y. 2013), the trustee sought to avoid a late payment made by the debtor to the creditor in the 90-day period. The debtor had generally paid the creditor late during the course of a lengthy relationship, so the court took into account the parties' routine practice of making and accepting late payments to establish a baseline for determining their ordinary course of business. In the pattern of dealing before the 90-day period, the debtor's average lateness in making payments was about 60 days. By comparison, the payment challenged by the trustee was made 90 days late. The court held that this delay went beyond a reasonable delay established by prior dealings and therefore did not qualify as within the ordinary course of business. In *In re Jan Weilert RV, Inc.*, 315 F. 3d 1192, *as amended*, 326 F. 3d 1028 (9th Cir. 2003), the court took a particularly flexible approach in deciding whether payments were on ordinary business terms. The court said that where a debtor is experiencing financial difficulty, the court should focus not merely on what would be ordinary patterns of dealing between financially secure parties but should also have regard to the usual way of dealing with financially distressed debtors. The transfer should only be avoided if it is so aberrant that it goes beyond the usual means by which a creditor might accommodate the needs of a financially shaky debtor.

Although a pattern of past dealings is helpful in establishing whether the transfer meets the test of §547(c)(2), this does not mean that the parties must have had an existing relationship to qualify a transfer as in the ordinary course. Where the transfer occurred in a first-time transaction, the test for deciding if it is in the ordinary course is whether the transaction would be ordinary for a person in the debtor's position and generally consistent with the debtor's prior practices.[24] In *In re Frey Mechanical*

23. See *In re Evergreen Oil, Inc.*, 2017 BL 125633, at *3 (B.A.P. 9th Cir. Apr. 10, 2017).
24. See *In re Ahaza Systems, Inc.*, 482 F.3d 1118 (9th Cir. 2007).

Group, Inc., 446 B.R. 208 (Bankr. E.D. Pa. 2011), after a commercial lender refused to extend a line of credit to the financially troubled debtor, the parents-in-law of the debtor's president extended a line of credit to the debtor under which they made loans to the debtor to enable it to continue operating. The court held that the §547(c)(2) exception was inapplicable. Not only were the lenders not in the business of lending money to companies, but an unsecured line of credit to a financially unsound debtor did not accord with ordinary business terms. (Example 5 deals with this exception.)

2. Ordinary Business Terms (§547(c)(2)(B)

A payment that was not made in the ordinary course of business for the debtor and the transferee may still be shielded by §547(c)(2)(B). This element is difficult to prove because the creditor must establish 1) the relevant industry in which the key parties operate and 2) the practices followed by third parties in that industry.

Establishing the applicable industry can be difficult. Imagine that Company, Inc. makes a variety of meat and vegetarian sausages. Company, Inc. sells its products to grocery stores, restaurants, caterers, and pizza parlors. Joe's Pizza Parlor files for bankruptcy and Company, Inc. seeks to invoke §547(c)(2)(B) to protect one of the payments it received from the debtor. What is the relevant industry? Should the focus be on the sale of sausage to any party, the sale of sausage to pizza parlors, the sale of food to pizza parlors, or some other niche in the market? Payment practices vary widely based on the industry. Consequently, the definition of the industry can be a dispositive issue. Unfortunately, courts have little guidance in this area and must invariably make a determination on a case-by-case basis.

Once the industry is established, the transferee will need to demonstrate customary payment practices by third parties in that industry. Courts have required defendants to provide "admissible, nonhearsay testimony related to industry credit, payment, and general business terms in order to support" this defense.[25] Expert testimony is generally the most effective way to establish an evidentiary basis. However, to the extent a transferee introduces evidence demonstrating the payment practices of other customers, the transferee should also establish that such parties were similarly situated to the debtor.[26]

---

25. *In re Conex Holdings, LLC*, 524 B.R. 55, 59 (Bankr. D. Del. 2015).
26. See id.

(3) Purchase-money security interests (§547(c)(3)). A purchase-money security interest is one granted by the debtor to secure a loan or credit used to acquire the very collateral subject to the interest. (*See* section 1.4.3.) An interest qualifies as a purchase-money interest for the purposes of §547(c)(3) to the extent that it secures new value given by the transferee to the debtor at or after the execution of a security agreement describing the collateral, and the new value is both intended to be used and is in fact used to acquire the collateral. The rationale for making an exception for purchase-money interests is that the holder of the interest has enabled the debtor to obtain the property that secures the debt and has not depleted the estate in some way.

Section 547(c)(3) does not absolutely except purchase-money security interests from avoidance. It merely creates a limited protection for the secured party by providing a special grace period for perfection. The interest is unavoidable provided that it is perfected within 30 days[27] from the date on which the debtor received possession of the collateral. It is important to understand the limited scope of §547(c)(3). Where a secured party does not perfect its security interest within 30 days of its attachment, the transfer dates from the date of perfection under §547(e)(3). Because the transfer occurs only on the perfection date, the debt becomes antecedent and the later perfection could push the transfer into the 90-day period, making it avoidable. Section 547(c)(3) provides that if this occurs, a purchase-money security interest will be protected if perfected 30 days after the debtor received possession of the property. Therefore, §547(c)(3) is only helpful to a secured party where 1) the debtor receives possession some time after the date on which the interest attaches, and 2) the perfection date is within 30 days of the possession date. (*See* Example 3.)

(4) Subsequent new value (§547(c)(4)). If, after receiving an avoidable transfer, the creditor gives to the debtor new value that is not itself secured or paid for by a new transfer, the otherwise avoidable transfer cannot be avoided to the extent of the new value.

The justification for this defense is that a creditor who extended new credit or other value to the debtor after payment of an older obligation was probably motivated by that payment to deal further with the debtor. Without the new value defense, the debtor's subsequent bankruptcy would cause the earlier payment to be reversed, and the creditor would suffer for having dealt with the debtor prepetition. The earlier payment would have to be returned and the creditor would have to make a claim

27. The grace period has increased over the years. It was originally 10 days but was amended to 20 days in 1994 and to 30 days by BAPCPA.

against the estate for both the old debt and the new one. Apart from being unfair to the creditor, a rule like this would discourage persons from dealing with a debtor in financial difficulty, because they would not be able to rely on the payment of earlier obligations as a basis for extending new credit. In addition, it could be argued that the later value, in effect, replenishes the estate by returning the preference to the estate, thereby reversing its prejudicial effect. The exception is commonly and appropriately applied where the debtor and creditor have an ongoing relationship in the form of a line of credit or a revolving credit transaction, under which the debtor makes periodic payments and withdrawals. For example, imagine that the debtor owes one of its creditors $50,000 for supplies. The debtor makes a $15,000 transfer to the creditor, but then obtains an additional prepetition, unsecured loan of $5,000 the following week. The debtor files for bankruptcy the next month, and the trustee seeks to recover the $15,000 payment. The creditor could rely on §547(c)(4). The trustee would only be able to recover $10,000 because the $5,000 "new value" loan shields a portion of the $15,000 payment.[28] The new value exception applies when the debtor has not 1) granted an unavoidable security interest to secure the new value or 2) made an "otherwise unavoidable transfer" to the creditor in exchange for it. Section 547(c)(4) applies in our example because the $5,000 loan is not secured and the debtor did not transfer any property to the creditor in exchange for the loan. Timing is important. In the example above, if the creditor had loaned the $5,000 first and the debtor had made the $15,000 payment the following week, §547(c)(4) would not protect the $15,000 payment because the creditor did not tender "new value" *after* the preference payment at issue.

Section 547(c)(4)(B) requires that the new value paid by the creditor must remain unpaid and has led to judicial dissension in some cases. In the example above, §547(c)(4)(B) is satisfied because the $5,000 unsecured loan is unpaid at the time the bankruptcy petition is filed. However, the new value defense may still be available if the debtor had paid the $5,000 loan prepetition but the payment is avoidable by the trustee (as a preference payment, for example) in bankruptcy. For example, imagine that the debtor owes one of its creditors $20,000 for supplies. The debtor makes a $10,000 payment to the creditor on March 1, and obtains an additional prepetition, unsecured loan of $12,000 on March 8. The debtor pays off this loan on March 30 and then files for bankruptcy the following month. Most courts would allow the creditor to rely on §547(c)(4) to protect the $10,000 payment it received because the $12,000 payment can be avoided by the trustee and recovered for the benefit of the estate. This renders the $12,000

---

28. Note that the creditor could not rely on the $5,000 "new value" loan to protect the full $15,000 payment she received.

new value unpaid, and "the debtor did not make an otherwise unavoidable transfer." Or, removing the double negative, the debtor made an avoidable transfer on March 8 (the $12,000 payment). The trustee will avoid the $12,000 payment as a preference, and the creditor will lose the payment, but she will gain the benefit of subsection (c)(4) to shield the $10,000 payment it received on March 1. *In re Frey Mechanical Group, Inc.*, 446 B.R. 208 (Bankr. E.D. Pa. 2011), illustrates this result. In that case, the court held that although the ordinary course exception in §547(c)(2) did not exempt the loan payments from avoidance, the payments could be partially exempted by §547(c)(4). The fact that the debtor had repaid the new value (the advances made to the debtor under the line of credit) before bankruptcy did not disqualify them from the exception because the payments were avoidable (or, in the double-negative suggested by the language of the section, were not unavoidable). In fact, the trustee was in the process of moving to avoid them as preferences. In other words, the new value cannot be counted if it was secured or repaid by the debtor and that security interest or payment cannot be avoided. However, if the security interest or payment is avoidable, the fact that it was made is irrelevant because it can be undone, resurrecting the unsecured debt for the new value.[29]

The scope of §547(c)(4) is narrow, and the protection given to creditors who deal with the debtor is quite restricted. Payments are protected only to the extent that new value is given by the creditor[30] after the payment without a corresponding new transfer by the debtor. The question of what constitutes new value involves an inquiry similar to that under §547(c)(1), and the definition of new value in §547(a)(2) applies here as well. For §547(c)(4) to be applicable, the value given must constitute a new benefit to the estate, which replenishes it after the transfer. A benefit that does not replenish the estate does not satisfy the exception. For example, in *In re ABC-Nabco, Inc.*, 483 F.3d 470 (7th Cir. 2007), a creditor's agreement to forbear from taking action against the debtor in return for the payment was held not to be new value because it added nothing to the estate. In *In re Armstrong*, 291 F.3d 517 (8th Cir. 2002), a casino's grant of new line of credit to the debtor was not new value for the payment of a debt to the casino because the line of credit did not replenish the estate but diminished it by enabling the debtor to incur more gambling debts. The operation of §547(c)(4) is illustrated by Example 6.

---

29. See also *Mosier v. Ever-Fresh Food Co. (In re IRFM, Inc.)*, 52 F.3d 228 (9th Cir. 1995); *In re Musicland Holding Corp.*, 462 B.R. 66 (Bankr. S.D.N.Y. 2011).

30. In *In re Musicland Holding Corp.* the court pointed out that the plain language of §547(c)(4) requires the new value to be given by "such creditor" and is not available where the new value is given to the debtor by a third party (an affiliate of the creditor in that case), rather than by the creditor who received the earlier transfer.

(5) Floating liens in inventory and receivables (§547(c)(5)). Floating liens were introduced in section 1.4.3 and Example 3 of Chapter 1. In this type of transaction, the security interest secures all advances made by the secured party in the future and automatically attaches to all new collateral of a particular kind (typically, accounts or inventory) acquired by the debtor in the future. The parties contemplate that the secured party will advance funds to the debtor when inventory or accounts come into existence. As the inventory is sold or the accounts are paid, the loan will be reduced by the proceeds. When a further batch of inventory is acquired or accounts are generated, the secured party will again make an advance in proportion to the value of the new collateral and the creditor's lien will attach to this new collateral. But floating liens raise unique problems in bankruptcy because a security interest in the newly acquired property that attaches within the 90 days before the petition date qualifies a preference under §547(b).[31]

To solve this problem, §547(c)(5) presents a simplified test for determining whether and to what extent the aggregation of all the transfers in the 90-day period should be avoided as a preference. The language of this section is convoluted, but the concept is quite straightforward: When a floating lien arrangement in accounts or inventory[32] has been validly created, each separate transaction in the 90-day period does not have to be examined. The transfers to the secured party are unavoidable except to the extent that all the transfers in the 90-day period caused a reduction in the shortfall between collateral and debt (i.e., in the deficiency) to the prejudice of unsecured creditors in the estate. If the secured party is an insider, the prebankruptcy period is, as usual, one year. If the transaction is first brought into effect within the applicable prebankruptcy period, the reduction of the shortfall must be measured from the time that new value was first given.

Therefore, the focus of §547(c)(5) is not on the individual transfers in the prebankruptcy period but on the transferee's overall improvement in position over the prebankruptcy period. If the collateral was worth less than the debt at the beginning of that period and transfers to the transferee during the period had the effect of eliminating or reducing that shortfall as of the petition date, the transfers are avoidable to the extent that they reduced the

31. Floating liens present other difficulties as well. For example, if the debtor becomes bankrupt in the course of such a continuing secured transaction, many transfers are likely to have been made to the secured party in the 90 days before bankruptcy. Every payment and every acquisition of new collateral would qualify as a transfer. To examine each one of these transfers for the purpose of determining avoidability would be an exhausting task because the total figures for each month may represent numerous transactions. Such a painstaking examination of the multitude of transfers under the floating lien could unfairly undermine the secured party's reliance on the routine activity in its continuing relationship with the debtor.
32. The section applies only to these two types of commercial collateral.

shortfall.[33] Although the two-point comparison can involve complex issues, such as valuation questions, it greatly simplifies what could be a very arduous examination of each transfer in an ongoing relationship that involves many individual transfers. It therefore assists a creditor who has been keeping an eye on the debtor's business and making sure that the value of the collateral never drops below the debt. For example, in *In re Smith's Home Furnishings, Inc.*, 265 F.3d 959 (9th Cir. 2001), the secured party had financed the debtor's inventory through a floating lien. When the debtor began operating at a loss, the secured party reduced its line of credit and required a substantial paydown of the debt. In the 90 days before bankruptcy, the debtor paid about $12 million to reduce the debt. The court held that the trustee could not recover these payments because he could not discharge his burden of showing that the creditor had been undersecured at the 90-day date.

In determining the transferee's improvement in position, transfers are not counted to the extent that they did not reduce the value of the estate to the prejudice of unsecured creditors. For example, if the collateral is inventory that appreciated in value due to market conditions, or if it is accounts that turned out to be more collectable than originally supposed, this augmentation of the value of the collateral could reduce any shortfall without harming the estate.

In summary, §547(c)(5) is applied by taking the following steps.

1. *Determine the first date for comparison.* This is 90 days before the petition for a noninsider, a year for an insider, or the date of the first advance, if that occurred after the start of the applicable prebankruptcy period.
2. *Determine the amount of the debt and value the collateral on this first date.* If the secured party is undersecured (i.e., the collateral is worth less than the debt), calculate the shortfall.
3. *Determine the amount of the debt and the value of the collateral on the date of filing the petition.* Calculate any shortfall.
4. *Compare the shortfall on the two dates.* There is a voidable preference to the extent that the shortfall has been reduced, provided that the reduction has reduced the value of the estate to the prejudice of other creditors.

Like the other exceptions to avoidance, §547(c)(5) is designed to protect legitimate, routine transactions that do not enable the creditor to obtain

33. Note that §547(c)(5) is concerned only with transfers within the prebankruptcy period. Under §552(a), acquisitions of collateral after the petition are not transfers because they are excluded from the floating lien and are estate property. Proceeds of prepetition collateral are also not transfers. They generally belong to the secured party, even if they are received postpetition, provided that nonbankruptcy law recognizes an interest in such proceeds, and the transfer of the proceeds is not otherwise avoidable. §522(b).

an impermissible advantage on the eve of bankruptcy. A holder of a floating lien who monitors the debtor's dealings with the collateral is able to reduce the risk of a shortfall. However, a lienholder who permits the debt to become undersecured takes the risk that any attempt to redress the deficiency by payment or new collateral could fall within the prebankruptcy period and be avoidable. Because the prebankruptcy avoidance period can only be ascertained once the petition has been filed, the lienholder will not know when it has begun until after the attempt at bolstering the interest has been made. Therefore, a careful lienholder should treat every day as the potential comparison date, and try to ensure that no shortfall ever occurs. *In re HovdeBray Enterprises*, 483 B.R. 187 (B.A.P. 8th Cir. 2012), illustrates how careful a secured creditor needs to be in setting up and monitoring its security interest. A bank granted an operating loan to the debtor about three years before its bankruptcy and took a security interest in inventory and accounts to secure the loan. However, the bank did not perfect its security interest by filing until the debtor defaulted on the loan. As it happened, this occurred within the 90-day prebankruptcy period. The value of the property covered by the security interest exceeded the debt as at the 90-day date so that there would have been no shortfall, and payments to the creditor in the 90-day period would have been protected by §547(c)(5). However, because the creditor had delayed perfecting its interest, the interest itself was avoidable under §547, which meant that all transfers pursuant to that interest within the 90-day period were outside of the protection of §547(c)(5).

Because §547(c)(5) requires a comparison of debt-collateral ratios at two points, valuation of the collateral at each stage is often an important issue on which the trustee and transferee may disagree. The extent of avoidance is enhanced by a lower value on the comparison date and a higher value on the bankruptcy date, and is reduced by contrary trend. (But bear in mind that valuation, on its own, is not the sole determinative factor. As noted above, to the extent that an increase in value results from an increase in market price or other facts not to the prejudice of creditors, there is no transfer.) As always, valuation is a factual issue to be determined under the circumstances of each case.

Before evidence can be received on value, the standard of valuation must be determined. Valuation of accounts could be based on their face value, collection value (the amount actually paid by customers), market value (the amount for which the accounts could be sold in a factoring transaction), book value (the amount at which they would be valued in accordance with accepted accounting practices), or contract value (the value placed on the accounts by the parties themselves when entering the transaction). Similarly, inventory could be valued based on its retail, wholesale, liquidation, or going-concern value. In deciding on the standard for valuation, the court must try to make a realistic assessment of the use or disposition of the collateral. Whatever standard of value is chosen, it must be applied to both the comparison date and the bankruptcy date.

(6) Statutory liens (§547(c)(6)). Section 547(c)(6) simply provides that statutory liens must be dealt with under §545, and they are beyond the scope of §547. If a statutory lien is unavoidable under §545, the trustee cannot try to avoid it under §547, even if it arose in the prebankruptcy period and satisfies all of §547(b)'s elements.

(7) Payment of debts for domestic support obligations (§547(c)(7)). As mentioned in sections 7.4.3 and 10.8.2, the Bankruptcy Reform Act of 1994 added a set of provisions designed to protect claims for family support obligations from the bankruptcy of a debtor spouse or parent. BAPCPA reinforced and refined these provisions. One of its refinements was to create a statutorily defined term, "domestic support obligation," in §101(14A) to cover a variety of domestic obligations owed to different parties. In essence the definition includes debts in the nature of alimony, maintenance, or support established by a separation agreement, divorce decree, property settlement agreement, court order, or determination of a governmental unit. The debt must be owed to or recoverable by a spouse, former spouse, child, the guardian or other person responsible for the child, or a governmental unit.

A transfer is not avoidable as a preference if it was the payment of a bona fide debt for a domestic support obligation. The statutory language makes it clear that the actual nature of the obligation—not merely the way that the parties have labeled or structured it—is determinative, and that the payment must relate to that obligation.

(8)-(9) Small-value transfers (§547(c)(8) and (9)). Where the debtor is an individual whose debts are primarily consumer debts, §547(c)(8) excludes a transfer from avoidance as a preference if the aggregate value of the property included in that transfer is less than $600. Section 547(c)(9) excludes avoidance of a transfer up to a total value of $6,225[34] where the debtor's debts are not primarily consumer debts. Section 547(c)(9) is not confined to individual debtors. Section 547(c)(8) was added to the Code in 1984 to prevent the recovery of small preferences in consumer cases. Following the recommendation of the 1994 National Bankruptcy Review Commission, BAPCPA enacted §547(c)(9) to expand the protection to cover nonconsumer debtors.

---

34. Section 547(c)(8) is not listed in §104, but §547(c)(9) is. Therefore, the dollar amount in §547(c)(9) is revised every three years, but the amount in §547(c)(8) is not. The figure in §547(c)(9) is that in effect from April 1, 2013. The next revision will take effect on April 1, 2016.

The Ninth Circuit Bankruptcy Appellate Panel explained the rationale for these sections in *Western States Glass Corp. v. Barris (In re Bay Area Glass, Inc.)*, 454 B.R. 86, 90 (B.A.P. 9th Cir. 2011):

> A policy that discourages litigation over relatively insignificant transfer amounts may promote commercial and judicial efficiency, not only by reducing litigation over nominal amounts, but also by preventing creditors with smaller claims from waiving otherwise meritorious defenses simply because the costs associated with defending against trustees' avoidance actions exceed any anticipated benefits.

The most frequent question raised in the case law addressing these sections is whether a court should aggregate all of the payments made to a single creditor during the preference period for purposes of determining whether that creditor may preclude avoidance. For example, imagine that Debtor rents furniture for her home from Company. She makes a $200 payment every month. After Debtor loses her job, Company demands that she start paying $400 each month to provide Company with a default cushion. She agrees. Three months later, Debtor files a Ch. 7 petition, and the trustee seeks to avoid three $400 payments to Company. Courts have held that Company cannot argue that §547(c)(8) precludes avoidance because each individual transfer at issue is less than $600. They have rejected this argument on the basis that the section's language and legislative history instruct courts to aggregate multiple transfers to a single creditor. Further, aggregation supports the policy rationale supporting §547(c)(8) and prevents creditors from manipulating the bankruptcy process by requiring debtors to make multiple, small-dollar transfers during the preference period.[35] Aggregation applies to §547(c)(9), as well.

§13.2 SETOFF UNDER §553

§13.2.1 Setoff in Nonbankruptcy Law

As a general principle of law, the debts of two persons who are mutually indebted may be set off against each other. For example, imagine that Company, Inc. owes Creditor $100,000 for materials, and Creditor owes Company, Inc. $50,000 based on an arbitration award stemming from a breach of contract. Both parties enjoy the right of setoff. For Creditor, the

35. See *Electric City Merchandise Co. v. Hailes (In re Hailes)*, 77 F.3d 873 (5th Cir. 1996) and *In re Transcontinental Refrigerated Lines, Inc.*, 438 B.R. 520 (Bankr. M.D. Pa. 2010).

setoff fully extinguishes its debt to Company, Inc. For Company, Inc., the setoff reduces to $50,000 the amount it owes to Creditor.

Section 553 recognizes a party's right to setoff under applicable nonbankruptcy law. The section does not create the right, though. Consequently, to exercise a right of setoff in a bankruptcy case, a creditor must 1) possess a right of setoff under applicable nonbankruptcy law; 2) satisfy the elements in §553(a); and 3) not be subject to any of the exceptions in §§553(a)(1), (a)(2), or (a)(3). However, the right to setoff is not absolute. The decision to allow a setoff lies within the discretion of the bankruptcy court.[36]

§13.2.2 Understanding Setoff Rights in Bankruptcy

When one of the mutually indebted parties becomes bankrupt, the other party's exercise of the right of setoff permitted by nonbankruptcy law results in full payment of the debt due from the bankrupt debtor to the extent that it is covered by the other debt. If §547 applied to setoffs, such a transaction could satisfy all its elements. For example, say that the debtor became indebted to the creditor for $1,000 four months before bankruptcy. Two months later, the debtor performed services for the creditor in an unrelated transaction for a fee of $1,000. Setoff simply cancels each debt. If the debtor was insolvent at the time of setoff, the transaction would satisfy all of the five elements of §547(b). It is a transfer to a creditor on account of an antecedent debt, made while the debtor was insolvent, during the 90-day prebankruptcy period. Except in the rare case where the estate has enough funds to pay all unsecured creditors in full, the setoff would prefer the creditor because it results in full payment of the debt. Had there been no setoff, the creditor would have had to pay the estate the $1,000 owed to the debtor and would have to prove claim for the $1,000 owed by the debtor. This claim would have been paid at the rate of distribution payable to general unsecured creditors. None of the exceptions in §547(c) apply.

Notwithstanding its potentially preferential effect, a right of setoff valid under nonbankruptcy law is not covered by §547 but is governed by §553, which generally upholds the setoff in bankruptcy provided that it does not fall within the limited grounds of avoidance under §553, which are addressed below. A valid right of setoff may be exercised at any time up to the petition, and may also be asserted thereafter following relief from stay. (Setoff is subject to the stay under §362(a)(7) and cannot be exercised postpetition without relief being obtained.)

---

36. See *Meyer Med. Physicians Grp., Ltd. v. Health Care Serv. Corp.*, 385 F.3d 1039, 1041 (7th Cir. 2004); see also *In re Kingsley*, 518 F.3d 874, 877 (11th Cir. 2008).

The policy of protecting the right of setoff is a longstanding one. It may seem like an exception to bankruptcy's general aim of evenhanded treatment of creditors because a creditor with a right of setoff is given more favorable treatment than one who just received payment of the debt during the pre-bankruptcy preference period. However, it is not really an exception at all because the right of setoff is treated as akin to a security interest—the mutual debt secures each party against the other's nonpayment. Section 506(a) expressly recognizes a right of setoff as a secured claim to the extent of the amount that is subject to setoff. (It is an unsecured claim to the extent that the amount due to the creditor is less than its claim.) For example, the debtor borrowed money from Bank, and the balance of the loan as at the petition dates is $10,000. The debtor also has a savings account at Bank, with a balance of $6,000 as at the petition date. A bank deposit is categorized in law as a debt due by the bank to its customer. Under nonbankruptcy law, if the debtor should default in repaying the loan, the bank would be entitled to set off the amount in the savings account against the debt due by the debtor. Section 553 upholds that setoff right in bankruptcy provided that none of the limitations in that section apply, and §506 treats the right of setoff as a secured claim. As a result, upon bankruptcy, Bank has a secured claim to the extent of the $6,000 deposit in the account, and an unsecured claim for the $4,000 balance of the loan in excess of that amount. *See* Example 7.

§13.2.3 §553(a)'s Requirements

Section 553(a) requires a creditor to satisfy four elements in order to exercise an existing right of setoff: 1) the creditor must hold a claim against the debtor under §101(5) of the Code; 2) the creditor's claim must have arisen prepetition; 3) the creditor must owe a prepetition debt to the debtor; and 4) the claim and the debt must be mutual obligations.[37] The first element is usually uncontroversial. The term "claim" is construed broadly and captures any right to payment, regardless of whether the right is "reduced to judgment, liquidated, unliquidated, fixed, contingent, matured, unmatured, disputed, undisputed, legal, equitable, secured, or unsecured."[38]

The second element requires that the creditor's claim against the debtor arose prepetition, and the third element requires that the creditor's debt to the debtor also arose prepetition. These elements are usually uncontested, but in cases where either is disputed, most courts rely on the "conduct test." The conduct test fixes the date that a claim arose by determining "the date of

37. See, e.g., *In re James River Coal Co.*, 534 B.R. 666, 669–70 (Bankr. E.D. Va.2015).
38. 11 U.S.C. §101(5)(A) (2010).

the conduct giving rise to the claim."[39] Courts that follow the conduct test hold that a claim arises "when the acts giving rise to [the defendant's] liability were performed, not when the harm caused by those acts was manifested."[40] In other words, a party seeking setoff must show that all transactions necessary for liability occurred prepetition.[41]

Finally, the fourth element requires that the claim and the debt must be mutual obligations. The condition is satisfied when the offsetting obligations are held by the same parties in the same capacity.[42] For example, imagine that the creditor holds a claim against the debtor, but the debtor's claim is against the creditor's corporate parent. The mutuality requirement would not be satisfied.[43]

§13.2.4 Limitations on the Right of Setoff

The limitations on setoff in §553 are designed to prevent abuses and to ensure that a creditor does not try to manipulate setoff rights to obtain an inappropriate advantage. The right of setoff may not be exercised by a creditor to the extent that any one of the following conditions is satisfied.

(1) §533(a)(1). The creditor's claim has been disallowed as a claim against the estate. This is the most obvious restriction on setoff. If the court disallows the creditor's claim, the effect must necessarily be that the creditor cannot use that claim to reduce any debt that the creditor owes to the estate.

(2) §533(a)(2). The creditor has acquired the claim by transfer from another entity either during the 90-day prebankruptcy period while the debtor was insolvent or after the commencement of the case. As in §547, there is a presumption of insolvency during the 90-day prebankruptcy period (§553(c)). This exception is aimed at transactions in

39. *In re Parker*, 313 F.3d 1267, 1269 (10th Cir. 2002) (citing *Grady v. A.H. Robins Co., Inc.*, 839 F.2d 198 (4th Cir. 1988)).

40. *In re Grossman's Inc.*, 607 F.3d 114, 122 (3d Cir. 2010).

41. See *In re Corporate Resource Services, Inc.*, 564 B.R. 196, 207 (Bankr. S.D.N.Y. 2017). Some courts have used a different test called the prepetition relationship test. This test imposes all the requirements of the conduct test but also requires that there must be a qualifying relationship — based on contract, exposure, impact, or privity — between the debtor and the creditor.

42. See *Meyer Med. Physicians Grp., Ltd. v. Health Care Serv. Corp.* (In re Meyer Med. Physicians Grp., Ltd.), 385 F.3d 1039, 1041 (7th Cir. 2004).

43. One exception to this general rule is that the U.S. government is considered a "unitary creditor" for purposes of meeting the mutuality requirement under §553(a), even if the claims at issue involve more than one agency. See *United States v. Maxwell*, 157 F.3d 1099, 1103 (7th Cir. 1998).

which a person who owes money to debtor of the estate takes over the claim of a creditor of the estate so that the debt and claim can be offset. Such a transaction would be prejudicial to the estate because the combination of the debt and claim in the hands of the estate's debtor has the effect of reducing or eliminating the debt that would otherwise be payable to the estate. For example, imagine that Finance Company made an unsecured prepetition loan of $10,000 to Debtor, Inc. Finance Company therefore has an unsecured claim of $10,000 against the estate. Buyer bought $10,000 of raw materials from Debtor on credit before the bankruptcy and had not paid the price of the goods by the time of the petition. Consequently, Buyer owes $10,000[44] to the estate. If these two transactions are kept separate, the trustee would be able to recover the full $10,000 from Buyer, but the estate would only pay Finance Company at the rate of distribution to unsecured creditors. If that rate is 10 percent, Finance Company would receive only $1,000 on its claim. The net result is that the estate would be enhanced by $9,000. However, further imagine that Finance Company and Buyer enter into a transaction whereby Finance Company sells its claim of $10,000 to Buyer for $5,000. Without §553(a)(2), Buyer could setoff its newly purchased $10,000 claim against the $10,000 it owes to the estate. The effect of this setoff is that the estate loses $9,000, to the detriment of the creditor body. To avoid this kind of manipulation, §553(a)(2) generally invalidates a setoff right 1) acquired from another entity within the 90 days before the petition and while the debtor was insolvent, or 2) after commencement of the case.

(3) §553(a)(3). The debt due from the creditor was incurred during the 90-day prebankruptcy period, while the debtor was insolvent, and for the purpose of obtaining a right of setoff against the claim owed to the creditor. This subsection may sound repetitious of §553(a)(2), but it deals with a different situation. It does not target a creditor's acquisition of a setoff right from a third party. Instead, the subsection invalidates the deliberate creation of a setoff right between the debtor and a creditor on the eve of bankruptcy. For example, imagine that the debtor owes Bank $10,000 as a result of a loan. Bank becomes concerned about the debtor's financial situation. To give itself some protection from default, Bank insists that the debtor open a savings account with it and maintain a deposit of not less than $4,000 in the account. A bank account constitutes a debt by Bank to the debtor, its depositor. The effect of this arrangement is that if the debtor became bankrupt, the bank would cut its losses by having a $4,000 right of setoff against the loan debt; in other words it would now have a partially

44. The debt to the debtor and claim against the debtor are in the same amount in this example. This need not be so. If the debts are not of equal amount, setoff operates to the extent of the lesser amount.

secured claim instead of a completely unsecured claim, and the secured claim would be paid in full. Section 533(a)(3) precludes a party from invoking setoff rights created 1) within 90 days of the petition, 2) while the debtor was insolvent, and 3) with the purpose of creating the setoff right. In most cases, the disputed element will be whether the creditor actually incurred the debt for the purpose of creating a right of setoff. Ultimately, this element entails a subjective inquiry as to whether the creditor's motive was to obtain a setoff and improve its position among the debtor's other creditors in the event of a bankruptcy filing.[45]

(4) §553(b). The setoff has enabled the creditor to improve its position in the 90-day prebankruptcy period by reducing an insufficiency between the claim against and the debt due to the debtor. This is an improvement-in-position test similar in concept to that in §547(c)(5). Although there are differences in the rules of the tests in §§553(b) and 547(c)(5), both tests use a two-point comparison. Stated in the simplest terms (and without its qualifications and refinements), the test in §553(b) is intended to prevent a creditor from using setoff in the 90 days before bankruptcy in order to recover more of its claim than it could have recovered if the mutual debts had been set off 90 days before the petition. The test requires measurement of the amount (if any) by which the creditor's claim exceeds its debt to the debtor on the 90-day date and on the date of setoff. If the insufficiency in the setoff—that is, the amount of the creditor's claim in excess of the debtor's claim—is reduced between the 90-day date and the setoff date, the offset is recoverable by the trustee to the extent of that reduction.

For example, imagine that the debtor filed bankruptcy on March 1. On December 1 (which is within the 90-day period prior to the petition date), the debtor owes Creditor $50,000 for accounting services. On that same date, Creditor owes the debtor $10,000 for raw materials supplied to Creditor. On February 1, after the debtor supplied an additional $25,000 in raw materials to Creditor, the debtor still owed Creditor $50,000, but now Creditor owes the debtor $35,000. Creditor decides to effectuate a setoff of the $35,000 on February 10. Section 553(b) would allow the trustee in the debtor's bankruptcy case to recover from Creditor. Creditor's insufficiency 90 days before the petition date was $40,000. Creditor's insufficiency as of the date of setoff (February 10) was only $15,000.

45. See *In re Southern Indus. Banking Corp.*, 809 F.2d 329, 332 (6th Cir. 1987). *In re HovdeBray Enterprises*, 483 B.R. 187 (B.A.P. 8th Cir. 2012), illustrates this situation. In that case, in addition to holding that the §547(c)(5) exception did not save the creditor bank's floating lien, the court invalidated a setoff created by an arrangement between the bank and the debtor within 90 days of the petition, under which the debtor made a deposit with the bank. The court found that the deposit was not an ordinary course transaction, but rather was deliberately arranged for the purpose of giving the bank a right of setoff.

The trustee can recover $25,000 from Creditor under §553(b) because Creditor improved its position by that amount during the 90-day period prior to the petition date.

Examples

EXAMPLES

1. On January 1, Binow & Palater, Inc. sold and delivered goods to Gloria Transit Co., Inc. The price of the goods, $2,000, was to be paid within 30 days of delivery. Gloria Transit failed to pay on the February 1 due date. After making demands for payment, Binow & Palater received a check for $2,000 from Gloria Transit on March 30. The check was deposited immediately and was paid by Gloria Transit's bank on April 5.

   Gloria Transit had been in financial difficulty for some time, and its liabilities had exceeded the value of its assets since November last year. On July 1, it filed a voluntary Ch. 7 petition. After secured and priority claims are paid, the fund remaining in the estate will be enough to pay 10 percent of unsecured general claims. Has there been a transfer avoidable under §547(b)?

2. On January 1, Gloria Transit Co., Inc. bought some other goods on credit from Prudential Purveyors, Inc. At the time of the sale, Prudential retained a security interest in the goods that was properly perfected by filing under UCC Article 9 on January 20. The price of the goods was $2,000. Gloria Transit was obliged to pay for the goods in two installments due at the end of February and March. It failed to make the payments on the due dates. Upon being threatened with foreclosure, it paid half the debt ($1,000) on April 10. No further payments were made, and Gloria Transit filed its Ch. 7 petition on July 1.

   If the collateral is worth $2,500 at the time of the petition, can the trustee avoid the payment of $1,000? What difference would it make if the collateral was worth $1,500 or $2,000?

3. On February 15, Gloria Transit Co., Inc. borrowed money from D. Laid Security, Inc. to purchase a piece of equipment. On that day, the parties executed a security agreement under which Gloria Transit gave a security interest in the equipment to D. Laid Security. D. Laid Security immediately remitted the loan funds to the supplier of the equipment, which delivered the equipment to Gloria Transit on the same day.

   D. Laid Security normally perfects its secured transactions immediately. However, because of an oversight, no filing was made at the time of the agreement. The omission was discovered during a routine audit in May, and the filing was made on May 3.

   Gloria Transit filed its bankruptcy petition on July 1. Is there an avoidable transfer here?

4. In January, a customer of Gloria Transit Co., Inc. commenced suit against it for damages arising out of a breach of contract. On January 15, the plaintiff obtained an order of attachment, and on January 20 it levied on a piece of equipment owned by Gloria Transit.[46] On June 1, the plaintiff obtained judgment against Gloria Transit. On June 10, it levied execution on the equipment that had been held in the sheriff's custody under the writ of attachment. A sale in execution was scheduled for July 3. On July 1, before the sale could take place, Gloria Transit filed its bankruptcy petition.

   Has there been a transfer avoidable under §547(b)?

5. On February 15, Annie C. Dent borrowed $5,000 from Fallshort Finance Co. for the purpose of paying for some orthodontic treatment for her son. To secure the loan, Annie executed a security agreement granting Fallshort Finance a security interest in an antique cabinet that had been appraised at $6,000. Fallshort Finance filed a financing statement in proper form on February 20. Unknown to both parties, the cabinet had been incorrectly appraised, and its true value was only $2,500. This fact was not discovered until Annie's trustee had the cabinet reappraised after her bankruptcy.

   In terms of the loan agreement, Annie was obliged to repay her debt to Fallshort Finance at the rate of $200 per month. She paid on time in the months of March, April, and May, and then defaulted, leaving a balance of $4,400 plus interest due to Fallshort Finance. Before Fallshort Finance could proceed to foreclose on its security interest, Annie filed her bankruptcy petition on July 1.

   Are any of the transfers to Fallshort Finance avoidable under §547(b)? Will any exception in §547(c) protect such transfers from avoidance?

6. In February Chex N. DeMail borrowed $5,000 from his friend, Annette Result, promising to repay the loan in a month. When he failed to pay on the due date, Annette began to nag him and eventually threatened never to speak to him again unless he repaid her. Eventually, on May 15, Chico sent Annette payment of the $5,000. Unknown to Annette, Chico was insolvent at this time.

   On June 1, Chico called on Annette with a hard luck story and a plea for another loan. Being softhearted, Annette loaned him $3,000, which he promised to repay in two weeks. As before, Chico failed to repay the loan on its due date and still owed the money to Annette when he filed a

46. Attachment is explained in section 2.3.2. It is a remedy that is available in some cases (as in this one for a debt on a contract) in the period before the plaintiff has obtained judgment. Levy of attachment creates a lien on the attached property that secures the judgment that is ultimately obtained.

voluntary Ch. 7 petition on July 1. Shortly thereafter, Chico's trustee in bankruptcy demanded that Annette pay to the estate the $5,000 received from Chico on May 15.

Is the trustee justified in making this demand?

7. Two years ago, Mutual Obligation Co., Inc. entered into a contract with the U.S. Air Force in which it undertook to construct buildings on an air base. It breached the contract and became liable to pay damages to the Air Force. The Air Force sued to recover the damages, and the parties settled the suit a few months ago. In terms of the settlement, Mutual agreed to pay the Air Force $500,000. Last month, Mutual obtained a judgment in a case that had been pending in the U.S. Tax Court, obliging the Internal Revenue Service to refund $300,000 in overpaid federal taxes. Mutual had been struggling financially for some time, and it has now filed a petition under Ch. 7. It is badly insolvent, can no longer conduct its business, and will be liquidated. At the date of filing, it had not paid the damages due to the Air Force and had not received a refund of its overpaid taxes from the I.R.S.

Immediately after the filing, the government applied for relief from stay so that it could offset the tax refund of $300,000 due to Mutual against the $500,000 damages due by Mutual. It would then prove an unsecured claim of $200,000 against the estate. The trustee has challenged the government's claim of setoff on the grounds that there is no mutual indebtedness because Mutual's claim is against the I.R.S., not the Air Force. In the alternative, the trustee argues that even if the indebtedness was mutual, the setoff right is avoidable because it arose within 90 days of bankruptcy. Are these good arguments?

Explanations

1. The chronology of the transaction is as follows:

				90-day period		
Jan. 1	Feb. 1	Feb./Mar.	Mar. 30	Apr. 2	Apr. 5	July 1
Goods sold on credit and delivered	Payment due	Demands made	Check received	Check paid		Bankruptcy filing

First determine if the transfer qualifies as a preference under §547(b). If it does, then consider if any of the exceptions to avoidance in §547(c) apply. It does satisfy all five of the requirements for avoidance. First, the payment is a transfer of property of the debtor to the creditor. When payment is made by check, it is not the delivery of the check, which is merely an order to the bank, but its payment by the drawee bank that constitutes the transfer for purposes of §547(b). This was settled by *Barnhill v. Johnson*, 503 U.S. 393 (1992), following general principles of nonbankruptcy law.[47]

Second, the transfer is on account of an antecedent debt. In a sale of goods, the debt of the buyer normally arises when the goods are delivered. See *In re Energy Co-Op, Inc.*, 832 F.2d 997 (7th Cir. 1987). Thus, the debt was created on January 1 and is antecedent to the transfer on April 15.

Third, Gloria Transit was insolvent at the time of the transfer. Under §101(32), insolvency is determined on the basis of the balance sheet test. The presumption of insolvency in §547(f) eases the trustee's burden of proving this element.

Fourth, the transfer—the payment of the check on April 2—occurred within the prepetition avoidance period. Because Binow & Palater is not an insider of Gloria Transit Co., the preference period is 90 days before the petition. Counted back from the bankruptcy date, the 90-day period begins on April 2.

Fifth, the transfer improves the position of Binow & Palater. The improvement-in-position test requires a comparison to be made between the total amount Binow & Palater would receive in a Ch. 7 distribution if the transfer had not been made, and the total satisfaction it receives (combining the transfer and the Ch. 7 distribution on any balance of its claim) if the transfer is left undisturbed. If the transfer is not avoided, Binow & Palater is paid in full; if it is avoided, Binow & Palater, as a general unsecured creditor, will receive approximately 10 percent of its claim. (The percentage will increase slightly over 10 percent because the fund available to unsecured creditors will be enlarged by the value of the returned transfer.) Hence, the transfer has improved the position of Binow & Palater. Section 547(b)(5) is almost always satisfied when the transfer has been made to a general unsecured (or partially secured) creditor and the estate has insufficient funds to pay general unsecured

47. *Barnhill* focused on the question of whether delivery or payment of the check constituted the transfer for the purposes of §547(b). The Court expressly confined its opinion to §547(b) and left open the issue of whether a different rule should apply where the date of transfer must be determined for the purpose of establishing an exception under §547(c). There is substantial lower court authority that the date of delivery, rather than the date of payment, should be determinative where the transferee seeks to show that a transfer was substantially contemporaneous under §547(c)(1), or is made in the ordinary course of business under §547(c)(2), or constitutes a post-transfer payment of new value to the debtor under §547(c)(4). The Supreme Court acknowledged that the policy of protecting regular commercial practices could justify a different rule under these subsections.

creditors in full. Any portion of the debt that is satisfied by a prebankruptcy transfer is paid at a higher rate than it would be in bankruptcy.

Having determined that §547(b) is satisfied, one must now consider if one of the exceptions in §547(c) applies. None of them do. Most are not even remotely relevant, but §547(c)(1) and (2) merit some discussion. Section 547(c)(1) does not save the transaction because the transfer is not a substantially contemporaneous exchange for new value. Although §547(c)(1) was drafted with check transactions in mind, the kind of exchange contemplated was the immediate delivery of a check in payment of the goods or services. In the present case, the parties intended a credit transaction. Section 547(c)(2) protects ordinary-course transactions and covers regular payments on ordinary debts. In the present case, the debt may have been incurred in the ordinary course of business, but the payment was not routine or regular. It was overdue, and followed some pressure by the creditor. This is not the kind of payment that should be excepted from avoidance under §547(c)(2).

2. Chronological diagram:

Jan. 1	Jan. 20	Apr. 2	Apr. 10	July 1
Sale and creation of security interest	Perfection of security interest	90-day date	Overdue partial payment of $1,000	Bankruptcy filing

Unlike Binow & Palater in Example 1, Prudential has a perfected secured claim. (Although the creation of a security interest is expressly included in the definition of transfer in §101(54), that transfer is not within the preference period, and its avoidance is not in issue.) The payment of $1,000 on April 10 is also a transfer. It satisfies the first four requirements of §547(b) (*see* the analysis in the Explanation to Example 1). However, the fact that Prudential has a secured claim affects the improvement-in-position test of §547(b)(5).

If the collateral is worth $2,500 on the date of the petition, the payment to Prudential did not enable it to do better than it would have done in the absence of the transfer: Prior to the transfer it had a secured claim of $2,000 which would have been paid in full from the proceeds of the collateral. The transfer reduces the claim to $1,000, which would still be paid in full, with a large surplus left over for the estate. Either way, Prudential is paid in full. Because one of the requirements of §547(b) is not satisfied, the transfer is unavoidable. This shows that a valid security interest, perfected before the 90-day preference period, fully protects the creditor, provided that the collateral is sufficiently valuable to accommodate the entire debt. (Example 3 deals with the creation of a security interest within the 90-day period.)

If the collateral is worth only $1,500 at the time of the petition, the improvement-in-position analysis changes. The transfer reduced the debt to $1,000, so that it became fully covered by the collateral. Without the transfer, the debt would have been undersecured with a deficiency of $500. As the deficiency would have been paid as a general unsecured claim, Prudential would not receive full payment unless the estate has sufficient funds to pay general unsecured claims in full. Thus, by eliminating the deficiency, the transfer improved Prudential's position and is avoidable. None of the exceptions in §547(c) apply. As a result, Prudential is obliged to return the $1,000 to the estate and to prove a claim for its secured debt of $1,500 and its unsecured debt of $500. (By agreement with the trustee, Prudential may be permitted to keep the $1,000 and to deduct it from the secured claim, leaving it with a secured claim of $500 and an unsecured claim of $500.)

If the collateral is worth $2,000, the result may seem to be the same as it was in the first example: The transfer did not improve Prudential's position, because the secured claim would have been paid in full out of the collateral even in the absence of the transfer. However, the exact equivalence of the debt and collateral does change the answer: A secured claimant is entitled to interest, legal costs and attorney's fees under §506(b), to the extent of any surplus value in the collateral. Without the transfer, there would be no such surplus, so no interest, costs, and fees could be claimed. However, payment of the $1,000 creates a surplus by reducing the debt in relation to the collateral value. The right to interest, costs, and fees improves Prudential's position and makes the transfer avoidable. This demonstrates that a secured creditor does well to ensure that an equity cushion exists in the collateral so that payments on the debt are fully protected.

3. Chronological diagram:

Feb. 15	Apr. 2	May 3	July 1
Security agreement executed. Loan funds remitted to seller. Equipment delivered to debtor.	90-day date	Perfection	Bankruptcy filing

The facts mention no payments to D. Laid Security, so the only transfer in issue is the grant of the security interest, which, as stated before, constitutes a transfer under §101(54). Although D. Laid Security discovered its error before the petition was filed, thereby preventing avoidance of its interest under §544(a),[48] the perfection in the 90-day period could make the transfer avoidable under §547(b). The crucial issue is the date of the transfer: If it occurred at the time of execution of the security agreement, it is outside of the 90-day period and is contemporaneous with the debt. However, if it occurred when the interest was perfected, it falls within the 90-day period and is some considerable time after the creation of the debt.

Section 547(e)(2) sets out the rules for fixing the date of the transfer:

(1) The transfer normally takes effect for bankruptcy purposes on its effective date as between the parties under nonbankruptcy law.

(2) If an act of perfection is required by nonbankruptcy law, that act must be completed within 30 days of the effective date as between the parties. If so, the effective date remains the date of the transfer for bankruptcy purposes. If perfection is delayed beyond the 30-day period, the date of perfection becomes the transfer date. (Under §547(e)(1), a transfer of real property is perfected when a bona fide purchaser of the property from the debtor cannot acquire an interest in the property superior to the transferee. A transfer of personal property is perfected when it is effective against an ordinary judicial lienholder.)

(3) If the transfer has not been perfected by the time the petition is filed, the transfer is deemed to have occurred immediately before the filing of the petition. However, if the 30-day period for perfection has not yet expired when the petition is filed, the transferee may complete the act of perfection within the 30-day period, in which case the transfer occurs on the date that it took effect between the parties.

Under UCC §9.203, a security interest takes effect between the parties (attaches) when the security agreement is authenticated in proper form, the debtor has rights in the collateral, and value is given by the secured party. This happened on February 15, when the agreement was executed, D. Laid Security advanced money to the seller, and the equipment was delivered to Gloria Transit. The perfection of the interest occurred on May 3, when the proper filing was made. Because the perfection is more than 30 days after the date on which the transfer took effect as between the parties, the transfer is deemed to have occurred on the perfection date. This places the transfer in the 90-day period, and it removes it in time from the debt, thereby making the debt antecedent. Therefore, assuming that the presumption of insolvency cannot be

48. *See* section 12.2.1 and Example 1 of Chapter 12.

rebutted, the elements of §547(b) are satisfied — there is a transfer to D. Laid Security on account of an antecedent debt within the 90-day period. Because D. Laid Security would be a general unsecured creditor in the absence of the transfer (its unperfected security interest would be avoided under §544), the transfer does improve its position unless the estate is solvent and can pay all creditors in full. The 30-day grace period in §547(e), like the avoidance power in §544, is a manifestation of the policy against unrecorded interests. By placing the security interest in jeopardy if there is a delay in perfection beyond the fairly short period of 30 days, it encourages secured parties to record their interests expeditiously.

None of the exceptions to avoidance in §547(c) are applicable. Section 547(c)(1) is not likely to save the transfer. It would be a real stretch to argue that a delay of nearly three months is substantially contemporaneous. Section 547(c)(3) also does not save the transfer. Even though the interest was a purchase-money security interest, the special grace period for perfection, measured 30 days from the debtor's receipt of possession of the collateral, does not extend the time for perfection on the present facts because the delivery of the collateral to the debtor coincided with, and was not later than the effective date of the transfer.

4. Chronological diagram:

Jan. 15	Jan. 20	Apr. 2	June 1	June 10	July 1
Attachment authorized	Attachment writ levied	90-day date	Judgment	Execution levied	Bankruptcy filing
	attachment lien			execution lien	

As discussed in section 2.3.2, under general principles of state law, attachment gives rise to an inchoate lien that is effective on the date of the levy of the writ of attachment. When execution is ultimately levied after judgment, the execution lien merges with the earlier attachment lien and backdates for priority purposes to the date of the levy of attachment. Therefore, although the execution lien is a transfer[49] within the 90-day period, the prior attachment lien has already secured the debt so that the execution lien does not prefer the lienholder in position. Section 547(b)(5) is not satisfied, and the lien is unavoidable.

49. The definition of *transfer* in §101(54) includes involuntary dispositions.

Although the execution lien backdates in priority, this example does not raise the issue dealt with by the Supreme Court in *Fidelity Financial Services, Inc. v. Fink*, 522 U.S. 211 (1998). As discussed in section 13.1.3, the court held that "perfection," as used in §547(e)(1)(B), means the act of perfection, not its retrospective priority date. For this reason, if a transfer was perfected outside the grace period allowed by that section, the perfection cannot be backdated to fit within the grace period, even if nonbankruptcy law permits such backdating for priority purposes. In the present case, we are not concerned with trying to backdate the perfection of the execution lien under §547(e) so as to avoid the problem of a transfer for a noncontemporaneous debt. This is simply a case in which the transfer of the execution lien does not prefer the creditor in position because the property is already secured by the preexisting, unavoidable, attachment lien. (Although the attachment lien is inchoate in the sense that it would lapse if the creditor failed to levy execution within the prescribed time after judgment, it did not in fact lapse and was immediately succeeded by the execution lien.)

5. There have been four transfers to Fallshort Finance in this case: the grant of the security interest and the three payments. The security interest and the first payment are outside the 90-day period and are not in issue. The payments for April and May are avoidable under §547(b) because they satisfy all the elements of that subsection. (Example 2 explains why the payment to an undersecured creditor satisfies the improvement-in-position test.)

   The payments were not contemporaneous exchanges for new value, so §547(c)(1) is not applicable. However, §547(c)(2) likely protects from avoidance the regularly scheduled installment payments due under the loan agreement. As noted in section 13.1.4(2), §547(c)(2) is applicable to payments on a long-term debt provided that the debt was incurred in the ordinary course of business or financial affairs of both the debtor and the transferee and payment was in the ordinary course or according to ordinary business terms. The loan here is probably a one-time transaction because Annie does not regularly borrow money to pay for orthodontic treatment. However, a one-time transaction can qualify as a debt incurred in the ordinary course as long as it fits in with Annie's ordinary patterns of domestic consumption and is a normal transaction for a person in her position. The payments on the debt made up to the time of Annie's default also qualify as in the ordinary course because they were routine and regular payments made in terms of the loan agreement.

6. If it were not for §547(c)(4), the trustee would be entitled to demand return of the payment of $5,000 because it satisfies all the elements of a preference under §547(b). Annette would be obliged to return the

money and prove a claim against the estate for the two loans totaling $8,000.

However, §547(c)(4) makes the transfer to Annette unavoidable to the extent that, after the transfer, Annette gave new value to Chex without receiving a new unavoidable transfer or security interest in exchange for it. After being paid the $5,000, Annette made a second loan of $3,000. Its value must be offset against the $5,000 preference, making only $2,000 of the payment avoidable. Annette may therefore keep $3,000 of the payment, but must return $2,000 to the estate. She must now prove a claim in the estate for $5,000—the $2,000 balance on the original loan plus the $3,000 on the second loan.

7. Before Mutual obtained the Tax Court judgment, the Air Force had an unsecured claim of $500,000 against it. If the government cannot offset the debt to the estate for the tax refund against the Air Force's claim against the estate, it will have to pay the full $300,000 to the estate, and will prove its general unsecured claim of $500,000. Because the estate is badly insolvent, it may receive nothing or only a small fraction of its claim. However, if it can set off the debts, it could keep the $300,000 that would otherwise have been payable to the estate and apply it to the payment of its claim, which would be treated as secured to the extent of the $300,000. Only the balance of $200,000 would be an unsecured claim. Given the insolvency of the estate, the setoff would surely improve the government's position.

   Setoff can only be used when the parties are mutually indebted. It may sound as if this requirement is not satisfied here because Mutual's debt is owed to the Air Force, but it is the I.R.S., not the Air Force, that is indebted to Mutual. However, the real creditor is the U.S. government, and the Air Force and I.R.S. are simply agencies of the creditor. They are not separate entities. In *In re HAL, Inc.*, 122 F.3d 851 (9th Cir. 1997), the court permitted the setoff of debts owed by the debtor to some federal agencies against debts due to the debtor by others. It held that for the purposes of setoff, all agencies of the federal government must be treated as parts of a single governmental unit—a unitary creditor—and that a debt due to one agency of this unit can be offset by a debt owed by another. (The same principle would apply to agencies of the government of a single state, but obviously would not apply when agencies of different states or state and federal governments are involved.)

   This conclusion makes sense as a matter of principle, because all these agencies derive their funding and authority from a centralized source and do not operate autonomously. It has some support in the language of §553, read with the definitions in §101, but there is an ambiguity in §101(27) which could also justify a contrary argument: Section 553 refers to the setoff right of a "creditor," which is defined in

§101(10) to be an entity with a claim against the debtor. "Entity" is in turn defined in §101(15) to include a governmental unit, which is defined in §101(27) to include the United States, states, and other local and regional authorities, as well as their departments, agencies, and instrumentalities. *HAL* read this as meaning that the U.S. government, including its agencies and constituent parts, must be deemed an indivisible governmental unit, but a glance at that section will demonstrate that it could just as easily be read to mean that each constituent part qualifies as a "governmental unit" on its own.

Once the issue of mutual indebtedness is resolved, we must look at §553 to see if any of its grounds for avoidance are satisfied. They are not. Contrary to the trustee's argument, there is no bar to setoff merely because the mutual debt was created within the 90 days before bankruptcy. For the setoff to be avoidable, the setoff must be tainted in one of the ways specified in §553, which involve a defect in the claim itself or conduct by the creditor designed to create an improper improvement in position in the 90 days before bankruptcy.

CHAPTER 14

Fraudulent Transfers (§548) and Postpetition Transfers (§549)

§14.1 OVERVIEW OF FRAUDULENT TRANSFER LAW

In 1570, the Statute of Elizabeth was enacted to address a basic form of creditor evasion: when a borrower is unable to pay debts as they come due or anticipates being in such an unenviable position, she will be tempted to place some or all of her valuable assets beyond the reach of creditors, with an eye towards subsequently recovering them.[1] Pursuant to the statute, any transfer by a debtor made with the actual intent to hinder, delay, or defraud the debtor's creditors was void. Fraudulent transfer law that appears in the Bankruptcy Code and state law is based on this fundamental premise. However, the law has evolved dramatically since the sixteenth century and now covers many types of wrongful conduct and complex business transactions. Trustees routinely use fraudulent transfer law to recover multimillion-dollar payments and transfers that squander estate assets.

Section 548 voids any transfer that was made

1. on or within two years before the petition date; and
2. with an actual intent to hinder, delay, or defraud creditors.

1. *See* Samir D. Parikh, *Saving Fraudulent Transfer Law*, 86 Am. Bankr. L. J. 305, 315 (2012).

Further, the section also voids any transfer:

1. that was made on or within two years before the petition date;
2. for which the debtor did not receive reasonably equivalent value; and
3a. made while the debtor was insolvent or caused the debtor to become insolvent;
3b. left the debtor with unreasonably small capital in relation to its business;
3c. caused the debtor to incur a debt that it would be unable to pay as such debt matured; or
3d. made to an insider under an employment contract and not in the ordinary course of business.

States have their own fraudulent transfer laws, as explained in section 14.2. The substantive provisions of these laws mirror §548. Before a bankruptcy case is filed, state law provides creditors the means to recover fraudulently transferred property. After a bankruptcy filing, the state law remedy becomes available to the bankruptcy trustee pursuant to §544—which allows the trustee to bring a fraudulent transfer action based on applicable state law.[2] Trustees will often rely on state fraudulent transfer law because, though the substantive law is extremely similar to §548, state law invariably has a much longer statute of limitations.

§14.2 STATE FRAUDULENT TRANSFER LAW

As explained in section 2.1, an unsecured creditor takes the risk that the debtor will have no executable property to satisfy a delinquent claim. If the absence of assets is the natural result of economic adversity, the creditor can do little about it. However, a creditor may be able to avoid the transfer and recover the property or its value if the creditor can show that the debtor disposed of assets under circumstances that improperly placed them beyond the reach of execution. The avoidance of fraudulent transfers in state collection proceedings is governed by state statutes. Most states have adopted a uniform model act on fraudulent transfers, the UFTA (introduced in Chapter 12), which was drafted by the National Conference of Commissioners on Uniform State Laws (the "National Conference") in 1984.[3] This model

2. The trustee's power under §544 to use state fraudulent transfer law to avoid a fraudulent transfer is discussed in section 12.2.2.
3. In 2014, the National Conference approved the Uniform Voidable Transactions Act (UVTA) to replace the UFTA. The substantive provisions of the UVTA and the UFTA are

statute is an update of a 1918 uniform model law, the *Uniform Fraudulent Conveyance Act* (UFCA). The widespread enactment of the UFTA has resulted in a relatively uniform state fraudulent transfer law. The discussion in this chapter is based on the UFTA, and the citations are to sections of that Act.

The action under state law to avoid a fraudulent transfer is available to unsecured creditors and is not used by a creditor who has a perfected lien or other interest in the transferred property, valid against third parties. Such perfected liens and interests are usually superior to the rights of a transferee, so the holder of the lien or interest does not need fraudulent transfer law to assert its interest or recover the property. By contrast, as explained in section 1.3 and Chapter 2, an unsecured creditor has no rights in the debtor's property and is vulnerable to the debtor's attempt to place executable property beyond its reach. Although an unsecured creditor normally has no power to interfere with the debtor's use or disposition of property, fraudulent transfer law qualifies this general rule to the extent that the debtor's transfer of property constitutes an abuse of the debtor's ownership rights, having the effect of defeating the justifiable recourse to that property by the unsecured creditor.

§14.2.1 An Overview of the Avoidance Suit

This overview sets the stage for consideration of the detailed rules of the UFTA by illustrating the circumstances that could give rise to an avoidance suit and sketching the broad outlines of the action. For example, imagine that after attempting execution and receiving a nulla bona return, a creditor discovers that the debtor recently transferred a valuable necklace to her cousin for a fraction of its fair market value. The creditor commences suit against the cousin. The debtor may be joined in the suit, but the cousin is the essential party. The relief sought by the creditor is a judgment ordering restoration of the property to the debtor so that it can be levied upon to satisfy the judgment. As an alternative, the creditor could claim damages from the cousin based on the value of the asset.

Because the cousin is not a party to the debtor/creditor relationship, the UFTA provides protection for her legitimate interests. Therefore, the grounds for avoidance require examination of the debtor's conduct and motives and the cousin's role in the sale of the necklace. If the cousin behaved honestly and gave value to the debtor, the transfer may not be

---

quite similar. One key change was the removal of the word "fraudulent" from the UVTA because 1) litigants and jurists mistakenly thought that a party had to establish actual fraud to gain relief under the UFTA; and 2) some courts required the clear and convincing standard of proof, even though the preponderance standard is the appropriate standard.

avoidable despite the debtor's ill motives in making it, or if the transaction is in fact avoided, the cousin may at least be compensated for the value she gave.

The UFTA is available to creditors of the transferee. Section 1(4), read with §1(3), defines "creditor" to include persons with a wide variety of claims against the debtor. The UFTA distinguishes between creditors whose claims existed at the time of transfer, who are given broader rights of avoidance, and those whose claims arose afterward, whose avoidance rights are more limited. The UFTA is aimed at avoiding "transfers," defined in §1(12) read with §1(2) to include all dispositions of an interest in assets. "Assets" include only property to the extent that it is nonexempt and not subject to a security interest.

The UFTA provides two different grounds for avoidance. The first is actual fraud, §4(a)(1), and the other is constructive fraud, which can take one of three different forms, §§4(a)(2) and 5(a). A creditor need only establish one of the grounds of avoidance to receive relief.

§14.2.2 Actual Fraud

a. Dishonest Intent

A creditor can avoid a transfer made by the debtor with actual intent to hinder, delay, or defraud any creditor. §4(a)(i). This ground of avoidance is available both to creditors whose claims existed at the time of transfer and to those whose claims arose afterward. The UFTA does not make a distinction between creditors in this context because all creditors should be able to respond to actual fraud. To avoid the transfer on the basis of actual fraud, the creditor must prove that the debtor made the transfer with the deliberate motive of removing the property from the reach of creditors.

b. Proof of Fraud — Badges of Fraud

A creditor cannot prove fraud by direct evidence of the debtor's state of mind unless a debtor has admitted dishonest intent. Therefore, fraudulent intent is usually shown by proof of the debtor's conduct in circumstances that reveal a dishonest motive. Over the centuries, courts have identified typical patterns of behavior — referred to as "badges of fraud" — that indicate conduct prohibited by §4.

Badges of fraud are not presumptions, so they do not relieve the creditor of the burden of proving actual fraud. They are simply inferences that help to establish the creditor's case. If the creditor can show that suspicious circumstances attended the disposition of property, the factfinder may draw an inference of fraud unless the debtor offers a plausible explanation to the contrary.

The term "badges of fraud" is traditional. It is not used in the UFTA. However, §4(b) recognizes the evidentiary value of inferences. It lists examples of suspicious behavior and states that such factors may be considered, together with any other circumstances, in deciding the question of fraudulent intent. The list in §4(b) is drawn from badges of fraud that have been recognized by courts. It is not intended to be definitive. The determination of fraud is a factual matter, and the conduct of the debtor must be evaluated in each case. Also, some indicia of fraud are more compelling than others, and a combination of several suspicious factors strengthens the inference.

Some of the examples selected from the list illustrate the kinds of activity or circumstances that may give rise to an inference of fraud: The transfer was to an insider or someone with close family or other connections with the debtor; the debtor sought to conceal the transfer; the transfer occurred just before litigation or in the face of other impending collection activity; the transfer was made just before a significant debt was incurred. (The use of inferences is illustrated by Examples 1 and 2.)

It is the debtor's state of mind, rather than the transferee's, that is relevant. However, as discussed in section 14.2.5, the absence or presence of good faith on the transferee's part has an impact on the creditor's avoidance rights.

§14.2.3 Constructive Fraud

a. General Principles

A fraudulent transfer harms a debtor's creditors regardless of whether the debtor actually intended such harm. Consequently, the concept of constructive fraud was placed alongside actual fraud in the debtor/creditor jurisprudence.

Constructive fraud is very different from actual fraud established by inference. If the facts constituting constructive fraud are established, a conclusive presumption of fraud is created, and inquiry into the debtor's state of mind is irrelevant. The word "constructive" indicates that fraud is construed as a matter of law rather than established by evidence of a guilty mind. The policy basis for recognizing this type of presumptive fraud is that a disposition under the defined circumstances unfairly diminishes the debtor's executable estate and should not be allowed, even if it was not deliberately dishonest. Constructive fraud was recognized by courts long before the drafting of the UFCA in 1918. The UFCA, and its successor, the UFTA, incorporate the concept of constructive fraud, even though the term "constructive fraud" is not used in the UFTA.

Constructive fraud has two basic elements: (1) the debtor did not receive reasonably equivalent value in exchange for the transfer, and (2) the debtor was in a shaky financial condition at the time of the transfer. This second element is only satisfied if the creditor can establish one of three specific factual situations at the time of transfer:

1. The debtor was involved in or was about to engage in a business venture, and the transfer left the debtor with insufficient capital for the project (§4(a)(2)(i));
2. the debtor was about to incur debts with the actual or imputed intention of not paying them when due (§4(a)(2)(ii)); <u>or</u>
3. the debtor was insolvent (§5(a)).

A creditor whose claim existed at the time of the transfer may use any one of the three forms of constructive fraud as grounds to avoid a transfer.

However, a creditor whose claim arose after the fraudulent transfer can rely only on §4(a)(2)(i) or §4(a)(2)(ii). The policy rationale for this distinction is that a creditor whose claim arose after the fraudulent transfer invariably could have performed due diligence, and uncovered the transfer at issue prior to entering into a transaction with the debtor. For example, imagine that Debtor has sought a loan from Lender. Lender reviews Debtor's credit history and notices that, for the last three years, she had been making payments on a boat. But she did not list the boat in her borrower application. Despite this discrepancy, Lender decides to make an unsecured loan to Debtor. Debtor subsequently defaults, and Lender learns that Debtor had fraudulently transferred the boat to her brother shortly before seeking a loan from Lender. Lender could have investigated the discrepancy and chosen not to lend to Debtor. Fraudulent transfer law can still protect Lender, but the protection is limited to the relief provided in §4.

A creditor that held a claim against the debtor prior to the fraudulent transfer can rely on §4 or §5 for relief. The main advantage of this option is that the necessary showing under §5 will be easier in most cases. Section 5 requires a showing of "insolvency." This term is defined in §2 and can be demonstrated by showing that 1) the debtor's debts are greater than its assets, or 2) the debtor is generally not paying debts as they become due. Both of these factors can be resolved with an objective inquiry. But §4 presents a more complicated inquiry; the creditor must prove either the debtor 1) was engaged or about to engage in a business or transaction for which the debtor's remaining assets were unreasonably small in relation to the business or transaction; or 2) intended to incur, or believed or reasonably should have believed that she would incur, debts beyond her ability to pay as they became due. Both elements require a subjective inquiry. In the vast majority of cases, the evidentiary burden under §5 is going to be far easier to carry than the burden under §4.

Further, §5(b) allows for avoidance on grounds of constructive fraud if 1) the transfer was made to an insider for an antecedent debt, 2) the transfer was made at a time that the debtor was insolvent, and 3) the insider had reasonable cause to believe that the debtor was insolvent.

b. Reasonable Equivalence in Value

Under §3(a), value is given by the transferee if the debtor receives property in exchange for the transfer or a prior debt of the debtor is satisfied or secured. The UFTA itself does not provide a formula for determining whether value is reasonably equivalent. This is left to the courts.

The test of reasonable equivalence would be easy if courts simply used a mechanical formula in which economic values were compared and the quid pro quo received by the debtor was required to be worth at least a fixed percentage of the property transferred by the debtor. However, this approach is too rigid. After all, the test requires not simply equivalent value but reasonably equivalent value.

Therefore, this element is not satisfied merely because the transaction was somewhat disadvantageous to the debtor. Of course, the values exchanged are highly relevant. The less that the debtor received for the transfer the greater the likelihood of avoidance. But courts examine entire context, taking into account the relationship of the parties, the market environment, and the apparent motive for the transfer. Even though constructive fraud is not premised on actual fraudulent intent, this does not mean that suspicious or unusual circumstances in the transfer are completely disregarded. The context may justify the lower value of the exchange, based on legitimate market considerations, or it may suggest that the return value was not reasonably equivalent. (*See also* section 14.2.4.)

It should also be noted that the value of property may be uncertain. Valuation is a factual issue on which there could be conflicting evidence. Where value is subject to doubt, it may be more difficult to be sure that the consideration received by the debtor was deficient.

c. Financial Condition

i. Insolvency

The UFTA provides two alternative tests for determining insolvency. The primary test, articulated in §2(a), is the balance sheet or bankruptcy test. Under this test, a debtor is insolvent when the sum of the debtor's debts exceeds the fair value of its assets. As mentioned before, the term "assets" is defined in §1(2) to exclude property to the extent of any exemption or encumbrance. It can be difficult for a creditor to prove insolvency under the balance sheet test, especially if it does not have access to the debtor's financial data. Therefore, §2(b) provides an alternative means of establishing insolvency, known as the equity test. Under this test, a presumption of insolvency is created if the creditor can prove that the debtor is not paying its debts as they become due. Upon such a showing, the burden shifts to the debtor to show that it is in fact solvent under the balance sheet test. To satisfy this initial burden, the creditor must establish that there is a general pattern of nonpayment of a significant portion of the debtor's undisputed debt.[4]

Insolvency is measured at the time of the transfer. This means that the debtor may already have been insolvent when the transfer was made or may have been rendered insolvent as a result of the disposition of the transferred property.

Proof of insolvency under either test may involve difficult issues. The balance sheet test requires assets to be given fair value, and the appraisal of assets can be a contentious matter. A creditor may similarly have difficulties in trying to establish insolvency on the equity test to take advantage of the §2(b) presumption. To determine whether a debtor is not generally paying debts as they become due, the court must consider the proportion of debts that are not being paid on time, the patterns of payment or nonpayment, and the reasons for nonpayment.

ii. Undercapitalization or Intent to Incur Debts That Will Not Be Paid

As an alternative to showing insolvency, a creditor can rely on one of two other forms of financial instability. These two alternative tests move the focus from the traditional measure of financial precariousness—liabilities in excess of assets—to the relationship between the debtor's financial condition and intended future business activity. In broad terms, the tests allow the creditor to impugn a transfer for inadequate value if it was reckless or irresponsible in light of the debtor's prospective commercial dealings or if it would likely doom the debtor's planned venture to fairly certain failure. In some cases, the debtor's transfer under such circumstances may be tantamount to deliberate fraud, but this is a variety of constructive fraud; no deliberate intent to cheat creditors need be shown. Because these tests involve debtor action subsequent to the transfer, they may be relied on by future creditors as well as existing ones.

The factual issues presented by these alternative tests can be even more daunting than those involved in establishing insolvency. In an obvious case, it may be easy to show that a debtor was undercapitalized or was incurring debts without the justifiable expectation of repaying them. However, in many situations there could be divergent opinions about the level of assets needed for a venture or the debtor's prospects of generating future earnings sufficient to support new debt.

---

4. As discussed in section 6.6.4, the debtor's general nonpayment of due debts is also grounds for the filing of an involuntary bankruptcy petition. Section 6.6.4 discusses the standards used for determining if the debtor is not generally paying due debts in that context.

§14.2.4 The Remedy of Avoidance and the Rights of the Transferee

Traditionally, the creditors' bill in equity had to be used to avoid a fraudulent transfer.[5] This cumbersome equitable suit[6] was replaced by a more efficient statutory cause of action under the UFCA. The statutory remedy has been further refined in §§7 and 8 of the UFTA. The creditor has a choice of two remedies:

1. recovery of the property from the transferee so that it can be subjected to levy and sold in execution, or
2. a money judgment against the transferee for the lesser of either the value of the property measured at the time of transfer or the amount of the debt due by the debtor.

Whichever course is selected, the court has the discretion to order prejudgment remedies or other appropriate ancillary relief.

Suit may be brought against the person who acquired the property from the debtor or against a subsequent transferee. However, the UFTA protects the rights of persons who acquired the property in good faith. Therefore, even though the debtor's conduct provides grounds for avoidance, the creditor's power to recover the property or to obtain damages from the transferee is subject to a number of limitations. The rules can be summarized as follows:

(1) A good faith transferee from the debtor who gave reasonably equivalent value for the property is fully protected. No matter how guilty the debtor's motives were in conveying the property, the creditor cannot recover the property or damages from a transferee who gave the debtor fair equivalent value for it and acted honestly and without knowledge or reason to know of the debtor's fraudulent purpose.

5. The creditor's bill was introduced in section 2.7 in connection with proceedings in aid of execution.

6. Although the creditors' bill was an equitable remedy, the creditor's power of avoidance is legal in derivation. Therefore, prior to the creation of the statutory remedy, a suit to avoid the transfer was equitable, but a suit to recover damages from the transferee was legal. This classification may sound esoteric, but it can have practical significance. In *Granfinanciera, S.A. v. Nordberg*, 492 U.S. 33 (1989), the U.S. Supreme Court held that the legal nature of a monetary claim against the transferee entitled the parties to a jury trial.

(2) A transferee who acquired the property from the debtor in good faith, but for a value that was less than reasonably equivalent, receives partial protection. Where the transferee from the debtor acted in good faith, but the value for the transfer is not reasonably equivalent, the transfer is avoidable. The creditor can recover the property or obtain a money judgment. However, the transferee is entitled to offset against that recovery the value that had been given to the debtor for the property. If the property is returned for execution, this offset is secured by a lien and must be paid to the transferee from the proceeds of the execution sale. If the creditor receives a money judgment, the transferee's liability under the judgment is reduced by the offset.

(3) A bad faith transferee from the debtor is given no protection against the creditor. A transferee who acted in bad faith by actively or passively colluding with the debtor receives no protection from avoidance. Even if the transferee gave value to the debtor for the property, that value is not deductible from the creditor's recovery. The transferee may try to obtain restitution from the debtor, but that is not likely to be a promising enterprise because the debtor is in financial difficulty, and the court may be disinclined to award restitution to one who participated in the debtor's fraud.

(4) A subsequent transferee (i.e., one who did not take directly from the debtor) who acquired the property in good faith and for value is fully protected. Because the subsequent transferee did not deal with the debtor, the qualifications for immunity are somewhat easier to satisfy than those for a transferee from the debtor. As long as the transferee acted in good faith and gave some value for the transfer, the equivalence of the value given for the property is not inquired into.

(5) A subsequent transferee, whether or not in good faith, shelters under the rights of a prior good faith transferee. A transferee who qualifies for protection from avoidance cuts off any rights that the creditor may have to recover the property. For that reason, the creditor has no right of avoidance against any person who acquired the property from the protected transferee, or later transferees.

(6) A subsequent transferee who did not act in good faith and did not derive rights through a good faith transferee has no protection. Like a bad faith transferee from the debtor, this transferee is subject to avoidance or a money judgment and has no offset for any value given for the property.

§14.3 FRAUDULENT TRANSFERS UNDER FEDERAL BANKRUPTCY LAW (§548)

§14.3.1 Avoidance Under §548 as an Alternative to §544 and State Law

The trustee may avoid fraudulent transfers in the prepetition period either by using state fraudulent transfer law, which is accessible to the trustee under §544(b) (*see* section 12.2.2), or by employing the Code's own avoidance provision in §548. There are some striking similarities in language between §548 and the UFTA, which has been enacted in many states and is representative of the typical state law that would be available to the trustee under §544(b). The similarity is deliberate. Section 548 was modeled on the UFCA, the predecessor to the UFTA, and when the UFCA was revised to become the UFTA, the revision was modeled on §548. The influence of the Code on the UFTA is particularly evident in the UFTA's defined terms such as "insider," "creditor," and "transfer," and in its provisions relating to the determination of the effective date of the transfer.

The trustee's choice to seek avoidance of a transfer under §548 or under §544(b) and state law will depend on which vehicle for avoidance gives the trustee stronger rights. Because the provisions of the UFTA and §548 are similar in so many ways, it may not make a significant difference which route the trustee selects. However, in some cases, there could be an important advantage to selecting one or the other. Bear in mind that not every state has enacted the UFTA, so the law of a particular state could be notably different from §548. Even where the state has enacted the UFTA, there are differences in detail (identified in the following discussion) between that statute and §548 that could be significant on the facts of a particular case. Overall, the most common reason for relying on §544(b) and applicable state law instead of §548 is because of the significantly longer statute of limitations. Section 12.2.2 explains this issue in more detail.

§14.3.2 Actual Fraud

Section 548(a)(1)(A) deals with actual fraud. It empowers the trustee to avoid any transfer made or obligation incurred by the debtor within two years before the petition, if the transfer was made or the obligation was incurred with the actual intent to hinder, delay, or defraud an entity to which the debtor was indebted on the date of the transfer or became indebted thereafter. Section 548(a)(1)(A) is similar to UFTA §4(a)(i). As explained in section 14.2.2, UFTA §4(b) lists indicia of fraud known as "badges of fraud." This is a nonexclusive codification of long-recognized inferences that have been recognized by courts as tending to prove actual fraud by circumstantial evidence. Unlike the UFTA, §548(a)(1)(A) does not expressly list badges of fraud. However, these inferences are recognized by judicial decision in the context of bankruptcy as well. Because fraudulent intent is seldom provable by direct evidence of the debtor's state of mind, the presence of conduct or circumstances that give rise to an inference of fraud are commonly used to establish that intent.

§14.3.3 Constructive Fraud

Section 548(a)(1)(B) covers constructive fraud. The subsection empowers the trustee to avoid a transfer made or obligation incurred by the debtor within the two years prior to filing, if the debtor received less than reasonably equivalent value in exchange for it and the transfer 1) was made while the debtor was insolvent or caused the debtor to become insolvent, 2) left the debtor with unreasonably small capital in relation to its business, or 3) caused the debtor to incur a debt that it would be unable to pay as such debt matured. Further, §548(a)(1)(B) allows the court to avoid a transfer made or obligation incurred by the debtor within two years prior to the filing if the debtor 1) received less than reasonably equivalent value and 2) made the transfer to or for the benefit of an insider[7] under an employment contract and not in the ordinary course of business.

a. Reasonably Equivalent Value (§548(a)(1)(B)(i))

The analysis under §548 to determine the absence or presence of reasonably equivalent value follows the same lines as that under the UFTA. *See* section 14.2.3. Although the comparison of economic values is an important consideration, courts go beyond this to look at all the circumstances of the transfer, including the parties' relationship, the economic environment, and the apparent motive for the transfer.

---

7. Section 101(31) provides in relevant part that "[t]he term "insider" includes—A) if the debtor is an individual—1) relative of the debtor or of a general partner of the debtor; 2) partnership in which the debtor is a general partner; 3) general partner of the debtor; or 4) corporation of which the debtor is a director, officer, or person in control; B) if the debtor is a corporation—1) director of the debtor; 2) officer of the debtor; 3) person in control of the debtor; 4) partnership in which the debtor is a general partner; 5) general partner of the debtor; or 6) relative of a general partner, director, officer, or person in control of the debtor. . . ."

b. Insolvency (§548(a)(1)(B)(ii)(I)–(III))

The other element of constructive fraud in §548 identifies four separate situations, detailed below, of which three are the same as in the UFTA. (*See* Example 2, which presents an issue of constructive fraud under §548.)

(1) Insolvency: §548(a)(1)(B)(ii)(I). The transfer is avoidable by the trustee if the debtor received less than reasonably equivalent value and was insolvent at the time that the transfer was made or the obligation was incurred, or became insolvent as a result of the transfer or obligation. This subsection mirrors UFTA §5. (*See* section 14.2.3.) The definitions of insolvency are similar in the UFTA and the Code, but under UFTA §2 equity insolvency creates a presumption of insolvency. Section 548 does not offer a similar presumption.

As explained in section 14.2.3, under the UFTA, while actual fraud and other forms of constructive fraud may be used as a basis of avoidance by any creditor, constructive fraud on grounds of insolvency may be used as a basis of avoidance only by a creditor whose claim was in existence at the time of the transfer. Section 548 does not make an equivalent distinction between existing and subsequent creditors, because such a distinction is irrelevant where the avoidance remedy is exercised by the trustee for the benefit of the estate.

(2) Undercapitalization: §548(a)(1)(B)(ii)(II). The transfer is avoidable by the trustee if the debtor received less than reasonably equivalent value and was engaged in, or was about to engage in, a business or transaction for which the debtor's remaining property was unreasonably small capital. This is equivalent to UFTA §4(A)(2)(i), discussed in section 14.2.3.

(3) Intent to incur debts that will not be paid: §548(a)(1)(B)(ii)(III). The transfer is avoidable by the trustee if the debtor received less than reasonably equivalent value and intended to incur, or believed that he would incur debts that would be beyond his ability to pay as they matured. This is equivalent to UFTA §4(A)(2)(ii), discussed in section 14.2.3.

(4) Payment to an insider under an employment contract, not in the ordinary course of business: §548(a)(1)(B)(ii)(IV). The transfer is avoidable by the trustee if the debtor received less than reasonably equivalent value and made the transfer or incurred the obligation to or for the benefit of an insider under an employment contract and not in the ordinary course of business.

The rules relating to constructive fraud where the transfer is to an insider are different in the UFTA and §548. UFTA §5(b) allows avoidance of the transfer to an insider on grounds of constructive fraud if the transfer was made for an antecedent debt, the debtor was insolvent at the time, and the insider had reasonable cause to believe that the debtor was insolvent. Section 548 does not have an equivalent provision but provides specifically in §548(a)(1)(IV) for payments to insiders under an employment contract. It states that the trustee may avoid a transfer made or an obligation incurred by the debtor to or for the benefit of an insider within the two-year pre-bankruptcy period "under an employment contract and not in the ordinary course of business." In *In re TransTexas Gas Corp.*, 597 F.3d 298 (5th Cir. 2010), the court upheld the trustee's right to avoid a large severance payment to its CEO as constructively fraudulent. The transferee argued that he had given reasonably equivalent value to the debtor by agreeing to resign and compromising his rights under the employment contract. However, the court held that because there were grounds to dismiss the CEO for cause, his resignation was not reasonably equivalent value. The CEO also argued that he was not an insider at the time of the transfer because he was no longer working for the debtor when the payment was made. The court rejected this argument because he was an insider at the time that the obligation was incurred.

§14.3.4 Reach-Back and the Effect of Avoidance

One of the most important differences between the UFTA and §548 is their temporal range. Section 548 allows the trustee to avoid transfers that occurred within two years preceding bankruptcy,[8] and the UFTA generally allows creditors a period of four years from the transfer in which to commence an avoidance suit.[9] As noted in sections 12.2.2 and 14.3.1 if the transfer occurred more than two years before the petition, the trustee may be able to avoid it by using state law under §544(b), even though it cannot be avoided under §548. Also, the avoidance remedy itself is different. Section 548 does not have the remedial alternatives of the UFTA, but it is

8. The Bankruptcy Abuse Prevention and Consumer Protection Act of 2005 (BAPCPA) increased the period from one year to two. As explained in sections 11.7 and 12.2.2, the two-year period in §548 is a reach-back period: It specifies the period of vulnerability of the transfer. It is not a statute of limitations (a period within which the trustee must act to avoid the transfer). The statute of limitations is provided in §546(a).

9. The four-year period under the UFTA is a statute of limitations, but it operates as a reach-back period for purposes of avoidance. Thus, the trustee can reach back four years to avoid the transfer if applicable nonbankruptcy law follows the UFTA statute of limitations and the trustee exercises the avoidance power under §544(b), or two years if the trustee seeks avoidance under §548. In either case, the trustee must commence suit within the limitations period under §546(a).

subject to the general rules (outlined in Chapter 15) governing the return of avoided transfers to the estate.

The UFTA contains detailed provisions for the protection of good faith transferees for value and subsequent transferees. Section 548(c) adopts a similar approach by granting lien rights in favor of a good faith transferee for value, and §550 protects good faith subsequent transferees.

§14.3.5 Defense to a Fraudulent Transfer Action (§548(c))

After a prima facie case has been established for avoidance of a transfer, a transferee may prevent avoidance if she can establish that, pursuant to §548(c), she took for value and in good faith. The transferee bears the burden of proof.

a. First Element: Value

Section 548(d)(2) defines "value" as capturing "property, or satisfaction or securing of a present or antecedent debt of the debtor, but does not include an unperformed promise to furnish support to the debtor or a relative of the debtor." Some courts have used the same standard in evaluating "value" under §548(c) as they have for "reasonably equivalent value" under §548(a).[10] This approach may be misguided. More recent opinions have held that the two terms have distinct meanings.

In *Williams v. FDIC (In re Positive Health Mgmt.)*, 769 F.3d 899 (5th Cir. 2014), the Fifth Circuit Court of Appeals explained that a §548(c) analysis should assess value from the transferee's perspective, with an emphasis on what value the transferee tendered. The first step is for the court to determine whether a good faith transferee gave any value. If value was given, the court should then decide whether the value received exceeded the consideration given. If so, the court should subtract the difference and grant the trustee the right to recover that amount. The court explained that "consideration need not be 'reasonably equivalent' to be valid. . . . Any value given by a transferee in return for a transfer is sufficient to meet the 'value' element, but the good faith transferee is protected only to the extent of the value."[11]

---

10. See, e.g., *In re Rosen Auto Leasing, Inc.*, 346 B.R. 798, 806 (B.A.P. 8th Cir.2006) ("To the extent [the transferee] did not give value for purposes [of a §548(a)(1)(B) determination] . . . , he likewise did not give value for purposes of asserting a defense under [§548(c)].").

11. *In re O'Neill*, No. 14-30569, 2016 BL 124184, at *14 (Bankr. D.N.D. Apr. 19, 2016) (citing *In re Positive Health Mgmt.*, 769 F.3d 899, 908).

b. Second Element: Good Faith

The Code does not define "good faith." In evaluating this term, courts have used either the "objective test" or the "subjective test." The objective test has two prongs. The first prong seeks to determine if the transferee had information that put it—or should have put it—on inquiry notice of the transferor's insolvency or fraudulent purpose.[12] If so, the test's second prong seeks to determine if the transferee engaged in a diligent investigation regarding the transfer's propriety.

The subjective test has three steps. The first two mirror what is required under the objective test. Primarily, the court must determine whether what the transferee knew would suggest insolvency or a fraudulent purpose and trigger inquiry notice. Second, the court must determine whether the transferee undertook a diligent inquiry and the results of that inquiry. Finally, the third prong is where the subjective test diverges from the objective test. Under the third prong, if the court determines that a transferee's diligent inquiry did not discover the fraud, the court must then determine whether any reasonable investigation would have disclosed the wrong.[13]

§14.4 FRAUDULENT TRANSFER LAW AND LEVERAGED BUYOUTS

A leveraged buyout (often referred to in abbreviated form as an LBO) is a complex acquisition structure in which the purchase of shares in a corporation is financed by the corporation itself or secured by the assets of the corporation. In essence, the corporation makes available its own funds or other assets to enable the buyer to finance the purchase of its shares. This is in the nature of a loan by the corporation, and the expectation is that the corporate assets will be restored over time from future profits that the buyer will make from the operation of the corporation's business.

LBOs are structured in many different ways. In a typical LBO, a buying group—traditionally a private equity firm or a consortium of private equity firms—identifies a target company that 1) owns a significant amount of

---

12. For inquiry notice, if the circumstances are "such that an ordinary investor would be led to investigate the matter further," the transferee is assumed to have been on inquiry notice. See *National W. Life Ins. Co. v. Merrill Lynch, Pierce, Fenner & Smith, Inc.*, 89 F. App'x 287, 291 (2d Cir. 2004). Ultimately, "inquiry notice is not knowledge of fraud or other wrongdoing but merely knowledge that would lead a reasonable, law-abiding person to inquire further—would make him [or her] . . . suspicious enough to conduct a diligent search for possible dirt." *In re Sentinel Mgmt. Grp., Inc.*, 809 F.3d 958, 962 (7th Cir. 2016).

13. See *GLC v. Hunter Miller Family, LLC*, No. 1:15-cv-23, 2015 BL 221851, at *3-4 (S.D. Ohio July 10, 2015).

unencumbered assets; and 2) has been — at least from the buying group's perspective — undervalued by the market.[14] The buying group works with the target company's directors and officers to reach an agreed sale price. The buying group will then borrow an amount that represents upwards of 90 percent of the purchase price, secured by first-priority liens on all the target company's unencumbered assets. The loan proceeds, along with the buying group's injection of capital, are used primarily to purchase the target company's stock. The obvious problem with this structure is that the target company receives no direct benefit from the transaction. In fact, after the transaction, the target company has a sizeable debt load and assets that are fully encumbered.

A transaction like this is intended to enable the buyer to purchase the shares by using the resources of the corporation to acquire funding that would otherwise not be accessible to the buyer. Its effect is to encumber the assets of the corporation for a debt that benefits not the corporation itself, but its buyer. If the corporation is successfully managed, this prejudice to the corporation will eventually be reversed as the buyer's profits generate funds to settle the debt and release the corporate assets from the encumbrance. However, if the business does not produce large enough profits, the corporation will be unable to service its debt obligations. The risk of failure is borne not only by the corporation, but also by its unsecured creditors who have lost the protection of recourse to unencumbered assets. Stated differently, before the LBO, the prior owner of the corporation had an equity interest that was junior to the claims of unsecured creditors. Following the LBO, this equity has been paid out and replaced by senior secured debt.

§14.4.1 The Application of Fraudulent Transfer Law to LBOs

The LBO structure makes the transaction extremely susceptible to attack under fraudulent transfer law. But LBOs are not per se fraudulent. Nevertheless, when a corporation fails to pay its debts after an LBO and the corporation files for bankruptcy, its unsecured creditors invariably look to fraudulent transfer law to avoid the transfer made by the corporation in connection with the LBO. In the type of transaction described above, this transfer is the grant of a security interest by the corporation. (The grant of a security interest is a disposition of rights in property that meets the definition of transfer under the UFTA.) To avoid the transfer, the creditor must establish either actual or constructive fraud in accordance with the general principles discussed above.

14. *See* Samir Parikh, *Saving Fraudulent Transfer Law*, 86 Am. Bankr. L.J. 305, 311 (2012).

Occasionally, actual fraud is present. However, in the vast majority of cases, the LBO is not the result of a fraudulent scheme. But the transaction still violates §548(a)(1)(B) and state fraudulent transfer law. Indeed, the grant of a security interest in the corporate assets increased the corporation's debt over its assets, rendering it insolvent. It is not relevant that the owner may have received equivalent value for the transfer. The corporation, which is the debtor, did not.

§14.4.2 The Fraudulent Transfer of Exempt Property

It is not clear if the transfer of exemptable property qualifies as a fraudulent transfer. Some courts have held that if the property is exemptable, its transfer does not harm creditors and should not be avoidable. Others (the majority, it seems) say that the fact that the debtor could have claimed the property as exempt should not be taken into account. For example, *Tavenner v. Smoot*, 257 F.3d 401 (4th Cir. 2001), followed this approach. The court based its reasoning on two factors. First, §522(g) contemplates the avoidance of transfers of property that could have been exempted and precludes assertion of the exemption after recovery of fraudulently transferred property unless the transfer was involuntary and the debtor did not conceal the property. Second, property is not inherently exempt, and the debtor has to claim it as exempt in her schedules. If she fails to claim an exemption, the property remains in the estate for the benefit of creditors. *In re Lumbar*, 457 B.R. 748 (B.A.P. 8th Cir. 2011) also found the transfer of exempt property to be available. It held that even if state exemption law treats the transfer of exempt property nonfraudulent, federal law governs avoidance under §548 and allows the trustee to avoid the transfer of property that the debtor may otherwise have claimed as exempt. In essence, by transferring the property voluntarily, the debtor abandons the exemption and loses the right to claim an exemption in it, even after it is recovered by the trustee.

§14.4.3 Charitable Contributions by an Individual Debtor

Similar to §544(b)(2),[15] §548(a)(2) specifically provides that a charitable contribution to a qualified religious or charitable entity or organization is not to be treated as a transfer for less than a reasonable equivalent value provided that the contribution does not exceed 15 percent of the debtor's

15. *See* section 12.2.2.

gross annual income for the year in which it was given, or if in excess of that percentage, the contribution was consistent with the debtor's practices in making such contributions. Sections 548(d)(3) and (4) define "charitable contribution"[16] and "qualified religious or charitable entity"[17] with reference to the definitions used for tax-deduction purposes. The exception relates only to constructive fraud, it does not shield a transfer made with fraudulent intent to a charity or religious organization.

These provisions were added to §548 in 1998 to resolve uncertainty about whether a charitable contribution should be treated as constructively fraudulent. Although they cover both charities and religious organizations, Congress was primarily concerned about protecting churches from having to return tithes and contributions upon the debtor's bankruptcy. By preventing the avoidance of gifts to charities and churches, §548(a)(2) allows an insolvent debtor to continue to be generous at the expense of creditors. Courts do not agree on the extent to which this generosity is to be allowed. Some courts read §548(a)(2) as applying to each individual contribution, not to the total of contributions that the debtor may make in a year. On this interpretation, the debtor could contribute all her income and assets as long as she did it in separate gifts, each of which is under 15 percent of her income. Other courts recognize the absurdity of this interpretation and hold that the intent of the section is that aggregate contributions in the year must not exceed 15 percent of the debtor's gross annual income. For example, this was so held in *Universal Church v. Geltzer*, 463 F.3d 218 (2d Cir. 2006) and in *In re McGough*, 467 B.R. 22 (B.A.P. 10th Cir. 2012). In *In re McGough*, the trustee argued that §548(a)(2)'s plain language required that the full amount of the contributions be avoided because the debtor's contributions exceeded the 15 percent cap in both of the two years before bankruptcy. The court disagreed that §548(a)(2)'s language is that clear. It therefore consulted the legislative history, which indicated that Congress intended to protect up to 15 percent of the contributions, so that only the excess over that amount was avoidable.[18]

---

16. Pursuant to §548(d)(3) a "charitable contribution" is merely a contribution or gift made by a natural person that consists of either 1) a financial instrument (as that term is defined in the Internal Revenue Code); or 2) cash.

17. The definition includes a host of organizations, but primarily captures corporations, trusts, funds, and foundations that are organized and operate exclusively for religious, charitable, scientific, literary, or educational purposes.

18. But see *In re Zohdi*, 234 B.R. 371, 373 (Bankr. M.D. La. 1999) ("[W]e find that if a transfer exceeds 15 percent of the debtor's gross income and is otherwise avoidable under §548, the entire transfer is avoidable, not merely that portion of the transfer exceeding 15 percent of the debtor's yearly income.").

§14.5 POSTPETITION TRANSFERS UNDER §549

The avoidance powers discussed up to now concern prepetition transfers. Section 549 gives the trustee the power to recoup estate property that has been transferred without authority *after* the petition has been filed. The section is conceptually different from the other avoidance provisions because it seeks to preserve estate property as opposed to reversing prepetition dissipation. Section 549's central basis for avoidance is lack of authority to make the disposition. Therefore, if after the case has been commenced the debtor makes an unauthorized transfer of estate property to settle a prepetition debt, the trustee does not need to establish the elements of §547 to avoid the transfer, but simply relies on lack of authority under §549. The trustee bears the burden of proving what may be recovered under §549. But once the trustee has established a prima facie case, the burden shifts to the transferee to establish the transfer's validity.

Section 549(a) allows the trustee to avoid postpetition transfers that are not authorized by the Code itself or by the court and to avoid transfers that are authorized only under §§303(f) and 542(c). The reference to the two other Code sections requires explanation.

Section 303(f) allows a debtor in an involuntary case to continue to operate its business and to use or dispose of estate property until the order for relief is granted. However, once the order for relief is granted and a trustee is appointed, the trustee can use §549(a)(2)(A) to overturn any transfers made by the debtor unless they were approved by the court or they satisfy the requirements of §549(b). Section 549(b) validates transfers during the gap period to the extent that the transferee gave something new of economic value in exchange for the transfer, whether or not the transferee knew of the bankruptcy.

Section 542 requires entities who have estate property or who owe debts to the debtor to turn over the property or to pay the debts to the estate. Section 542(c) protects an entity who, acting in good faith and without actual knowledge or notice of the commencement of the case, transfers the property or pays the debt to someone other than the trustee. The transfer is treated as fully effective for the purpose of discharging the transferor's obligations to the debtor, and the transferor is not liable to the estate as a result of the inadvertent disposition. Although the good faith transferor is protected by §542(c), the person who receives the payment or the property is not covered by that section. Section 549(a)(2)(A) makes that transferee vulnerable to attack by the trustee. For example, immediately after a petition is filed, and before the trustee takes control of the estate, the debtor draws a check in favor of a creditor. Upon presentment, the bank pays the check in good faith and without notice or knowledge of the filing. Section 542(c) excuses the bank from liability to the estate for the improper payment of funds that had become property of the estate. However, this protection does not extend to the payee of the check, who has received an unauthorized postpetition transfer avoidable under §549(a).

In addition to these avoidance powers, §549 contains two other provisions. First, §549(c) protects certain transferees from avoidance. The subsection requires a copy or notice of the petition to be recorded with the title records pertaining to real property in the estate. If a bona fide purchaser (i.e., one who purchases the property for fair equivalent value, in good faith, and without knowledge of the bankruptcy) purchases the property under an unauthorized sale from the debtor, and that interest is perfected prior to the recording of the notice of bankruptcy, the transfer may not be avoided. If less than equivalent value was given, but the purchaser otherwise meets the standards of bona fide purchaser and the transfer was perfected before notice of the bankruptcy was recorded, the transfer is avoidable but the purchaser acquires a lien on the property to secure reimbursement of the value given.

The second provision is §549(d), which is a statute of limitations governing the avoidance of postpetition transfers. The trustee must commence avoidance proceedings before the earlier of two years after the transfer or the time that the bankruptcy case is closed or dismissed.

EXAMPLES

Examples

1. Some years ago, when Awful Artful was a successful entrepreneur, he bought a painting by Claude Monet. Awful's business collapsed, and he personally is deeply in debt. He owes more than $25 million to his creditors. The painting, worth $10 million, is his only remaining valuable asset. To ensure that his creditors could not get their hands on the painting, Awful sold it to his friend Hyde Hastily for $500 with the understanding that Hyde would not dispose of the painting to anyone else and that Awful had the right to buy it back whenever he wished for $600.

   Six months after the sale, one of Awful's unsecured creditors obtained judgment against him for $12 million. The creditor tried to levy on Awful's property, but the sheriff could not find any property of value at Awful's home and rendered a nulla bona return. The creditor investigated and found out about the painting. Does the creditor have grounds under the UFTA to avoid the transfer from Awful to Hyde?

2. Assume that Awful did not sell the painting to Hyde as described in Example 1. Instead, he decided to sell the painting on the market and to use the proceeds to maintain the lavish lifestyle to which he had become accustomed. He therefore hired an art dealer and instructed him to find a buyer. Awful told the dealer to act quickly and discreetly and to insist on a cash sale. The dealer found a buyer, Rob Grave. But Rob is

somewhat suspicious and therefore only offered $8 million for the painting. Awful accepted, and the painting was exchanged for the cash. It did not take long for Awful to fritter away every cent of the $8 million on ludicrous extravagances. He is now destitute and has no executable assets. One of his unsecured creditors has found out about the sale of the painting. Does the creditor have grounds to recover the painting from Rob?

3. Marc Ruckerberg is the founder and CEO of PictureWall. His salary is $1 million a year. Unfortunately, the business has been performing poorly and the board of directors asks Marc to resign. Marc is willing to consider the request but demands that the board provide him a large golden parachute. The board grudgingly agrees, and he and the company enter into an agreement pursuant to which Marc agrees to work for 30 days to ensure an orderly transition. Further, Marc is to receive $20 million in severance but waives all future claims against the company. Marc received his $20 million payment in March, 30 days after signing the agreement. Unfortunately, PictureWall's primary server farm was destroyed by fire in June, and the company was forced to file for bankruptcy. There is no indication that the company was insolvent prior to the fire. Can the bankruptcy trustee avoid the $20 million payment to Marc?

4. After a wildly successful legal career, Atticus Rich decides to donate $2 million in cash to his alma mater, Maize & Blue Law School. He normally does not donate money, but believes he is ready to become a philanthropist. He reaches the $2 million figure after meeting with his accountant, who tells him that his gross income for the year was $10 million. Atticus has invested all of his money with Bernard Charles. Shortly after making the donation, Atticus learns that Bernard has been running a Ponzi scheme and all investor money has been lost. Atticus is unable to pay his bills and files for bankruptcy. Assume that the bankruptcy trustee is able to establish that the donation to the law school is a fraudulent transfer under §548(a)(1)(B). Does the law school have a defense? How much money will the law school have to relinquish, if any?

5. Tim Harbaugh owns all 100,000 outstanding shares of Wolverine Electronics, Inc. The company owns a number of manufacturing facilities around the country. The vast majority of the facilities are owned outright by the company and there are no liens against them. Each share of the company is valued between $140 and $160. Tim is approached by Private Equity Firm that wants to purchase the company for $150 a share. Tim is concerned when the firm explains that they intend to make the acquisition through a leveraged buyout. But the price is too good for Tim to pass up. Tim agrees to sell his company. At the direction of Private Equity Firm, Wolverine Electronics receives a $15 million loan from Big Bank. The loan is secured by a lien on all of Wolverine Electronics' manufacturing

facilities. Private Equity Firm directs the loan funds directly to Tim's bank account and purchases all 100,000 outstanding shares of the company, becoming the new owner of Wolverine Electronics.

Unfortunately, there is a slight downturn in the economy shortly after the acquisition closes. Despite the fact that the correction is relatively minor, the company is unable to pay the new monthly debt payments that it owes to Big Bank. The company defaults and promptly files for bankruptcy. At first glance, there is not much for the bankruptcy trustee to do. The company has very little cash on hand, its revenue is declining, and all of its assets have liens that are in excess of the value of the asset. What do you recommend the trustee do?

6. Several years ago, Erstwhile Enterprises, Inc. purchased a plot of land as an investment. To finance the purchase, it borrowed money from Promised Land Co. and granted a mortgage on the property to Promised Land to secure the loan. The mortgage was properly recorded at the time. After suffering losses on its investments for some years, Erstwhile Enterprises became insolvent and could not raise the funds necessary to pay its debts. In January of this year it ceased payment of installments due on its mortgage. Promised Land commenced suit, obtained judgment, and foreclosed on the property. After complying fully with statutory notice and advertising requirements under state law, Promised Land held a foreclosure sale on April 15. The sale was conducted in all respects in accordance with the law.

   Shrewd Investment Co., a land speculator, attended the sale. Because bidding was light, it managed to buy the property for $30,000. At the time its fair market value was $50,000. The proceeds of the foreclosure sale were paid to Promised Land by the sheriff. They were just sufficient to settle the balance owing under the mortgage plus the costs of foreclosure.

   Erstwhile Enterprises filed a bankruptcy petition on July 1. Can the foreclosure sale be avoided?

Explanations

1. This question is meant to illustrate a clear case of actual fraud under UFTA. The creditor (defined in §1(4)) should succeed in avoiding the transfer under UFTA §4(a)(i). The sale of the painting is a transfer as defined in §1(12). The painting is an asset of Awful's under §1(2).[19]

19. Assume, for the sake of simplicity, that Awful has no claim to an exemption in the painting under the state exemption statute. If he did have an exemption that covered the painting, it would likely be subject to a value limitation that would make the exemption minuscule in relation to the worth of the painting. Where fraudulently transferred property is only partially exempt, the creditor may still recover and execute on it, but the debtor may be able to claim the amount of the exemption from the proceeds of the execution sale. Note,

The grounds of actual fraud are satisfied because Awful made the transfer with the intent of hindering, delaying, or defrauding creditors. The creditor must prove fraudulent intent, but can do so by offering circumstantial evidence of intent—badges of fraud. The transaction exhibits several badges of fraud: It occurred while Awful was besieged by creditors, and shortly before this creditor's unsuccessful levy, Awful was insolvent on the balance sheet test, the painting was his last remaining asset, he received laughably inadequate consideration for it, Hyde is a close friend, and Awful had an understanding with Hyde for the return of the painting for a nominal sum in the future. Because the creditor can likely prove actual fraud, it does not have to rely on constructive fraud grounds, but under the circumstances of the case, the elements of constructive fraud are present. Awful was insolvent at the time of the transfer, and the painting was disposed of for an amount that does not even come close to reasonably equivalent value. (Note that the two grounds for constructive fraud also count as badges of fraud for the purposes of proving actual intent to defraud.) The creditor can therefore rely on constructive fraud as an alternative ground of avoidance. Note that only a creditor whose claim was in existence at the time of the transfer can use constructive fraud as a basis of avoidance. The facts indicate that this claim was in existence at the time of the transfer.

Even where a debtor has acted with fraudulent intent, the transferee is protected from avoidance if he is a good faith transferee for reasonably equivalent value. If he acted in good faith, but the value was not reasonably equivalent, he may be entitled to a lien for the value that he gave the debtor. In this case, Hyde appears to have knowingly collaborated with Awful in attempting to hide the painting, and therefore does not qualify for any protection.

2. Analysis of this problem can be broken up as follows:
   (a) Actual fraud. Awful's disposition is motivated here, as it was in Example 1, by the desire to keep the painting from his creditors. This case has several indicia of fraud in common with Example 1, but there are a few differences: Awful does not have a close relationship with the transferee, and the value received for the painting is much closer to being equivalent. On the other hand, Awful speedily dissipated the proceeds of the painting. There are surely enough suspicious circumstances to provide a solid case for actual fraud.

---

however, that a court may hold that the debtor waived any exemption in the property by fraudulently transferring it.

(b) Constructive fraud. The facts make it clear that Awful was already insolvent before the transfer, which aggravated this condition. However, the question of whether he received reasonably equivalent value is less clear. The consideration for the painting is much closer to its true value. (Although the value of the transferred property is stated in the Example, remember that value can be a difficult factual issue, often requiring expert testimony.) Eighty percent of the painting's value may or may not be a reasonably equivalent value in exchange for the painting. This decision should not be made solely on an arithmetical comparison, but should be determined in light of all the circumstances of the transaction. If the disposition was a fairly bargained, regular market transaction, there may be a justification for the buyer's offering and the seller accepting less than the market price. However, where the price is depressed as a result of a hasty clandestine disposition and is paid in cash, a good case can be made that 80 percent of the market value was not a reasonably equivalent exchange.

(c) The transferee's defense or offset. To be completely protected from avoidance of the transfer, Rob must qualify as a good faith purchaser for value under §548(c). To receive the lesser protection of a lien or offset for the consideration paid, Rob must at least have acted in good faith. It has already been suggested that the price may not be reasonably equivalent value. If this is so, there is a likelihood that the transfer will be avoided and the issue of the lien or offset arises.

There is a good argument that Rob did not act in good faith. Although there was no express collusion and the parties did not know each other, the transaction is unsavory. The problem notes that Rob is suspicious of the sale. He may not have known the specifics of Awful's situation, but a court could determine that Rob was on inquiry notice, and he failed to undertake a diligent inquiry as required by §548(c). Courts often attribute knowledge to one who avoids inquiry under circumstances that strongly suggest fraud. If Rob is found to have lacked good faith, he receives no offset or lien. His restitution claim against Awful is valueless because Awful has no assets.

3. The bankruptcy trustee has a good chance of avoiding the $20 million transfer to Marc. There is no indication that there is actual intent to defraud PictureWall's creditors. The trustee will not be able to rely on §548(a)(1)(A). The trustee's best option is an avoidance premised on a §548(a)(1)(B) constructive fraud claim.

Primarily, the $20 million transfer occurred within two years before the petition date.[20] Further, it does not appear that the company received reasonably equivalent value for the transfer (§548(a)(1)(B)(i)). Marc's yearly salary is $1 million. The agreement entitled him to receive $20 million for an additional 30 days of employment. Marc did agree to waive all future claims against the company, but it is unlikely that the value of these claims could be anything more than a fraction of the transfer amount. The trustee's problem with a traditional constructive fraudulent transfer claim is that there is no indication that 1) the company was insolvent on the date of the transfer (§548(a)(1)(B)(ii)(I)), 2) the company was left with unreasonably small capital after the transfer (§548(a)(1)(B)(ii)(II), or 3) the company incurred debts beyond its ability to repay as such debts matured (§548(a)(1)(B)(ii)(III).

Consequently, the trustee's best argument is that Marc is an insider, and the transfer was made pursuant to an employment contract not in the ordinary course of business (§548(a)(1)(B)(ii)(IV)). Section 101(31) of the Code defines the term "insider." Marc qualifies because—at the time of the agreement establishing the transfer was executed—Marc was an officer of the company (§101(31)(B)(ii)). Marc may argue that he was not an insider at the time he *received the transfer*, but courts have rejected this argument.[21] The agreement qualifies as an employment contract as courts have defined that term broadly. Finally, the transfer was not in the ordinary course of business. Marc's ouster from the company was an unusual, isolated event. The transfer was made pursuant to an agreement prepared specifically to provide the framework for his departure. There is nothing customary or reoccurring about the transfer.

4. In this Example we are assuming that the bankruptcy trustee has a claim under §548(a)(1)(B). Section 548(a)(2) provides the law school with a possible defense. The section creates a safe harbor for certain charitable contributions. The first question is whether the $2 million contribution is a "charitable contribution." Atticus's contribution appears to qualify because it is a gift and, pursuant to §548(d)(3), it was made by an individual in the form of cash. The next question is whether the law school is a "qualified religious or charitable entity or organization." Section 548(d)(4) defines the term as an entity described in section 170(c)(1) or (c)(2) of the Internal Revenue Code of 1986. Educational institutions like law schools are included in the definition (*see* section 14.3.6, *supra*).

---

20. Even if the payment had occurred outside of the two-year window, the trustee could still invoke §544 and rely on a longer statute of limitations period under applicable state law.
21. See, e.g., *In re TransTexas Gas Corp.*, 597 F.3d 298 (5th Cir. 2010).

Because the law school and the donation qualify under §548(a)(2), the next question is what portion of the contribution is protected. Section 548(a)(2)(A) provides that the Code only protects the amount of the contribution that does not exceed 15 percent of Atticus's gross annual income for the year in which the transfer of the contribution was made. The problem tells us that Atticus's gross annual income is $10 million. The contribution represents 20 percent of his gross annual income. The law school could try to argue that §548(a)(2)(B) protects the $2 million contribution, but the problem states that Atticus has not engaged in this type of gift-giving in the past so it is unlikely §548(a)(2)(B) will apply.

The final question is what portion of the contribution the trustee can avoid. Some courts have ruled that the trustee can avoid the entire contribution, but the majority position is that the trustee can only avoid that portion of the contribution that exceeds 15 percent of Atticus's gross annual income. Consequently, the law school will most likely have to disgorge $500,000.

5. The trustee should rely on §548(a)(1)(B) and consider avoiding the $15 million transfer to Tim. The problem describes a fairly typical leveraged buyout. These types of acquisition models are extremely susceptible to attack as fraudulent transfers. Primarily, the transaction is within the two-year statute of limitations period prescribed by §548(a)(1)(A). The next question is whether Wolverine Electronics, the debtor in the case, received less than reasonably equivalent value. Remember Tim received $15 million for his shares in the company. That transfer was probably for reasonably equivalent value, but that is not the focus of the inquiry here. The question here is whether Wolverine Electronics received reasonably equivalent value for incurring $15 million in debt and giving Big Bank liens on its assets. The answer is that the company did not receive reasonably equivalent value. In fact, the company did not receive any value. The loan funds did not benefit the debtor; the funds went directly to Tim. Consequently, §548(a)(1)(B)(i) is satisfied. The final issue is whether the company was in a state of insolvency at the time of the transfer or fell into such a state because of the transfer. Any one of the three insolvency subsections — §§548(a)(1)(B)(i)(I), (II), or (III) — could apply. Because of the company's new debt obligations, even a minor downturn in the market immediately drove the company in bankruptcy. Consequently, it's likely that the company was insolvent at the time of the transfer. Even if this was not the case, it appears that the company became insolvent as a result of the transfer. Further, the company's property and assets after the transfer were unreasonably small for the business in which they are involved. Finally, the trustee can most

likely establish that the company incurred debts that it should have known it was unable to satisfy.

The trustee may be able to avoid the $15 million share purchase. If so, Tim could be forced to disgorge the funds in exchange for the shares of the company that he sold. Naturally, the shares are not worth much with the company in bankruptcy. Keep in mind that the bankruptcy court has discretion in prescribing a remedy in this case and may be disinclined to order such a harsh result, but it certainly has the authority to do so under the Code.

6. The foreclosure sale is a transfer of the debtor's property. It is expressly included in the definition of "transfer" in §101(54). The foreclosure sale in fact constitutes two transfers: the payment of the sale proceeds to Promised Land and the conveyance of the property to Shrewd Investment. The transfer to Promised Land was on account of an antecedent debt and was made while the debtor was insolvent within the 90-day prebankruptcy period. However, Promised Land is a fully secured claimant. It received from the sale no more than the value of its perfected secured claim, and did no better than it would have done in a Ch. 7 distribution if the transfer had not been made. Therefore the improvement-in-position test is not satisfied, and the transfer is not avoidable under §547.

   The transfer to Shrewd Investment is not a preferential transfer to a creditor and is therefore not avoidable under §547. However, because the sale occurred within two years of the bankruptcy filing, it is vulnerable under §548. It is not suggested that the debtor, Erstwhile Enterprises, was guilty of actual fraud in this involuntary disposition. However, it was insolvent, so that if the foreclosure proceeds are less than reasonably equivalent value, the grounds of constructive fraud in §548(2) are satisfied. There had been some doubt over whether a low price received at a foreclosure sale should be treated as inadequate value, but this question was settled by the U.S. Supreme Court in *BFP v. Resolution Trust Corp.*, 511 U.S. 531 (1994). The Court ruled that as long as the foreclosure sale is conducted in compliance with state law, the proceeds received from the sale are conclusively deemed to be reasonably equivalent value. The majority reasoned that as distress sales are seldom at market price, §548 could not be intended to allow courts to use a market standard of any kind to evaluate the price received at a foreclosure sale. The court found this interpretation to be supported by Congress's choice of wording in §548, which uses "reasonably equivalent value," and not "fair market value," as the basis of measuring adequacy of consideration for §548 purposes.

   BFP is expressly confined to the treatment of foreclosure sales under §548. Although its reasoning could persuade lower courts to adopt a similar rule in other distress sales, the case does not settle the divergence of views among courts of appeal in cases other than foreclosure.[22] As the proceeding under which Shrewd Investment acquired the property is a foreclosure sale, *BFP* governs. The sale fully complied with state law and cannot be avoided as a fraudulent transfer.

---

22. It is also not clear if *BFP* applies outside of §548. For example, under defined circumstances, §549 precludes the avoidance of a postpetition transfer for which "present fair equivalent value" was given. Some courts have held that *BFP* should be applied to a foreclosure sale under §549 as well. However, others, such as *In re Miller*, 454 F.3d 899 (8th Cir. 2006), have held that *BFP* is inapplicable because "present fair equivalent value" in §549 is not the same as "reasonably equivalent value" in §548.

CHAPTER 15

The Trustee's Power to Use, Sell, or Lease Estate Property (§363) and to Obtain Credit (§364)

§15.1 OVERVIEW

Sections 363 and 364 are concerned with two central administrative functions of the trustee: the power to 1) use, sell, or lease estate property and 2) enter into credit transactions on behalf of the estate. The powers are not equally relevant nor used the same way in every case but can be an invaluable form of relief when applicable. The sections are designed to enable the trustee to conduct the affairs of the estate to maximize creditor recoveries and reorganize a business. Section 363 addresses the use, sale, and lease of estate property. The section distinguishes between actions that are in the ordinary course of the debtor's business and those that are not. Subsection (b) provides that a trustee may use, sell, or lease estate property not in the ordinary course of business only with court authority obtained after notice and a hearing.[1] Subsection (c)(1) provides that, in certain instances, the trustee has discretion to enter into ordinary-course transactions without special permission of the court or notice and a hearing. However, subsection (c)(2) places restrictions on subsection (c)(1)'s grant of power in instances where the trustee seeks to use "cash collateral" — defined in §363(a). Subsection (e) applies to any use of estate assets and provides that before any

1. As stated before, "notice and a hearing" is defined in §102 to mean that parties in interest must receive notice, but that a hearing need not be held unless a party in interest requests it.

use, the trustee must provide adequate protection[2] of any interest in the asset held by a third party if that party does not consent to the trustee's use of the asset. Subsection (f) addresses instances where the trustee seeks to sell estate assets and allows for a sale free and clear of any interest in the property if certain conditions are met. Finally, subsection (m) provides that a sale of estate assets involving a purchaser who acted in good faith pursuant to a court-approved sale process may not be overturned on appeal, unless the court authorizing the sale agreed to stay the sale pending appeal. This protection is referred to as "mootness" and is another unique provision rarely seen outside of bankruptcy.

Section 363's scope is broad and contains a number of subsections that are rarely invoked. This chapter focuses on the section's overarching principles and key facets but does not attempt to explore the entire labyrinth of §363's subsections.

Section 364 authorizes the trustee to obtain credit and incur debt on behalf of the estate. The section offers the trustees a hierarchy of options for obtaining postpetition credit. Pursuant to §364(a), a trustee is authorized — unless otherwise restricted by the court — to obtain unsecured credit in the ordinary course of business without court approval. Pursuant to §364(b), with prior court approval, unsecured credit also may be obtained outside the ordinary course of business and the resulting debt treated as an administrative expense. If the trustee cannot entice a lender to offer credit by agreeing to recognize the debt as an administrative expense, §364(c) allows the trustee, subject to prior court approval, to obtain financing that provides the postpetition lender with 1) administrative expense "superpriority" status; 2) a lien on any unencumbered property of the estate; and/or 3) a junior lien over property of the estate subject to existing liens.

In some cases, a trustee cannot obtain credit based on any of the foregoing terms. Consequently, §364(d) allows the trustee to provide a postpetition lender with a lien on encumbered property of the estate that has a superior priority to any existing lien on that property. This is referred to as a "priming lien." The primary protection offered to existing lienholders in these cases is that the bankruptcy court must determine that the existing lienholder's interest is adequately protected, a term defined by §361. Bankruptcy courts will generally defer to a debtor's business judgment when evaluating financing requests under §364.

Section 364(e) is similar to §363(m)'s mootness provision. Indeed, the appeal of an order authorizing postpetition financing will not adversely affect the position of a postpetition creditor acting in good faith, unless the financing order was stayed by the court pending appeal.

---

2. Section 361 defines the term "adequate protection."

§15.2 THE USE, SALE, OR LEASE OF ESTATE PROPERTY UNDER §363

Section 363 provides authority for the trustee's dealings with estate property, sets out some general principles governing the exercise of this power, and places limits on the trustee's discretion for the protection of creditors and other parties whose interests may be affected by the trustee's activities. Section 363 encompasses a wide range of activity, including the disposition of estate assets, the operation of equipment, the use of resources and premises, and the routine conduct of daily operations.

§15.2.1 Ordinary Course Transactions

As noted above, §363 makes a fundamental distinction between transactions in the ordinary course of business, which may be conducted within the trustee's discretion, and those outside the ordinary course, which require notice to interested parties and, where requested, a hearing and court approval. The basic idea behind this distinction is that the trustee should be able to maintain routine business operations with a minimum of interference but should not be permitted to enter extraordinary transactions without giving notice to creditors and other interested parties and, if need be, justifying the transaction to the court.

The trustee may enter into ordinary-course transactions without notice and a hearing under §363, but only if the debtor had been engaged in business at the time of the petition and the postpetition conduct of business operations is generally allowed in the chapter under which the petition has been filed. Section 363(c)(1) is expressly premised on the trustee's underlying statutory authorization to operate the debtor's business under §§721, 1108, or 1304. In rehabilitation cases, if the debtor had a business at the time of the petition, authority to continue its operation is normal. Sections 1108 and 1304 allow the trustee to continue business activities unless the court orders otherwise. Therefore, in rehabilitation cases, the trustee may continue the debtor's ordinary business operations under §363(c)(1) without notice or court approval unless such activity has been curtailed by court order. Section 15.2.3 discusses the "cash collateral" exception to this rule.

The opposite is true in liquidation cases. Ch. 7 is aimed at the expeditious liquidation of the estate, and continuation of the debtor's business is not normally contemplated. Section 721 requires court approval for any business activity by the trustee, and stipulates that such approval should be granted only for a limited time and only upon a showing that further business operations are in the best interests of the estate and consistent with orderly liquidation. In a Ch. 7 case, therefore, there can be no ordinary-course business activity without notice and a hearing under §363(c)(1) unless the conduct of the business has first been authorized by the court under §721.

In short, unless the debtor-conducted business at the time of the petition and the continuation of the business is permitted under the chapter governing the petition, notice and a hearing is required for any use, sale, or lease of estate property, whether or not in the ordinary course of business. If the continuation of ordinary business operations is authorized, ordinary-course transactions may proceed at the trustee's discretion, but any transaction involving the extraordinary use, sale, or lease of estate property must be preceded by notice and a hearing. (*See* Example 1.)

To know if notice must be given, the trustee must decide if a transaction fits within the scope of ordinary business operations. In some situations this is not a difficult question to resolve. For example, a routine sale of inventory to a customer is obviously in the ordinary course of business if the debtor's business is the retail sale of goods. But the sale of all the debtor's inventory or the disposition of one of its branches is not ordinary.

In instances where the nature of a transaction is not entirely clear, the assessment is a factual question to be resolved in light of the particular circumstances of the case. Courts apply two complementary tests—the "vertical dimension" test and the "horizontal dimension" test—to determine if a transaction is in the ordinary course of the debtor's business. A transaction in within the debtor's ordinary course of business if both tests are satisfied. Under the vertical dimension test, courts evaluate the transaction from the perspective of a hypothetical creditor and determine if that creditor would reasonably expect the debtor to undertake the transaction at issue in the ordinary course of the debtor's business. The test compares the debtor's prepetition and postpetition practices to determine if "the transaction subjects a creditor to economic risks of a nature different from those [it] accepted when [it] decided to extend credit."[3]

Under the horizontal dimension" test, courts look more broadly at the commercial context in which the debtor's business is operated, and ask whether the postpetition transaction is of a type that may be expected in a business similar to the debtor's. Overall, the purpose of the two-pronged inquiry is to ascertain whether parties in interest could reasonably have anticipated a transaction of this type, given the range and scope of the debtor's business and the normal practices in the business environment in which the debtor participates. If not, the transaction is outside the

---

3. *In re Johns-Manville Corp.*, 60 B.R. 612, 616 (Bankr. S.D.N.Y. 1986).

ordinary course of the debtor's business, and interested parties must be informed of it and given an opportunity to demand a hearing.[4]

§15.2.2 Transactions Outside the Ordinary Course of Business Under §363(b)(1)

a. Use, Sale, or Lease of an Estate Asset

The use, sale, or lease of property outside the ordinary course of business may be approved by the court pursuant to §363(b)(1). The standard for approval is that the transaction maximizes the value of the estate and furthers the legitimate ends of the bankruptcy case. This is a factual determination to be made in the context of the case as a whole. The factors evaluated by the court include the adequacy of the price, the business efficacy of the transaction, and its overall benefit to the estate.[5] The terms of the transaction are usually left to the trustee's discretion and judgment.

In a Ch. 11 case, the court will view the transaction in light of the larger scheme of rehabilitation envisioned for the estate to determine if the transaction is likely to further or hamper the debtor's rehabilitation strategy. Section 363 is meant to be used for extraordinary dealings with estate property prior to the confirmation of the Ch. 11 plan. Therefore, if there is no need for immediate action, or the transaction involves the sale of a significant portion of the debtor's assets, the court may refuse approval under §363 and require the transaction to be dealt with in the plan of reorganization, which is subject to a confirmation process that has a variety of creditor protections.[6] Example 1(e) illustrates the factors to be considered by a court in approving sales outside the ordinary course of business.

b. Sale of Substantially All Estate Assets (§363(b)) and Mootness (§363(m))

In many cases, a company files a bankruptcy petition intending to reorganize its business but discovers that its prospects for a successful reorganization are slim. Instead of converting the case to one under Ch. 7 and relinquishing control, the debtor may wish to sell its entire business pursuant to §363. This is a dramatic disposition and presents a different set of issues than a §363 sale involving a single estate asset. In fact, some scholars have argued

4. See *Aalfs v. Wirum (In re Straightline Invs.)*, 525 F.3d 870 (9th Cir. 2008). *See also* Example 1.
5. See *In re Exaeris, Inc.*, 380 B.R. 741 (Bankr. D. Del. 2008).
6. These safeguards are explained in Chapter 20. They include the publication of a disclosure statement detailing plan provisions, voting on the plan by creditors, and compliance with statutory confirmation requirements. The notice and hearing process in §363(b)(1) does not provide safeguards of equal strength.

that a sale of substantially all estate assets should not be permitted under §363; rather, such a sale should be effectuated through a plan of reorganization, which — as noted above — is subject to a confirmation process that provides a variety of creditor protections. Nevertheless, courts uniformly agree that a debtor can sell substantially all of its assets pursuant to §363, and these types of sales are frequently sought in Ch. 11 cases.

In *In re Lionel Corp.*, 722 F.2d 1063 (2d Cir. 1983), the leading case on this issue, the Second Circuit held that a debtor can sell substantially all estate assets if a sound business reason supports the sale and the decision is an exercise of business judgment. In determining if a sound business reason exists, courts consider:

1. the proportionate value of the asset to the estate as a whole;[7]
2. the amount of elapsed time since the filing;[8]
3. the likelihood that a plan of reorganization will be proposed and confirmed in the near future;
4. the effect of the proposed disposition on future plans of reorganization;
5. the proceeds to be obtained from the disposition vis-a-vis any appraisals of the property;
6. which of the alternatives of use, sale, or lease the proposal envisions;
7. whether the asset is increasing or decreasing in value;
8. whether the sale opportunity still exists at the time of plan confirmation — if not, what is the probability of a comparable opportunity existing at that time; and
9. whether the estate has the liquidity to survive until confirmation of a plan.[9]

This list is not exhaustive and courts are not obligated to consider every factor or give the factors equal weight. If the court believes that the debtor is authorized to make the requested sale, the court enters an order allowing the debtor to sell substantially all estate assets pursuant to an auction and defining procedures for that auction (the "Sale Procedures Order").

The court's order is the precursor to an auction process that is unique to bankruptcy. Asset sales of this kind are invariably initiated by a debtor in possession, which has actively marketed its business and identified a potential buyer prior to requesting court approval of a sale. This potential buyer is identified as the "stalking horse bidder." The stalking horse bidder has already conducted due diligence and agreed to the material terms for the purchase of substantially all estate assets. The Sale Procedures Order

---

7. Sales of all or substantially all estate property will receive additional scrutiny.
8. Asset sales proposed shortly after the petition date will receive additional scrutiny.
9. See, e.g., *In re Boston Generating, LLC*, 440 B.R. 302, 322 (Bankr. S.D.N.Y. 2010).

recognizes the stalking horse bidder's bid for the assets. The order also sets up procedures for other parties to become qualified bidders and bid at an auction for estate assets. Assuming other parties become qualified bidders and wish to bid on the estate assets, an auction will occur before the court.

The court manages the auction on the predetermined date. There is an opening bid, usually set by the stalking horse bidder, and then qualified bidders are able to submit overbids. The bidding occurs pursuant to the Sale Procedures Order. Though the court oversees the process, the debtor in possession has the discretion to select the bid that it deems to be optimal. The debtor has a statutory and fiduciary duty to select the offer that most benefits the estate. However, the highest bid may not be the winning bid due to a variety of reasons, including unfavorable variations in the proposed payment schedule or concerns about a bidder's ability to close the transaction and successfully tender payment.

After the winning bid is selected, the court will enter an order confirming the sale. As part of this order, the debtor and the winning bidder will invariably ask the court to order that §363(m) has been satisfied. Section 363(m) is often referred to as the "mootness" provision. The subsection provides that any reversal or modification of the sale order on appeal does not affect the validity of the sale. Therefore, the subsection renders an appeal attacking the validity of the sale moot. In order to secure this relief, the court must 1) find that the purchaser entered into the transaction in good faith; and 2) not stay the sale pending an appeal. This dramatic protection is premised on the idea that without this level of finality, potential bidders would either submit significantly discounted prices to account for the risk that the sale will be overturned on appeal or refuse to participate in the auction process at all.[10] This phenomenon would suppress the value received from §363 sales and materially disadvantage creditors.

§15.2.3 Restrictions on Dealing with Cash Collateral (§363(c))

Section 363 treats cash collateral differently from other property of the estate. The essential difference is that cash collateral may not be dealt with by the trustee, even in the ordinary course of business, unless the holder of the interest in that collateral consents or the court authorizes the transaction after notice and a hearing. "Cash collateral" is defined in §363(a) to mean cash or a cash equivalent that is subject to an interest held

10. See, e.g., *Adeli v. Barclay (In re Berkeley Del. Court, LLC)*, 2016 BL 273132, at *3 (9th Cir. Aug. 23, 2016) and *Chamberlain v. Stanziale (In re Chamberlain)*, 545 B.R. 827, 844 (D. Del.2016).

by someone other than the estate. The most common form that this interest takes is a security interest in the cash collateral, either as original collateral or as proceeds of original collateral. Of course, the security interest must be valid under nonbankruptcy law, and if the cash collateral is proceeds of original collateral, the security interest must validly extend to such proceeds under nonbankruptcy law. Quite a wide range of property is considered to be the equivalent of cash under §363(a). The definition includes not only banknotes and bank accounts, but also various kinds of negotiable or readily transferable commercial paper such as negotiable instruments, documents, and securities. These are treated as cash equivalents because they can be liquidated easily by being sold to purchasers who take free of the rights of the secured party. Example 3 illustrates different types of cash collateral.

The liquid nature of cash and cash equivalents explains the stricter approach in §363 to the trustee's dealings with cash collateral. The debtor's business needs cash to operate. Consequently, debtors face the temptation to utilize cash on hand in the ongoing conduct of the business. A creditor that has a security interest in such assets faces a significant risk that its collateral will evaporate in the payment of daily business expenses. For this reason, §363(c)(2) freezes the use of cash collateral, even when this normally would be in the ordinary course of running the business, until the trustee either obtains 1) permission from the interest holder or 2) a court order authorizing the use. In addition, §363(c)(4) obliges the trustee to keep cash collateral separate and to account for it, unless the creditor or court dispenses with this requirement. Sections 363(d) and (e) specify that the authorization to deal with cash collateral is subject to any relief from stay that has been granted and is conditional upon adequate protection of the interest.

The cash needed to continue operating the debtor's business invariably constitutes "cash collateral," and the debtor will need access to this cash immediately after filing its bankruptcy petition. It is therefore common for the debtor to negotiate an agreement with the secured party under which it gives permission to the debtor to use the cash collateral, but the debtor agrees to operate pursuant to a budget formulated by the secured creditor and place cash collateral in a restricted bank account. If the debtor cannot obtain creditor consent, it must apply to court for authorization.

In many Ch. 11 cases, debtors in possession are unable to obtain creditor consent to use cash collateral when the bankruptcy petition is filed. At the same time, the debtor's business is unable to operate without use of the cash collateral. Section 363(c)(3) is designed to address this situation. The subsection allows a court to authorize interim use of cash collateral, usually for a few weeks. This type of relief is invariably sought at the beginning of a case under emergency circumstances.

§15.2.4 Adequate Protection (§363(e))

Where a proposed use or disposition of estate property jeopardizes a party's interest in that property, the party may seek adequate protection of its interest under §363(e). Under §363(o), the party who demands adequate protection bears the burden of proving the interest, but the trustee must prove that the interest is adequately protected. The right to adequate protection applies to all proposed transactions under §363, whether or not they are in the ordinary course of business and irrespective of the nature of the property.

Section 361 defines the term "adequate protection" and section 363(e) is designed to protect a creditor against diminution of the value of its collateral during the bankruptcy case. The request for adequate protection is most frequently made by a secured creditor concerned by the debtor's continued use of collateral. More specifically, a debtor in possession is entitled to use estate property in the ordinary course of its business without court approval, but a creditor that holds a valid lien on that property can argue that its interest is not adequately protected. If the court agrees with this claim, then the debtor must provide adequate protection or the court will restrict the debtor's use.

Section 361 provides a nonexhaustive list of ways that adequate protection can be provided, including providing a creditor with: 1) cash payments; 2) an additional or replacement lien; or 3) other relief as will result in the creditor realizing the indubitable equivalent of its interest. Courts determine whether adequate protection has been provided by 1) valuing the secured creditor's interest; 2) identifying the risks to the collateral that flow from the debtor's proposed use; and 3) determining whether the debtor's proposal of adequate protection protects the secured creditor's interest to an extent consistent with the value of the creditor's bargained-for rights. Courts frequently focus on if there is an equity cushion[11] in the collateral and the debtor's prospects for a successful reorganization. Consequently, in instances where a debtor has significant equity in a creditor's collateral, the court may reject that creditor's request for adequate protection.

§15.2.5 Sales Free and Clear of Interests (§363(f))

Section 363 asset sales are attractive in part because of the prospect of a sale occurring free and clear of any lien or encumbrance. Section 363(f)

11. An "equity cushion" is a term of art defined as the amount by which the value of the collateral exceeds the liens encumbering the collateral. The amount is referred to as a cushion because it protects the creditor's interest if the property value declines during the bankruptcy case.

authorizes the transfer of estate property unencumbered by "any interest in such property" if at least one the following occurs: 1) applicable nonbankruptcy law permits sale of such property free and clear of such interest; 2) such entity consents; 3) such interest is a lien and the price at which such property is to be sold is greater than the aggregate value of all liens on such property; 4) such interest is in bona fide dispute; or 5) such entity could be compelled, in a legal or equitable proceeding, to accept a money satisfaction of such interest. Each of these criteria are explored in depth in the following section.

This sale provision is particularly attractive to buyers because the risk of the buyer being responsible for an unexpected legacy obligation related to the purchase is reduced significantly. The estate benefits because this provision tends to put upward pressure on the sale price the estate receives.

The term "interest" certainly captures property interests such as liens and money judgments. But courts have adopted a broader reading of the term and found it to also include tort, statutory, and contractual claims against the debtor.[12]

a. Sales Permitted by Applicable Nonbankruptcy Law

Section 363(f)(1) allows for a sale free and clear of an interest if applicable nonbankruptcy law permits such a sale. This subsection is designed to avoid a situation in which creditors receive additional sale protections in bankruptcy that they would not have been able to enjoy if the sale had occurred outside of the federal bankruptcy process. For example, imagine that a real estate developer files for bankruptcy. State law applicable to the property owned by the debtor is subject to a "changed circumstances" doctrine that provides that covenants affecting real property transfers may be terminated when changes within the covenanted area are so radical that they practically destroy the covenant's purpose. The debtor seeks to sell the real property free and clear of any covenants affecting the property and beneficiaries of the covenants at issue object. The bankruptcy court could order such a sale pursuant to section 363(f)(1) if the court determined that 1) the changed circumstances doctrine would have allowed for the sale free and clear of any covenants if the sale had been proposed outside of bankruptcy court;

12. See *In re Trans World Airlines, Inc.*, 322 F.3d 283, 289 (3d Cir. 2003) (finding that Equal Employment Opportunity Commission claims pending against the debtor were "interests" under §363(f)); *UMW Combined Benefit Fund v. Walter Energy, Inc.*, 551 B.R. 631, 640–41 (N.D. Ala. 2016) (ruling that debtor's future liability under the Coal Act was an "interest"); and *Faulkner v. Bethlehem Steel/Int'l Steel Grp.*, No. 2:04-CV-34, 2005 BL 5649, at *3–4 (N.D. Ind. Apr. 27, 2005) (barring successor liability for racial discrimination claims). Note that parties holding these interests may be able to seek recourse from the proceeds of the sale.

and 2) the debtor proved that the changed circumstances doctrine applied based on the facts of the case.[13]

b. Third Party Consents to Sale Free of Its Interest

Section 363(f)(2) permits a sale of property free and clear of an interest if the entity that holds the interest consents. A party will generally consent in instances where it holds a lien, and the lien will attach to the proceeds of the sale. Consent is customarily made expressly and conveyed to the court by an agent for the party holding the interest. However, some courts have ruled that consent can be implied where the debtor has provided proper notice of the proposed sale and the affected party fails to object.[14]

c. Asset Sold for Price Greater than Aggregate Value of All Liens

Section 363(f)(3) allows the court to order a sale of estate property free and clear of any interest when the "interest [at issue] is a lien and the price at which such property is to be sold is greater than the aggregate value of all liens on such property." In these circumstances, the obligation owed to the lienholder can be satisfied in full from the proceeds received from the sale. Consequently, there is no reason to prevent a sale free and clear of the lien.

d. Interest in Bona Fide Dispute

Section 363(f)(4) allows for a sale of property free and clear of an interest if there is a bona fide dispute as to the interest. The term "bona fide dispute" is not defined in the Code, but courts have defined it to capture some sort of meritorious, existing conflict where there are substantial factual or legal questions that bear upon the debtor's liability.[15] The bankruptcy court must determine if a bona fide dispute exists, but does not need to resolve the merits of the dispute for purposes of §363(f)(4).

e. Interest Holder Could Be Compelled to Accept Money Satisfaction

Section 363(f)(5) allows a court to order a sale free and clear of an interest if the interest holder could be compelled—pursuant to bankruptcy or non-bankruptcy law—to accept money to extinguish its interest. In order for the

---

13. See *In re Midsouth Golf, LLC*, 549 B.R. 156 (Bankr. E.D.N.C. 2016) (explaining the changed circumstances doctrine that existed under North Carolina law and ordering a sale free and clear of covenants pursuant to §363(f)(1)).

14. See *FutureSource LLC v. Reuters Ltd.*, 312 F.3d 281, 285–86 (7th Cir. 2002) (finding that implied consent is sufficient under §363(f)(2) because transaction costs could be prohibitive if express consent had to be procured from all interested parties prior to a sale).

15. See *Key Mech. Inc. v. BDC 56 LLC (In re BDC 56 LLC)*, 330 F.3d 111, 117–18 (2d Cir. 2003).

court to invoke this subsection, the debtor must establish that 1) a legal or equitable proceeding is pending or could be brought; 2) the interest holder holds an interest in the estate asset; and 3) the interest holder could be compelled to accept a money satisfaction in exchange for its interest.

The last criterion is the most controversial. For this criterion, debtors have pointed to various state court proceedings pursuant to which a lienholder may be compelled to accept a money satisfaction, including receivership proceedings, liquidations of a probate estate, and tax sales.[16] Further, courts have ruled that §363(f)(5) can be used to compel an interest holder to accept less than full payment.[17]

§15.2.6 Insolvency or Bankruptcy Clauses in Prepetition Contracts or Nonbankruptcy Law (§363(l))

In dealing with property of the estate, section 9.3.2 indicated that §541(c) invalidates ipso facto clauses — provisions in contracts or nonbankruptcy law that restrict transfer or provide for the forfeiture of property rights on bankruptcy — so that private parties or states cannot circumvent bankruptcy law by making the debtor's property interests nonassignable to the trustee. Similar considerations exist with regard to the trustee's power to use, sell, or lease property. To prevent states or private parties from negating the trustee's power to deal with property under §363, §363(l) disregards contractual or statutory provisions that provide for the forfeiture or modification of the debtor's property rights upon insolvency or bankruptcy.

§15.3 POSTPETITION CREDIT UNDER §364

§15.3.1 §364's Rationale

Section 364 deals with credit given to the estate after the petition has been filed. In these transactions the estate is the debtor, and is liable for payment

16. See *In re Jolan, Inc.*, 403 B.R. 866, 870 (Bankr. W.D. Wash. 2009).
17. See, e.g., *In re Boston Generating, LLC*, 440 B.R. 302, 333 n.29 (Bankr. S.D.N.Y. 2010) ("For example, under New York law, a junior lienholder [either in a foreclosure of real property or of collateral under the Uniform Commercial Code] is entitled to nothing more than the surplus cash generated in a sale. See, e.g., N.Y. U.C.C. §§9–608, 9–615."); but see *In re Stroud Wholesale, Inc.*, 47 B.R. 999, 1002–04 (E.D.N.C. 1985) (ruling that lienholder must receive full satisfaction of its claim under §363(f)(5)).

of the debt.[18] A Ch. 7 estate does not usually need to borrow money. However, corporate reorganization is an expensive, time-consuming process. A Ch. 11 debtor that is undergoing rehabilitation and is attempting to operate and reorganize its business requires access to capital. Remember, the entity has invariably sought bankruptcy protection because of some form of liquidity crisis. Postpetition financing will be vital to the debtor's survival and successful reorganization. To obtain credit, the debtor needs to convince a prospective financer that it has good prospects of rehabilitation. In addition, because of the risk that the debtor will not overcome its financial difficulties, the postpetition lender is likely to require some security or an assurance of priority if the debt cannot be repaid. Section 364 assists the trustee in obtaining postpetition credit by providing the means for securing or otherwise protecting financial transactions entered into by the estate.

Like the ordinary use, sale, or lease of estate property, the routine creation of postpetition unsecured debt is within the trustee's discretion. However, credit transactions outside the ordinary course of business and the creation of secured debt must be authorized by the court following notice and a hearing. The assumption of new debt by the estate is potentially detrimental to existing unsecured creditors. If the reorganization ultimately fails, new creditors with secured or priority claims will consume assets or funds that would have been available to pay the prepetition claims. Thus, postpetition financing creates a dilemma: If the debtor obtains new credit, its chances of successful rehabilitation are improved, and prepetition unsecured creditors have a chance to receive a higher level of payment than they would have received in liquidation. However, if new credit is obtained and the debtor still fails, the estate's assets will have been further encumbered, the expenses of administration will have increased, and the source of funds formerly available to unsecured creditors will have been reduced or eliminated. Because prepetition creditors bear a large part of the risk of failure, courts are usually careful to try to protect their interests when called upon to approve a postpetition credit transaction. Fully secured prepetition creditors are not as vulnerable as unsecured creditors because their claims are protected by their liens. However, proposed postpetition financing can, under some circumstances, affect the security of a prepetition secured creditor. If this is a possibility, the prepetition creditor is entitled to receive adequate protection of its interest as a precondition to the court approving the financing.

---

18. These estate debts qualify as administrative expenses with top priority for payment.

§15.3.2 The Credit Arrangements Permitted by §364

Section 364 is based on the policy that the trustee should be required to find the least onerous financing available. For example, if unsecured credit is available, it is to be preferred to secured credit. If secured credit is necessary, unencumbered property should be used as collateral rather than property subject to an existing interest. This policy is expressed in the section's hierarchical organization, which offers four different levels of credit transaction that are progressively more burdensome for the estate. Courts will not approve a postpetition financing arrangement if one with less onerous terms is available.

The four levels of transaction are as follows:

(1) Unsecured debt incurred in the ordinary course of business (§364(a)). If continuation of the debtor's business is authorized under §721, 1108, or 1304, the trustee has the power to obtain unsecured credit in the ordinary course of business. The debt obligation is given the priority of an administrative expense designed to be paid before most other unsecured claims. (*See* Chapter 17.) This provision is similar in concept to §363(c)(1), which was discussed in section 15.2.1. Unless the court orders otherwise, these routine credit transactions do not require notice or a hearing. The test for deciding whether a transaction is in the ordinary course of business is the same as when evaluating a request to use, sale, or lease estate property. *See* section 15.2.1.

(2) Unsecured debt outside the ordinary course of business (§364(b)). If the unsecured credit transaction does not fall within the normal course of the debtor's business (or if there is no authority to operate a business under the applicable chapter of the Code), the trustee must obtain court permission, following notice and a hearing, to incur the unsecured credit. The approved credit is given administrative expense priority. The general grounds for approving the credit transaction are similar to those for approving the use, sale, or lease of estate property outside the ordinary course of business: The court must be satisfied that the transaction is on fair and reasonable terms, that it is likely to further the interests of the estate, and that it will not impose an unjustifiable burden or risk on parties in interest.

(3) Secured or superpriority credit (§364(c)). If the trustee cannot obtain unsecured credit allowable as an administrative expense, §364(c) allows the court, after notice and a hearing, to approve security or special priority for the debt. Section 364(c) provides the court with three alternatives 1) authorize superpriority for the debt, placing it ahead of administrative expenses so that it is paid in preference over priority and general unsecured claims,[19] 2) allow the trustee to secure the debt by a lien on unencumbered property, or 3) allow the trustee to secure the debt by a junior lien on encumbered property. The court is not confined to any one of the alternatives and can approve a transaction that combines them. In addition to determining that unsecured credit is unavailable, the court takes into account the same factors as those identified for §364(b) in deciding whether to approve a transaction under §364(c).

(4) Credit secured by a senior or equal lien on encumbered property (§364(d)). Subsection (d) presents dramatic financing terms. The credit terms in the prior categories do not infringe upon the rights of existing secured claimants. Under this subsection, a court (after notice and a hearing) can approve credit that is secured by a lien senior or equal to an existing lien on estate property if the credit is unobtainable by any other means and the need for it is demonstrated by the trustee. This kind of lien is commonly called a "priming lien' because it primes an existing lien on the property.

The grant of such a lien endangers the valid preexisting security interest in the property and the holder's legitimate expectation of full satisfaction of its secured claim. Therefore, priming is only approved in compelling circumstances. For a party that is primed, §364(d) requires the existing interest to be adequately protected. The trustee has the burden of proving adequate protection, and the principles discussed in sections 8.4 and 15.2.4 apply. Section 361 defines "adequate protection" and states that it may be provided by the debtor offering the affected creditor either 1) cash payments; 2) an additional or replacement lien; or 3) other relief as will result in the creditor realizing the indubitable equivalent of its interest. Adequate protection is generally found to exist where the collateral has a significant equity cushion. However, the fact that the equity cushion is large enough to accommodate both the existing and the proposed liens may not, on its own, be enough to adequately protect the existing interest. For example, in *In re Stoney Creek Technologies, LLC*, 364 B.R. 882 (Bankr. E.D. Pa. 2007), the court refused to approve credit secured by a senior lien despite an adequate equity cushion because the Ch. 11 debtor's prospects of successful reorganization were poor and the proposed financing would not have improved

19. Prior to 2005, administrative expenses were a first-priority claim, paid before all other categories of priority claims. The Bankruptcy Abuse Prevention and Consumer Protection Act of 2005 (BAPCPA) elevated domestic support obligations to first priority, so administrative expenses are now in second place. (*See* Chapter 17.) Because postpetition credit is more commonly used in business bankruptcy cases, this change in the priority structure will often have no impact on the rank of a superpriority claim. However, if postpetition credit is given to an individual debtor who owes domestic support obligations, superpriority is no longer as super as it was.

them. In other words, when the effect of the priming lien is "merely to pass the risk of loss to the holder of the existing lien, the request for authorization should be denied."[20]

§15.3.3 Unique Lending Terms in Debtor in Possession Financing

a. Cross-Collateralization

In many cases, the Ch. 11 debtor is a poor credit risk and may not be able to entice a new lender to extend credit. Consequently, the debtor will be forced to approach an existing creditor for further advances. The existing creditor has a stake in the debtor's rehabilitation and some incentive to provide new financing if it believes that the debtor's reorganization may be successful. The creditor has an even stronger incentive to provide postpetition financing if its prepetition claim is unsecured or undersecured, and the debtor is willing to provide collateral to secure both the new credit and the unsecured prepetition credit. Such an arrangement is known as "cross-collateralization." In short, cross-collateralization is a provision of a postpetition financing arrangement where the collateral securing newly incurred postpetition debt also secures the lender's unsecured or undersecured prepetition claim. For cross-collateralization to benefit the lender, there must be a present or anticipated excess equity in the collateral beyond the amount of the new debt. For example, suppose a creditor is owed a prepetition debt of $5 million, secured by collateral worth $4 million. The creditor agrees to make a new postpetition loan of $2 million to the debtor to enable it to reorganize. As a condition of this postpetition loan, the creditor demands a security interest in unencumbered property of the estate worth $3 million, which will secure both the postpetition loan and the prepetition debt. If this arrangement is authorized by the court, the creditor not only secures the new financing, but also bolsters the security for its prepetition debt and eliminates its unsecured deficiency. In essence, the creditor uses its bargaining power in negotiating postpetition financing to improve the position of its undersecured prepetition debt at the expense of other unsecured creditors. Cross-collateralization is controversial because it results in an undersecured creditor having the unsecured portion of its claim become fully secured.

Cross-collateralization is certainly a disfavored means of financing, but the term is allowed by the majority of courts as a last resort. Courts have allowed the provision where the debtor in possession has shown that 1) the

---

20. In re *Windsor Hotel, L.L.C.*, 295 B.R. 307, 314 (Bankr. C.D. Ill. 2003).

business will not survive without the proposed financing, 2) the estate cannot obtain better financing, 3) the proposed lender will not agree to better terms, and 4) the transaction is in the best interests of the estate and creditors.[21]

b. Roll-Ups

A roll-up occurs when a prepetition lender agrees to be the debtor's post-petition lender on the condition that the proceeds of the postpetition financing will be used first to repay the prepetition debt in full. For example, imagine that a bank is owed $100 million prepetition debt that is secured, and the debtor in possession needs $20 million in postpetition financing. Pursuant to a roll-up, the bank would lend the debtor in possession $120 million with $100 million going to satisfy the prepetition debt.

As with cross-collateralization provisions, roll-ups are a disfavored financing term. Courts are skeptical of roll-ups because the provision transforms the obligation owed to the lender into an administrative claim. A debtor's plan of reorganization cannot "cram down" a prepetition lender under §1129(b) of the Code if the lender's prepetition claims are elevated to the status of administrative claims. *See* Chapter 20. In utilizing a cram down, the debtor in possession could, under certain circumstances, modify the interest rate, maturity date, or repayment terms of the prepetition claim over the lender's objection. But administrative claims may not be crammed down. These claims must be paid in full in cash on the effective date of a confirmed plan of reorganization, unless otherwise agreed to by the holders of such claims. Ultimately, roll-ups elevate the priority of prepetition claims to administrative priority status, making this debt immune from §1129(b)'s cram-down provisions.

§15.3.4 Protection on Appeal (Mootness Under §364(e))

A party in interest may appeal the court's approval of postpetition credit. If the estate needs the advance urgently, the delay resulting from an appeal could be damaging. Therefore, provided that the court has not stayed action pending appeal, §364(e) allows the parties to proceed with the transaction

---

21. See, e.g., *In re Vanguard Diversified*, 31 B.R. 364 (Bankr. E.D.N.Y. 1983); but see *Shapiro v. Saybrook Mfg. Co. (In re Saybrook Mfg. Co.)*, 963 F.2d 1490, 1494–95 (11th Cir. 1992) (ruling cross-collateralization to be per se impermissible because, although bankruptcy courts do have general equitable powers to adjust claims to avoid unfairness, they cannot authorize the preferential treatment of a claim in contravention of the Code's priority scheme and the fundamental policy of evenhanded treatment of creditors).

immediately after approval, notwithstanding an appeal. As long as the creditor has acted in good faith, the debt and its supporting lien or priority authorized by the court remain valid and enforceable even if the approval is reversed or modified on appeal. This protection is described as mootness and mirrors the relief discussed under section 363(m). *See* §15.2.2. Section 364(e) is designed to incentivize lenders to lend to debtors in possession by offering finality and certainty.

A lender fails to act in good faith if it commits fraud, attempts to take unfair advantage of others, or acts with an improper purpose, but the mere fact that the creditor knows that an appeal is pending does not constitute bad faith. In *In re Foreside Management Co., LLC*, 402 B.R. 446 (B.A.P. 1st Cir. 2009), the court noted that the protection afforded to a good faith lender under §364(e) is broad and substantial, so the appellate court cannot second-guess or modify the bankruptcy court's approval. The sole issues for consideration on appeal are whether the lower court stayed action pending appeal, and if not, whether the lender acted in good faith in extending the credit.

Examples

EXAMPLES

1. Carrion Business, Inc., which operates a chain of three retail stores, has recently filed a voluntary Ch. 11 petition. Are the following proposed transactions within the ordinary course of the debtor's business?
   a. The debtor keeps the stores open and continues selling inventory to customers.
   b. The debtor proposes to conduct a mammoth clearance sale at which it plans to sell all its slow-moving inventory at greatly reduced prices to reduce stock and improve its cash flow.
   c. The debtor proposes to use the cash generated by its sale of inventory to pay salaries, rent for its premises, and other operating expenses.
   d. One of the debtor's three stores has never made a profit. The debtor enters into an agreement with one of its competitors under which it proposes to sell the unprofitable store to the competitor for cash.
   e. The debtor has filed the petition under Ch. 7 rather than Ch. 11. The trustee wishes to keep the stores open for a few months and to continue selling inventory to customers to liquidate the inventory at its retail value.

2. Joyful Trifles, Inc. is a toy manufacturer. Its toys contain electronic components manufactured by Sound Bytes, Inc., a profitable and financially stable company in which Joyful Trifles is the majority shareholder. These shares are Joyful Trifle's most valuable asset. After suffering losses for several years, Joyful Trifles filed a Ch. 11 petition in an attempt to restructure its business. While it was formulating its plan of reorganization, it received an offer for the purchase of its shares in Sound Bytes, Inc.

The prospective buyer has offered a very good price for the shares, provided that the sale can be executed speedily. Joyful Trifles wishes to accept the offer so that it can use the proceeds in the reorganization of its manufacturing business, but some creditors objected upon being notified of the proposed sale. What factors should the court take into account in deciding whether or not to approve the sale?

3. Fiscal Jam Co., Inc. operates a berry farm, makes its produce into jam, and sells the finished product to supermarkets. Fiscal Jam owns its farm, a cannery, and a warehouse building. It does not need the entire warehouse for its own product, and leases a portion of the building to a tenant.

   Fiscal Jam has filed a petition under Ch. 11. At the time of filing the petition, Fiscal Jam's estate included the property listed below. Which of these assets satisfies the definition of cash collateral?

   a. The debtor's inventory of jam, subject to a security interest in favor of a lender.
   b. Proceeds of the sale of jam, received prior to the bankruptcy filing and deposited in a special proceeds account, as required by the security agreement between the debtor and the inventory financer.
   c. Proceeds of the sale of jam, received after the bankruptcy filing and deposited in the special account.
   d. Accounts receivable, representing debts due to the debtor by its customers for jam sold on credit.
   e. Undeposited checks received from customers in payment of jam sold.
   f. Other funds in the general bank account, derived from sources other than sales of inventory and rent. The bank in which this account is maintained had made a loan to the debtor prior to the petition, and the loan remains unpaid.

4. Charlton's Tacos filed a Ch. 11 petition, and is being operated by the debtor in possession. The debtor's restaurant is located on an extremely valuable piece of property. The debtor owns the property, but it is encumbered by three interests: a senior lien securing a $200,000 debt owed to Maize & Blue Bank, a $150,000 junior lien to secure a loan made by a consortium of lenders, and a $100,000 judicial lien for a judgment obtained by Richard Rodriguez, who was injured inside the restaurant last year. Rodriguez's lien attached to the property just three weeks prior to the petition date. The debtor acknowledges that these liens are valid. The agent for the consortium has informed the debtor that the consortium will not consent to the sale, but will not object to the sale motion either. The property is valued at $400,000. Can the debtor sell the property free and clear of these encumbrances?

5. Last year, Receding Airlines, Inc. filed a Ch. 11 petition. Shortly thereafter, one of its secured creditors, Mayday, Mayday & Co., applied for relief from stay on the grounds that its collateral (some equipment owned by the debtor) was not adequately protected. In response to the application, the debtor augmented the collateral by including some additional equipment. The court found that the increase in collateral adequately protected Mayday's interest, and it refused relief from stay. A few months ago, the court approved a loan to the estate from Mortimer Post, Inc. and authorized its payment in priority over all administrative expenses, as provided for in §364(c)(1).

   Receding Airline's attempt at reorganization has failed and the company is in liquidation. It now appears that the additional collateral given to Mayday was not enough to offset depreciation. Although it was fully secured at the time that it applied for relief from stay, its collateral now falls short of its debt by $200,000. The balance due to Mortimer Post on its loan is $2 million.

   After secured claims are paid, the fund remaining in the estate for distribution to all creditors is $1.5 million. How will this fund be distributed?

6. a. State Street Bank made a loan to Winged Helmet, Inc. and received a security interest in all of the company's assets. The following year, the company filed a Ch. 11 petition, citing declining sales. At the time of the filing, the bank was owed $2 million, but the debt was secured by collateral worth only $1 million. Winged Helmet has approached State Street Bank and sought $3 million in postpetition financing, secured by a lien on unencumbered real property worth approximately $5 million. The president of the bank is open to making the loan but is most concerned about the $2 million in prepetition debt that is woefully undersecured. The bank's failure to properly assess the collateral securing that debt makes the bank look bad, and the president does not want to write-down the debt. What do you suggest?
   b. State Street Bank has a change of heart and decides to accept a simplified postpetition financing agreement, offering the debtor $3 million in postpetition financing but demanding a first-priority lien on a manufacturing facility owned by the debtor. The bank views the value of the facility being far more stable than that of the property considered before. The facility has only one encumbrance: a $500,000 lien held by Banner Bank. The debtor files a motion seeking authorization from the court for postpetition financing and authority to prime Banner Bank's lien pursuant to §364(d). The court grants the motion, valuing the facility at $4 million and deeming Banner Bank's interest to be adequately protected due to the significant equity cushion. Banner Bank asks the court to stay the order pending appeal,

but the court refuses. Nevertheless, Banner Bank appeals the order. The bank produces compelling evidence that the bankruptcy court overvalued the facility by $2 million, and Banner Bank's interest is not in fact adequately protected, precluding relief under §364(d). In the interim, State Street Bank allows the debtor to borrow $1 million, and the debtor intends to borrow another $200,000 every month until it has exhausted its $3 million credit facility. Should Banner Bank pursue the appeal or is it a futile effort?

EXPLANATIONS

Explanations

1. a. The continued routine operation of the retail stores is clearly in the ordinary course of its business. Unless the court has ordered otherwise, this activity is authorized by §1108 and encompassed within §363(c)(1). The debtor's ability to conduct its business in the usual way is often central to the Ch. 11 debtor's effort to reorganize and revitalize its business. Therefore, unless there is some good reason to restrict the debtor's normal income-producing endeavors, the debtor should be able to get on with its business without the disruption and inefficiency of notifying interested parties of its routine activities and seeking court approval in the event of objection.

   b. The mammoth clearance sale is not as obviously in the ordinary course of business as the day-to-day dealings with customers. To decide whether this transaction is in the ordinary course of business, the court must consider the reasonable expectations of parties in interest in light of the commercial context in which the debtor operates. If periodic clearance sales are part of the debtor's business practice, and such sales are not inconsistent with expected activity in the debtor's trade, this may qualify as an ordinary-course transaction. In addition, the degree of markdown, the inventory included in the sale, and the period of the sale should not be dramatically different from usual.

   c. The use of proceeds of inventory to pay business expenses qualifies as an ordinary-course transaction provided that the payments are not abnormal or accelerated. See, for example, *In re James A. Phillips, Inc.*, 29 B.R. 391 (S.D.N.Y. 1983). Note, however, that if the inventory was subject to a security interest, the funds generated by the sale of inventory would be cash collateral, and cannot be used even to pay ordinary-course business expenses without notice and a hearing or the consent of the secured party.

   d. The sale of the unprofitable store is not in the ordinary course of business. Although it may be a good idea for the debtor to dispose of the unprofitable store as part of its Ch. 11 reorganization, this must, at a minimum, be done with notice and an opportunity for a hearing under §363(b). Even this procedure may not be appropriate. Unless there is a good reason to authorize the sale under §363 because, for example, the debtor needs to dispose of the store without delay, it is more appropriate for the debtor to provide for the sale in the plan of reorganization so that it is subject to the safeguards of the plan-confirmation process.

e. The operation of the stores by a Ch. 7 trustee does require court approval. Even though the operation of the stores is in the ordinary course of the debtor's business, §363(c)(1) only allows the trustee to conduct the business of the debtor without notice and a hearing if continued operation is authorized in the chapter under which the bankruptcy is filed. In Ch. 7 cases, §721 allows the short-term operation of the business only if the court authorizes it as being in the best interests of the estate and consistent with orderly liquidation. Therefore, in a Ch. 7 case, the trustee may not continue running the stores, even in the ordinary course of business, unless the court has given permission to keep the stores open for a limited period in order to realize the most advantageous price for the inventory.

2. This question is inspired by *In re Lionel Corp.*, 722 F.2d 1063 (2d Cir. 1983). Like Joyful Trifles, Lionel Corp.'s most valuable asset was stock that it owned in a profitable corporation that manufactured electronic components for its toys. In the *Lionel* case, the proposed sale was motivated not by an attractive offer to buy the shares but by pressure exerted by major creditors to sell the shares for the purpose of realizing a substantial cash fund. The proposed sale was objected to by stockholders in the debtor and by the Securities and Exchange Commission (SEC) which is also an interested party in Ch. 11 cases involving public corporations. The court of appeals reversed the bankruptcy court's approval of the sale on the grounds that there was no articulated business justification for selling the shares at this stage instead of dealing with the disposition of the shares in the Ch. 11 plan, subject to the safeguards of the plan-confirmation process.

   The court articulated the factors to be considered in deciding when it is appropriate for a sale of a significant asset to be conducted under §363, rather than in the Ch. 11 plan. The court must be concerned not only with the merits of the transaction (i.e., whether it is advantageous, represents good business judgment, and will further the ends of successful reorganization) but also with its timing: Under all the circumstances of the case, an immediate sale must be based on a reasonable business judgment and must be likely to further the best interests of the estate. Some of the questions to be asked in making this determination are the following: Is the proposed sale on such attractive terms that they are not likely to be repeated if the sale is not executed? Is the asset likely to depreciate or appreciate? Will the management of the asset constitute a drain on the resources of the estate? Is the sale of the asset at this stage consistent with the debtor's plans for rehabilitation? The court concluded that there was no good business reason to sell the shares in the electronics company at that time: They were not depreciating, the price was not adequate, and no emergency required disposition. By contrast, in *Stephens Industries, Inc. v. McClung*, 789 F.2d 386 (6th Cir. 1986), the court did permit the sale under §363 of all the debtor's assets. The debtor was a radio station and one of its principal assets was a Federal Communications Commission (FCC) license. The estate no longer had the capacity to keep its radio station operational and risked revocation of its license for going off the air. The immediate sale was therefore necessary to prevent loss of the license which was the estate's most valuable asset. In effect, the sale amounted to the liquidation of the estate, which is not an appropriate use of §363 except in the most pressing circumstances.

The facts of this question do not suggest a dire emergency like that in *Stephens Industries* but they do suggest some business justification that was absent in *Lionel*—an advantageous price. However, this may not, on its own, be enough to justify an immediate sale in advance of plan confirmation.

3. The classification of the collateral is as follows:
   a. The inventory, although readily disposable property, is not cash collateral. It is neither commercial paper nor a cash equivalent as required by §363(a). Therefore, because the debtor is authorized to continue its business under §1108, sales of inventory in the ordinary course of business may continue without notice and a hearing under §363(c)(1).
   b. The funds in the special bank account are identified as proceeds of inventory. The inventory is subject to a security interest. UCC Article 9, which governs such security interests, automatically extends the interest to identifiable proceeds received by the debtor in exchange for the original collateral. Hence, the funds in the special account are cash collateral under §363(a). They cannot be used by the debtor unless court authority or creditor consent is given under §363(2).
   c. The only difference between these proceeds and those described in question (b) is that these were received after the petition was filed. Postpetition proceeds of estate property are included in the estate. §541(a)(6). In terms of §552(b), they are subject to the security interest because they are proceeds of prepetition collateral under a valid prepetition interest that extends to proceeds under nonbankruptcy law. In defining cash collateral, §363(a) expressly includes postpetition proceeds in which a security interest is recognized by §552(b). Therefore, like the funds deposited in the special account

before commencement of the case, these identifiable cash proceeds of inventory, received after the filing of the petition, are cash collateral.

d. Like the inventory in question (a), these accounts are not commercial paper or cash equivalents. They are simply intangible claims that the debtor has against its customers. They do not fall within the definition of cash collateral. However, the accounts are identifiable proceeds of original collateral in which the security interest continues under §552(b). When the accounts are paid, the payments are likewise identifiable proceeds and will be cash collateral.

e. The checks are negotiable instruments under UCC Article 3, and are cash collateral under §363(a).

f. These funds are not proceeds of original collateral. However, because the debtor is indebted to the bank, and the bank has a right of setoff against the account, the funds are treated as collateral of the bank to the extent of its unpaid claim. (*See*§553, discussed in section 16.2.) A deposit account is included in the definition of cash collateral in §363(a). This question illustrates one of the ways in which an original interest in cash collateral may arise.

4. This question explores §363(f), which allows the debtor in possession to sell estate assets free and clear of any interest if at least one of five conditions is met: 1) applicable nonbankruptcy law permits sale of such property free and clear of such interest; 2) such entity consents; 3) such interest is a lien and the price at which such property is to be sold is greater than the aggregate value of all liens on such property; 4) such interest is in bona fide dispute; or 5) such entity could be compelled, in a legal or equitable proceeding, to accept a money satisfaction of such interest.

   The first interest is the $200,000 lien held by Maize & Blue Bank. The property is valued at $400,000 so the debtor could attempt to rely on §363(f)(3) in selling the property free and clear of this lien. That subsection states that an estate asset can be sold free and clear of an interest if that interest is a lien and the price at which the property is to be sold is greater than the aggregate value of all liens on such property. Unfortunately, aggregate value of the liens on the property is $450,000 so the debtor cannot rely on §363(f)(3). The debtor could attempt to gain the bank's consent to allow the sale to proceed on the condition that its lien would attach to the proceeds of the sale. There is a high likelihood that the bank would accept this proposal.

   The second encumbrance is the $150,000 junior lien held by a consortium of banks. The agent for the consortium has refused to consent to the sale, but has also stated that the consortium will not object to the sale. Section 363(f)(2) provides that an estate asset can be sold free and clear of an interest if the entity that owns that interest consents.

The debtor can probably rely on §363(f)(2) because most courts hold that the consent required by §363(f)(2) can be either explicit—an affirmative statement from an authorized representative of the interest holder consenting to the sale—or implicit—a failure to object to the sale after receipt of proper notice. Assuming the debtor properly serves notice on the consortium and the consortium fails to object to the sale, the debtor can argue that §363(f)(2) allows the debtor to sell the property free and clear of the consortium's lien, which would attach to the proceeds of the sale.

The third encumbrance is best attacked by relying on §363(f)(4), which allows the debtor to sell estate property free and clear of an interest if that interest is in bona fide dispute. It may be difficult for the debtor to attack the substance of the judgment at this stage. It does not appear that the debtor has appealed the judgment, and the debtor cannot use the bankruptcy courts as a forum to relitigate a state court judgment. However, the judicial lien attached to the property just three weeks prior to the petition date. Therefore, the debtor is able to attack the lien as a preference under §547. *See* Chapter 13. The debtor would need to demonstrate that there is an objective basis for a legal dispute as to the lien's validity. If successful, the debtor would be able to sell the property free and clear of this lien. Richard Rodriguez would still hold a tort claim against the bankruptcy estate, but the claim would be a general unsecured claim.

There is one final item to note. If the debtor were to delay the sale of the property and first avoid Richard Rodriguez's claim under §547, the total aggregate value of the liens against the property would be reduced to $350,000. At that point, the property's value would be greater than the aggregate value of all the liens on the property. Consequently, the debtor would be able to sell the property free and clear of both the senior and junior liens by relying on §363(f)(3).

5. If adequate protection is provided, and it later turns out to have been inadequate to protect the interest, the shortfall is given superpriority by §507(b). It takes precedence over all other claims allowable as administrative expenses.

   However, Mortimer Post's claim has also been given a heightened level of priority under §364(c)(1), and this priority is senior to that granted by §507(b). This is apparent from a comparison of the wording of §§507(b) and 364(c)(1). While §507(b) gives Mayday's claim "priority over every other claim allowable under [§507(a)(2)],"§364(c)(1) gives Mortimer Post's claim "priority over any or all administrative expenses of the kind specified in . . . §507(b)." In other words, Mortimer Post's claim is placed above all administrative expenses, including Mayday's superpriority claim. The fund of $1.5 million is less than

Mortimer Post's $2 million claim. As a result, the full fund is paid to Mortimer Post, leaving an unsatisfied balance of $500,000. Mayday receives no payment at all on its deficiency of $200,000, so the backup to its adequate protection failed. In addition, unsecured creditors of the estate, both priority[22] and general, have borne the risk of the debtor's failure, because the payment of the postpetition loan has consumed the entire fund and left nothing for the payment of claims.

6. a. State Street Bank could demand the inclusion of a cross-collateralization or a roll-up provision in its financing agreement. As to the former, the bank could agree to lend the debtor $3 million, but the lien on the real property would secure the $3 million of postpetition lending and the $2 million of prepetition lending. In the alternative, the bank could simply lend the debtor $5 million with the agreement that $2 million of those funds will be used to satisfy the prepetition lending obligation in full. Both provisions elevate the bank's undersecured creditor status, and courts will be reluctant to grant either provision. The debtor in possession will need to demonstrate that 1) the business will not survive without the proposed financing, 2) the estate cannot obtain better financing, 3) State Street Bank will not agree to better terms, and 4) the transaction is in the best interests of the estate and creditors.

   b. Section 364(e) provides that the reversal or modification on appeal of any authorization under §364 to obtain credit or incur debt, or of a grant of priority or lien, does not affect the validity of any debt, priority, or lien if the lender extended credit in good faith. Section 364(e) can be invoked if State Street Bank acted in good faith and the bankruptcy court refused to stay its postpetition financing order. Both criteria appear to be satisfied here. However, the appeal may not be futile. Courts have disagreed on the scope of §364(e)'s protection. Some courts follow the Ninth Circuit's decision in *In re Cooper Commons*, 430 F.3d 1215, 1219 (9th Cir. 2005), where the court held that the subsection "broadly protects any requirement or obligation that was part of a postpetition creditor's agreement to finance." For example, *Boullioun Aircraft Holding Co. v. Smith Mgmt. (In re Western Pac. Airlines, Inc.)*, 181 F.3d 1191, 1195-96 (10th Cir. 1999) expressed the view that §364(e) "prohibits not only outright invalidation of a lien or priority where the challenging party has failed to seek a stay, but also

22. As noted in section 17.3.2, BAPCPA elevated domestic support obligations to first priority over administrative expenses. This has no impact in this case because the debtor is a corporation. However, if the debtor had been an individual who owes domestic support obligations, both superpriority claims would have ranked below those obligations.

modification of the *terms* of a postpetition lender's bargained-for collateral . . . ." (emphasis in original).

But many courts have advocated for a limited scope to the doctrine of equitable mootness. See, e.g., *In re City of Detroit, Michigan*, 838 F.3d 792 (6th Cir. 2016) (acknowledging that recent judicial opinions have advocated for a limited scope to the doctrine of equitable mootness); *In re One2One Commc'ns, LLC*, 805 F.3d 428 (3d. Cir. 2015) (Kraus, concurring). The facts of this problem mirror those found in *Resolution Trust Corp. v. Swedeland Dev. Grp., Inc. (In re Swedeland Dev. Grp., Inc.)*, 16 F.3d 552 (3d Cir. 1994). In that case, the Third Circuit advocated for a limited scope for §364(e) and ruled that the subsection protected a lender as to funds it had already disbursed, but not necessarily as to funds it still held. Consequently, an appellate court could modify terms found in a postpetition financing order as to those undisbursed funds, notwithstanding §364(e).

As to the Example, an appellate court could hear Banner Bank's appeal as to whether the bank's interest was adequately protected. The appellate court would have to review the bankruptcy court's finding of adequate protection under the clearly erroneous standard. Since a finding of adequate protection is a prerequisite to the court authorizing a priming of the bank's interest, the financing order could be modified. The problem states that Banner Bank has compelling evidence that the value of the facility is only $2 million, not $4 million. If true, the appellate court could determine that the bankruptcy court's findings were clearly erroneous. If Banner Bank is not adequately protected, State Bank would not be entitled to a priming lien. A court following the *Swedeland* ruling, would not be able to alter the rights delineated in the financing order as to the $1 million in funds that State Bank has already disbursed to the debtor. Those funds would enjoy all the rights granted by the bankruptcy court, including the priming lien. However, the appellate court could rule that any future funds would not be secured by a priming lien on the manufacturing facility. This is certainly an odd result but would ostensibly honor the bankruptcy court's financing order and the terms agreed to by the debtor and State Street Bank while limiting the damage to Banner Bank for the bankruptcy court's error as to adequate protection.

CHAPTER 16

Executory Contracts and Unexpired Leases

§16.1 OVERVIEW

Section 365 is a vital component of successful restructurings. The section empowers trustees to breach executory contracts and unexpired leases, while paying affected counterparties a fraction of their damage claims. Unadulterated contract rejection is a defining characteristic of the federal reorganization process and is a power virtually unavailable in other contexts.

Section 365 delineates a trustee's duties and powers in dealing with executory contracts and unexpired leases. Unfortunately, the section is long and confusing, full of detail, subtleties, and gaps. It consists of general provisions and subsections that relate to an array of contracts and leases. Nevertheless, section 365's essential goal is to empower the trustee[1] to optimize the rights and assets of the estate while affording some protection to the countervailing interests held by other parties. Many §365 provisions attempt to balance the good of the estate against a third party's right to receive the benefit of its bargain.

Being part of Ch. 3, §365 applies in all forms of bankruptcy, but its operation and importance in each case depends on the nature of the debtor's prepetition affairs and the form of bankruptcy relief sought. Section 365 is particularly significant in Ch. 11 cases, because Ch. 11 debtors often have

1. In a Ch. 11 case, the word "trustee" commonly refers to a debtor in possession. As noted in §1107, the debtor in possession enjoys much of the same rights, powers, and duties as a bankruptcy trustee.

many outstanding contractual relationships and have specifically filed for bankruptcy in order to modify these obligations.

Courts must approve the assumption or rejection of an executory contract. In deciding whether to approve a trustee's request to assume or reject, a court will generally defer to the trustee's business judgment.[2] The estate is obliged to notify the other contracting party of its election, and the other party has the opportunity to object to the proposed action.

Section 365(a) delineates the trustees' assumption and rejection powers. Section 365(b) provides that in cases where the debtor has already defaulted under an executory contract or unexpired lease, the trustee cannot assume the contract or lease unless she can 1) cure all defaults — or provide adequate assurance that the trustee will promptly cure such defaults — other than certain enumerated types of defaults for which cure is not required, 2) compensate — or provide adequate assurance that the trustee will promptly compensate — the injured party for any pecuniary loss resulting from the default, and 3) provide adequate assurance of future performance.

Pursuant to section 365(f) but subject to section 365(c), the trustee may assign an executory contract or unexpired lease that has been assumed, notwithstanding most contractual limitations on assignment. Upon assignment, neither the debtor nor the estate is liable on the contract. The counterparty may look only to the assignee for future performance. Section 365(f) requires that 1) the trustee assume the contract or lease at issue, and 2) the assignee provide adequate assurance of future performance.

Section 365(h) offers unique rights to tenants whose landlord files for bankruptcy and seeks to reject the unexpired lease of real property. Section 365(n) offers similar rights to licensees under an intellectual property contract whose licensor files for bankruptcy and seeks to reject the contract.

Section 365's scope is broad and captures a diverse set of contracts and leases. This chapter focuses on the section's overarching principles and key facets but does not attempt to explore the entire labyrinth of §365's subsections.

§16.2 THE MEANING OF "EXECUTORY CONTRACT" AND "UNEXPIRED LEASE"

The Code does not define "executory contract" or "unexpired lease." The standard definition of executory contract, known as the "Countryman

2. See *In re Sabine Oil & Gas Corp.*, 547 B.R. 66 (Bankr. S.D.N.Y.2016) (explaining that bankruptcy courts generally defer to the debtor's determination of whether rejection of an executory contract is advantageous, unless the decision to reject is the product of bad faith, whim, or caprice).

definition," derives from a test expounded by Professor Countryman in a 1973 law review article: A contract is executory if the obligations of both parties are so far unperformed that the failure of either to perform would be a material breach. In other words, a contract only qualifies as executory for bankruptcy purposes if, at the time of bankruptcy, both parties had material obligations outstanding. If either had fully or substantially performed, the contract is no longer executory and should not be dealt with under §365. Similarly, if the contract had terminated prior to bankruptcy, either because its term had ended or because one of the parties rightfully canceled it, it is not executory. The Countryman definition can be difficult to apply and its results can be unpredictable where the materiality of the outstanding obligations is unclear. A contract is less likely to be treated as executory where one of the parties has paid its monetary obligations in full, but this is not dispositive. As the court pointed out in *In re Aerobox Composite Structures, LLC*, 373 B.R. 135 (Bankr. D.N.M. 2007), that party may still have significant nonmonetary obligations outstanding.

The Countryman definition is approved in §365's legislative history and is the standard test for executory contracts in the majority of circuits.[3] However, some courts have moved away from the test in favor of a more functional approach that looks not only at the materiality of the unperformed portion of the contract, but also takes into account the impact on the estate of allowing the trustee to assume or reject.[4] This approach is premised on the concern that a rigid test of materiality — one that examines only the contractual significance of outstanding mutual performances — may make some contracts unassumable because one side has substantially performed. As the principal goal of assumption or rejection of an executory contract is to benefit the estate, a court should consider not merely if there has been substantial performance, but also what effect the determination of executoriness will have on the estate, the interests of creditors, and the debtor's prospect of rehabilitation. This thinking is expressed, for example, in *In re Riodizio, Inc.*, 204 B.R. 417 (Bankr. S.D.N.Y. 1997). (*See* Example 4.)

---

3. See *Olah v. Baird (In re Baird)*, 567 F.3d 1207, 1211 (10th Cir. 2009); *Lifemark Hosps., Inc. v. Liljeberg Enters (In re Liljeberg Enters.)*, 304 F.3d 410, 436 (5th Cir. 2002); *Enterprise Energy Corp. v. U.S. (In re Columbia Gas Sys. Inc.)*, 50 F.3d 233, 239 (3d Cir. 1995); *Cameron v. Pfaff Plumbing & Heating, Inc.*, 966 F.2d 414, 416 (8th Cir. 1992); *Mitchell v. Streets (In re Streets & Beard Farm P'ship)*, 882 F.2d 233, 235 (7th Cir. 1989); *Pacific Express, Inc. v. Teknekron Infoswitch Corp. (In re Pacific Express, Inc.)*, 780 F.2d 1482, 1487 (9th Cir. 1986); and *Gloria Mfg. Corp v. International Ladies' Garment Workers' Union*, 734 F.2d 1020, 1021–22 (4th Cir. 1984).

4. See *Sipes v. Atlantic Gulf Cmtys. Corp. (In re General Dev. Corp.)*, 84 F.3d 1364, 1375 (11th Cir. 1996) (affirming bankruptcy court decision applying functional approach in determining that real estate purchase agreement was executory); *La Electronica, Inc. v. Capo-Roman (In re La Electronica, Inc.)*, 995 F.2d 320, 322 n.3 (1st Cir. 1993); *Chattanooga Mem'l Park v. Still (In re Jolly)*, 574 F.2d 349, 351 (6th Cir.), *cert. denied*, 439 U.S. 929 (1978).

§16.3 THE ESTATE'S RIGHT TO ASSUME OR REJECT EXECUTORY CONTRACTS[5]

In making provision for executory contracts, the Code distinguishes bilateral contractual relationships from unilateral contract rights. If one party to a contract has fully or substantially performed, all that remains is the other party's claim for counterperformance. Therefore, if the debtor had fully performed its contractual obligations by the time of bankruptcy, the outstanding performance due by the other party is simply a right of the debtor's which becomes property of the estate under §541. Conversely, if the other party has fully performed, the debtor's remaining obligation gives rise to a prepetition claim, to be proved in the estate and paid at whatever rate of distribution is due to claims of that class.

However, when material performance is due on both sides at the time of the petition — so that the contract qualifies as executory under the Countryman definition — the Code recognizes this as a live relationship between the debtor and the other party, not simply as a set of claims by and against the estate. Section 365 gives the trustee the option of honoring this relationship or repudiating it. If the trustee elects to keep the relationship in existence, the estate assumes the contract, thereby adopting it so that it becomes the estate's contract. The estate is entitled to receive the other party's performance and is liable for the obligations undertaken by the debtor. The performance due by the estate qualifies as an administrative expense and is thus entitled to priority under §507(a)(2). *See* section 17.5.4.

An executory contract or unexpired lease must be assumed or rejected in its entirety.[6] Subject to certain exceptions outlined in §365, the trustee cannot receive the benefits of the contract but reject the burdens. The trustee's election to reject a contract constitutes a breach that is treated by §365(g)(1) as a prepetition breach by the debtor. Upon rejection, the other party to the contract becomes a creditor (it is specifically included in the definition of "creditor" in §101(10)(B)), and its claim for damages for breach of contract is classed by §502(g) as a general unsecured prepetition claim. It is paid in the bankruptcy distribution at whatever fractional rate is due to such claims. Some claimants receive less: §502(b)(6) and (7) limit damage claims for the unexpired period of real property leases and

5. Section 365 refers to both executory contracts and unexpired leases, which is redundant because an unexpired lease is a form of executory contract. Some specific types of leases are given special treatment, as mentioned in section 16.9, but aside from that, the same general principles apply whether the executory contract is a lease or some other kind of agreement. To avoid constant repetition of the phrase "executory contracts and unexpired leases," this chapter will occasionally use the term "executory contracts" to include both leases and contracts.

6. *In re Fleming Cos.*, 499 F.3d 300, 308 (3d Cir. 2007).

employment contracts so that the rejection of these long-term contracts does not result in excessive claims against the general fund of the estate. Because the estate pays damages at the reduced rate payable to unsecured claims, the estate is able to commit a more profitable breach than the debtor would have been able to do outside of bankruptcy.

If the estate first assumes a contract and later rejects it, the rejection is the estate's breach and the other party's damages are treated as an administrative expense under §365(g)(2). These damages are measured at the time of rejection or, if a rehabilitation case was converted to Ch. 7 between assumption and rejection, at the time of conversion.

In deciding whether to assume or reject the contract, the trustee tries to serve the best interests of the estate. The trustee will invariably assume a contract if the contract is 1) advantageous and profitable or 2) advances the debtor's plans for economic recovery. Conversely, the trustee will invariably reject a contract if the 1) terms are not favorable, 2) the estate could do better by using its resources elsewhere, or 3) the contract imposes an unacceptable burden or risk on the estate. It should be noted, however, that the trustee does not have absolute discretion to adopt an opportunistic approach to the contract. As indicated below, courts sometimes refuse to approve a rejection unless it is clear that performance would place an undue burden on the estate.

§16.4 THE PROCEDURE AND STANDARDS FOR ASSUMPTION OR REJECTION

Section 365(d)(1) requires the Ch. 7 trustee to assume or reject a contract within 60 days of the order for relief or in such extended period as the court may for cause allow. If the trustee does not act by the end of that period, the Code deems the contract to be rejected. In cases under Chs. 11 and 13, the trustee may make the decision to assume or reject at any time up to confirmation of the plan, unless the contract is a lease of nonresidential real estate. Nonresidential real estate leases are deemed rejected unless the trustee acts by the earlier of 1) 120 days after the order for relief is entered and 2) the date the order confirming a plan of reorganization is entered. Upon application, the court extend these deadlines or order the trustee to make an earlier decision.

An affirmative decision to assume or reject must be approved by the court following a motion by the trustee on notice. However, if the contract is deemed rejected because of the trustee's failure to act within the prescribed period, the rejection is automatic and does not require court approval.

The business judgment rule is the most widely accepted standard for the court's approval of the trustee's decision to assume or reject. The court will not interfere with the trustee's decision if it was based on a good faith, reasonable business judgment that appears beneficial to the estate.[7] *See* Example 5. In *In re Pomona Valley Medical Group, Inc.*, 476 F.3d 665 (9th Cir. 2007), the court said that the bankruptcy court's review of the trustee's rejection of the contract under the business judgment standard should be cursory, and focused merely on ensuring that the decision benefited the estate, and was not capricious or in bad faith. A more exacting review would put the court in the position of having to second-guess the trustee's judgment, which it is not equipped to do. Other courts have engaged in a more stringent review, particularly where the trustee seeks to reject a contract. They have refused to approve rejection unless assumption of the contract would be unduly burdensome to the estate. Where the bankruptcy filing was motivated primarily by the desire to use the rejection power to escape an unwanted contract, rejection may well not satisfy the good faith test. *See* Example 6.

§16.5 THE ASSUMPTION OF CONTRACTS IN DEFAULT (§365(b))

§16.5.1 General Overview of §§365(b)(1) and (2)[8]

To assume a contract that is in default, the trustee must comply with §365(b)(1) by 1) curing all defaults—or providing adequate assurance that the trustee will promptly cure such defaults—other than certain enumerated types of defaults for which cure is not required, 2) compensating—or providing adequate assurance that the trustee will promptly compensate—the injured party for any pecuniary loss resulting from the default, and 3) giving the party adequate assurance of future performance under the contract. The question of whether there has been a default is determined with reference to the contract terms and nonbankruptcy law. Section 365(b) applies regardless of whether the default occurred before or after the petition date.

7. Section 1113 provides special rules for the rejection of collective bargaining agreements in a Ch. 11 case.

8. Section 365(b)(3) goes to some length in expressing what is required for adequate assurance of performance in connection with leases of premises in shopping centers. This subsection addresses a niche issue and is not explored further.

Under §365(b)(2) two types of default need not be cured:

1. If the default is simply the violation of an ipso facto clause (explained in section 16.7), the default really cannot be cured without the debtor dismissing the bankruptcy case and becoming solvent. It would, therefore, be an absurdity to demand such cure, and §365(b)(2) does not require it.
2. If the default consists of the failure to pay a penalty rate relating to some nonmonetary default (for example, the debtor's failure to maintain insurance coverage specified in the contract), cure of that default is not needed for assumption.

§16.5.2 The Requirements for Assumption Under §365(b)(1)

Section 365(b)(1) delineates the three requirements for assumption of a contract or lease where there has been either a prepetition or postpetition default by the debtor.

a. §365(b)(1)(A): The Cure Requirement

Section 365(b)(1)(A) captures the first requirement but contains language that is terribly confusing. As originally enacted, the subsection presented a simple cure requirement that required the debtor to cure all defaults under the contract or provide adequate assurance[9] of a prompt cure. But the section was modified by the Bankruptcy Abuse Prevention and Consumer Protection Act of 2005 (BAPCPA) amendments in 2005 and an extremely long and convoluted exception to section 365(b)(1)(A)'s cure requirement was enacted. The new language excepts from the cure requirement certain non-monetary obligations under an unexpired lease of real property that are virtually impossible to cure. Indeed, with respect to any breach related to the failure to operate in accordance with a nonresidential real property lease, section 365(b)(1)(A) provides that "such default shall be cured by performance at and after the time of assumption in accordance with such lease, and pecuniary losses resulting from such default shall be compensated. . . ." However, the exception to the cure requirement only applies to leases of real property. Other types of leases — including those involving personal property — are still subject to the cure requirements even if the default at issue is impossible to cure.

9. Section 16.5.2(c), *infra*, provides additional insight into the phrase "adequate assurance."

For example, imagine that Bo owns Big House Apparel, which sells college football apparel and memorabilia. The store is located in a home that has been converted into commercial space. The store rents the space and also leases a t-shirt stamping machine. The store lease requires that Big House Apparel must close by no later than 6:00 p.m. every night. In addition, the equipment lease requires that the machine can only be operated by someone who is certified by the manufacturer. The store is struggling. To increase sales the store begins staying open until 8:00 p.m. on most nights. Further, Bo fires an employee and replaces her with his son, Jack. On some nights, Bo asks Jack to run the t-shirt stamping machine even though Jack hasn't been certified by the manufacturer. Despite these efforts, Big House Apparel is forced to file for bankruptcy. Will the store be able to assume the store lease or the equipment lease?

The store has committed a default under the store lease. Section 365(b)(1)(A) requires the store to cure the default or provide adequate assurance that it will promptly cure. But Bo cannot go back in time and make sure that the store closes at 6:00 p.m. However, because the store has committed a nonmonetary default under an unexpired lease of real property that is impossible to cure, it can rely on the exception to §365(b)(1)(A)'s cure requirement and assume the lease by providing the landlord adequate assurance that the store will no longer stay open past 6:00 p.m.

Unfortunately for the store, the equipment lease is a lease of personal property and is excluded from the exception to the cure requirement. An incurable nonmonetary default can prevent assumption in this context. To ameliorate this potentially harsh result, courts have held that a nonmonetary default in this context must only be cured if it is material and economically substantial.[10] In evaluating this requirement, courts focus on the default term at issue and the "importance of the term within the overall bargained-for exchange; that is, whether the term is integral to the bargain struck between the parties (its materiality) and whether performance of that term gives a party the full benefit of his bargain (its economic significance)."[11] Going back to our example, Big House Apparel may be able to argue that the requirement that the machine be only operated by someone who has been certified by the manufacturer is neither a material nor economically substantial part of the lease. It does not appear that Jack's operation of the machine caused any damage. Consequently, the store will most likely be allowed to assume the equipment lease.

---

10. See, e.g., *In re New Breed Realty Enters., Inc.*, 278 B.R. 314, 321 (Bankr. E.D.N.Y. 2002) ("Where the default is non-monetary and is not curable, the debtor is precluded from assuming an executory contract only if the default was material or if the default caused 'substantial economic detriment.'").

11. *In re Fleming Cos.*, 499 F.3d 300, 306 (3d Cir. 2007).

b. §365(b)(1)(B): Compensation of Actual Pecuniary Loss

Section 365(b)(1)(B) requires the trustee to provide compensation—or adequate assurance[12] of prompt compensation—for the counterparty's pecuniary losses. Section 365(b)(1)(A) requires the trustee to cure all defaults under the contract or lease. Subsection (b)(1)(B) requires the trustee to compensate the counterparty for pecuniary losses arising from such default.

Section 365(b)(1)(B) does not create an independent basis for quantifying pecuniary losses. Courts rely on terms of the contract or lease and applicable state law in determining the appropriate amount of compensation.

c. §365(b)(1)(C): Adequate Assurance of Future Performance

Section 365(b)(1)(C) requires the trustee to provide adequate assurance of future performance. But the Code does not define "adequate assurance." Instead, courts employ a factual analysis and evaluate the phrase on a case-by-case basis.

The concept of adequate assurance is taken from UCC §2-609, which entitles a party to a sales agreement to demand such assurances when there are grounds for insecurity about the other party's ability to perform. Both under the UCC and in §365(b)(1)(C), assurance is provided by showing that resources are likely to be available for the discharge of the contractual obligations and performance appears to be commercially feasible. Factors that affect a court's adequate assurance assessment include 1) the debtor's history of performance;[13] 2) available cash on hand;[14] 3) data showing that the debtor could generate sufficient revenues in the future;[15] and 4) provision of a security deposit.[16]

---

12. Section 16.5.2(c) explains the phrase "adequate assurance."

13. *Texas Health Enters., Inc. v. Lythe Nursing Home (In re Texas Health Enters. Inc.)*, 72 F. App'x 122, 127 (5th Cir. 2003) (explaining that the debtor's history of defaults and poor performance led to conclusion that it could not provide adequate assurance).

14. *In re 2300 Xtra Wholesalers, Inc.*, 445 B.R. 113, 123–24 (S.D.N.Y. 2011) (noting that the court's finding of adequate assurance was influenced by the fact that the debtor had $3 million in available cash on hand).

15. *Richmond Leasing Co. v. Capital Bank, N.A.*, 762 F.2d 1303, 1309 (5th Cir. 1985) (ruling that showing that debtor could generate sufficient revenues in the future was sufficient adequate assurance).

16. *Park Ave. Assocs., L.L.C. v. Park Ave. Garage, L.L.C. (In re Park Ave. Garage, L.L.C.)*, 403 F. App'x 555, 557 (2d Cir. 2010) (ruling that the debtor's resources and financial wherewithal, as well as a security deposit and certain conditions placed on the lease, provided adequate assurance).

§16.5.3 Ipso Facto Clauses and Penalty Provisions Under §365(b)(2)

a. Ipso Facto Clauses

Section 365(b)(2) states that §365(b)(1)'s cure requirements do not apply to defaults relating to the 1) debtor's insolvency or financial condition, 2) commencement of the bankruptcy case, or 3) appointment of a bankruptcy trustee or a prepetition custodian. Collectively, these types of provision are designed to penalize the debtor for exercising the right to file for federal bankruptcy and are commonly referred to as "ipso facto" or "bankruptcy" clauses. Section 365(e) renders these types of provisions unenforceable in bankruptcy. Section 365(b)(2) reinforces this prohibition by stating that the debtor does not have to cure any defaults premised on ipso facto clauses. A customary ipso facto contractual provision provides that the debtor commits a default under the contract by filing a bankruptcy petition and entitles the counterparty to terminate the contract in its entirety without penalty. This provision is unenforceable in bankruptcy, and §365(b)(2) absolves the trustee of any obligation to cure this type of default.

b. Penalty Rate or Provision

Section 365(b)(2)(D) provides that §365(b)(1)'s cure requirements do not require the debtor to satisfy "any penalty rate or penalty provision relating to a default arising from any failure by the debtor to perform nonmonetary obligations. . . ."[17] It is important to note that the subsection does not excuse the debtor from having to cure a *default* related to a nonmonetary obligation. Rather, the subsection merely excuses the debtor from having to cure a *penalty rate or penalty provision* related to such a default.

---

§16.6 NONASSUMABLE CONTRACTS (§365(c))

Section 365(c) denotes three types of executory contracts that may not be assumed. The bar on assumption arises as a matter of law and does not depend on the existence of a clause in the contract forbidding or restricting assignment.

---

17. 11 U.S.C. §365(b)(2)(D).

§16.6.1 §365(c)(1), the Hypothetical Test, and Contracts That Are Unassignable under Nonbankruptcy Law

In the absence of consent by the other party, §365(c)(1) prevents the assumption of a contract if applicable nonbankruptcy law—including federal and state law—excuses the other party from accepting performance from or rendering performance to someone other than the debtor or the debtor in possession.[18] Section 365(c)(1) therefore is intended to respect rights of nontransferability under nonbankruptcy law and to enable the other party to resist assumption by the estate if transfer of the contract could have been prevented outside of bankruptcy.

It is a general rule of contract law that contractual rights and duties can be transferred. The transfer of rights is called "assignment," and the transfer of duties, "delegation." However, federal and state laws recognize exceptions to this rule. For example:

- Licenses. Under certain applicable federal and state intellectual property laws, agreements to license trademarks, copyrighted material, and other intellectual property may not be assigned absent the non-assignor-counterparty's consent.
- Personal service contracts. Under most state laws, a contract that contemplates personal performance by a party cannot be delegated. Similarly, rights to performance cannot be assigned if this would reduce the other party's expectation of proper counter-performance.
- Contracts with the U.S. Government. The Federal Anti-Assignment Act renders contracts with the government unassignable.[19]
- Franchise agreements. Most states have laws that permit a franchisor to prohibit assignment of a franchise agreement.[20]

Unfortunately, §365(c) has a material textual error that alters Congress's original design. The section's initial phrase reads, "The trustee may not assume **or** assign any executory contract or unexpired lease. . . ." But the phrase should read, "The trustee may not assume **and** assign any executory contract or unexpired lease. . . ." The inclusion of the word "or" distorts §365(c). Indeed, imagine that George Pitt is a famous actor, who recently

---

18. Note that this section does not conflict with section 365(f)(1), explored in section 16.8. Section 365(f)(1) renders unenforceable any provision in *a contract or lease* that attempts to prohibit assignment. Section 365(c)(1) enforces restrictions on assignment that appear in *applicable nonbankruptcy law*, including other federal statutes and state law.

19. See *In re West Electronics, Inc.*, 852 F.2d 79, 83 (3d Cir. 1988).

20. See *In re Pioneer Ford Sales, Inc.*, 729 F.3d 27, 28 (1st Cir. 1984) (ruling that §365(c) prohibited the debtor from assigning its Ford dealership).

signed a contract with Gigantic Studios to play the role of Batman in an upcoming movie. Unfortunately, George is in some financial distress and has to file for bankruptcy in order to prevent foreclosure of his ranch in Colorado. After filing, George is approached by Marc Ruckerberg, a 30-year old technology entrepreneur. Marc has always dreamed of playing Batman on the big screen and is undaunted by the fact that he is only 5 feet 6 inches tall and has no acting experience. Marc is willing to pay George $20 million to assign the contract. Section 365(c)(1) would prevent George from assigning the contract to Marc without Gigantic Studios' consent if applicable state law prevented the assignment of a personal service contract.

However, what if George merely wanted to assume the contract and fulfill his contractual obligations? Could George assume the contract in bankruptcy and perform? Surprisingly, the answer is "no" in the majority of jurisdictions. Despite §365(c)(1)'s obvious drafting error, most courts have relied on a strict reading of the statute and ruled that assumption of an executory contract can be prohibited if the debtor wants to assume **or** assign the contract.[21] George would not be allowed to assume the contract without Gigantic Studios' consent even if he had no intention of assigning the contract and merely wanted to perform under the contract as all parties had intended. This approach is referred to as the "hypothetical test" because it prohibits debtors from assuming a contract if applicable nonbankruptcy law would prevent a hypothetical assignment of the agreement to a third party.

§16.6.2 Loan and Financing Transactions

Section 365(c)(2) forbids the trustee from assuming a contract to make a loan, to extend other debt financing or financial accommodations to the debtor, or to issue a security of the debtor. Limited in its scope, it does not cover all credit transactions but is confined to loan and financing contracts. For example, the subsection does not include many types of transactions in which the debtor is given credit, such as leases or credit sales of goods or services. Courts construe §365(c)(2) strictly and refuse to extend it to contracts whose primary purpose is not the provision of a loan or financing. For example, in *In re UAL*, 368 F.3d 720 (7th Cir. 2004), the court held that a credit card processing agreement between the debtor (United Airlines) and

21. See, e.g., *EBC I, Inc. v. America Online, Inc. (In re EBC I, Inc.)*, 382 F. App'x 135, 136 (3d Cir. 2010); *RCI Tech. Corp. v. Sunterra Corp. (In re Sunterra Corp.)*, 361 F.3d 257, 267 (4th Cir. 2004); *Perlman v. Catapult Entm't, Inc. (In re Catapult Entm't, Inc.)*, 165 F.3d 747, 752 (9th Cir. 1999); but see *Bonneville Power Admin. v. Mirant Corp. (In re Mirant Corp.)*, 440 F.3d 238, 248-49 (5th Cir. 2006) (rejecting the hypothetical test and employing the "actual test," which sought to determine whether the debtor actually intended to assign the contract at issue); *Summit Investment & Development Corp. v. Leroux*, 69 F.3d 608, 609 (1st Cir. 1995) (adopting the "actual test" of assignment).

a bank was not a contract that extended financial accommodations to the debtor and therefore was assumable. Although some extension of credit was involved, it was incidental to the contract's primary purpose of enabling the debtor to make credit card sales of tickets to its customers.

You may wonder why §365(c)(2) is necessary, because most financing contracts would probably be nonassumable under §365(c)(1); the identity of the debtor is material, and a lender would be excused from accepting transfer of the contract. However, the rule against assumption in §365(c)(2) is stricter than that in §362(c)(1) because it does not even allow assumption with the consent of the other party. The reason for this is that the assumption of a financing contract is tantamount to postpetition credit, and assumption under §365 cannot be allowed to circumvent the creditor protections in §364.[22]

§16.7 BANKRUPTCY TERMINATION OR IPSO FACTO CLAUSES

As discussed in section 16.5.3, a provision in a contract that allows the nondebtor to declare default or to terminate the contract on the grounds of the insolvency, financial condition, or bankruptcy of the debtor (a bankruptcy termination or ipso facto clause) is ineffective in bankruptcy. The disregard of such clauses and provisions of nonbankruptcy law has already been discussed in connection with property of the estate (section 9.3.2), the avoidance of statutory liens (section 12.3), and the trustee's power to deal with estate property (section 15.2.6). These provisions reflect the general policy of preventing states or private parties from undermining the bankruptcy process through laws or contractual terms that are designed to take effect on bankruptcy.

Section 365 refers to ipso facto provisions four times: §365(b)(2) does not require cure of a breach of an ipso facto clause in a contract: §365(c)(1) makes such contract terms ineffective in deciding whether contract rights are transferable under nonbankruptcy law; §365(e)(1) prevents termination or modification of an executory contract after the petition on grounds of an ipso facto clause in the contract or in nonbankruptcy law; §365(f)(3) prevents termination or modification under such a clause or provision of nonbankruptcy law when the trustee assigns an executory contract after assuming it. Note that §§365(b)(2) and 365(c)(1) apply only to contractual clauses, while §§365(e)(1) and 365(f)(3) cover provisions of nonbankruptcy law as well. The bar on enforcing ipso facto termination rights

22. See *In re Sun Runner Marine, Inc.*, 945 F.2d 1089 (9th Cir. 1991).

comes into effect once the petition has been filed. If the ipso facto clause covered the debtor's insolvency or other adverse financial circumstances, and the other party validly exercised the termination right on those grounds prior to bankruptcy, the termination is effective to end the contract so that it is no longer executory when the bankruptcy case is commenced.

§16.8 ASSIGNMENT OF A CONTRACT OR LEASE (§365(f))

In some cases, the optimal way for the estate to realize the value of a contract is to sell it. Contract rights are property, and as a general rule, the debtor would have had the right to transfer property of this kind under nonbankruptcy law. This transfer is referred to as an "assignment."[23] Section 365(f)(1) allows for an assignment notwithstanding any contractual or statutory restrictions on assignment. Upon assignment of the contract, the purchaser of the contract (the assignee) acquires all the estate's rights under the contract, and assumes all its duties of future performance. Section 365(f)(2) allows for assignment if the trustee 1) has properly assumed the contract or lease at issue; and 2) provides adequate assurance of future performance by the assignee of the contract or lease. Section 365(f)(3) invalidates ipso facto provisions that may restrict assignment or otherwise prevent the estate from realizing the full value of the assignment.

§16.8.1 The Assignment Power (§365(f)(1))

Section 365(f)(1) invalidates contractual and statutory antiassignment provisions. However, creditors are well aware of this restriction and have modified contracts and leases so that assignment is allowed but the economic benefit of the assignment has been diminished. Courts have invalidated these de facto antiassignment provisions. Sharing clauses are a good example of these types of provisions. Sharing clauses require that—as a prerequisite to assignment—the debtor remit to the landlord a significant portion of the value received from the assignment or the increased value of the lease at the time of assignment.[24] In determining if such a provision is unenforceable pursuant to §365(f)(1), courts consider: 1) the extent to

23. The word "assignment" is used to describe the transfer of a contract in its entirety. The assignment of a contract includes both the assignment of rights due under the contract and the delegation of duties owed under the contract.

24. See, e.g., *South Coast Plaza v. Standor Jewelers W., Inc. (In re Standor Jewelers W., Inc.)*, 129 B.R. 200, 202 (B.A.P. 9th Cir. 1991) (invalidating a sharing clause that required the assignee to remit

which the provision hampers a debtor's ability to assign the contract or lease; 2) if the provision prevents the estate from realizing the full economic value of the assignment; and 3) the economic detriment to the nondebtor party.

As stated in section 16.6, §365(c)(1) prohibits assumption (and consequent assignment) of a contract by the trustee if applicable nonbankruptcy law excuses the nondebtor party from accepting performance from or rendering it to a person other than the debtor. Section 365(f)(1) is expressly made subject to §365(c), yet it appears to contradict §365(c) by making a contract assignable notwithstanding a provision in the contract or in applicable nonbankruptcy law that prohibits assignment. Courts have been able to craft a fragile reconciliation of these two sections. In broad terms, the difference between the sections lies in the distinction between the general and the specific. Section 365(f) invalidates contractual antiassignment clauses, and also overrides nonbankruptcy laws that generally uphold antiassignment clauses in contracts. By contrast, section 365(c) gives effect to nonbankruptcy laws that makes certain specific types of contracts unassignable, whether or not the contract contains an antiassignment clause. Although §365(f) protects the estate by rendering ineffective antiassignment clauses and nonbankruptcy laws that preclude assignment, this disregard of nonbankruptcy law is not absolute. The protection is qualified by §365(c), which respects the antiassignment provisions that appear in nonbankruptcy law under certain circumstances. In other words, §365(f)(1) lays out a broad rule regarding antiassignment provisions while §365(c)(1) embraces legal justifications for a counterparty refusing to render or accept performance, irrespective of assignability.[25]

§16.8.2 The Prerequisites to Assignment (§365(f)(2))

To assign a contract or lease, the estate must 1) assume the contract or lease in compliance with §365's requirements (§365(f)(2)(A)); and 2) provide adequate assurance of future performance by the assignee, regardless of whether there has been a default under the contract or lease (§365(f)(2)(B)).

The second requirement is necessary because §365(k) relieves the estate of all liability for postassignment breaches.[26] As noted above, the Code does not define "adequate assurance." Courts evaluate this phrase on

---

75 percent of the appreciation in value of the lease to the landlord as a prerequisite to gaining the landlord's consent to the assignment).

25. See *Reiser v. Dayton Country Club Co. (In re Magness)*, 972 F.2d 689, 695 (6th Cir. 1992); see also *In re CFLC, Inc.*, 89 F.3d 673 (9th Cir. 1996); *In re Claremont Acquisition Corp.*, 186 B.R. 977 (C.D. Cal. 1995); *In re Pioneer Ford Sales, Inc.*, 729 F.2d 27 (1st Cir. 1984).

26. The estate is therefore in a better position than a delegating party would be under nonbankruptcy law. Outside of bankruptcy, delegation does not usually release the delegator

a case-by-case basis. Consequently, the assignee will have to demonstrate that it has the wherewithal to fulfill its contractual obligations. More specifically, courts have required a showing by the assignee that it will be able to satisfy all material and economically significant terms in the contract or lease. This requirement protects the other party from being forced into a contractual relationship with an assignee who is financially unstable or otherwise unlikely to provide a performance that conforms to the contract. This is important because, as noted above (unlike the general rule in nonbankruptcy law), the other party to the contract has no recourse against the estate if the assignee breaches.

Adequate assurance of performance covers the monetary provisions of the contract and all of the debtor's material future obligations under the contract. This is necessary in order to assure the counterparty that it will receive the full benefit of the bargain.[27] The assurance does not have to be an absolute guarantee of performance but is merely a showing, on the preponderance of the evidence, that the assignee is likely to perform.[28]

Once the assignment of an executory contract or unexpired lease is approved by a bankruptcy court, an assignee is bound by all contractual provisions contained in the agreement, including any antiassignment clauses that were previously invalidated by a bankruptcy court. Ultimately "[a]n assignment is intended to change only who performs an obligation, not the obligation to be performed."[29]

§16.9 DEBTOR-LESSOR'S REJECTION OF REAL PROPERTY LEASE AND LESSEE RIGHTS (§365(h))

In instances where the trustee rejects an unexpired lease of real property under which the debtor is the lessor, §365(h) provides the lessee two options. Primarily, the lessee may accept the rejection, deem the lease terminated, and file a claim with the bankruptcy estate for damages.

The lessee's second option is to disregard the rejection and retain its rights under the lease. If the lessee chooses to continue in occupation, §365(h)(1)(A)(ii) preserves key terms under the lease, including 1) rental payments and the due dates for such payments; 2) the right to occupy and

---

from its responsibility under the contract, and it could be liable for damages if the delegate fails to perform properly.

27. See *In re Fleming Companies, Inc.*, 499 F.3d 300 (3d Cir. 2007).

28. See *In re Resource Technology Corp.*, 624 F.3d 376 (7th Cir. 2010) (finding that there was no adequate assurance of performance where the assignee would have to secure substantial funds to perform the contract, and it could not be shown that the assignee would be able to secure such funds).

29. *Medtronic Ave., Inc. v. Advanced Cardiovascular Sys., Inc.*, 247 F.3d 44, 60 (3d Cir. 2001).

use the premises, 3) the right to sublet the premises; and 4), the lessee's ability to exercise any unilateral rights to extend the term of the rental. However, even though all the lessee's rights remain intact, the debtor-lessor is relieved from performing any of its future obligations such as the provision of services and the maintenance of the premises. Further, a lessee that invokes §365(h)(1)(A)(ii) loses the right to file a claim in the debtor-lessor's bankruptcy case. The lessee must still pay rent, but rental amounts can be offset against any damages suffered as a result of the debtor-lessor's nonperformance of contractual duties. Similar protection is made available by §365(i) to a possessory vendee who purchased real property from the debtor under an installment sale.[30] (*See* Example 14.)

§16.10 DEBTOR-LESSOR'S REJECTION OF INTELLECTUAL PROPERTY CONTRACT AND LICENSEE RIGHTS (§365(n))

Section 365(n) addresses a situation quite similar to §365(h). Indeed, in instances where the trustee rejects an unexpired lease under which the debtor is the licensor of a right to intellectual property,[31] §365(n) provides the licensee two options. Primarily, the licensee may accept the rejection, deem the license terminated, and file a claim with the bankruptcy estate for damages.

The licensee's second option is to disregard the rejection and retain its rights under the license. The licensee is entitled to retain the rights included in the license and any supplement to the license, including 1) the continued use of the license; 2) the enjoyment of exclusive use of the intellectual property if provided in the applicable agreement(s); and 3) the right to exercise any term that extends the licensee's time period to use the license. The estate benefits because the licensee does not retain any right to specific performance, and the licensee must continue to make all royalty payments. Under §365(n)(2)(C), a licensee waives any setoff right and any administrative expense claim, but the licensee can file a general unsecured claim for

30. *See also* §365(i), which contain a similar provision for time-share properties.

31. Section 101(35A) defines intellectual property as a "(A) trade secret; (B) invention, process, design, or plant protected under title 35 [which involves patentable inventions]; (C) patent application; (D) plant variety; (E) work of authorship protected under title 17 [, which involves copyrightable work]; or (F) mask work protected under chapter 9 of title 17." Noticeably missing from the definition of intellectual property are trademarks, trade names, or service marks. Because of this omission, courts have concluded that §365(n) does not apply to license agreements involving trademarks, trade names, and service marks. See, e.g., *In re Deel, LLC*, No. 10-11310, 2011 BL 351659, at *8 (Bankr. D. Del. Feb. 8, 2011) (finding that §365(n) did not apply to the rejected franchise agreement containing permission to use the franchisor's trademark).

damages in the bankruptcy case. Finally, §365(n)(3)(A) requires the debtor to provide to the licensee, upon the licensee's written request, any intellectual property held by the trustee, to the extent this demand right appears in the license agreement. Further, §365(n)(3)(B) requires that the debtor not interfere with the rights provided to the licensee in the license agreement.

EXAMPLES

Examples

1. Howard Grocers supplies fruits and vegetables to Mega Market pursuant to an agreement between the parties. The contract requires Howard to ship all items from its main Ann Arbor facility, which is located just two miles from the Mega Market store. The contract does not allow for any variance from this term, because it ensures that Mega Market is receiving fresh produce. Howard is paid 30 days after delivery. However, Mega Market allows its customers to return purchased items up to 45 days after purchase. Returned produce is picked up by Howard at every delivery and it then credits Mega Market's account. The Grocery Contract specifies that if more than 10 percent of Howard's delivered produce is returned by Mega Market customers in a given month, Howard must pay Mega Market a $15,000 penalty within 48 hours or Mega Market may terminate the Grocery Contract. Howard's legal counsel is not sure if the penalty is enforceable but Howard does not care because its business would collapse if Mega Market stopped selling Howard's produce.

   Mega Market informed Howard that 12 percent of Howard's produce was returned during the previous month. Howard was unable to make the lump sum payment. Howard attempted to negotiate a delay in payment, but Mega Market refused to make any concessions. Howard was forced to file for bankruptcy.

   In bankruptcy, Howard, as the debtor in possession, wishes to assign the lucrative Grocery Contract to Peppers Grocers. Peppers Grocers is able to deliver produce on the schedule and at the price delineated in the contract. However, Peppers is not able to use Howard Grocer's Ann Arbor facility. Nevertheless, Peppers has a comparable facility just 30 miles away from Mega Market's store. Can the debtor assign this contract?

2. Woodson Manufacturing has contracted with the federal government to build new judicial benches for the federal courts in its area. Woodson begins purchasing the materials and hiring the employees necessary to complete the project. Unfortunately, a water pipe burst at its main storage facility and most of its materials were damaged. Woodson was forced to file for bankruptcy. Woodson, as the debtor in possession, wishes to assume the contract, but learns that the federal government will not consent. The contract has an antiassignment clause, but the debtor is not seeking to assign the contract. Further, the debtor has not committed

a default under the contract so it is not subject to §365(b). Is there anything that could prevent the debtor in possession from assuming the contract?

3. Carr Technologies is party to two contracts with Brady Software. The first contract allows Carr to use software owned by Brady as part of a new type of voice-activated desktop phone. The contract affords Carr an exclusive license to the software for five years and the option to extend that right for another three years (the "License Contract"). The contract also requires Brady to update the software every six months and provide annual training to Carr employees. The second contract allows Carr to use Brady Software's logo on boxes of the phones it sells (the "Logo Contract"). Under the Logo Contract, Brady is obligated to protect its brand from unlawful infringement and periodically provide Carr with updated logos.

   Brady Software has been sued in a class action proceeding for systemic gender discrimination. The company has lost key clients and has no choice but to file for bankruptcy. In bankruptcy, Brady, as the debtor in possession, seeks to reject its two contracts with Carr Technologies, but Carr wishes to continue using Brady's software and logo. Is there anything Carr can do to preserve the rights it enjoys under the contracts? If so, which rights can be preserved?

4. Alice N. Vendorland sold a house to Wendy Vendee under a land sale contract. The contract provides that Wendy is obliged to pay the price of the land in installments over several years. Wendy occupied the property immediately after execution of the contract. Alice has no duty under the contract to maintain the property or perform other services. Her only outstanding obligation is to transfer title to the property when all payments have been made.

   Alice has become bankrupt. Wendy is a few years away from completing her payments on the house. The property has appreciated since the sale, and Alice's trustee wishes to reject the contract so that the property can be recovered by the estate and resold at a higher price.
   a. Is this contract executory?
   b. If so, can the trustee reacquire the property by rejecting the contract?

5. Jack Pott, Inc. owned some land on which it decided to build a house. The company entered into a construction financing contract with Fairweather Funding, Inc., under which Fairweather agreed to lend Jack Pott, Inc. funds to pay for the building. The contract provided for advances to be made in the form of direct payments to the contractor as work progressed. Fairweather recorded a mortgage on the property at the time of the contract to secure the advances to be made. Jack Pott, Inc. then contracted with Housebound, Inc. for construction of the house.

   After the house had been half built and Fairweather had advanced about half of the loan, Jack Pott, Inc. filed a Ch. 11 petition. Property values have appreciated, and if the house is completed, the property can be sold for a good profit. Jack Pott, Inc., as debtor in possession, would like to assume both the financing contract and the construction contract so that it can finish the house. May it do so?

6. Martin A. Idle is an actor. He recently contracted with a public broadcasting station to perform the role of Hamlet in a television production of that play. Shortly before filming was to begin, Martin received an irresistible offer to play the principal heartthrob in a prime-time soap opera, which would give him national exposure, fame, and fortune. He cannot work on both productions at the same time.

   Martin filed a Ch. 11 petition and, as debtor in possession, he immediately rejected the contract with the public broadcasting station so that he can accept the offer of the other contract. Can he do this?

7. Sandy Trapp is a member of a country club. To avoid congestion on its golf course, the club distinguishes general membership from golf membership and restricts golf privileges to a strictly limited number of people. Golf membership has been fully subscribed for decades, and new admissions can only occur when existing members leave. As a result, golf privileges are prized, and people who desire them have to wait for years. To ensure an equitable and orderly succession to vacancies, the club maintains a waiting list and fills openings in golf membership in order of seniority.

   Sandy holds a coveted golf membership. He has filed a Ch. 7 petition. His trustee has discovered that several people who are not near the top of the list are eager to buy Sandy's membership and are willing to bid against each other for it. The trustee realizes that the sale of the membership will bring substantial funds into the estate. The trustee seeks to assume Sandy's golf membership and to sell it to the highest bidder. The country club objects.

   May the trustee assume and assign Sandy's golf membership?

EXPLANATIONS

Explanations

1. Howard Grocers has defaulted under the contract. The contract is certainly executory so the debtor can assign the contract if it can satisfy §365(f)'s requirements. Primarily, under §365(f)(2)(A), the debtor must be able to assume the contract under §365(b). The first requirement is that the debtor cure its monetary default by making the $15,000 payment or providing adequate assurance that it will be able to make the payment promptly. Based on the facts in the example, it appears that the debtor will have the funds necessary to cure the default. The debtor will also need to compensate—or provide adequate assurance that it will

promptly compensate—Mega Market for any pecuniary damages stemming from the failure to pay the penalty. The case was filed promptly after default and the cure should occur shortly after the filing. Consequently, Mega Market's pecuniary damages should be limited.

Finally, the debtor will need to provide adequate assurance of future performance under §365(b)(1)(C) in order to assume the contract. But since the debtor is seeking to assign the contract, courts tend to replace this element with an analysis of whether the *assignee* of the contract can provide adequate performance of future performance under §365(f)(2)(B).

There is some doubt whether Peppers Grocers will be able to demonstrate that it has the wherewithal to fulfill the contractual obligations at issue. Peppers Grocery may be able to show that it can deliver produce on the schedule and at the price delineated in the contract, but that may not be sufficient. The contract requires that produce be delivered from Howard Grocer's Ann Arbor facility. Peppers Grocers would not necessarily be expected to comply with the specifics of this provision, but a court may require Peppers to comply with the spirit of the provision. Indeed, Mega Market included this provision in the contract because it believed that the facility's proximity to the store provided customers with fresh produce. This appears to be a material and economically significant term in the contract. Peppers Grocers has a facility that is 30 miles away from the store, but that may not be comparable. In order to be assigned the contract, Peppers may need to find a facility that is closer to the Mega Market store or be able to establish that the difference in proximity between its facility and the Howard Grocer facility has no effect on the freshness of its produce.

2. The debtor in possession is not subject to §365(b), but it is subject to §365(c). Though the section's language may be a result of a drafting error, §365(c) states that Woodson may not assume **or** assign the contract if 1) the federal government does not consent to the assumption and 2) applicable nonbankruptcy law precludes assignment of the contract without the federal government's consent. In this example, the federal government will not consent to the assumption. Further, the contract is subject to the Federal Anti-Assignment Act, which precludes assignment of a contract with the federal government without the government's consent. Consequently, §365(c) would preclude assumption.

   The debtor could attempt to argue that strict application of §365(c)'s language leads to an absurd result, which would allow the court to rely on legislative history and other external sources to interpret the section. However, most courts have rejected this argument.

3. Both contracts are executory so Carr Technologies can rely on §365(n) and attempt to maintain its rights under the contracts. Section 365(n)

affords licensees certain protections when a debtor-licensor files for bankruptcy and seeks to reject an intellectual property agreement. Section 101(31A) defines the term "intellectual property." The definition includes patentable inventions, including software. But the definition does not include trademarks. Consequently, Brady Software will be allowed to reject the Logo Contract, and Carr's only recourse will be to file a damage claim with the estate. However, §365(n) does apply to the License Contract, and allows Carr to retain some rights. Primarily, Carr will be allowed to continue its exclusive use of the software and extend that use for three years after the initial term ends. But §365(n)(2)(C) precludes specific performance, and Brady Software does not have to provide Carr with updates to the software or annual employee training. Following Brady's termination of its performance under §365(n)(2)(C), Carr can file a general unsecured claim for any resulting damages. Finally, Carr must continue to make royalty payments under the License Contract.

4. a. The standard traditional test for deciding whether a contract is executory is that there are material unperformed obligations on both sides. In this contract, Wendy still has to pay the balance of the purchase price and probably has other obligations as well concerning the maintenance and protection of the property. Her outstanding performance is surely material. Alice's only remaining obligation is to transfer title to the property when payment is complete. Some courts have held that the transfer of title is a legal formality that is not significant enough to make the contract executory.[32] Other courts have disagreed, and have held that because a failure to deliver title would be a material breach, the duty to transfer title makes the contract executory.[33] This difference of opinion shows that the materiality of an outstanding performance is a matter of contract interpretation on which courts can differ.

Because a focus on nothing more than the materiality of the outstanding obligations can be very rigid, some courts have moved away from the traditional test in favor of a more flexible "functional approach." This continues to take the materiality of outstanding obligations into account, but treats this as a guideline rather than a firm test, and also examines the nature of the contract and the impact on the estate of classifying it as executed or executory.

It has been argued that a land sale contract should not be treated as an executory contract at all because it is analogous to a credit sale of the property secured by a mortgage and should therefore be regarded

32. See, e.g., *In re Streets & Beard Farm Partnership*, 882 F.2d 233 (7th Cir. 1989).
33. See, e.g., *In re Ravenswood Apartments, Ltd.*, 338 B.R. 307 (B.A.P. 6th Cir. 2006).

simply as a secured claim by or against the estate and not be dealt with under §365. Some courts have accepted this argument, and others have not. In *In re Terrel*, 892 F.2d 469 (6th Cir. 1989), the court, while conceding the merit of the analogy, pointed out that the transactions are legally quite distinct and should not be treated alike in the absence of Code authority. Whatever approach is taken, if the contract is executory, it must be dealt with under §365. If not, the contract rights are property of the estate.

b. If the contract is executory, it falls within the special rule in §365(i) for the protection of a possessory purchaser of real property. Even if the trustee rejects the contract, Wendy is entitled to remain in possession of it and to complete her purchase under the terms of the contract. Therefore, in the present case the characterization of the contract as executory does not enable the trustee to reacquire the property.

5. Both contracts are unquestionably executory. The estate cannot assume the financing contract; it clearly falls within the exception to assumption in §365(c)(2). As the financing contract cannot be assumed, Fairweather cannot be compelled to provide further funds. The advances already made are a secured prepetition claim against the estate. Section 365(c)(2) does not authorize assumption, even with the consent of Fairweather. However, if the property has in fact appreciated so that Fairweather is assured of the full benefit of its bargain, Jack Pott, Inc. may be able to persuade it to provide the remaining funds under a new credit agreement negotiated and approved in terms of §364.

   The construction contract is assumable, but if the estate cannot obtain the needed financing it may not be able to perform its obligations to Housebound. There apparently has not been a default in the contract, so Housebound is not entitled to adequate assurance of performance under §365(b). However, to obtain court approval of the assumption on the business judgment standard, Jack Pott, Inc. must show that the estate has the means to perform its obligations under the contract and that assumption is likely to benefit the estate. Ultimate benefit to the estate can be established by evidence of appreciating value, but unless Jack Pott, Inc. can arrange postpetition financing—either with Fairweather or with another lender—he cannot demonstrate a source of funding for progress payments under the contract. In assuming the contract, the estate cannot modify terms of the contract, so Jack Pott, Inc. cannot force Housebound to defer payment until the property is sold.

6. Good try, sweet prince, but this tactic may not work. Martin, in his capacity as debtor in possession, is using §365 to reject the *Hamlet*

contract so that he can accept the offer, in his personal capacity, to star in the soap opera. The issue is whether it should be treated as an abuse of the Code for a debtor to file bankruptcy for the primary purpose of using §365 to escape an unwanted contract. In *In re Carrere*, 64 B.R. 156 (Bankr. C.D. Cal. 1986), which inspired this Example, the court refused to approve the rejection. Although the court relied on a rather technical analysis to find that the trustee had no standing to reject a personal services contract, the underlying principle of the decision is that §365 is supposed to be used to benefit the estate, not to let the debtor out of a contract for personal services. Other courts have allowed the estate to reject such contracts, at least where the debtor was genuinely in need of relief from financial adversity and was not solely motivated by the purpose of getting rid of the contractual obligation.[34] BAPCPA did not make any amendment to the Code to address this issue. However, a court may find some guidance in §707(b)(3).[35] That section includes, as one of the factors to be considered in deciding if a Ch. 7 consumer case should be dismissed for abuse, whether the debtor seeks to reject a personal services contract and the financial need for such rejection. Although this provision is not directly relevant here because Martin's debts may not be primarily consumer debts, it does signal Congress's approach to this kind of conduct.

7. This question is a simplified version of the facts in *In re Magness*, 972 F.2d 689 (6th Cir. 1992). In that case, the court characterized the debtor's golf membership as an executory contract in which both parties had material outstanding obligations: the debtor's payment of dues and the club's provision of golfing facilities. The court's central focus was the reconciliation of §362(c)(1), which upholds rules of nonbankruptcy law excusing the nondebtor party from accepting the assignment and assumption of a contract, and §362(f)(1) which overrides anti-assignment provisions in contracts and nonbankruptcy law. The court held that while §362(f) sets out the general rule disregarding barriers to assignment in bankruptcy, §362(c) recognizes an exception to this rule where the assignment of the contract in question would have an adverse impact on the rights of the nondebtor party, and nonbankruptcy law protects those rights by permitting the nondebtor party to refuse assignment.

---

34. See, e.g., *In re Taylor*, 913 F.2d 102 (3d Cir. 1990) and *All Blacks B.V. v. Gruntruck*, 199 B.R. 970 (W.D. Wash. 1996).

35. Section 707(b)(3) is discussed in section 6.8.5. It deals with the grounds for dismissing a Ch. 7 consumer case for abuse where the presumption of abuse (the means test) is inapplicable or rebutted.

The court found that assignment of the golf membership would adversely affect the club's maintenance of an orderly method of filling golf vacancies, and would force it into a breach of its obligations to members on the waiting list. State law upholds reasonable rules developed by voluntary associations and hence would excuse the club from accepting the assignment of a golf club membership. Therefore, the court concluded, §362(c)(1) precludes the trustee's assumption and assignment of the debtor's golf membership without the club's consent.

CHAPTER 17

Claims Against the Estate

§17.1 OVERVIEW

The subject of creditor claims and their ranking has arisen frequently in earlier chapters. This chapter focuses more systematically on the rules and principles governing the assertion of claims against the estate and the distribution of estate funds or property to creditors. Beginning with an explanation of the different types of claim that may be proved against the estate, the discussion then explores the process of claim submission and allowance, and claim priority.

Section 501 provides details on the logistics involved in filing a proof of claim in a bankruptcy case. Section 502 explores the process for the allowance or disallowance of a claim and is the basis for the burden-shifting framework that courts use in evaluating disputed claims. Section 502(b) explores the primary bases for disallowance or reduction of a claim. Section 502(c) allows the bankruptcy court to estimate the value of certain claims in order to avoid an undue delay in the administration of a bankruptcy case. Finally, §507 delineates an elaborate hierarchy for claims in order to prioritize distributions from the estate.

§17.2 WHAT IS A CLAIM?

§17.2.1 The Definition of "Claim"

Section 101(5) defines "claim" very broadly to include any secured or unsecured right to payment arising in law or equity. The claim need not be fixed, settled, and due at the time of the petition, but it may be unliquidated, contingent, unmatured, or disputed. The term's broad scope establishes that all legal obligations of the debtor—no matter how remote or contingent—can be addressed in the bankruptcy case.[1] To qualify as a claim, the obligation must give rise to a right to payment. A nonmonetary right—such as an injunction that merely mandates or restrains some conduct of the debtor without any alternative for a monetary remedy—is not a claim. Of course, many injunctions and other judicial and administrative orders do provide for a payment alternative because they might permit recourse to compensation if the debtor fails to obey the order. The question of whether an obligation of the debtor represents a right to payment, thereby qualifying as a claim, has two important consequences. First, if the obligation is not a claim, the obligee has no right to participate in the bankruptcy distribution. Second, liability on a claim is dischargeable in bankruptcy, but obligations that are not claims are not subject to the discharge. Therefore, the debtor's ongoing responsibility to perform the obligation after bankruptcy is dependent on the determination of whether the obligation is classified as a claim.

The significance of determining whether an obligation is a claim is illustrated by the problem of dealing with the debtor's liability for environmental pollution. In *Ohio v. Kovacs*, 469 U.S. 274 (1985), a state agency had obtained a court order, prior to the debtor's bankruptcy, authorizing it to clean up pollution caused by the debtor and to claim the cleanup cost from the debtor. The Supreme Court held that the debtor's liability to the state for the cost of remedying pollution qualified as a claim because it constituted a right to payment under §101(5). The situation in which the debtor has monetary liability to the government arising from environmental harm must be distinguished from that in which the government has obtained an injunction against the debtor prohibiting future pollution. The bar on prospective action is not a claim because it cannot be translated into money. Indeed, the state agency does not have the authority to permit the pollution to continue in exchange for compensation. In applying *Kovacs*, courts have developed refinements on the question of when liability for pollution translates into a claim. In *In re Industrial Salvage, Inc.*, 196 B.R. 784 (Bankr. S.D. Ill. 1996), state law did not empower the agency to perform the cleanup itself and claim reimbursement, but confined the state to seeking a cleanup order. The cleanup order did not give rise to a claim, even though the estate would have to spend money to comply with the order. However, in *In re Torwico Electronics, Inc.*, 8 F.3d 146 (3d Cir. 1993), the agency had the power either to

1. See *In re Dubois*, 834 F.3d 522, 529 (4th Cir. 2016); see also *Kipp Flores Architects, LLC v. Mid-Continent Cas. Co.*, 852 F.3d 405, 410 (5th Cir. 2017).

obtain a cleanup order or to perform the work itself and seek reimbursement. The state's option of performing the cleanup and claiming reimbursement qualified the obligation as a claim. In *In re Mark IV Industries, Inc.*, 459 B.R. 173 (S.D.N.Y. 2011), the state statute under which the agency ordered the debtor to perform environmental remediation did not provide for the alternative remedy of a monetary compensation. The debtor argued that its obligation to remedy the pollution nevertheless constituted a claim because the agency had a choice of statutes under which to proceed, and some of the applicable statutes did permit the agency to remedy the pollution and claim reimbursement. The court rejected this argument, explaining that the question of whether monetary relief is available as an alternative to a cleanup order must be based on the statute used by the agency, not on remedies that might be available under different statutes that the agency could have used but did not invoke. Examples 2 and 3 deal with the determination of whether an obligation is a claim, and this issue is also discussed in connection with the discharge in Chapter 21.

§17.2.2 Unliquidated, Contingent, Unmatured, and Disputed Claims

Section 101(5) expressly includes unliquidated, contingent, unmatured, and disputed claims. A claim is unliquidated if its amount is not fixed and certain and cannot be calculated arithmetically from known data. For example, a tort claim arises upon commission of the tort, but is unliquidated until determined by adjudication or settlement. A claim is contingent if the debtor's liability is conditional upon the happening of a future, uncertain event. The possibility of this contingency occurring is in the actual or presumed contemplation of the parties when their relationship is created. For example, when a surety guarantees the debt of the principal debtor, the surety's debt comes into existence upon execution of the suretyship, but liability on the debt only arises if the principal debtor defaults. (*See also* Examples 2 and 3.) A claim is unmatured until the time for payment comes about. For example, when goods are purchased on 30-days' credit, the debt is created on delivery of the goods, but it only matures at the end of the 30-day credit period.[2] A claim is disputed if the debtor challenges the existence or extent of liability. The fact that a debt is disputed does not, in itself, make the debt unliquidated or contingent if the underlying debt itself is of fixed amount and unconditional.[3]

2. Note that the debt cannot be considered contingent because the mere passage of time is a certainty and, therefore, cannot represent a contingency.
3. For example, the fact that a final judgment is on appeal does not render the amount owed pursuant to that judgment "disputed."

A debt that is subject to one or more of these barriers to enforcement at the time of the petition is nevertheless a claim against the estate. During the course of the case, the issue or issues affecting enforcement will be resolved by negotiation or litigation. Disputes will be settled or adjudicated, and a value will be placed on unliquidated or contingent claims, as discussed in section 17.4. Bankruptcy inevitably alters contractual due dates for unmatured debts, and some debts may be accelerated, especially in liquidation cases, while others may be extended through a plan of reorganization.

In re Rodriguez, 629 F.3d 136 (3d Cir. 2010) illustrates how a claim might exist even though there is no right to payment on the petition date. The holder of a mortgage on the debtor's property argued that the debtor's obligation to pay funds into an escrow account to cover future disbursements by the mortgagee for tax and insurance payments was not a claim. The basis of this argument was that until the disbursements were made by the mortgagee, there was no debt due to it, and hence no claim. The court rejected that argument, explaining that although the debt had not yet arisen, the terms of the mortgage obliged the debtor to make the payment into escrow. Therefore, although the mortgagee's right to payment out of the escrow account was contingent on its paying the taxes and insurance premium, the debtor's obligation was nevertheless a claim in existence at the time of the petition.

§17.2.3 Prepetition and Postpetition

Section 17.2.2 explained that a creditor may be able to assert a claim in the bankruptcy case even if that claim is not enforceable on the petition date. Nevertheless, the right to assert the claim must exist on the petition date. Consequently, as a general rule, only the debtor's prepetition debts are claims against the estate. In the case of an individual debtor, postpetition debts incurred by the debtor are charges against the debtor's fresh start estate. However, postpetition debts incurred by the estate itself are debts of the estate and are treated as an administrative expense. Postpetition debts in a corporate bankruptcy are always debts of the estate, and, provided that they were authorized, are paid from the estate as second-priority administrative expenses. (This is explained in section 17.5.4.)

There are some claims that arise after the petition date but are treated as prepetition claims because they are linked to a prepetition transaction. For example, the rejection of an executory contract occurs after the petition, but it gives rise to a claim deemed by §365(g)(1) to have arisen prepetition. Similarly, a claim created by the avoidance of a transfer is deemed to be a prepetition claim by §502(h).

There are two situations, applicable only in Ch. 13 cases, where the debtor's personal postpetition debts may be included as claims against the estate. In the first, §1305(a)(1) permits governmental units to prove claims in the estate for postpetition taxes owing by the debtor.

In the second situation, §1305(a)(2) enables a proof of claim to be filed by a creditor who has extended credit to the debtor in a postpetition consumer transaction for the debtor's purchase of "property or services necessary for the debtor's performance under the plan." The property or services must be essentials such as medical treatment or the repair of vital property, and they must relate to the debtor's personal or domestic affairs, not to business activity. The creditor does not have to prove this postpetition claim against the estate. The creditor has the option of treating the debt as a nondischargeable claim against the debtor's fresh start estate and collecting it from the debtor personally. However, the claim may be hard to collect. The debtor may have little cash to spare after making payments to the trustee under the plan, and the creditor cannot enforce the debt against estate property until the close of the case, by virtue of the stay under §362(a)(3). Therefore, the creditor may elect to prove the claim in the estate to ensure payment under the plan. The drawback to the creditor is that if the debtor obtained prior approval of the transaction from the trustee, or such approval was impractical, any balance of the debt unpaid in the Ch. 13 distribution is discharged by §1328(d). The creditor is barred from proving a claim in the estate if the creditor knew or should have known that the debtor could have obtained the trustee's advance approval and failed to do so.

§17.2.4 Claims Against the Debtor's Property

When one thinks of prepetition claims against the estate, one usually assumes these are debts on which the debtor was personally liable at the time of bankruptcy. In most cases this assumption is correct, but §102(2) extends "claim" to cover not only the debtor's personal obligations but also claims against the debtor's property. It is possible that a right to payment constitutes a charge on property of the debtor even though the debtor has no personal liability on it. This may happen, for example, when a secured party holds a nonrecourse[4] security interest in the debtor's property. It could also occur with some statutory liens — such as construction liens — which attach to real property even though the work was ordered by the prime contractor rather than the owner. Because the lienholder and owner have no contractual relationship, the owner has no personal debt to the lienholder. However, if the claim is not paid, the lienholder is entitled to foreclose

4. The term "nonrecourse" describes a situation where the secured party's claim can be asserted only against the collateral identified in the relevant agreement between the parties, and the debtor is not responsible for any deficiency.

on the property to recover payment. Section 102(2) makes it clear that such claims against the debtor's property are to be treated as claims in bankruptcy.

§17.2.5 Determining When a Claim Arises

As explained in section 17.2.3, the date on which a claim arises is important. If the claim arose prepetition, it is a claim against the estate. If it arose postpetition it may be either an administrative expense in the debtor's bankruptcy case[5] or a claim against the debtor's postbankruptcy estate.[6] The Code does not prescribe any specific test for deciding when a claim arises, and this issue must be resolved by referencing nonbankruptcy law. The general rule under nonbankruptcy law is that a claim comes into existence as soon as the act giving rise to liability takes place. In most situations, it is not difficult to determine the date on which liability was created. However, the question can occasionally be quite complex, particularly where the conduct that creates potential liability occurs some time earlier than the date on which liability actually arises. For example, say that the debtor, an industrial corporation, causes pollution prior to its bankruptcy. At the time of filing the petition, the pollution has not been rectified, and a government agency intends to clean it up during the course of the administration of the estate. If the government's claim for the cleanup costs arose at the time that the pollution occurred (the act giving rise to liability), it is an unsecured prepetition claim, but if it arises only when the cleanup work is performed, it is a postpetition claim.

Liability for potential injury from a hazardous product provides a second example. Imagine that a customer bought a rug from the debtor prior to the debtor's bankruptcy filing. Unknown to the customer, the rug was impregnated with a toxic chemical that made the customer ill. However, the illness only manifested postpetition. The claim is a prepetition claim if it arises at the time of exposure; but the claim is a postpetition injury and not a claim against the estate if it arises at the time of the onset of the illness. Courts have struggled with the question of when the claim arose in situations like this. Most courts believe that a test based simply on the date liability was created, or on the date that the debt was actually incurred, is not sophisticated enough to balance the fresh start policy of bankruptcy against the policy of holding the debtor accountable for injurious acts. To fix the claim at too early a date tends to favor the debtor's fresh start too heavily by making most liability for prepetition wrongs into dischargeable general

5. Invariably the case in a corporate bankruptcy in Ch. 7 or Ch. 11.

6. As noted in section 17.2.3, in an individual bankruptcy, postpetition debts incurred by the debtor, rather than by the trustee in the administration of the estate, are debts of the debtor's postbankruptcy estate.

unsecured claims. Conversely, to fix the claim as arising only when the debt is actually incurred tends to give special preference to the claim, either by treating it as an administrative expense or by treating it as a nondischargeable charge against the fresh start estate. To attempt a better policy balance, these courts have favored a more complex test under which the claim comes into existence at some point between these poles.

In re Chateaugay Corp., 944 F.2d 997 (2d Cir. 1991), involved a claim for cleanup costs by the Environmental Protection Agency (EPA). The court drew an analogy to contract law, because it felt that the EPA as regulator has a relationship with the debtor similar to that between parties to a contract. On this theory, the claim arises as soon as EPA becomes aware of the problem site and can reasonably contemplate the need for cleanup. Since *Chateauqay* was decided, many other courts have adopted a test based on relationship and reasonable contemplation to find that the claim arose at some point in the prepetition period. For the debt to arise prepetition, there must have been some identifiable prepetition relationship between the claimant and the debtor, either because they had a contract or were in some other form of privity or because the claimant had already been exposed to tortious conduct by the debtor before the filing. This was the test adopted in *In re Piper Aircraft Corp.*, 58 F.3d 1573 (11th Cir. 1995), and followed in relation to future sex abuse claimants in *In re Roman Catholic Archbishop of Portland in Oregon*, 2005 WL 148775 (Bankr. D. Or. Jan. 10, 2005). Some courts have refined the test further by adding a requirement of fairness. For example, in *Signature Combs, Inc. v. U.S.*, 253 F. Supp. 2d 1028 (W.D. Tenn. 2003), the court held that a claim for environmental cleanup arose, not when the EPA had a general awareness that there was a pollution problem, but when it became aware and could fairly have contemplated that the site would require remediation. In *In re Zilog, Inc.*, 450 F.3d 996 (9th Cir. 2006), the court applied the "fair contemplation" test to a sex discrimination claim. (*See also* Example 3.)

The problem of fixing the date on which a claim arose is particularly difficult where it is not clear, on the petition date, whether a claim will actually come into being. That is, there is a potential liability, but that liability is contingent on an injury that has not yet manifested itself and may never do so. For example, in *In re Grossman's, Inc.*, 607 F.3d 114 (3d Cir. 2010), the court had to determine when the debtor's liability to its customer arose. The customer's claim was for personal injury caused by asbestos in building products. The products were sold to her by the debtor some years prepetition, but the asbestos-related disease only manifested itself about ten years after the debtor's Ch. 11 plan had been confirmed. The court, overruling its precedent that a claim arises only when the injury manifests itself, and adopting the "relationship" test, held that the claim arose prepetition. Because the customer and the debtor had a prepetition relationship under which the product was sold, the claim arose when the customer was exposed to the harmful product.

§17.3 ALLOWANCE AND DISALLOWANCE OF CLAIMS

§17.3.1 General Claim Procedures, Timing, and Amendments

A creditor files a proof of claim in a bankruptcy case pursuant to §501. The claim must be allowed under §502 for a creditor to participate in the distribution of the debtor's assets. A proof of claim is the creditor's formal submission of a claim against the estate. In a Ch. 11 case, a creditor need not prove a claim unless its claim is 1) listed as disputed, contingent, or unliquidated; or 2) unlisted and the creditor otherwise comes to know of the bankruptcy. In cases under all other chapters, an unsecured creditor must prove its claim to be included in the distribution.

Rules 3002 and 3003 of the Federal Rules of Bankruptcy Procedure establish the filing deadlines. Rule 3002(c) provides that, in cases under Chs. 7 and 13, a claim should generally be filed within 90 days after the first date set for the §341 meeting of creditors.[7] In cases under Chs. 9 and 11, Rule 3003 requires that a creditor file a proof of claim within the time prescribed by the bankruptcy court.

Because a secured claim encumbers specific property of the estate, almost all courts have held that a secured claimant need not prove a claim to protect its lien. Even though the debtor's personal liability is discharged in bankruptcy, the lien—which constitutes a right in the property—survives the discharge. Section 506(d) codifies this principle and provides the general rule that a lien is void to the extent that it secures a claim that is not allowed. Further, §506(d)(2) validates a claim that was not allowed only because it was not proved. An undersecured creditor must prove a claim to receive a distribution on its deficiency.

Courts generally allow amendments to a proof of claim where the purpose is to 1) cure a defect in the claim as originally filed, 2) describe the claim with greater particularity, or 3) plead a new theory of recovery on the facts set forth in the original claim.[8] However, courts scrutinize post-bar

7. Governmental units are afforded special treatment under the rules and §502(b)(9) of the Code and may file a proof of claim within 180 days from the date the order of relief is entered.

8. *United States v. International Horizons, Inc. (In re International Horizons, Inc.)*, 751 F.2d 1213, 1216 (11th Cir. 1985).

date amendment requests to ensure that a creditor is not attempting to file a new claim under the pretense of an amendment.

Even after a claim has been allowed or disallowed, §502(j) permits it to be reconsidered for cause, so that the objector or the claimant can apply for a new ruling if new evidence, fraud of the other party, or other grounds exist for reopening the matter.

§17.3.2 Claim Review and the Burden-Shifting Framework

Once a claim is proved, it is allowed automatically unless a party in interest files a timely objection to the claim. When such an objection is filed, the Code employs a "burden-shifting framework"[9] for the task of determining a claim's amount and validity.

Filing a proof of claim in accordance with the applicable rules and court orders constitutes prima facie evidence of the amount and validity of the claim. A creditor that is able to gain this presumption[10] shifts the burden to the party objecting to the claim—invariably a bankruptcy trustee or the debtor in possession. To rebut the presumption of validity, the objecting party "must come forward with sufficient evidence and show facts tending to defeat the claim by probative force equal to that of the allegations of the proofs of claim themselves."[11] This burden of proof requires, the objecting party to produce "evidence which, if believed, would refute at least one of the allegations that is essential to the claim's legal sufficiency."[12] If the objecting party satisfies this burden and rebuts the claim's presumptive validity, the burden then reverts back to the claimant to prove the amount and validity of the claim by a preponderance of the evidence. Applicable nonbankruptcy law guides a court's evaluation of the claim's underlying merits, subject to any applicable Code provisions.

As a general rule, claims in a Ch. 7 case are paid near the end of the bankruptcy proceedings, after claims have been determined and assets liquidated. In rehabilitation cases, most payments begin after confirmation of

9. Under this framework, the burden rests on different parties at different points in the evidentiary process.

10. A proof of claim has no prima facie validity if it fails to comply with the applicable rules, including the supporting documentation requirements of Bankruptcy Rule 3001(c). With respect to such claim, an objecting party has no evidentiary burden to overcome and merely needs to object to the claim on some good faith grounds other than the mere assertion that the proof of claim is not supported by documentation. See *Sears v. Sears (In re Sears)*, No. 15-3352, 2017 BL 246854, at *4 (8th Cir. July 18, 2017).

11. *Margulies Law Firm, APLC v. Placide (In re Placide)*, 459 B.R. 64, 72 (B.A.P. 9th Cir. 2011).

12. *In re Allegheny Int'l, Inc.*, 954 F.2d 167, 173-74 (3d Cir. 1992).

the plan, and continue over time as provided for in the plan but payments could be made earlier if appropriate. For example, administrative expenses are often paid for when incurred, and payments to a secured party may be needed to ensure adequate protection.

§17.3.3 Claim Disallowance (§502(b) and (d))

a. §502(b)

Section 502(b) sets forth the nine primary bases for claim disallowance. Courts have held that these nine subsections are "the sole grounds for objecting to a claim and [a court must allow a claim] unless one of the exceptions applies."[13] Most of the grounds listed in §502(b) apply only to the extent that the claim falls within its terms. Consequently, a claim can be reduced, rather than completely disallowed.

Subsection 502(b)(1) invalidates claims that are unenforceable against the debtor and the debtor's property under an agreement or applicable law. This is the most comprehensive exception and allows a party to attack the merits of a claim under nonbankruptcy law. The other subsections are invoked less frequently, but three are worthy of discussion.

Primarily, §502(b)(5) provides for the disallowance of unmatured debts that are excepted from discharge pursuant to §523(a)(5). Section 523(a)(5) exempts from an individual debtor's discharge "domestic support obligations." This phrase captures postpetition debts owed to a spouse, a former spouse, or a child of the debtor that are in the nature of alimony, maintenance, or support of such person. By disallowing such claims, subsection (b)(5) prevents claimants with nondischargeable future domestic support obligations from participating in distributions of estate property. The reason for this exclusion is that these claimants hold non-dischargeable claims and are able to seek payment from the debtor's post-petition property.[14] Section 502(b)(6) is a complicated provision with a relatively simple objective. According to the legislative history, the subsection is meant to prevent landlords from receiving a windfall as a result of the termination in bankruptcy of a long-term nonresidential real property lease. The provision is "designed to compensate the landlord for [her] loss while not permitting a claim so large . . . as to prevent other general unsecured

---

13. See *In re Dove–Nation*, 318 B.R. 147, 150 (B.A.P. 8th Cir. 2004); see also *In re Norris*, No. 16-44297-BDL, 2017 BL 143225, at *2 (Bankr. W.D. Wash. Apr. 19, 2017).

14. Keep in mind that section 502(b)(5) applies only to "unmatured" debts, which is generally considered to mean those arising postpetition. In contrast, to the extent that a claim is a "matured" claim at the time of the bankruptcy filing, it will be allowed against the estate's assets and entitled to first priority under section 507(a)(1).

creditors from recovering a dividend from the estate."[15] To be clear, claims for unpaid prepetition rent are allowed in full under §502(b)(6)(B). But the subsection creates a cap on a landlord's claims based on damages resulting from termination of a nonresidential real property lease, including destruction of property, real estate taxes, insurance, and property maintenance fees.[16] The landlord bears the burden of establishing the validity of the damages claimed.

Section 502(b)(7) is similar to subsection (b)(6), and caps an employee's claim for damages arising from a terminated employment contract to the lesser of 1) one year's salary, or 2) the salary that accrues from the date of the employee's termination to the petition date.[17] Subsection (b)(7)'s purpose has been understood to "limit the claims of key executives who have been able to negotiate contracts with very beneficial terms," including generous severance packages.[18] But courts have interpreted the subsection more broadly. Indeed, courts have held that the subsection caps a full range of damages that result from termination of an employment contract, including claims in tort and contract. For example, imagine a company decides to terminate the employment agreement entered into with one of its executives. Pursuant to the agreement, the employee makes $150,000 per year. The employee believes that the termination was a result of age discrimination, and brings a suit alleging that claim, amongst others, under the Age Discrimination in Employment Act and applicable state law. After eight months, the employee wins a $1 million judgment against the company. The company appeals the judgment, which is affirmed on appeal. The company files for bankruptcy shortly thereafter, approximately 18 months after the employee was terminated. To the extent that the court determined that the employee's claim for damages results from the termination of his employment agreement, §502(b)(7) would cap the employee's claim to the lesser of 1) $150,000—one year's salary under the employment agreement—or 2) $225,000—the salary that accrued during the 18 months from the date of the employee's termination to the petition date. Ultimately, the employee's claim would be capped at $150,000.

---

15. H.R. Rep. No. 95-595, at 353 (1977), *reprinted in* 1978 U.S.C.C.A.N. 6309; see also *EOP-Colonnade of Dallas Ltd. P'ship v. Faulkner (In re Stonebridge Techs., Inc.)*, 430 F.3d 260, 268–69 (5th Cir. 2005).

16. See *In re Kupfer*, 852 F.3d 853, 858-59 (9th Cir. 2016) ("§502(b)(6) does not cap damages resulting from every breach of contract—only those claims for 'damages resulting from the termination of a lease.'") (citation omitted).

17. Courts have held that the subsection caps claims arising from the termination of the employee contract whether the claim arises from breach of contract or some other cause of action, such as one based on a violation of the National Labor Relations Act.

18. See *In re VeraSun Energy Corp.*, 467 B.R. 757, 765 (Bankr. D. Del. 2012).

b. §502(d)

As explored in Chapters 13 and 14, where a debtor has transferred property in a manner that renders the transfer avoidable under the Code, a trustee is entitled to recover such property. A creditor who is facing this type of avoidance action cannot participate in any distribution from the bankruptcy estate until it is resolved. Section 502(d) delineates this requirement, explaining that a transferee of a voidable transfer must return property or the value of the property transferred to the estate or its claims against the estate will be disallowed. Under §502(d), a failure to turn over property will result in a complete disallowance of the proof of claim as opposed to a mere reduction in the value of the claim by the amount of transferred property.

§17.4 ESTIMATING CONTINGENT AND UNLIQUIDATED CLAIMS (§502(c))

In the normal course of events outside of bankruptcy, liability on an unliquidated or contingent claim is settled with the passage of time. An unliquidated debt will be made certain by negotiation or litigation, and a contingent debt will either become due or fall away, depending upon whether or not the future contingency occurs. In bankruptcy it is not always possible to allow the resolution of contingent or unliquidated liability to take its normal course, because the process may delay resolution of the bankruptcy case. Therefore, §502(c) requires contingent or unliquidated claims to be estimated[19] where necessary to prevent undue delay in the administration of the estate. Further, the section provides for estimation of any right to payment arising from a right to an equitable remedy for breach of performance.

In some situations, the estimation can be provisional—for example, where the claim is likely to be resolved by normal means during the future course of a Ch. 11 case but an immediate determination of the claim is needed to fix the claimant's voting rights. In other situations, when the prospect of timely resolution is poor, estimation may have to be a final determination that fixes the claimant's distribution from the estate.[20] For example, imagine that Big House Retirement Fund (BHRF) manages

19. More specifically, §502(c) requires that all qualifying claims against the debtor be converted into dollar amounts.

20. A provisional estimation for voting purposes is a core proceeding, but the final estimation for distribution purposes is noncore and must be finally decided by the district court unless all parties consent to the bankruptcy court's jurisdiction. See *In re Roman Catholic Archbishop of Portland in Oregon*, 339 B.R. 215 (Bankr. D. Or. 2006).

the retirement accounts for employees of Brady Industries. Brady Industries is experiencing some financial distress and files a Ch. 11 petition. BHRF files a consolidated proof of claim in the bankruptcy case alleging that the debtor owes $25 million as a withdrawal liability pursuant to the Employee Retirement Security Act of 1974 (ERISA). This is one of the largest claims in the case. This dispute is subject to a mandatory arbitration provision. However, the average time expended on this type of arbitration dispute is two years. The debtor could rely on §502(c) and seek estimation of the claim. The claim is unliquidated because the value of the claim could not be ascertained before resolution of substantial disputed issues. Further, a two-year delay would certainly frustrate the debtor's bankruptcy proceedings and potentially preclude a successful reorganization.

If estimation is required, §502(c) leaves it to the court to decide the most efficient and reliable means of making the estimation. More specifically, the court has broad discretion to employ "whatever method is best suited to the case as long as the procedure is consistent with fundamental bankruptcy policies, which require speed and efficiency."[21] Consequently, the method may involve a truncated trial,[22] arbitration,[23] a summary evaluation by the court based on briefs and oral argument,[24] or otherwise facilitating negotiation between the parties. The goal is to make an accurate estimate based on the circumstances while avoiding unnecessary delay that could compromise the debtor's successful reorganization. When estimating claims, the bankruptcy court is "required to evaluate claims pursuant to the [applicable nonbankruptcy law] which may govern the ultimate value of the claim. . . ."[25]

To liquidate an unliquidated claim, the court evaluates testimony on the debt or loss. The fixing of a contingent claim can be more awkward, because a contingent claim by its nature depends on the occurrence of an uncertain future event. Even if the amount of the contingent claim is certain (i.e., it is liquidated), the ultimate liability could be for the full debt or nothing, depending upon whether or not the event occurs. The court has to decide on the probability of the event occurring and must try to value the contingent claimant's chance of having a realized claim against the estate. If the contingent claim is also unliquidated, the uncertainty is greater still, and the court must resolve both the probability of actualization and the extent of the debt. Ultimately, courts avoid making definitive findings in these instances; rather, they

21. *In re Pac. Sunwear of Cal., Inc.*, No. Chapter 11, 2016 BL 262403, at *3 (Bankr. D. Del. Aug. 08, 2016).
22. See *In re Baldwin-United Corp.*, 55 B.R. 885, 899 (Bankr. S.D. Ohio 1985).
23. See *Maxwell v. Seaman Furniture Co. (In re Seaman Furniture Co. of Union Square, Inc.)*, 160 B.R. 40, 42 (S.D.N.Y. 1993).
24. See *In re Perry*, 425 B.R. 323, 343 (Bankr. S.D. Tex. 2010).
25. See id. at 342.

assess the possibilities of the various contentions and apply the appropriate discount to reflect the uncertainties of the contingencies.[26]

§17.5 CLAIM CLASSIFICATION AND PRIORITIES (§507)

§17.5.1 General Principles

The dichotomy between secured and unsecured claims is thoroughly familiar by now. In summary, secured claims are satisfied by the collateral or its proceeds. If there is more than one lien on a piece of property, the secured claims are ranked in accordance with priority prescribed by non-bankruptcy law, as discussed in Chapter 1. The general rule is that the most senior lien (usually measured by date of perfection) has first claim to the collateral, and junior liens are covered by the collateral only to the extent that there is any value left in it after more senior claims have been paid. In bankruptcy, ranking is not confined to secured claims. Unsecured claims are also divided into different priority categories. Section 507(a) lists ten priority classes in descending order. They are followed by general (that is, nonpriority) unsecured claims, which are in turn followed by low-priority categories such as unmatured interest on unsecured claims.

The ranking of claims is the same in all forms of bankruptcy, whether under Chs. 7, 11, or 13, but the rules governing the treatment of claims in Ch. 7 are different from those applicable in other chapters. In a Ch. 7 case, the fund realized from the liquidation of estate property is applied in turn to each class of priority claims in order of rank. A senior class must be paid in full before the next class is entitled to any distribution. The fund travels down the hierarchy until it is exhausted. If the fund is insufficient to pay all claims in a class in full, it is shared pro rata in that class.[27] Because most bankrupt estates are insolvent, the fund is seldom large enough to cover all claims. Often, the insolvency is so severe that only claims in the top priority class or classes receive payment. Because general unsecured claims are fairly low in the order of priority, it is quite usual for them to receive only minimal payment or no payment at all from an insolvent estate.

---

26. See *In re Innovasystems, Inc.*, 2014 BL 357352, at *7 (Bankr. D.N.J. Dec. 18, 2014).

27. For example, imagine that the fourth class of creditors in a bankruptcy case is comprised of Creditor A, who holds a $10,000 claim; Creditor B, who holds a $5,000 claim; and Creditor C, who holds a $3,000 claim. The estate can only distribute a total of $9,000 to this class of creditors. A pro rata distribution occurs where each creditor receives a distribution in proportion to the amount of its claim. The class has $18,000 in claims, but the estate only has $9,000 available for distribution. $9,000/$18,000 = $.50 for every dollar claimed. This means that a creditor in this class is going to receive 50 cents for every dollar of its claim. Creditor A receives $5,000. Creditor B receives $2,500. Creditor C receives $1,500.

The standards for plan confirmation in Chs. 11 and 13 require all §507 priority claims to be paid in full unless holders of the claims agree to the contrary. Therefore, the ranking of different classes of priority claims does not have the same significance in rehabilitation cases as it has in Ch. 7. In the absence of the agreement of the holders of priority claims, a plan cannot be confirmed unless it proposes to pay them in full. However, this does not mean that the priority ranking of claims is unimportant in a rehabilitation case. The rate of distribution under Ch. 7 has an impact on the question of whether full payment is made at face value or present value. Even if the plan provides for full payment of priority claims and it is confirmed, the ranking of priority claims could later become directly relevant if the rehabilitation fails and the debtor is ultimately liquidated.

The existence of priority claims has a further impact on a rehabilitation case, in that it affects the minimum payment required for unsecured claims. The amount that would have been paid on unsecured claims, if the debtor had been liquidated, is used as one of the yardsticks to decide if the plan may be confirmed: General unsecured claims must receive at least as much under the plan as the present value of what they would have received in a Ch. 7 liquidation. This means that if priority claims would have consumed all or a significant portion of the fund if the debtor had been liquidated, the minimum payment required for general unsecured claims in the plan is correspondingly lessened.

§17.5.2 The Order of Distribution

Diagram 17a summarizes the order of distribution. The different categories of claim are explained thereafter. (*See also* Example 5.) Secured and priority claims are governed by §§506 and 507, respectively. The order of distribution for general unsecured claims and lower-ranking orders is provided for in §726, which, as noted earlier, only applies to Ch. 7 cases, but is indirectly applicable in other cases.

The Order of Distribution in Bankruptcy

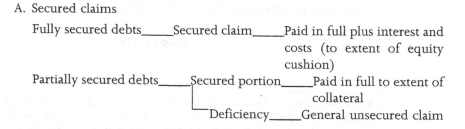

A. Secured claims

Fully secured debts____Secured claim____Paid in full plus interest and costs (to extent of equity cushion)

Partially secured debts____Secured portion____Paid in full to extent of collateral

Deficiency____General unsecured claim

B. Priority claims

Note that the priority classes denoted with an asterisk have dollar limits. To the extent that the claim exceeds the limit, it is a general unsecured claim.

(1) Domestic support obligations and any administrative expenses incurred by a bankruptcy trustee.[28]

(2) Administrative expenses
First rank—superpriority claims under §364(c)(1)
Second rank—superpriority claims under §507(b)
Third rank—other admin. expenses under §503

(3) In an involuntary bankruptcy case under §303, the ordinary-course business expenses incurred in the gap period between filing and order for relief

(4) Wages and salaries (limited)*

(5) Employee benefits (limited)*

(6) Grain producers and fishermen—claims against processor or storehouse (limited)*

(7) Deposits for consumer goods or services (limited)*

(8) Various taxes (limited)*

(9) Claims arising out of federal depository insurance

(10) Claims for wrongful death or personal injury resulting from debtor's driving while intoxicated

C. General unsecured claims

(Includes the balance of undersecured or limited priority claims together with all other claims proved and allowed and not covered by a priority category)

(1) Timely filed general unsecured claims and late claims where creditor had no notice or knowledge of the case to file in time but filed early enough to be able to participate

(2) Other tardily filed general unsecured claims

D. Claims for fines, penalties, forfeiture, or punitive damages, which are not compensation for actual pecuniary loss

E. Interest on priority and general unsecured claims

F. Any surplus remaining goes to the debtor

Diagram 17a

28. Domestic Support Obligations are listed first under 507(a)(1), but §507(a)(1)(C) provides that these expenses shall be subordinate to any administrative expenses incurred by a bankruptcy trustee to the extent that the trustee administers assets otherwise available for the payment of the domestic support obligation claims.

§17.5.3 Secured Claims (§506)

a. The Definition and Nature of Secured Claims

The nature and effect of security has been given much attention in prior chapters. In summary, a lien that is valid under nonbankruptcy law and unavoidable under the Code is fully effective in bankruptcy, and is satisfied in full to the extent of the value of the collateral. Although the lienholder's right to foreclose is subject to the automatic stay, and the estate may retain the collateral in furtherance of its efforts at rehabilitation, the lienholder is entitled to adequate protection of its interest and to ultimate full payment of its secured claim. Nonbankruptcy law dictates the priority between competing liens in the same property.

Section 506(a)(1) defines "secured claim" as "[a]n allowed claim of a creditor secured by a lien on property in which the estate has an interest," or an allowed claim that is subject to setoff under §553. "Lien" is expansively defined in §101(37) to include any "charge against or interest in property to secure payment of a debt or performance of an obligation" The definition therefore encompasses all encumbrances, whether consensual or not. The requirement that the underlying claim be allowed reflects the principles introduced in Chapter 2 that a lien cannot exist in the abstract; it must secure a valid debt. Therefore, if the claim supporting the lien is invalid and therefore disallowed, the lien that purported to secure that debt cannot be treated as a secured claim. Section 506(d) reinforces this by voiding the lien on a claim that was proved but disallowed. However, a lien cannot be voided solely because the claim was not proved. A lienholder may decide not to prove a claim against the estate. In that case, an enforceable lien survives as a charge against the property even though personal liability of the debtor is discharged. (*See* Example 1.)

b. Deficiency in Collateral Value: "Strip Down" and "Strip Off"

Section 506(a)(1) states that a claim is secured to the extent of the collateral's value and is unsecured as to any deficiency. Because security is necessarily limited by the value of collateral, §506(a)(1) splits an undersecured debt into a secured and unsecured claim. If a secured party forecloses on collateral under nonbankruptcy law, the value of the collateral at the time of foreclosure determines how much of the debt is secured. It does not matter that at some time before foreclosure the collateral held a different value. In bankruptcy, however, the court will invariably determine the value of the collateral at some time before foreclosure, and there is a delay between the judicial determination of value and the price actually received at the ultimate foreclosure sale. Where that happens and the collateral has increased in value since the valuation, the issue is whether the increase in value benefits the creditor by increasing the secured amount of the claim. In other words, if the debt was undersecured at the time of the valuation, the Code would bifurcate the claim into a secured debt to the extent of the value of the collateral and an unsecured debt for the deficiency. But sale of the property rarely coincides with the moment of valuation. Therefore, where foreclosure does not occur immediately, and the property increases in value between the time of the valuation and the foreclosure, courts must determine how to deal with this increase in value. The increase could be added to the secured claim, thereby reducing the unsecured deficiency, or the secured claim could be treated as having been pegged at the value fixed by the court, so that the appreciation redounds to the debtor's benefit. To illustrate this, imagine the collateral is a sculpture securing a claim of $6,000. Based on an appraisal, the court fixes the value of the sculpture at $5,000, which gives the creditor a secured claim of $5,000 and an unsecured claim of $1,000. Because the sculpture has no value for the estate, the Ch. 7 trustee abandons it to the debtor. The creditor has the right to apply for relief from stay and to foreclose on the security interest immediately, but it does not do this for six months. In the interim, the value of the sculpture has risen to $5,500. If the increase in value is added to the secured claim, it reduces the unsecured deficiency to $500. However, if the secured claim is pegged at the $5,000 value of the collateral originally fixed by the bankruptcy court, the appreciation of $500 belongs to the debtor. This is known as "lien stripping" or "strip down."

In *Dewsnup v. Timm*, 502 U.S. 410 (1992), the U.S. Supreme Court held that a debtor cannot strip down a consensual lien in a Ch. 7 case. The Ch. 7 debtor argued that because §506(a)(1) bifurcates an undersecured claim, the deficiency cannot be classified as an "allowed secured claim." This means that it must be void under §506(d), which voids a lien "[t]o the extent that [it] secures a claim . . . that is not an allowed secured claim." The court rejected this argument and found that the language of §506(d) was only intended to cover situations in which the secured claim itself had been disallowed, not where the secured claim was allowed, but a deficiency remains that becomes an unsecured claim. In reaching its decision, the court was influenced by the fact that pre-Code law treated liens as passing through bankruptcy unaffected, and that if Congress had intended to change that result, it would have more clearly provided so. The effect of *Dewsnup* is that a Ch. 7 debtor cannot use §506(d) to reduce an undersecured claim to the present value of the collateral as judicially determined in the bankruptcy case. However, the court was concerned only with a consensual lien in a Ch. 7 case and did not indicate if the same rule would apply outside of Ch. 7 or to a nonconsensual lien. Most subsequent lower court decisions have extended it to nonconsensual liens in Ch. 7 cases.[29] However, subsequent

29. See *In re Concannon*, 338 B.R. 90 (B.A.P. 9th Cir 2006).

case law has not generally applied *Dewsnup* to rehabilitation cases. Courts have pointed out that *Dewsnup* is not reconcilable with the different approach to undersecured claims in a Ch. 11 case and should therefore not be extended beyond its Ch. 7 context.[30]

Since *Dewsnup*, a number of courts have grappled with its impact on secured claims that have completely lost all the value of their collateral. This occurs where there are two liens on property, and the value of the property is so low that it is sufficient to pay only the senior interest (in whole or in part) so that there is no value remaining to cover the junior interest. Debtors have argued that *Dewsnup* applies only to an undersecured lien, and that if a lien is totally unsecured on the debtor's bankruptcy the claim cannot be treated as secured at all and the lien must be void. (This is known as "strip off," as opposed to "strip down.") Courts have reacted differently to this argument. Some courts have accepted it, but others have held that there is no principled distinction between this situation and that addressed by *Dewsnup*. Therefore, provided the lien is otherwise valid and unavoidable, the debtor should not be able to strip it off merely because the collateral does not have enough value to support it at the time of bankruptcy.[31]

c. Interest, Costs, and Fees on Secured Claims

We have already encountered the principle that if the collateral is worth more than the debt, the surplus is applied to any junior claims to the property or, if there are none, belongs to the estate. This principle is subject to the oversecured claimant's right to interest and costs under §506(b). Once the surplus is exhausted, the secured claim's right to interest, fees, and costs ends.

Under §506(b) a secured claimant is entitled to postpetition interest[32] on its claim to the extent of any surplus value in the collateral. Since *United States v. Ron Pair Enterprises*, 489 U.S. 235 (1989), it is clear that interest is not confined to consensual lienholders but is also available to oversecured nonconsensual liens. The rate of interest is the contract rate. In *In re Payless Cashways, Inc.*, 287 B.R. 482 (Bankr. W.D. Mo. 2002), the court noted that while §506(b) applies a reasonableness standard to costs and fees, it says nothing about reasonable interest. Therefore, the court should apply the contract rate, and as long as that rate is permissible under nonbankruptcy law, should not inquire into its reasonableness.

---

30. See *In re Heritage Highgate, Inc.*, 679 F.3d 132 (3d Cir. 2012); In re Johnson, 386 B.R. 171 (Bankr. W.D. Pa. 2008).

31. See *Ryan v. Homecomings Financial Network*, 253 F.3d 778 (4th Cir. 2001).

32. Although it does not expressly say so, §506(b) applies only to postpetition interest. Interest that had accrued prior to the petition is added to the claim regardless of whether the claimant is oversecured. If the underlying contract or statute so provides, and if the collateral is valuable enough to accommodate it, the prepetition interest forms part of the secured debt.

If the lien is consensual and the agreement so provides, the claimant can also recover reasonable postpetition costs and fees from the surplus. Unlike interest, these costs and fees are subject to a test of reasonableness, and the court can reduce them even if the contract authorizes them in the amount claimed. In *In re Welzel*, 275 F.3d 1308 (11th Cir. 2001), the court said that even if fees provided for in the contract are reduced as unreasonable, this does not mean that they are disallowed. The unreasonable portion of the costs and fees cannot be paid out of the surplus, but they can be proved in the estate as an unsecured claim.

d. Surcharge: The Costs of Realizing or Preserving the Collateral

The trustee may need to take action to preserve or realize collateral. If so, §506(c) permits the reasonable and necessary costs and expenses of doing so to be recovered from the collateral to the extent of any benefit to the secured claimant. To be recoverable from the collateral, the expenses must be directly related to its preservation or disposition so that the secured claimant benefits by the protection or realization of its interest. (*See* Example 4.) If the expenditure benefits the claimant in part, a pro rata share of it is chargeable against the collateral. Expenses payable under §506(c) take precedence over the claimant's right to recover interest and costs and reduce any surplus that would otherwise be available for those charges.

Although the trustee is able to recover these costs from the secured party, the U.S. Supreme Court held in *Hartford Underwriters Ins. Co. v. Union Planters Bank*, 530 U.S. 1 (2000), that §506(c), by its clear terms, is only available to the trustee. Therefore, if the trustee does not claim the expenses, the party who provided the services has no direct cause of action against the secured party for their recovery.

e. Valuation of the Collateral

The valuation of collateral is obviously crucial to the extent and treatment of a secured claim. Section 506(a)(1) states the general principle that collateral must be valued in light of the purpose of the valuation and of the proposed disposition or use of the property. That is, §502(a)(1) prescribes a rational, fact-based valuation that takes the circumstances and purpose of the valuation into account. For example, if it is apparent that the property is to be liquidated, liquidation value should be used, but if the property is to be used by the debtor or sold on the market, a market-based value makes more sense. Although this general principle is easy to grasp in the abstract, it has proved very difficult to apply. It is not always obvious how the proposed disposition or use is to be defined. Even where a market standard is appropriate, there is often no single market standard, which raises the question of which market standard to use. Finally, once the standard is determined, value is a factual question on which experts can differ.

The U.S. Supreme Court tackled the issue of valuation in *Associates Commercial Corp. v. Rash*, 520 U.S. 953 (1997). In *Rash*, the Ch. 13 debtor proposed to keep a truck that was subject to a security interest. Under Ch. 13, the plan must provide for the payment of the present value of the secured claim. To peg the truck's present value as low as possible, the debtor argued that the liquidation value of the truck was the proper measure because if the debtor's Ch. 13 plan did not provide for his retention of the truck, the creditor would foreclose on it and would sell it at a distress sale. The Court rejected this argument. Because the debtor proposed to keep the truck, the "proposed disposition" under §506(a) was the truck's replacement value—a market standard based on what the debtor would have to pay to acquire the truck on the market. The Court suggested that in calculating the replacement value, it may be appropriate to deduct the seller's costs of sale because the debtor already owned the truck and would not actually be buying it. The opinion in *Rash* was confined to the valuation of collateral in a Ch. 13 case for the purpose of determining the amount to be paid on the claim in the Ch. 13 plan. Although its standard of valuation is based on the general guideline set out in §506(a)(1) and is therefore potentially applicable in all cases, it is not clear how far it extends beyond those facts.

The Bankruptcy Abuse Prevention and Consumer Protection Act of 2005 (BAPCPA) further confused the scope of *Rash* by adding a new subsection (2) to §506(a). Subsection (a)(2) partially codifies *Rash* and partly deviates from it. Also, the subsection is confined to a narrow situation—where the valuation relates to personal property that is collateral for a secured claim in an individual debtor's case under Ch. 7 or 13. It follows *Rash* by providing that the value of property in those circumstances must be based on the replacement value of the property at the date of the petition. However, it does not accept the suggestion in *Rash* that it may be appropriate to deduct the costs of sale and marketing from the replacement value. That is, in the situations in which it applies, §506(a)(2) calls for the use of the actual replacement cost on the market, without any deduction for the costs of sale or marketing. Notwithstanding, some lower courts have taken the saving of these costs into account to some extent by pointing out that "replacement value" is not synonymous with "retail value." Therefore, where the property could be replaced in the market through purchase from a private individual, rather than a dealer, the replacement value could be lower than what a dealer would have to charge to cover its overhead.[33] Section 506(a)(2) does not contain a generally applicable definition of "replacement value," but it does define that term in relation to personal property acquired for personal,

33. See e.g., *In re Henry*, 457 B.R. 402 (Bankr. E.D. Pa. 2011).

family, or household purposes (consumer goods). Where the property securing the debt is consumer goods, replacement value is the price that a retail merchant would charge for property of that kind considering its age and condition at the time of valuation. This has led courts to conclude that the valuation standard differs, depending on whether or not the personal property collateral was bought by the individual Chs. 7 or 13 debtor for personal, family, or household purposes: If the property is not consumer goods, the replacement value must be determined from the debtor's perspective—the price must be based on what a willing debtor would pay to obtain the property on the market. However, if it is consumer goods, the replacement value must be measured from the seller's perspective.[34] This could lead to different values, depending on the purpose for which the debtor purchased the property.

Because §506(a)(2) is only a partial codification of *Rash*, and does not cover exactly the same ground, it leads to the confusing situation in which rules have been established for valuations in some circumstances that may or may not apply in others. In essence, the combined effect of *Rash* and §506(a)(2) seems to be that in cases under Ch. 7 or 13 involving an individual debtor, personal property collateral must be valued under §502(a)(2) by replacement value, not taking costs of sale into account. (*Rash* involved an individual debtor in Ch. 13, so §502(a)(2) affirms the holding but parts company with the Court on the deduction of the seller's costs of sale.) In all other cases, such as those involving real property in a Ch. 13 case, or real or personal property in a case under Chs. 7 or 11 where the debtor is not an individual, §502(a)(2) does not apply, but *Rash* might. Because *Rash* interprets the meaning of the words "intended disposition or use" in §502(a)(1), a good argument can be made that its interpretation is relevant beyond the narrow confines of the facts of the case. Nevertheless, some courts have applied *Rash* narrowly and have held that replacement value is not always the correct standard. For example, in *In re Henderson*, 235 B.R. 425 (Bankr. C.D. Ill. 1999), the court used liquidation value to decide the redemption price of goods under §722 because if the debtor did not redeem, the property would be foreclosed upon.[35]

§17.5.4 Priority Claims

While secured claims are satisfied by the collateral or its proceeds, all other claims are paid from the general fund of the estate. The Code recognizes ten classes of priority unsecured claims that are payable, in descending order,

34. *In re Henry*, *supra*.
35. See also *In re Zell*, 284 B.R. 569 (Bankr. D. Md. 2002).

before general unsecured claims are entitled to any share in the estate. It is worth stressing again that the general rule is that all claims in a class rank equally and are paid pro rata if estate funds are insufficient to pay them in full. As you will see when we look more closely at the various priority categories, there are two exceptions to this general rule in relation to domestic support obligations and administrative expenses.

Prior to 2005, the expenses of administering the estate were given the highest priority. However, BAPCPA elevated claims for domestic support obligations, which formerly had seventh priority, to the position of first priority. As explained in sections 10.8.2 and 13.1.4(7), the Bankruptcy Reform Act of 1994 enacted a set of provisions designed to ensure that a debtor cannot use bankruptcy to escape domestic support obligations. As part of that package of protections, debts due to a spouse, ex-spouse, or children for alimony, maintenance, or support were given a seventh priority. BAPCPA enhanced this protection by ranking those debts (now encompassed within the statutory definition of "domestic support obligations" in §101(14A)) as a first-priority claim, alongside certain claims of the bankruptcy trustee (discussed in the following section).

Administrative expenses occupy the second priority level. As discussed in the following section and in section 15.3, superpriority claims for post-petition financing under §364(c)(1) are at the top of this category and are paid first, followed by superpriority claims under §507(b) to compensate for a failure of adequate protection, followed by other administrative expenses.

Section 507(a) ranks the remaining nine priority categories in order. Every subsection of §507(a) uses the word "allowed" to qualify the claims in each priority class. If a claim is disallowed, it does not participate in the estate as a priority claim or otherwise. Also, many of the priority categories have monetary limits. To the extent that a claim exceeds the limit, the overage is a general unsecured claim. It is therefore possible for a single debt to be partly a priority claim and partly a general claim. Where a priority category has a dollar limit, that limit is administratively adjusted every three years based on changes in the Consumer Price Index. Section 507(a) is one of the sections included in §104, which provides for these periodic administrative adjustments. The amounts were last adjusted on April 1, 2016, and will be adjusted again on April 1, 2019.[36]

The more common and important priority categories are explained below.[37] Congress has chosen to give these claims priority because it believes that the claims are worthier of payment than claims in a lower

---

36. *See* section 3.4.3 for an explanation of the periodic adjustment of dollar amounts in the Code.

37. Other priority categories that are not discussed further are sixth-priority claims of grain farmers and fishermen for produce deposited with the debtor; seventh-priority claims for a

class. The policy of preferring administrative expenses makes practical sense because if they were not given a high priority it would be difficult to find people who would be willing to perform services for the estate. The other classes of priority claims are given priority because Congress decided that these types of claims should be singled out from other unsecured claims and given special treatment. Although these priority claims are surely deserving, the reason for prioritizing some claims over others is not always entirely clear. Further, Congress's rationale for ranking claims in a particular order is similarly opaque.

Priority rules interact with the provisions relating to discharge, discussed in Chapter 21. Where a priority debt is also nondischargeable, the debtor is benefited by the priority status of the debt. Because the debt has priority, it is more likely to be paid in the bankruptcy, which means that there is a better chance that the debtor will not have responsibility for it after the case.

(1) First-priority domestic support obligations (§507(a)(1)). As noted above, §101(14A) defines "domestic support obligation," which covers debts in the nature of alimony, maintenance, or support, established by a separation agreement, divorce decree, property settlement agreement, court order, or determination of a governmental unit. The debt must be owed to or recoverable by a spouse, former spouse, child, the guardian or other person responsible for the child, or a governmental unit. The definition makes it clear that it is a question of fact whether a debt qualifies as a domestic support obligation irrespective of how the parties may have labeled or structured it. The types of obligation covered by the definition of "domestic support obligation" are quite wide. They extend beyond obligations payable directly to the spouse or dependent to include obligations to governmental agencies and others who have furnished support or assistance to the dependents. Courts have tended to read the definition broadly. For example, in *Wisconsin Dept. of Workforce Development v. Ratliff*, 390 B.R. 607 (E.D. Wis. 2008), the court granted first-priority status to the government agency's claim for repayment of food stamp overpayments made to the debtor, and used for the support of the debtor's dependent children. Further, the section affords first-priority status to the fees of a guardian ad litem appointed to represent the debtor's minor child and "other identified relationships standing in loco parentis to the child of the debtor."[38]

---

deposit paid by a consumer to the debtor for future goods or services that were not provided (for example, a down payment or possibly even a full advance payment to a retailer or provider of services); ninth-priority claims based on a debtor depository institution's commitment to governmental units that insure deposits; and tenth-priority claims for death or personal injury resulting from the debtor's driving of a vehicle while under the influence of alcohol or drugs.

38. *In re Etnire*, 568 B.R. 80, 83 (Bankr. C.D. Ill. 2017).

Section 507(a)(1) does not follow the usual principle of treating all claims in the same-priority category equally. It breaks the first priority into three subcategories, (A), (B), and (C), and prioritizes those categories. The claims that must be satisfied first are those listed last in subsection (C)—administrative expenses under §503(b)(1)(A), (2), and (6)—that is, the actual necessary costs and expenses of the trustee and the trustee's fee "to the extent that the trustee administers assets that are otherwise available for the payment of . . ." claims in subsections (A) and (B). While the exact meaning of this convoluted language is elusive, the idea seems to be that although other administrative expenses are paid after domestic support obligations, the trustee's fees and expenses that are directly related to the administration of assets used to pay domestic support obligations must be paid as a very top priority. Therefore, a trustee is incentivized to administer assets to pay for domestic support obligations. Claims under subsection (A) are paid next. These are, in essence, allowed claims for domestic support obligations owed directly to the spouse, ex-spouse, child, or the child's legal guardian or responsible relative. Claims under subsection (B) are paid last. These are allowed claims for domestic support obligations that are assigned to or owed directly to a governmental unit.

(2) Second-priority administrative expenses (§507(a)(2)). Unlike most other claims against the estate, administrative expenses are incurred after the petition has been filed. They are given high priority because the costs of administering the estate are meant to benefit creditors as a whole, and also because it would be difficult to find anyone to provide services or supplies to the estate without a reasonable assurance of being paid. The kinds of claims that are entitled to administrative priority are described in §503(b). The broadest group of expenses are the actual and necessary costs of preserving the estate referred to in §503(b)(1)(A). This encompasses all manner of expenditures deemed by the court to be reasonable in advancing the estate's interests, preserving or enhancing its assets, or furthering the debtor's efforts at rehabilitation. In addition to this general species of expense, §503(b) includes items such as trustee compensation, fees for professional services, and postpetition taxes due by the estate. Also, as mentioned in Chapters 15 and 16, the estate's obligations for postpetition credit and the performance of executory contracts are administrative expenses. The list in §503(b) is not definitive, and the court has the discretion to approve other expenses for inclusion in this category.[39] Administrative expense claims are illustrated in Examples 4 and 5(f).

39. Civil liabilities for wrongful acts by the estate's representative are commonly treated as administrative expenses because they are committed in the course of the estate's business. However, it is unclear that every liability for wrongful conduct by the estate's representatives should be treated as an administrative expense. For example, in *Pennsylvania Dept. of Environmental*

For the most part, all administrative expenses rank equally in accordance with the general principle that all claims in a class are of equal rank. However, recall that there are two classes of superpriority claim that take precedence over administrative expenses. Superpriority claims for postpetition financing under §364(c)(1) occupy the most senior position, and are given "priority over any or all administrative expenses." Next in line are superpriority claims under §507(b), which have "priority over every other claim allowable under [§507(a)(2)]."[40] Thereafter, all administrative expenses are of equal rank.

The ranking of administrative expenses breaks into two priority categories where a rehabilitation case under Chs. 11, 12 or 13 is converted to Ch. 7. Section 726(b) subordinates the preconversion administrative expenses to the postconversion Ch. 7 administrative expenses. The reason for this is that the administrative expenses of the failed reorganization could be significant, and unless the expenses of liquidating the estate are given preference, there may not be enough funds in the estate to cover them. Most courts that have considered the question have held that when a case is converted to Ch. 7, the priority given to the Ch. 7 administrative expenses by §726(b) takes precedence over all priority claims arising prior to the conversion, including superpriority claims under §§364(c)(1) and 507(b).[41] However, some courts read the language of §§726(b) and 364(c)(1) differently.[42]

(3) Third-priority "gap" administrative expenses (§§502(f) and 507(a)(3)). In an involuntary case, the debtor is entitled to continue operating its business or conducting its financial affairs in the period between the petition and the order for relief or appointment of a trustee. Section 502(f) allows as a claim against the estate expenses incurred by the debtor in the ordinary course of business or financial affairs. Section 503(b) expressly excludes these expenses from second-priority administrative expenses, but §507(a)(3) gives them third priority so they are paid immediately after administrative expenses. (*See* Example 5(c).)

Resources v. Tri-State Clinical Laboratories, Inc., 178 F.3d 685 (3d Cir. 1999), the court refused to give administrative expense priority to a fine imposed on the estate for the unlawful disposal of waste, because this would have the effect of making junior creditors pay the penalty for the estate's unlawful activity.

40. These superpriority categories are explained in section 17.6.2.

41. See *In re Visionaire Corp.*, 290 B.R. 348 (Bankr. E.D. Mo. 2003) *aff'd as to this aspect of the opinion by* 299 B.R. 530 (B.A.P. 8th Cir. 2003) (holding that §726(b)'s language is absolute in giving postconversion expenses priority over a preconversion superpriority claim under §364(c)(1)).

42. See *In re Mayco Plastics, Inc.*, 379 B.R. 691 (Bankr. E.D. Mich. 2008) (explaining that by giving a superpriority claim priority over all administrative expenses, §364(c)(1) elevates the claim over both preconversion and postconversion administrative expenses).

(4) Fourth-priority salary and wage claims (§507(a)(4)). The fourth priority provides limited protection to claims of the debtor's employees[43] for wages, salary, or commission (including vacation, severance, or sick-leave pay) that was unpaid at the time of bankruptcy. The Bankruptcy Reform Act of 1994 added to this category individuals (or corporations with only one employee) who, while they are independent contractors and not technically employees, earn a large portion of their livelihood (75 percent or more of their income) from commissions paid to them by the debtor for the sale of goods or services.

The extent of fourth-priority claims is curtailed by both time period and amount. The modest dollar limit and relatively short temporal limit mean that the protection of priority will provide only a modicum of security to workers whose wages are unpaid at the time of bankruptcy. There is a $12,850[44] limit on each claim, and the remuneration must have been earned within 180 days of the petition or, if the debtor ceased business before that, within 180 days of the closing of the business. To the extent that the employee's claim exceeds these limits, it is a general unsecured claim. The fourth priority includes not only the employee's net earnings but also taxes due by the employee on those earnings, which should be withheld from her pay. These fourth-priority taxes due by the employee must be distinguished from employment taxes due by the debtor-employer and taxes that have already been withheld by the debtor-employer, both of which fall into the eighth-priority category. The fourth priority covers only prepetition earnings. If the debtor's business is operated by the trustee after the petition, the salary of employees for that period is an administrative expense entitled to first priority. (*See* Example 5(c).)

(5) Fifth-priority contributions to employee benefit plans (§507(a)(5)). The fifth priority must be taken in conjunction with the fourth. The purpose of the fifth priority is to cover fringe benefits that complete an employee's pay package, but which do not count as wages or salary under the fourth priority. The priority includes contributions to employee benefit plans, such as pensions, life insurance, or health insurance. It is not always clear if a particular program provided by an employer for its employees qualifies as an employee benefit plan. For example, prior to 2006, several bankruptcy courts had looked to the ERISA to determine if a program qualified. However, in *In re Howard Delivery*

---

43. Whether an employer/employee relationship exists is a fact-intensive inquiry, invariably requiring the court to look to state law. Most courts have held that for a claim to qualify for §507(a)(4)(A) wage priority, the debtor-employer must exert a substantial measure of control over the claimant's conduct.

44. This is the amount adjusted under §104 on April 1, 2016. It will be adjusted again on April 1, 2019.

Service, Inc., 547 U.S. 651 (2006), the Supreme Court held that if Congress had intended for courts to reference ERISA, the statute would have unequivocally referred to ERISA in §507(a)(5). The court held that ERISA is not to be the source in determining whether a claim falls within the confines of the phrase "contributions to an employee benefit plan." Indeed, this evaluation should be dictated by the essential character of the workers' compensation regime. Ultimately, the Court ruled that premiums owed to an employment compensation insurer did not qualify as contributions to an employee benefit plan because the insurance primarily benefited the employer by indemnifying it from liability to its workers for employment-related injuries.

Payments to employees for salary or wages under the fourth priority reduces the amount payable under the fifth because the fourth- and fifth-priority categories have a combined $12,850[45] cap per employee, with wage and salary claims paid first. Each plan's priority is limited to contributions relating to services rendered by covered employees in the 180 days before the earlier of the filing of the petition or the cessation of the debtor's business. The priority is also limited in amount. It cannot exceed $12,850 multiplied by the number of employees covered by the plan, less the aggregate amount paid to covered employees as salary or wages under the fourth priority. If there is more than one employee benefit plan, then the total payable to all plans under the fifth priority, together with amounts paid to covered employees under the fourth priority, cannot exceed the number of covered employees multiplied by $12,850.

(6) Eighth-priority taxes (§507(a)(8)). The eighth priority covers a variety of taxes due to governmental units, defined in §101(27) to include federal, state, and local governments. Taxes that receive priority under §507(a)(8) are nondischargeable under §523(a)(1). In rehabilitation cases, these priority taxes must be paid in full under the plan unless the taxing authority agrees otherwise. In a Ch. 7 case, if the fund is inadequate to pay eighth-priority taxes in full, the debtor remains liable after bankruptcy for any unpaid balance. When there are sufficient estate funds to pay claims through the eighth priority, but not enough to pay general unsecured claims as well, the debtor benefits and general creditors are prejudiced by this priority for nondischargeable taxes. Indeed, payment of the taxes from the estate exhausts the fund that would otherwise have been distributed to the general creditors, while eliminating or reducing the debtor's nondischargeable liability for the taxes. Under the right circumstances, the

45. This is the amount under §104 adjusted on April 1, 2016. It will be adjusted again on April 1, 2019.

debtor's taxes are, in effect, paid by unsecured creditors. Although this may sound outrageous, bear in mind that federal and state governments have powerful collection rights under nonbankruptcy law too, and can usually trump unsecured creditors by perfecting a statutory lien on all the debtor's property.

A number of different taxes are included in the eighth priority. Many of them have priority only to the extent that they became due within a specified time before bankruptcy. Generally, eighth priority is given to income taxes for three to four years prior to the petition; property taxes payable in the year before bankruptcy; "trust fund" taxes that the debtor withheld from its employees' salaries but failed to transmit to the taxing authority; employment taxes due by the debtor itself and payable by the debtor within approximately three years of bankruptcy (which differ from withholding taxes in that the debtor, rather than the employee, is liable for them); certain excise and customs duties; and compensatory penalties due on other eighth-priority taxes. (Example 5(e) illustrates the tax priority.)

One of three alternative timing conditions must be met for a tax claim measured on income or gross receipts to be afforded priority. The first one is where a tax return, for the tax claim in question, was last due (including extensions) at some point after three years before the petition date.[46] The subsection's focus is on the date that a return is last due (including extensions, if any). For example, imagine that March 1, 2016 is the debtor's petition date. The debtor has unpaid taxes for the years 2011 and 2012. The debtor's federal income tax returns for 2011 and 2012 were last due (including extensions) on April 17, 2012, and April 15, 2013, respectively. Are both tax claims entitled to priority? The answer is no. The 2012 tax return was due within three years before the petition date, and the taxes associated with that return would be entitled to priority treatment. On the other hand, the 2011 tax return was due outside of the three-year look-back period described above. The taxes associated with that year would not be entitled to priority treatment, but they may qualify as nondischargeable debt.

The second possible timing condition for a tax claim measured on income or gross receipts to qualify for section 507(a)(8)(A) status is where the taxes were assessed within 240 days before the petition date. This 240-day period is then increased by any time during which an offer in compromise with respect to the tax was pending or in effect during the 240 days after which the assessment was pending, plus 30 days, and any time during which a stay of

46. Section 507(a)(8)(A)(i) refers to when a tax return is "due." However, should the debtor obtain any type of extension, the relative due date would be the extended filing date and not the original due date. See *In re Carlin*, 318 B.R. 556, 561 (Bankr. D. Kan. 2004), *aff'd* 328 B.R. 221 (B.A.P. 10th Cir. 2005).

proceedings against collections was in effect in a prior bankruptcy case during the 240-day period, plus 90 days. Unlike the first timing condition prescribed by §507(a)(8)(A)(i), under §507(a)(8)(A)(ii) the tax return due date is immaterial. The dispositive date is when the tax was first assessed against the debtor.[47]

Finally, §507(a)(8)(A)(iii) also grants priority status to a tax claim on or measured by income or gross receipts for a taxable year ending on or before the petition date if the tax was not assessed previously and the tax is assessable under applicable law or by agreement after the commencement of the case, *except* for a tax of the kind specified in section 523(a)(1)(B) and (C).[48] This final provision addresses those taxes where taxable activities or events actually occurred prepetition, but taxes were not able to be assessed until after the case was commenced. This provision addresses situations where an audit is being undertaken even though the taxes themselves were assessable prior to the petition date. Further, where an audit goes on for many years, §507(a)(8)(A)(iii) would then be able to capture those taxes that may otherwise be far outside of §507(a)(8)(i)'s three-year look-back period.

§17.5.5 General Unsecured Claims and Lower Classes

As stated already, general unsecured claims share pro rata in any fund remaining after all priority claims have been paid. All unsecured claims that do not qualify for priority fit into this category, as well as any deficiency due on undersecured claims and any amount over the limit on priority claims. (*See* Example 5.) Because most bankrupt estates are insolvent, general unsecured claims often receive only a partial distribution or are discharged with no payment at all. When the estate is solvent and general claims are paid in full, any remaining funds are distributed to the lowest-priority claims listed in Diagram 17a.

---

47. Consequently, there is a possibility of overlap between sections 507(a)(8)(A)(i) and 507(a)(8)(A)(ii). Indeed, a tax return could be due within the three years prior to bankruptcy and also involve a tax that was assessed within the 240-day period prior to the petition date.

48. Section 523 sets forth various claims that are nondischargeable in bankruptcy. Section 523(a)(1)(B) addresses taxes or custom duties with respect to which a required return was not filed or was filed after its due date and within the two years preceding the petition date. Section 523(a)(1)(C) are taxes or custom duties with respect to which the debtor made a fraudulent return or willfully attempted in any manner to evade or defeat the tax. These two types of taxes are specifically not granted priority under §507(a)(8)(A)(iii).

§17.6 SUBORDINATION OF CLAIMS

Subordination is the demotion of a claim. In nonbankruptcy law, subordination may result from agreement or it may be imposed upon a claimant by a court of equity. Section 510 recognizes both these forms of subordination in bankruptcy.[49]

§17.6.1 Consensual Subordination

A senior claimant may agree to subordinate its claim to induce another person to enter into a desirable transaction with the debtor. Say, for example, that a secured party has a security interest in the debtor's equipment. The debtor wishes to borrow money from another lender to upgrade the equipment, and the second lender will only advance the funds if it is given a first-priority security interest in the equipment to secure the loan. If the senior secured party believes that the equipment in its present state may not be worth enough to fully cover its loan, and that the renovations will enhance the equipment's value beyond the amount of the second secured loan, it may be willing to make an agreement with the second lender to subordinate its otherwise senior lien to that of the second lender. Section 510(a) recognizes such subordination agreements and makes them enforceable in bankruptcy to the extent that they are enforceable in nonbankruptcy law. Courts have held that subordination agreements do not need to be in any particular form or even in writing.[50]

---

49. Subordination must be distinguished from recharacterization. Recharacterization of a claim could have a similar impact as subordination, but it is a distinct remedy. Recharacterization focuses on the underlying substance of a disputed transaction to determine whether the party advancing funds is properly characterized as holding a debt or an equity investment in the debtor. More specifically, recharacterization is a determination by the court that a claim asserted by a claimant is improperly characterized as a claim but is more appropriately treated as an investment in the debtor. Recharacterization does not lower the rank of a claim because of the claimant's conduct; rather, it is the result of the court finding that the claimant is not a creditor at all because the underlying purpose of the transaction was not a loan to the debtor, but an investment in the debtor. The focus here is not on inequitable conduct, but on the underlying substance of the transaction. As discussed below, subordination applies where equity demands that the payment priority of one claim be altered to fall behind those of other claimants.

50. See, e.g., *Advanced Analytics Labs., Inc. v. Environmental Aspecs, Inc. of N.C. (In re Environmental Aspecs, Inc.)*, 235 B.R. 378, 396–97 (E.D.N.C. 1999) and *In re Howland*, 545 B.R. 653, 659 (Bankr. D. Or. 2015).

§17.6.2 Equitable Subordination

Courts of equity have the power to subordinate a claim where the equities so dictate. Section 510(c) authorizes the bankruptcy court to use principles of equitable subordination to reduce the rank of all or part of an allowed claim. Subordination is a drastic and unusual remedy that should be applied only to address "seriously" inequitable conduct.[51] If the subordinated claim is secured, the court may transfer the lien to the estate.

Courts generally require the satisfaction of three conditions before considering equitable subordination: 1) the claimant must have engaged in some type of "seriously" inequitable conduct; 2) the misconduct must have resulted in injury to the creditors of the debtor or conferred an unfair advantage on the claimant; and 3) subordination must not be inconsistent with the express provisions of the Code. Subordination is meant to be an adjustment of rank to correct inequitable conduct that will produce injustice or unfairness to the creditor body in a case; the relief is not intended to simply penalize the claimant. Consequently, the general rule is that a claim is subordinated only to the extent necessary to rectify harm. For example, if a senior secured claimant caused harm to a junior lienholder by making a misrepresentation to it, the appropriate remedy is to subordinate the senior claim to the junior one. However, particularly harmful and inequitable conduct could justify a dramatic reduction in rank.[52] Although the use of equitable subordination is clearly warranted where harm is caused by inequitable conduct, it is not clear if a court has the discretion to subordinate a claim on general equitable considerations in the absence of wrongful conduct by the subordinated creditor.

In *United States v. Noland*, 517 U.S. 535 (1996), the U.S. Supreme Court cast doubt on the propriety of equitable subordination in the absence of inequitable conduct by the creditor. The claim subordinated by the bankruptcy court was an administrative expense claim for nonpecuniary tax penalties owed by the estate to the I.R.S. The I.R.S. had not acted inequitably. Nevertheless, the bankruptcy court subordinated its claim on the premise that it was unfair to pay nonpecuniary penalties ahead of the claims of general creditors. Although the Court did not decide if creditor misconduct must always be found as a basis for equitable subordination, it did hold that a court should not simply subordinate a claim because it considers it unfair to pay it in priority over claims in a lower class. Congress has set the priorities for payment, and it is not up to a court to use the equity powers recognized by §510(c) to reorder these priorities because it perceives the Code's ranking to be unfair.

---

51. See *Carhart v. Carhart–Halaska Int'l, LLC*, 788 F.3d 687, 692 (7th Cir. 2015).

52. See, e.g., *In re Fabricators, Inc.*, 926 F.2d 1458 (5th Cir. 1991); *In re Lemco Gypsum, Inc.*, 911 F.2d 1553 (11th Cir. 1990); and *In re Giorgio*, 862 F.2d 933 (1st Cir. 1988).

EXAMPLES

Examples

1. Included in the Ch. 7 estate of Lester Pay is a house worth $100,000, subject to a mortgage held by Mori Bond Co. securing a debt of $120,000.
   a. Must Mori Bond Co. prove a claim in the estate to preserve its rights or to receive payment of its claim?
   b. Assume that the trustee abandoned the property as having no value or benefit to the estate. Because the property has been abandoned, Mori Bond may apply for relief from stay and foreclose on it immediately, or wait to foreclose after the case is closed. Lester commences proceedings to have the mortgage declared void under §506(d) to the extent that the debt exceeds the value of the collateral (i.e., by $20,000), and to peg the value of the secured claim at $100,000. Can Lester do this?
2. Cess Pools, Inc. manufactures pool chemicals. Some years ago it developed a revolutionary chemical that kept water clearer and brighter than any competing product. After the chemical had been marketed successfully for several years, it was discovered to be carcinogenic. Because it had been so popular, countless people had been exposed to it. Several hundred had already become ill, and an unknown number of people will probably develop cancer in the future as a result of contact with the chemical. In the face of this widespread tort liability, Cess Pools, Inc. has filed a Ch. 11 petition. Do the people with cancer have claims against the estate? How about the people who have been exposed to the chemical but do not have cancer?
3. In the course of manufacturing the chemicals described in Example 2, Cess Pools, Inc. discharged hazardous substances into the ground. These discharges occurred prior to Cess Pools' bankruptcy and have since ceased because Cess Pools no longer makes the chemicals. Shortly before Cess Pools filed its Ch. 11 petition, the EPA identified the polluted land as requiring cleanup. Although the EPA could have ordered Cess Pools to clean up the waste, it exercised its statutory right to restore the site itself and to claim reimbursement from Cess Pools. No cleanup work had begun by the time of Cess Pools's bankruptcy, and the exact extent of the pollution and the cost of restoration are not yet known.

   The EPA contends that its future claim for reimbursement following cleanup is not a dischargeable claim against Cess Pools's Ch. 11 estate, but will become a debt payable in full from the assets of the reorganized debtor. Is the EPA correct?
4. Prior to its bankruptcy under Ch. 7, Withering Heights, Inc. owned and operated an office building. The property is subject to a mortgage securing a debt that exceeds the building's market value. The trustee continued to manage the building for a few months after the petition was filed,

pending a determination of its value and a decision on what should be done with it. Eventually the building was abandoned to the mortgagee as having no value or benefit to the estate. During the period that the estate operated the building, the power company continued to supply electricity that was needed to keep the building habitable by tenants and to allow its electronic security system to function. The electricity bills for this period have not been paid. How should they be treated?

5. Trickle Downs, Inc. owned and managed an apartment complex. A group of its creditors petitioned to place it in Ch. 7 bankruptcy. A week after the petition, an interim trustee was appointed. The order for relief was granted a few weeks later. The trustee has sold the apartment complex as well as other estate property, and the estate will soon be distributed. Rank the following claims that have been proved and allowed in the case:
   a. A first mortgage on the apartment complex, recorded ten years ago.
   b. A second mortgage on the complex, recorded five years ago.
   c. Salary due to the manager of the complex for the month prior to the petition and the month thereafter.
   d. The manager's claim for breach of contract, arising from the estate's termination of his employment contract a month after the petition. At that time, the term of the contract had two more years to run.
   e. Property taxes on the complex for the two years prior to the petition.
   f. An attorney's fee for services rendered to the trustee in connection with the sale of the complex.
   g. A claim by a landscaping service company for maintenance work done in the months before the petition and for damages for breach of contract arising out of the trustee's rejection of the contract for future services.
   h. Various claims by trade creditors that provided services and supplies to Trickle Downs in the months before bankruptcy.

Explanations

EXPLANATIONS

1. a. Must Mori Bond prove a claim? A secured claim need not be proved to preserve the lien. Even though the debtor's personal obligation is dischargeable, the lien survives the bankruptcy provided that it is valid and not disallowed on grounds other than the lienholder's failure to prove a claim. However, Mori Bond is undersecured. If it wishes to receive a distribution on its deficiency (provided, of course, that nonbankruptcy law permits a mortgagee to claim a deficiency), it must prove a claim.
   b. Is the mortgage void under §506(d) to the extent of the deficiency? Lester's purpose is to peg the mortgage debt at the level of the current value of the property—that is, to have the court declare that the undischarged mortgage survives the bankruptcy only to the extent

of $100,000, not to the full extent of the debt of $120,000. The advantage to Lester is that if the property appreciates before foreclosure so that it realizes more than $100,000, any surplus will belong to Lester and cannot be claimed by the mortgagee up to the amount of $120,000. Another advantage would be that if Lester was able to redeem the property, the redemption price would be $100,000 rather than $120,000, irrespective of any appreciation in the property. The tactic being tried by Lester is called "lien stripping." As discussed in section 17.5.3, *Dewsnup v. Timm* precludes a Ch. 7 debtor from stripping down a consensual mortgage. Even though the reach of the case is uncertain beyond that, it clearly applies here, and the mortgage survives to the full extent of $120,000, even though Lester's personal liability is discharged.

2. The people who are already stricken clearly have claims against the estate. These claims may still be unliquidated or disputed, but they qualify as claims under §101(5). During the course of the case, their claims will be resolved by litigation or negotiation. Under §502(c), the claims can be estimated if the normal process of resolution would cause undue delay in the administration of the case.

   The people who have been exposed to the chemical but are still healthy are potential claimants: The harmful act has been committed, but it has not yet caused physical injury. Some of these people will become ill, and others will not. As explained in section 17.4, they could be treated as the holders of contingent claims against the estate, but they might be treated as having no claim against the estate at all, which would leave them with a postbankruptcy claim against the debtor if and when they do become ill. Different courts have developed the different tests identified in section 17.4 for trying to resolve this issue.

   The decision on whether to treat potential liability as a prepetition contingent claim or a postbankruptcy claim has significant consequences for claimants, the estate, and the debtor. If Cess Pools, Inc. has a good prospect of successful reorganization, potential victims may do better if their claims are treated as arising postpetition, because they can be asserted against the rehabilitated debtor when they arise, and need not be proved in the estate for fractional distribution. This classification creates serious trouble for Cess Pools, Inc., which cannot settle its liability in the bankruptcy case. If Cess Pools's prospects of survival following reorganization are not good, potential claimants are better served by having their claims treated as contingent. This allows them to prove claims in the estate so that they can share in the fund. (The same would be true if the debtor is to be liquidated: Because it will not survive the bankruptcy, the characterization of the incipient claims as contingent prepetition claims allows the potential victims to participate in the estate.) If the claims are treated as contingent, they must be estimated by taking into account both the likely extent of injury and the probability of contracting the disease.

3. Because the EPA has chosen to restore the site and claim the costs of doing so, its reimbursement claim is a right to payment under §101(5), and therefore a claim as determined by the U.S. Supreme Court in *Ohio v. Kovacs*, discussed in section 17.2.1. If the EPA's claim is treated as a prepetition claim, it is a general unsecured claim against the estate. However, if it arose postpetition, it could be classified as an administrative expense or a post-petition claim against the reorganized debtor. It is therefore important to determine when the claim arose. As explained in section 17.2.5, the dating of the claim can be difficult in situations like this. It could be seen as arising postpetition, when the cleanup costs are incurred, or it could arise pre-petition, when liability was created by the act of pollution. If it arises prepetition, it is a contingent claim (conditional on the EPA performing the cleanup), but a contingent claim does qualify as a claim under §101(5). In deciding when a claim such as this arises, most courts do not use a mechanical test to select one or the other of these times, but use a more sophisticated test based on the reasonable or fair contemplation of the parties, as explained in section 17.2.5: The claim arose when the EPA became aware of the pollution and could reasonably or fairly have contemplated that the site would require remediation. Our facts are not full enough to enable us to decide at what point the EPA can be taken to have contemplated that Cess Pools's site would require remediation, which shows that this standard is much more complex than a test based on an identifiable, discrete event. To answer the question, the court will have to conduct a factual inquiry into the history of the EPA's relationship with the debtor and the site, including the extent of its investigation and the action taken over a period of time.

   The court's effort to date the claim performs the kind of policy balancing that was mentioned in Example 2 of Chapter 3 and in section 3.5: When bankruptcy policy pulls in a different direction from the policies served by another federal statute, the court must try to balance and reconcile the conflicting aims of the statutes as well as it can. The inclusion of the cleanup obligation as a claim in the estate serves at least two bankruptcy goals. It permits the debtor a fresh start by discharging the claim, and it advances the aim of evenhanded treatment of creditors by according the environmental claim no higher status than any other claim of its class. This must be balanced against the dominant goal of environmental legislation to ensure that the person responsible for pollution, rather than the public treasury, pays for its remediation. Treating the cleanup responsibility as a postbankruptcy claim will usually best serve this goal unless the debtor has no assets and no likelihood of rehabilitation.

4. Provided that the trustee had court authority to operate the debtor's business under §721 for the purpose of orderly liquidation, the electricity charges qualify as an administrative expense under §§364(a), 503(b)(1), and 507(a)(2). However, the trustee may argue that the consumption of electricity was a reasonable, necessary expense for the preservation of the building that was incurred for the benefit of the mortgagee. As such, it is recoverable from the property under §506(c).

   In *In re Delta Towers, Ltd.*, 924 F.2d 74 (5th Cir. 1991), the case on which this question is based, it was conceded that the expenses were necessary and reasonable, which is probably true in the present case as well. The focus was therefore on the issue of whether they were beneficial to the mortgagee. The court emphasized that the expenses must be primarily for the benefit of the secured claimant, and that the benefit must be quantifiable and direct—it is not enough that some tangential or speculative benefit is conferred. The court concluded that no such direct benefit was received by the mortgagee. Its interest extended only to the property itself and was not enhanced or protected by the continued supply of utilities that were not needed to prevent deterioration of the property or to maintain its realizable value.

   The question of benefit is a factual one, and it does not inevitably follow that the present case would be resolved the same way as *Delta Towers* was. The facts indicate that power was needed to operate a security system and to allow tenants to inhabit the building. It could be argued that the security system protected the building itself (rather than only the tenants), and that failure to provide the tenants with services would have resulted in lease cancellations that would have reduced the building's value. The facts would need to be examined more fully to decide if these arguments are tenable. If the electricity costs were partially beneficial to the mortgagee, they must be apportioned so that only those attributable to the preservation of the property are charged against it.

5. These claims should be ranked as follows.

   a.-b. The first and second mortgages are secured claims that will both be paid in full out of the proceeds of the apartment complex—provided that the property realizes enough to cover them both. If the property's proceeds are sufficient to cover both mortgages, their relative priority is not practically significant because they are both paid in full. As there do not appear to be interests in the property junior to the mortgages, any surplus goes into the general fund of the estate for ultimate distribution to unsecured creditors. However, if the property is not valuable enough to pay both claims in full, they must be ranked. The order of priority between them is determined by nonbankruptcy law, which most likely follows the first-in-time rule based on the date of recording the mortgages. Therefore, for example, if the proceeds are sufficient to pay the first mortgage in full but only to satisfy the second in part, the deficiency due to the second mortgagee is a general unsecured claim. Of course, the claims set out in (c) through (h) will only be paid to the extent that there are funds in the estate. Therefore, once the priority rank of the claims is determined, each class will be paid in order until the fund runs out.

c. The manager's salary for the month prior to the petition is a fourth-priority claim under §507(a)(4), but only to the extent of $12,850. If the claim is larger than that, the excess is a general unsecured claim. The manager's salary for the month after the petition should be split into two. The salary for the week between the petition and the appointment of the trustee is a claim under §502(f). It seems to be an ordinary-course expense incurred by the debtor in operating its business before the trustee's appointment in an involuntary case. As such, it is excluded from administrative expenses by §503(b) and is given third priority by §507(a)(3).

   The claim for salary for the period following the trustee's appointment arises out of the trustee's short-term operation of the debtor's business in the course of liquidation. Provided that the court authorized this operation under §721, the claim results from the ordinary course of operating the debtor's business as permitted by §364(a), and it is a second-priority administrative expense claim under §507(a)(2).

   In summary, the salary debt due to the manager splits into three separate claims, having second, third, and fourth priority. In addition, if the prepetition claim exceeds $12,850, the debt also produces a fourth claim that is a nonpriority general claim.

d. The manager's damages claim for breach of contract arises out of the estate's rejection of the executory employment contract. As discussed in Chapter 16, §365(g) treats the rejection as a prepetition breach and §502(g) provides for the damages claim to be handled as if it arose prepetition. Section 502(b)(7) disallows the claim for damages to the extent that it exceeds one year's compensation measured from the petition date or the date on which the employee's performance terminated. Therefore, not only is this claim a general unsecured claim, but it will also be reduced to the extent that it exceeds the limits imposed by §502(b)(7).

e. Property taxes qualify for eighth priority under §507(a)(8)(B) provided that they were assessed before the petition and were last payable, without penalty, within a year of the petition. The tax claim represents two years' unpaid property taxes. Although the latest year probably satisfies the conditions for priority, the tax for the prior year only does so if the debtor could have paid it in the year before bankruptcy without being liable for a penalty. The state tax statute must be consulted to determine this. To the extent that the tax claim does not qualify for eighth priority, it is a general unsecured claim. (The exception to discharge in §523(a)(1) does not apply to the portion of the tax that does not qualify for priority status.)

f. The attorney's fee relating to the sale of the complex is a cost of administering and liquidating the estate. It qualifies as an administrative expense under §503(b)(2), provided that the trustee's employment of the attorney is authorized under §327 and the fee is awarded by the court under §330. As an administrative expense, it is given second priority under §507(a)(2).

g. The landscape company's claim for prepetition work fits into no priority category. It is a general unsecured claim. The same is true of the damages claim for breach arising out of the rejection of the executory contract which, like the manager's claim, is deemed to be a general unsecured prepetition claim. Unlike the manager's claim, there is no limit imposed by §502 on the extent of damages claimable.

h. The trade claims are all general unsecured claims.

In summary, the claims are ranked in the following order:

Secured Claims (to the extent of the proceeds of the collateral):

1. First mortgage
2. Second mortgage

Priority Claims:

Second	Manager's salary for period after trustee's appointment attorney's fee
Third	Manager's salary during gap between petition and trustee's appointment
Fourth	Manager's prepetition salary, up to $12,850
Eighth	Property taxes, to the extent that they qualify under §507(a)(8)(B)

General Unsecured Claims (all of equal rank):

Deficiency on mortgages, if any
Property taxes, to the extent not qualified for eighth priority
Manager's prepetition salary above $12,850
Manager's claim for breach of contract, subject to limit in §507(b)(7) Landscape company's claims for prepetition work and for damages for breach of contract
Trade claims

CHAPTER 18

Debt Adjustment Under Chapter 13

§18.1 OVERVIEW

Many of the general principles of bankruptcy law, discussed in previous chapters, are applicable in a Ch. 13 case. However, the focus of this chapter is on the details of Ch. 13 bankruptcy, especially on the proceedings themselves and the mandatory and permissive standards for confirming a Ch. 13 plan. Unlike Ch. 7, in which the debtor's nonexempt assets are liquidated and the proceeds distributed to creditors, Ch. 13 is designed to enable the debtor to keep all or most of her property and to use part of future income over a period of years to pay creditors at least as much as — and ideally more than — they would have received from the liquidation of prepetition assets.[1]

The debtor commences a Ch. 13 case by filing a plan and schedules under §1321. An estate is created immediately under §1306 and a trustee is appointed under §1302. Sections 1322 and 1325 set out the required and permissive contents of the plan and the standards for its confirmation. These sections are the core of Ch. 13. The principal provisions of §1322, governing the content of the plan, provide for what the plan must include (§1322(a)) and what it may include (§1322(b)). Section 1322(c) permits

1. Refer back to section 5.8 for a summary of the principal differences between Ch. 13 and the other forms of bankruptcy. It is a general policy of bankruptcy law to favor rehabilitation under Ch. 13 over liquidation under Ch. 7, on the theory that creditors are likely to do better in a Ch. 13 case. Whether or not this assumption is correct, it motivates the means test of §707(b), discussed in section 6.8, which restricts the use of Ch. 7 as an alternative to Ch. 13 where a consumer debtor is deemed able to afford a Ch. 13 plan.

the plan to modify the rights of certain claimants and to cure prepetition default. Section 1322(d) specifies the maximum and minimum payout period allowed for the plan.

Section 1325 sets out the standards for confirmation of the plan, so it also, in essence, operates to prescribe the required content of a plan — that is, the plan will not likely be confirmed unless it satisfies the confirmation standards in §1325. Section 1325(a) provides that the court shall confirm a plan that complies with the provisions of Ch. 13 and the specific standards set out in the subsection. The most important of these standards is that the plan must be proposed in good faith, it must provide for payments to creditors over the life of the plan that meet the required level of total payment, and it must show that the debtor has a reasonable prospect of consummating the plan. Even if the plan meets the requirements of §1325(a), the court has the discretion not to approve the plan under §1325(b) if the trustee or the holder of an unsecured claim justifiably objects to the plan on the ground that the plan does not provide for the application of all the debtor's disposable income to payments under the plan. This disposable income test is tied to the substantial abuse provision in §707(b), discussed in section 6.8. The confirmation of the plan and objections to it are handled at a confirmation hearing under §1324.

The debtor does not wait until plan confirmation to begin payments called for by the plan. Under §1326(a)(1), the debtor must begin to make payments under the plan within 30 days of filing the petition, even if the plan has not yet been confirmed. Section 1326(a)(2) defers the trustee's distribution of these payments to creditors until the plan is confirmed.

Section 1327 sets out the effects of confirmation. Section 1327(a) states that the plan binds the debtor and all creditors, including those creditors whose claims are not provided for in the plan. Section 1327(b) revests in the debtor all estate property that is not required for performance of the plan. That is, all the prepetition and postpetition property that entered the estate is released back to the debtor upon confirmation of the plan except to the extent that it is needed for effectuating the plan.

Finally, §1328 grants a discharge to the debtor upon completion of all payments under the plan. Discussion of the detailed provisions of §1328 is deferred to Chapter 21.

§18.2 THE INITIAL STAGES OF THE CH. 13 CASE

§18.2.1 Commencement of the Ch. 13 Case

As discussed in section 5.5, eligibility for Ch. 13 relief is restricted. Only an individual with regular income, whose debts fall within the limitations of

§109(e), may be a debtor under Ch. 13. While most Ch. 13 debtors are wage-earning consumers,[2] Ch. 13 relief is not confined to them. Any individual debtor with a source of regular income and debts below the maximum total amounts specified §109(e) can file under Ch.13, including self-employed individuals, business owners, and people whose debts are primarily business-related.

A Ch. 13 case begins much like the Ch. 7 case, as described in section 6.3, with a voluntary petition[3] and similar supporting documents. The plan is also usually filed with the petition. The automatic stay takes effect on the filing of the petition, and in a Ch. 13 case, §1301 extends it to any individual who is a codebtor or surety of the debtor on a consumer debt.

§18.2.2 Property of the Ch. 13 Estate

Upon filing of the petition, the debtor's property becomes property of the estate.[4] Under §1306, the Ch. 13 estate consists not only of prepetition property of the debtor covered by §541 but also of all such property, including postpetition earnings, acquired by the debtor between the commencement of the case and its close. Postpetition property is included in the Ch. 13 estate because the debtor's performance under the plan is typically dependent on it. However, upon confirmation of the plan, some of this property is returned to the debtor under §1327(b), which revests in the debtor estate property that is not required for the performance of the plan.

§18.2.3 The Ch. 13 Trustee

In all Ch. 13 cases, a trustee is appointed[5] under §1302 after the petition has been filed. Unlike a Ch. 11 debtor, the Ch. 13 debtor cannot exercise the functions of a trustee as a debtor in possession. However, a debtor who operated a business at the time of the petition is permitted by §1304 to

2. In the bankruptcy context, a consumer debtor is a person whose debts are primarily incurred for personal, family, or household purposes.
3. A Ch. 13 case must be commenced voluntarily. Creditors have no right to petition for an involuntary Ch. 13 bankruptcy. Similarly, only the debtor may convert a case to Ch. 13.
4. The debtor may claim exemptions in property in a Ch. 13 case, as in a Ch. 7 case. However, exemptions are not directly applicable in Ch. 13 because the general effect of Ch. 13 is to enable the debtor to keep all property that is not designated for liquidation in the plan. However, exemptions are relevant in a Ch. 13 case, in that they are taken into account in deciding how much the debtor must pay under the plan to meet minimum requirements for confirmation, as explained in section 18.8.
5. There is no provision for the trustee's election by creditors, as there is in a Ch. 7 case. In districts with a large volume of cases, individual trustee appointments are not made for each case because a standing trustee handles all Ch. 13 cases.

continue to run it after bankruptcy, subject to monitoring by the trustee under §1302(c) read with §1106(a)(3) and (4).

The Ch. 13 trustee's principal duty is to collect and disburse payments under the plan. In addition, under §1302, the trustee must account for property of the estate, investigate the debtor's affairs, examine and object to proofs of claim, help the debtor to formulate the plan, and participate in the confirmation and discharge hearings.

§18.2.4 Commencing Payments Under the Ch. 13 Plan

Unless the court orders otherwise, §1326(a)(1) requires the debtor to begin making payments within 30 days of the order for relief or the filing of the plan, whichever is earlier. The debtor must make payments to the trustee in the amount proposed by the plan, except for 1) any current lease payments for personal property leased and 2) any payments to ensure adequate protection of a purchase-money security interest in personal property, which must be made directly to the lessor or secured party. Section 1302(b)(5) imposes the duty on the trustee to ensure that the debtor makes the payments. Under §1326(a)(2), the trustee retains the payments made to her until the plan is confirmed, and then, as soon as practicable after confirmation, the trustee transmits payments to creditors in accordance with the plan. If the plan is not confirmed, the trustee refunds the payments that she has been holding to the debtor, less administrative costs.

§18.3 THE CH. 13 PLAN AND THE PREREQUISITES FOR CONFIRMATION

Section 1321 requires the debtor to file a plan, which is the debtor's proposal for the resolution of the Ch. 13 case. Under Rule 3015(b), the plan must be filed with the petition or within 14 days thereafter unless the court extends the time. Only the debtor may file a plan.[6] Section 1323 allows the debtor to modify the plan before confirmation without court approval. This enables the debtor to respond to any objections informally before the plan is submitted to the court for confirmation.

Broadly speaking, the plan has three components: It states what income and assets will be used to fund the plan, it proposes the treatment to be given to claims, and it provides for various optional matters, such as the election

6. Unlike a Ch. 11 case, creditors have no right to file competing plans. *See* section 20.2.

on whether to assume or reject executory contracts. Sections 1322 and 1325 provide for the contents of the plan and the standards for its confirmation. These provisions are listed here and are discussed more fully in later sections.

(1) Optional provisions under §1322(b). Section 1322(b) lists optional provisions that may be included in the plan. It covers matters such as the classification of unsecured claims, the modification of claims, the cure of default, and other terms that may be useful to the debtor and appropriate in the case. The list in §1322(b) is not exclusive: §1322(b)(11) allows the debtor to include in the plan any provision that is not inconsistent with the Code.

(2) Mandatory provisions under §1322(a). Section 1322(a)(1), (2), and (3) state that the plan "shall" contain the following provisions:

1. Section 1322(a)(1) — it must bind the debtor to pay future earnings in an amount sufficient to execute the plan. (*See* section 18.5.)
2. Section 1322(a)(2) — it must provide for the full payment of priority claims unless the claimant agrees otherwise. This rule is qualified by §1322(a)(4).[7] The plan may provide for less than full payment of those first priority domestic support obligations that are assigned to or owed directly to a governmental unit (that is, claims under §507(a)(1)(B)), but only if the plan commits all the debtor's disposable income for the five years of the plan. (*See* section 18.8.2.)
3. Section 1322(a)(3) — if the plan classifies claims, it must treat claims in the same class equally. (*See* section 18.8.3.)

(3) Confirmation requirements under §1325(a). Section 1325(a) states that the court "shall" confirm a plan if it meets the criteria set out in the section and if confirmation is not precluded by §1325(b). In its plain meaning, the section appears to give the court no discretion to refuse confirmation of a plan that meets all of the requirements of §1325. However, the court does have considerable discretion in determining whether each of the individual requirements set out in §1325(a) is satisfied, and therefore can refuse confirmation on the basis that the plan failed to meet one or more of the listed requirements. Similarly, §1325(a)'s language does not indicate whether a court has the discretion to confirm a plan that falls short of those criteria. This has led some courts to hold that they have the discretion to confirm a plan that does not fully meet the requirements of §1325(a),

7. This provision was added to the Code by the Bankruptcy Abuse Prevention and Consumer Protection Act of 2005 (BAPCPA).

provided that the deviation from the requirements is trivial or the parties whose rights are infringed acquiesce.[8] Other courts have reached the opposite conclusion, and have held that the requirements of §1325(a) are mandatory and should be understood as requirements for confirmation.[9]

In summary, §1325(a)'s criteria are:

1. §1325(a)(1). The plan must comply with Ch. 13 and all other applicable provisions of the Code.
2. §1325(a)(2). All fees required to be paid before confirmation must have been paid.
3. §1325(a)(3) and (7). The debtor must both have filed the petition and proposed the plan in good faith, and the plan must not violate the law. (*See* section 18.7.)
4. §1325(a)(4). The distribution to be paid to each unsecured claimant under the plan must be at least equal to what it would have received had the estate been liquidated under Ch. 7. Because the payments under the plan will be made over time, interest must be added to the amount distributed to each claimant so that the claimant receives the present value of its hypothetical Ch. 7 distribution. (*See* section 18.8.3.)
5. §1325(a)(5). Unless a secured claimant accepts different treatment, the plan must either provide for the collateral to be surrendered to the claimant, or it must preserve the claimant's lien and provide for full payment of the present value of the secured claim. Present value is determined by adding interest to the face amount of the claim. (*See* section 18.8.1.)
6. §1325(a)(6). The plan must be feasible. Based on the financial data furnished in the schedules, it must be apparent that the debtor will be able to make all payments under the plan and to comply with it. (*See* section 18.5.)
7. §1325(a)(8). The debtor must have paid all domestic support obligations required to be paid, by court or administrative order or by statute, that became due after the petition was filed.

(4) Confirmation requirements under §1325(b). Section 1325(b) contains a further requirement for confirmation that can only be enforced by the court if a trustee or unsecured claimant files an objection. In the simplest terms, the trustee or an unsecured creditor who would receive less than full payment under the plan may object to the plan if the debtor has not committed to payment of unsecured claims under the plan all of her disposable

---

8. See, e.g., *In re Escobedo*, 28 F.3d 34 (7th Cir. 1994).
9. See, e.g., *Shaw v. Aurgroup Financial Credit Union*, 552 F.3d 447 (6th Cir. 2009).

income for the "applicable commitment period," which is up to five years. This disposable income test is explained in section 18.8.3.

§18.4 CONFIRMATION OF THE PLAN AND ITS EFFECTS

Section 1324 deals with the confirmation hearing. It provides that the hearing must take place not less than 20 days nor more than 45 days after the meeting of creditors. The court is able to hold the hearing earlier if it determines this to be in the best interests of creditors and the estate and there is no objection to the earlier date. Rules 2002(b) and 3015(d) provide for notice of the hearing and the transmission of the plan or a summary of it to creditors. Even if no one objects to the plan, the hearing must be held, and the court must scrutinize the plan to ensure that it complies with the statutory standards. The term of art "after notice and a hearing" is not used in §1324, so the hearing is not dispensed with in the absence of objections. If confirmation is refused, the debtor has the opportunity to correct objectionable elements in the plan by amendment. If the plan is not satisfactorily amended, a party in interest can apply under §1307 for dismissal of the case or its conversion to Ch. 7.

Upon confirmation of the plan, the trustee distributes the debtor's preconfirmation payments under §1326(a)(2), and the debtor begins the course of payments required by the confirmed plan. If necessary, the court is able to issue a form of garnishment order under §1325(c), compelling the person from whom the debtor receives income to transmit the plan payments to the trustee. Section 1326 contemplates that the debtor makes payments provided for in the plan to the trustee, who disburses them in accordance with the plan after deducting trustee's fees and other administrative expenses. However, in appropriate circumstances the court has the discretion to confirm a plan that provides for the debtor to make some payments directly to particular creditors. The debtor's default in the performance required under the plan is grounds for dismissal or conversion under §1307.

Section 1327(a) states the effect of confirmation: The plan binds the debtor and each creditor, whether or not the creditor's claim is provided for by the plan and whether or not the creditor has "objected to, has accepted, or has rejected the plan." The reference to acceptance or rejection of the plan by creditors is misleading. Aside from a narrow exception,[10] creditors do not vote on the Ch. 13 plan and they are not called on to accept or reject it.

10. The narrow exception applies where the plan proposes to give a secured or priority claim less than its statutory entitlement. The creditor's consent is then required for confirmation of the plan.

A creditor's primary opportunity to challenge the plan is to try to prevent its confirmation through an objection on the grounds that the plan does not meet statutory standards. Nevertheless, the basic point is that if the plan is confirmed, it binds creditors whether they like it or not. It is imposed on them — "crammed down" in bankruptcy jargon — provided that it satisfies the prerequisites for confirmation.

Under §1327(b) and (c), confirmation of the plan vests all property of the estate in the debtor, free and clear of any claim or interest in it, except as otherwise provided in the plan or the order of confirmation. Although the debtor's postpetition property continues to enter the estate under §§1306 and 541, all the estate property passes back to the debtor upon confirmation except for that property or income committed to performance of the plan. The estate continues to exist as a legal entity, separate from the debtor, even though the bulk of its property vests in the debtor.

The Ch. 13 confirmation does not operate as a discharge. The debtor is only discharged under §1328 after the plan has been consummated, unless cause exists for an earlier discharge on grounds of hardship (discussed more fully in Chapter 21). Therefore, if the debtor defaults on the plan and the case is dismissed, the balance of the claims against the debtor remains recoverable. If the case is converted to Ch. 7, the discharge is as provided for in a Ch. 7 case.

In appropriate circumstances, the plan may be revoked or modified after confirmation. Revocation may be ordered under §1330 after notice and a hearing if a party in interest applies for it within 180 days after the entry of the order of confirmation and shows that the confirmation was fraudulently procured. Modification may be applied for under §1329 by the debtor, the trustee, or an unsecured claimant.

§18.5 THE FUNDING OF THE PLAN AND THE DEBTOR'S OBLIGATION TO MAKE PAYMENTS

As stated before, the Ch. 13 debtor usually seeks to keep the property that would otherwise have been liquidated under Ch. 7 and to substitute a series of payments to be distributed by the trustee to creditors. Although the premise of Ch. 13 is that the plan will be funded from the debtor's future income, it does not have to rely exclusively on that source. The debtor may liquidate some property to supplement the monies contributed from income, and is authorized to do so by §1322(b)(8). Also, §1325(a) permits the debtor to surrender property subject to a security interest, rather than retain the property and pay off the debt. Whatever the source of funding may be, the plan must specify it as well as set out the proposed periodic payments to be made by the debtor and the length of the payment period. Section 1322(a) requires the plan to provide for income to be submitted to the trustee sufficient to support the plan, §1302 obliges the trustee to ensure that payments are commenced, and §1326 regulates payments by the trustee.

Because the debtor's payments are the lifeblood of the plan, the court must be satisfied at the outset that the debtor can afford to make the payments. As stated in section 5.5.3, a debtor must have regular income to be eligible for Ch. 13 relief. A debtor with unpredictable or unstable income cannot be permitted to undertake Ch. 13 bankruptcy. This principle is also reflected in §1325(a)(6), which includes as one of the criteria for confirmation that the debtor appears to be able to make payments under the plan. Sections 109(e) and 1325(a)(b) impose a minimum standard of affordability on the debtor. At the other end of the scale, §1325(b) enables the trustee or an unsecured creditor to insist that the debtor commits all disposable income to the plan. This is discussed in section 18.8.3.

§18.6 THE LENGTH OF THE PLAN

Section §1322(d) limits the length of time that a debtor can be committed to payments under a Ch. 13 plan. The maximum length of the plan payment period is either three or five years, depending on the financial resources of the debtor,[11] as measured by a formula derived from the §707(b) means test.[12] If the combined current annual income of the debtor and spouse[13] is less than the median family income for a household of the debtor's size,[14]

11. Prior to the enactment of BAPCPA in 2005, the maximum payment period for all Ch. 13 debtors was three years. When it added the means test to §707(b), BAPCPA amended §1322(d) to extend the period to five years for higher-earning debtors, but retained the three-year maximum length for debtors who qualify as low-earning debtors, based on the concepts of current monthly income and median family income that are used in the means test of §707(b).

12. Although the Ch. 7 means test applies only to consumer debtors, the rule in this section applies to all Ch. 13 debtors, whether or not their debt is primarily consumer debt. The means test of §707(b) is explained in section 6.8.

13. Section 101(10A) defines "current monthly income" to mean the average income that the debtor receives from all sources for the six-month period ending on the last day of the calendar month preceding the petition. (*See* section 6.8.3.) The median family income is an annual figure, so the debtor's income must be annualized for comparison purposes. Therefore, the current monthly income must be multiplied by 12 to get the current annual income. Note that for purposes of §1322(d), the current annual income is the combined income of the debtor and spouse, even though the case is not a joint case and the debtor's spouse has not also filed for bankruptcy.

14. "Median family income" is defined in §101(39A) to mean the median family income as reported by the Census Bureau for the most recent year for the "applicable state," which is presumably the state in which the debtor resides. If the Bureau has not reported the median

the plan cannot go beyond three years without the court's approval for cause. However, if the combined current annual income of the debtor and spouse is higher than the median family income for a household of the debtor's size, the plan may extend to a maximum of five years. Section 1322(d) absolutely forbids payments under a plan to extend beyond this maximum five-year period. Although a plan may be modified after it is confirmed (see section 18.11), the modification cannot extend the payment period beyond the statutory limit, which continues to be measured from the original date, not from the modification date.

No minimum period of payment is prescribed. Courts disagree on whether the disposable income test has the effect of making the maximum payment period into a minimum period as well by requiring the debtor to make payments for the full three- or five-year period. (This is discussed in section 18.8.3.) Quite apart from this, a debtor who proposes to pay relatively small amounts over a short period will probably not satisfy the good faith and best interests tests described below.

§18.7 GOOD FAITH

Section 1325(a)(7)[15] requires that the filing of the petition must be in good faith and §1325(a)(3) requires that the plan must be proposed in good faith and not by any means forbidden by law. That is, there is a pervasive requirement of good faith in Ch. 13, so that the court may refuse to confirm a Ch. 13 plan if the debtor lacked good faith either in filing the case or in proposing the plan. Section 1325(a)(7) makes it clear that a lack of good faith in filing the case is grounds not only for dismissing a Ch. 13 case under §1307, but also for refusing confirmation of the plan. The practical difference between dismissal and refusal to confirm the plan is that dismissal terminates the bankruptcy case, while refusal of confirmation allows the debtor the opportunity of coming forward with an amended plan that cures the problem of lack of good faith.[16] Courts have used the same standards to measure good faith, whether they are dealing with a motion to dismiss or to convert the case or an objection to plan confirmation.

The scope and meaning of good faith is not defined by the Code, but it has been developed judicially. The inquiry is directed at the debtor's state of mind in seeking Ch. 13 relief or in proposing the plan. The debtor's honesty

income for the current year, the figure for the most recent year is used, with adjustments to reflect changes in the Consumer Price Index. (*See* section 6.8.3.)

15. Section 1325(a)(7) was enacted by BAPCPA, but even before that courts recognized a good faith requirement in relation to both the filing of the case and the proposal of the plan.

16. See *In re Lancaster*, 280 B.R. 468 (Bankr. W.D. Mo. 2002).

is a factual issue to be decided under all the circumstances of the case. There is no definitive list of factors to be considered. However, the following are some of the areas that are often the subject of inquiry: the accuracy and honesty of the debtor's financial disclosures; the circumstances under which debts were incurred (e.g., whether they arose from tortious or dishonest conduct); the debtor's prepetition dealings with creditors (e.g., whether the debtor had used delaying tactics to avoid payment or had otherwise misled or deceived creditors); the debtor's dealings with property (e.g., whether there had been avoidable preferences, fraudulent transfers, or attempts to conceal assets); the reason for the debtor's financial distress (e.g., whether it was caused by unfortunate circumstances or by irresponsible or dishonest dealings); the advantages sought by the debtor in choosing relief under Ch. 13 instead of under Ch. 7 (e.g., whether there is a substantial debt that is dischargeable under Ch. 13 but not under Ch. 7, as illustrated by Example 2); and the debtor's financial history (including, for example, the frequency with which the debtor has sought bankruptcy relief in the past).

Courts differ on whether and to what extent a court should take into account in the good faith evaluation the degree of effort undertaken by the debtor to pay claims as fully as possible. As discussed in section 18.8, §1325 has objective criteria—the best interests test and the disposable income test—for deciding if the debtor's proposed payments under the plan are sufficient. If the payments are not enough to satisfy these minimum standards, that is in itself grounds for refusing confirmation of the plan, so an inquiry into the debtor's good faith is not needed. However, these payment standards prescribe a minimum commitment and, as explained in section 18.8.3, the formula used in the disposable income test could underestimate the amount of disposable income that the debtor might actually have. Where the debtor declines to pay any more than mandated by §1325, the argument has been made that the debtor is not making a sincere effort to treat creditors fairly, and this should be taken into account in deciding if the debtor is acting in good faith. Some courts have been willing to consider this factor in deciding good faith in the totality of the circumstances.[17]

Other courts have held that §1325 imposes objective criteria to determine the amount that the debtor is required to pay under the plan, and therefore the fact that the debtor may be able to pay more is not pertinent to the inquiry into good faith. For example, in *In re Welsh*, 711 F.3d 1120 (9th Cir. 2012), the above-median debtor's plan proposed payments that were fully in compliance with the disposable income test (discussed in section 18.8.3). Despite this, the trustee objected to the plan on good faith grounds, arguing that the plan was not a sincere effort to pay what the debtor could

17. See, e.g., *In re LeMaire*, 898 F.2d 1346 (8th Cir. 1990); *In re Keach*, 243 B.R. 851 (B.A.P. 1st Cir. 2000); and *In re Lancaster*, 280 B.R. 468 (Bankr. W.D. Mo. 2002).

afford. The formula for calculating disposable income excludes Social Security payments and amounts paid to secured creditors. However, the debtor was in fact receiving Social Security payments and also could have reduced the amounts paid to secured creditors by giving up some of the assets (several motor vehicles) subject to the security interests. The trustee therefore contended that the debtor actually had more disposable income than the formula required him to commit to the payments under the plan, and should, in good faith, provide for greater payments under the plan. The court rejected the trustee's objection, stating that by enacting an objective formula for the calculation of the payments required of a debtor, Congress had chosen to reduce the courts' discretion to determine what the debtor could afford to pay. This narrows the good faith inquiry and precludes the court from taking into account a debtor's ability to pay more than the amount determined under the disposable income formula.

§18.8 THE CLASSIFICATION OF CLAIMS AND THE STANDARDS APPLICABLE TO EACH CLASS

The plan deals with secured, priority, and general claims separately. In addition, §1322(b)(1) allows the debtor to divide unsecured claims into classes. The treatment of claims in each of the three principal classifications is subject to different rules.

§18.8.1 Secured Claims

a. The Debtor's Three Alternatives for the Treatment of Secured Claims Under §1325(a)(5)

The debtor has three alternatives for the treatment of secured claims[18] in a Ch. 13 plan:[19] consensual treatment under §1325(a)(5)(A), payment of the claim and preservation of the lien while payment is pending under §1325(a)(5)(B), or surrender of the collateral under §1325(a)(5)(C).

18. Recall that under §506, a partially secured claim bifurcates. The claim is secured only to the extent of the collateral's value and is unsecured as to the deficiency. This rule applies fully in Ch. 13. However, in the case of a mortgage on the debtor's principal residence, it is a precondition to the debtor's retention of the home under the plan that the actual debt, not just the secured portion of it, be fully paid. *See* section 18.9.3. As discussed in section 18.8.1b, the obscure "hanging paragraph" of §1325(a)(9) may extend this principle to certain purchase-money mortgages in personal property.

19. As a fourth alternative, the debtor can simply not provide for the claim in the plan, in which case it is not affected by the bankruptcy and survives the discharge.

The last two do not require the creditor's acquiescence and can be crammed down, provided that the plan meets the statutory requirements.

i. The consensual treatment of a secured claim under §1325(a)(5)(A).

Section 1325(a)(5)(A) allows the debtor to handle the secured claim in a manner different from that provided for in §1325(a)(5)(B) or (C) if the holder of the claim accepts the plan. Acceptance is indicated most clearly by an affirmative act, but the claimant may be held to have accepted the plan if it fails to object.

ii. Payment of the claim and preservation of the lien while payment is pending under §1325(a)(5)(B).

The amount to be paid is the allowed amount of the secured claim, valued as at the effective date of the plan. As noted in section 17.5.3(e), *Associates Commercial Corp. v. Rash*, 520 U.S. 953 (1997), requires replacement value, not foreclosure value, to be used in determining the value of the collateral, which will in turn determine if the claim is fully secured, and if it is not, the amount of the secured portion of the claim. (*See* section 17.6.3(e) for a fuller discussion of the determination of replacement value.) The value as of the effective date of the plan (present value) is calculated by adding interest to the face value of the claim to compensate for the payment over time under the plan. The calculation of the amount of interest to be added to reach present value must also be based on a market standard. Disagreement among courts on how to calculate market interest was settled by *Till v. S.C.S. Credit Corp.*, 541 U.S. 465 (2004), in which the Court adopted a "formula" approach that uses an objective interest rate (the national prime rate) adjusted to take the creditor's risk into account.[20]

If the plan provides for the payment of the secured claim, it must also preserve the holder's lien to secure payment. Section 1325(a)(5)(B) makes it clear that the secured claimant retains the lien until the grant of the discharge under §1328, or the full payment of the debt under nonbankruptcy law, whichever is earlier. This provision, added by BAPCPA, overrules cases that allowed the debtor to get the lien released as soon as the secured portion of a bifurcated claim was paid. The creditor therefore becomes entitled to foreclose to the extent of the full balance of the debt if the debtor should default before consummation of the plan, and the case is converted or dismissed without completion of the plan.

---

20. Note that *Till* was a Ch. 13 case, so the court's choice of rate is clearly applicable in a Ch. 13 case, but is not necessarily applicable in a Ch. 11 case. See *In re American Homepatient, Inc.*, 420 F.3d 559 (6th Cir. 2006) and section 20.4.3(b).

Except in the case of home mortgages, the payment schedule under the plan may be different from the original payment terms governing the secured debt. Also, the plan may provide for the cure of default and for the payment of long-term debt beyond the period of the plan. This is discussed in sections 18.9 and 18.10. Section 1325(a)(5)(B) requires periodic payments under the plan to be in equal monthly installments. If the collateral securing the claim is personal property, the amount of the periodic payments must be enough to provide the secured claimant with adequate protection during the period of the plan.

iii. Surrender of the collateral under §1325(a)(5)(C).

If the debtor so choses, she may surrender the collateral to the holder of the claim, thereby disposing of the secured claim and freeing the debtor of the obligation to pay it under the plan. Of course, if the collateral is worth less than the debt, the deficiency is provable as an unsecured claim, provided that the creditor is entitled to claim the deficiency under nonbankruptcy law.

b. Restrictions on Strip Down Under the "Hanging Paragraph" of §1325(a)

BAPCPA added some obscure language following §1325(a)(9), which is not part of subsection (9) but rather floats at the end of §1325(a). This poorly drafted and sloppily incorporated provision therefore has no subsection number and has come to be called the "hanging paragraph." The exact intent of this language is unclear. It says that §506 will not apply to a claim for purposes of §1325(a)(5) in two separate situations: The first is where the claim is secured by a purchase-money interest in a vehicle acquired by the debtor for personal use, and the debt was incurred within the 910 days prior to the petition. The second is where the claim is secured by a purchase-money interest in "any other thing of value," and the debt was incurred within the one-year period before the petition.

The apparent purpose of this provision is to protect the rights of secured creditors who entered into secured personal property transactions with the debtor within a fairly recent time before the petition — 910 days (about two and a half years) for purchase-money security interests in a motor vehicle bought for personal use, or one year in the case of a purchase money interest in other personal property of value. Because the transaction occurred relatively close to the bankruptcy and the motor vehicle or other valuable personal property could depreciate quite quickly, the debtor is not permitted to strip down the lien. For example, the debtor bought a car for personal use on secured credit two years before the petition and financed the purchase by a secured loan, repayable over four years. Because cars depreciate relatively quickly after being removed from the showroom, the car's value at the date of the petition has dropped below the outstanding amount of the debt — for example, the car is worth $20,000, but the debtor still owes $23,000 on the loan. In the absence of the hanging paragraph, the amount owed to the creditor would be bifurcated under §506 into a secured claim of $20,000 and an unsecured deficiency of $3,000. The debtor would thereby strip down the lien to the car's current value. The hanging paragraph is intended to prevent this by excluding the application of §506 in this situation. The problem with the hanging paragraph is that its clumsy drafting has raised questions on how to apply it in some situations. It seems to be clear that where the debtor elects to retain the collateral under §1325(a)(5)(B), the claim cannot be bifurcated and has to be treated in its entirety as secured, even if the collateral is worth less than the debt. It seems, furthermore, that because the entire claim is treated as secured, the creditor is entitled to present-value interest calculated on the whole claim.[21] However, where the debtor elects to surrender the collateral under §1325(a)(5)(C), courts disagree on the effect of excluding the application of §506. Some courts have held that because the hanging paragraph eliminates recourse to §506, there is no bifurcation of the claim, so that the surrender of the vehicle extinguishes the claim for a deficiency. Other courts have disagreed, reasoning that §506 merely defines the nature of a secured claim, but it does not create the creditor's right to a deficiency. That right derives from nonbankruptcy law, so that if the creditor is entitled to a deficiency under the contract and state law, the creditor may prove a claim for it even though the collateral has been surrendered.[22]

While the one-year rule for other things of value applies to a purchase money interest any type of collateral, the 910-day rule applies only to purchase-money interests in motor vehicles bought for personal use. The creditor must establish each of these elements to prevent strip down. One of the crucial elements is whether a security interest qualifies as a purchase-money interest. Although it is usually quite easy to establish whether the debt was incurred to enable the debtor to acquire the collateral, this is not always clear. For example, in *In re Trejos*, 374 B.R. 210 (B.A.P. 9th Cir. 2007), the debtor argued that a car loan lost its status as a purchase-money interest when the original lender assigned it to the creditor who held it at the time of the petition. The court rejected the argument. In *In re Penrod*, 802 F.3d 1084 (9th Cir. 2015), the lender's security interest in the debtor's car did not qualify for protection under the hanging paragraph because the amount lent covered not only the purchase price of the car, but also an

---

21. See *In re Dean*, 537 F.3d 1315 (11th Cir. 2008) and *In re Jones*, 530 F.3d 1284 (10th Cir. 2008).
22. See, e.g., *Capital One Auto Finance v. Osborne*, 515 F.3d 817 (8th Cir. 2008) and *In re Rodriguez*, 375 B.R. 535 (B.A.P. 9th Cir. 2007).

amount allocated to paying off the balance of the loan outstanding on the vehicle traded in by the debtor.

§18.8.2 Priority Claims

Section 1322(a)(2) requires all priority claims to be paid in full by deferred cash payments unless the holder agrees to different treatment. As mentioned in section 18.3, there is a narrow exception to this rule in §1322(a)(4), which allows less than full payment of first priority domestic support obligations that are assigned to or owed directly to a governmental unit (that is, claims under §507(a)(1)(B)), but only on condition that the plan commits all the debtor's disposable income for the five years of the plan. The purpose of this rule is to alleviate the burden on a debtor who owes such a significant amount to a governmental agency for support obligations that it would be impossible for the debtor to pay this debt in full over the period of the plan. Provided that the debtor commits all disposable income to the plan for five years, the plan can reduce the total payment on this support debt by the appropriate amount.

Because priority claims must be paid in full, the order of priority in §507 is not as directly relevant in a Ch. 13 case as it is in Ch. 7. However, the ranking has some impact on the treatment of claims. If a class of priority claims would have received nothing had the case been filed under Ch. 7 (because the fund would have been exhausted by senior classes), the plan need provide only for full payment of the face amount of claims in that class. However, if the class would have been paid in full under Ch. 7, the best interests test described in section 18.8.3 requires that the class receives the present value of the Ch. 7 distribution, which includes interest on the face amount of the claims. If the priority class would have been treated somewhere between these extremes had the case been filed under Ch. 7 so that the claims would have received a pro rata payment, the amount paid under the plan must be the greater of the face value of the claims and the present value of the hypothetical pro rata Ch. 7 distribution. That is, if the Ch. 7 distribution plus interest is higher than the face value of the claim, this higher amount must be provided for in the plan to satisfy the best interests test.

§18.8.3 Unsecured Claims

The standards for confirmation relating to unsecured claims are prescribed by §1325(a)(4) and (b). Section 1325(a)(4) sets a minimum level of payment for unsecured claims — unsecured creditors must receive at least as much under the plan as they would have received if the debtor had filed for liquidation under Ch. 7. This requirement has traditionally been called the "best interests" test. Section 1325(b), added to the Code in 1984 and significantly amended by BAPCPA, requires the debtor to commit to payments under the plan all disposable income for an "applicable commitment period" not to exceed five years. As mentioned before, this requirement only applies if invoked by the trustee or by an unsecured claimant whose claim is not to be paid in full under the plan.

a. The Best Interests Test

Section 1325(a)(4) requires that the amount paid on each allowed unsecured claim have a value as of the effective date of the plan that is no lower than what would have been paid on the claim had the estate been liquidated under Ch. 7. To determine present value, a hypothetical Ch. 7 distribution must be calculated based on the value of estate property at the petition date, and to that amount a market interest rate for the period of payments under the plan must be added. The principle here is similar to that applicable to secured claims, in that interest must be added to compensate the claimant for payment over time. Note, however, that the formula for calculating present value differs between secured and unsecured claims. The present value of a secured claim is determined by adding interest to the allowed amount of the claim (i.e., its face value); the present value of an unsecured claim is confined to the Ch. 7 distribution plus interest. This is because secured claims are paid in full out of the collateral in a Ch. 7 case, but unsecured claims receive only a partial distribution unless the estate is solvent.

If the Ch. 7 estate would have been so badly insolvent that general unsecured claims would have received no distribution, the best interests test provides no relief to them. As they would have received nothing under Ch. 7, a plan that provides for no distribution to general creditors satisfies the test. In such a case, a creditor cannot complain of inadequate payments unless there are grounds for invoking the disposable income test or the good faith standard.

b. The Disposable Income Test

The disposable income test is brought into effect on the objection of the holder of an allowed unsecured claim that is not to be paid in full under the plan, or the objection of the trustee. In essence, §1325(b) forbids court approval of the plan unless the plan commits all the debtor's projected disposable income for a three-year period, or in some cases a five-year period, to the payment of unsecured claims. The calculation of the debtor's disposable income is based on a formula set out in §1325(b). This formula was added to the Code by BAPCPA at the same time that it enacted the means test of §707(b), and is intended as a companion measure.[23] You may therefore find it helpful to reread the discussion of the means test in section 6.8. The disposable income test in §1325(b) is subject to the same criticism as the means test in §707(b). First, it is badly drafted and difficult to interpret. Second, its method of calculating disposable income can lead to unrealistic results, making it an unreliable solution to the problem of inadequate payment efforts by debtors. Although the toughening of standards may help to prevent some abuse of the Code, the more rigorous approach and the use of quite rigid and artificial formulae make it more difficult for the debtor to propose a confirmable plan with reasonable prospects of consummation. The following discussion explains the rules set out in §1325(b) for applying the disposable income test and then shows how the formula must be applied.

(1) The total amount of money committed to the plan: the "applicable commitment period." Section 1325(b) provides a two-tiered commitment period, called the "applicable commitment period," which distinguishes between debtors whose income exceeds or is less than the family median income.[24] "Applicable commitment period" is defined in §1325(b)(4). In essence, the period is three years unless the combined current annual income of the debtor and spouse exceeds the median family income for a household of the debtor's size in the "applicable state," in which case it is five years. Although "applicable state" is not defined, §707(b)(2)(A)(ii) indicates that this is the state in which the debtor resides.

For example, say that the debtor's monthly disposable income is calculated to be $200. If the debtor's current annual income is over the state median, he must pay a total of $200 × 60 months ($12,000) over the term of the plan. If his current annual income is under the state median, he must pay a total of $200 × 36 months ($7,200).

Subsection (b)(4)(B) allows the applicable commitment period to be less than the three- or five-year period (whichever is applicable) only if the plan provides for payment in full of allowed unsecured claims over a shorter period. This provision has caused confusion over the relationship between the "applicable commitment period" and the maximum length of the

---

23. Prior to 2005, the court had wider discretion to determine the debtor's disposable income by conducting a factual evaluation of the debtor's budget and deducting the debtor's projected reasonable expenses from projected income. Although the court based the determination of the debtor's monthly income on her current and historic earnings, the concept of projected disposable income allowed the court to take into account how the debtor's income might change over the period of the plan. The current test, enacted by BAPCPA, makes the disposable income test more rigid and rigorous.

24. Prior to the BAPCPA amendments to§1325(b), the section simply required the debtor to commit all disposable income for three years to payments under the plan. It did not distinguish debtors of higher and lower income.

payment period under the plan, provided for in §1322(d) and discussed in section 18.6. Section 1322(d) prescribes the maximum plan length, but does not set out any minimum payment period. Some courts have held that §1325(b)(4) does not change this. It is merely a monetary provision—that is, it simply prescribes the total amount that the debtor must pay under the plan, but does not require the plan to last the full three or five years. That is, as long as the plan provides for the payment of the total amount of disposable income projected to be received over the three- or five-year period, it does not actually need to last for that amount of time.[25] Other courts have held that §1325(b)(4) is both a monetary and a temporal provision—that is, it not only requires the debtor to pay the amount calculated under the test, but also that the "applicable commitment period" is a temporal concept that also requires the plan to last no less than the three- or five-year period unless unsecured payments are to be paid in full under the plan. For example, *Baud v. Carroll*, 634 F.3d 327 (6th Cir. 2011) followed this approach and explained the impact of treating §1325(b)(4) as temporal: Although the amount that the debtor has to pay is the same under both interpretations, requiring the plan to go for the full term increases the period during which a creditor may seek to modify the plan under §1329 on the grounds that the debtor's income has increased beyond the amount anticipated when projected disposable income was originally calculated.[26]

Some courts have adopted a hybrid approach, in which the "applicable commitment period" does normally set the minimum temporal duration of the plan, but this does not apply where the calculation of the debtor's projected disposable income shows that the debtor will have no disposable income to make any payment to unsecured creditors. For example, in *In re Flores*, 692 F.3d 1021 (9th Cir. 2012), the calculation of projected disposable income showed that the above-median debtors had a negative disposable income after payments to secured and priority creditors. The debtors proposed to pay 1 percent of allowed general unsecured claims for 36 months, but the trustee objected on the grounds that the plan had to last 60 months. The court, reaffirming its own precedent, held that the "applicable commitment period" applied only to payments of projected disposable income, and that if the debtor proposed to make some payments to unsecured creditors beyond that mandated by the disposable income test, they were not required to have the plan extend to the full "applicable commitment period."

25. See, e.g, *In re Fuger*, 347 B.R. 94 (Bankr. D. Utah 2006) (§1325(b)(4) (merely requires a set return, but does not require the debtor to commit to a specific time period for payment).
26. See also *Pliler v. Stearns*, 747 F.3d 260 (4th Cir. 2014). Postconfirmation plan modification is discussed in section 18.11.

(2) The debtor's projected monthly income. Although §1325(b)(2) requires the calculation of "projected disposable income," it does not define that term. It does, however, define "disposable income" in §1325(b)(2) to mean the "current monthly income received by the debtor" (excluding certain payments such as child support or other payments made on account of a child, to the extent reasonably necessary for expenditure on the child)[27] less reasonably necessary expenses as explained in (3) below. As we have seen, "current monthly income" is defined in §101(10A) to mean the average income that the debtor receives from all sources for the six-month period ending on the last day of the calendar month preceding the petition. It includes amounts contributed regularly by someone else for the debtor's household expenses but excludes various government benefits such as Social Security payments.[28] Sometimes this snapshot of the debtor's income in the six months immediately preceding the bankruptcy will be a reasonably reliable basis for making a projection of the debtor's prospective income over the period of the plan, but sometimes it will not be. For example, it does not take into account whether the debtor's earnings in that period were atypical (say, because the debtor did not work for part of the period, or conversely, because he worked more than usual or received income from sources that are not likely to continue into the future).

In essence, §1325(b)(2) has a gap—it tells us what current monthly income is, but does not articulate the meaning of projected disposable income. However, unlike current monthly income, projected disposable income is forward looking, and requires some assessment of the possible changes to the debtor's income over the period of the plan. Lower courts had differed on whether §1325(b)(2) permitted some adjustment to current monthly income to take into account the debtor's actual income potential over the term of the plan. This question was settled by the Supreme Court in *Hamilton v. Lanning*, 560 U.S. 505 (2010). The Court rejected a purely mechanical approach to the determination of projected disposable income. The debtor had received a lump sum payment from her former employer during the six-month prepetition period, which inflated her current monthly income. If a mechanical approach was followed, this would have resulted in an unrealistically high projected disposable income that would have required plan payments that the debtor clearly could not afford. The court noted that

---

27. The exclusion from the debtor's income calculation of child support and other payments made on account of a child follows the Code's general policy of protecting the integrity of child support. See *In re Brooks*, 784 F.3d 380 (7th Cir. 2015) (holding that the payments must not be included in the debtor's current monthly income, provided that they did not greatly exceed the amount reasonably necessary for the support of the child).

28. The definition of current monthly income applies to both above- and below-median debtors. The distinction between these two types of debtor is relevant to the expense side of the calculation of disposable income, not to the income side. See *Mort Ranta v. Gorman*, 721 F.3d 241 (4th Cir. 2013).

although §1325(b) defines "disposable income," it does not define "projected disposable income." In ordinary usage, a projection, while based on current data, must take anticipated future circumstances into account. Therefore, while the debtor's disposable income, based on the deduction of reasonably necessary expenses from current monthly income, is the starting point for calculating projected disposable income, the court may take into account changes in the debtor's income or expenses that are known or virtually certain at the time of confirmation. To hold otherwise would lead to a senseless situation in which an abnormally low current monthly income would deprive creditors of higher payments, and an abnormally high current monthly income would make it impossible for the debtor to propose a realistic plan. The court noted that this interpretation is in accord with other language in §1325 and with practice prior to the enactment of BAPCPA. It is not to be assumed that Congress intended to overturn established practice in the absence of a clear indication that it meant to do so.

Note that the definition of current monthly income in §101(10A) excludes Social Security benefits received by the debtor. That is, any Social Security payments that the debtor receives in the six-month prepetition period are not counted in determining current monthly income, and hence are not included in the calculation of projected disposable income. In *Mort Ranta v. Gorman*, 721 F.3d 241 (4th Cir. 2013), the debtor excluded Social Security payments from his current monthly income, which resulted in his disposable monthly income being insufficient to make any payment to unsecured creditors. Nevertheless, so that the debtor could meet the feasibility standard, he proposed in the plan to use some of his Social Security income to make a minimal payment on unsecured debts. The bankruptcy court (affirmed by the district court) refused to confirm the plan because it felt that the debtor could afford to make a greater payment. If the debtor declined to include Social Security income in his disposable income, it could not be taken into account in the determination of whether the plan was feasible. Therefore, if the Social Security income was disregarded, the plan did not meet the feasibility standard. The court of appeals reversed. It held that because Social Security income was statutorily excluded from current monthly income, it was necessarily excluded from projected disposable income. This was not affected by the forward-looking approach mandated by *Hamilton*, which recognizes the court's discretion to take into account foreseeable changes in the debtor's income but does not permit the court to ignore the statutory formula for determining that income. The court also held that the lower courts erred in refusing to take the Social Security income into account in the feasibility determination: Nothing in the Code precluded the debtor from funding the plan from a source other than his disposable income. In *In re Ragos*, 700F.3d 220 (5th Cir. 2012), the court likewise held that the debtor properly excluded Social Security benefits from current monthly income, and that *Hamilton* was inapposite because it involved the entirely different circumstance of a disparity between current monthly income and anticipated actual disposable income. The court affirmed the bankruptcy court's confirmation of the plan, rejecting the trustee's argument that the debtor failed to propose a plan in good faith by refusing to use Social Security income to pay creditors.

(3) The debtor's reasonably necessary expenses. To calculate the debtor's projected disposable income, the amounts necessary to be expended for the maintenance or support of the debtor or a dependent must be deducted from income. As amended by BAPCPA, §1325(b) curtails the factual inquiry into expenses where a debtor earns more than the median family income by imposing a formula for determining those expenses. This formula is essentially the same as that used in deciding if a presumption of abuse applies for the purpose of dismissing a Ch. 7 case under §707(b).

Sections 1325(b)(2) and (3) must be combined to determine what amounts qualify as necessary to be expended for the maintenance or support of the debtor or any dependents. Section 1325(b)(2) sets out three types of expenses that are claimable in all cases. They include domestic support obligations that first become payable postpetition, qualifying charitable contributions, and if the debtor is in business, any amounts reasonably necessary to pay the expenses of continuing, preserving, or operating the business.

Section 1325(b)(3) sets out the basis of determining other expenses. If the debtor's current annual income is less than the applicable family median income, the court determines the debtor's remaining allowable monthly expenses by evaluating the debtor's budget and deciding, using its discretion, whether the claimed expenses are appropriate. If the debtor's current annual income exceeds the applicable family median income, §1325(b)(3) adopts the expense formula used in §707(b)(2)(A) and (B). That is the list of expenses based on the National and Local Standards promulgated by the I.R.S. for the area of the debtor's residence, combined with those additional expenses authorized by §707(b)(2)(A) and adjusted for special circumstances established by the debtor under §707(b)(2)(B). (*See* section 6.8.5 for a fuller explanation of these provisions.)

As discussed in section 18.8.3(2), above, in *Hamilton v. Lanning* the U.S. Supreme Court rejected a mechanical calculation of projected disposable income in favor of a forward-looking approach that allows the court to take into account known or virtually certain changes in income. Although *Hamilton* focused on the income side of the calculation, the court indicated that the same approach should be adopted with regard to expenses. Therefore, although the formula prescribed by §707(b)(2) is the starting point for calculating expenses, and it creates a presumption that expenses will be as determined under the formula, the court has some discretion to make adjustments based on realities that are known or strongly anticipated.

The awkward drafting of §§707(b) and 1325(b) has led to uncertainty about the treatment of priority claims. Section 1325(b)(1)(b) requires that the disposable income be applied to the claims of unsecured creditors. It does not specify that this means general unsecured creditors, so it could include priority claims, which are also unsecured. However, the calculation under §707(b) allows the debtor to deduct payments on priority claims as an expense. In *In re Wilbur*, 344 B.R. 650 (Bankr. D. Utah 2006), the court held that the reference to unsecured creditors must mean only general unsecured creditors because to include priority claims would result in these claims being taken into account twice, which would be absurd. However, in *In re Williams*, 394 B.R. 550 (Bankr. N.D. Colo. 2008), the court reached the opposite conclusion. It noted that an approach that avoids double-counting for above-median debtors would have a negative impact on below-median debtors because the formula in §707(b) does not apply to them, and they do not deduct priority claims as expenses. *In re Puetz*, 370 B.R. 386 (Bankr. D. Kan. 2007) opted for a more flexible approach to "unsecured claims" that would include priority claims that are not deducted as expenses.

Courts had disagreed on whether the above-median debtor's calculation of disposable income may include expenses allowed under §707(b) where the debtor's actual expenses in that category are less than the allowed amount, or are nonexistent. For example, §707(b) makes an allowance, based on I.R.S. standards, for transportation expenses relating to vehicle ownership. The question is whether the debtor can claim this expense in full even though her actual expenses are less than the allowed amount, or she has no such expenses at all. The U.S. Supreme Court settled this question with regard to a debtor who has no such expenses in *Ransom v. F.I.A. Card Services, N.A.*, 562 U.S. 61 (2011). The court held that a debtor who has no actual loan or lease expenses on a car cannot claim the car ownership expense. The court based its decision on the use of the word "applicable" in §707(b), which confined expense claims to those that corresponded to the debtor's actual circumstances.[29] The court also made it clear that a debtor whose actual expenses exceeded the I.R.S. standards is confined to the standard amount and cannot claim more. However, the court did not decide if a debtor whose actual expenses are less than the standard could claim the full standard amount. Courts have disagreed on the approach to be taken in this situation. In *In re Scott*, 457 B.R. 740 (Bankr. S.D. Ill. 2011), the court held that as long as the debtor had some car ownership expenses, the I.R.S. standard is "applicable," as required by *Ransom*, so that the debtor is entitled

29. Although the court resolved this issue in relation to the disposable income calculation under §1325(b), its holding extends to the same calculation that is required for the presumption of abuse under §707(b). (*See* section 6.8.5.)

to claim the full standard expense, even if his actual expense is lower. However, in *In re Schultz*, 463 B.R. 492 (Bankr. W.D. Mo. 2011), the court said that the essence of *Ransom* is that a debtor should not be allowed to claim expenses that were essentially fictional, so that debtors whose car operating expenses[30] were lower than the standard amount were confined to their actual expenses.

(4) The formula, in summary. In simple terms, the formula for determining projected disposable income can be charted as follows.

> **STEP 1**
>
> Calculate the debtor's **current monthly income** as defined in §101(10A):
>
> This is calculated by taking the debtor's actual earnings from all sources for the six months before bankruptcy, divided by six to get the average monthly income. Then multiply the monthly figure by 12 to compare the debtor's income to the annual median income.

> **STEP 2**
>
> Ascertain the **median family income** for a household of the debtor's size in the state of the debtor's residence.
>
> This is an annual income figure obtained from the Census Bureau report.

> **STEP 3**
>
> **If the debtor's current annual income is less than the median family income, do the following:**
>
> ***(a) The disposable monthly income calculation:***
>
> (1) Calculate the debtor's monthly income. This is presumptively the debtor's current monthly income (excluding child support payments received), but where it is known or virtually certain that the debtor's prospective monthly income will be higher or lower, the court has the discretion to take the anticipated increase or decrease into account.

30. This case involved car operating expenses, as opposed to ownership expenses. Both types of expense are covered in the standards.

(2) Calculate the actual expenses reasonably necessary to support the debtor and any dependents, as well as postpetition expenses for domestic support, charitable contributions, and running a business. There is no statutory formula for calculating these expenses, which the court must evaluate on the facts, using its discretion to allow, reduce, or disallow claimed expenses.

(3) Deduct the expenses from the income. This gives the debtor's monthly disposable income.

(b) Determine disposable income for three years:

Multiply the debtor's monthly disposable income by 36 to determine the debtor's projected disposable income for three years. This is the total amount that the debtor must commit to the plan to satisfy the disposable income test.

If the debtor's current annual income is more than the median family income, do the following:

(a) The disposable monthly income calculation:

(1) Calculate the debtor's monthly income. This is presumptively the debtor's current monthly income (excluding child support payments received), but where it is known or virtually certain that the debtor's prospective monthly income will be higher or lower, the court has the discretion to take the anticipated increase or decrease into account.

(2) Determine the debtor's allowed expenses. The debtor is entitled to deduct only those expenses allowed under §707(b)(2)(A) and (B) as well as postpetition expenses for domestic support, charitable contributions, and running a business. The debtor may only deduct §707(b)(2)(A) expenses that he actually incurs. Although expenses calculated under the formula are presumptively applicable, where it is clear that they are not realistic, given the debtor's circumstances, the court has discretion to make adjustments.

(3) Deduct the expenses from the income. This gives the debtor's monthly disposable income.

(b) Determine disposable income for five years:

Multiply the debtor's monthly disposable income by 60 to determine the debtor's projected disposable income for five years. This is the total amount that the debtor must commit to the plan to satisfy the disposable income test.

One of the items that can be claimed as an expense is a bit odd. Although the debtor is in severe financial trouble, is struggling to pay creditors, and is held to a stringent budget for her living expenses, §1325(b)(2)(A) permits her to include charitable contributions up to an amount of 15 percent of the debtor's annual gross income made to a charitable or religious organization that meets the qualifications of §548(d)(4) and the Internal Revenue Code. Because these contributions come out of the disposable income that would otherwise go to the payment of creditors, the debtor is permitted to be charitable at their expense. This subsection was part of a set of provisions enacted in 1998 for the primary purpose of protecting tithes and other contributions to churches and other religious organizations. Other charities were included to avoid First Amendment problems. (These contributions are also protected from avoidance as prepetition transfers under §544(b)(2) or as fraudulent transfers under §548(a)(2), and are not to be taken into account by the court in deciding whether to dismiss a debtor's Ch. 7 cases for abuse under §707(b)(1).) The language of §1325(b)(2)(A)(ii) gives the court very little flexibility to question the reasonableness of contributions of up to 15 percent of the debtor's gross income, but the court is able to examine the debtor's motive in making the contribution under the good faith requirement of §1325(a)(3). For example, in *In re Cavanagh*, 250 B.R. 107 (B.A.P. 9th Cir. 2000), the court inquired into the debtor's good faith where the debtor, who had not previously paid church tithes, amended his Ch. 13 plan to reflect an increase in earnings offset by a new contribution of tithes to his church. (Despite these suspicious circumstances, the court concluded that the debtor had undergone a genuine religious conversion.)

c. The Classification of Unsecured Claims

Section 1322(b)(1) gives the debtor the discretion to place unsecured claims in separate classes. There are three guidelines that apply to claim classification: Claims in the same class must be treated alike (§1322(a)(3)), the plan must not discriminate unfairly against any class (§1322(b)(1)), and claims can only be classed together if they are substantially similar (§1322(b)(1) read with §1122). In addition, the best interests and disposable income tests require that even the class of claims that is treated least generously in the plan receives the level of payment required by §1325.

Section 1322(b)(1) expresses only one justification for separate classification: If an individual is liable with the debtor on a consumer debt, that claim may be separated from other unsecured claims. The purpose of this provision is to allow the debtor to treat a consumer debt preferentially to eliminate or reduce the liability of a friend or relative who is codebtor or surety. The rationale behind the provision is that it prevents financial hardship to the codebtor and eliminates any pressure that the debtor would otherwise feel to pay the debt outside the plan, thereby endangering his rehabilitation.

The separate classification of guaranteed or joint consumer debts is presumptively fair, since §1322(b) specifically mentions this basis for discrimination. However, this does not mean that it is conclusively fair, so it is still subject to scrutiny by the court. There is no statutorily recognized justification for other types of claim, so the debtor must provide a good reason for any classification and discriminatory treatment. A court is likely to approve a claim classification only if it is necessary to the execution of the plan and the debtor's rehabilitation, it is reasonable and proposed in good faith, and the degree of discrimination is no greater than it needs to be to achieve its purposes. Most courts adopt an evaluation that centers around these questions, recognizing that the determination of whether discrimination is fair involves the exercise of reasonable court discretion.[31] For example, courts have generally held that discrimination based purely on nondischargeability is unfair. That is, the debtor may not devote a disproportionate amount of her disposable income toward the payment of the nondischargeable claim, thereby reducing the fund that would otherwise be available to pay other creditors. However, this is not an invariable conclusion because there may be other factors that persuade a court that there is a justification for the separate classification of a nondischargeable debt.[32]

§18.9 THE MODIFICATION OF A CLAIMANT'S RIGHTS AND THE CURE OF DEFAULT

§18.9.1 Introduction and General Note on Cure

Section 1322(b)(2) allows the plan to modify the rights of all claimants except those whose claims are secured only by a security interest in real property used by the debtor as a principal residence. Section 1322(b)(3) allows the plan to provide for the cure or waiver of any default; this cure or waiver of default applies to all debts, including an otherwise nonmodifiable home mortgage.

The cure of default is a pervasive concept in §1322. It is permitted both by §1322(b)(3), which covers claims to be fully disposed of during the plan

31. See *In re Crawford*, 324 F.3d 539 (7th Cir. 2003) and *In re Pracht*, 464 B.R. 486 (Bankr. M.D. Ga. 2012).

32. For example, in *In re Pracht*, *supra*, the court found that the debtor's separate classification and higher rate of payment of a nondischargeable student loan debt was fair discrimination. The reduction on payments to other creditors was modest but the maintenance of contract payments on the student loan during her Ch. 13 case would make the debtor eligible for a student loan forgiveness program that would allow her to write off a significant amount of the otherwise nondischargeable debt.

period, and by §1322(b)(5), which covers long-term debt to be paid off beyond the period of the plan. (Long-term debt is discussed in section 18.10.) This note states some general principles of cure, but the subject recurs in the remainder of this section and in section 18.10. As noted earlier, the cure of default is not regarded as a modification of the contract, so it applies, both under §1322(b)(3) and §1322(b)(5), to specially protected, nonmodifiable home mortgages. Although §1322(b)(3) provides in general terms for the cure of any default, its primary use is in connection with a secured debt in default. The debtor's motivation to propose the cure is her desire to retain property subject to a security interest. To do this, she is obliged, not only to pay the amounts due prospectively on the secured claim, but also to pay arrears or to remedy other breaches. That is, if the debtor has fallen into arrears in payments or has otherwise breached the contract, the right to cure enables her to reinstate the agreement by providing in the plan for payments or performance to remedy the breach. That is, of course, in addition to provisions in the plan (or in and beyond the plan for long-term debt) for the payment of future installments.

There is a difference of opinion among courts on whether §1322(b)(3) and (5) apply only to prepetition defaults, or if they can also be used by a debtor who defaults during the course of the case by failing to perform the obligations assumed in the plan. If the cure right is available postpetition, a debtor who stumbles in making plan payments could then apply for a modification of the plan to include a cure of the default, thereby preventing dismissal or conversion to Ch. 7. *In re Mendoza*, 111 F.3d 1264 (5th Cir. 1997), is one of the cases that interpreted the cure provisions as applicable to postpetition default. The court noted that the general policy of §1322 is to encourage and facilitate the cure of default, and there is nothing in the language of the section that confines it to prepetition defaults. The court did recognize, however, that the debtor would be precluded from curing a postpetition default if the plan contained a "drop-dead" clause, which allows the creditor to foreclose in the event of default.

§18.9.2 The Modification and Cure of Claims Other Than Specially Protected Home Mortgages

The ability to modify rights enables the debtor to extend contractual installment periods that would otherwise have ended before the proposed period of the plan. This is most helpful when the debtor wishes to keep property subject to a security interest. Say, for example, that the debtor purchased a car on secured credit prior to bankruptcy, and the contractual payment period has two years to run. If the debtor proposes a three-year plan, §1322(b)(2) allows the payment period to be extended an extra year, thereby reducing the size of the monthly payments. In addition, if the debtor defaulted on the contract, §1322(b)(3) permits cure of the default so that the plan may provide for the payment of arrears as well as future installments. In effect, §1322(b)(2) and (3) give the debtor the opportunity to redeem collateral by installments—something that cannot be done in a Ch. 7 case. The debtor's ability to modify a claimant's rights is limited by the confirmation criteria in §§1322 and 1325. So, for example, unless the claimant accepts the plan, the debtor cannot modify a security agreement by canceling the lien, substituting collateral, or giving the secured claimant less than it is entitled to receive under §1325(a)(5).

§18.9.3 The Special Treatment of Claims Secured Only by a Security Interest in Real Property That Is the Debtor's Principal Residence

Section 1322(b)(2) excludes from the debtor's ability to modify secured claims, a claim that is "secured only by a security interest in real property that is the debtor's principal residence." Section 101(13A) defines "debtor's principal residence" to mean a residential structure and incidental property used by the debtor as a principal residence. The structure may or may not be attached to real property, and it could be an individual condominium, a co-operative unit, a manufactured or mobile home, or a trailer. However, because §1322(b)(2) applies only to real property, a security interest in a mobile home, trailer or other unattached property would not be subject to the bar on modification if state law did not classify the structure as real property. It also does not apply to property that is not the debtor's principal residence, such as a summer beach cottage.

The bar on the modification of a security interest in the debtor's principal residence is intended to protect home mortgagees on the theory that its absence would discourage them from providing home financing to individuals. Even though the debtor has some flexibility in restructuring other debts, the terms of the debtor's home mortgage must be complied with if the debtor wishes to keep the home. The plan cannot alter the payment schedule or otherwise propose to ease the debtor's commitments under the security agreement.

The prohibition on modification applies only to future payments. Default on the mortgage may be cured under §1322(b)(3) and (c)(1) by providing in the plan for payment of the arrears by installments. Section 1322(c)(1), added by the Bankruptcy Reform Act of 1994, makes it clear that the cure provisions in §1322(b)(3) and (5) are not affected by the antimodification rule in §1322(b)(2). Section 1322(c)(1) also specifies that the right to cure is not cut off by foreclosure until such time as the foreclosure sale has been completed. In states that recognize a statutory redemption period, courts have held that the right to cure extends even beyond the sale, until the end of the redemption period. (*See* Example 4.) The debtor has the right to cure defaults whether the mortgage is a short-term loan payable within a period of the plan, or a long-term loan that may be dealt with under §1322(b)(5), as discussed in section 18.10.

The language used in §1322(b)(2) to exclude home mortgages from the debtor's modification power covers claims that are "secured only by a security interest in real property that is the debtor's principal residence." The word "only" means that if the mortgage covers other property in addition to the debtor's home (such as a second piece of real property, or personal property and appliances on the premises) or a multifamily dwelling, the antimodification rule does not apply. In *In re Scarborough*, 461 F.3d 406 (3d Cir. 2006) the court held that the antimodification provision did not apply to a two-unit residence where the debtor lived in one unit and rented the other. However, in *In re Ferandos*, 402 F.3d 147 (3d Cir. 2005), the court held that the inclusion in the mortgage of rents arising from the property did not change it from being secured only by a security interest in the home. The rents were merely incidental to and stemmed from the property itself and were not separate collateral.

Section 1322(c)(2), also added in 1994, creates another situation in which the antimodification rule is inapplicable. If the final payment under the mortgage falls due within the period of the plan (that is, the original contractual due date for the final payment occurs within the plan period), the payment schedule can be amended by the plan so as to stretch out the mortgage payments over the entire length of the plan.

Section 1322(b)(2) refers to "secured claims," and does not indicate how an undersecured claim (where the value of the home is worth less than the debt) should be treated. Under §506(a), an undersecured claim bifurcates into a secured claim to the extent of the collateral's value and an unsecured claim for the deficiency. This question was settled by *Nobelman v. American Savings Bank*, 508 U.S. 324 (1993), in which the Court held that an undersecured mortgage on the debtor's principal residence is protected to the full amount of the debt. The Court based this conclusion on the wording of §1322(b)(2), which prohibits modification of the *rights* of the holder of the mortgage, not merely of the claim secured by the mortgage. The effect of *Nobelman* is to extend the principle of *Dewsnup v. Tim*, 502 U.S. 410 (1992), to a mortgage on the debtor's principal residence under Ch. 13. (*Dewsnup*, discussed in section 17.6.3b, held that a debtor cannot use §506(d) to strip down an undersecured lien on real property in Ch. 7 by pegging its value at the judicially determined valuation at the time of bankruptcy.) The combined effect of *Nobelman* and *Dewsnup* is that a debtor cannot strip a lien on real property in a Ch. 7 case, or a mortgage on his principal residence in a Ch. 13 case. The U.S. Supreme Court has not addressed lien stripping with regard to other secured claims, and lower courts have generally held it to be permissible.[33]

Although *Nobelman* settles the issue of strip down in relation to a partially secured mortgage on the debtor's principal residence, it does not cover the question of whether a debtor may "strip off" a completely unsecured second mortgage. A second mortgage becomes completely unsecured if the home has no excess value after the senior mortgage has been paid. The strip-off issue was discussed in relation to *Dewsnup* in section 17.6.3b, in which it was noted that courts have been divided on whether *Dewsnup* extends to strip off. Courts dealing with the issue under §1322(b)(2) have likewise been divided, but the weight of opinion is that *Nobelman* was premised on the creditor having at least some interest in the property at the time of bankruptcy, so that if there is no equity left in the property to support the mortgage, it cannot qualify as a secured claim entitled to protection under §1322(b)(2).[34]

§18.10 LONG-TERM DEBT

While §1322(b)(2) enables the plan to extend payments on short-term debt, §1322(b)(5) allows the debtor to take advantage of a contract payment period that is longer than the period of the plan. Section 1322(b)(5) applies to all long-term debts, including those secured by a home mortgage. Note, however, it applies only to long-term debts — that is, debts whose last payment is due after the date of the final payment on the plan. If the due date of the debt is within the plan payment period, the debtor may not use §1322(b)(5) to extend the payments beyond the plan period. For example, in *In re Pierotti*, 645 F.3d 277 (5th Cir. 2011), the debtor owed arrear taxes to the IRS, secured by a tax lien on the debtor's real property. The debtor proposed to pay off the arrear taxes over a 15-year period. The court held this to be impermissible because the tax debt was already mature, payable, and in default. It was therefore not a debt due only after the final payment under the plan.

The following example illustrates how §1322(b)(5) operates where the final payment of the debt is due, under the original contract, only after the final payment under the plan. The debtor bought a piece of equipment on credit two years before bankruptcy. Under the contract of sale, the seller retained a security interest in the equipment, which the debtor undertook to pay off in installments over ten years. The debtor proposes a five-year plan,

33. See *In re Davis*, 716 F.3d 331 (4th Cir. 2013).
34. See id.; *In re Zimmer*, 313 F.3d 1220 (9th Cir. 2002) and *In re Samala*, 295 B.R. 380 (Bankr. D.N.M. 2003).

but the remaining contractual payment period is eight years. This is so even if the debtor had defaulted on the payments, and the contract allows the creditor to accelerate payments under nonbankruptcy law. The debtor's right to cure the default reverses any acceleration, so that the final date of payment is the unaccelerated contractual due date. Section 1322(b)(5) allows the debtor to adhere to the contractual payment schedule, rather than accelerating it to bring it within the term of the plan. The debtor maintains regular installment payments while the plan is pending (these may be paid through the trustee or directly to the claimant) and continues to make contract payments after the conclusion of the plan until the debt is satisfied. Because payments on the claim will extend beyond the period of the plan, §1328(a)(1) excludes the debt from the Ch. 13 discharge. (For a further illustration of the use of §1322(b)(5), *see* Example 4.)

If the debtor had defaulted on the debt, §1322(b)(5) requires cure of the default within a reasonable time. Therefore, in addition to paying the regular installments as they become due, the debtor must provide in the plan for payments to be made on the arrears. The question of what time is reasonable for affecting the cure depends upon the circumstances of the case. The debtor is not necessarily entitled to spread the cure payments over the whole length of the plan.

§18.11 MODIFICATION OF A CONFIRMED PLAN

As mentioned in section 18.3, before confirmation, §1323 permits the debtor to modify the plan easily, and without court approval. Modification after confirmation is a more onerous process that does require an application to court. Section 1329 provides for the modification of a confirmed plan, at any time before completion of payments, on request of the debtor, the trustee or the holder of an unsecured claim. Under §1329(a), the modification may either increase or reduce payments to a particular class, alter the time period for such payments, change the amount of the distribution to a creditor to take account of payments outside of the plan, or to allow the debtor to reduce payments for the purpose of buying health insurance under specified circumstances. For the modification to be approved, §1329(b) states that the plan as modified must satisfy the same standards and requirements under §§1322 and 1325(a) as govern the original confirmation of a plan (such as the full payment of priority claims, the good faith and feasibility standards, and best interests test—as discussed in sections 18.3 through 18.8). Section 1329(b) does not say that the modified plan must also satisfy §1325(b)—the disposable income test. This is odd, especially because a creditor's right to apply for modification under §1329 was added to the Code in 1984, at the same time as the disposable income test. (Prior to

1984, §1329 allowed only a debtor to seek modification of the plan.) The effect of this omission is unclear. For example, in *In re Sunahara*, 326 B.R. 786 (B.A.P. 9th Cir. 2005), the court held that on the plain language of §1329(b), the disposable income test in §1325(b) is not directly applicable in a modification, but a change in the debtor's disposable income could be taken into account in the analysis of the debtor's good faith. *In re Keller*, 329 B.R. 697 (Bankr. E.D. Cal. 2005), disagreed with this approach, holding that even though §1329(b) does not expressly mention §1325(b), it does not exclude it either.

Upon approval of the modification, the modified plan substitutes for and supersedes the original. Under §1329(c), even if a plan is extended by modification, it cannot exceed the permissible length measured from the date of the first payment under the original plan. That is, the modification cannot increase the payment period beyond the maximum applicable commitment period prescribed by §1322(d) from the time of the first payment made in the case.

Most applications for modification are brought by debtors who seek to reduce or extend the payment of obligations undertaken in the original plan on the basis that the commitments in the confirmed plan are too onerous or have become so as a result of changed circumstances. However, it is not uncommon for a creditor or trustee to apply for modification on the grounds that the debtor's financial situation has improved. Some courts treat the confirmed plan as res judicata with regard to any circumstances that existed or were foreseeable at the time of confirmation, so they require a substantial unanticipated change to justify modification. Other courts adopt a more lenient test, and do not require the applicant to demonstrate a significant unexpected change in circumstances.[35]

Section 1329(a) expressly permits modifications to adjust the amount or period of payments, but it does not say whether or not a debtor may modify the substantive provisions of the plan to achieve other purposes. Some courts have held that the debtor's ability to use §1329 to make substantive changes to the confirmed Ch. 13 plan is restricted, especially where the modification would result in unfairness to a creditor. For example, in *In re Nolan*, 232 F.3d 528 (6th Cir. 2000), the court held that where collateral has depreciated in value, the debtor cannot modify the plan to surrender the collateral and reduce the amount of the secured claim based on the lower value. In *In re Adkins*, 425 F.3d 296 (6th Cir. 2005), the court applied this same rule where the debtor had defaulted on plan payments and the collateral had been repossessed and sold at a lower value following relief from stay. That is, the court held in these cases that once a claim has been

---

35. See, e.g., *Germeraad v. Powers*, 826 F.3d 962 (7th Cir. 2016); *Barbosa v. Soloman*, 235 F.3d 31 (1st Cir. 2000); and *In re Thomas*, 291 B.R. 189 (Bankr. M.D. Ala. 2003).

classified as secured in a fixed amount in the original plan, the plan cannot be later modified to reduce the amount of the secured claim and increase the unsecured deficiency. Not all courts agree with this approach. For example, in *In re Disney*, 386 B.R. 292 (Bankr. D. Colo. 2008) and *In re Mellors*, 372 B.R. 763 (Bankr. W.D. Pa. 2007), the courts held that because §502(j) allows reconsideration of an allowed claim for cause, it is permissible to reduce the amount of a secured claim under §1329 where cause for the modification is shown.

§18.12 SUCCESSIVE FILINGS UNDER CHS. 7 AND 13: THE "CHAPTER 20" TACTIC

Under certain circumstances, a debtor may benefit from the tactic of first filing a Ch. 7 case to gain advantages available under Ch. 7 and, immediately thereafter, filing a Ch. 13 case to obtain advantages under Ch. 13 that were not available under Ch. 7. Because this tactic involves the combination of Chs. 7 and 13, it has come to be called "Chapter 20." BAPCPA made some amendments to the Code that, while they do not directly prevent a "Chapter 20" serial filing, erect three significant barriers to the "Chapter 20" strategy.

First, a consumer debtor has greater difficulty in filing the initial Ch. 7 case because §707(b) makes the debtor more vulnerable to dismissal of the Ch. 7 case, either because the presumption of abuse applies or because the court finds abuse under the totality of the circumstances.

Second, BAPCPA amended §1328 to prevent a debtor from getting a Ch. 13 discharge within four years of getting a discharge in another case filed under Ch. 7 or 11. It thereby eliminated a strategy, previously used by some debtors, under which the debtor would successively file cases under Ch. 7 and 13 to get the advantages of both chapters. As discussed in Chapter 21, some debts are nondischargeable in a Ch. 7 case but can be discharged in Ch. 13. A debtor who wished to liquidate under Ch. 7 but needed Ch. 13 to handle a debt that was dischargeable only in Ch. 13 could file a case under Ch. 7 to handle the bulk of his debt by liquidation, and then file a Ch. 13 case to dispose of the debt that could not be discharged in Ch. 7. By preventing a debtor from getting a Ch. 13 discharge within four years of a Ch. 7 or Ch. 11 discharge, §1328 eliminates the use of "Chapter 20" for this purpose.

Third, BAPCPA added a ground for relief from stay under §362(d)(4)(b) which authorizes the court to grant relief from stay to a creditor whose claim is secured by real property where the court finds that the filing of the petition was part of a scheme to hinder, delay, or defraud creditors that involved multiple bankruptcy filings against the property. (*See* section 8.3.4.)

Although the debtor is not able, under §1328, to receive successive discharges in Ch. 7 and 13 within a four-year period, there are other reasons why a debtor may choose the "Chapter 20" strategy: One is that if the debtor wishes to file under Ch. 13, but his debt exceeds the Ch. 13 debt ceiling, he can make himself eligible for Ch. 13 relief by reducing his debt through a Ch. 7 discharge. The other is that "Chapter 20" may help a debtor to handle liens that survive a Ch. 7 discharge. The use of "Chapter 20" to deal with a lien that survived the Ch. 7 discharge works as follows: The debtor first files a Ch. 7 case and receives a discharge of personal liability on her debts. One of these discharged debts is secured by a mortgage on real property. Although the debtor's personal liability on the claim is discharged, the security interest is not affected by the discharge. After the close of the Ch. 7 case, the mortgagee commences foreclosure proceedings, but before the foreclosure sale is held, the debtor files a Ch. 13 petition in which she proposes to retain the property and pay off the mortgage claim in installments. The debtor is thereby able to use Ch. 13 to force the secured claimant into accepting the equivalent of a redemption by installments, which she would not have been able to do in the Ch. 7 case. The prior Ch. 7 discharge also gives the debtor the advantage of keeping her payments under the Ch. 13 plan to a minimum because she has shed her dischargeable debt in the prior Ch. 7 case.

The U.S. Supreme Court held in *Johnson v. Home State Bank*, 501 U.S. 78 (1991), that this practice is permitted by the Code. The court said that a mortgage still qualifies as a claim under §101(5), even after the debtor's personal liability has been discharged, and the Code has no restriction on filing a Ch. 13 case immediately after receiving a Ch. 7 discharge. The Court did recognize, however, that the good faith standard in §1325 could be used to refuse confirmation of the plan if, under the totality of the circumstances, the Ch. 13 plan was filed as part of a scheme to undermine the policy and purposes of the Code. Since *Johnson*, several lower courts have applied the good faith standard to "Chapter 20" serial filings. For example, *In re Cushman*, 217 B.R. 470 (Bankr. E.D. Va. 1998), found a lack of good faith where, in the totality of the circumstances, the debtor had planned the Ch. 13 filing before he filed the Ch. 7 case to force the secured claimant to accept what amounted to a redemption by installments, he discharged all his debt under Ch. 7 without making any payment to unsecured creditors, and he planned to pay the secured claim off over four years even though he could have afforded to pay the debt more quickly.

A debtor may also use "Chapter 20" to strip down a partially secured claim or to strip off a formerly secured claim that is no longer backed with any collateral value. As explained in section 17.5.3, under §506(a)(1) a claim is treated as secured to the extent of the value of the collateral and is unsecured as to any deficiency. Strip down is the process whereby the debtor uses §506(a)(1) to fix the amount of the secured claim at the value of the collateral at the time of bankruptcy. As a result, any increase in the value of the collateral thereafter will not be added to the secured claim, which is pegged at the original value determined by the court. Strip off is similar to strip down, but it relates to situations where the value of the collateral at the time of determining secured status is so low, that there is nothing to secure the claim. This typically occurs where the claim is a junior lien on the property, and the collateral value is less than the amount of the senior lien. *Dewsnup v. Timm*, 502 U.S. 410 (1992) held that a debtor cannot strip down an undersecured consensual lien in a Ch. 7 case. Courts have differing views on whether *Dewsnup* applies to nonconsensual liens, or to strip off, so it is possible that a court in a particular venue will treat all strip downs and strip offs as impermissible in a Ch. 7 case. Where the debtor wishes to file under Ch. 7, but is precluded from stripping down or stripping off a lien under Ch. 7, the debtor may seek to use the "Chapter 20" tactic to first dispose of debt under Ch. 7, and then to use §1322(b)(2) to strip down or strip off surviving liens in Ch. 13. Some cases, such as *In re Gerardin*, 447 B.R. 342 (Bankr. S.D. Fla. 2011), have refused to allow a debtor to use "Chapter 20" to strip down or strip off liens. However, others have held that this use of "Chapter 20" is permissible. In *In re Scantling*, 754 F.3d 1323 (11th Cir. 2014), the court allowed strip off, describing this as the majority view. *In re Davis*, 348 B.R. 449 (Bankr. E.D. Mich. 2006) held that debtors who had discharged personal liability in a previous Ch. 7 case could strip off junior liens on property[36] in the subsequent Ch. 13 case where those liens had become completely unsecured because the senior lien exceeded the value of the collateral. The court held that even though the amendment of §1328 precluded the debtors from getting a discharge in the Ch. 13 case, this did not prevent the debtors from using the "Chapter 20" tactic to strip off liens that had become valueless. The court rejected the trustee's argument that the debtors were using "Chapter 20" to evade *Dewsnup's* bar on Ch. 7 lien stripping and concluded that the debtors were merely taking advantage of a mechanism made available under the Code.

Although *Johnson* holds that the Code does not prohibit serial filings, it does not address the situation in which a debtor files Ch. 7 and then files a Ch. 13 case while the Ch. 7 case is still pending. Some courts have permitted this where, even though the Ch. 7 case was still pending at the time of the Ch. 13 petition, the Ch. 7 discharge had already been granted. However, courts generally agree that the Ch. 13 petition cannot be filed before the Ch. 7 discharge because a debtor may not maintain two concurrent cases relating to the same debts.[37]

---

36. The property in question was the debtor's principal residence, but the court held that *Nobelman* did not bar strip off because the lien did not qualify as a secured claim entitled to protection from modification under §1322(b)(2). See section 18.9.3.

37. See *In re Sidebottom*, 430 F.3d 893 (7th Cir. 2005).

Examples

1. Buster Budgett has filed a petition under Ch. 13. He works as the manager of a store and earns a gross salary of $5,000 per month ($60,000 per year). However, three months before he filed his petition, he took two months' unpaid leave to care for his father, who had been seriously ill. Buster is unmarried and lives alone. The applicable median family income in Buster's state is $40,000 per annum. Buster's schedules reflect his current monthly income as $3,333. As required by §1325(b)(2), this is based on his average income for the six months prior to the petition (four month's earnings of $5,000) divided by six. His schedules show monthly expenses of $2,733, which include payments on his house and car, utilities, property taxes, insurance, gas, parking, food, clothing, entertainment, medical and dental expenses (including the cost of health insurance), and state and federal taxes. The monthly expenses of $2,733 are well supported and documented, entirely reasonable, and not in excess of appropriate living standards. After his monthly expenses are deducted from his current monthly income, Buster is left with $600 a month, which he proposes to allocate for five years to the payment of unsecured claims under his Ch. 13 plan. There are no priority claims in Buster's estate except for administrative expenses. Had Buster filed under Ch. 7, the realizable value of his nonexempt property after the full payment of administrative expenses would have been $36,000, which would have been enough to pay 10 percent of the claims of general unsecured creditors.
   a. Does Buster need court approval for a five-year payment period?
   b. Based on the figures given above, does the proposed plan satisfy the financial standards for plan confirmation in §1325?
   c. Change the facts of this Example to the following extent: Buster did not take the two months' unpaid leave, and earned the full $5,000 a month for the six months prior to filing. In addition, because his employer was temporarily short-staffed during two of those six months, Buster was called upon to work overtime, for which he received additional salary of $2,000 for each of those two months (that is, $4,000 in total overtime pay). This was an unusual circumstance. Buster's employer does not normally ask staff to work overtime. The addition of his overtime pay makes his current monthly income $5666 ($30,000 plus $4,000 divided by six). Buster's actual reasonable expenses are $4,000, but the standardized expenses allowed under §707(b)(2)(A) and (B) are $3,500. Buster asserts that his projected disposable income is $1,000 per month ($5,000 income less $4,000 reasonable expenses), and he proposes a plan

under which he will allocate this amount for 60 months, with a total payout of $60,000 to general unsecured creditors. The trustee objects, arguing that Buster has not committed all his disposable income to payments under the plan. In the trustee's view, Buster's disposable income is actually $2,166 ($5,666 current monthly income less $3,500 standardized monthly expenses), so he is required to make a total 60-month commitment of $129,960 to the payment of unsecured creditors. Can Buster's proposed plan be confirmed over the trustee's objection?

2. Fido Semper had been fired by his ex-employer, Fire and Casualty Co., Inc. and bore a deep grudge against the company. One night Fido broke into the offices of Fire and Casualty Co. and set a fire that destroyed furniture and equipment worth $100,000. Shortly afterward, Fido filed a Ch. 13 petition. His plan proposes to pay 20 percent of his monthly income over 30 months in payment of his debts. His largest debt by far is the tort claim of Fire and Casualty Co. Fido's annualized current monthly income is far below the applicable median family income, and it is clear that Fido cannot pay more than the 20 percent of his income that he proposes in his plan. This amount will pay general unsecured creditors, including Fire and Casualty Co., 2 percent of their claims.

   Fido has so few assets that if his nonexempt property had been liquidated under Ch. 7, there would not have been enough proceeds to pay anything to general unsecured creditors. However, the claim of Fire and Casualty Co. would not have been discharged in the Ch. 7 case because it arose from willful and malicious injury to property and would have been excluded from the discharge under §523(a)(6). This claim is dischargeable in a Ch. 13 case because §1328, the discharge provision of Ch. 13, does not apply the exclusion to willful and malicious injury to property in a Ch. 13 case.[38] As a result, Fido will be able to discharge Fire and Casualty Co.'s claim after paying 2 percent of it under the plan. (*See* Chapter 21 for a fuller discussion of this discharge issue.)

   What grounds, if any, does Fire and Casualty Co. have for objecting to Fido's plan?

3. Mo DeFied filed a Ch. 13 petition two years ago. At the time, he was employed as a sales representative and earned $50,000 per annum in salary and commission. He proposed a plan under which general

38. A claim for damages arising out of a judgment for willful and malicious action resulting in personal injury or death is excluded from the Ch. 13 discharge, as discussed in Chapter 21. However, a claim for willful and malicious damage to property is not excepted from the Ch. 13 discharge.

unsecured creditors would receive payment of 20 percent of their claims. The plan met the standards of §§1322 and 1325 and was confirmed.

One of Mo's unsecured creditors has now discovered that Mo was recently promoted to sales manager, and that his annual earnings have increased to $100,000. The creditor has applied for modification of the plan under §1329, asking for the size of the payments to be doubled. Mo opposes the modification. He argues that the modification would be unfair because he earned the extra income by working hard. He also says that if modification is allowed under these circumstances, debtors would have no incentive to better themselves because any increase in income simply enlarges the commitment under the preexisting plan.

Should the court approve the modification?

4. Bill Overdew owns a home subject to a mortgage. The home is his principal residence. He defaulted on his monthly mortgage payments, and the mortgagee accelerated the debt, initiated foreclosure proceedings, and eventually obtained a judgment of foreclosure. The mortgage would have had 20 more years to run had it not been accelerated. The house is worth considerably more than the balance of the debt.

   Shortly after the judgment, and before a foreclosure sale took place, Bill filed a Ch. 13 petition. In his plan, he proposes to pay the arrears owing on the mortgage over a few months. (Assume that the period of the proposed cure is reasonable.) He will also pay the current installments on the mortgage as required in the mortgage note. These payments will extend beyond the period of the plan, for the remaining term of the mortgage.

   Is this provision in the plan acceptable?

5. Sal Vage borrowed money secured by a mortgage on a piece of land. Sal defaulted on the loan, and the mortgagee began suit to foreclose on the collateral. While the foreclosure proceedings were pending, Sal filed a Ch. 7 petition. The value of Sal's nonexempt property was sufficient to pay general unsecured creditors 5 percent of their claims. The rest of his unsecured debt was discharged. In addition, he discharged his personal liability on the loan, but the mortgage on the property was not affected by the discharge. (*See* section 17.3.1.) After the close of the Ch. 7 case, the mortgagee resumed its foreclosure action. However, before the foreclosure sale could be held, Sal filed a Ch. 13 petition. In his Ch. 13 plan, Sal proposes to retain the property and to pay off the mortgage claim in installments. Is this permissible?

6. Katie Gorize, a debtor under Ch. 13, has proposed a plan that meets the best interests and disposable income tests. The lowest class of unsecured

claims will receive a total distribution of 10 percent of the value of their claims. These claims would have received no payment in a Ch. 7 liquidation. Although the plan seems to be acceptable in other respects, the treatment of three claims raises questions. Is there a basis for objecting to this treatment?

a. Three years ago, Katie bought a car on credit, and gave the seller a security interest to secure the debt. The term of the loan is five years, so it has two years to run. The car is worth less than the balance of the debt. Katie proposes to keep the car. The plan provides for the seller's retention of its lien, and for payment of the full balance owing on the car over the five years of the plan.
b. Katie failed to pay the property taxes due on her house for the tax year ending prior to her petition. The taxes had been assessed, and they should have been paid a few months before the petition to avoid penalties. The state did not file a lien, so the claim is unsecured. Katie has classified it with other unsecured claims, and will pay 10 percent of it over the five years of the plan.
c. A short time before Katie's bankruptcy, a friend loaned her some money to help her cope with her financial difficulties. Katie is grateful to the friend, and feels bad about not having repaid the loan. She has therefore classified the friend's claim separately and proposes to pay 100 percent of it over the five years of the plan.

7. a. Prior to Leanne Stripper's bankruptcy, Junior Loan Co. lent her \$25,000, secured by a second mortgage on her home. At the time of the transaction, the home, Leanne's principal residence, was subject to a first mortgage in favor of Senior Security Co. Leanne has now filed a petition under Ch. 13. The balance due to Senior under the first mortgage is \$180,000, and the balance of the debt due to Junior is \$20,000. The value of the home has been reliably appraised at \$160,000. In her plan, Leanne proposes to treat Senior's first mortgage as a secured claim to the extent of \$160,000, and an unsecured claim to the extent of the deficiency of \$20,000. The proposed plan treats Junior's claim in its entirety as a general unsecured claim. The plan provides for a 10 percent distribution on general unsecured claims. Does either Senior Security Co. or Junior Loan Co. have grounds to object to the plan?
   b. Would your answer change if, at the time of the transactions, Leanne was using the home as her principal residence, but by the time of the petition, she had moved out of the house to live elsewhere, and was renting it to a tenant?

EXPLANATIONS

Explanations

1. Although Buster's actual monthly income is $5,000, his current monthly income as defined in §101(10A), calculated as the average of his earnings over the six months before the petition, is only $3,333. (He earned salary for only four of the last six months, so his average income for the period is $20,000 divided by six.) To compare this with the family median income, an annual figure, his current monthly income must be multiplied by 12, which comes to $39,996. This leads to the strange result that Buster's income, according to the statutory definition, is below the median, even though his real income is above it. Under the plain meaning of the provision, the confirmation standards that apply to him are therefore those applicable to a debtor who earns below the median family income. *Hamilton v. Lanning*, 560 U.S. 505 (2010)[39] allows for a court to exercise discretion in adjusting projected disposable income to accord with reality, but it does not extend to determining current monthly income, which must conform to the statutorily-prescribed calculation.
   a. ***The five-year payment period***. Had Buster's current monthly income exceeded the median, §1322(d)(1) would have authorized a five-year plan without the court needing to approve the period for cause. However, because Buster's income is below the median, §1322(d)(2) applies, and Buster can only propose a plan with a payout period of more than three years if the court approves the longer period for cause. If Buster's projected disposable income is based purely on a mechanical multiplication of his current monthly income, his payments of disposable income over three years would have been insufficient to satisfy the best interests test. However, because (as explained in (b) below) a court is likely to find that Buster's projected disposable income is higher than it would be under a mechanical calculation based on current monthly income, the amount that he is required to pay under the disposable income test over three years will satisfy the best interests test, and his plan will also satisfy the feasibility test. Therefore, there does not appear to be cause to extend the plan to five years.
   b. ***The financial standards***. In this question we are not interested in secured claims, which you should assume are properly dealt with under the standards of §1325(a)(5). Also, the priority administrative expenses would have been paid in full had Buster filed under Ch. 7, and §1322(a)(2) requires them to be paid in full in the Ch. 13 case. Assume that they will be. We are therefore concerned only with the financial standards relating to the payment of general unsecured claims. There are three financial standards for confirmation in §1325:

39. *See* section 18.8.3b for a discussion of this case.

the best interests test in §1325(a)(4), the feasibility test in §1325(a)(6), and the disposable income test in §1325(b).

The best interests test — §1325(a)(4). To satisfy the best interests test, the total amount of payments to unsecured claims under the plan must be not less than the present value of amounts that would have been paid on those claims had the debtor filed under Ch. 7. Had Buster filed under Ch. 7, there would have been a fund of $36,000 to distribute to his unsecured creditors, paying 10 percent of their claims. Therefore, to satisfy the best interests test, the total payments to unsecured creditors under the plan must be at least $36,000 plus interest to compensate the unsecured creditors for having to wait for their money over the plan payout period. Buster's proposed payment to general unsecured creditors of $36,000 over the proposed five years of the plan ($600 multiplied by 60) is exactly equal to the face value of the Ch. 7 payment to unsecured claims. This is not enough because it does not include the interest necessary to give the claims their present value. To satisfy this test, Buster's payments must be high enough to cover interest.

The feasibility test — §1325(a)(6). The court should not confirm a plan unless it is apparent that the debtor will be able to make all payments and comply with the plan. Had Buster's actual projected earnings been no more than $3,333 a month, he would have had trouble meeting the feasibility standard, because his disposable income would not realistically have been enough to support the plan payments including interest. However, the reality is that Buster has more actual disposable income than the amount based on current monthly income. A plan that uses his actual disposable income should satisfy the feasibility test.

The disposable income test — §1325(b). Buster's projected disposable income must be determined by deducting his projected expenses from his projected income. Where, as in Buster's case, the debtor's current monthly income is lower than the median, actual expenses are used, rather than the standardized expenses allowed by §707(b).[40] Buster's expenses sound reasonable and are likely to be approved. However, the income figure is the problem here. If the court allowed the use of the current monthly income figure to determine projected income, the disposable income test would not require Buster to pay more than the $600 per month that he proposes. However, *Hamilton* calls for a

---

40. Had Buster been an above-median debtor, his expenses would have been based on the standardized expenses allowed under §707(b)(2)(A) and (B). Most of his expenses seem to be of the kind and may be in the amount allowed by the National Standards and Local Standards promulgated by the I.R.S., supplemented by the other expenses allowed by §707(b)(2)(A) and (B). This is illustrated in Example 1c.

forward-looking approach to projected disposable income that allows the court to take into account known or virtually certain changes in income. As in *Hamilton*, the debtor's current monthly income is artificial because it is skewed by circumstances that are not likely to recur, so the court is likely to adjust Buster's projected monthly income upwards to reflect the expectation that he will earn $5,000 per month, rather than $3,333. Because he is a below-median debtor, his actual reasonable expenses are used, rather than the standardized expenses. Because his expenses are stated to be reasonable, assume that the court approves them. This gives him a monthly projected disposable income of $2,267 (income of $5,000 less actual reasonable expenses of $2,733). The total that he would be obliged to pay under a 3-year plan as a below-median debtor is $81,612 ($2,267 multiplied by 36). This is more than enough to satisfy the best interests test—it will pay unsecured creditors a considerably higher percentage of their claims than the present value of what they would have received under a Ch. 7 distribution. In short, the court is not likely to approve Buster's proposed plan because it satisfies neither the best interests test nor the disposable income test. To have his plan confirmed, Buster will have to make the greater commitment of projected disposable income for three years, as indicated above.

c. Buster's current monthly income now exceeds the median, so he is subject to the confirmation standards applicable to above-median debtors. He may propose a plan with a five-year payment period without court approval. (As noted in section 18.8.3b, some courts hold that he is obliged to commit to a five-year payment period.) As in the original version of the facts, there is an obvious discrepancy between his projected disposable income in reality and as determined mechanically from his current monthly income. In this case, his earnings in the six-month prepetition period are inflated by unusual income, rather than reduced by an unusual loss of earnings. Nevertheless, the principle is the same, and this is an appropriate case for a court to use its discretion to disregard the unusual earnings in projecting his disposable income, which should be $5,000 per month. Because Buster is an above-median debtor, he cannot deduct his actual expenses of $4,000, even if the court finds them reasonable, but is confined to the standardized expenses of $3,500. (There do not seem to be facts that suggest that the standardized expenses are so obviously not an accurate predictor of future expenses that the court should use its discretion to increase them.) This means that the projected disposable income that he must commit to the plan is $90,000 ($5,000 - $3,500 = $1,500 × 60). Because this is more than the present value that general unsecured creditors would receive in a Ch. 7 distribution, the best interest test is also satisfied.

2. There are three possible grounds on which Fire and Casualty Co. could object to confirmation of the plan.
   a. The best interests test. Fido's proposed plan satisfies the best interests test because the plan unquestionably pays more than the present value of zero, which is what unsecured creditors would have received had the case been filed under Ch. 7. Even though the claim of Fire and Casualty Co. would have been nondischargeable under Ch. 7, §1325(4) requires only that the claim receive what it would have been paid by the estate on liquidation. It does not take into account what the creditor may have ultimately recovered from the debtor's fresh start estate on an undischarged debt.
   b. The disposable income test. The facts state that Fido earns below the median income and that his disposable income has been properly determined. The only issue here is that Fido proposes a 30-month plan. Section 1325(b)(1)(B) requires the debtor to apply all his disposable income in the applicable commitment period to payment under the plan. Where the debtor earns less than the median income, §1325(b)(4)(A) prescribes a three-year commitment period. To satisfy the disposable income test, Fido would have to pay the equivalent of 36 months of disposable income. Some courts would allow him to do this over 30 months if he can afford it, but others read §1325(b)(4)(A) to require a 36-month commitment period.
   c. Good faith. Sections 1325(a)(3) and (7) require the debtor to have been in good faith both in filing the petition and in proposing the plan. Good faith is a factual matter to be decided under all the circumstances of the case. It is not necessarily bad faith for a debtor to select Ch. 13 to take advantage of its broader discharge—this is just the exercise of a choice that Congress has conferred. However, where a Ch. 13 plan proposes to pay only a small portion of a debt that would not have been discharged under Ch. 7, the plan must be given particular scrutiny to decide if it is in good faith. See *In re Caldwell*, 895 F.2d 1123 (6th Cir. 1990); *In re Francis*, 273 B.R. 87 (B.A.P. 6th Cir. 2002).

      Section 18.7 sets out the considerations that courts take into account in deciding whether the totality of the circumstances demonstrates a lack of good faith. The relevant facts here are that Fido filed his petition very soon after he had deliberately and maliciously done extensive property damage; had he filed under Ch. 7, he could not have escaped liability for this debt, which constituted the greater part of his indebtedness; and his payments under the plan are a tiny fraction of what he owes.[41]

---

41. For examples of cases that apply the totality of the circumstances test, see *In re Sidebottom*, 430 F.3d 893 (7th Cir. 2005); *In re Lancaster*, 280 B.R. 468 (Bankr. W.D. Mo. 2002); *In re Norwood*, 178 B.R. 683 (Bankr. E.D. Pa. 1995); and *In re Schaitz*, 913 F.2d 452 (7th Cir. 1990).

3. Section 1329(a)(1) allows an unsecured creditor to apply for modification of the plan to increase the amount of the payments. As noted in section 18.11, §1329(b) applies the standards of confirmation in §1322(a) and (b) and §1325(a) to a modification but fails to mention the disposable income test in §1325(b), which suggests that the disposable income test does not apply to a modification. Notwithstanding, courts have not hesitated to approve modifications where the debtor's income has increased significantly under circumstances that were not anticipated in the plan. Mo's argument that the modification would be unfair and would create a disincentive to betterment is not persuasive. Similar arguments were rejected by the court in *In re Arnold*, 869 F.2d 240 (4th Cir. 1989). The court pointed out that the fresh start is supposed to begin after the debtor has consummated the plan, and that a responsible debtor should be willing to increase payments to creditors if she can afford it.

4. Although the home is Bill's principal residence, §1322(b)(2) is not implicated because Bill does not seek to modify the rights of the mortgagee. Under §1322(b)(5), the curing of a default is not treated as a modification of the mortgagee's rights. In addition, §1322(c)(1) (enacted in 1994 to overturn case law to the contrary) makes it clear that cure is possible until such time as the property has been sold at a properly conducted foreclosure sale. This provision overrides any rule of state law that would have the effect of extinguishing the debtor's right to cure at a stage before the completion of the foreclosure sale.[42]

5. Sal is using the "Chapter 20" tactic described in section 18.12. He seeks to first discharge his personal liability on the debt in the Ch. 7 case, and then to use Ch. 13 to prevent foreclosure on the surviving lien so that he can keep the property and force the lienholder to accept payment of the secured claim under the plan. Had he simply filed the initial petition under Ch. 13, he would have been able to prevent the foreclosure, cure the default, and cram down the installment payments. However, by discharging all his unsecured debt in the previous Ch. 7 case, Sal gets the additional advantage of having eliminated the need to provide in the plan for any payment of that unsecured debt. This frees him from the need to commit his future disposable income to the payment of those debts. Although the U.S. Supreme Court held "Chapter 20" to be

---

42. The impact of §1322(c)(1) is not clear where state law gives the debtor a postsale right of redemption. Some courts have held that the debtor has the right to cure up to the end of the state law redemption period. See, e.g., *In re Sims*, 185 B.R. 853 (Bankr. N.D. Ala. 1995). Other courts have disagreed and have held that §1322(c)(1) unambiguously designates the completion of the foreclosure sale as the termination of the debtor's right to cure. See, e.g., *In re Cain*, 423 F.3d 617 (6th Cir. 2005).

permissible in *Johnson v. Home State Bank*, the debtor's conduct and motivation in filing the successive petitions are subject to evaluation under the good faith test. (Because Sal does not seek a Ch. 13 discharge, but is using it to manage his mortgage, the restriction on successive discharges in §1328 is not applicable.)

6. a. The claim secured by the car. This claim is not covered by the hanging paragraph of §1325(b). Although this is a purchase-money security interest in a car bought for personal use, the transaction occurred more than 910 days before the petition. Katie proposes to pay this claim under §1325(a)(5)(B) after modifying the payment period under §1322(b)(2). If the claim was fully secured, this treatment would be unobjectionable, provided that the full payment amount is adjusted to present value. The problem with the proposal is that the car is worth less than the debt, so part of the claim is unsecured. Katie has in fact classified the seller's secured and unsecured claims together and is proposing full payment of both. This could be challenged under §1322(b)(1) by another creditor or the trustee, or disapproved by the court of its own accord. The secured and unsecured claims are not substantially similar as required by §1122, and the discrimination is unfair because there is no appropriate justification for treating this unsecured claim differently from others.
   b. The property taxes. The property tax meets the qualifications for priority under §507(a)(8)(B): It was assessed before the petition and was last payable without penalty within a year before the petition. Section 1322(a)(2) requires full payment of priority claims unless the holder agrees to a different treatment. This claim has been misclassified, and the proposed payment is inadequate.
   c. The friend's loan. The friend's claim is a general unsecured claim which Katie has placed in a separate class. She is entitled to do this by §1322(b)(1), as long as the discrimination is not unfair. For discrimination to be fair, there must be a reasonable basis for the separate classification, and the discrimination should serve some legitimate purpose in the debtor's attempt at rehabilitation. The desire to favor a friend should not be adequate justification for paying him more at the expense of other creditors, who are being paid only a tenth of their claims, and whose distribution will be reduced by the higher payment to the friend.

7. a. Leanne's proposal to bifurcate Senior's mortgage and to treat the deficiency as an unsecured claim, payable at the rate of 10 percent, is a clear contravention of *Nobelman v. American Savings Bank*, 508 U.S. 324 (1993). The mortgage is a claim secured only by a security interest in real property that is the debtor's principal residence, and §1322(b)(2) forbids any modification of the rights of the holder. *Nobelman* held that

the section's use of the word "rights" extends the protection beyond the portion of the debt that qualifies as a secured claim, and includes any deficiency that would otherwise qualify as an unsecured claim. Leanne's attempt to strip Senior's lien to correspond to the present appraised value of the property is not allowed, and Senior has grounds to object.

Junior's position is less clear because the senior lien covers the entire value of the property, leaving nothing over for Junior. Its mortgage is therefore not merely undersecured, but completely unsecured. As noted in section 18.9.3, courts differ on whether a completely unsecured mortgage is protected from "strip off" by §1322(b)(2).

b. Section 1322(b)(2) gives no indication of the point in time at which the use of the property must be determined. This issue had to be resolved in *In re Smart*, 214 B.R. 63 (Bankr. D. Conn. 1997), in which the court held that the time of the original transaction, not the time of the petition, was the proper point for determining the property's use. The court reasoned that the purpose of §1322(b)(2) was to encourage lenders to make home loans, and this incentive would be undermined if they could not rely on the state of affairs that existed at the time of the loan. It imports a risk, inconsistent with the goals of the section, to deprive a lender of the protection from modification if, after the transaction, the debtor converts the use of the property from that of principal residence. On this reasoning, the answer to question (a) would not change merely because Leanne was no longer using the home as her principal residence at the time of her bankruptcy.

CHAPTER 19

Understanding Chapter 11

§19.1 AN OVERVIEW OF CH. 11

Chapter 11's primary design is to offer corporations and other businesses the means to preserve going concern value, thereby maximizing the amount that creditors receive and minimizing harm to employees and communities.[1] The Code offers a variety of tools — many of which we have already addressed — to achieve this objective. The vast majority of Ch. 11 debtors file for bankruptcy with the intention of using these tools and ultimately formulating and confirming a plan of reorganization, which will allow the business to exit bankruptcy and continue as a going concern.[2] However, in recent years, many Ch. 11 debtors have decided that they can best maximize creditor value by selling the debtor's business through a §363 asset sale.

One of the defining characteristics of the Ch. 11 process is that a trustee is not appointed automatically. Rather, the presumption is that the existing management team will continue to run the business in Ch. 11 as the debtor in possession.[3] However, a variety of safeguards ensure that the debtor fulfills its fiduciary duty to creditors. Primarily, the debtor in possession

1. As discussed below, Ch. 11 is also available to small businesses, individuals, and businesses owning a single real estate asset. Specialized Code provisions apply to these debtors.

2. Chapter 20 contains a full description of plans of reorganization and the confirmation process.

3. This structure is somewhat unique to the U.S. bankruptcy system. Indeed, insolvent companies in other countries are invariably taken over by a trustee or similar third party who is merely tasked with liquidating the company.

is monitored by the bankruptcy court and the U.S. Trustee. In most cases, the bankruptcy court will appoint an official committee of unsecured creditors to provide additional monitoring. Further, other official committees—including ones to represent retirees and even shareholders—may be appointed to provide additional input. In cases where corporate officers have committed malfeasance or exhibited gross incompetence, bankruptcy courts have the power to appoint a trustee to assume management of the debtor in possession. In the alternative, courts can appoint an examiner to assess the cause of the debtor in possession's decline and determine who may be liable before deciding whether to appoint a trustee.

Ch. 11 cases involve a staggering number of affected stakeholders with claims against the estate, including secured creditors, unsecured creditors, current employees, former employees, contractual counterparties, and governmental agencies. At the same time, there are often times sufficient assets to address many—thought not all—of these claims. Consequently, Ch. 11 cases produce extremely interesting legal and policy discussions that are litigated aggressively.

U.S. history is marked by economic recessions that forced iconic companies into bankruptcy, including General Motors, Lehman Brothers, MGM, Delta Airlines, Chrysler, American Airlines, the Los Angeles Dodgers, and Toys 'R Us. Ch. 11 is the optimal venue for these types of rehabilitation efforts.

§19.2 CH. 11'S OBJECTIVE AND TOOLS

As noted in section 19.1, the goal of a Ch. 11 case is the debtor's rehabilitation and the maximization of creditor recovery. By filing a Ch. 11 petition, the debtor is able to continue the operation of its business under the shelter of the automatic stay. It is thereby able to preserve its profitable activities and assets while it negotiates with creditors and attempts to develop a strategy for the satisfaction of debts and the revitalization of its failing enterprise. If the negotiations are fruitful, the debtor formulates a plan, which is the blueprint for its rehabilitation. The plan contains proposals for the treatment of debt and sets out the course to be taken by the debtor in seeking financial recovery.

If the plan satisfies the requirements of the Code, it is confirmed by the court. The debtor then tries to implement the plan. A successful consummation depends on the accuracy of the business judgments underlying the plan, the competence of the debtor's management, and the prevailing economic conditions. If all these factors are favorable, the terms of the plan will be performed, the Ch. 11 case will eventually be closed, and the debtor will emerge from bankruptcy fiscally healthy and freed of the bulk of its prepetition debts. From the creditors' perspective, a successful reorganization holds the promise of a greater recovery on their claims. For the owners of the debtor, rehabilitation offers a chance of preserving some or all of an investment that would have been lost in liquidation. Society as a whole is benefited by the preservation of the profitable elements of the enterprise with its jobs and products. Of course, not all Ch. 11 debtors can be rehabilitated. Many debtors in possession are sold through a §363 asset sale; others end up in liquidation, which may be accomplished by converting the case to Ch. 7 or by remaining in Ch. 11 and modifying the plan to provide for the debtor's liquidation.[4]

The Code offers debtors in possession a host of tools to effectuate a successful reorganization. The general provisions in Chs. 1, 3, and 5 are applicable in all forms of bankruptcy and the discussion throughout this book on topics covered by those Chapters has relevance to a case under Ch. 11.

This diverse list of Ch. 11 tools is the reason why a number of different motivations spur businesses to file a Ch. 11 petition. Some businesses are in an industry that has historically provided goods or services through brick-and-mortar retail stores but is now transitioning to online sales. A company in that industry may need to seek bankruptcy protection to reject the commercial leases to which it is a party and then adjust its business model to focus on sales through the Internet. Blockbuster Video's 2010 and Toys 'R Us's 2017 bankruptcy cases are just two examples of this phenomenon. In other instances, a company may have issued too much corporate debt at a prevailing interest rate that is well above market. This company may need to rely on specialized Code provisions that allow debtors to replace existing debt with debt issued at a lower interest rate. MGM's 2010 bankruptcy case is an example of this phenomenon. Other debtors file for Ch. 11 because there are significant contingent liabilities that can be uniformly addressed in Ch. 11. Asarco's 2005 bankruptcy case involving billions of dollars of asbestos liability is an example. Some debtors have defaulted on key obligations and face having all key assets seized. These debtors file for Ch. 11 because there is no other option. Lehman Brothers' 2008 and the Los Angeles Dodgers' 2011 bankruptcy cases are just two examples of this fairly common phenomenon. Finally, some debtors file for Ch. 11 because they plan to sell the company to another party through a

---

4. Apart from liquidation following an unsuccessful attempt at reorganization, a debtor can choose from the outset to liquidate under Ch. 11. Section 1123(a)(5)(D) expressly permits liquidating plans. Although the end result of liquidation under Ch. 11 is legally the same as liquidation under Ch. 7, a Ch. 11 liquidation can provide practical advantages to the debtor and creditors. For example, the debtor can usually retain greater control of the liquidation process, take more time to wind up its affairs, and enhance the ultimate liquidation value of its estate.

§363 asset sale. General Motors' 2009 and the Texas Rangers' 2010 bankruptcy cases are two examples.

On many occasions in previous chapters of this book, there have been specific references to the operation of sections in Chs. 1, 3, and 5 in a Ch. 11 case. In this chapter, we provide an overview of the Ch. 11 process. Chapter 20 addresses formulating and confirming a plan of reorganization.

§19.3 TREATMENT OF SPECIAL TYPES OF DEBTORS

Ch. 11 is designed to address the issues of a particular type of debtor: large corporate debtors and other commercial entities. Nevertheless, a variety of debtors can file a Ch. 11 petition, and it is important to understand the unique treatment of these debtors.

§19.3.1 Small Business Debtors

When the Code was enacted in 1978, Congress decided that Ch. 11 should consist of a single set of rules applicable to all debtors irrespective of their size. This was a change from the old Bankruptcy Act, which had provided separate chapters for large public corporations (Ch. X) and smaller businesses (Ch. XI). This unitary approach has never been entirely satisfactory because Ch. 11 was drafted to cater for the reorganization of large enterprises, and many of its rules and procedures were too complex for smaller ones. Congress recognized this when it enacted Ch. 12, which provided a simpler, expedited reorganization process for smaller family-owned farm operations with relatively low amounts of debt. Although Ch. 12 has been successful at creating a streamlined procedure for small farming businesses, it is confined to family farmers and is not available to other small businesses. There was an attempt in the early 1990s to enact an equivalent of Ch. 12 for other small businesses, but a proposed bill to create a new chapter of general application to small businesses (which would have been numbered Ch. 10) turned out to be too controversial and failed.

The Bankruptcy Reform Act of 1994 enacted a more modest and limited set of amendments to Ch. 11, designed to make simpler procedures available to small businesses in Ch. 11. If a debtor satisfied the definition of a small business, an expedited procedure was followed in the Ch. 11 case. The problem was that most of the small business procedures only applied if the debtor elected to be treated as a small business. As a result, a small business that did not want to subject itself to speedier procedures did not exercise the election. The 1994 National Bankruptcy Review Commission recommended strengthening the small business provisions enacted in 1994, making them mandatory, and expanding the U.S. Trustee's supervisory role in small business cases to compensate for less active creditors' committees in small cases. Congress accepted these recommendations. The Bankruptcy Abuse Prevention and Consumer Protection Act of 2005 (BAPCPA) amended the small business provisions of Ch. 11 to 1) eliminate the debtor's election, 2) greatly expand the statutory oversight of the U.S. Trustee in small business bankruptcies, and 3) reinforce the simplified small business procedures enacted in 1994.

Section 101(51C) defines "small business case" to mean a Ch. 11 case in which the debtor is a "small business debtor," which is in turn defined in §101(51D). In simplified terms (disregarding some qualifications and limits in the definition), a "small business debtor" is a person engaged in commercial or business activities whose noncontingent, liquidated secured and unsecured debt at the time of the petition is less than $2,556,050.[5] (Note that the definition uses the term "person," which is defined in §101(41) to include individuals, partnerships, and corporations.) For the small business provisions of Ch. 11 to apply, there must be no committee of unsecured creditors appointed in the case, or the court must have decided that the committee has not been active enough to provide effective oversight of the debtor.

§19.3.2 Individual Debtors

Individuals are also allowed to file a Ch. 11 petition. Ch. 13 is generally more appropriate for an individual than Ch. 11 but in some cases the individual's liabilities exceed the Ch. 13 limitations or the debtor has affairs that are complex enough to necessitate Ch. 11's tools and flexible structure.

Although many of the rules and procedures in Ch. 11 apply equally to individuals and to corporate debtors, there are some provisions — many enacted by BAPCPA) — that treat individuals differently. These rules are generally intended to cut down on the differences between Chs. 11 and 13 in cases involving individual debtors and to ensure that an individual debtor does not use Ch. 11 to evade duties or to nullify creditor protections that are provided for in Chs. 7 and 13. The different rules applicable to individual debtors are the following.

(1) Property of the estate. Where the Ch. 11 debtor is not an individual, property of the Ch. 11 estate is determined by the general rule in §541: estate property consists of property in which the debtor had a legal or

5. This number is subject to adjustment under §104. The dollar amount in the text is as adjusted with effect from April 1, 2016. It will be next adjusted with effect from April 1, 2019.

equitable interest at the time of the petition. However, where the debtor is an individual, §1115 adopts the same approach mandated in Ch. 13. The debtor's postpetition property continues to enter the estate after the petition until the case is closed, dismissed, or converted. The debtor remains in possession of estate property while the case is pending except to the extent provided for in the plan, or unless a trustee is appointed.

(2) Domestic support obligations. As noted before, the Bankruptcy Reform Act of 1994 enacted several provisions of the Code to enhance the protection of the debtor's spouse, ex-spouse, and children to whom the debtor owes domestic support obligations. In addition to the other provisions that give special treatment to domestic support obligations—for example, in relation to the automatic stay, exemptions, and discharge—§1129(a)(14) provides that if a debtor fails to pay any domestic support obligation that first became due after the petition was filed (that is, current payments, as opposed to arrears), the debtor's plan does not qualify for confirmation under §1129(a)(14), and §1112(b)(4)(P) allows for dismissal of the case on this ground.

(3) The disposable income test. BAPCPA introduced the disposable income test of Ch. 13 to an individual's Ch. 11 case. It added a rather cryptic requirement in §1123(a)(8) that an individual debtor must commit earnings from personal services to the payment of creditors under the plan to the extent necessary for execution of the plan. More directly, if the holder of an unsecured claim objects to confirmation of the plan, §1129(a)(15) subjects the plan to the disposable income test of §1325(b).

(4) Plan modification. BAPCPA added a provision to §1127 that is similar to §1329. Where the debtor is an individual, the plan may be modified at any time between confirmation and the completion of payments, at the request of the debtor, the trustee, the U.S. Trustee, or an unsecured creditor, to increase or reduce the amount of payments or the time period for payments.[6]

(5) Discharge. Section 1141(d)(2) specifies that the Ch. 11 discharge of an individual debtor is fully subject to the exclusions from discharge in §523. The general rule in §1141(d) is that the Ch. 11 discharge takes effect on confirmation of the plan. Section 1141(d)(5), added by BAPCPA, changes the timing of the Ch. 11 discharge of an individual. The section postpones the discharge—unless the court otherwise orders for cause—until the debtor has completed all payments under the plan. Section

6. *See* section 20.2.5.

1141(d)(5) includes a discharge on grounds of hardship similar to that provided for in Ch. 13.

§19.3.3 Single Asset Real Estate Cases

Single asset real estate cases are ones where 1) the debtor owns a single commercial property or project, 2) ostensibly all of the debtor's income comes from this asset, and 3) the debtor is not conducting any other business aside from managing the asset.[7]

These types of filings are characterized by a high likelihood of abuse. In most cases, the owner of the real estate has defaulted to its lenders and files for bankruptcy hoping to prevent foreclosure and delay adjudication of the case long enough to allow the owner to secure favorable financing or for improvement in the real estate market. Consequently, the Code places a number of unique restrictions on these cases. The automatic stay as to the property terminates on the later of 90 days after the order for relief or 30 days after the court determines that the debtor qualifies as a single assets real estate case, unless the debtor, prior to that time, has 1) "filed a plan of reorganization that has a reasonable possibility of being confirmed within a reasonable time"; or 2) started making monthly payments to the secured creditor equal to the amount of interest due under the applicable nondefault contract rate.[8]

§19.4 MANAGEMENT OF THE BANKRUPTCY CASE AND APPOINTMENT OF A CH.11 TRUSTEE AND EXAMINER

§19.4.1 The Debtor in Possession

Upon the filing of a Ch. 11 petition, the company that existed prior to the petition date automatically becomes the "debtor in possession." The debtor-in-possession concept is a legal fiction necessary to differentiate between the company that existed prepetition and the postpetition entity responsible for operating the business during the bankruptcy case. The debtor in possession has all the powers, rights, obligations, and duties of a trustee under the Code, including obtaining postpetition credit;[9] using, selling, or leasing

7. *See* 11 U.S.C. §101(51B).
8. 11 U.S.C. §362(d)(3).
9. Delineated in §364; *see* Chapter 15.

estate property;[10] avoiding preference payments;[11] avoiding fraudulent transfers;[12] and assuming and rejecting executory contracts and leases.[13] The debtor in possession and the individuals tasked with running the debtor in possession must represent and act in the best interests of creditors.

But why allow existing management to continue running the company in bankruptcy? Couldn't one argue that the existing management team made the decisions that drove the company into bankruptcy? Few countries have bankruptcy systems that allow existing management to stay in power after insolvency. There are a number of reasons for this Ch. 11 structure. Primarily, current management has a familiarity with the business and is generally best suited to orchestrate the rehabilitation process.[14] For debtors in possession that represent complex, highly sophisticated corporate enterprises, the proposition that an uninitiated trustee could be appointed to run a multinational business is anathema — "a curse on the debtor's creditors, shareholders, and employees."[15] But in addition to the threat of poor decision-making, the trustee and her professionals would require significant time to familiarize themselves with the business before beginning any meaningful efforts. That delay could prevent a successful reorganization. And the familiarization process will be costly. The additional cost of this education could potentially be staggering and threaten the debtor's successful reorganization. Finally, if appointment of a trustee was not considered an extraordinary and rare remedy, managers and officers of troubled companies would resist filing for bankruptcy out of fear of losing control of the company. This delay would diminish the prospects of a successful reorganization.[16] For all these reasons, a strong presumption exists that the debtor in possession should be permitted to remain in control of its Ch. 11 case. An alternative presumption would prove disadvantageous to most constituencies.[17]

§19.4.2 Appointment of a Ch. 11 Trustee

Despite the strong presumption noted above, the bankruptcy court can order the appointment of a Ch.11 trustee to displace the debtor in possession's

10. Delineated in §363; *see* Chapter 15.
11. Delineated in §547; *see* Chapter 13.
12. Delineated in §548; *see* Chapter 14.
13. Delineated in §365; *see* Chapter 16
14. *See* H.R. Rep. No. 95-595, 232 (1977).
15. *See* Samir D. Parikh, *The Improper Application of the Clear and Convincing Standard of Proof: Are Bankruptcy Courts Distorting Accepted Risk Allocation Schemes?* 78 U. Cin. L. Rev. 271, 302 (2009).
16. *See* Commission on the Bankruptcy Laws of the United States, Report of the Commission on the Bankruptcy Laws of the United States, H.R. Doc. No. 93-137, pt. I, at 190-91.
17. See, e.g., *In re Marvel Entm't Group, Inc.*, 140 F.3d 463 (3d Cir. 1998).

management team.[18] Section 1104 provides that this appointment can be made for cause, which includes "fraud, dishonesty, incompetence, or gross mismanagement of the affairs of the debtor by current management, either before or after the commencement of the case."[19] In determining whether to appoint a trustee, courts have demanded something more aggravated than simple mismanagement.

Criteria courts have considered include: 1) conflicts of interest, including inappropriate dealings between corporate parents and subsidiaries; 2) various instances of conduct found to establish fraud or dishonesty; 3) evenhandedness in dealings with insiders or affiliated entities vis-a-vis other creditors or customers; 4) the existence of prepetition preferences or fraudulent transfers; 5) management's unwillingness to pursue estate causes of action; 6) inadequate or irregular recordkeeping and reporting or various transgressions as to taxes; and 7) self-dealing by management or waste of corporate assets. For example, imagine that the CEO of a company is the sole owner of an affiliated corporation that owns valuable commercial real estate. At the CEO's direction, the company has leased commercial space from the affiliated corporation at a rate that is well above fair market value. Further, shortly before filing for bankruptcy, the company prepaid for the upcoming six months under the lease. Once in bankruptcy, the CEO is automatically part of the management team for the debtor in possession, but the appointment of a Ch.11 trustee may be appropriate. The debtor in possession has fraudulent transfer and preference claims against the affiliated corporation, and it is unlikely that those claims will be pursued by current management.

A trustee can also be appointed if the appointment is in the interests of creditors, any equity security holders, and other interests of the estate.[20] For example, imagine that the management team of the debtor in possession has a long history with the debtor's sole employee union. The inability to negotiate a new collective bargaining agreement prepetition led to a strike that ultimately forced the company into bankruptcy. Unfortunately, the bankruptcy filing has only exacerbated relations between the company and the union. The debtor's creditors may decide that though the debtor's management team has not committed any malfeasance or gross mismanagement, the prospect of a successful reorganization improves dramatically

---

18. Note that the presumption against the appointment of a trustee is so strong many courts require that the necessary showing be made by clear and convincing evidence. See *Official Comm. of Asbestos Claimants v. G-I Holdings, Inc. (In re G-I Holdings, Inc.)*, 385 F.3d 313, 317-18 (3d Cir.2004); *Marvel Entm't Group.*, 140 F.3d 463, 471 (3d. Cir. 1998); *In re Adelphia Commc'ns Corp.*, 336 B.R. 610, 655-56 (Bankr. S.D.N.Y. 2006); *In re Bellevue Place Assocs.*, 171 B.R. 615, 623 (Bankr. N.D. Ill. 1994)); *In re Nautilus of N.M. Inc.*, 83 B.R. 784, 788 (Bankr. D.N.M. 1988); and *In re William A. Smith Constr. Co.*, 77 B.R. 124, 126 (Bankr. N.D. Ohio 1987).
19. *See* 11 U.S.C. §1104(a)(1).
20. See 11 U.S.C. §1104(a)(2).

with a new management team. These facts may support appointing a Ch. 11 trustee under §1104(a)(2).

Finally, §1104(e) instructs the U.S. Trustee to "move for the appointment of a Chapter 11 Trustee if there are reasonable grounds to suspect that current members of the [debtor's management group] . . . participated in actual fraud, dishonesty, or criminal conduct in the management of the debtor or the debtor's public financial reporting." For example, imagine that the CEO and the CFO of a publicly traded company have been altering the numbers in the company's financial statements to artificially inflate the company's profits. This conduct allows the company to meet previously established profit projections and keeps the stock price at historically high levels. If the accounting fraud is subsequently discovered and the company files a Ch. 11 petition, §1104(e) compels the U.S. Trustee to seek appointment of a Ch. 11 trustee. This subsection was enacted in 2005 and sought to remove the U.S. Trustee's discretion in cases involving a wide range of corporate malfeasance.

§19.4.3 Appointment of a Ch. 11 Examiner

As noted above, a strong presumption exists against the appointment of a Ch. 11 trustee. Further, even if the appointment is justified, the harm from the shift in management may actually ensure the debtor's demise. Consequently, the appointment of an examiner pursuant to §1104(c) is sought far more frequently. Under the subsection, the court is required to order an examiner if 1) such appointment is in the best interests of creditors, any equity security holders, and other interests of the estate; or 2) the debtor's fixed, liquidated, unsecured debts, other than debts for goods, services, or taxes, or owing to an insider, exceed $5,000,000.[21] Courts can give specific direction as to what issues are to be investigated.

An examiner is invariably appointed in large Ch. 11 cases. In those cases, the examiner is tasked with investigating the events and decisions that precipitated the bankruptcy and determining the estate's most viable causes of action. For example, the examiner may identify breaches of fiduciary duties by senior officers and theorize potential causes of action against creditors. In many cases, a motion seeking to appoint a Ch. 11 trustee may be much easier to substantiate after an examiner has investigated the debtor's prepetition activities.

21. The second criteria are satisfied in the vast majority of Ch. 11 cases, but aside from large-scale bankruptcy cases, examiners are often not sought. The reason for this dichotomy is that creditors realize that examiners and their teams of legal and financial professionals can be extremely expensive but provide the estate with limited new avenues to recover funds.

§19.5 ADDITIONAL STAKEHOLDERS AND DEBTOR OVERSIGHT

§19.5.1 Official Committee of Unsecured Creditors and Unofficial Committees

Individual unsecured creditors rarely have the incentive to participate actively in a Ch. 11 case; their claims are much smaller than secured creditors, and they face the prospect of a limited recovery. Nevertheless, the bankruptcy system is designed to protect the interests of these creditors. The primary means to do so is creating an aggregate group of general unsecured creditors and appointing representatives to advocate on behalf of the group. The official committee of unsecured creditors (the "Creditors' Committee") plays a significant role in many Ch. 11 cases, particularly when the case is large enough to warrant the attention and interest of an influential group of creditors. The Creditors' Committee's function is to "aid, assist and monitor the debtor to ensure that the unsecured creditors' views are heard and their interests promoted and protected."[22]

Section 1102 requires the U.S. Trustee to appoint at least one committee of unsecured creditors as soon as practicable after the order for relief. The Creditors' Committee is generally populated with 3 to 7 of the debtor's 20 largest creditors. Service on the committee is voluntary but can be attractive in many cases. The committee is one of the most prominent and vocal actors in a bankruptcy case, and bankruptcy judges are influenced by the committee's perspective. In other words, the committee has significant influence on the direction of the case, and a committee representative can influence the position that the committee takes on various issues. Despite the fact that representatives on the committee are self-motivated, they still owe a fiduciary duty to the creditor body that they represent.[23]

In carrying out its duties, the Creditors' Committee retains its own attorneys, accountants, financial advisors, and other professionals. The committee is not represented by the professionals representing the debtor in possession. The committee's professionals are compensated by the bankruptcy estate.

---

22. *Pan Am Corp. v. Delta Air Lines, Inc.*, 175 B.R. 438, 514 (S.D.N.Y. 1994). In smaller cases, especially where creditors do not have large debts at stake or have little optimism about getting substantial payment, it can be difficult to establish and maintain an active committee. When the debtor qualifies as a small business (*see* section 19.3.1), the U.S. Trustee's duty to appoint a committee is qualified by §1102(a)(3), which allows the court to dispense with the appointment of a committee on request of a party in interest and for cause.
23. See *In re Refco, Inc.*, 336 B.R. 187, 195-96 (Bankr. S.D.N.Y. 2006).

Pursuant to §1102, the U.S. Trustee may appoint additional committees of creditors and equity security holders if parties have a material stake in the bankruptcy case but their interests are not being adequately represented. For example, imagine a large Ch.11 case where the primary issue is the need for the debtor to make significant modifications to their pension and health care obligations owed to current and retired employees. The primary employee union has a representative on the Creditors' Committee, but retirees may believe that the union is representing the interests of current employees, not former ones. In that case, retirees may request that a committee for retirees be formed. Section 1102 authorizes the U.S. Trustee to approve that request.

Further, creditors can decide to form unofficial—or ad hoc—committees in order to influence the direction of the case. The bankruptcy estate does not pay for the professionals employed by an ad hoc committee, but the committee can request reimbursement from the estate if it can prove that it provided substantial contribution to the case.[24] Courts rarely grant these reimbursement requests.

Unofficial committees must comply with Bankruptcy Rule 2019's requirement to file a statement delineating 1) the names and addresses of the creditors or equity holders represented by the committee; 2) the facts and circumstances surrounding the committee's formation; 3) the nature and current amount of each claim held by each committee member, including the acquisition date if less than a year before the petition date; and 4) the amount of each member's claim at the time of committee formation, the time those interests were acquired, the amounts paid, and the sale of any interest. Many creditors avoid participating in ad hoc committees because of these disclosure requirements.

§19.5.2 U.S. Trustee

a. General Duties

The United States Trustee Program is a component of the Department of Justice. U.S. Trustees plays a meaningful role in Ch. 11 cases. 28 U.S.C. §586 delineates the U.S. Trustees' duties. Primarily, U.S. Trustees are tasked with monitoring the bankruptcy cases filed in their region and overseeing the professionals retained by each estate. More specifically, the U.S. Trustees 1) review plans of reorganization and disclosure statements, ensuring compliance with Code requirements; 2) ensure that the debtor's required reports, schedules, and fees are properly and timely filed; 3) monitor the

24. See 11 U.S.C. §503(b)(3) and (4).

progress of each Ch. 11 case to ensure that there is no undue delay; and 4) review employment applications.

As noted above, the professionals' fees incurred by the debtor in possession and official committees are paid by the bankruptcy estate. The U.S. Trustees are tasked with objecting to fees that are exorbitant or unsubstantiated and ensuring that professionals with conflicts of interest are not retained by the estate or official committees. The U.S. Trustees also appoint and monitor official committees and can petition for the appointment of a Ch. 11 trustee or an examiner.

b. Duties as to Small Business Debtors

Section 1116 and 28 U.S.C. §586(a)(3)(H) and (6) set out the additional duties of the U.S. Trustee and the debtor in possession in a small business case. In each case, the U.S. Trustee's supervisory function can be divided into two stages:

i. The U.S. Trustee's duties at the outset of the case.

One of the principal underlying goals of the small business procedures is to have the U.S. Trustee focus on a small business case at its initial stages and to identify as early as possible those cases in which the debtor does not have a reasonable prospect of reorganization. The U.S. Trustee must conduct an initial interview with the debtor, investigate the debtor's viability, and generally counsel and supervise the debtor. If the U.S. Trustee finds that the debtor will not be able to get a Ch. 11 plan confirmed, she must move for dismissal of the case. The debtor is required to attach financial information to its petition and must attend meetings scheduled by the court or the U.S. Trustee.

ii. The U.S. Trustee's oversight of the debtor in possession while the case is pending.

As the definition of "small business debtor" indicates, a Ch. 11 case only qualifies as a small business case if the court authorizes the U.S. Trustee not to appoint an unsecured creditors' committee, or the court finds it to be ineffectual. One of the rationales for creating small business procedures is that unsecured creditors are generally not likely to participate actively in a small business case, so unsecured creditors' committees are seldom effective in such cases and do not exercise adequate supervision of the debtor in possession. The U.S. Trustee's supervisory role, once the case has passed the initial stage and proceeds through plan confirmation and consummation, is therefore largely intended to substitute for the role that would normally be exercised by a creditors' committee. To aid the U.S. Trustee in her supervision, the debtor has extensive reporting requirements during the course of the case, which are intended to reveal the state of the debtor's management of the business and its financial affairs. These reports include information on such matters as cash receipts and disbursements, tax payments, and profitability.

§19.6 COMMENCEMENT OF THE CASE AND FIRST DAY MOTIONS

§19.6.1 Commencement of the Case

A Ch. 11 case may be commenced either voluntarily or involuntarily. Under Rule 1007, the debtor must file a schedule of assets and liabilities, a statement of financial affairs, and a statement of executory contracts, as described in section 9.3. In addition, a corporate debtor must file a list of equity security holders, and all Ch. 11 debtors must file a list of the 20 largest unsecured creditors. This filing allows the U.S. Trustee to appoint a creditors' committee.

A case can be converted involuntarily to Ch. 11 only from Ch. 7, and it can be dismissed or converted to Ch. 7 by a party other than the debtor for cause. Section 1112 gives the debtor broader rights of conversion to and from Ch. 11.

§19.6.2 First Day Motions

The filing of a Ch. 11 petition invariably sends a seismic shock through the debtor's business. Code provisions affect all facets of the company and, in many cases, threaten the debtor's viability. Fortunately, the Code allows the bankruptcy court to grant relief that will ensure the debtor's access to capital and normalize operations and customer interactions. Ch. 11 debtors would like to secure this relief immediately. Consequently, along with the filing of the Ch. 11 petition, debtors invariably file a host of "first day motions" that seek immediate relief to allow the debtor's business to continue with minimal disruption.

The majority of first day motions are procedural and uncontroversial, allowing the debtor to continue operating as before.[25] Stakeholders

25. Examples of which include 1) maintenance of customer programs, 2) payment of prepetition, nonexecutive employee wages and benefits, 3) retention of debtor's counsel and other key professionals, 4) maintenance of cash management system, 5) extension of the deadlines to file schedules and other documents, and 6) joint administration of all cases filed by affiliated entities.

generally support these procedural motions because they seek to preserve the debtor's going concern value. However, coupled with these simple procedural motions are other first day motions that impact stakeholders' rights and distributions in ways that are significant and inveterate. For example, debtors in possession invariably need significant postpetition financing to move through the bankruptcy process. Section 15.3.2 explores the details of postpetition financing under §364. The need for postpetition financing is uncontroversial, but the protections most postpetition lenders seek can be injurious to the interests of other stakeholders, and courts will need to hear objections to the proposed financing arrangement. At the same time, delays in securing financing can irreparably undermine the debtor's rehabilitation efforts. A similar dynamic emerges with first day motions seeking to use cash collateral. Section 15.2.3 explores the details of the debtor's use of cash collateral under §363. Courts invariably grant temporary relief in these cases that allows the debtor to continue operating as it had prepetition but affords stakeholders time to review proposed action and file the appropriate objections — if any — prior to a final hearing on the relief requested.[26]

§19.7 THE IMPORTANCE OF NEGOTIATION AND BUSINESS JUDGMENT IN A CH. 11 CASE

Ch. 11 is much more intricate than Ch. 13 because the affairs of a Ch. 11 debtor can be very complex and require greater flexibility and more extensive participation by parties in interest. Two aspects of a Ch. 11 case stand out and distinguish it dramatically from the other forms of bankruptcy. The first is the great leeway given to the debtor and other parties in interest to negotiate during the case for the purpose of reaching agreement on the terms of the plan of reorganization, explored fully in Chapter 20. Provision is made for representative committees, for the communication of information, and for voting. Ideally, a Ch. 11 plan should be a consensual document, although Ch. 11 does have some mechanisms for overriding opposition to it and imposing its terms on unwilling parties. The role played by Code provisions in encouraging negotiation or providing bargaining leverage to one or another party is a constant theme in any discussion of Ch. 11.

The second distinguishing feature of Ch. 11 is the extent to which it interacts with difficult issues of corporate and business law and business strategy. Particularly in corporate reorganizations, the Code provisions, complex as they may be, are mere skeletal structures. They are augmented

26. See 11 U.S.C. §363(c)(3) (contemplating interim use of cash collateral).

by nonbankruptcy laws such as those governing corporations, labor relations, commercial law, securities, and taxation. Of course, nonbankruptcy law and economic considerations are relevant in all forms of bankruptcy, as has often been pointed out before. However, the scope and scale of the application of nonbankruptcy business law and business judgment is typically much greater in a complex Ch. 11 case.

Examples

EXAMPLES

1. M.C. Young wishes to acquire the Big Banana Casino. To make this acquisition, he has to secure the approval of the state casino control commission. In testifying before the commission, Young assures the commission that he does not intend to fire more than 2 percent of staff or make other dramatic changes if he is allowed to acquire the casino. The commission approves the sale to Young, who becomes president and CEO of the casino. Immediately after securing approval, Young begins making dramatic changes to improve profits. Young decides that cleaning rooms daily is gratuitous. Instead, the Big Banana cleans rooms only as requested by guests. This change allows Young to fire half of his cleaning staff. Young also fires a quarter of his dealers and floor managers, relying on automated gambling machines. These actions prompt the employee union representing these employees to file a number of complaints alleging violation of the collective bargaining agreement. Undeterred, Young goes on to eliminate most of the landscaping and maintenance crew. Not surprisingly, Big Banana Casino falls into disrepair. Patrons begin complaining about mold growing in the rooms and small rats stealing water bottles. Gambling revenues begin to fall and eclipse the cost savings Young achieved through his cost-cutting measures. Later that year, the Big Banana Casino's gambling license is up for renewal. The state commission undertakes an extensive review and issues a preliminary denial of the license-renewal request, finding that Young was dishonest in his testimony during the sale approval process and has exhibited a lack of good character, integrity, and competence.
   a. Young decides he wants to have Big Banana Casino file for bankruptcy to allow him to maintain control of the casino and perhaps negotiate a sale. If you are Young's bankruptcy counsel, what primary deficiency do you see with Young's plan?

2. Assume the same facts as in Example 1. After listening to your concerns, Young decides that he will step down as president and CEO, and his son Ricky will be promoted into those roles. Ricky decides that he will otherwise keep the management team the same but will now run the casino according to the highest standards and undo the decisions his father made. Since there will not be any postpetition malfeasance,

Young believes that the concerns you raised earlier have been addressed. Is he right?

3. Thericorn has developed a new drug — Stasis — that will allow individuals to stop blinking for five hours at a time. Individuals seeking uninterrupted screen-time on their mobile devices have been touting the product on social networks and sales have been strong. Unfortunately, sales have not been as strong as investors expected. To address this deficiency, Thericorn has been undertaking some creative accounting: for every bottle of Stasis shipped, Thericorn's accounting department recognizes that bottle as being sold. The accounting department then counts that bottle as being sold again when it is actually sells. The good news is that when the sales figures were reported, Thericorn's stock price increased significantly. The bad news is that employees revealed the accounting fraud, and the company wound up in bankruptcy.

   Surprisingly, Thericorn's management team is able to convince all stakeholders that it is best suited to manage the company's reorganization and no creditor has sought the appointment of a Ch. 11 trustee. Should Thericorn worry about another party requesting that the bankruptcy court appoint a Ch. 11 trustee?

Explanations

EXPLANATIONS

1. a. Young plans to file a Ch.11 petition to maintain control of the casino. The primary threat to his objective is that §1104(a)(1) allows for the court to appoint a Ch. 11 trustee to take over the debtor in possession if "cause" exists. "Cause" includes, but is not limited to, fraud, dishonesty, incompetence, or gross mismanagement of the affairs of the debtor. Section 1104 does not require that more than one of these elements need be present for the court to order the appointment of a Ch. 11 trustee. In most cases, the bankruptcy court will need to make its own assessment of whether any of these elements exist. However, in this case, the court can rely on the conclusions of the state casino commission.

   The commission has already undertaken an extensive review of Young's management and determined that he acted dishonestly and incompetently. Further, his decisions could easily be characterized as gross mismanagement. The court will need to review the commission's process and findings but a factual record already exists establishing the propriety of the appointment of a Ch. 11 trustee.

   Section 1104(a)(2) is also implicated. The subsection allows the court to appoint a Ch. 11 trustee if the appointment is in the interests of creditors, any equity security holders, and other interests of the estate. This subsection is applicable as well. Young's conduct has caused the casino to lose its gambling license—one of the most disastrous results a casino can experience. The casino's viability is in doubt, and all stakeholders have been harmed by Young's management. Appointment of a Ch.11 trustee would be in the best interests of all stakeholders.

It is important to make Young aware of the fact that if the casino files a Ch. 11 petition, there is a high probability that the casino's existing management team will be replaced by a Ch. 11 trustee.

2. Young believes that by stepping down as president and CEO, he materially reduces the odds of a Ch. 11 trustee being appointed, but he is wrong. Primarily, §1104(a)(1) makes clear that in evaluating "cause" courts are to consider both prepetition and postpetition conduct. Consequently, Young's prepetition conduct is sufficient to substantiate the appointment, and his departure from the management ranks is not enough to alter this result. In *In re Sharon Steel*, 871 F.2d 1217 (3d Cir. 1989), the Third Circuit held that a partial change in management does not prevent the appointment of a Ch. 11 trustee if other officers who were in management during the misconduct at issue are still involved in the debtor's operations. In this case, Ricky is taking over for his father, but the management team is otherwise unaffected. These officers are tainted by Young's conduct and their continued involvement in the debtor's management justifies appointment of a Ch. 11 trustee.

   That being said, in instances where the entire former management team is replaced, courts have denied requests to appoint a Ch. 11 trustee. For example, in *In re Adelphia Communications*, 336 B.R. 610 (Bankr. S.D.N.Y. 2006), the founder of the company and various family members were found to have engaged in egregious and extensive fraudulent conduct. After the company filed for bankruptcy, all individuals involved in the malfeasance resigned from management and the board of directors. New independent directors were appointed to the board, and these directors reconstituted the management team at the debtor and the debtor's subsidiaries and affiliates. The bankruptcy court in that case denied a motion seeking appointment of a Ch. 11 trustee. The new management team had not been tainted by the old management team, and there was no evidence of self-dealing or misconduct perpetrated by new management. Similar sweeps of management occurred in the *Worldcom* bankruptcy and the motion seeking appointment of a Ch.11 trustee was denied in that case, as well.[27] Ultimately, "where current management

27. In re WorldCom, Inc., *Memorandum Decision and Order Denying Motions for Appointment of a Chapter 11 Trustee and Examiner*, Docket No. 02-13533 #5923 (Bankr. S.D.N.Y. May 16, 2003); see also *In re The 1031 Tax Group, LLC*, 374 B.R. 78 (Bankr. S.D.N.Y. 2007).

is not implicated by a debtor's prior misdeeds, there may be no legal basis for the imposition of a trustee. . . ."[28]

3. In most cases, a creditor brings the motion seeking appointment of a Ch.11 trustee. However, in this context, §1104(e) specifically instructs the U.S. Trustee to move for the appointment of a Ch.11 trustee under subsection (a) "if there are reasonable grounds to suspect that current members of the governing body of the debtor, the debtor's chief executive or chief financial officer, or members of the governing body who selected the debtor's chief executive or chief financial officer, participated in actual fraud, dishonesty, or criminal conduct in the management of the debtor or the debtor's public financial reporting." Thericorn's management team has engaged in criminal misconduct in the company's public financial reporting by altering the company's sales figures. It appears that reasonable grounds exist to suspect the misconduct. Consequently, the U.S. Trustee is compelled to bring a motion for appointment, even if the U.S. Trustee may disagree with the course of conduct.

28. *Id.* at 10.

CHAPTER 20

The Chapter 11 Plan of Reorganization

§20.1 OVERVIEW OF THE PLAN PROCESS

Ch. 11 offers a debtor in possession the opportunity to rehabilitate its business and continue as a going concern. In many respects, this is Ch. 11's ultimate design. But the path to a successful formulation and confirmation of a plan of reorganization is a labyrinth (see Diagram 20a on page 561), and many debtors are unsuccessful. Indeed, myriad requirements must be satisfied for a debtor to matriculate through each stage of confirmation. The debtor must build consensus among groups of creditors that have suffered a variety of different injuries due to the debtor's financial distress. The process culminates with creditors who hold recognized claims against the estate voting to either approve or deny confirmation of the plan. Those who approve the plan accept the treatment of their claims delineated in the plan. But even if all claimants approve the plan, the bankruptcy court must still evaluate the plan and determine if it satisfies certain specific Code requirements. Further, despite unanimity among creditors, the U.S. Trustee may still object to confirmation based on a belief that the debtor has failed to satisfy the Code's requirements. The debtor is invariably attempting to balance a host of competing interests while still running its business and fending off parties that believe they have a better formulation for how the debtor should be rehabilitated.

The process begins with the disclosure statement, which is intended to provide all stakeholders with comprehensive details about the debtor's past, current, and future operations. Before the disclosure statement is disseminated to creditors, the bankruptcy court must rule that the statement complies with §1125's requirements.

If the disclosure statement is approved, the debtor is allowed to distribute it to creditors and begin the balloting process. Creditors will generally have between 30 to 60 days to review the disclosure statement and submit their votes on whether the plan should be approved or denied.

The plan of reorganization places creditors into distinct classes based on the nature of each recognized claim against the estate. Claimants who are not receiving a full satisfaction of their claim through the plan are considered "impaired" and entitled to vote on the plan. Section 1129(a)(8) requires that in order to confirm the plan each impaired class must "accept" the plan. Section 1126 provides that a class has accepted a plan if the plan is approved by 1) more than one-half in number of allowed claimants or interest holders; and 2) creditors holding at least two-thirds in amount.

But gaining consent from each creditor class is difficult. Policymakers recognized this and drafted §1129(b)(1) to provide debtors an alternative, referred to colorfully as "cramdown." A court can confirm a plan of reorganization even if §1126 is unsatisfied by cramming down secured, unsecured, and equity classes if the debtor can satisfy a host of requirements designed to protect these creditors. The effect of this provision is profound. Indeed, the debtor is allowed to modify the crammed down creditor's rights over the creditor's objections and invariably in violation of an existing agreement between the parties.

If the Ch. 11 labyrinth is successfully navigated, the bankruptcy court will confirm the plan of reorganization and set a date for the plan to take effect. On that date, the debtor will begin performing as delineated in the plan and ultimately exit the safe confines of bankruptcy to reacclimate to the business world.

§20.2 FORMULATING THE PLAN

§20.2.1 The Debtor's Exclusive Period to Propose a Plan of Reorganization

For debtors in possession seeking to use Ch.11 to reorganize their company, the formulation of a plan of reorganization begins immediately after the decision to file for bankruptcy is made.[1] The Code affords the debtor a

1. In some cases, the plan is actually prepared and voted on prior to the filing of the bankruptcy petition. *See* section 20.5, *infra*.

The Progress of a Ch. 11 Case

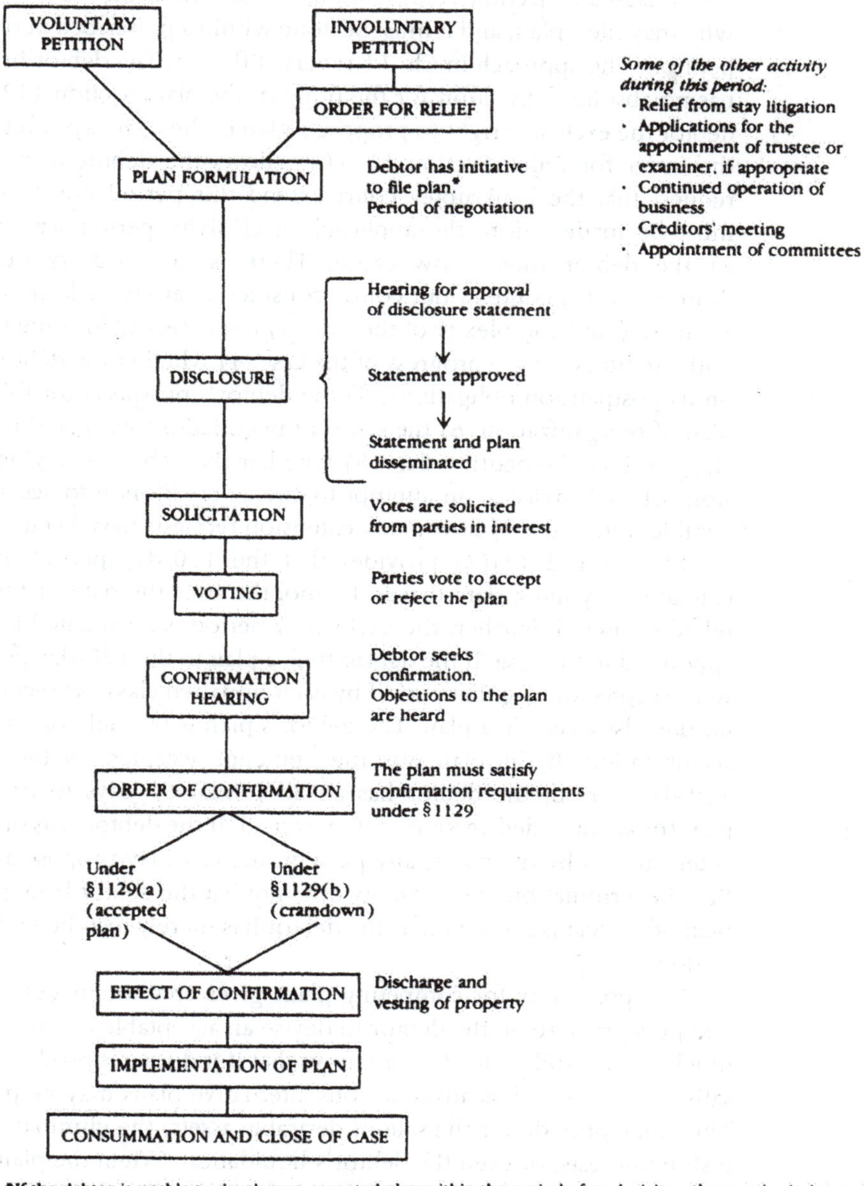
VOLUNTARY PETITION
INVOLUNTARY PETITION
ORDER FOR RELIEF
Some of the other activity during this period:
· Relief from stay litigation
· Applications for the appointment of trustee or examiner, if appropriate
· Continued operation of business
· Creditors' meeting
· Appointment of committees
PLAN FORMULATION
Debtor has initiative to file plan.*
Period of negotiation
Hearing for approval of disclosure statement
DISCLOSURE
Statement approved
Statement and plan disseminated
SOLICITATION
Votes are solicited from parties in interest
VOTING
Parties vote to accept or reject the plan
CONFIRMATION HEARING
Debtor seeks confirmation.
Objections to the plan are heard
ORDER OF CONFIRMATION
The plan must satisfy confirmation requirements under § 1129
Under §1129(a) (accepted plan)
Under §1129(b) (cramdown)
EFFECT OF CONFIRMATION
Discharge and vesting of property
IMPLEMENTATION OF PLAN
CONSUMMATION AND CLOSE OF CASE

*If the debtor is unable to develop an accepted plan within the period of exclusivity, other parties in interest may file plans. This diagram does not reflect the possibility of competing plans.

Diagram 20a

period of time — referred to as the exclusivity period — during which only the debtor is allowed to submit a plan of reorganization.

As stated in section 18.3, in a Ch. 13 case the debtor is the only person who may file a plan, and it must be done within a prescribed period after the petition. The approach in Ch. 11 is very different. The debtor in possession has no absolute time limit for the filing of the plan. Section 1121 gives the debtor the exclusive right to propose a plan in the 120 days after the date of the order for relief. Section 1121(d) allows the debtor in possession to request that the bankruptcy court extend this period but 1) the request must be made before the applicable exclusivity period has expired and 2) the debtor must show cause. There is no statutory definition of "cause" in this context, but courts consider a variety of factors, including 1) the size and complexity of the case; 2) the necessity for time to negotiate with creditors; 3) the progress of the case; 4) whether the debtor is current on its postpetition obligations; 5) the debtor's prospects for filing a viable plan of reorganization; 6) the status of negotiations with creditors; 7) time elapsed since the petition date; 8) whether the debtor is relying on extensions of exclusivity in an attempt to coerce creditors into accepting unfavorable terms; and 9) how many extension requests have been filed to date.

Section 1121(d)(2) provides that the 120-day period may not be extended beyond a date that is 18 months after the date of the order for relief is entered. Further, the exclusivity period is terminated if a trustee is appointed in the case. If the debtor filed a plan in the 120-day period, and it was accepted during that period by each impaired class (*see* section 20.3.2), no one else may file a plan. The debtor's plan is the only one available for confirmation. If the plan was filed but not accepted by the end of the 120-day period, the debtor has an additional 60 days to try to get the plan (or an amended version of it) accepted. If the debtor fails or exclusivity is terminated by the court, any party in interest may propose a plan. Note that the termination of exclusivity does not bar the debtor from proposing a plan of reorganization; rather, the debtor has merely lost the exclusive right to do so.

The possibility for competing plans gives creditors negotiating power and puts pressure on the debtor to devise an acceptable and feasible plan as quickly as possible. The debtor knows that if it does not produce a plan that satisfies creditors, less advantageous alternative plans may be put forward. They may provide for the sale of desirable assets, the elimination of ownership interests, or even the debtor's liquidation. When the plans are voted on, dissatisfied creditors may favor a plan that the debtor does not want. Therefore, even if no competing plan emerges, the threat of alternative plans has an impact on the debtor's thinking as it deals with creditors in the negotiating process.

If competing plans are proposed, each must comply with the disclosure requirements and confirmation standards discussed below. If, in the end, there are two or more plans that satisfy the requirements for confirmation, §1129(c) requires the court to consider the preferences of creditors and equity security holders in deciding which to confirm. Only one plan can be confirmed.

Where the debtor qualifies as a small business, §1121(e) provides a shorter exclusivity period. This provision was added in 1994 for the purpose of expediting bankruptcies involving business debtors with relatively small liabilities. As enacted in 1994, the provision applied only if the debtor elected to be treated as a small business. The Bankruptcy Abuse Prevention and Consumer Protection Act of 2005 (BAPCPA) eliminated the debtor's power to elect application of the section and made it mandatory if the debtor meets the definition of a "small business debtor" in §101(51C). Section 1121(e), as amended by BAPCPA, gives the debtor an exclusivity period of 180 days and imposes an outer limit for the proposal of all plans, whether by the debtor or otherwise, of 300 days from the order for relief. Section 1129(e) requires the plan to be confirmed within 45 days after a plan complying with the Code is filed. The court's power to extend these time limits is circumscribed. It may grant an extension only if the application is made before the end of the time limit, for cause, and upon a showing that a confirmable plan will be proposed within a reasonable time. If the court does grant an extension, it must impose a new deadline.

§20.2.2 The Disclosure Statement

a. The Approval Process

In a Ch. 11 case, creditors and equity security holders vote to accept or reject the plan. These parties need detailed information about the debtor's past, current, and future operations to make an informed decision. Consequently, before the debtor can propose a plan of reorganization, the debtor must submit a disclosure statement to the court for approval.

Section 1125 requires that the disclosure statement contain "adequate information" — which is specifically defined to capture "information of a kind and in sufficient detail, as far as is reasonably practicable in light of the nature and history of the debtor and the condition of the debtor's books and records . . . that would enable . . . a hypothetical investor of the relevant class to make an informed judgment about the plan. . . ."[2] The statement must be approved by the court after notice and a hearing, and it must then be transmitted to all creditors and equity security holders, together with a copy

2. 11 U.S.C. §1125(a).

of the plan or a summary of it. Section 1125 prohibits the postpetition[3] solicitation of acceptances or rejections of a plan prior to the dissemination of the plan and the court-approved disclosure statement.

Typically, a disclosure statement provides a history of the debtor and a description of its business operations. It explains the plan and alerts parties to any options available under the plan. It describes the proposed course of consummation of the plan and provides financial information so that the debtor's prospects of rehabilitation can be evaluated and its liquidation value assessed. In determining whether to approve a disclosure statement, most courts consider if the statement contains the following elements: 1) a summary of the plan; 2) the circumstances that precipitated the bankruptcy filing; 3) a summary of key postpetition events; 4) a complete description of all available estate assets; 5) a complete list of all potential causes of action, including ones that the debtor intends to bring after confirmation; 6) the anticipated future of the debtor, including future management and risks inherent in the business model and capital structure proposed by the plan; 7) the source of the information provided in the disclosure statement; 8) alternatives to confirmation of the plan, including a full liquidation analysis; and 9) the tax consequences of the plan.

The disclosure statement is analogous to the prospectus published by a corporation in connection with the issuance of stock. If the Ch. 11 case involves a corporation and the plan is complex, the disclosure statement could be as lengthy and intricate as a prospectus. If the debtor is an individual or a smaller business, the statement is likely to be considerably shorter and simpler.

Section 1144 provides that the court may revoke confirmation at any time before 180 days after the date of entry of the confirmation order if confirmation of a plan of reorganization was based on a disclosure statement that contained a material fraudulent statement or statements.

A debtor that qualifies as a small business (*see* section 20.2.1), §1125(f), as amended by BAPCPA, provides for a less stringent process for approval of the disclosure statement. If the court concludes that the plan itself provides adequate information, it can dispense with a separate disclosure statement, or the court can approve a standard form disclosure statement. The statement can be conditionally approved by the court, and the debtor can immediately begin to solicit acceptances and rejections based on the conditionally approved disclosure, as long as the debtor provides adequate information to those holders of claims and interests who are solicited. Final approval of the statement may be combined with the confirmation hearing.

3. Section 1125 applies only to postpetition solicitation of votes. Sometimes the debtor may negotiate a plan with creditors before filing the petition. BAPCPA added §1125(g) to make this clear by permitting prepetition solicitation if it complies with nonbankruptcy law. This is discussed in section 20.5.

b. The Disclosure Statement and Securities Regulations

Outside of bankruptcy, the disclosure required by a corporate prospectus is subject to securities regulation. Section 1125(d) allows regulatory agencies such as the Securities and Exchange Commission (SEC) to address the court on the adequacy of disclosure, but makes it clear that the standards of bankruptcy law ultimately determine the extent of disclosure required. A statement that does not fully satisfy nonbankruptcy standards could be adequate for Ch. 11 purposes.

Section 1125(c) allows different statements to be approved for different classes, but all members of a particular class must receive the same statement. Variations in the statement sent to different classes may be appropriate based on the nature of the claims or interests in that class and the depth of information that they require to exercise informed judgment.

Section 1125(e) contains what is called a "safe harbor" provision, which protects persons who violate nonbankruptcy regulations in the solicitation of votes or the issuance of securities under the plan, provided that they act in good faith and in accordance with the Code. The effect of this provision is to protect parties, such as creditors' committees, attorneys, or creditors, who solicit votes on the plan by using the court-approved disclosure statement. The protection only applies if the party acts in good faith, without knowledge of some defect or omission in the statement, and in compliance with the solicitation requirements of the Code.

§20.2.3 Voting on the Plan

When the court approves the disclosure statement, it fixes the period for voting on the plan. Holders of claims or interests who are eligible to vote on the plan receive ballots with the disclosure statement and must return them within the prescribed time, indicating acceptance or rejection of the plan.[4] Acceptance of the plan is not based on a simple majority of all the votes. Instead, all claims and interests are divided into classes as explained in section 20.3.2. Each class forms a voting block. If the requisite majority of members of that class votes in favor of the plan, the class as a whole accepts it, even though some of its members may have voted to reject the plan. It is the vote of the class that is significant for confirmation purposes, and the outvoted dissenters are bound by the majority. However, when the class has accepted the plan, the minority who favored rejection is given some protection by provisions that set minimum standards for the treatment of their claims and interests. (This is discussed in section 20.4.2.)

---

4. *See* Rules 3017 and 3018 of the Federal Rules of Bankruptcy Procedure.

The voting majority for acceptance by a class of claims is slightly different from that for a class of interests. Under §1126(c), a class of claims accepts the plan if at least two-thirds in amount and more than half in number of the voting creditors with allowed claims in that class have accepted the plan. (Voting majorities are illustrated in Examples 2, 3, and 4.) Note that the majority is determined on the basis of voting members of the class and does not take into account the claims of members who decline to vote. Therefore, for example, if the class consists of twenty creditors, but only one of them votes, that vote will carry the class, irrespective of the size of the claim. Under §1126(d), a class of interests accepts the plan if at least two-thirds in amount of the voting holders of allowed interests in that class have accepted the plan. Section 1126(e) allows the court, on request of a party in interest and after notice and a hearing, to exclude from the vote any entity whose acceptance or rejection was not in good faith or was not solicited or procured in good faith or in accordance with the provisions of the Code.

In two situations, the vote of a class is presumed as a matter of law, so no actual voting takes place. First, a class that is unimpaired does not vote on the plan, but is conclusively deemed by §1126(f) to have accepted the plan.[5] Second, a class of claims or interests that will receive or retain no property under the plan is deemed under §1126(g) to have rejected the plan and is not required to vote.

§20.2.4 Confirmation

After the period for voting has closed and notice of hearing has been given, §1128 requires a confirmation hearing to be held. Parties in interest may object to confirmation. An objection to confirmation differs from a vote to reject the plan: Rejection is motivated by the preference of the holder, and its perception of its best interests; objection must be based on the legal ground that the plan fails to meet the requirements for confirmation prescribed by §1129. (*See* section 20.4.) If the plan satisfies those requirements, the objection fails and the court issues an order of confirmation under Rule 3020. As noted in section 20.2.1, in a small business case, §1129(e), enacted by BAPCPA, requires the court to confirm a plan that complies with the provisions of the Code not later that 45 days after the plan is filed, unless the court has approved a time extension under §1121(e)(3).

---

5. As explained in section 20.3.2, a class is impaired unless the rights of its members are left unaltered by the plan, except for the cure of default.

§20.2.5 Modification of the Plan

Section 1127 permits the proponent of a plan to modify it before or after confirmation. Any modification must comply with the requirements applicable to the original plan under §§1122 and 1123, and a disclosure statement must be approved by the court and disseminated for the modified plan in accordance with §1125. A holder of a claim or interest who accepted or rejected the original plan is deemed to have voted the same way on the modified plan unless the holder changes its vote.

Prior to confirmation, §1127(a) allows the proponent to modify the plan simply by filing a modified plan with the court. This gives the proponent some flexibility to make changes in the plan to overcome opposition and achieve a higher degree of acceptance. The modified plan must comply with all the provisions of §§1121 through 1129, and there must be disclosure of the modified plan under §1125. Modification after confirmation is more disruptive, so §1127(b) imposes restrictions on postconfirmation modification. The plan may only be modified with court approval following notice and a hearing and upon a showing that circumstances warrant modification. In addition, the modification must be made before "substantial consummation" of the plan. This is defined in §1101(2) to mean the transfer of all or substantially all of the property proposed to be transferred by the plan, assumption by the debtor or its successor of the business or of the management of all or substantially all of the property dealt with by the plan, and commencement of distribution under the plan.

Where the debtor is an individual, BAPCPA added §1127(e), which is similar to §1329(a). The plan can be modified at the request of the debtor, the trustee, the U.S. Trustee, or the holder of an unsecured claim to reduce or increase the amount of payments or to alter the length of the payment period. As in Ch. 13, payments under a Ch. 11 plan can be changed to take into account a significant unforeseen change in the debtor's financial circumstances.

§20.2.6 The Effect of Confirmation

Section 1141 delineates the effect of confirmation. In general, §1141(a) makes the provisions of the confirmed plan binding on all parties in interest—including the debtor, creditors, and shareholders—whether or not their claims were impaired and whether or not they accepted the plan. This general rule is subject to the exceptions to discharge mentioned below. Under §1141(b) and (c), confirmation also vests all the estate's property in the debtor, free and clear of all claims and interests except to the extent that the plan provides otherwise. The plan may provide otherwise for the purpose of preserving liens pending payment of secured claims or because some property is to be transferred or liquidated to settle claims.

Where the debtor is not an individual, §1141(d)(1) discharges the debtor upon confirmation of the plan, so that the debtor's original obligations fall away and are replaced by the commitments under the plan. This used to be the rule for all debtors, but BAPCPA changed it for individuals in Ch. 11, apparently to conform more closely to the Ch. 13 discharge. Where the debtor is an individual, §1141(d)(5) states that unless the court, after notice and a hearing, orders otherwise for cause, confirmation of the plan does not discharge any debt provided for in the plan until the court grants a discharge on completion of all payments under the plan. The language of §1141(d) is different from that of §1328(a). Section 1328(a) says that the court "shall" grant a discharge to the debtor as soon as practicable after the completion of payments under the plan. By contrast, §1141(d)(5) states that confirmation of the plan does not discharge debts "until the court grants a discharge on completion of all payments under the plan," but it gives the court some discretion to grant an earlier discharge under specified circumstances.

A Ch. 11 discharge is extremely broad in scope and relates to all prepetition debts as well as postpetition debts allowed under §502(g), (h), and (i), regardless of whether a proof of claim was filed, the claim was allowed, or the plan was accepted by the holder. The discharge is subject to the provisions of the plan and the confirmation order, which may curtail its scope and exclude otherwise dischargeable debts.

Quite apart from the provisions of the plan, §1141(d)(2) and (3) contain exceptions to discharge. Section 1141(d)(2) excepts from the discharge of an individual debtor any debts that are nondischargeable under §523. Section 1141(d)(3) denies a discharge to the debtor—whether it is an individual or a corporation—if 1) the plan liquidates all or substantially all of its property; 2) the debtor does not engage in business after consummation of the plan; and 3) it would not have been entitled to a discharge if the case had been filed under Ch. 7.

Section 1141(d)(1)(B) deals with the effect of confirmation on ownership interests in the debtor: Except as otherwise provided in the plan or the confirmation order, confirmation terminates the rights and interests of equity security holders and general partners provided for by the plan. In other words, §1141(d)(1)(B) sets out a general rule that ownership interests in the debtor cannot survive Ch. 11 bankruptcy unless the debtor is able to have a plan confirmed that preserves them in whole or in part. To achieve confirmation of a plan with such provisions, the debtor must provide sufficient payment to gain acceptance of the plan by creditors, or to meet the stringent cramdown standards explained in section 20.4.3.

§20.2.7 The Effective Date of the Plan, Performance, and Consummation

Unlike Ch. 13, Ch. 11 prescribes no time limit for performance of the obligations under the plan. The payment periods and the timetable for implementation of the plan are stipulated by the plan itself. These periods are settled in the preconfirmation negotiation process and are based on the business realities of the debtor's situation. Section 1142 requires the debtor to proceed with implementation of the plan following its confirmation. The plan takes effect on a specified date shortly after confirmation, referred to in several sections of Ch. 11 as the "effective date" of the plan. If the plan is successfully consummated, the case is closed. Otherwise, the debtor's failure to perform is grounds for dismissal or conversion to a Ch. 7 under §1112.

§20.3 THE CONTENT OF THE PLAN

§20.3.1 Overview

Ch. 11 is designed to facilitate consensual plans of reorganization formulated through negotiation amongst all key stakeholders. Section 1123(a) therefore gives the debtor considerable flexibility to develop a plan that best meets its needs while accommodating the legitimate demands of creditors and other parties in interest. Section 1123 contains eight mandatory provisions for the plan, and §1123(b) sets out a range of permissive provisions that may be included in it. The content of the plan is also affected by §1129, which prescribes the standards that it must meet for confirmation. While some of the mandatory provisions and standards are absolute, others may be varied by consent so that they give bargaining power to a party whose consent is sought.

§20.3.2 The Mandatory Plan Provisions Under §1123(a)

Section 1123(a) requires the plan to deal with the following matters.

a. Designation of Classes of Claims and Interests (§1123(a)(1))

The basic principles of claim classification were addressed in Chapter 17, which described the tripartite classification into secured, priority, and general claims, and in Chapter 18, which discussed the classification of unsecured claims in a Ch. 13 plan. The classification of claims and interests assumes a particularly important role in the Ch. 11 case because it not only affects the distribution to be received, but also the voting power of the creditor or interest holder.

Section 1123(a)(1) requires the plan to designate classes of claims. All secured and unsecured claims — except for those that qualify for second, third, and eighth priority under §507(a)[6] — must be placed in classes. The principles governing classification are set out in §1122 and in case law (and are illustrated in Examples 1 and 2).

The classification decision has an impact on the substantive and voting rights of parties and can ultimately affect whether a plan is confirmed. For example, imagine that a Ch. 11 debtor faces considerable opposition to its plan of reorganization from one of its primary suppliers. This supplier has a significant claim. Other similar creditors have all been placed in Class 5. Assume that if this creditor is placed in Class 5 and votes against the plan, that vote is sufficient by itself to cause the class to vote against the plan. At the same time, Class 6 is composed of a group of creditors that each have large claims and overwhelmingly support the plan. Assume that the debtor knows that if it places the disgruntled supplier in Class 6, the impact of its vote would be diluted and the class would vote in favor of the plan regardless of how the disgruntled supplier voted. Naturally, the debtor will be tempted to place the disgruntled supplier in Class 6 even though the decision is based on pure gamesmanship. Consequently, the Code attempts to control the debtor's discretion in establishing classes to prevent unfair discrimination and manipulation of voting power. The following principles apply to the debtor's classification decision:

1. Section 1122 requires claims and interests in a class to be substantially similar. The Code does not say what constitutes substantial similarity, but this is generally taken to mean that the claims must be of the same priority and quality. For example, a debtor cannot place in the same class a secured and an unsecured claim, or claims having different priorities. Although unsecured claims of equal rank are often placed in the same class, each secured claim is usually given a class of its own because secured claims are not substantially similar to each other — they are either secured by different collateral or have a different priority in the same collateral.

   One group of dissimilar claims may be combined in a single class under §1122(b). Unsecured claims of relatively low value may be classed together for convenience, so that they can be dealt with in the same way. This classification requires court approval, which is granted only if the ceiling amount is reasonable and the classification is necessary for administrative convenience.

6. More specifically, §507(a)(2) addresses administrative expenses, §507(a)(3) addresses gap administrative expenses in an involuntary case, and §507(a)(3) addresses priority taxes.

2. Although §1122 prevents the inclusion of dissimilar claims in a class, neither §1122 nor any other section of Ch. 11 forbids the debtor from placing similar claims in different classes. However, courts have held that the debtor's ability to classify similar claims separately is subject to the requirement that the classification has a reasonable basis, comports with the best interests of creditors, and facilitates the debtor's legitimate efforts to reorganize. This is intended to prevent manipulation of the classification process for the purpose of diluting the votes of unsympathetic creditors or providing preferential treatment for favored creditors.
3. Three types of priority claims are not subject to classification in the plan. Administrative expenses of the Ch. 11 case, given second priority by §507(a)(2); operating expenses incurred by the debtor in the gap period in an involuntary case, given third priority under §507(a)(3); and tax claims given eighth priority under §507(a)(8) are not classified. Claims under §507(a)(2) and (3) are not classified because §1129(a)(9)(A) requires all these claims to be fully paid in cash on the effective date of the plan. Because they are settled before the plan goes into effect, no purpose is served by classifying them. The rights of the holders of such claims cannot be impaired without their consent, and they do not vote on the plan. Eighth-priority tax claims are not classified either because §1129(a)(9)(C) permits their full payment in installments, subject to controls on the period and terms of payment. As with administrative expenses, the debtor has no discretion to impair these claims without the consent of the holder, so classification serves no purpose. Other priority claims may be classified because, as explained in section 20.4.2, §1129(a)(9)(B) contemplates the possibility that claims in other priority categories may accept a plan that provides for installment payments, rather than immediate cash payment.
4. Like claims, interests may also be divided into classes. For example, a corporate debtor may have issued preferred stock that has priority over common stock. The same rules apply to prevent the placing of dissimilar interests in the same class or dividing up similar interests into arbitrary or manipulative classifications.

b. Specification of Unimpaired Classes of Claims and Interests (§1123(a)(2))

Impairment is a central concept in Ch. 11. It has already been referred to in connection with voting, and its significance in the confirmation of the plan is discussed in section 20.4. Section 1123(a)(2) requires the plan to specify any class of claims or interests that is not impaired under the plan. It follows that it will also be apparent from the plan which classes are impaired.

Section 1124 delineates the meaning of impairment. A class of claims or interests is impaired unless each claim or interest in the class is treated in one of the two ways specified in the section. Notice that although it is the class that is impaired, the test for nonimpairment is applied to each claim or interest in the class. In short, for a claim or interest to be unimpaired, the rights of the holder must be unaltered, or they must be unaltered except for cure of a default and deceleration of the debt, with full compensation for any damages incurred in reasonable reliance on the default or acceleration clause.[7] More specifically, these requirements mean the following:

1. *No alteration of rights* (§1124(1)). A claim or interest is not impaired under the plan if the legal, equitable, and contractual rights of the holder are left unaltered. In other words, the plan proposes to give the holder exactly what it is entitled to receive under the terms of its contract or applicable nonbankruptcy law. Any change in those rights (apart from those described in the next paragraph) is an impairment.
2. *No alteration of rights except for the cure of a default and deceleration with compensation for loss* (§1124(2)). If the debtor defaulted on an obligation prior to bankruptcy, §1124(2) allows it to provide in the plan for cure of the default and reversal of the acceleration. If the holder of the claim or interest is compensated for any damages resulting from reasonable reliance on the term of the contract or on nonbankruptcy law that permitted acceleration, and if all other rights of the holder of the claim or interest are left intact, the provision for cure and reinstatement of the original maturity date does not constitute an impairment.

c. Specification of the Treatment of Impaired Classes of Claims or Interests (§1123(a)(3))

The preceding explanation of impairment shows that, as a general matter, almost every deviation from the nonbankruptcy rights of a claimant or interest-holder results in impairment of the claim or interest. Because impaired parties will not receive exactly what they had the right to expect under nonbankruptcy law, the plan must set out precisely how they are to be treated, including what value they will receive, if any, and when and in what form they will receive it. A plan that fails to do this cannot be confirmed.

Section 1123(a)(3) merely requires the plan to specify the treatment of the impaired classes. Section 1129 sets out some minimum standards for that treatment, which are discussed in section 20.4. Subject to those standards, the debtor, as proponent of the plan, decides how impaired claims are to be treated. Of course, to secure confirmation of the plan, the debtor needs

7. Impairment is illustrated in Example 3.

to consult and negotiate with impaired parties in devising provisions that are practicable, affordable, and acceptable.

There are many different ways in which impaired claims could be treated. For example, the plan may undertake full or partial payment over an extended time or in a lump sum; it may propose that a class of claims be paid pro rata out of a particular fund or the proceeds of specified property; it may propose to issue stock or to transfer property to creditors in satisfaction of their claims; it may even provide for no distribution at all to a particular class or classes.

d. Equal Treatment of Claims or Interests in a Class (§1123(a)(4))

The principle of equal treatment of members of a class was introduced previously in the Ch. 13 context in Chapter 18. Once claims or interests have been classified together, they must be treated the same unless the holder of a particular claim or interest agrees to a less favorable treatment.

e. Adequate Means for the Plan's Implementation (§1123(a)(5))

A plan is meaningless unless it has provisions for its implementation. Section 1123(a)(5) requires the plan to set out the manner in which the plan will be funded and the course that will be followed to bring the reorganization to a successful conclusion. Section 1123(a)(5) has a nonexclusive list of some of the implementation provisions that may be included in the plan. Creation of the means of implementation is one of the important areas of flexibility in Ch. 11. It gives a wide range of options to the debtor for devising a reorganization scheme that best satisfies claims, while allowing the debtor to take advantage of resources available for the salvation of its business. The plan's implementation provisions can range from a simple funding scheme derived from future income and the liquidation of unwanted assets to a much more complex arrangement involving such strategies as the issuance of new stock, the creation of new investment or credit, or merger with another entity.

f. Voting Powers for Corporate Debtors (§1123(a)(6))

If the debtor is a corporation, the plan must provide for matters of voting power in the charter of the debtor and of any corporations with which it proposes to become associated. The charter of the reorganized debtor must forbid the issuance of nonvoting securities. If there are different classes of security, the voting power among them must be appropriately distributed.

g. The Selection of Officers (§1123(a)(7))

The provisions in the plan concerning the selection of any officer, director or trustee must be consistent with public policy and the interests of creditors and equity security holders.

h. The Commitment of Earnings of an Individual Debtor (§1123(a)(8))

BAPCPA added subsection (a)(8) to the mandatory requirements for a plan in a case where the debtor is an individual. The subsection is rather vague. It states that the debtor must "provide for the payment to creditors under the plan of all or such portion of earnings from personal services performed by the debtor after the commencement of the case, or other future income of the debtor as is necessary for the execution of the plan." Note that the provision does not require the commitment of all disposable income, or indeed of any particular portion of the debtor's income. It requires these payments only to the extent necessary to execute the plan. Although the enactment of this subsection at the same time as the means test in §707(b) and the toughened version of the disposable income test in §1325(b) would suggest that it must have some relationship to those tests, the relationship is hard to see. On its face, all this provision says is that to the extent necessary, the debtor must fund the plan from postpetition income. Notwithstanding the vagueness of this subsection, BAPCPA also added a new subsection (15) to §1129(a) that makes it clear that the disposable income test is a confirmation requirement for an individual Ch. 11 debtor. (*See* section 20.4.2.)

§20.3.3 Permissive Plan Provisions Under §1123(b)

Section 1123(b) is similar in tone to §1322(b) in that it provides a broadly drafted list of provisions that can be included in the plan if the proponent so desires. The decision on which classes of claims to impair or leave unimpaired is one example. Other matters that may be provided for include the assumption or rejection of executory contracts or the sale of property.

In short, the plan may deal with any appropriate matters that are not inconsistent with the Code. As mentioned before, the range and detail of these optional provisions can be far-reaching in the reorganization of a large debtor.

Section 1123(b)(5) duplicates in a Ch. 11 case the modification-of-rights provision of §1322(b)(5). Section 1123(b)(5) was added by the Bankruptcy Reform Act of 1994 to incorporate into the Ch. 11 case of an individual the same rule as applies in Ch. 13: The debtor can modify the rights of holders of unsecured claims and secured claims, except for the rights of the holder of a claim secured only by a security interest in real property that is the debtor's principal residence. The addition of §1123(b)(5) overrules case law that held that the protection from strip down, available to home mortgagees under Ch. 13, was not available in a Ch. 11 case. An individual debtor may therefore not use Ch. 11 to get around the prohibition on modification discussed in section 18.9.3.

§20.4 CONFIRMATION REQUIREMENTS

§20.4.1 Overview

Section 1129 imposes the standards and requirements for plan confirmation. It provides for two alternative means of confirmation: 1) §1129(a), which sets out the prerequisites for confirmation when the plan has been accepted by all impaired classes; and 2) §1129(b), which governs confirmation in the absence of universal acceptance by all impaired classes, known as "cramdown." Cramdown confirmation under §1129(b) is subject to all the requirements of §1129(a), except for §1129(a)(8), which specifies acceptance by all classes. In addition, the further requirements of §1129(b) must be satisfied. Diagram 20b shows these alternative means of confirmation.

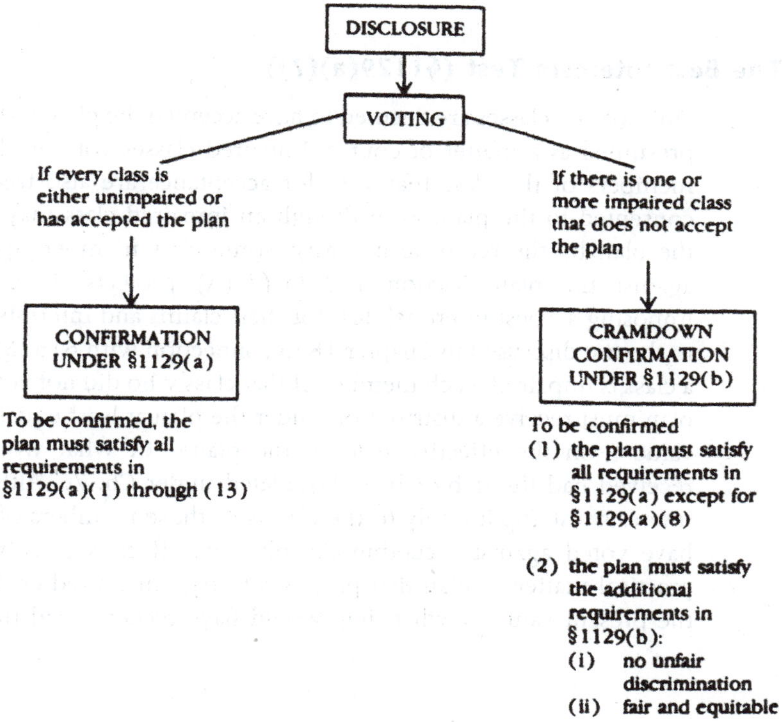

Diagram 20b

§20.4.2 Confirmation Under §1129(a) Where All Impaired Classes Have Accepted the Plan

There are 16 requirements for confirmation in §1129(a).[8] Some are applicable to all Ch. 11 plans, but some apply only in particular cases. For example, §1129(a)(14) and (15), added by BAPCPA, apply only to individual debtors. Some of the requirements are quite technical, and are omitted from this chapter. Coverage is confined to those that are necessary to an understanding of confirmation under §1129(a).

a. Lawfulness and Good Faith (§§1129(a)(1), (2), and (3))

Both the plan itself and the proponent's conduct in proposing it must comply with the Code. In addition, the standard of good faith that was discussed in connection with the Ch. 13 plan applies to a Ch. 11 plan as well. The court has the power to refuse confirmation of a plan that is abusive, manipulative, or counter to the spirit and purpose of Ch. 11.

b. The Best Interests Test (§1129(a)(7))

Unimpaired classes are deemed to have accepted the plan, so their consent is presumed as a matter of course. Impaired classes vote on the plan. Those members of the class that vote for acceptance are also treated as having consented to the plan. Even though an impaired class may have accepted the plan by the requisite majority, some class members may have voted against the plan. Section 1129(a)(7)(A) protects these dissenters by imposing a "best interests" test for their claims and interests that is similar to the test discussed in Chapter 18 in connection with §1325(a). Namely, if a class is impaired, each member of that class who did not vote to accept the plan must receive a distribution under the plan at least equal to the present value—on the effective date of the plan—of what would have been received had the debtor been liquidated under Ch. 7.[9] Although the best interests test applies only to the claims of those members of the class who have voted against accepting the plan, its effect is usually broader as a practical matter. A plan that proposes to pay unsecured creditors less than the present value of what they would have received had the debtor been

---

8. Section 1129(d) sets out a seventeenth requirement that allows a governmental unit to object to the plan if the plan's principal purpose is the avoidance of taxes or the application of security laws. This requirement is not discussed further here.
9. *See* Chapter 17 for a discussion of valuation.

liquidated is not likely to be well received by creditors in that class, and will probably not gain enough votes to be accepted by the class.[10]

c. Acceptance by Classes of Claims and Interests (§1129(a)(8))

Section 1129(a)(8) sets out the acceptance requirements that must be satisfied for a plan to be confirmed under the consensual standards of §1129(a). Each class of claims or interests must either be unimpaired or must have accepted the plan. Remember that an unimpaired class does not vote because its acceptance is presumed, and a class that receives no value under the plan is deemed to have rejected it. Section 1129(a)(8) is unsatisfied if even one impaired class does not accept the plan. At that point, confirmation can only be achieved by complying with the additional requirements for cramdown confirmation under §1129(b).

d. The Required Treatment for Priority Claims (§1129(a)(9))

Except to the extent that the holder of a particular claim has agreed to a different treatment, §1129(a)(9) specifies how priority claims must be treated. Section 1129(a)(9) breaks priority claims into three categories, each with a different rule, as explained below. (*See also* Example 1.)

1. Administrative expenses (that is, second priority claims under §507(a)(2)) and claims arising out of the conduct of the debtor's business during the gap period in an involuntary case (that is, third-priority claims under §507(a)(3)) must be paid in cash, to the extent of the allowed amount of the claim, on the effective date of the plan.
2. All other priority claims, apart from priority tax claims, must be paid in full. If a class of priority claims has accepted the plan, the claims in that class may be paid in installments.[11] The amount paid must equal the present value of the allowed claim as at the effective date of the plan. If a class does not accept the plan, claims in that class must be paid in cash on the effective date of the plan.
3. The present value of priority tax claims under §507(a)(8) must be paid in full in installments. Although priority tax claims are entitled to be paid in full, the holders of those claims cannot insist on cash payment, but must accept payments by installments if the plan so provides. Section 1129(a)(9) sets a limit of five years from the order for relief for the installment payment of priority tax claims.

---

10. As discussed further below, §1129(a)(7)(B) prescribes the minimum distribution to be provided for undersecured claims that have made the election under §1111(b).
11. Note that it is the class as a whole that must agree to accept the plan.

e. Acceptance by at Least One Impaired Class (§1129(a)(10))

(1) Impairment Generally. Section 1129(a)(10) requires that at least one impaired class of claims has accepted the plan if any class of claims is impaired under the plan. In counting votes for this purpose, the affirmative votes of any insiders in that class are disregarded. (*See* Example 3.)

This provision is of limited effect in a confirmation under §1129(a), because §1129(a)(8) requires acceptance by all impaired classes. In most cases, compliance with §1129(a)(10) follows as a matter of course from satisfaction of the requirements of §1129(a)(8), but this is not always so. Section 1129(a)(10) excludes the acceptance votes of any insiders in the class. Therefore, the plan cannot be confirmed if the acceptance of impaired classes was achieved only by the affirmative vote of insiders in those classes.

In cramdown under §1129(b), §1129(a)(10) serves as a control by ensuring that there is some modicum of creditor support for the plan. Although dissenting classes may exist, at least the majority of noninsider creditors in one impaired class has voted in favor of the plan.

(2) Debtor Gamesmanship and Artificial Impairment. In some Ch. 11 cases—and quite frequently in single asset bankruptcy cases—a debtor may not be able to satisfy §1129(a)(10) because the only truly impaired class of creditors intends to vote against the plan of reorganization, and the debtor plans to cramdown that class to confirm the plan. In these cases, the debtor has two primary options: either work with the impaired class of creditors to secure class approval of the plan or create a separate impaired class of creditors who will vote to approve the plan. This latter option is referred to "artificial impairment." In this form of debtor gamesmanship, the debtor has the ability to pay a class of unsecured creditors in full on the effective date. Invariably, this class has a relatively small amount of claims against the estate. If the debtor were to pay this class in full, the class would be deemed unimpaired. However, to satisfy §1129(a)(10), the debtor decides to pay this class in a few staggered installments commencing on the effective date of the plan. The class is willing to vote for the plan even with this change because it is a minor deviation. But the change is sufficient to render the class "impaired." By this simple maneuver, the debtor has satisfied §1129(a)(10) and can now seek to cramdown the other unsecured creditor class.

The Code does not prohibit this gamesmanship, but courts are split on whether this conduct violates §1129(a)(3)'s requirement that the plan be proposed in good faith. Ultimately, the majority view is that §1129(a)(10) does not distinguish between discretionary and economically driven impairment, and artificial impairment is permissible as long as there is no alliance between the debtor and the impaired creditors that would violate §1129(a)(3)'s good faith requirement.[12]

f. The Feasibility Standard: The Plan Must Have a Reasonable Prospect of Success (§1129(a)(11))

Section 1129(a)(11) requires, as a condition of confirmation, that the plan is not likely to be followed by liquidation or further financial reorganization, except as provided for by the plan.[13] The subsection contains two related but independent determinations: 1) the debtor is able to consummate the provisions of the plan; and 2) if consummated, the plan will enable the debtor to emerge from bankruptcy as a viable entity. Section 1129(a)(10) places the burden on the proponent to satisfy the court that the plan has a reasonable prospect of achieving its goals and allows the court to refuse confirmation if the plan is impracticable or over-optimistic.

To satisfy this requirement, the debtor will generally produce detailed, five-year financial projections. These projections are usually reviewed by advisors to the key stakeholders in the case. In some cases, parties may object to the debtor's financial projections and produce projections of their own. In assessing feasibility, courts will consider myriad factors, including — but not limited to — the following: 1) the debtor's past business and financial performance, including its performance during the pendency of bankruptcy case; 2) prospective earnings and the adequacy of the debtor's capital structure; 3) the probability of necessary financing or funding;[14] 4) the earning power of the debtor's business; 5) the economic conditions in the debtor's area of business; 6) the ability of the debtor's management; and 7) the probability of continuation of the same management.

Ultimately, the court is not required to find a certainty that plan payments will be made. Rather, the court is looking for an evidentiary basis that will support a finding that the reorganized debtor has a reasonable assurance of commercial viability. This requirement must be satisfied even where all parties have accepted the plan and no party objects to confirmation.

---

12. *See, e.g.*, *Vill. Green 1, GP v. Fannie Mae (In re Vill. Green I. GP)*, 811 F.3d 816 (6th Cir. 2016) (holding that artificial impairment is generally permissible but affirming the district court's ruling that §1129(a)(3) had been violated in that case due to the debtor's improper relationship with the artificially impaired class of creditors); *see also Western Real Estate Equities, LLC v. Vill. At Camp Bowie I, L.P. (In re Vill. at Camp Bowie I, L.P.)*, 710 F.3d 239 (5th Cir. 2013); *Matter of L&J Anaheim Assocs.*, 995 F.2d 940 (9th Cir. 1993); *but see In re Windsor on the River Assocs., Ltd.*, 7 F.3d 127 (8th Cir. 1993).

13. The caveat makes it clear that this standard does not prevent a liquidating plan when that is the resolution contemplated by the plan.

14. A showing of exit financing to fund a plan of reorganization in whole or in part has been found to represent substantial evidence of debtor feasibility.

However, courts will often accept that feasibility is not an issue in cases where no party has objected to the plan on that basis.

g. Domestic Support Obligations of an Individual Debtor (§1129(a)(14))

BAPCPA added this additional prerequisite to plan confirmation for an individual in Ch. 11 as part of the set of provisions intended to ensure that the debtor cannot use bankruptcy to evade domestic support obligations, as defined in §101(14A). (*See* section 10.4.3 for background.) In essence, §1129(a)(14) makes it a condition of plan confirmation that the debtor is current on all postpetition domestic support obligations that the debtor is required to pay by court or administrative order or by statute. (If there are any domestic support obligations owing in arrears from the prepetition period, they may be provided for in the plan.)

h. The Disposable Income Test for an Individual Debtor (§1129(a)(15))

Prior to 2005, the disposable income test was confined to Ch. 13. In addition to making that test tougher in Ch. 13 cases, BAPCPA added §1129(a)(15), which adopts the test where the Ch. 11 debtor is an individual. The effect is to prevent a debtor from filing under Ch. 11 to avoid the application of the disposable income test. The disposable income test is only applied upon objection to confirmation by the holder of an allowed unsecured claim that is not to be paid in full under the plan. If such an objection is made, §1129(a)(15) requires that the debtor commit all projected disposable income, as defined in §1325(b)(2), for the longer of five years from the due date of the first payment under the plan or the duration of the plan payments.

The disposable income test may not operate in exactly the same way under Ch. 11 as it does under Ch. 13. Section 1129(a)(15) cross-references only to the definition of "disposable income" in §1325(b)(2). That section defines "disposable income" to mean current monthly income less amounts reasonably necessary to be expended for the maintenance and support of the debtor or a dependent, as well as necessary business expenses and allowable charitable contributions. Section 1129(a)(15) does not specifically refer to §1325(b)(3), which requires expenses to be calculated on the basis of the standardized expenses formula of §707(b) where the debtor's current monthly earnings exceed the median income. (For further details on the calculation of disposable income under §1325(b)(2), *see* section 20.4.2.) It is therefore not clear if the standardized expenses are to be used in a Ch. 11 case. The cross reference to §1325(b)(2) may include §1325(b)(3) by implication, but the inference to be drawn from the omission of

§1325(b)(3) suggests that in a Ch. 11 case, the debtor's expenses are determined on the basis of actual, reasonably necessary expenses. This was the conclusion reached in *In re Roedemeier*, 374 B.R. 264 (Bankr. D. Kan. 2007).

The amount of disposable income that the debtor has to commit to the plan under §1129(a)(15) is potentially greater than under §1325(b) because if the plan payments are to extend beyond five years (which may occur in Ch. 11, but not in Ch. 13), the disposable income for the entire plan payment period must be committed to the plan.

§20.4.3 Cramdown Confirmation Under §1129(b)

As noted above, §1129(a)(10) requires that every impaired class must vote to approve the plan. But unanimity can be elusive. Section 1129(b) is designed to give the debtor a means of confirmation even though one or more creditor classes have refused to accept the plan. Essentially, §1129(b) prescribes a minimum level of treatment for claims and interests that was considered by Congress to be fair enough to justify imposition of the plan on unwilling classes. This process is premised on compelled compliance and is universally referred to as "cramdown." Needless to say, the term strikes fear in the heart of creditors.

In order for a court to allow a debtor to cramdown a creditor class and confirm a plan of reorganization, the debtor must be able to demonstrate the following:[15]

1. All the standards of confirmation in §1129(a) are satisfied except for §1129(a)(8), which requires acceptance by all impaired classes.
2. The plan does not discriminate unfairly against any impaired class that has not accepted the plan.
3. The plan is fair and equitable with respect to each impaired class that has not accepted the plan.

The latter two requirements require far more explanation.

a. Unfair Discrimination (§1129(b)(1))

The Code does not provide any insight into the question of whether a dissenting class has been unfairly discriminated against. The inquiry is largely a factual one that involves some degree of discretionary evaluation by the court. Generally, the term seeks to "ensure that a dissenting class will receive relative value equal to the value given to all other similarly situated

15. *See also* Examples 2, 3, and 4 for illustrations of the general standards for cramdown.

classes."[16] Naturally, the plan must provide creditors within the same class the same treatment. But variations in treatment exist among different classes. The "unfair discrimination" requirement accepts that classes will be treated differently but disparate treatment of the dissenting class of creditors in a cramdown must not reach the level of unfair discrimination.

Generally, the question of fairness is resolved by evaluating the need and motive for the discrimination. In making this determination, most courts consider "(1) whether the discrimination is supported by a reasonable basis; (2) whether the debtor could consummate the plan without the discrimination; (3) whether the discrimination is proposed in good faith; and (4) the relationship between the discrimination and its basis or rationale."[17]

Recently, some courts have adopted a rebuttable presumption test that seeks to determine if the disparate treatment between the dissenting class and a comparable class of equal priority results in either "(a) a materially lower percentage recovery for the dissenting class (measure in terms of net present value of all payments), or (b) regardless of percentage recovery, an allocation under the plan of materially greater risk to the dissenting class in connection with its proposed distribution."[18] The debtor may rebut the presumption of unfairness if it can demonstrate "that a lower recovery for the dissenting class is consistent with the results that [would be obtained] outside of bankruptcy, or that a greater recovery for the other class is offset by contributions from that class to the reorganization."[19]

b. Fair and Equitable (§§1129(b)(1) and (2))

The requirement that impaired classes must be treated fairly and equitably covers an even broader range of considerations than the unfair discrimination standard. However, the Code offers some specific guidance in assessing if this requirement has been satisfied. Section 1129(b)(2) prescribes the minimum level of treatment that must be given to secured claims, unsecured claims, and interests for the plan to qualify as fair and equitable. Note that these are minimum standards. A plan is not fair and equitable if the standards are not satisfied. At the same time, even satisfying the minimum standards may not resolve the issue. Other factors may lead to the conclusion that the plan is still not fair and equitable to an impaired class that has not accepted the plan.

16. In re *Johns-Manville Corp.*, 68 B.R. 618, 636 (Bankr. S.D.N.Y. 1986).
17. In re *Armstrong World Indus., Inc.*, 348 B.R. 111, 121 (D. Del. 2006).
18. *See id.*
19. In re *Sentry Operating Co. of Tex., Inc.*, 264 B.R. 850, 864 (Bankr. S.D. Tex. 2001).

i. Secured Claims

To be fair and equitable to an impaired class of secured claims,[20] the plan must at a minimum contain provisions that satisfy one of three alternative tests:

(1) Retention of the lien and deferred payments (§1129(b)(2)(A)(i)). To satisfy the first alternative test, the liens of the claimants in the class must be preserved to the full allowed amount of their secured claims. In addition, each claimant in the class must receive deferred cash payments totaling at least the allowed amount of its secured claim having a value, as at the effective date of the plan, at least equal to the value of the holder's interest in the property.

More specifically, the Supreme Court has interpreted §1129(b)(2)(A)(i) to mean that the plan must provide that the affected secured creditor receive payments that assure it of receiving the value of its collateral as of the effective date of the plan.[21] Inherent in this interpretation is an instruction to the bankruptcy court to employ a present value analysis to determine value. A creditor can only receive the present value of its claim "if the total amount of the deferred payments includes the amount of the underlying claim *plus an appropriate amount of interest to compensate the creditor for the decreased value of the claim caused by the delayed payments.*"[22] This interest requirement ensures that the creditor receives the present value of the claim.[23]

In other words, the first alternative test requires that claimants in the class retain their liens and also receive periodic payments that cannot be less than the allowed amount of the claim, adjusted upward to compensate for deferred payment. When the claimant is fully secured, these two tests mean that it must receive deferred payments equal to the present value of its fully secured claim. If the claimant is undersecured, matters become a little more complicated because of an election provided for under §1111(b). That is dealt with in section 20.6.

To calculate the deferred cash payments, the bankruptcy court must 1) value the secured party's collateral; and 2) determine the appropriate interest rate for the debtor to pay on the obligation.

---

20. Plans of reorganization invariably place each secured claim in its own separate class. Therefore, although §1129(b)(2) applies to a class of secured claims and refers to claims in the plural, there is often only one claim in each class.

21. See *United Sav. Ass'n of Tex v. Timbers of Inwood Forest Assocs.*, 484 U.S. 365, 377 (1988).

22. *In re Airadigm Commc'ns, Inc.* 547 F.3d 763, 768-69 (7th Cir. 2008) (emphasis added).

23. See *In re Weinstein*, 227 B.R. 284, 294 n.11 (B.A.P. 9th Cir. 1998).

A. Valuing Collateral

Section 17.5.3 addresses the issue of valuing collateral in cases under Chs. 7 and 13 and explores *Assocs. Comm. Corp. v. Rash*, 520 U.S. 953 (1997), the seminal Supreme Court case. Section 506(c)(2) codifies aspects of *Rash*, but the section is inapplicable in Ch. 11 cases. Consequently, Ch. 11 debtors in possession seeking to invoke §1129(b)(2)(A)(i) take a unique approach. Debtors retain financial professionals to opine on the valuation issue, and the court makes the final determination.

The professionals invariably use one of four valuation methodologies that have been widely accepted outside of the bankruptcy context to value the debtor or one of the debtor's assets: 1) asset-based valuation—where a company's value is determined by estimating the current value of a company's assets and subtracting its liabilities. 2) earnings-based valuation—where value is determined by taking historical earnings figures (often on a rolling three-year average) and dividing that number by the expected rate of return in a given year. 3) discounted cash flow—where value is determined by estimating future cash flows from the operation and potential future sale of the company and then discounting that aggregate number to present value, and 4) relative valuation—where value is determined based on how comparable assets and businesses are priced or valued.

Ultimately, the court will be presented with expert testimony as to the value of the collateral implicated in the cramdown and will make an assessment of the appropriate valuation number.

B. Appropriate Rate of Interest

The Code does not instruct courts on how to assess the appropriate rate of interest under §1129(b)(2)(A)(i). As noted in section 18.8.1, *Till v. S.C.S. Credit Corp.*, 541 U.S. 465 (2004), provides significant insight as to this issue in the Ch. 13 context. In that case, the Supreme Court adopted what has been commonly referred to as the "formula approach." Under this approach, courts are instructed to start with the current national prime rate of interest as a baseline.[24] However, the Supreme Court went on to note that "[b]ecause bankruptcy debtors typically pose a greater risk of nonpayment than solvent commercial borrowers," the interest rate should be adjusted upward to account for the risk.[25] The amount of the adjustment depends

24. The national prime rate is an optimal starting point because it "reflects the financial market's estimate of the amount a commercial bank should charge a creditworthy borrower to compensate for the opportunity costs of the loan, the risk of inflation, and the relatively slight risk of default." *Id.* at 466.
25. *Id.* at 479.

"on such factors as the circumstances of the estate, the nature of the security, and the duration and feasibility of the reorganization plan."[26]

The *Till* ruling's precedential effect is limited to the Ch. 13 context but the opinion still informs Ch. 11 cases, and courts have built on the formula approach. For example, the Sixth Circuit Court of Appeals recently held that in determining the appropriate cramdown rate in a Ch. 11 case, the bankruptcy court should determine whether an efficient market exists for lending in the specific cramdown context before the court.[27] If so, the court should use the rates dictated by the market. To the extent an efficient market does not exist, the court should use *Till*'s formula approach.[28]

(2) Sale free and clear of liens, and a lien on the proceeds (§1129(b)(2)(A)(ii)). The second alternative test applies if the debtor wishes to sell the property free and clear of liens, so that the lien cannot be preserved as required by §1129(b)(2)(A)(i). Section 363(i) allows the debtor to sell the property free and clear of the lien, but the lienholder enjoys unique protections. Primarily, the lien of the secured creditor subject to cramdown attaches to the proceeds of the sale. The claimant is given the same rights to preservation of the lien in the proceeds and to payment as are provided in §1129(b)(2)(A)(i) and (iii). Further, unless the court for cause orders otherwise,[29] the secured creditor has the right to credit bid its claim — which means that the creditor may bid at the sale of the collateral and then offset its claim against the purchase price.

(3) Indubitable equivalent (§1129(b)(2)(A)(iii)). The third alternative gives the court discretion to approve some other treatment of the secured claim that assures the claimant that it will receive the indubitable equivalent of its claim. This term is also used in §361(3). *See* section 8.4.4. As in that context, the question to be decided is whether some alternative treatment proposed in the plan will result in the holder of the claim receiving value that is unquestionably equal to its claim. For example, a proposal to surrender the collateral may satisfy this test. Further, a replacement lien on similar

---

26. In re *American Trailer & Storage, Inc.*, 419 B.R. 412, 434 (Bankr. W.D. Mo. 2009).

27. See In re *American HomePatient, Inc.*, 420 F.3d 559 (6th Cir. 2005). This starting point is based on footnote 14 in *Till*, which explains that "[b]ecause every cramdown loan is imposed by a court over the objection of the secured creditor, there is no free market of willing cramdown lenders [in the Ch. 13 context]. Interestingly, the same is not true in the [Ch. 11] context, as numerous lenders advertise financing for [Ch. 11] debtors in possession." *Till*, 541 U.S. at 477.

28. *American HomePatient*, 420 F.3d at 568. Various other courts have adopted a similar approach. See In re *MPM Silicones, LLC*, 2017 BL 376794 (2d Cir. Oct. 20 2017); *American Trailer & Storage*, 419 B.R. at 436; In re *Cantwell*, 336 B.R. 688 (Bankr. D.N.J. 2006); In re *Northwest Timberline Enters., Inc.*, 348 B.R. 412 (Bankr. N.D. Tex. 2006); see also *General Elec. Credit Equities, Inc. v. Brice Rd. Dev., L.L.C.* (In re *Brice Rd. Dev., L.L.C.*), 392 B.R. 274, 280 (B.A.P. 6th Cir. 2008).

29. Courts rarely deny secured creditors the right to credit bid.

collateral or an exchange of existing collateral with other collateral may suffice.[30]

However, this alternative captures a limited universe of treatment. Courts have been reluctant to allow debtors in possession unable to satisfy either §§1129(b)(2)(A)(i) or (ii) to invoke §1129(b)(2)(A)(iii) instead. For example, in *RadLAX Gateway Hotel, LLC v. Amalgamated Bank*. 132 S.Ct. 2065 (2012), the Ch. 11 plan proposed to sell the debtor's assets at auction but provided that the bank, which had a security interest in the property, could not bid at the auction. The debtor believed that the bank's ability to credit bid would chill bidding. The debtor argued that §1129(b)(2)(A)(iii) was satisfied because the bank's lien would attach to the proceeds of the sale. The bank objected. The Supreme Court held that if a debtor chooses to satisfy the fair and equitable standard by a sale free and clear of the lien, it is bound by the requirements of §1129(b)(2)(A)(ii), which, when read with §363(k), entitles the secured party to bid at the sale. The court rejected the debtor's argument that, because proceeds of the sale would be applied to paying off the lien, the proposed sale process would give the bank the indubitable equivalent of its claim under §1129(b)(2)(A)(iii). The court held that the alternative of indubitable equivalence in subsection (iii) is a general provision, which applies only to situations not covered by the more specific provisions of subsections (i) and (ii).[31]

ii. Unsecured Claims

For the plan to be fair and equitable to a dissenting class of unsecured claims, it must satisfy one of two alternative requirements:

(1) Payment of the allowed amount of the claim (§1129(b)(2)(B)(i)). The plan must provide that each holder of a claim in the class receives property of a value, as of the effective date of the plan, equal to the allowed amount of the claim. This is the present value test again. If deferred payments are to be made, the amount of the distribution must equal the full face amount of the claim plus interest.

(2) The absolute priority rule: No junior claim or interest receives or retains any property on account of its claim or interest (§1129(b)(2)(B)(ii)). As an alternative to full payment of the claims in the class, the plan can satisfy the fair-and-equitable standard by providing for no distribution or retention of property by anyone whose claim or interest is junior to the dissenting impaired class. This alternative is

30. See *In re Pine Mountain*, 80 B.R. 171 (B.A.P. 9th Cir. 1997) (plan that substituted new promissory note for old promissory note satisfied the "indubitable equivalent" test).
31. *See id.* at 2070-71.

known as the "absolute priority rule." The rule is a judicial invention that predates the Code. The rule arose from the concern that insiders would manipulate the reorganization process—the debtor is tasked with formulating the plan of reorganization and may propose a plan that is too generous to the debtor's owners and other insiders. The initial iterations of the absolute priority rule required that creditors must be paid before the owners of the debtor could retain equity interests under any circumstances. Section 1129(b)(2)(B) codified the rule, which now provides that in a cramdown, if the dissenting class is not receiving property equal to the allowed amount of their claims, then the class can only be crammed down if the plan provides that claims junior to claims of that dissenting class will not receive or retain any property under the plan on account of their interest.

The effect of the rule is that if the senior nonaccepting class is not paid in full, the plan can only be crammed down if the debtor is willing to deprive all junior classes of all value. For example, if the debtor wishes to cramdown a class of general unsecured creditors, equity holders cannot receive property under the plan based on account of their interest.

The impact of the absolute priority rule on ownership interests. Shareholders and other holders of ownership interests in the debtor are junior to creditors. Under the absolute priority rule, holders of equity in the debtor cannot remain owners unless general unsecured creditors are paid in full. In other words, equity holders are "wiped out." Because cramdown results in the sacrifice of ownership equity, the debtor usually has a strong incentive to avoid this course, and to try to negotiate acceptance of the plan. However, if the debtor is willing to pay this price, or if no other alternative is feasible, the absolute priority rule allows cramdown of a plan that pays the nonaccepting class little or nothing on its claims. (*See* Example 4.) Even where equity holders sacrifice their investment in the debtor because of inability to satisfy the absolute priority rule, dissenting unsecured claimants are still protected by the best interests test of §1129(a)(7). Therefore, the amount paid to dissenting unsecured creditors in the class must be at least the present value of what they would have received in a Ch. 7 liquidation.

The applicability of the absolute priority rule to individual debtors. Where the debtor is an individual, BAPCPA amended §1129(b)(2)(B)(ii) by adding a qualification to the absolute priority rule. It states that an individual debtor "may retain property included in the estate under section 1115" provided that the debtor has paid all domestic support obligations that arose postpetition, as required by §1129(a)(14). Section 1115 alters the general rule relating to property of the estate where the debtor is an individual. The general rule is that property of the Ch. 11 estate consists of that property in which the debtor had a legal or equitable interest at the time of the petition. However, if the Ch. 11 debtor is an individual, §1115 expands the property of the estate to include property acquired by the debtor postpetition, including earnings from services. The purpose of the provision is to bring Ch. 11 more closely in accord with Ch. 13 with regard to the individual debtor's postpetition property and earnings.

The problem is that the impact of the proviso to §1129(b)(2)(B)(ii) is not clear. Some courts have held that it abolishes the absolute priority rule with regard to the entire estate where the debtor is an individual. This basis of this interpretation is that §1115 states that property of the estate consists of property under §541 as well as postpetition property. Therefore, the reference to property "included in the estate under §1115" in §1129(b)(2)(B)(ii) covers all the property of the estate. This interpretation is plausible because Congress intended to bring an individual Ch. 11 case more closely in accord with Ch. 13, which has no absolute priority rule. Creditors have the protection of the disposable income test in an individual Ch. 11 case, and it would be too harsh to subject the debtor to the rule in light of the expansion of property of the estate to include postpetition property and earnings.[32] However, the view that now seems more prevalent is that the proviso does not completely abolish the absolute priority rule with regard to an individual debtor, but, by its terms, applies only to postpetition property and earnings brought into the estate by §1115. Therefore, the plan may provide for the debtor's retention of postpetition property, to the extent not needed for implementation of the plan, even if a dissenting class of unsecured creditors is not paid in full.[33] *In re Maharaj*, 681 F.3d 558 (4th Cir. 2012), illustrates the impact of interpreting §1129(b)(2)(B)(ii) to apply only to postpetition property. At the time of the petition, the debtors owned an auto body repair shop. Their plan proposed to retain the business and to use income from the business to fund payments under the plan, which would pay general unsecured creditors 1.7 cents on the dollar. Because the unsecured class voted against the plan, the debtors could only gain confirmation by cramdown and could not have the plan confirmed under the absolute priority rule if they retained the auto body repair business, which was prepetition property.

The new value exception to the absolute priority rule.
There is one cramdown situation in which some courts have allowed equity holders to retain their interests even though a senior nonaccepting class has not received full payment: where equity holders contribute new capital to the debtor that is equal to or greater than the value of their interests. In this

32. See *In re Shat*, 424 B.R. 854 (Bankr. D. Nev. 2010) and *In re Roedemeier*, 374 B.R. 264 (Bankr. D. Kan. 2007).
33. See *In re Lively*, 717 F.3d 406 (5th Cir. 2013) and *In re Stephens*, 704 F.3d 1279 (10th Cir. 2013).

case, courts have allowed equity holders to retain stock in the debtor in exchange for this new value. This is known as the "new value exception."[34] The new contribution must be in money or money's worth; it cannot take the form of a promise of managerial services or other intangible benefits. The effect of the exception is that equity holders can preserve their equity by making a contribution of capital reasonably equivalent to the value of their interests in the debtor.

The new value exception was recognized under the Bankruptcy Act, but it is not expressly adopted in the Code. Courts have disagreed as to the viability of the new value exception. The Supreme Court has had opportunities to resolve this conflict, but it has not done so. In *Bank of Am. v. 203 N. LaSalle St. P'ship*, 526 U.S. 434 (1999), the Court skirted the question of finally deciding if the new value exception exists under the Code. Instead, the Court held that even if the exception did exist, the plan had not created a process by which equity holders could be found to have given new value. The Court explained that to satisfy §1129(b)'s language, the equity holders must allow others to bid on the equity position that the equity holders had reserved for themselves. In other words, the opportunity to bid on the new equity was a property right that had value. Offering the right to bid exclusively to old equity holders was impermissible. The Court explained that there must be some means to test the value of this property right; the best way to determine value is exposure to the market. But the Court did not explain the best way for a debtor to do this.

In an attempt to fill this void, the National Bankruptcy Review Commission proposed two amendments to the Code: one recognizing the new value exception and allowing a junior class to purchase a new interest; and a second one providing that if the debtor is seeking to cramdown and provide for the sale of an interest in the business to old equity, then the debtor's exclusive right to propose a plan should terminate and other parties should be allowed to propose a plan and conceivably offer more for the equity stake. Unfortunately, Congress has not acted on this proposal. Most courts have agreed that the new value exception can only be invoked if the court allows for some sort of competitive bidding on the new equity interest.[35]

iii. Interests

The fair-and-equitable standard applicable to classes of interests that have not accepted the plan is similar to that relating to unsecured claims. If the class does not receive the present value of its interest, no junior interest may receive or retain any property under the plan. The present value of the

34. Some commentators argue that it is not an exception at all, but a corollary to the rule that is implicit in the wording of §1129(b).
35. *See, e.g., In the Matter of Castleton Plaza, LP*, 707 F.3d 821 (7th Cir. 2013).

interest must be based on the greater of the fixed liquidation preference or the fixed redemption price to which the holder is entitled, or the value of the interest. §1129(b)(2)(C)(i) and (ii).

§20.5 PREPACKAGED AND PRENEGOTIATED PLANS

The above outline presupposes that the plan is developed and votes are solicited after the petition has been filed. This is the conventional approach, but the debtor may be able to work out a plan with creditors before filing the petition. The Code recognizes this possibility and accommodates it in §1121(a), which allows the debtor to file a plan with the petition; §1125(g), which allows for prepetition solicitation; and §1126(b), which treats prepetition acceptances and rejections as valid, provided that proper disclosure was made under nonbankruptcy disclosure regulations or, if none exist, under the "adequate information" standard of §1125(a).

A plan that is wholly or substantially settled prior to the petition is called a "prepackaged plan." It is essentially an out-of-court settlement between the debtor and creditors (or at least the most important creditors), followed by a Ch. 11 filing so that the Code can be used to effectuate the settlement, to deal with dissenters, and to obtain the court's imprimatur. If a prepackaged plan can be formulated, the reorganization usually proceeds much more quickly, which reduces the risk, delay, cost, and uncertainty of the post-petition process. A relatively short reorganization process minimizes disruption to the debtor's business and harm to the debtor's brand. Further, parties that would otherwise oppose the debtor's preferred reorganization approach have less time to formulate their strategy and build opposition.

Of course, a prepackaged plan is not a possibility for every debtor. The prospect of settling the reorganization before filing is only open to those debtors who are in a position to approach creditors without the protection of the bankruptcy stay. In addition, the feasibility of prepetition resolution of the plan is affected by factors such as the scope and complexity of what is to be achieved in the reorganization and the range of claims and interests to be accommodated. Section 1126(b) allows for prepetition solicitation, but only honors prepetition votes if the disclosure statement complies with Code requirements. To the extent that parties object to the disclosure statement postpetition, a bankruptcy court may find it deficient and force the debtor to start over. Finally, prior to the filing of a bankruptcy petition, the debtor must prepare and file a registration statement with the SEC if creditors are receiving securities through the plan of reorganization. The debtor may not have enough time to do so.

Ultimately, prepackaged plans pose obstacles that arguably eclipse their benefits. Today, "prenegotiated" plans are far more prevalent. Under a prenegotiated plan, the debtor works with key stakeholders prepetition and receives support on crucial pieces of a plan of reorganization. Often, these parties enter into "lock up" agreements with the debtor in which they agree to support — and in some cases agree to vote in favor of — a plan of reorganization that is substantially similar to the one the parties contemplated prepetition. Solicitation and voting occurs postpetition.

§20.6 UNDERSECURED CREDITORS AND §1111(b)

Section 1111(b) provides a protective device for undersecured creditors that is not available under any other chapter of the Code. You cannot discern the meaning of §1111(b) by reading it. In essence, its purpose is to provide a strategy for undersecured creditors that will allow them, under some circumstances, to gain greater bargaining leverage in the Ch. 11 case and to prevent the stripping of their liens. For example, imagine that a Ch.11 corporate debtor owns a commercial building that the court values at $5 million. A secured creditor has a valid lien on the building — which is its sole piece of collateral — but is owed $10 million by the debtor. The debtor is offering general unsecured creditors 20 cents on the dollar. The secured creditor believes that the court has undervalued the building and the real estate values in that area are going to increase rapidly in the next few years. Further, the secured creditor believes that the debtor is not addressing its fundamental business problems through the reorganization process and will default on its key payments shortly after it exits bankruptcy. Based on these facts, the secured creditor could make a §1111(b) election. Instead of maintaining its lien at $5 million and accepting $1 million for the unsecured portion of its claim, the secured creditor maintains a $10 million lien on the property. The plan proposes that the debtor will make payments to the secured creditor over the course of the next 15 years for the balance owed. But imagine that the debtor defaults on these payments after 18 months. The property is foreclosed and sold for $11 million. Because of the election, the secured creditor has a $10 million claim — subtracting any payments that have been made postconfirmation — and has the prospect of a full recovery.

As is often the case in Ch. 11, it is not necessarily the exercise of the election but the possibility of its exercise that is important. Indeed, the election is rarely made. However, the debtor's realization that the election is available could make the debtor more amenable to negotiating a consensual plan. Section 1111(b) does two things. First, it treats an undersecured nonrecourse claim as if it were a recourse claim. Second, it allows any class of undersecured claims (whether or not with recourse) to elect to be treated as fully secured for the purpose of applying the "fair and equitable" standard. The operation of §1111(b) is complex and is subject to a number of restrictions that are not detailed here. This overview is merely intended to explain its basic operation and purpose.

i. Nonrecourse undersecured claims.

A nonrecourse claim is one for which the debtor has no personal liability. The holder of the lien is confined (usually by contract or by a rule of state law) to the collateral for payment and has no recourse against the debtor to recover any deficiency. A nonrecourse claim would therefore not normally bifurcate under §506. The creditor has a secured claim only to the extent of the collateral's value but has no unsecured claim for the balance. Section 1111(b) disregards nonrecourse provisions in contract and under nonbankruptcy law and gives the nonrecourse creditor a deficiency claim. The reason for this is that the nonrecourse creditor is particularly vulnerable to a low appraisal of the property in the Ch. 11 case, which would strip down its lien to the current value and prevent it from recovering any enhanced value of the collateral if the debtor ultimately defaults. (Under nonbankruptcy law the nonrecourse creditor can better protect itself by bidding at the foreclosure sale and acquiring the property at current depressed value, which it could later resell once the value increases.)

ii. The election under §1111(b).

The election under §1111(b) must be made by the class as a whole. (Often, the requirement that the class as a whole makes the election is not important because the claim is placed in a class by itself.) A class of undersecured creditors can make the election, whether the claims in that class have recourse under nonbankruptcy law or are nonrecourse claims treated as having recourse under §1111(b). Where the class of undersecured creditors makes the election, the unsecured deficiency is eliminated and the claim is treated as secured to the full amount of the debt. As a result, the class of creditors loses its unsecured claims, which means that it loses its right to vote as a class of unsecured claims and to receive any distribution on those claims. In exchange, the members of the class now have secured claims for the full amount of the debt. As a result, the debtor cannot satisfy the "fair and equitable" test of §1129(b)(2)(A) by paying only the present value of the collateral. Instead, the debtor must pay at least the full face value of the secured claims in the class, having a present value equal to the value of the collateral. (Note that this treatment differs from that accorded to a fully secured claim, which must be paid at the present value of the allowed secured claim. Upon the §1111(b) election, the undersecured claim must be paid the greater of the face value of the allowed secured claim, or the present value of the collateral.) By adding the deficiency to the claim, its face value is increased, so if the deficiency is large enough it can inflate the face value of the claim beyond the present value of the collateral, and the plan can meet the "fair and equitable" standard only if the debtor provides for the full payment of this amount.

As noted previously, the election is particularly useful to avoid strip down where the collateral is temporarily depressed in value or undervalued. If the reorganization is unsuccessful and the collateral is ultimately liquidated, the election preserves the claim for the full amount of the debt and is not confined to the value of the collateral at the effective date of the plan.

The election will not always benefit a class of undersecured creditors. The loss of the distribution that would have been made on the unsecured deficiency claims, and the loss of voting power on those claims (which could have given the class the power to reject the plan and to force a cramdown) must be weighed against the benefit of enhancing the value of the secured claims. Example 5 illustrates the basic operation of §1111(b).

Examples

EXAMPLES

1. The debtor, a small corporation, is seeking to reorganize under Ch. 11. The following are some of its debts:
   a. $50,000 in administrative expenses incurred to date in the Ch. 11 case.
   b. $40,000 owed to five employees for salary earned the month before the petition. None of the five claims exceeds $12,850.
   c. $100,000 owed to the I.R.S. for income taxes due for the tax year that ended just before the petition
   d. $500,000 due to six trade creditors who sold inventory to the debtor on credit in the three months before the petition.

   What general rules does Ch. 11 prescribe for the treatment of these claims in the plan?

2. A corporate Ch. 11 debtor owes a total amount of $600,000 to three finance companies from whom it had received unsecured lines of credit for operating expenses. One of these creditors, Co-operative Credit Co., is owed $220,000 of this total debt. It has become apparent that Co-operative is very hostile to the debtor and will not accept the debtor's proposed reorganization plan, under which creditors in the class will receive payment of 60 percent of their claims. The other two finance companies are sympathetic and have indicated that they will support the plan. Assume that the three claims are substantially similar and can be placed in the same class under §1122. If the plan places all three of these creditors into a class, does it seem that the debtor can gain the vote of the class to accept the plan? If not, what is the debtor's best option to confirm its plan?

3. The corporate Ch. 11 debtor's plan classifies claims and proposes the following treatment of each class of creditor:
   a. Class 1. A secured creditor that has a fully secured mortgage on real property. The creditor will retain its lien and will be paid in accordance with the original loan agreement.
   b. Class 2. The president and major shareholder in the debtor who made a loan to the debtor, secured by a security interest in the debtor's equipment. The equipment is worth less than the balance of the loan, so the plan proposes to bifurcate the claim. Class 2 consists of the secured claim, which will be paid in full to the value of the collateral. The unsecured deficiency is included in class 5, with other general unsecured claims.
   c. Class 3. A secured creditor that has a security interest in the debtor's truck, which is worth more than the balance of the debt. The creditor will retain its lien and will be paid in full, with interest. However, the plan proposes to extend the payment period, so that is a year longer than provided for in the original loan agreement.
   d. Class 4. Administrative expenses, to be paid in cash on the effective date of the plan.
   e. Class 5. General unsecured claims, which will receive a distribution of 20 percent of their claims.

   Classes 1, 2, and 4 voted to accept the plan, but classes 3 and 5 voted not to accept. What steps can the debtor take to confirm its plan of reorganization?

4. A corporate Ch. 11 debtor has proposed a plan under which general unsecured creditors are classified together and will receive installment payments equal to 60 percent of their claims. This amount is quite generous, and it satisfies the best interests test because general unsecured creditors would not receive anything close to that if the debtor was liquidated under Ch. 7. Therefore, some of the creditors in the class are willing to vote in favor of the plan. However, the two largest creditors in the class, whose claims together constitute half of the amount of claims in the class, refuse to accept anything less than full payment, and will not vote to accept a plan that provides for anything less. These two creditors are the only dissenters in the entire creditor body. All other classes are willing to accept the plan. The president of the debtor, who is also the principal shareholder in the debtor, does not believe that the debtor can afford to pay unsecured claims in full. What will happen if the debtor declines to increase the proposed distribution?

5. The real property of a Ch. 11 debtor is subject to a nonrecourse mortgage that secures a debt of $500,000. Because of a slump in property values, the collateral is appraised at $400,000, but it will likely appreciate in the future. The debt owed to the mortgagee therefore bifurcates into a

secured claim of $400,000 and an unsecured claim of $100,000. Under nonbankruptcy law, because this is a nonrecourse mortgage, the unsecured deficiency is not recoverable from the debtor. Under §1111(b) a class of creditors that is undersecured is entitled to elect under §1111(b) to eliminate the deficiency and to have the entire $500,000 claim treated as secured. (Assume that the mortgagee is the only creditor in this class.) What are the advantages and drawbacks of so electing?

6. A local software company had to file a Ch. 11 petition. Luckily, the case has progressed smoothly, and the debtor in possession was able to confirm a plan of reorganization in January. The plan proposed to pay general unsecured creditors 40 cents on the dollar and give the class 10 percent of the equity in the reorganized debtor. The general unsecured creditors accepted equity in the reorganized debtor because even though the debtor's liquidation value was considerable, the creditors believed that the debtor's future prospects were extremely promising. The debtor owned an extremely valuable patent. The disclosure statement explained that the debtor's exclusive ownership of the technology protected by the patent would serve as the foundation for the company's future software endeavors.

   In the summer of that year, one of the general unsecured creditors learned that despite the debtor's representations in its disclosure statement, the debtor had given its postpetition lender the right to license the technology protected by the valuable patent. The loss of its exclusive right affects the debtor's future prospects. The general unsecured creditors would not have voted in favor of the plan if they had known about this misrepresentation. Is there anything they can do?

EXPLANATIONS

Explanations

1. a. The administrative expenses are entitled to second priority under §507(a)(2), but in a corporate Ch. 11 case they are actually first-priority claims because the claims entitled to first priority under §507—domestic support obligations—are not implicated. Unless the holder of the claim has agreed to different treatment, §1129(a)(9)(A) requires the allowed amount of administrative expense claims to be paid in full in cash on the effective date of the plan.
   b. The $40,000 owed to the employees qualifies as a fourth priority claim under §507(a)(4) because the salary was earned within 180 days before the petition and no claim exceeds the maximum priority amount of $12,850. Under §1129(a)(9)(B) the allowed amount of these claims must also be paid in cash on the effective date of the plan unless the plan provides for payment by installments and the class has

accepted the plan. Because the claims of the five employees are similar, the debtor is likely to be required to classify them together and treat them equally under §1122 and 1123(a)(4). The class as a whole must accept the plan, for which §1126(c) requires an affirmative vote of two-thirds of the claims in amount and more than half in number.

c. The tax debt is an eighth priority claim under §507(a)(8) because it is for a tax measured by income for a taxable year ending before the petition for which a return was last due after three years before the filing of the petition. Section 1129(a)(9)(c) treats priority tax claims differently from other priority claims. Unless the I.R.S. has agreed to a different treatment, the claim must receive the present value of the full allowed amount of the claim. However, the claim can be paid in installments over a period not to exceed five years and need not be paid in cash on the effective date of the plan.

d. The trade creditors have general unsecured claims. If the claims are similar, the debtor may classify them together under §1122, but may place them in separate classes provided that the classification has a reasonable basis and is not for the purpose of manipulation. The plan will propose the treatment of these claims, and if the class is impaired (that is, it its members will receive less than their entitlement under nonbankruptcy law) the class will vote on whether to accept the plan. If the class votes not to accept the plan, the debtor can only have the plan confirmed by the cramdown method, which will require compliance with the requirements of §1129(b) that the plan must not discriminate unfairly against the dissenting class, and must be fair and equitable. (*See* section 20.4.3.) If the class as a whole votes to accept the plan, any dissenting members of the class have the protection of the best interests test under §1129(a)(7)(A).

2. If Co-operative refuses to accept the plan, the debtor will lose the favorable vote of the entire class. For a class of creditors to accept the plan, §1126(c) requires that at least two-thirds in amount and more than one-half in number of creditors in the class must vote to accept it. Although more than half in number of the creditors in the class appear willing to accept the plan, the total of their claims comes to $380,000, which falls $20,000 short of the necessary two-thirds of the total amount of claims in the class.

   It is not clear if the debtor would be permitted to classify Co-operative's claim separately. There is no provision in Ch. 11 that forbids the placing of similar claims into separate classes, but courts refuse to allow this if the purpose of the separate classification is to manipulate voting or to achieve some end that is contrary to the interests of creditors and not reasonably needed to achieve the legitimate goals of reorganization. The debtor's principal benefit from classifying the claim separately would be to ensure that at least one class of impaired claims accepts the plan, which is required for confirmation under §1129(a)(10). This will be an important benefit if there is no other class of claims that has voted to accept the plan. Whether Co-operative is classified with the other two claims and its negative vote prevents that class from accepting, or it is placed in its own class and votes against the plan, its refusal to accept the plan creates a dissenting class that will preclude consensual confirmation under §1129(a) and require the debtor to satisfy the cramdown requirements of §1129(b).

3. We begin by determining which of these classes is impaired. Section 1124(1) states that a class is impaired unless the plan "leaves unaltered the legal, equitable, and contractual rights" to which each claim in the class is entitled. Therefore, the only unimpaired classes are class 1, the secured claim that will be treated exactly as provided for in the loan agreement, and class 4, the administrative expenses to be paid in cash on the effective date of the plan. Because it is unimpaired, class 1 is deemed to accept the plan and does not vote on it. Class 4 does not vote on the plan either. As explained in section 20.3.2, the administrative expense claim does not even have to be classified at all because it has to be paid in cash on the effective date of the plan. This leaves classes 2, 3, and 5, all of which are impaired because there has been an alteration of the legal rights that they have under nonbankruptcy law. Class 2 is impaired because the lien has been stripped down; the claim has been bifurcated and only the secured portion will be paid in full. Class 3 has been impaired. Even though the claim will be paid in full, the payment period will be longer than provided for in the loan agreement. Class 5 is impaired because creditors in that class will not be paid in full.

   Because two classes (3 and 5) voted not to accept the plan, it does not qualify for consensual confirmation under §1129(a). Consensual confirmation is only possible under §1129(a)(8) if each class is either unimpaired or has accepted the plan. If §1129(a)(8) is not satisfied, the plan can only be confirmed by cramdown under §1129(b). However, all the requirements of §1129(a), apart from (a)(8), must be satisfied for a cramdown confirmation. One of those standards is that at least one class of impaired claims has accepted the plan, determined without including any acceptance of the plan by an insider. The only impaired class that has accepted the plan is class 2, but the creditor in that class is the president of the debtor, and as an officer of the debtor, qualifies as an insider under §101(31). Therefore, there is insufficient support of the plan by noninsider impaired classes to allow for confirmation under §1129(b).

4. If the debtor does not meet the demands of the holdout creditors, and cannot persuade them to accept a plan that pays less than they demand,

their negative votes on the plan will preclude acceptance by the class under §1126(c). The rest of the creditors in the class hold only one-half in amount of the claims in the class. This will prevent the debtor from confirming the plan as consensual under §1129(a), and will require a cramdown confirmation under §1129(b). The plan can only be confirmed in a cramdown if it qualifies as fair and equitable. To satisfy this test with regard to a class of unsecured claims, §1129(b)(2)(b) requires either that each holder of a claim that class receives the present value of the allowed amount of its claim, or if not, that no claim or interest junior to that class receives any property under the plan. This is the absolute priority rule. The effect of this is that if the debtor declines to pay the unsecured claims in full, equity interests, which are junior to debt, are wiped out. That is, the president will lose his ownership interest in the debtor.

5. Under §1111(b) the unsecured deficiency is recognized in the Ch. 11 case even if the mortgage was without recourse.

   If the mortgagee does not make the §1111(b) election and the debtor proposes to keep the property, §1129(b)(2)(A) requires the debtor to pay at least the full value of the secured claim ($400,000), having a present value equal to the value of the collateral ($400,000 plus interest). The unsecured claim of $100,000 is entitled to a distribution and to a vote, so there may be both economic and strategic value to the claim. However, the drawback to not making the election is that if the Ch. 11 case is not successfully consummated and the collateral is liquidated, the secured claim is confined to payment of the balance of the $400,000 collateral value fixed in the plan, and gets no advantage of any appreciation of the collateral's value.

   If the mortgagee makes the election under §1111(b), it loses the $100,000 deficiency claim as well as its voting rights as an unsecured claimant and has a secured claim for the full amount of $500,000. The plan must now provide for the greater of the face value of the claim ($500,000) or the present value of the collateral ($400,000 plus interest). If the Ch. 11 reorganization fails, the mortgagee's claim to the liquidation proceeds of the property is the balance of the $500,000 secured claim. Thus, the effect of the election is to prevent the debtor from stripping the lien.

6. Section 1144 provides for the revocation of an order of plan confirmation if the order was procured by fraud. The general unsecured creditors would have to prove that the debtor relinquished its exclusive ownership rights in the patent but left this material fact out of the disclosure statement to cause the creditors to rely on the misrepresentation and vote in favor of the plan to their detriment.

However, it is unclear how many days have passed since the confirmation order was entered. Section 1144 allows a party to consider a revocation request "at any time before 180 days after the date of the entry of the order of confirmation." It is possible that the creditors are outside of this 180-day period. If so, the bankruptcy court would not grant the request based on a strict reading of the statute. In that case, the creditors may have to make an equitable argument. In light of the apparent inequity, the creditors may be able to convince the bankruptcy court to consider taking action under §105, which provides the court the power to issue any order necessary to prevent an abuse of process.

CHAPTER 21

The Debtor's Discharge

§21.1 OVERVIEW

The debtor's discharge has been referred to frequently in prior chapters. The discharge is the statutory forgiveness of the balance of debts that are not paid in full in the bankruptcy case. The debtor's right to receive a discharge as a matter of law, even in the absence of creditor assent, is one of the features that distinguishes bankruptcy from insolvency proceedings under state law. For many debtors, it is the principal incentive for seeking bankruptcy relief. The discharge is one of the most important manifestations of bankruptcy's fresh start policy

The general discussion of bankruptcy policy in Chapter 3 explains that the goal of the discharge is to provide the debtor a fresh start, but this goal must be balanced against other public policies sought by the Code. To give due deference to these policies, limits and qualifications are imposed on the debtor's right to a discharge. For this reason, there are provisions in the Code that deny or limit the discharge as a penalty for dishonest or improper debtor conduct; in other instances Congress has determined—as a matter of policy or practicality—that the discharge is not appropriate or that particular types of debt should not be dischargeable. The nondischargeability of selected types of debt is exemplified by provisions that exclude from the discharge domestic support obligations, student loans, and certain taxes. These exclusions from dischargeability are very specific and only apply to debts that fall within the statutory qualifications.

The discharge applies differently to individuals and to corporate entities. Unless there are grounds for denial of the discharge (and subject to any applicable exclusions from the discharge), an individual may obtain a discharge irrespective of which form of bankruptcy relief has been chosen. However, a corporation can only receive a discharge if it undergoes rehabilitation under Ch. 11. If it is liquidated under Ch. 7 or 11, it becomes a mere shell. Bankruptcy does not actually terminate its existence, which is left to nonbankruptcy law. But if the corporation is not deregistered under nonbankruptcy law, the Code provides a strong disincentive to the revitalization of the corporate shell: Its undischarged prepetition debts remain in existence and are claimable from its new assets.[1]

A discharge under Ch. 7 is granted to the debtor by §727, under Ch. 11 by §1141, and under Ch. 13 by §1328. However, in addition to these discharge provisions applicable to each of the Code chapters governing the case, there are three general provisions in Ch. 5—§§523, 524, and 525—which apply generally to discharges under all Code chapters, except to the extent that they are excluded by the specific provisions of a particular chapter. Therefore, the rules applicable to the debtor's discharge under a particular form of bankruptcy, whether liquidation under Ch. 7 or Ch. 11, or rehabilitation under Ch. 11 or Ch. 13, are to be found in the discharge provision of that chapter, read in conjunction with the general provisions of §§523, 524, and 525. The effect of the specific provisions Chs. 7, 11, and 13 is to vary the extent and scope of the discharge in cases under each of those chapters. In part, these variations in the discharge reflect the policy favoring rehabilitation over liquidation. This is most strikingly apparent in the comparison between discharge under Chs. 7 and 13. However, divergence in the discharge provisions also reflects the particular structure of each chapter and the premises on which it is based.

Section 727(a) requires the court to grant a discharge to an individual Ch. 7 debtor unless the debtor is subject to the grounds for denial of the discharge set out in the subsection. Section 727(b) provides for the scope of the Ch. 7 discharge, and §727(c) permits creditors, the trustee, and the U.S. Trustee to object to the discharge or seek revocation of it on the grounds enumerated in the subsection. Section 1141(d) provides for the Ch. 11 discharge. Except as otherwise provided in the plan or order confirming it, a corporate debtor's discharge goes into effect upon confirmation of the plan. By contrast, unless the court orders otherwise, an individual Ch. 11 debtor only receives the discharge on completion of payments under the plan. Section 1328(a) requires the court to grant a discharge to a Ch. 13 debtor upon completion of payments under the plan, the payment of any

1. *See, e.g.*, *In re Goodman*, 873 F.2d 598 (2d Cir. 1989) (the successor to a defunct corporation was held liable for its prepetition debt).

domestic support obligations that are due, and compliance with §1328(g) (completion of an instructional course on personal financial management) and (h) (establishing that §522(q)(1)[2] is inapplicable). Section 1328(b), (c), and (d) exclude certain debts from the discharge. Section 1328(b) gives the court discretion to grant a "hardship discharge" to a debtor who has not completed plan payments if the requirements of the subsection are satisfied. Section 1328(e) allows the court to revoke a discharge if a party in interest shows cause under the subsection.

Section 523 lists debts that are excluded from an individual debtor's discharge. The purpose of the section is to exclude those debts from the discharge that Congress has decided, for reasons of fairness or policy, should not be dischargeable in the individual debtor's bankruptcy case. These exclusions are fully applicable in an individual bankruptcy under Ch. 7 or Ch. 11, but some of them are not applicable in a Ch. 13 case because they are overridden by §1328. Section 524(a) and (b) deals with the effect of the discharge. Section 524(c), (d), (k), and (l) prescribes detailed requirements for reaffirmation agreements, which are discussed in section 10.10. Section 524(g) provides for the court's supplementation of a Ch. 11 discharge by injunction. Section 525 prohibits governmental units, private employers, and lenders engaged in a government supported student loan program from discriminating against debtor solely on the ground that the debtor was bankrupt or discharged debts.

§21.2 THE SCOPE OF THE DISCHARGE

The discharge applies only to debts that fall within the bankruptcy case. As a general rule, this covers only prepetition debts that were or could have been proved in the estate. The estate itself incurs debts in the course of administration. These postpetition debts are obligations of the estate and are handled in the bankruptcy case. Depending on the chapter under which the debtor has filed, these estate debts may or may not be dischargeable if unpaid in the course of the case, but this issue does not often come up because administrative expenses are usually paid in full as a priority out of the estate. Most postpetition debts incurred by the individual debtor (as opposed to debts incurred by the estate itself) are obligations of the debtor's fresh start estate and are not affected by the discharge. There are exceptions to this rule. In an involuntary Ch. 7 case, §727(b) includes in the discharge all debts incurred in the gap period between the petition and the adjudication of bankruptcy; in a Ch. 11 case, §1141(d)(1) includes in the discharge

2. *See* sections 21.5.2(7) and 21.7.2

all debts that arose before the order of confirmation; and in a Ch. 13 case, the discharge covers all claims provided for in the plan (§1328).

Only debts are discharged. Sections 727, 1141, and 1328 all specifically refer to "debt" in providing for the discharge. "Debt" is defined in §101(12) to mean liability on a claim, which is in turn defined, in very broad terms, in §101(5). (*See* section 17.2.1.) Although most obligations are encompassed by this broad definition, some prepetition obligations of the debtors do not qualify as claims. If they are not claims, they are not covered by the discharge. The Supreme Court dealt with this issue in *Ohio v. Kovacs*, 469 U.S. 274 (1985). (*See* section 17.2.1.) In *Kovacs* the court held that a prepetition court order directing the debtor to clean up hazardous waste was a claim because the state agency had the alternative, under the state environmental statute, to conduct the cleanup itself and to seek reimbursement from the debtor. The court indicated that if there had been no alternative of a monetary remedy, the order compelling the debtor to clean up the site would not have been a claim. In *Pennsylvania Department of Public Welfare v. Davenport*, 495 U.S. 552 (1990), the Supreme Court held that the debtor's obligation to make restitution as a condition of probation in a criminal case is a right to payment and hence a debt.[3] Since *Kovacs* and *Davenport*, lower courts have followed this distinction in a variety of different cases. For example, in *Kennedy v. Medicap Pharmacies, Inc.*, 267 F.3d 493 (6th Cir. 2001), the court held that an injunction to enforce a covenant not to compete did not constitute a claim under *Kovacs* because the plaintiff had no alternative right to payment. The equitable relief of an injunction was premised on the absence of an adequate legal remedy for damages.

As explained in sections 17.3.1 and 17.5.3, because the discharge only covers debts, it affects only the debtor's personal liability on a secured claim. It does not terminate any lien on the debtor's property. Therefore the lien survives the discharge, although a debt secured by a lien is discharged and cannot be collected from the debtor as a personal liability. Once the automatic stay is lifted, the lienholder is able to foreclose on the property to satisfy the discharged debt to the extent of the collateral's value.

§21.3 THE EFFECT OF THE DISCHARGE

The discharge eliminates all the debtor's liability on the discharged debts. Section 524(e) makes it clear that the discharge covers only the debtor's liability for the debt and does not operate as a discharge in favor of any other

3. Congress responded to *Davenport* by making the debt nondischargeable in a Ch.13 case, as discussed in section 21.7.3. *See also* Example 2.

person who is also liable on the debt. Section 524(a) enjoins all further proceedings and activity to collect or recover the debt. The injunction created by the discharge succeeds the automatic stay that had been in effect during the case and turns the temporary bar of the stay into a permanent prohibition on collection activity in respect of a discharged debt.

The enforcement of the injunction is by means of the court's civil contempt power under §105. This is because the injunction, although imposed by statute, is equated to an order of court. Therefore, deliberate and knowing violation of the injunction subjects the creditor to civil sanctions, if it is established on a clear and convincing standard that the creditor knew or should have known of the injunction and failed to make reasonably diligent efforts to comply with it.[4] The sanctions could be coercive in nature (that is, designed to compel obedience) as well as compensatory in nature, including compensatory damages, attorney's fees, and in an egregious cases, even punitive damages. In *In re Sandburg Financial Corp.*, 446 B.R. 793 (S.D. Tex. 2011) the creditor sought to enforce a reaffirmation agreement that did not comply with §524.[5] The court found this to be a willful violation of the stay and awarded the Ch. 11 debtor compensatory contempt damages of $500,000. In *Walls v. Wells Fargo Bank, N.A.*, 276 F.3d 502 (9th Cir. 2002), the court held that a civil contempt order is the only remedy available to the debtor, who is granted no independent private right of action under §524. However, the court pointed out that no remedy beyond a contempt order is needed because the court can make a compensatory contempt order to reimburse the debtor for any loss suffered as a result of the violation. *In re Vivian*, 150 B.R. 832 (Bankr. S.D. Fla. 1992), illustrates the awesome power of the contempt remedy. Although the creditor knew of and tried to obey the discharge, it apparently could not get its computer to stop sending monthly dunning letters to the debtor. The court found the creditor's computer to be in contempt and fined it 50 megabytes of hard drive memory and 10 megabytes of R.A.M.

As is true with the automatic stay, the discharge injunction does not forbid all creditor communication with the debtor. The stay is violated only if the purpose of the communication is to harass the debtor or seek to recover the discharged debt. The coercive or harassing effect of the communication is determined objectively. In *Bates v. CitiMortgage, Inc.*, 844 F.3d 300 (1st Cir. 2016), the creditor, who had foreclosed on a mortgage on the debtors' home in the course of the bankruptcy, sent a communication to the debtors to the effect that forgiveness of the debtors' personal liability on the loan might have tax consequences. The debtors claimed that the notification violated the discharge injunction because it was an attempt to collect

4. *See, e.g., In re Covelli*, 550 B.R.256 (S.D. N. Y. 2016).
5. *See* section 10.10.

on the discharged mortgage debt. The court held that the communication was not an attempt to collect on the debt, but merely informational. Although the debtors may subjectively have felt threatened by the communication, there was no evidence that it was objectively coercive.

Section 525(a) prohibits discrimination by governmental units against a person that is or has been a debtor, or a person associated with the debtor, and §525(b) prohibits discrimination by a private employer against an individual debtor or an individual associated with the debtor, solely on the ground of the debtor's bankruptcy, insolvency, or nonpayment of a discharged debt. The bar on discrimination by a governmental unit in §525(a) covers "persons" (so includes corporate debtors) and encompasses licenses, permits, and other grants as well as the denial of employment and termination or discrimination in employment. The bar on discrimination by a private employer in §525(b) is worded differently. It covers only individuals and is confined to termination of employment or discrimination with respect to employment. In *In re Burnett*, 635 F.3d 169 (5th Cir. 2011), the court held that different language relating to the scope of prohibited discrimination means that while a governmental unit cannot discriminate against a debtor in both hiring and employment, the bar on discrimination by a private employer covers only existing employees, and does not preclude discrimination in hiring.[6] A private employer is therefore entitled to refuse to hire a person solely on the ground of bankruptcy, insolvency, or failure to pay a discharged debt.

The word "solely" allows a governmental unit or employer to justify adverse treatment by showing that it was based on grounds other than the debtor's bankruptcy or the nonpayment of a discharged debt. Courts have disagreed on the meaning and effect of "solely." Some have given it an interpretation favoring the debtor, and find discrimination if the bankruptcy played a significant role in the decision to refuse government services or to dismiss an employee. Others have adopted a plain-meaning approach and require only that the government or employer shows that the action was motivated by legitimate reasons other than the debtor's bankruptcy. For a discussion of these two approaches, see *Laracuente v. Chase Manhattan Bank*, 891 F.2d 17 (1st Cir. 1989), in which the court adopted the latter interpretation of §525. There is some difference of opinion about whether §525 extends to discrimination against a debtor who intends to file bankruptcy. In *In re Majewski*, 310 F.3d 653 (9th Cir. 2002), the court held that §525 does not preclude an employer from dismissing an employee who revealed that he was in financial difficulty and planned to file a petition.

Section 525(c) was added to the Code in 1994 and clarifies that a debtor, ex-debtor, or person associated with a debtor who seeks a student

---

6. See also *Murdock v. Esperanza, Inc.*, 529 B.R. 834 (E.D. Pa. 2015).

loan or loan guarantee is included in §525's protection from discrimination. Section 525(c) merely clarifies that applications for student loans are included in the protection against discrimination, and does not confer any higher level of protection on them. Therefore, although the debtor cannot be discriminated against solely because of the bankruptcy or discharge, the loan or guarantee can still be denied for other, legitimate, reasons. That is, the debtor's eligibility for the loan or guarantee must be evaluated as if the bankruptcy or discharge never existed.

§21.4 WAIVER OF THE DISCHARGE AND REAFFIRMATION OF THE DEBT

Section 524(a)(2) states that the injunctive force of the discharge and the release of the debtor from liability is not affected by any waiver of the discharge. This provision generally invalidates waivers, but it is qualified by §§727(a)(10) and 1328(a), which give effect to a waiver executed by the debtor in writing after the order for relief and approved by the court. Although Ch. 11 does not have a provision with the same wording, §1141(d) has the same effect, in that it permits the debtor to waive a discharge in the plan. The discharge relating to a specific debt can also be waived by a reaffirmation agreement covering that debt, discussed in section 10.10. Reaffirmation is subject to controls even more stringent than waiver. Although waiver or reaffirmation is unenforceable unless the prescribed requirements are satisfied, §524(f) allows the debtor to repay a debt voluntarily. Of course, if the creditor puts undue pressure on the debtor to pay, this would violate the injunction.

§21.5 THE CH. 7 DISCHARGE

§21.5.1 Procedure and Scope

As stated before, the Ch. 7 discharge is available only to an individual debtor. Unlike other chapters of the Code, Ch. 7 does not specify the point in the proceedings at which the discharge occurs. Rule 4004 requires objections to the discharge to be filed within 60 days of the creditors' meeting. If an objection is filed, or there is a motion pending to dismiss the case for abuse, the discharge is granted only after the court hears the matter and determines the debtor's right to a discharge. In the absence of such challenges, the discharge is granted as soon as possible after the expiry of that period.

Under §524(d), after the court grants or denies the discharge, it may hold a discharge and reaffirmation hearing at which the court deals with any reaffirmation agreement that the debtor has made.

Under §727(b), the discharge covers all prepetition debts as well as postpetition claims treated as prepetition debts by §502. This includes, for example, claims arising out of the rejection of an executory contract or the avoidance of a transfer, as explained in section 17.2. A creditor cannot avoid the discharge by not proving a claim. The discharge covers all debts, whether or not proved, subject to an exception noted in section 21.5.4(3) for debts omitted from the schedule. The debtor's right to a discharge is qualified by §727, which deprives the debtor of a discharge completely, and by §523, which excludes certain debts from it.

§21.5.2 Denial of the Discharge Under §727

The denial of a discharge deprives the debtor of one of the most important benefits of bankruptcy: forgiveness of the unpaid balance of debts provable against the estate. The grounds for denial of a discharge are set out in §727(a), which states that the court "shall grant the debtor a discharge unless" one of the grounds for denial applies. If any one of them is applicable, the trustee, a creditor, or the U.S. Trustee may object to the grant of the discharge. Many of the grounds for denial are intended to penalize wrongful conduct or to prevent abuse of the fresh start policy, but some are motivated by other concerns. The grounds for denying the Ch. 7 discharge can be grouped into the following categories.

(1) Debtors who are not individuals cannot receive a discharge under Ch. 7. As noted before, §727(a)(1) precludes the Ch. 7 discharge of a debtor that is not an individual. A corporation, association, or other legal entity must reorganize to obtain a discharge. If the entity is liquidated, the debt that was not paid in the liquidation remains with the corporate shell.

(2) Waiver. Section 727(a)(10) validates a written waiver of discharge executed by the debtor after the order for relief and approved by the court.

(3) Improper debtor conduct in or in anticipation of the Ch. 7 case. Section 727(a)(2) through (6) require the court to deny the discharge if the debtor has been guilty of specified dishonest, unlawful, or uncooperative conduct either during the case or in anticipation of it. The conduct listed in these subsections includes the fraudulent transfer of property, concealment of or damage to property, unjustified failure to keep records, destruction or falsification of records, inability to explain a loss or deficiency in assets, refusal to obey a court order or to answer questions, or unjustified refusal to testify. In *In re Petersen*, 564 B.R. 636 (Bankr. D. Minn. 2017), the court acknowledged the extreme nature of the denial of discharge and explained the judicial reluctance to grant this type of request. In assessing a denial request, courts invariably 1) construe §727(a)(2)'s provisions narrowly; 2) require that the objections be real and substantial, not merely technical; and 3) place on the party seeking denial of the discharge the burden to prove each element of the denial claim by a preponderance of the evidence.

A debtor has the affirmative duty to document business dealings and to preserve records, so the debtor's unjustified failure to produce proper and complete business records is a common basis for denial of the discharge. The denial of the discharge on this ground is usually reserved for cases of serious inadequacy that makes it difficult or impossible to ascertain the debtor's financial situation or relevant financial history, or calls into question the debtor's honesty in conducting and disclosing his affairs. In determining what constitute adequate records, courts take into account the degree and seriousness of the deficiency as well as the nature and complexity of the debtor's financial affairs and the debtor's business sophistication.[7] The creditor makes out a prima facie case for denial of the discharge by showing the lack of adequate records, upon which the burden shifts to the debtor to justify his failure to produce the documentation.[8] (Examples 1 and 3 illustrate some of the grounds for denial of the discharge under §727(a) through (6).)

(4) Improper conduct in relation to another case. Where the debtor's financial affairs are tied up with those of another entity, their fortunes may be so closely linked that the bankruptcy of one of them could lead to the bankruptcy of the other. For example, the failure of a corporation could lead not only to its bankruptcy, but to the bankruptcy of its principal shareholder as well. Section 727 recognizes that where two cases are closely related, the debtor in the one case may have the ability to influence what happens in the other and may use that power for improper ends. Therefore, §727(a)(7) authorizes the court to deny a discharge to a debtor who has committed any of the acts specified in §727(a)(2) through (6) in connection with the bankruptcy of an insider while the debtor's own case is pending or within a year before the debtor's petition.

(5) Successive bankruptcy filings. Ideally, once a debtor has received a discharge, he should not need bankruptcy relief again, especially in the near future. Serial bankruptcy filings within a short period are likely to be more than the result of just bad management or economic misfortune; they begin

---

7. *See*, e.g., *In re Simmons*, 810 F.3d 852 (1st. Cir. 2016) and *In re Schifano*, 378 F.3d 60 (1st Cir. 2004).

8. See *In re Caneva*, 550 F.2d 755 (9th Cir 2008).

to look like an abuse of the system. To discourage abuse of this kind, §707(a)(8) and (9) preclude the debtor from getting successive discharges within a relatively short period of years. The approach of §707(a)(8) and (9) is therefore not to prohibit successive bankruptcy filings but rather to discourage them by precluding the discharge in the later filing, thereby depriving the debtor of that important advantage of bankruptcy.[9] Section 727(a)(8) precludes a debtor from a Ch. 7 discharge in a case commenced within eight years of the filing of an earlier case under either Ch. 7 or Ch. 11 in which the debtor received a discharge. Section 727(a)(9) bars the debtor from a discharge under Ch. 7 for a period of six years after the commencement of a case under Ch. 13 in which the debtor received a discharge unless the Ch. 13 plan paid unsecured claims in full, or paid at least 70 percent of unsecured claims, was proposed in good faith, and was the debtor's best effort.

(6) Failure to take the required course on financial management. The Bankruptcy Abuse Prevention and Consumer Protection Act of 2005 (BAPCPA) added §727(a)(11), which denies a Ch. 7 discharge to a debtor until she has completed the instructional course on personal financial management required by §111 and approved by the U.S. Trustee. Section 5.4.3describes the prepetition debt counseling required of an individual debtor under §109(h). The financial management course required by §727(a)(11) is different and must be taken subsequent to filing the petition. (BAPCPA added the same language to §1328(a), making this a condition to the grant of the Ch. 13 discharge as well.) Section 727(a)(11) excuses the debtor from this requirement if the U.S. Trustee has determined that there are not sufficient courses available for "additional individuals" who are required to take the course, or if the debtor is excused from taking the course under §109(h)(4) because of severe incapacity or disability, or because of active military duty in a combat zone.

(7) Pending proceedings to determine reduction of the homestead exemption. BAPCPA added §727(a)(12), which forbids the granting of a Ch. 7 discharge until the court finds, after notice and the opportunity for a hearing, that there is no reasonable cause to believe that §552(q)(1) is

9. As discussed in section 5.4.2, there is a situation in which the Code does prohibit successive bankruptcy filings. Section 109(g)(1) and (2) preclude an individual debtor from being a debtor in a successive case if, within 180 days of the filing, the debtor's prior case was dismissed for willful failure to obey a court order or to appear before the court in proper prosecution of the case, or the debtor requested and obtained a voluntary dismissal of the case following the filing of a request for relief from stay. Section 109(g) makes the debtor temporarily ineligible to file a petition for the for the 180-day period following the dismissal. By contrast, even where §109(g) does not bar the debtor from filing, §727(a)(8) and (9) provide for the denial of a discharge in a successive case under the stated circumstances.

applicable, or that there is any proceeding pending in which a debtor may be found guilty of a felony of the kind described in §522(q)(1)(A) or liable for as debt of the kind described in §522(q)(1)(B). The primary purpose of §522(q), enacted by BAPCPA, is to cut down on the size of the homestead exemption where the state of the debtor's domicile allows a large or unlimited exemption and the debtor has been guilty of improper conduct. Section 522(q) places a limit of $160,375[10] on the homestead exemption where the debtor has been convicted of a felony that demonstrates that the filing of the bankruptcy case was an abuse of the Code or where the debtor owes a debt arising from various wrongful, criminal, or tortious acts. (The limitation on the homestead exemption is discussed in section 10.7.) Section 727(a)(12) is awkwardly and inconclusively worded. It seems to provide merely that before granting the discharge, the court must be satisfied that it is not likely that §522(q)(1) is applicable to the debtor and that there is no reasonable basis for believing that a proceeding under §522(q)(1) is pending. Section 727(a)(12) does not preclude the discharge if the debtor has been guilty of the conduct covered by §522(q)(1). The effect of that conduct is dealt with by limiting the homestead exemption, and §727(a)(12) delays the discharge, rather than denying it permanently. If there is cause to believe that §522(q)(1) is applicable, the discharge must be suspended until the §522(q)(1) question is resolved and the extent of the homestead exemption is settled.

§21.5.3 Revocation of the Discharge

Section 727(d) allows a creditor, the trustee, or the U.S. Trustee to apply for revocation of the debtor's discharge on various grounds. The most general grounds are that the debtor obtained the discharge through fraud that was not discovered by the applicant until after the discharge was granted;[11] the debtor deliberately withheld or concealed property that would have been property of the estate; or the debtor committed an act specified in §727(a)(6)—that is, disobeyed a court order or refused to testify or respond to a material question without justification based on the privilege against self-incrimination. Section 727(e) requires an application for revocation for fraud to be made within a year after the grant of the discharge, and an application on either the grounds of withholding property or of disobedience to a court order to be made within the later of one year after the grant of the discharge or the close of the case.

---

10. This is one of the dollar amounts adjusted every three years under §104. This amount is in effect from April 1, 2016. The next adjustment will be made with effect from April 1, 2019.
11. *See, e.g., Jones v. U.S. Trustee*, 736 F.3d 897 (9th Cir. 2013).

§21.5.4 Exclusions from the Individual Debtor's Ch. 7 Discharge by §523

Even when the debtor is entitled to a discharge under §727, the discharge may not include all the debts that are provable against the estate. Section 523 excludes several types of debt from the individual debtor's discharge. The reasons for these exclusions differ. Some of them are primarily aimed at penalizing wrongful conduct by the debtor, while others are more concerned with the protection of debts which Congress felt should not be reduced or eliminated in bankruptcy. There are several categories of nondischargeable debts listed in §523(a). The most generally applicable exclusions are summarized below, and some of them are illustrated by Examples 2, 3, 4, and 5.

All the exclusions in §523 are applicable in a Ch. 7 case.[12] Most of the exclusions do not have to be adjudicated during the bankruptcy case and simply take effect if the debt meets the criteria for exclusion. This means that, with regard to many of the types of debt that qualify for exclusion from the discharge under §523, the debt automatically survives the bankruptcy and can be enforced by the creditor in the normal course, even after the debtor has received the discharge. In fact, disputes over whether a debt qualifies as nondischargeable often arise, not in the bankruptcy case itself, but at some time afterwards, when the creditor takes action to enforce it. However, this general rule is subject to an important qualification with regard to three types of nondischargeable debt. Section 523(c)(1) requires creditors whose debts qualify for exclusion under §523(a)(2), (4), or (6)[13] to apply to the court on notice for a determination of dischargeability. Rule 4007 governs this application, which must normally be filed within 60 days of the creditors' meeting unless the court grants an extension of the time. When a determination of nondischargeability is required, the debt is not automatically excluded from the discharge, and its exclusion from the discharge must be determined by the court. The creditor loses the right to exclude the debt from the discharge if the matter is not brought before the court for determination in time. The creditor's responsibility to make timely application for a dischargeability determination presupposes that the creditor knew or should have known of the bankruptcy. If the debt was not scheduled or listed and the creditor did not otherwise obtain knowledge of the bankruptcy in time to apply for the determination, §523(a)(3) excludes the debt from the discharge despite the lack of a court determination.

Some of the categories of exclusion are quite narrow and specialized. The following are those that are most likely to arise. The heading for each

---

12. Their applicability under other chapters is discussed in sections 21.6 and 21.7.3.

13. These sections generally relate to fraud or intentional wrongs.

category indicates whether or not the creditor needs to seek a determination of nondischargeability for that category of debt.

(1) Priority taxes (§523(a)(1)). (A nondischargeability determination is not required.) Taxes that are entitled to priority under §507(a) (*see* section 17.5.4) are not discharged. In addition, taxes are excluded from the discharge if a required return was not filed, if it was filed late within two years before bankruptcy, or if the debtor filed a fraudulent return or tried to evade the tax. Under §523(a)(14), if the debtor borrows money to pay a nondischargeable tax, the loan itself becomes nondischargeable.

(2) Obligations incurred fraudulently (§523(a)(2)). (A nondischargeability determination is required.) This exception to discharge is frequently invoked. It has different rules for two distinct types of fraudulent conduct of the debtor in relation to the debt. The first, dealt with in subsection (A), is the more general ground of fraud covering the debtor's fraud and false representations, whether made orally or in writing. In cases involving last-minute consumer spending sprees, subsection (A) is augmented by a presumption set out in subsection (C). The second, dealt with in subsection (B), is a more specific basis for nondischargeability when the debt was induced by a materially false written financial statement.

Section 523(a)(2) is one of the subsections listed in §523(c)(1), so the debt is not automatically excluded from the discharge, and the creditor must seek a determination of dischargeability from the court following notice and a hearing. At the hearing, the creditor has the burden of proving that the debt qualifies for exclusion from the discharge.[14] In *Grogan v. Garner*, 498 U.S. 279 (1991), the Supreme Court made it clear that fraud must be proved on the normal preponderance-of-the-evidence standard, and need not be established on the more rigorous clear-and-convincing standard.

Where the debt in question is a consumer debt, the creditor faces a hazard in seeking to have it excluded from the discharge on grounds of fraud. To discourage creditors from making vexatious or groundless applications under §523(a)(2) for the nondischargeability of consumer debts, §523(d) gives the court the discretion to award costs and attorneys' fees for the proceedings to the debtor if the creditor's application for nondischargeability was not substantially justified and there are no special circumstances that would make the award unjust.

In *Cohen v. De La Cruz*, 523 U.S. 213 (1998), the Supreme Court held that if a debt is excluded from the discharge under §523(a)(2), the exclusion

---

14. This burden is relieved by the presumption of fraud in §523(a)(2)(C) where the debtor has engaged in a last-minute consumer spending spree, as explained below.

covers full liability on the debt — which includes both the original debt and any award of punitive damages traceable to the fraud and made by a court to penalize the debtor for the fraudulent conduct. Because *Cohen* requires the penal award to be traceable to the fraud, it must arise from the fraud. Therefore, in *In re Sabban*, 600 F.3d 1219 (9th Cir. 2010), the court found that a statutory penalty that required an unlicensed contractor to disgorge his fee did not arise from the debtor's fraud. Although the debtor had fraudulently misrepresented that he was licensed, the disgorgement penalty under the statute punished the lack of a license and was not dependent on a finding of fraud.

In *Archer v. Warner*, 538 U.S. 314 (2003), the Supreme Court held that a fraudulently induced debt does not change character where it is later included in a settlement agreement and released in exchange for a promise to pay the amount stipulated in the settlement. The settlement is not a novation. The debt retains its fraudulent character and is not extinguished and replaced by a mere contract claim.

On a literal reading, §523(a)(2) does not actually say that the debtor must have himself been guilty of the fraud. The language of the section focuses on the character of the debt, not necessarily on the conduct of the debtor. As a result, the debt may be nondischargeable where it was induced by the fraud of another person — such as an agent or a partner of the debtor — whose conduct can be imputed to the debtor.[15] This is so even if the debtor was not himself guilty of the fraud, had no knowledge of it, and did not benefit from it. For example, in *In re M.M. Winkler & Associates*, 239 F.3d 746 (5th Cir. 2001) the debt was held to be nondischargeable as a result of the fraud of the debtor's partner because of the partnership relationship and the joint and several liability of the partners.

The following discussion of §523(a)(2) is divided into four parts: Nondischargeability for actual fraud (including false representation, false pretenses) under §523(a)(2)(A), the presumption of fraud in a last-minute consumer spending spree under §523(a)(2)(C), nondischargeability for materially false financial statements under §523(a)(2)(B), and oral misrepresentations of financial condition that are not covered by either §523(a)(2)(A) or (B).

§523(a)(2)(A): Nondischargeability for actual fraud.

Section 523(a)(2)(A) excludes from the discharge a debt for money, property, services, or new or renewed credit to the extent that it was obtained by false pretenses, a false representation, or actual fraud. Although §523(a)(2)(A) broadly covers a wide range of fraudulent representations and conduct, it

15. See *In re Quinlivan*, 434 F. 3d 314 (5th Cir. 2005) (a debt induced by the fraud of another is only nondischargeable if the other party is the debtor's partner or agent, as determined under principles of state law).

does not cover a statement representing the debtor's or an insider's financial condition, which is explicitly excluded from subsection (a)(2)(A), and is dealt with separately in subsection (a)(2)(B), discussed below. The effect of separating fraud generally from fraudulent statements relating to financial condition means that certain types of fraudulent misrepresentations are not covered by §523(a)(2) at all. This is explained below. 523(a)(2)(A) specifies three types of fraud—false pretenses, false representation, and actual fraud.

False representation.

The type of conduct that will make a debt nondischargeable for false representation is determined with reference to the elements of fraud in the inducement (that is, fraud that induces the transaction) under nonbankruptcy law. The false representation could be by affirmative statement, or by silence where the debtor has a duty of disclosure.[16] A debtor's false representation is fraudulent if the misrepresentation is material, the debtor made it with knowledge of its falsity and intent to deceive, and it justifiably induced the creditor to provide the debtor with money, property, services, or credit, resulting in loss to the creditor. There must be a causal link between the fraudulent misrepresentation and the creditor's loss. Intent to defraud is determined under the totality of the circumstances. Some of the relevant factors are 1) the length of time between the creation of the debt and the petition; 2) whether the debtor had been contemplating bankruptcy at the time of incurring the debt; 3) the debtor's employment status and prospects; 4) whether the charges were for luxuries or necessities; 5) whether the spending was unusual or frenetic; and 6) the degree of the debtor's financial sophistication.

For example, courts have found fraud in cases where 1) the debtor went on a buying spree on receiving a credit card;[17] 2) the debtor made 47 purchases of luxury goods totaling about $8,600 a few weeks before her petition, when she was not earning enough to cover her living expenses;[18] and 3) the debtor charged $60,000 to her card for a six-week European vacation at a time when she already owed $300,000 on other credit cards.[19]

By contrast, the court did not find fraud where 1) the debtor incurred $67,000 in credit card debt to buy necessities to support herself after losing her job, and while she was trying to find new employment;[20] nor 2) where the debtor incurred about $3,800 in credit card charges in the three weeks

16. See *In re Juve*, 761 F.3d 847(8th Cir. 2014).
17. See *In re Ward*, 857 F.2d 1082 (6th Cir. 1988).
18. See *In re Burdge*, 198 B.R. 773 (B.A.P. 9th Cir. 1996).
19. See *In re Hashemi*, 104 F.3d 1122 (9th Cir. 1996).
20. See *In re Shartz*, 221 B.R. 397 (B.A.P. 6th Cir. 1998).

before her bankruptcy in an honest — but unrealistic — effort to keep her struggling business in operation.[21]

Sometimes a court may give too much credence to a debtor's optimism. In *In re Rembert*, 141 F.3d 277 (6th Cir. 1998), the court found that dishonest intent was not established where the debtor used his credit card to obtain a cash advance so that he could gamble. The debtor hoped that he would win and would use some of his winnings to repay the debt. The debtor in *In re Herrig*, 217 B.R. 891 (Bankr. N.D. Okla. 1998), was not so lucky. The court found fraudulent intent where the debtor used his card to its credit limit in a short period of time to fund his gambling.

Even if fraudulent intent is established, the debt is not excluded from the discharge under §523(a)(2)(A) unless the creditor justifiably relied on the false representation. According to *Field v. Mans*, 516 U.S. 59 (1995), justifiable reliance is not as strict a test as the purely objective reasonable reliance standard, and it does allow account to be taken of some subjective attributes of the creditor, such as knowledge, experience, and other circumstances. (Example 5 raises the issue of nondischargeability for fraudulent misrepresentation.)

False pretenses and actual fraud.

By listing not only false representations, but also false pretenses and actual fraud, §523(a)(2)(A) goes beyond the kind of dishonest misstatements that fall within the common law concept of fraud by the inducement. The Supreme Court in *Husky International Electronics, Inc. v. Ritz*, 136 S.Ct. 1581 (2016), considered the scope of the term "actual fraud." In that case, a creditor sought to exclude a debt from the discharge on the grounds that the debtor had made a fraudulent transfer to hinder the collection of a debt. The Court held that the reference to actual fraud in §523(a)(2)(A) encompasses not only fraudulent statements that originally induce the debt, but also other fraudulent conduct in relation to the debt. The court noted that the predecessor of §523(a)(2)(A) in the Bankruptcy Act referred only to false pretenses and false representations. By adding "actual fraud" when it enacted the Code, Congress must have intended to expand the section's reach. Therefore, §523(a)(2)(A) is broad enough to cover not only a false representation in the form of an affirmative untrue statement inducing the debt, but also deliberately dishonest conduct intended to impair or hinder the collection of a debt. The Court rejected the argument that a debtor does not "obtain" the benefit or credit as a result of the fraudulent transfer. The Court held that §523(a)(2)(A) covered a fraudulent transfer, even

21. See *In re Kountry Korner Store*, 221 B.R. 265 (Bankr. N.D. Okla. 1998).

though the debtor did not make an actual fraudulent statement or representation to the creditor.

§523(a)(2)(C): The presumption of fraud in a last-minute consumer spending spree.

The creditor normally bears the burden of proving fraud. However, §523(a)(2)(C) makes one exception to this by creating a presumption of fraud for the purposes of §523(a)(2)(A) when, shortly before filing the petition, the debtor went on a consumer spending splurge. The presumption only applies to consumer debt incurred by an individual. It takes effect in one of two alternative circumstances.

First, the presumption applies if, within 90 days before the order for relief, the debtor incurred consumer debts for luxury goods or services[22] aggregating more than $675 owed to a single creditor.[23] There can be an interpretational issue about what constitute luxuries, and one debtor's luxury may be another's necessity. For example, in *In re Hall*, 228 B.R. 483 (Bankr. M.D. Ga. 1998), the court held that while credit given to a debtor by a casino is a luxury when the gambling is recreational, it does not so qualify when the debtor is a long-time, high-stakes gambler trying to save his business by making a big win.

Second, fraud is presumed if within 70 days before the order for relief, the debtor obtained cash advances aggregating more than $950 and constituting an extension of consumer credit under an open-end credit plan.[24] This is a plan under which the debtor is given a line of credit and repeated transactions are contemplated. This provision is worded so as not to include the requirements that the advances be used to buy luxury goods or services, or that they all be obtained from the same creditor.

It is worth stressing that §523(a)(2)(C) does not make debts incurred under the stated circumstances automatically nondischargeable; it merely establishes a presumption that a debt so incurred is fraudulent. This places the burden on the debtor to prove that the elements of fraud are not satisfied despite the suspicious circumstances.

---

22. Defined in the subsection as those not reasonably necessary for the support or maintenance of the debtor or her dependent.

23. BAPCPA lowered the threshold for the presumption to take effect by increasing the period of the presumption from 60 days to 90 days and decreasing the amount of the debt. Section 523(a)(2)(c) is one of the sections subject to §104(b), so the amount of the debt is adjusted administratively every three years. It was last adjusted with effect from April 1, 2016. The next adjustment will be made with effect from April 1, 2019.

24. BAPCPA expanded the scope of this presumption as well, by increasing its period from 60 to 70 days and decreasing the amount of the debt. This subsection is also subject to periodic adjustment in amount under §104.

§523(a)(2)(B): Nondischargeability for materially false financial statements.

Section 523(a)(2)(B) applies only to situations in which money, property, services, or new or renewed credit is obtained by a materially false written statement "respecting the debtor's or an insider's financial condition." This subsection is only applicable to statements respecting financial condition, so courts often have to grapple with the question of whether a false statement relates to financial condition. As noted above, some courts define "financial condition" narrowly, to include only statements relating to the debtor's overall financial situation or net worth. If the statement does not meet this narrow definition, its nondischargeability for fraud should be evaluated under §523(a)(2)(A) rather than (a)(2)(B). In *In re Kosinski*, 424 B.R. 599 (B.A.P. 1st Cir. 2010), the creditor was induced to lend money to the debtor for the development of a nightclub project on the strength of a profit and loss projection furnished by the debtor. The court held that this did not qualify as a statement respecting the debtor's financial condition. The statement covered by §523(a)(2)(B) must at least describe the debtor's financial condition in some way, although it need not be a formal financial statement.

Unlike subsection (a)(2)(A), this subsection does set out the required elements: 1) the statement must be written; 2) it must be materially false; 3) the debtor must have published it or caused it to be published with intent to deceive; and 4) the creditor must have reasonably relied on it. As you can see, the elements are quite similar to those for common law fraud, with two differences: Only written statements are covered, and the test for reliance is the more stringently objective reasonableness standard. The legislative history of §523(a)(2)(B) and *Field v. Mans* (above) explain why this subsection articulates the elements of a false financial statement and imposes the stricter reasonable reliance standard; namely, Congress did not want a creditor to claim nondischargeability on the basis of some unimportant misstatement or inaccuracy in a credit application or financial statement.

Because the elements of the subsections are similar in many respects, it may often not matter which of the two apply. However, in some cases, one of these two differences in the subsections could have a significant effect. For example, in *In re Sharpe*, 351 B.R. 409 (Bankr. N.D. Tex. 2006), the court's determination that the oral misrepresentation related to financial condition excluded it from §523(a)(2)(A), and because it was oral, it failed to meet §523(a)(2)(B)'s requirements. This is explained further below.

The difference between the more subjective "justifiable reliance" standard and more objective "reasonable reliance" standard could also be important. *In re Kosinski* points out the impact of this difference. The test of reasonable reliance is more stringent than justifiable reliance because it focuses factors that would alert a reasonable creditor to the falsity of the representation, rather than on the individual attributes of this particular creditor, which may justify him in being less vigilant. Section §523(a)(2)(B) does not differ from §523(a)(2)(A) in the extent to which the debt will be excluded from the discharge. Both subsections are subject to the prefatory language that the debt is excluded from the discharge "to the extent obtained by" the fraud. Therefore, although *Cohen v. De La Cruz* was concerned with a case involving §523(a)(2)(A), its interpretation that the exclusion covers full liability on the debt, including punitive damages, is equally applicable to §523(a)(2)(B).

Oral misrepresentations of financial condition which fit under neither §523(a)(2)(A) or (B).
An oral misrepresentation of financial condition is not covered in either subsection (a)(2)(A) or (a)(2)(B) and is therefore not a basis for exclusion from the discharge under §523(a)(2). The reason for confining nondischargeability to written misrepresentations of financial condition is because oral representations of financial condition lack the formality necessary for financial statements. Because there is no basis for finding a debt nondischargeable based on an oral misrepresentation of financial condition, courts have made some fine distinctions to decide if an oral misrepresentation relates to financial condition (so the debt is dischargeable) or to some other inducing factor (so that it is excluded from the discharge under §523(a)(2)(A)). For example, in *In re Joelson*, 427 F.3d 700 (10th Cir. 2005), and *In re Bandi*, 683 F.3d 671 (5th Cir. 2012), the court gave the narrowest possible meaning to "financial condition," confining it to statements relating to the debtor's overall financial situation or net worth. As a result, in both these cases the court found that the debtors' misrepresentations about their ownership of assets and ability to repay did not constitute statements relating to financial condition. The misrepresentations were therefore not excluded from §523(a)(2)(A), and qualified as fraudulent misrepresentations under that subsection. In *In re Sharpe*, above, the court gave a more expansive meaning to "financial condition." It held that the debtor's ostentatiously extravagant lifestyle, combined with oral misrepresentations of wealth, did constitute false representations of financial condition, and the debt induced by that representation was not covered by the exclusion from the discharge in §523(a)(2)(A). Further, §523(a)(2)(B) did not exclude the debt from the discharge because the representations were not in writing.

(3) Unlisted or unscheduled debts (§523(a)(3)). (A dischargeability determination is not required.) Although the discharge normally extends even to those debts for which no proof of claim was filed, §523(a)(3) protects creditors who did not know of the bankruptcy in time to file a claim. If the debtor did not timely list or schedule the debt, so that the creditor did not receive notice of the bankruptcy and did not otherwise find out about it in time to file a proof of claim, the debt is excluded from the discharge.

As mentioned earlier, §523(a)(3) also precludes discharge of a debt covered by §523(a)(2), (4), or (6) where the creditor's failure to make timely application for a nondischargeability determination resulted from lack of knowledge of the bankruptcy because the debtor failed to list or schedule the debt.

(4) Debts arising out of the debtor's dishonesty as a fiduciary, or from embezzlement or larceny (§523(a)(4)). (A dischargeability determination is required.) If, while acting in a fiduciary capacity, the debtor committed fraud or defalcation or if, acting in any capacity, the debtor embezzled money or committed larceny, the liability arising from that wrongful act is excluded from the discharge. This is one of the exclusions for which a determination of dischargeability must be requested. Note that the requirement that the debtor was acting in a fiduciary capacity is applicable only to the acts of fraud and defalcation. The requirement that the debtor was acting as a fiduciary does not apply to the exclusion from the discharge of debts arising from embezzlement[25] or larceny. Therefore, if fiduciary capacity cannot be established, embezzlement may be an alternative ground for nondischargeability under §523(a)(4). This does not always work. In *In re Thompson*, 686 F.3d 940 (8th Cir. 2012), a general contractor failed to remit to a subcontractor funds that the owner had paid to the contractor on account of the subcontractor's work. The subcontractor sought to have the contractor's debt excluded from the discharge under §523(a)(4), but the court held that the debt was dischargeable: The debtor was not acting in a fiduciary capacity because, although a state statute declared such funds to be held in trust by the contractor, the obligation to remit the funds was merely contractual and the statute did not actually create a real trust relationship. The debtor could also not be treated as having embezzled the fund because the payment from the owner was the debtor's property, and he had merely a contractual obligation to pay the subcontractor. A person cannot embezzle his own funds.[26] (*See also* Example 2.)

Courts disagree on the scope of that portion of §523(a)(4) that applies to fraud or defalcation committed in a fiduciary capacity. Some restrict it to trusts in the formal sense—that is, express or technical trusts.[27] Other courts interpret "fiduciary capacity" more broadly to include any relationship in which the debtor stands in a position of trust and confidence toward

---

25. Embezzlement is determined under principles of nonbankruptcy law and consists of the misappropriation of funds with fraudulent intent or deceit. See *In re Carpenter*, 2017 WL 1194701 (S.D.N.Y.).

26. See also *In re Carpenter*, *supra*, in which the creditor failed to establish either that the debtor was a fiduciary or that her conduct satisfied the common law elements of embezzlement.

27. *See, e.g.*, *In re Thompson*, 686 F.3d 940, *supra*; *Hunter v. Philpott*, 373 F.3d 873 (8th Cir. 2004); and *In re Burress*, 245 B.R. 871 (Bankr. D. Colo. 2000).

the creditor which demands a duty of loyalty and care.[28] An attorney-client relationship is an example, and some courts have been willing to apply §523(a)(4) when the debt arose as a result of the attorney's faithless conduct, even if the wrong did not involve the misappropriation of trust funds. However, even among courts that adopt the broader approach, there seems to be general agreement that there must at least be some kind of actual relationship of trust between the parties, so it is not appropriate to apply §523(a)(4) when the debtor is deemed by equity or statute to be a constructive trustee purely for the sake of affording a remedy to the victim of the fraud or defalcation. As mentioned above, this was the conclusion reached by the court in *In re Thompson*. *In re Marchiando*, 13 F.3d 1111 (7th Cir. 1994), was to the same effect. The debtor, who owned a convenience store, failed to remit to the state the proceeds of lottery tickets that she had sold. The state statute provided that the proceeds of ticket sales would constitute a trust fund until paid to the state. The state sought to have the debt for the unpaid proceeds excluded from the debtor's discharge under §523(a)(4), but the court found the section inapplicable. Although the court agreed with a wider definition of fiduciary capacity, the debtor here was merely a ticket agent without any special power, expertise, or duty of loyalty. The statutory device of deeming the funds to be in trust was really nothing more than the creation of a constructive trust as a collection device.

There had been some confusion in the case law over the meaning of "defalcation." Some courts interpreted it broadly to cover all misappropriations or failures to account, whether or not deliberate. Others required the conduct to have been consciously wrongful, or even egregiously wrongful. The U.S. Supreme Court settled this conflict in the case law in *Bullock v. BankChampaign, N.A.*, 569 U.S. 267 (2013), in which it held that "defalcation" requires an intentional wrong. This includes not only conduct that the fiduciary knows to be improper, but also reckless conduct of the kind commonly treated as equivalent in criminal law. To qualify as defalcation where the trustee acts recklessly without actual knowledge of wrongfulness, the trustee must have grossly deviated from the conduct that a law-abiding person would observe, and must have been willfully blind to the substantial and justifiable risk that his conduct would violate his fiduciary duty.

Because §523(a)(4) covers fraud and defalcation, it has some commonality with §523(a)(2), which excludes fraudulently incurred obligations from the discharge. Therefore, where the facts satisfy the elements of §523(a)(2), that ground for excluding the debt from the discharge could be an alternative to §523(a)(4). If the exclusion is sought under §523(a)(2), the creditor does not need to show fiduciary capacity, but does need to show that money, property, services, or credit was obtained

28. *See, e.g.*, *In re McDade*, 282 B.R. 650 (Bankr. N.D. Ill. 2002).

by the fraud. The question of which of these two bases for nondischargeability fits best will depend on the relative difficulty of proving fiduciary capacity or the link between the fraud and the giving of value.

(5) Domestic support obligations (§523(a)(5)). (A dischargeability determination is not required.) Section 523(a)(5) excludes domestic support obligations, defined in §101(14A), from the discharge. Domestic support obligations have been discussed several times before.[29] Unlike the other provisions that prevent the debtor from evading domestic support obligations, §523(a)(5) was not created by the Bankruptcy Reform Act of 1994; it has been part of the Code since its enactment in 1978. It was amended by BAPCPA, which substituted the newly defined term "domestic support obligation" for the prior language "alimony, maintenance, or support." In essence, the definition covers prepetition and postpetition support debts established by court or administrative order or by divorce decree or separation or property settlement agreement, and owing to a spouse, ex-spouse, child, person responsible for a child, or a governmental unit.

The debt must actually be for support. The protection does not extend to a debt arising from some other obligation merely because it has been characterized or labeled as for support. The way in which the parties have chosen to label the debt may be relevant to showing their intent, but it is merely one factor to consider, and is not dispositive. The issue of whether the debt is actually for support is a factual one, determined under federal bankruptcy law, not state law. The determination is made on all the facts, taking into account factors such as the mutual intent of the parties, their respective financial situations, and the purpose to be served by the obligation. *In re Johnson*, 397 B.R. 289 (Bankr. M.D.N.C. 2008), applied this test and also held that a debt payable to a third party, other than the dependent or a governmental unit, could qualify as domestic support. The debt in that case was the debtor's obligation, incorporated into a divorce decree, to pay to the mortgagee installments due under a deed of trust on the former marital home. The court said that this was in the nature of domestic support because the debtor's payments were intended to relieve his ex-wife of the obligation to pay.

(6) Debts for willful and malicious injury (§523(a)(6)). (A dischargeability determination is required.) A debt resulting from the debtor's willful and malicious injury to another entity or the property of another entity is excluded from the discharge. This is one of the exclusions for which a determination of dischargeability must be requested.

Although the precise scope of the term "willful and malicious" is subject to doubt, it is clear that this exclusion applies to liability for

29. *See, e.g.*, sections 7.4.3, 10.8.2, 13.1.4(7), and 17.5.4.

deliberate wrongful conduct. It is concerned with intentional rather than negligent behavior. Any doubt on this issue was settled by the Supreme Court in *Kawaauhau v. Geiger*, 523 U.S. 57 (1998), in which the claim arose from the debtor's medical malpractice. It was apparent that the debtor's conduct had been reckless. The court stressed that §523(a)(6) requires that the injury be both willful (that is, deliberate and intentional rather than reckless or negligent) and malicious (that is, inflicted with the intent to harm or with the callous realization that harm would be caused). These are separate and distinct elements. Willfulness encompasses the debtor's volition in taking the action, and malice focuses on the debtor's motivation in acting. The court found that it would violate the plain meaning of §523(a)(6) to read the subsection as covering reckless conduct, or even intentional conduct that is not accompanied by the intent to do the harm. The court said that such a reading would also render superfluous other subsections that cover reckless injury, namely §523(a)(9) (debts for injury caused by driving while intoxicated) and §523(a)(12) (malicious or reckless failure to fulfill commitments due to a federal depository institution regulatory agency). In applying *Kawaauhau* lower courts have emphasized the need to find both the elements of intent to commit the act and intent to cause harm.[30] In *In re Patch*, 526 F.3d 1176 (8th Cir. 2008), the court held that although reckless or negligent injury is not enough, it is not necessary that the debtor desires to bring about the harmful consequences, provided that the act is done deliberately and the debtor realizes that the resulting harm is substantially certain.

Willful and malicious injury is normally associated with intentional tortious conduct that causes physical harm, and some courts have read a reference in *Kawaauhau* to intentional torts as confining nondischargeability to tortious conduct. For example, in *Lockerby v. Sierra*, 535 F.3d 1038 (9th Cir. 2008), the court refused to apply §523(a)(6) to a deliberate breach of contract unless there was tortious conduct involved in the breach. However, several courts have had no difficulty in applying §523(a)(6) to deliberate and malicious conduct in relation to a commercial transaction, that causes economic injury. In *In re Smith*, 555 B.R. 96 (Bankr. D. mass 2016), the court pointed out that neither the *Kawaauhau* holding nor §523(a)(6) confines the injury to tortious conduct, so §523(a)(6) applies also to contractual debts, provided the elements of intent to commit the act and intent to cause harm are present. In *In re Jercich*, 238 F.3d 1202 (9th Cir. 2001), the court applied

30. *See, e.g.*, *Ball v. A.O. Smith Corp.*, 451 F.3d 66 (2d Cir. 2006) (an attorney committed willful and malicious injury by bringing a suit that he knew to be unreasonable and without prospect of success); *In re Sicroff*, 401 F.3d 1101 (9th Cir. 2005) (defamation was both deliberate and with malicious motive); *In re Moore*, 357 F.3d 1125 (10th Cir. 2004) (the debtor's false representation to an employee that the debtor carried liability insurance was deliberately intended to deceive but was not malicious, so the employee's claim for uninsured personal injury was not excluded from the discharge).

§523(a)(6) to a breach of contract that was both deliberate and motivated by a desire to harm the other party, and in *In re Trantham*, 304 B.R. 298 (B.A.P. 6th Cir. 2004), the court applied it to a purposeful and malicious infringement of patent rights.

If the claim has already been adjudicated in state court, and that court had made a finding as to willfulness and malice, the bankruptcy court may adopt that finding on the principle of collateral estoppel, so that the creditor does not have to prove these elements again in the dischargeability hearing. For example, in *In re Braen*, 900 F.2d 621 (3d Cir. 1990), damages for malicious prosecution were held nondischargeable without further evidence because the necessary elements had already been proven in the tort case. However, for collateral estoppel to apply, the prior state court judgment must have disposed of all the elements required for nondischargeability. In *In re Stage*, 321 B.R. 486 (B.A.P. 8th Cir. 2005), the state court judgment settled the question of whether an injury arising from deliberate tort was willful but did not address whether it was malicious because malice was not an element of the tort. The court therefore held that the creditor did not have to prove willfulness in the discharge hearing but did have to establish malice to have the debt excluded from the discharge.

As noted in the discussion of §523(a)(2), *Cohen v. De La Cruz* held that the language of §523(a)(2) covered punitive damages as well as the original debt. Although the court did not address whether the same result would be called for by §523(a)(6), its reasoning, based on a grammatical interpretation of §523(a)(2), would be equally applicable to §523(a)(6) because the structure of the language is the same. In fact, if anything, the language of §523(a)(6) even more strongly leads to the conclusion that punitive damages are covered, because it simply excludes from the discharge "any debt . . . for willful and malicious injury," without the qualifying "to the extent" language found in §523(a)(2). In *Jendusa-Nicolai v. Larson*, 677 F.3d 320 (7th Cir. 2012), the debtor physically attacked his ex-wife and had been convicted of attempting to murder her. In addition to the criminal conviction, the ex-wife obtained a civil tort judgment against the debtor in state court for compensatory and punitive damages arising out of the assault, and her current husband and daughter obtained judgments against him for loss of consortium. In the debtor's subsequent bankruptcy, the bankruptcy court held that all these claims were nondischargeable under §523(a)(6). The court of appeals affirmed. There was no question that the injury qualified as both willful and malicious, and all the damages were nondischargeable. The ex-wife's damages were due to the debtor's conduct and were the consequence of willful and malicious injury. Further, the court held that the damages claimed by the ex-wife's husband and daughter were also nondischargeable, because the fact that the debtor did not intend to harm these parties is irrelevant in this context. The damages for loss of consortium were suffered as a result of the debtor's willful and malicious act and derivative from the injury to the ex-wife. Section 523(a)(6) is illustrated in Examples 3 and 4.

(7) Governmental fines, penalties, and forfeitures (§523(a)(7)). (A dischargeability determination is not required.) Debts due to the government for fines, penalties, or forfeitures that are not compensation for actual pecuniary loss are excluded from the discharge. This category includes penalties on taxes that are nondischargeable under §523(a)(7), but does not include penalties on dischargeable taxes or on a transaction that occurred more than three years before the petition.

Section 523(a)(7) sets out four conditions for a debt to qualify as nondischargeable under the subsection: the debt must be a fine, penalty, or forfeiture; it must be payable to a governmental unit; it must be payable for the benefit of the governmental unit; and it must not be compensation for actual pecuniary loss. It can be a difficult factual question to decide whether a debt due to the government qualifies for exclusion from the discharge under §523(a)(7). *Kelley v. Robinson*, 479 U.S. 36 (1986), examined this question in relation to restitution payments imposed by a court as a condition of the debtor's probation following conviction of welfare fraud.[31] Although the restitutionary obligation did have the purpose of compensating the state for the loss caused by the fraud, the Court nevertheless found that the restitution obligation was excluded from the discharge under §523(a)(7). The Court characterized the claim as a noncompensatory penalty because a criminal restitution obligation goes beyond mere compensation of the victim and serves the state's broader goal of punishing and rehabilitating offenders and enforcing its criminal law.[32] (*See* Example 2.)

Since *Kelley*, lower courts have continued to grapple with the question of when a debt to the government is a penalty or forfeiture, rather than compensation for pecuniary loss. For example, *In re Taggart*, 249 F.3d 987 (9th Cir. 2001), a California statute allowed the state bar to collect the costs and fees of disciplinary proceedings from an attorney who was disciplined. The court found the claim for the costs and fees to be dischargeable because it was for compensation of pecuniary loss—a simple fee-shifting provision—and not a punishment. The court distinguished cases that interpreted statutes from other states, in which the payment of costs had a punitive purpose. After the case was decided, the California legislature amended the statute to recharacterize the award of costs and fees as a

---

31. In a dictum, the Court expressed doubt that a restitution obligation is a debt at all under §101(12). If it does not qualify as a debt, it cannot be discharged, even if none of the exclusions in §523 apply. However, in *Pennsylvania Department of Public Welfare v. Davenport*, 495 U.S. 552 (1990), the Court reversed itself on its dictum in *Kelley* and held that a restitution obligation is a debt and is therefore dischargeable unless one of the grounds for nondischargeability in §523 applies.

32. See also *In re Thompson*, 418 F.3d 362 (3d Cir. 2005).

punishment to protect the public. In *In re Findley*, 593 F.3d 1048 (9th Cir. 2010), the court found that the statutory amendments focused the statute on the protection of the public and the maintenance of standards in the profession, and therefore moved the costs and fees beyond mere compensation for pecuniary loss and rendered them nondischargeable.

In *Kelley* the restitutionary obligation was for the repayment of fraudulently obtained welfare benefits, so restitution was payable to the state. Some courts have therefore distinguished cases where the restitution imposed in the criminal sentence or the other financial award is payable to a private party, rather than the government. Applying the plain meaning of the subsection, which uses the words "payable to and for the benefit of a governmental unit," these courts have held that the debt is dischargeable where payment is due to a private party.[33] Other courts have adopted a more flexible approach and have been willing to apply §523(a)(7) to an award to a private litigant where the award has a penal basis or is criminal in nature.[34]

Section 523(a)(7) refers to forfeitures in addition to fines and penalties. The meaning and extent of this word is not entirely clear. In *In re Nam*, 273 F.3d 281 (3d Cir. 2001), the debtor had posted bail for his son, who jumped bail and fled the country. The court held that the bail bond in favor of the city was excluded from the discharge as a forfeiture. By using the word "forfeiture" in the section, Congress indicates that it is not necessary that the debt arise from punishment. It was clear that the bond was not compensation for pecuniary loss. The court confined its decision to bonds given by family members, recognizing that different considerations may apply to a professional bail bond agent.

(8) Educational loans and benefits (§523(a)(8)). (A dischargeability determination is not required.) Section 523(a)(8) excludes from the discharge educational loans and other repayable educational benefits if they were made, insured, or guaranteed by the government, were made under a program wholly or partially funded by the government or a nonprofit institution, or otherwise qualify as educational loans or benefits as enumerated in the section. The obvious intent of this provision is to protect governmental and institutional student loan programs by preventing graduates from using bankruptcy to discharge liability for loans. Section 523(a)(8) used to be confined to loans whose first payment date occurred

---

33. *See, e.g.*, *In re Griffin*, 491 B.R. 602 (Bankr. S.D. Ga. 2013) (although the purpose of civil contempt sanctions is to uphold the court's authority, the award of monetary sanctions in favor of the creditor is not payable to a governmental unit, and therefore not covered by §523(a)(7)). and *In re Rashid*, 210 F.3d 201 (3d Cir. 2000) (a restitution obligation payable directly to the victim is not within §523(a)(7)).
34. *See, e.g.*, *In re Verola*, 446 F.3d 1206 (11th Cir. 2006).

within seven years of bankruptcy. This was eliminated by an amendment in 1998, which bars the discharge of student loans, no matter how old they may be, in all cases commenced after the effective date of the amendment.

Even if the debt is nondischargeable under §523(a)(8), the section gives the court the discretion to discharge the debt if exclusion from the discharge would cause undue hardship to the debtor or dependents. The hardship determination is an adversary proceeding to be initiated by the debtor seeking the discharge, and the court should not discharge any part of nondischargeable student debt in the absence of a hardship determination. In *United Student Aid Funds, Inc. v. Espinosa*, 559 U.S. 260 (2010), the debtor's Ch. 13 plan proposed to pay the principal of a student loan and to discharge the accrued interest. The debtor did not file a complaint to initiate a hardship hearing, but the bankruptcy court nevertheless confirmed the plan. The debtor paid off the principal of the debt over five years, following which the court discharged the debt for accrued interest. About three years after the discharge, the creditor sought to enforce payment of the discharged portion of the debt, and the debtor moved for an order holding the creditor in contempt for violating the discharge injunction. The Supreme Court held that the bankruptcy court should not have confirmed the plan. However, its error was not jurisdictional, and the creditor's due process rights had not been violated because it had received notice of the filing and contents of the plan. Therefore, despite the bankruptcy court's error, its confirmation of the plan was not void, and the discharge was effective.

The Code does not indicate what constitutes undue hardship. *Brunner v. New York State Higher Educ. Services Corp.*, 831 F.2d 395 (2d Cir. 1987), establishes the predominant test for determining undue hardship. The *Brunner* test sets out three factors that must be satisfied to invoke undue hardship. The first factor assesses the debtor's current circumstances and inquires if she can repay the loans and still maintain a minimal standard of living. Courts undertake a comprehensive evaluation of the debtor's living situation to determine if the debtor can reduce expenses or increase income. Courts scrutinize expenditures but there is no expectation that the debtor should live in "abject poverty" to satisfy this factor.[35] The second factor requires the debtor to demonstrate that the current state of affairs is likely to persist over the payment period of the loan. In evaluating this factor, some courts have ruled that a "certainty of hopelessness" must be found[36]

35. *Tennessee Student Assistance Corp. v. Hornsby (In re Hornsby)*, 144 F.3d 433, 438 (6th Cir. 1998) and *Pennsylvania Higher Educ. Assistance Agency v. Faish (In re Faish)*, 72 F.3d 298, 305 (3d Cir. 1995).
36. *Spence v. Educational Credit Mgmt. Corp. (In re Spence)*, 541 F.3d 538, 544 (4th Cir. 2008); *Educational Credit Mgmt. Corp. v. Mosley (In re Mosley)*, 494 F.3d 1320, 1326 (11th Cir. 2007); *Barrett v. Educational Credit Mgmt. Corp. (In re Barrett)*, 487 F.3d 353, 359 (6th Cir. 2007); *In re Frushour*, 433 F.3d 393, 401 (4th Cir. 2005); *Brightful v. Pennsylvania Higher Educ. Assistance Agency (In re Brightful)*, 267 F.3d 324, 328 (3d Cir. 2001); but see *Educational Credit Mgmt. Corp. v. Polleys*,

and consider a host of elements, including 1) serious mental or physical disability of the debtor or the debtor's dependents, preventing employment or advancement; 2) the debtor's obligation to care for dependents; 3) lack of, or severely limited education; 4) poor quality of education; 5) lack marketable job skills; 6) underemployment; 7) maximized income potential in the chosen educational field, and no other lucrative job skills; 8) limited number of years remaining in work life to allow payment of the loan; 9) age or other factors that prevent retraining or relocation as a means for payment of the loan; 10) lack of assets, whether or not exempt, that could be used to pay the loan; and 11) potentially increasing expenses that outweigh any potential appreciation in the value of assets and/or likely increases in income.[37]

The third factor demands that the debtor must have made a good faith effort to repay the loan and the forces precluding repayment are beyond her reasonable control. For this factor, courts put considerable weight on whether the debtor participated in an alternative repayment program[38] prepetition.[39]

The *Brunner* test has been applied in numerous subsequent cases. For example, in *In re Gerhardt*, 348 F.3d 89 (5th Cir. 2003), the court found no undue hardship where the debtor chose to work as a cellist in an orchestra for a low salary, but had the qualifications, ability, and free time to supplement her income, and in *In re Oyler*, 397 F.3d 282 (6th Cir. 2005) the court found no undue hardship where the debtor chose to work for a low salary as the pastor of a small church, but was qualified for a higher-paying job. By contrast, in *Educational Credit Management Corp. v. Polleys*, 356 F.3d 1302 (10th Cir. 2004) the court found undue hardship where the debtor had debilitating emotional problems that prevented him from taking jobs commensurate with his qualifications. In *In re Reynolds*, 425 F.3d 526 (8th Cir. 2005) the court found undue hardship where the debtor, a qualified lawyer, worked in a secretarial job because she could not find employment as an attorney despite diligent efforts, had longstanding serious mental health problems that made it unlikely that she would improve her position, and her fragile mental equilibrium was threatened by the stress of trying to cope

---

356 F.3d 1302, 1310 (10th Cir. 2004) ("[I]n applying this prong, courts need not require a 'certainty of hopelessness.'").

37. See *Educational Credit Management Corp. v. Nys (In re Nys)*, 446 F.3d 938 (9th Cir. 2006).

38. The Income Contingent Repayment Plan (ICRP) — established by the Department of Education — is the most common example.

39. *Tirch v. Pennsylvania Higher Educ. Assistance Agency (In re Tirch)*, 409 F.3d 677, 682 (6th Cir. 2005) (the debtor's decision not to take advantage of the IRCP was probative evidence of her lack of good faith intent to repay her loans); but see *Krieger v. Educational Credit Management Corp.*, 713 F.3d 882 (7th Cir. 2013) (finding that the debtor had demonstrated good faith because, although she had not enrolled in the ICRP, she had made some payments on her loans and tried aggressively to find work).

with the loan payments. In *Krieger v. Educational Credit Management Corp.*, 713 F.3d 882 (7th Cir. 2013) the court found undue hardship where the debtor, a 53-year-old paralegal, lived with her mother in a rural area, had not been successful in job searches over a 10-year period, and had little prospect of improving her situation.

Some courts find the *Brunner* three-pronged test too restrictive, and prefer a broader evaluation under the totality of the circumstances.[40] This test considers "(1) the debtor's past, present, and reasonably reliable future financial resources; (2) a calculation of the debtor's and her dependent's reasonable necessary living expenses; and (3) any other relevant facts and circumstances surrounding each particular bankruptcy case."[41] Although this test is more wide ranging and not as predictable, it has the advantage of identifying circumstances that may not be taken into account in the narrower test. (*See* Example 6.)

Where hardship may not warrant discharge of the entire debt, the court has the power, under its general discretion granted by §105, to discharge part of the debt to the extent necessary to relieve the hardship.[42] Even a partial discharge must satisfy the undue hardship test under §523(a)(8).[43]

(9) Liability for driving under the influence of drugs or alcohol (§523(a)(9)). (A dischargeability determination is not required.) If the debtor incurred liability for death or personal injury, caused by the unlawful operation of a vehicle while under the influence of drugs, alcohol, or another substance, such liability is nondischargeable. This subsection formerly applied only to judgments and consent decrees relating to such liability, but it was amended in 1990 to make it clear that the liability is nondischargeable even if no judgment had been obtained by the time of the petition.

(10) Debts from a prior case in which a discharge was waived or denied (§523(a)(10)). (A dischargeability determination is not required.) Section 523(a)(10) deals with the situation of a debtor who has been bankrupt before and waived the discharge in the prior case or was denied it under any of the grounds in §727(a)(2) through (7). Such a waiver or denial makes all debts in that case permanently nondischargeable. Therefore,

---

40. See *Long v. Educational Credit Management Corp. (In re Long)*, 322 F.3d 549 (8th Cir. 2003); see also *In re Roth*, 490 B.R. 908 (B.A.P. 9th Cir. 2013) (labeling the *Brunner* test labeled *Brunner* a "relic of times long gone").

41. *In re Long*, 322 F.3d at 544-55; see also *In re Dufresne*, 341 B.R. 391 (Bankr. D. Mass. 2006) (there was hardship where the debtor, after amassing large debt for college and law school tuition, could not pass the bar after multiple attempts and was in a precarious financial situation).

42. See *In re Saxman*, 325 F.3d 1168 (9th Cir. 2003).

43. *In re Miller*, 377 F.3d 616 (6th Cir. 2004); *In re Tirch*, 409 F.3d 677 (6th Cir 2005).

if the debtor subsequently seeks bankruptcy relief again, the discharge in the later case does not cover any balance still owing on undischarged debts from the earlier case. Note that §523(a)(10) refers only to §727(a)(2) to (7). The section does not prevent the discharge in a current bankruptcy of debts that survived an earlier case because a discharge was denied under the eight-year rule of §727(a)(8) or the six-year rule of §727(a)(9). Therefore, in the debtor's third or later bankruptcy, debts from the preceding bankruptcy may be discharged if a discharge had been denied in that case solely on the grounds of §727(a)(8) or (9). These surviving debts are treated differently because the denial of the earlier discharge was based on an objective time period, rather than on the debtor's dishonest or obstructive behavior, or on the debtor's consensual waiver of the right to discharge.

Section 523(a)(10) only applies where the earlier discharge was denied in its entirety under §727. It is not applicable to debts that survived an earlier discharge under §523. The treatment of such debts is discussed in section 21.5.5.

(11) Payments under an order of restitution in federal cases (§523(a)(13)). (A dischargeability determination is not required.) The discussion of §523(a)(7), above, noted that *Kelley v. Robinson* found a criminal restitution order to be excluded from the discharge by §523(a)(7) because it could properly be characterized as a penalty, notwithstanding its compensatory aspect. The debt giving rise to the restitution order might also qualify for exclusion under §523(a)(6) as arising from willful and malicious injury. *Kelley* did not entirely clear up the confusion in the treatment of criminal restitution obligations, so Congress added §523(a)(13) in the 1994 Bankruptcy Reform Act in an attempt to clarify that criminal restitution obligations are not dischargeable. However, §523(a)(13) has not been entirely successful in settling this issue because it only covers restitution orders in federal cases. A debt arising from a restitution order under state law is therefore not covered by §523(a)(13) and is dischargeable unless it can be made to fit within the exclusions of §523(a)(6) or (7). In *In re Verola*, 446 F.3d 1206 (11th Cir. 2006), the court did exclude a state court restitution order under §523(a)(7) on the basis there was no indication that Congress did not intend state court orders to be covered under §523(a)(7), although §523(a)(13) does not include them.

(12) Matrimonial debts that do not qualify as domestic support obligations (§523(a)(15)). (A dischargeability determination is not required.) The Bankruptcy Reform Act of 1994 added §523(a)(15) to give some protection to matrimonial debts (such as debts arising out of a property settlement on divorce or separation) that do not qualify for exclusion from the discharge as domestic support obligations under §523(a)(5). To be nondischargeable under §523(a)(15), the debt must have been incurred in the course of a divorce or separation or in connection with a separation agreement, divorce decree, or other order of a court or government agency. Prior to the enactment of BAPCPA in 2005, §523(a)(15) did not exclude debts of this kind from the discharge in all cases. Instead, it imposed a balancing test to be used by the court in deciding if the debt should be excluded from the discharge. The court was required to conduct an inquiry into the debtor's ability to pay the debt and to balance the relative hardship and need of the debtor (and his dependents) and the creditor spouse. BAPCPA removed this limitation, making the debt absolutely nondischargeable as a matter of course. Because the evaluation of hardship and need has been eliminated, §523(a)(15) has been removed from the list of sections for which a dischargeability hearing is required under §523(c).

§21.5.5 The Discharge of Nondischargeable Debts in a Subsequent Case

As discussed above, if the debtor was denied a discharge entirely under §727(a)(2) through (7) in a prior bankruptcy, or waived the discharge, the surviving debts are excluded from the discharge in the later bankruptcy by §523(a)(10). Surviving debts that were excluded from a prior discharge under §523 are not covered by §523(a)(10), but are dealt with in §523(b). Provided that the grounds for exclusion no longer apply, §523(b) allows the discharge in a later bankruptcy of three types of debt that were excluded from the discharge in an earlier case: nondischargeable tax debts under §523(a)(1), unscheduled debts under §523(a)(3), and education loans under §528(a)(8). Because these are the only debts included in §523(b), all other debts that were not discharged in the prior case are excluded from the discharge in the later case as well. The basis for the exclusion from the subsequent discharge is that the exclusion in the prior case is res judicata. Once the debt is held nondischargeable, it is always nondischargeable.[44]

§21.6 THE CH. 11 DISCHARGE

Unlike Ch. 7, the Ch. 11 discharge is available to both individuals and corporate entities. If the debtor is not an individual, §1141(d) brings the discharge into effect upon confirmation of the plan. This used to be true of an individual debtor as well, but BAPCPA added §1141(d)(5). That subsection postpones an individual Ch. 11 debtor's discharge until the

---

44. See *In re Paine*, 283 B.R. 33 (B.A.P. 9th Cir. 2002).

completion of all payments under the plan unless the court orders otherwise for cause after notice and a hearing. Section 1141(d)(5) brings the Ch. 11 discharge of an individual more closely in line with the Ch. 13 discharge, which is granted only after consummation of the plan. However, §1141(d)(5)'s language differs from that of §1328(a) in two respects. First, §1141(d)(5) lacks §1328(a)'s mandatory language. While §1328(a) says that the court "shall" grant a Ch. 13 discharge on completion of plan payments, §1141(d)(5) says no debts are discharged in an individual Ch. 11 case "until the court grants a discharge" on completion of plan payments. The significance of this difference in language is unclear. It could simply reflect the fact that Ch. 11 gives the debtor and creditors more flexibility to agree on the scope and terms of the discharge and to record this in the plan. Second, §1141(d)(5) contemplates the possibility of an earlier discharge for cause. The section gives no indication of what constitutes cause. *In re Sheridan*, 391 B.R. 287 (Bankr. E.D.N.C. 2008), provides an example of what a court might accept as cause. In that case, the court found cause because the debtor had fully complied with the plan-confirmation requirements. Further, he had given notice in the disclosure statement of his intent to apply for a discharge on plan confirmation, and there was a strong likelihood that the plan would be successfully consummated.

The Ch. 11 discharge covers all debts that arose before the date of confirmation, including debts deemed under §502(g), (h), and (i) to have arisen prepetition. The discharge of a debt is not dependent on the proof or allowance of the claim or on the holder's acceptance of the plan. The plan itself may contain provisions that expand or reduce the extent of the discharge.

Ch. 11 does not have a §727 equivalent. However, §727 applies in a Ch. 11 case where the debtor is being liquidated under the plan. Section 1141(d)(3) states that confirmation of the plan does not discharge the debtor if the plan provides for the liquidation of all or substantially all of the debtor's estate, the debtor does not engage in business after consummation of the plan, and the debtor would have been denied a discharge under §727(a) if the case had been filed under Ch. 7. The simple point of this provision is that if the debtor is to be liquidated under Ch. 11 and will not remain in business, there is no reason to treat the Ch. 11 discharge differently from that under Ch. 7. Therefore, if the debtor is a corporation, the discharge is precluded by §727(a)(1). If the debtor is an individual, any grounds for the denial of a discharge under any other provision of §727 apply in the Ch. 11 case.

If the debtor is an individual, §1141(d)(2) excludes from the discharge all debts that are nondischargeable under §523, so that the exceptions to the individual debtor's discharge are the same in Chs. 7 and 11—with one qualification: Under §1141(d) the plan may provide for the discharge of a debt that would otherwise be excluded from the discharge under §523. Of course, a provision of this kind is only feasible where the debtor has enough negotiating leverage to include it in the confirmed plan and the plan satisfies the confirmation standards discussed in Chapter 20. When the Ch. 11 debtor is not an individual, the exclusions from discharge in §523 are not applicable.

Section 1144 permits the court to revoke an order of confirmation, including the grant of the discharge, if the confirmation order was obtained by fraud. Revocation must be requested by a party in interest within 180 days from the entry of the order and can be granted only after notice and a hearing.

§21.7 THE CH. 13 DISCHARGE

§21.7.1 Procedure and Scope

Section 1328(a) requires the court to grant the discharge only after the debtor has completed payments under the plan. However, an earlier discharge can be granted on the grounds of hardship, as discussed in section 21.7.6. The Ch. 13 discharge includes all debts provided for by the plan or disallowed under §502. "Provided for" means not that payment must be provided for in the plan, but merely that the debt is dealt with, even if no payment will be made.

§21.7.2 Preconditions to the Grant of the Ch. 13 Discharge

BAPCPA added three provisions to §1328 that impose additional conditions on the grant of a Ch. 13 discharge. First, under §1328(a), to receive the discharge the debtor must certify that he has paid all domestic support obligations that are due at the time of the discharge. The certification must cover all domestic support obligations required to be paid by court or administrative order or by statute as of the date of the certification, including not only current postpetition obligations, but also prepetition obligations to the extent that they are provided for by the plan.

Second, under §1328(g), the debtor is not entitled to the Ch. 13 discharge until he has completed the instructional course on personal financial management required by §111 and approved by the U.S. Trustee. This provision is identical to §727(a)(11), explained in section 21.5.2.

Third, §1328(h) forbids the granting of a Ch. 13 discharge until the court finds, after notice and the opportunity for a hearing, that there is no reasonable cause to believe that §552(q)(1) is applicable, or that there is any proceeding pending in which the debtor may be found guilty of a felony of the kind described in §522(q)(1)(A) or liable for a debt of the kind described in §522(q)(1)(B). This provision is the same as §727(a)(12), discussed in section 21.5.2.[45]

§21.7.3 Exclusions from the Ch. 13 Discharge

When Congress enacted the Code in 1978, it created a number of incentives designed to encourage debtors to choose Ch. 13 over Ch. 7. One of the incentives conceived of in 1978 was to give the Ch. 13 debtor a broader discharge than under Ch. 7 by limiting the applicability of the exclusions from discharge under §523(a) in a Ch. 13 case. Section 1328(a)(2) provides that only the selected exclusions from the discharge specified in the section are applicable in a Ch. 13 case. Over the years since 1978, Congress has gradually whittled away at the broader Ch. 13 discharge and has periodically increased the number of §523 exclusions that apply in a Ch. 13 case. Congress came to realize that it was not good policy to continue some of the original §523 exclusions from Ch. 13, because they related to debts for wrongful conduct, from which the debtor should not be released under any chapter. Therefore, amendments to §1328(a)(2) since 1978 have excluded from the Ch. 13 discharge almost all of categories of §523 exclusions that relate to debts incurred under wrongful circumstances. Only a small vestigial exclusion remains for debts arising out of willful and malicious injury, as explained later in this section. As a result, the Ch. 13 discharge has become less generous than it used to be, reducing the dischargeability incentive of Ch. 13. Another reason why the dischargeability incentive is not appealing to many debtors is that some of the debts that are discharged in Ch. 13, but not in Chs. 7 and 11 are fairly unusual and are not likely to be owed by most debtors. As a result, the discharge advantage of Ch. 13 now seems so marginal that it is likely irrelevant to most debtors.

The narrowing of the Ch. 13 discharge seems to accord with the general approach of BAPCPA, which tends to favor pressing debtors into Ch. 13 rather than merely encouraging them to use it. This is particularly evident in §707(b)'s means test. Of course, it is important to remember that the means test does not apply to all individual debtors who are eligible for Ch. 13.

---

45. There is one subtle difference in the wording of these two sections. Section 727(a)(12) states that the court "shall grant the debtor a discharge unless" the court has found reasonable cause to believe that proceedings under §522(q) are applicable and pending. Section §1328(h) says that the court "may not grant a discharge . . . unless" the court has found no reasonable cause to believe that proceedings under §522(q) are applicable and pending. Presumably, the difference in wording is nothing more than an attempt to accommodate the provision to the existing grammatical structure of the sections.

Section 707(b) provides grounds for dismissing a Ch. 7 case only where the debtor owes primarily consumer debts and the court finds grounds for abuse, either because the debtor's level of disposable income is high enough to give rise to the presumption or because abuse is otherwise established. This means that some debtors still have the relatively unrestricted choice of filing under Ch. 7 or Ch. 13, and in some situations, a debtor may find an advantage in the Ch. 13 discharge.

As discussed in section 18.7, a Ch. 13 debtor must be in good faith both in filing the case and in proposing the plan. Courts have frequently had to consider whether a debtor violates this obligation of good faith by choosing Ch. 13 for the primary purpose of discharging a debt that would be excluded from the discharge under Chs. 7 and 11. Because Congress has provided for a broader discharge in Ch. 13, courts generally adopt the approach that it is not per se bad faith for a debtor to choose Ch. 13 to take advantage of it. However, the debtor may fail the good faith test where the dominant purpose of the Ch. 13 filing is to discharge an otherwise nondischargeable debt, the plan provides no substantial advantage to creditors, and there is no sincere effort to pay to the best of the debtor's ability. (*See* section 18.7 and Example 2 of Chapter 18.) This issue affects fewer cases since the passage of BAPCPA because, as explained above, the opportunity for using Ch. 13 to discharge debts that are otherwise nondischargeable has shrunk dramatically.

Section 1328(a)(2) specifies that the only §523 exclusions from discharge applicable in a Ch. 13 case are those in §523(a)(2), (3), (4), (5), (8), and (9). (Subsections (a)(2), (3), and (4) were added to the list by BAPCPA.) The listed subsections are explained in section 21.5.4. In summary, they cover debts for money, property, or credit obtained by fraud or false pretenses (§523(a)(2)); unscheduled debts (§523(a)(3)); debts for fiduciary fraud, embezzlement, or larceny (§523(a)(4)); domestic support obligations (§523(a)(5)); educational loans (§523(a)(8)); and debts for death or personal injury caused by the debtor while driving under the influence of drugs or alcohol (§523(a)(9)).

The exclusion of priority taxes in §523(a)(1) is not mentioned in §1328(a)(2), but because priority tax claims must be paid in full under the plan unless the holder agrees to different treatment, the discharge of any unpaid balance of the claim does not arise at all or else relates only to the present value enhancement of the claim. (*See* sections 17.5.4 and 18.8.2.)

Neither §523(a)(7) (the exclusion of a noncompensatory fine, penalty, or forfeiture to a governmental unit) nor §523(a)(6) (the exclusion for debts incurred for willful and malicious injury) is listed in §1328(a)(2), so they do not apply in a Ch. 13 case. However, some debts of this kind may qualify for exclusion in a Ch. 13 case under §1328(a)(3) or §1328(a)(4). The exclusions in these sections are narrower than the more general exclusions in §523(a)(6) and (7). Therefore, while the exclusions for the type of wrongful conduct covered by §523(a)(6) and (7) are not fully applicable in a Ch. 13 case, §1328(a)(3) and §1328(a)(4) bring the extent of the Ch. 13 discharge for this kind of wrongful conduct closer to that in a Ch. 7 case.

Section 1328(a)(3) applies to exclude a fine or restitutionary obligation if the willful and malicious act was a crime and the debtor was prosecuted and convicted of it, and was fined or ordered to pay restitution as part of his sentence.[46] This section is confined to restitution or a criminal fine that is part of the debtor's sentence in a criminal case. It would not be applicable if the creditor had obtained a civil judgment of restitution, or the debtor made a voluntary commitment to repay.

Section 1328(a)(4), added by BAPCPA, fills part of the gap left by §1328(a)(3). It excludes from the Ch. 13 discharge a debt for restitution or damages awarded against the debtor in a civil action for personal injury or death caused by the debtor's willful and malicious conduct. In *In re Grossman*, 538 B.R. 34 (Bankr. E.D. Ca. 2015), the creditor and the debtor lived together for two years. During that time, the creditor allowed the debtor to make a video of the parties engaging in sexual acts. The debtor had promised that he would keep the video private, but broke that promise after the relationship ended by posting the video on a pornography site. The creditor sued the debtor in state court for invasion of privacy and intentional infliction of emotional distress. The debtor countered by filing a Ch. 13 petition. After the bankruptcy court granted relief from stay, the state court action proceeded and was settled for $25,000. The settlement was made an order of the state court. In a motion to dismiss the claim of nondischargeability, the bankruptcy court held that the creditor had asserted a valid claim that the debt was nondischargeable under §1328(a)(4). The injury was both willful and malicious, and intentional infliction of emotional distress qualifies as personal injury. The court said that had Congress intended to restrict the provision to bodily injury, it would have used the words "bodily" or "physical" to qualify "injury."

Section 1328 contains two exclusions from the Ch. 13 discharge that relate to particular features of the Ch. 13 process. Section 1328(a)(1) excludes from the discharge any debt provided for by §1322(b)(5). These are long-term debts to be paid beyond the period of the plan (*see* section 18.10). Because the plan contemplates that they will continue to be paid after the consummation of the plan, they necessarily remain enforceable after the discharge. Section 1328(d) excludes from the discharge any

46. Section 1328(a)(3) was added to the Code in response to *Pennsylvania Department of Public Welfare v. Davenport*, 495 U.S. 552 (1990), in which the Supreme Court rejected the argument that a criminal restitution order does not qualify as a claim. Because the court characterized the restitution obligation as a claim, there was no barrier to discharging it in a Ch. 13 case under the provisions existing at the time. Congress therefore added §1328(a)(3) to exclude from the Ch. 13 discharge any debt for restitution included in a sentence on the debtor's conviction of a crime.

debts based on an allowed claim filed under §1305(a)(2) if the trustee's prior approval of the debt was practicable but not obtained. As explained in section 17.2.3, §1305(a)(2) allows a creditor to prove a claim for a post-petition consumer debt incurred by the debtor for household or personal necessities, so that the debt can be handled in the estate. If the debtor obtained the trustee's prior approval or if the prior approval was not practicable, any balance on the debt unpaid in the Ch. 13 distribution is discharged. However, if the trustee's approval could have been obtained and the debtor failed to get it, the debt is excluded from the discharge. (If the creditor knew that trustee approval was practicable but not obtained, the claim is disallowed under §1305(c), so its dischargeability would not be an issue.)

§21.7.4 Discharge in Successive Cases

The grounds for denial of a discharge in §727 are not applicable in a Ch. 13 case, so dishonest, manipulative, or uncooperative debtor conduct is policed under the good faith standard. Sections 727(a)(8) and (9), which bar a discharge in successive bankruptcy filings, are also not applicable in Ch. 13. Before BAPCPA there was no prohibition of a discharge in a subsequent Ch. 13 case filed within a relatively short time of a prior bankruptcy. However, BAPCPA changed that by enacting §1328(f), which precludes the grant of a Ch. 13 discharge if the debtor received a discharge in a prior Ch. 7 or Ch. 12 case filed in the four-year period before the petition or in a prior Ch. 13 case filed within the two-year period before the petition.

Note that §1328(f) bars only successive discharges. It does not preclude the debtor from filing a Ch. 13 petition after getting a discharge in Ch. 7 (a so-called "Chapter 20") for the purpose of preventing foreclosure on collateral and forcing a secured creditor into accepting payment by installments. (This strategy is explained in section 18.12.) In *Johnson v. Home State Bank*, 501 U.S. 78 (1991), the U.S. Supreme Court held that there was no statutory bar to "Chapter 20." Therefore, provided that the debtor complied with the general requirement of good faith, he could first file under Ch. 7 to discharge personal liability on debt and then file under Ch. 13 to prevent foreclosure of a mortgage and to force the mortgagee to accept payments in installments. Section 1328(f), enacted after *Johnson* was decided, now precludes a Ch. 13 discharge in a "Chapter 20" situation. However, this limits only successive discharges, not successive filings. Therefore the central holding in *Johnson* has not been overturned. Subject to the requirement of good faith, the debtor may file a Ch. 13 case immediately after having received a Ch. 7 discharge if the purpose is not to obtain a Ch. 13 discharge but to take advantage of the ability to prevent foreclosure and continue paying the secured debt by installments.

§21.7.5 Waiver or Revocation of the Ch. 13 Discharge

Section 1328(a) recognizes a written waiver of discharge, executed by the debtor after the order for relief and approved by the court.

Section 1328(e) permits the court to revoke the discharge on grounds of the debtor's fraud if the applicant for revocation did not know of the fraud until after the discharge was granted. The application for revocation must be made within a year of the discharge and can only be granted after notice and a hearing.

§21.7.6 The Hardship Discharge

As stated in section 21.7.1, the debtor must normally complete payments under the plan to receive the discharge. However, §1328(b) gives the court the discretion, after notice and a hearing, to grant a hardship discharge to a debtor who has not been able to complete payments under the plan. A hardship discharge may only be granted to the debtor if three conditions are satisfied: The failure to complete payments must result from factors beyond the debtor's control; the distribution actually made to unsecured claims must satisfy the best interests test (i.e., the payments actually made to unsecured creditors under the plan up to the time of discharge must be at least equal to the present value of what unsecured creditors would have received in a Ch. 7 liquidation); and modification of the plan must be impracticable. Because the hardship discharge is given to a debtor who has not consummated the plan, it is not as generous as the normal Ch. 13 discharge and is fully subject to the exclusions in §523(a). In sum, under §1328(c) and (d), the hardship discharge does not extend to secured debts, debts excluded from the plan under §1322(b)(5), postpetition debts for consumer necessities incurred without trustee approval, and all debts excluded from the discharge by §523(a).

Examples

1. Hippocrates Oaf is a successful physician whose hobby was real estate speculation. He embarked upon a large suburban development project, using all his savings as well as borrowed funds. The venture failed, rendering Dr. Oaf insolvent and forcing him into default on his loan. Dr. Oaf plans to seek Ch. 7 relief. Dr. Oaf's state of domicile has enacted legislation under §522(b), making nonbankruptcy exemptions applicable in bankruptcy cases. Under the state's exemption law, most exemptions are subject to low dollar limits. However, because the state has a strong policy of encouraging its citizens to compose and perform fine music,

the state legislature has granted an unlimited exemption in musical instruments.

Dr. Oaf is tone-deaf and has never owned a musical instrument. In the few weeks before filing his Ch. 7 petition Dr. Oaf sold a number of valuable nonexempt assets, realizing $450,000, which is the market value of the assets sold. He used the $450,000 to buy an antique grand piano. He then filed his Ch. 7 petition. Would or should Dr. Oaf's pre-petition conduct have any impact on his discharge?

2. While employed as a personnel manager, Penny Tentiary padded the company's payroll by adding fictitious names to it. When checks were issued to these nonexistent employees, Penny cashed them and kept the money. She did this for a few months, until her employer discovered her subterfuge, dismissed her, and filed criminal charges. Penny was convicted and was sentenced to a term of imprisonment, suspended on condition that she pay back the stolen funds by specified monthly installments over three years. Under the state's probation statute, Penny was required to make payments to the probation department, which would transmit the funds to the victim of the crime. Penny paid the installments for about six months, and then filed a petition under Ch. 7. She listed the restitution obligation as an unsecured debt. Is the restitution obligation excluded from the Ch. 7 discharge? Would it be excluded from the discharge if she had filed under Ch. 13 instead of Ch. 7?

3. Will Fully owned and operated a retail store as a sole proprietor. He recently filed a Ch. 7 petition. In the months prior to his bankruptcy, Will fell behind in payments due to his suppliers and could no longer buy inventory on credit. To raise cash to buy new inventory, Will sold all his office equipment and furnishings. This property was subject to a valid and perfected security interest in favor of a bank that had financed its purchase. Will realized that the sale was a violation of an express term of the security agreement.

   Will sold the new inventory in the course of business and used its proceeds to pay expenses. This enabled him to operate for a while longer, but his business eventually failed and he filed his Ch. 7 petition. It was only after the filing that the bank discovered that its collateral had been sold and the proceeds dissipated, leaving the bank with an unsecured claim against the estate. (The buyer of the collateral cannot be found, so the bank cannot recover it from him.)

   The bank has applied for a determination of nondischargeability under §523(c).

   a. Should the debt be excluded from Will's discharge?
   b. Would the answer be different if Will had filed under Ch. 13?

4. Comic Kazi has a wonderful sense of humor. He is employed by an auto parts and tire store. One day, as a prank, he threw a lighted firework into the store's basement for the purpose of scaring a fellow employee. Because there were gas fumes in the basement, the firework set off an explosion that injured the coworker. The coworker sued Comic for damages and obtained a judgment for actual damages of $1,000,000 and punitive damages of $500,000.

   Comic filed a petition under Ch. 7. Is the tort judgment dischargeable?

5. Falsus N. Omnibus applied for a credit card from Reliance Bank. He completed a short and simple application form that asked for no information about the applicant's financial affairs. A few weeks later, the card arrived in the mail. Reliance had not checked Falsus's credit. Had it done so, it would have found that he was heavily in debt and had a poor credit record. Upon receiving the card, Falsus immediately went to the mall and bought a variety of consumer electronics to the full credit limit on the card. Falsus never made any payments to Reliance, which eventually sued him to recover the debt and obtained default judgment against him. Before Reliance could execute on its judgment, Falsus filed a Ch. 7 petition. Six months had elapsed between the purchases and the bankruptcy filing.

   Reliance filed an application for a nondischargeability determination on the grounds that Falsus had made a false representation under §523(a)(2)(A). Reliance conceded that Falsus had made no express misrepresentations, but argued that his application and subsequent use of the card constituted an implied representation that he was financially responsible and would pay for purchases charged to the account. Should the debt be excluded from the discharge?

6. Hardy Schipp graduated near the top of his law school class and immediately went to work for a large law firm. Although he earned an excellent salary, he hated the work and found it very unsatisfying. One day he realized that he would never find fulfillment representing rich clients in large commercial transactions. Hardy therefore resigned from the law firm and went to work for a nonprofit public interest firm that provided legal assistance to indigent people. Hardy's earnings dropped to 20 percent of what he had earned at the large law firm, but he did not mind because he was not materialistic and did not need much to live on. The problem was his huge debt for student loans from college and law school. He struggled for about a year to maintain payments on the loans, but it was impossible to survive on what he had left over each month after making those payments. Can Hardy get rid of the loans if he files for bankruptcy?

Explanations

1. Apart from §522(o), which is applicable only to the homestead exemption and therefore not pertinent here,[47] the Code does not forbid debtors from ordering their affairs to take advantage of exemptions in anticipation of filing a petition. In fact, the legislative history of §522 indicates that Congress expected debtors to engage in reasonable prepetition planning to maximize exemptions. (This issue is also discussed in section 10.6 and Example 5 of Chapter 10.) However, if a debtor's prepetition planning is abusive or in bad faith, the court has the power to sanction that conduct either by dismissing the case or by denying the debtor a discharge. Because this is a Ch. 7 case, the basis for denying the discharge must be found in §727(a). (Section 523(a) is not applicable because that section applies only where there are grounds for excluding a particular debt from the discharge because of the nature of the debt or the circumstances of its creation.)

   Where the debtor has improperly converted nonexempt property into exempt property in anticipation of bankruptcy, the only provision of §727(a) that might be applicable to deny the debtor a discharge is §727(a)(2)—that the debtor transferred property within a year before the petition with the intent to hinder, delay, or defraud creditors. Dr. Oaf's sale of nonexempt assets clearly was a transfer of property within a year of the petition. The issue is whether the disposition had those additional elements of dishonesty that make it fraudulent. This "extrinsic fraud," as it is sometimes called, can take many forms. For example, the debtor may have used new credit to acquire the exempt property, or may have taken steps to conceal the conversion from creditors, or may have sold nonexempt property at sacrifice prices to get rid of it quickly and complete the conversion before creditors could find out about it.[48] Although extrinsic fraud is usually required for denial of the discharge under §727(a)(2), there is also some case authority that dispenses with the need to establish extrinsic fraud where the conversion is on a great enough scale. For example, in *Norwest Bank Nebraska v. Tveten*, 848 F.2d 871 (8th Cir. 1988), the court denied a discharge to the debtor, who converted $700,000 worth of nonexempt property into fully exempt insurance and annuity policies. Although there was no evidence of extrinsic fraud, the court considered that the excessive size of the

47. As discussed in section 10.7, BAPCPA enacted §522(o), which creates some controls on the conversion of nonexempt assets into a homestead where the state has opted out of federal exemptions and has an unlimited or very generous homestead exemption. However, these controls apply only to the homestead exemption. They are not relevant to the conversion of nonexempt property into some type of exempt property other than a homestead.

48. *See, e.g.*, *In re Armstrong*, 931 F.2d 1233 (8th Cir. 1991); *In re Smiley*, 864 F.2d 562 (7th Cir. 1989); and *In re Reed*, 700 F.2d 986 (5th Cir. 1983).

conversion so perverted the Code's fresh start policy that it could not be tolerated.

There is no indication of extrinsic fraud in Dr. Oaf's case, so his prepetition planning is likely effective and will not cause him to be denied a discharge. However, this conclusion is subject to the possibility that the wholesale conversion may go beyond the acceptable to constitute an abuse of the Code, subjecting the debtor to §727(a)(2). Advising a prospective debtor on this kind of prepetition activity requires careful judgment by the debtor's attorney, who must inform the client of his legal rights so that he can make legitimate planning choices, but must not participate in or encourage fraudulent manipulations.

2. *Kelley v. Robinson* (discussed in section 21.5.4) dealt with issues similar to those presented by these facts and held that a restitution obligation, imposed as a condition of probation in a criminal sentence, is a non-compensatory penalty, excluded from the discharge by §523(a)(7). Penny's restitution obligation arises from the embezzlement of funds, so it could also be excluded under §523(a)(2) or (4). However, from the creditor's perspective, §523(a)(7) is a more advantageous basis for excluding the debt from the discharge because a §523(c) determination of dischargeability is required for §523(a)(2) and (4), but is not required for §523(a)(7).

   Had Penny filed under Ch. 13, the creditor would not have been able to exclude the debt from the discharge under §523(a)(7) because it is not one of the provisions of §523 listed in §1328(a)(2). However, §1328(a)(3) provides a partial substitute for §527(a)(7) in a Ch. 13 case, in that it excludes the debt from the Ch. 13 discharge if it is for restitution or a criminal fine included in a sentence on the debtor's conviction of a crime. Although §1328(a)(3) is narrower than §523(a)(7), it does cover Penny's debt and excludes it from the discharge. As an alternative, the creditor could seek the debt's exclusion from the discharge under §523(a)(2) or (4), which were added to the list in §1328(a)(2) by BAPCPA and are therefore available as a basis for excluding a debt from the Ch. 13 discharge, as they are in a Ch. 7 case.

3. a. *Exclusion from the Ch. 7 discharge.* Although the willful and malicious injury that excludes a debt from the discharge under §523(a)(6) is often associated with intentional tortious conduct that causes physical injury to property or person, the section's range is broader than that, and can encompass commercial injury. Will's wrongful disposal of collateral is both a breach of contract and a conversion of the secured party's property interest in the collateral. If the disposal is both willful and malicious, it could constitute an injury to the creditor's property as contemplated by §523(a)(6).

Will's sale of the collateral was a deliberate act. There has clearly been a willful injury to the property interest of the bank. The circumstances strongly indicate that malice was present as well. Will knew that the sale was a breach of the security agreement, and he intended to spend the proceeds, rather than to remit them to the bank. Given his financial circumstances, he must have realized, as a person with some business experience, that he was depriving the bank of its protection against nonpayment at a time when default was a definite possibility. Malice does not require a motive or desire to inflict harm, but is present where the debtor deliberately persists in the injurious conduct, knowing that the consequences are substantially certain to follow. Therefore, even though the bank has lost its security, it may obtain some consolation by having its unsecured debt excepted from the discharge.

Apart from the possibility of excluding the debt from the discharge under §523, Will's conduct could be bad enough to disqualify him from the Ch. 7 discharge in its entirety under §727. The sale of the collateral may constitute the transfer of property with the intent to hinder, delay, or defraud a creditor as contemplated by §727(a)(2), and his inability to identify the buyer of the collateral could be attributable to a failure to keep and preserve proper records under §727(a)(3).

b. *Exclusion from the discharge if Will had filed under Ch. 13*. Section 523(a)(6) is not one of the exclusions incorporated into Ch. 13 by §1328(a). Will's debt is therefore dischargeable in Ch. 13 even though he was guilty of willful and malicious injury to the bank's property interest. BAPCPA enacted §1328(a)(4), which deals with debts resulting from willful and malicious injury in a Ch. 13 case but provides for a much narrower exclusion from the discharge than §523(a)(6). Under §1328(a)(4) a debt for willful and malicious injury is nondischargeable in a Ch. 13 case only where the willful and malicious conduct resulted in death or personal injury and a court has awarded restitution or damages in a civil action against the debtor. Section 1328(a)(4) is therefore inapplicable on these facts.

4. Unlike Example 3, in which the harm arose out of a commercial transaction, the injury here is caused by a physical tortious act that causes personal injury. Under *Kawaauhau* (discussed in section 21.5.4), both willfulness and malice must be proved, and recklessness is not enough. Comic's act was clearly willful—it was deliberate and intentional. Malice is more difficult to decide. For malice to be present, the creditor does not have to show that the debtor had the motive to injure. It is enough to show that the debtor acted deliberately, realizing that harm was substantially certain. Comic may not have intended to harm his coworker, and his behavior may have been idiotic rather than motivated by the desire to

cause injury. However, it is on the dividing line of a subtle distinction. This is shown by the disposition of *In re Hartley*, 869 F.2d 394, *reversed on rehearing*, 874 F.2d 1254 (8th Cir. 1989), on which this Example is based. The bankruptcy court and district court found that throwing a firework into a room containing gas fumes was so certain to cause injury that it was malicious. The majority of the court of appeals, with one judge dissenting, found that although the act was reckless, it did not amount to malice. However, in a subsequent en banc hearing, the court of appeals panel was reversed. The conduct was found to be malicious, and the district court judgment was affirmed.

In this case, the coworker's claim has already been adjudicated in state court. If the state court made a finding as to willfulness and malice (which the court likely has done, because it awarded punitive damages), the bankruptcy court may adopt that finding on the principle of collateral estoppel, so that the creditor does not have to prove these elements again in the dischargeability hearing.

The coworker was awarded both compensatory and punitive damages. If the injury is found to have been inflicted willfully and maliciously, the exclusion from discharge should include not only the compensatory damages, but the punitive damages as well. *Cohen v. De La Cruz* (cited in section 21.5.4) found that the grammatical meaning of the language of §523(a)(2) covered punitive damages as well as the original debt. This same reasoning should apply to §523(a)(6) because the structure of its language is even more conducive to this interpretation than the language in §523(a)(2). It excludes from the discharge "any debt . . . for willful and malicious injury."

5. During difficult economic times, credit card issuers may become more cautious in issuing credit cards without checking the applicant's creditworthiness. However, under more exuberant economic conditions, issuers may tend to become less risk averse and less finicky about the fiscal means or responsibility of their customers. Reliance has been careless in vetting its applications, and Falsus has taken advantage of this by incurring debt on the card beyond his ability to pay. Falsus has not made any express fraudulent misrepresentation, so if Reliance seeks to exclude the debt from the discharge under §523(a)(2), it must make the argument indicated in the Example — that by using the card, Falsus made a false representation by conduct that he had the means and intent to pay the debt incurred. Most courts are willing to find an implied misrepresentation under these circumstances. However, Reliance must prove all the elements of fraud on the preponderance of the evidence. Reliance is not aided by the presumption of fraud in §523(a)(2)(C). Although the spending spree apparently involved consumer transactions, it occurred beyond the periods specified in that section.

For the implied representation of ability and intent to repay to qualify as fraudulent, it must have been false and made with intent to deceive. Fraudulent intent to breach a contract in the future is difficult to establish. It is not enough that the debtor knows he has financial trouble or that he does not have a clear idea of how he will pay the debt. He must have intended, when using the card, never to pay the debt. At least where the misrepresentation is implied, rather than express, the test is subjective—based on what the debtor intended—not objective and based on what he should have realized.[49] Fraudulent intent is judged on the totality of the circumstances, and takes into account such factors as the debtor's financial circumstances and prospects at the time that the debt was incurred, and the extent to which the debtor had the capacity to comprehend those circumstances; whether the debtor had been contemplating bankruptcy at that time; whether the charges were for luxuries or necessities; and whether the spending was unusual or frenetic. Falsus's poor credit record and his immediate purchase of nonnecessities to the full credit limit of his new card, at a time that he had no realistic prospects of paying the debt, suggest fraudulent intent.

Fraudulent intent is not the only element to be established for exclusion from the discharge under §523(a)(2). The creditor must also show that it was justified in relying on the misrepresentation. While some courts are intolerant of credit card issuers that do not conduct sufficient inquiry into the creditworthiness of prospective customers, other courts are somewhat more sympathetic and weigh the debtor's dishonesty against the creditor's lack of diligence. They hold that as long as the creditor has conducted a reasonable level of investigation and monitoring, it is entitled to assume, in the absence of suspicious indications to the contrary, that the debtor will use the card honestly.[50] However, because Reliance conducted no inquiry into Falsus's creditworthiness before issuing the card to him, even a more sympathetic court is unlikely to find that it had any justification for reliance on the representation.

6. Section 523(a)(8) excludes qualified educational loans from the discharge. This exclusion applies whether the debtor has filed under Ch. 7, Ch. 11 (*see* §1123(b)(2)), or Ch. 13 (*see* §1328(a)(2)). However, §523(a)(8) gives the court the power to discharge the debt if excepting it from the discharge would impose an undue hardship on the debtor or his dependents. The issue is therefore whether Hardy's circumstances constitute undue hardship. The three-part *Brunner* test, described in section 21.5.4, is the predominant test for determining undue hardship, but

---

49. See *In re Mercer*, 246 F.3d 391 (5th Cir. 2001) and *In re Moore*, 365 B.R. 589 (Bankr. D. Md. 2007).

50. *See, e.g., In re Mercer, supra.*

some courts use a wider-ranging totality of the circumstances test. Under the *Brunner* test, undue hardship is present where the debtor could not maintain a minimal standard of living if he is required to repay the loan, his financial circumstances are not likely to improve, and he has made a good faith effort to repay the loan.

Hardy's circumstances do not demonstrate undue hardship. He does not satisfy the first two prongs of the test because his lower level of earnings, while nobly motivated, is self-imposed, and could be substantially increased. He does not satisfy the third prong either. Although he has made some attempt at repaying the loan, he has apparently made no effort to negotiate an adjustment of payments and contemplates bankruptcy relatively soon after graduating from law school, with the primary purpose of discharging the loan debt. Congress has made it clear that it considers the protection of education loan programs to be of great importance, so a debtor cannot escape liability for repayment merely by electing to earn less than he is able to earn. It is hard to imagine that the totality of the circumstances test would reveal any additional factors that might change the conclusion reached under the *Brunner* test.

Glossary

Abandonment. In relation to estate property, abandonment is the trustee's relinquishment of estate property that is burdensome to the estate or of inconsequential value or benefit to the estate (§554). In relation to the debtor's homestead, abandonment is the debtor's permanent termination of residence in the property, so that it no longer qualifies for the exemption.

Absolute priority rule. In a Ch. 11 case, it is the principle that in a cramdown confirmation, no junior class of claims or interests may receive anything of value from the estate unless a more senior nonaccepting class of unsecured claims or interests is paid in full (§1129(b)(2)(B) and (C)).

Abstention. The court's dismissal or suspension of a bankruptcy case, or its refusal to entertain related proceedings, on grounds of fairness or in deference to another court (§305; 28 U.S.C. §1334(c)).

Acceleration. The termination of the debtor's right to pay a debt in installments or at a future maturity date, so that the debt becomes immediately payable. The payment of a debt may be accelerated under an acceleration clause in a contract upon the happening of a specified event, usually the debtor's default.

Acceptance of a Ch. 11 plan. The determination, by a majority vote of the members of a class of claims or interests, to acquiesce in a proposed Ch. 11 plan (§1126).

Account, or an account receivable. A right to payment for goods sold or services rendered (sometimes abbreviated to "receivable").

Adequate protection. If the estate retains property in which a person other than the debtor has an interest, that interest is entitled to adequate protection. That is, the value of the interest must be maintained during the period of retention, so that if the interest is ultimately foreclosed, the holder will receive no less than would have been received had the property been surrendered or liquidated immediately (§§361, 363, and 364).

Administrative expenses. Expenses incurred by the trustee or debtor in possession in the conduct of the estate's affairs or the preservation of its property. If allowed under §503, these expenses are paid as a second priority under §507.

Adversary proceedings. Litigation in the bankruptcy case that is required by Rule 7001 to take the form of a civil suit, initiated by complaint; a full civil lawsuit within the bankruptcy case. *Compare* Contested matter.

After-acquired collateral. Property acquired by the debtor that, by contract or operation of law, automatically becomes subject to a lien created in advance of the debtor's acquisition of the property. *See also* Floating lien.

Alias writ. A second writ of execution, issued after the first writ failed to generate sufficient proceeds to satisfy the judgment.

Allowed claim. A claim that is accepted as owing by the estate under §502 either because it is not objected to or because the court has upheld it following a hearing on the objection.

Antecedent debt. A debt due by the debtor that arose before the debtor made a transfer to the creditor in respect of the debt.

Antiassignment provision. A provision in a contract or in law that prohibits the transfer of rights or the delegation of duties by the original holder of those rights and duties. *See* Assignment.

Artisan's or Repairer's lien. A common law lien (now codified in many states) that may be asserted in personal property by a person who has repaired or improved it. The lien secures the agreed or reasonable cost of the work performed. In common law, it must be perfected by possession, but a statutory alternative of perfection by filing may be available.

Assignment for the benefit of creditors. An insolvency procedure under state law under which the debtor makes a voluntary transfer of property in trust to another person (the assignee), with instructions to liquidate the property and to distribute its proceeds to creditors who have elected to participate.

Assignment of contract. Strictly speaking, assignment is the transfer of rights under a contract. The transfer of contractual duties is called "delegation." However, "assignment" is often used to mean the transfer of both rights and duties by one of the parties to a contract. It is used in this sense in §365, which empowers the trustee to assume an executory contract of the debtor and then to realize its value by assigning (i.e., selling) the debtor's package of rights and obligations to a third party. *See* Assumption of contract.

Assumption of contract. The estate's adoption of an executory contract entered into by the debtor prior to bankruptcy, so that the estate is substituted for the debtor as party to the contract (§365). *Compare* Rejection of contract.

Attachment of a lien. Attachment is the creation of the lien, valid and enforceable as between the lienholder and the debtor. (Once the lien becomes effective against third parties as well, it is said to be "perfected.")

Attachment remedy and lien. The prejudgment remedy of attachment is the sheriff's seizure and retention of property of the defendant pending final resolution of the case. Upon attachment, the creditor obtains an attachment lien on the property that has been seized. This judicial lien secures the plaintiff's claim while the case is pending. If the plaintiff ultimately obtains judgment, the plaintiff has the right to sell the property in execution to satisfy the judgment.

Automatic perfection. The perfection of a lien immediately upon its attachment, without the need for any further action by the lienholder.

Automatic stay. The injunction that arises by operation of law, without the need for a court order, immediately upon the filing of a bankruptcy petition. The stay bars creditors from initiating or continuing with efforts to collect or enforce prepetition secured or unsecured debts, or to enforce prepetition claims against estate property or the debtor's property (§362).

Avoidance. Avoidance is the overturning of a debt or obligation. In bankruptcy, the trustee has the power under §§544 to 553 to avoid certain prepetition dispositions or obligations of the debtor, as well as certain unauthorized postpetition dispositions of estate property. The debtor has the right under §522(f) to avoid specified interests to the extent that they impair qualified exemptions in property.

Backdating. Upon timely completion of the prescribed act of perfection, some liens are given retrospective effect so that their priority will date from some specified earlier time.

Badges of fraud. Suspicious circumstances leading to the inference that a transfer made by the debtor was motivated by the actual intent to defraud creditors.

BAFJA. The Bankruptcy Amendments and Federal Judgeship Act of 1984, which made several significant amendments to the Code.

Balance sheet test. *See* Insolvency.

Bankruptcy Act. The predecessor to the present Code, which was enacted in 1898 and repealed in 1978.

Bankruptcy Appellate Panel (BAP). A court, consisting of three bankruptcy judges, established in some circuits to hear appeals from bankruptcy courts.

Bankruptcy Reform Act. The 1978 statute which, with amendments, forms the present Code. (The same name was given to the act that amended the Code in 1994.)

Bankruptcy test. *See* Insolvency.

BAPCPA. The Bankruptcy Abuse Prevention and Consumer Protection Act of 2005, which made many significant amendments to the Code.

Best interests test. One of the standards for plan confirmation, which requires that the total amount to be paid on a claim under the plan has a present value at least equal to what the claimant would have received had the estate been liquidated under Ch. 7. The requirement of present value is intended to compensate the claimant for having to await distribution over time instead of receiving immediate payment upon liquidation of the estate. The present value of the distribution is determined by adding interest at the market rate to the face value of the hypothetical Ch. 7 payment (§§1129(a)(7), 1125(a)(4), and 1325(a)(4)).

Bifurcation of claim. *See* Claim bifurcation.

Bona fide purchaser. (Latin: "Good faith") A person who, in a consensual transaction, acquires rights in property in good faith (i.e., with subjective honesty) for value and without actual or constructive notice that the purchase violates rights in the property held by a person other than the transferor. *Compare* Good faith purchaser.

Business judgment rule. A standard for court approval of a business decision (such as a trustee's decision to assume or reject an executory contract) under which the court declines to interfere with the decision if it was made (1) in good faith; (2) in the best interests of the company or the bankruptcy estate; (3) after a reasonable investigation; and (4) by an individual not interested in the subject at issue.

Cash collateral. Cash or cash equivalent that is subject to an interest (such as a security interest) held by a person other than the estate (§363(a)).

Chapter 20. An unofficial name for the debtor's tactic of filing sequentially under Chs. 7 and 13. A debtor may use this tactic to discharge personal liability on debts in the Ch. 7 case and thereafter prevent foreclosure of a lien on property (which is not discharged) by providing for payment of it with installments in the Ch. 13 plan.

Claim. Any secured or unsecured right to payment arising in law or equity (§101(5)).

Claim and delivery. *See* Replevin.

Claim bifurcation. The splitting of an undersecured debt into a secured claim to the extent of the collateral's value and an unsecured claim for the deficiency. This division is required by §506.

Class of claims or interests. Claims or interests that have been placed in the same category for treatment in bankruptcy, either because they fall within one of the statutory priority classifications or because the debtor has properly grouped them together in a plan under Ch. 11 or 13.

Codebtors. Persons who are liable on the same debt (also called "joint debtors," not to be confused with debtors in joint cases).

Cognovit note. (Latin: "Acknowledgment") *See* Confession to judgment.

Collateral. The property subject to a lien or security interest.

Collective proceedings. General name for proceedings such as assignments for the benefit of creditors, compositions, and bankruptcy, under which the claims of creditors are dealt with collectively to avoid the disruption and inequality of individual creditor action.

Common law lien. A lien arising by operation of common law, not dependent on agreement, statute, or judicial process. Common law liens are typically intended to provide security for the agreed or reasonable charges owing to a person who has repaired, improved, or preserved personal property or provided personal services at the owner's request. They must usually be perfected by possession.

Composition. A contract between a debtor and creditors, under which partial payment is promised and accepted in full settlement of claims. A composition may be combined with an extension — an agreement to extend the time in which to pay off the debt.

Confession to judgment. The debtor's waiver of the right to contest a collection suit, authorizing the creditor to obtain judgment by consent. A confession during the course of litigation (also called a "stipulation") is enforceable if freely made. However, a confession made before default, particularly one contained in the instrument of debt itself (called a "cognovit note" or "warrant of attorney") is subject to particular scrutiny and is usually unenforceable in a consumer transaction.

Confirmation of a plan. The confirmation of a plan under Ch. 11 or Ch. 13 is the court's determination that the plan meets the requirements of the Code, and that it will form the basis for the treatment of claims, disposition of estate property, and conduct of the estate's affairs.

Confirmation of a sale in execution. Where real property is sold in execution, state law usually requires that the court approves (confirms) the sale.

Consensual lien. A lien granted in a contract between the lienholder and the debtor, such as a mortgage or a UCC Article 9 security interest.

Consolidation of cases. *Procedural consolidation* is the consolidation of two separate petitions filed in relation to the same debtor. *Substantive consolidation* is the combination of the estates of two closely related debtors, so that assets are pooled and creditors of each become creditors of the combined estate. *Compare* Joint administration.

Construction lien. *See* Mechanic's lien.

Constructive fraud. Fraud established not by proof of actual dishonest intent but by facts that are, as a matter of legal policy, treated as giving rise to an irrebuttable presumption of fraud.

Constructive notice. *See* Notice.

Constructive trust. An equitable remedy under which a person who has acquired property by a wrongful act is deemed to hold the property in trust for the victim of the wrong.

Consumer debt. A debt incurred by an individual primarily for personal, family, or household purposes (§101(8)).

Contested matter. A proceeding within the bankruptcy case, initiated by motion or objection rather than by the filing of a complaint. *Compare* Adversary proceedings.

Contingent claim. A claim in which the debtor's potential liability has been created (usually by contract or wrongful act), but actual liability will only arise upon the happening of a future event that may not occur.

Conversion of case. A change in the Code chapter governing the case, altering the form of bankruptcy relief sought. For example, a case originally filed under Ch. 13 may be converted into a liquidation under Ch. 7 if the debtor's attempt at debt adjustment fails.

Conversion of nonexempt property. The realization of nonexempt property and the use of the proceeds to acquire exempt property. *See also* Prepetition planning.

Core proceeding. A proceeding in a bankruptcy case that involves the adjudication of rights created by the Code, or concerns issues that, by their nature, could only arise in a bankruptcy case. Because core proceedings involve substantive rights granted under the Code, they may be finally determined by the bankruptcy court itself. *Contrast to* Related proceedings.

Cramdown. The confirmation of a plan despite opposition from some creditors, where the plan satisfies the Code's prerequisites for non-consensual confirmation (§§1129(b) and 1325).

Credit bid. The secured creditor bids at the foreclosure auction of its collateral, and if it is successful in buying the property, it sets off the debt against the price that it bid at the auction.

Creditor's bill. An equitable suit available to a creditor for the purpose of locating and recovering executable property that has been concealed or wrongfully transferred by the debtor or for reaching assets that otherwise cannot be executed upon using procedures at law.

Creditors' committee. A committee of creditors appointed by the U.S. Trustee in Ch. 11 cases, and sometimes in Ch. 7 cases, to represent the interests of the creditor body as a whole or, if more than one committee is appropriate, a class of creditors.

Creditors' meeting. The statutory meeting of creditors required in all bankruptcy cases by §341. The meeting must be convened by the U.S. Trustee within a prescribed time following the order for relief. Its primary business is the examination of the debtor.

Cross-collateralization. In the context of postpetition financing, a term in the financing contract under which collateral furnished by the estate to secure the new credit also covers an unsecured or undersecured prepetition claim of the lender.

Cure of default. The payment of arrears or the rectification of any other breach of contractual obligations, so that the party's performance is brought into compliance with the terms of the contract.

Custodian. Any person appointed to take charge of the debtor's property under nonbankruptcy law, such as a receiver or an assignee for the benefit of creditors (§101(11)).

Debt. An obligation to pay money. In §101(12), "debt" is defined as liability on a "claim," which is defined in §101(5) as a right to payment.

Debt adjustment. A case under Ch. 13.

Debtor. In general, a person liable on a debt. In bankruptcy, the debtor is the person concerning whom the bankruptcy case was filed (§101(13)).

Debtor in possession. The new legal personality acquired by the debtor in a Ch. 11 case, under which the debtor administers the estate and fulfills the role of trustee for most purposes (§§1101(1) and 1107).

Debtor's equity. The debtor's unencumbered ownership interest in property.

Default. The debtor's material breach of contract, such as the failure to pay a debt on the due date. Some contracts provide that the insolvency or bankruptcy of the debtor constitutes ipso facto default. Such a provision is not enforceable in bankruptcy.

Default judgment. A judgment granted on application of the plaintiff when the defendant has failed to file an answer or other required pleading.

Deficiency. The shortfall that results when a debt is undersecured, that is, when the collateral securing the debt is worth less than the amount owing, so that realization of the collateral does not fully satisfy the debt. *See* Equity cushion; Surplus.

Delegation. *See* Assignment.

Delivery bond. *See* Redelivery bond.

Delivery of writ. The transmission of a writ to the sheriff with instructions to execute it.

Discharge. The debtor's release from liability for the unpaid balance of all debts that are provable in bankruptcy and that are not excluded from discharge under the Code.

Discharging/dissolution bond. A bond posted by the debtor for the purpose of releasing property from attachment. The bond is an undertaking by the debtor, supported by a surety, to pay any judgment ultimately obtained by the creditor. Its effect is to terminate the attachment and restore the property to the debtor. *Compare* Redelivery bond.

Disclosure statement. The statement required by §1123 to be disseminated by the proponent of a Ch. 11 plan, providing sufficient information on the plan to enable the holders of claims and interests to make an informed judgment on it.

Dismissal. The court's termination of the bankruptcy case upon voluntary withdrawal by the petitioner or on the motion of a party in interest or the court's own motion.

Disposable income test. A requirement for plan confirmation that the debtor must commit all his or her disposable income to payments under the plan for a period of three or five years. "Disposable income" is that portion of the debtor's income not reasonably necessary for the maintenance and support of the debtor or a dependent, and not necessary for the operation and preservation of any business in which the debtor is engaged. The test is only applied upon objection to confirmation by a competent party.

Distraint/Distress. The seizure of property to secure or satisfy a debt. For example, a landlord's right to seize a tenant's goods on the leased premises to satisfy a claim for unpaid arrear rent.

Distress sale. A forced sale, such as an execution or foreclosure sale. Because of the circumstances of the sale, the price obtained for the property is usually depressed.

Docket. A record of proceedings in court or the act of making an entry in such record.

Dormant judgment. A judgment that has become unenforceable because it has not been executed upon within the prescribed time. It can be revived by application. (*Dormancy* must be distinguished from *expiry* of a judgment: When a judgment reaches the end of its statutory lifespan, it becomes ineffective and cannot be revived.)

"Drop-dead" clause. A provision in a contract or rehabilitation plan that requires exact compliance with the debtor's obligations and gives the creditor an immediate right of action (for example, to accelerate the debt or to foreclose) in the event of default.

Elegit. An early common law writ, available as an alternative to *fieri facias*, that enabled a judgment creditor to obtain personal property of the debtor or to receive revenues from a portion of the debtor's lands. *Compare* *Fieri facias*.

Enabling loan. *See* Purchase money security interest.

Encumbrance. A right to or interest in property, such as a lien, which diminishes the extent of the owner's title.

Entity. A general term used in the Code to encompass a wide variety of legal persons, including individuals, corporations, and governmental units (§101(15)).

Equitable lien. A lien recognized under principles of equity in the absence of legal lien rights, in order to do justice between the parties and to provide effective relief to an otherwise unsecured creditor.

Equitable subordination. *See* Subordination.

Equity. In addition to its general meaning of fairness or justice, "equity" denotes the body or rules and principles developed by Courts of Chancery (and now applied by courts of combined legal and equitable jurisdiction) to afford relief where remedies at law are inadequate. The word "equity" is also used to refer to an owner's unencumbered interest in property. *See* Debtor's equity.

Equity cushion. The amount of equity held by the debtor in collateral in excess of the value of the claim of a lienholder and any encumbrances senior to the secured claim. This excess value in the collateral is called an "equity cushion" because it provides a margin of safety for the lienholder to cover any adverse change in the collateral-debt ratio caused by future depreciation of the property or the accumulation of interest or costs.

Equity of redemption. The mortgagor's right to save property from foreclosure by paying the mortgage debt before the foreclosure sale. The equity of redemption arises from principles of equity and applies only in the presale period. It must be distinguished from statutory redemption, which extends beyond the sale date and may be exercised against the purchaser of the property. *See also* Redemption.

Equity receivership. *See* Receiver.

Equity security. A share in a corporation or a limited partner's interest in a partnership (§101(16)).

Equity test. *See* Insolvency.

Estate. In general terms, a person's estate is all the property held by that person. In the bankruptcy context, the estate is the legal entity created by the filing of the petition, which succeeds to the debtor's property rights under §541.

Examiner. A person appointed by the court under §1104(b) to investigate the management or conduct of the debtor in a Ch.11 case.

Exception to discharge. A debt that is excluded from the debtor's discharge on one of the grounds enumerated in §523 or §1328.

Exclusivity period. The period following the filing of a Ch. 11 petition, during which the debtor has the exclusive right to file a plan (§1121).

Executable property. Property of the debtor that is not exempt or otherwise immune from execution, so that it can be subjected to the claims of creditors.

Execution. The enforcement of a judgment by the seizure and sale of nonexempt property of the debtor.

Execution lien. A judicial lien created in property of the debtor levied upon under a writ of execution.

Executory contract. In general, a contract is executory if it has not been fully performed. Upon the bankruptcy of one of the parties, a contract that qualifies as executory for bankruptcy purposes may be assumed by the estate. In bankruptcy, the most widely used test for deciding if a contract is executory is whether the obligations of both parties are so far unperformed that the failure of either to complete performance would be a material breach. The trustee must elect to reject or assume the executory contract under §365.

Exemption. A right granted by statute to an individual debtor to hold specified property free from the claims of creditors (§522).

Extension. A contract between a debtor and a creditor or creditors, under which the debtor is allowed additional time in which to pay debts. *See also* Composition.

Fair and equitable standard. A Ch. 11 plan can only be confirmed by the cramdown method if classes of claims and interests are treated in a fair and equitable manner. This requires not only fair treatment in the usual sense, but also that the specific requirements of §1129(b) (such as the absolute priority rule) are satisfied.

Family farmer. A debtor (including an individual, spouse, or a family-held corporation or partnership) that is engaged in farming operations and meets the other eligibility requirements for Ch. 12 relief (§101(18), (19), (20), and (21)).

Feasibility standard. The requirement for plan confirmation that the debtor has demonstrated a reasonable prospect of being able to make the payments and meet the rehabilitative goals set out in the plan.

Fieri facias. Originally, a common law writ commanding the sheriff to seize chattels of the debtor to satisfy a judgment. The term is still used in some jurisdictions as the name for the writ of execution (abbreviated as "fi fa") *Compare* Elegit.

Financing statement. The document filed in public records to perfect a security interest under UCC Article 9.

First day motions. Motions filed with a Ch. 11 petition in which the debtor seeks various forms of immediate relief aimed at minimizing disruption to the debtor's business.

First-in-time rule. The general rule of priority under which an earlier perfected lien or interest in property takes precedence over a later one.

Floating lien. A security interest that extends to collateral of a specified type acquired by the debtor, or to advances made to the debtor after the execution of the security agreement, or to both. *See* After-acquired collateral; Future advance.

Foreclosure. The process whereby a lienholder enforces the lien following the debtor's default and subjects the collateral to satisfaction of the debt. Following seizure, the collateral is normally sold and its proceeds applied to payment of the debt. However, strict foreclosure (forfeiture of the property to the lienholder in full satisfaction of the debt) is permitted as an alternative in the case of some liens.

Fraudulent transfer/conveyance. A disposition of property by a debtor with the actual or constructive intent to defraud creditors, or to delay or hinder their collection efforts.

Fresh start. The rehabilitation of a debtor through the process of bankruptcy, achieved by the resolution and discharge of prepetition debt.

Future advance. A loan or credit advanced to the debtor after a security interest has been created and secured by such preexisting security interest. *See also* Floating lien.

Gap creditor. A person who extends credit or financing to the debtor during the period between two legally significant events, such as between the attachment and perfection of a security interest or between the filing of an involuntary petition and the order for relief.

Garnishment. A creditor's (garnishor's) levy on property of the debtor in the possession of a third party (garnishee), or on a debt or obligation due by the garnishee to the debtor.

Garnishment lien. A judicial lien that arises in property upon which garnishment has been levied.

Going concern value. The value of a business based on its sale as a continuing operation, rather than on the proceeds that would be realized upon the liquidation of its assets.

Good faith. Honesty, usually measured under a subjective test, and (in the bankruptcy context) compliance with the spirit of the Code.

Good faith purchaser. This term is sometimes used synonymously with bona fide purchaser. However, it is also sometimes used to denote a purchaser who acts honestly, but does not satisfy all of the other elements necessary to qualify as a bona fide purchaser. *Compare* Bona fide purchaser.

Holder of a claim. A creditor of the debtor whose claim is provable in the estate.

Homestead exemption. An exemption granted under state law or §522(d)(1) in an individual debtor's interest in property in which the debtor or a dependent resides.

Hypothetical status of trustee. The legal fictions created by §544, permitting the trustee to exercise avoidance rights that would have been available to a bona fide purchaser of real property, a lien creditor, and an execution creditor, had such persons existed on the date that the bankruptcy petition was filed.

Illiquid. Inability to convert assets into cash. *See* Insolvency.

Impaired class of claims or interests. In a Ch. 11 case, a class is impaired unless the rights of each member are unaltered except for the cure of any default and deceleration of the debt (§1124).

Improvement in position test. One of the requirements for the avoidance of a transfer under §547 is that the transfer enabled the creditor to improve on the position that it would have occupied without the transfer. Improvement in position occurs where the transfer has enabled the creditor to receive more on its claim than it would have been paid in a hypothetical Ch. 7 distribution in the absence of the transfer.

In custodia legis. (Latin: "In the custody of the law") The retention of property for safekeeping by the sheriff, a receiver, or some other person with legal authority.

Individual. A natural person, as distinct from a corporate entity.

Indubitable equivalent. A broad standard for measuring adequate protection under §361(3). The court must be satisfied that a proposed method of protecting an interest in property will undoubtedly provide the claimant with value equal to the value of the interest. The form of indubitable equivalence that courts are most likely to recognize is the existence of a substantial equity cushion. Indubitable equivalence is also used as a standard for determining whether a secured claim has been treated fairly and equitably in a cramdown confirmation (§1129(b)(2)(A)(iii)).

Insider. A person who has such a close relationship with another that he or she has special access to information and opportunities for favorable treatment. Several provisions of the Code treat insiders of the debtor differently from other parties. "Insider" is defined in §101(31) to include relatives of an individual debtor and persons in control of a corporate debtor.

Insolvency. Inability to pay debts, determined by one of two tests: inability to pay debts as they fall due (called the "equity test") or an excess of liabilities over assets (called the "bankruptcy" or "balance sheet" test) (§101(32)).

Interim trustee. A trustee appointed under §701 following the order for relief in a Ch. 7 case, to serve until a permanent trustee is appointed or elected at the meeting of creditors.

Involuntary case. A case under Ch. 7 or Ch. 11 initiated against the debtor by a creditor or creditors who qualify to seek bankruptcy relief (§303).

Ipso facto clause/provision. (Latin: "By the fact itself") A provision in a contract or in nonbankruptcy law under which the insolvency or bankruptcy of the debtor is treated as a default.

Joint administration. The administration of the estates of closely related debtors for the purpose of convenience and the reduction of administrative costs. *Compare* Consolidation of cases.

Joint case. A bankruptcy case in which a single voluntary petition is filed by both spouses, placing both their estates in bankruptcy. Although the estates are administered jointly, their assets and liabilities are not consolidated unless appropriate (§302).

Joint debtors. *See* Codebtors.

Judgment lien. A judicial lien arising on all the real property owned by the debtor in the county in which the judgment is docketed or recorded. In some states, a judgment recorded in UCC filing records creates a judgment lien on the debtor's personal property.

Judicial lien. Any lien arising out of court proceedings (§101(36)).

Knowledge. *See* Notice.

Leverage. In negotiations, leverage is bargaining power or the ability to exert pressure on the other party to obtain a desired resolution. "Leverage" also has an alternative meaning that relates to debt; for example, the making of an investment consisting largely of borrowed funds or the use of borrowed funds instead of capital.

Leveraged buyout. The purchase of stock in a corporation with borrowed funds, financed by the corporation itself or secured by its assets.

Levy. The sheriff's seizure or taking control of property pursuant to a writ.

Lien. Used broadly, any charge against or interest in property to secure a creditor's right to payment, so that if the debt is not paid, the creditor may have recourse to the property to satisfy the debt. (*See* §101(32).) "Lien" is sometimes used more narrowly to denote only such interests that arise by operation of law or court order, as distinct from interests created by contract, called "security interests."

Lienholder/Lienor. The holder of a lien. (Note: The person who grants the lien is simply called a debtor; there is no such thing as a "lienee.")

Lien stripping. A strategy whereby the debtor attempts to peg an undersecured debt or a debt that has become unsecured at the value of the collateral as determined by the bankruptcy court, so that if the collateral appreciates after the bankruptcy case, the lien (which survives the bankruptcy) cannot extend to the increase in equity but is frozen at the bankruptcy valuation. Where the lien is undersecured, the fixing of the amount of the lien at the current value of the collateral is called "strip down." If the lien has become fully unsecured (because it is a junior lien, and the senior lien has taken up the full value of the collateral), the fixing of the lien value at zero is called "strip off."

Liquidated claim. *See* Unliquidated claim.

Liquidating plan. A Ch. 11 plan that provides for the liquidation of the debtor, rather than its rehabilitation.

Liquidation. The realization of the debtor's executable assets for the purpose of generating proceeds to be applied to the payment of debts.

Lis pendens. (Latin: "Pending suit") The doctrine, deriving from common law, that a person who acquires an interest in realty while litigation is pending concerning title, possession, or other rights to it, is bound by the court's ultimate resolution of the controversy. A party wishing to be protected by the doctrine must file a notice of pendency in the real estate records to give constructive notice of the litigation to any potential transferee.

Marshalling of assets. An equitable doctrine that applies when two creditors are competing for satisfaction of their claims from the same fund, and one of them has another fund available for application to its debt. Marshalling requires that creditor resort to the other fund before having recourse to the shared fund.

Materialman's lien. *See* Mechanic's lien.

Mature claim. *See* Unmatured claim.

Means test. A nonstatutory term describing the standard for dismissing a Ch. 7 consumer case on the grounds of abuse where the debtor's disposable income, calculated under the formula set out in §707(b), is deemed sufficient to support payments under a plan of rehabilitation. A version of the means test is also used to measure the debtor's disposable income in a Ch. 13 case.

Mechanic's lien. A statutory lien on real property available to a person who, at the request of the owner or the owner's agent, has furnished services or labor on credit in connection with the improvement of the property. The supplier of materials used in the construction may assert a similar statutory lien called a "materialman's lien." These traditional names for the liens have been abandoned in some states in favor of the more modern "construction lien."

Net result rule. A traditional but inaccurate name for the exception to the avoidance of transfers under §547(c)(4), which validates an otherwise avoidable transfer to the extent that the creditor-transferee gave new unsecured value to the debtor after receiving the transfer.

New value exception. An exception (or corollary) to the absolute priority rule that enables equity holders to retain their interests in the debtor, even though a senior nonaccepting class has not been paid in full, if the equity holders contribute new capital to the debtor equal to or greater than the value of their interests.

No-asset case. A liquidation case in which there are insufficient assets to allow for a distribution.

Nonbankruptcy law. The term used in the Code to describe the entire body of law prevailing in the jurisdiction, both state and federal, apart from bankruptcy law.

Noncore proceedings. *See* Related proceedings.

Nondischargeable debt. A debt that is excluded from the discharge under §523 or §1328.

Nonrecourse secured debt. A secured debt for which the debtor has no liability beyond the value of the collateral, so that the debtor cannot be held responsible for any deficiency following foreclosure or surrender of the collateral.

Notice. Information concerning a fact, whether deriving from actual knowledge or imputed as a legal consequence of proper recording or other publicity. Imputed knowledge is called "constructive notice."

Notice and a hearing. When a Code provision states that particular action can only be taken after notice and a hearing, this means that appropriate notice must be given, but a hearing is only required if a party in interest requests it (§102(2)).

Nulla bona return. (Latin: "No goods") The report returned by the sheriff following an attempt at levy in which no executable property could be found.

Objection. A written response required by the Bankruptcy Rules to challenge certain actions or assertions by another party, such as a claim, a claim of exemption, a proposed plan, or the discharge of a debt.

Order for relief. In an involuntary case, the court's grant of the petition for bankruptcy relief. In a voluntary case, no actual adjudication of bankruptcy is required. The filing of the petition itself constitutes the order for relief.

Party in interest. Although used frequently in the Code, this term has no general statutory definition. It is described in §1109(b) for Ch. 11

purposes to include the debtor, trustee, creditors, equity security holders, and their committees. Courts usually treat the term as having the same meaning elsewhere in the Code. It is usually mentioned in the context of standing to initiate motions or other proceedings.

Perfection. The process of making a lien effective against persons other than the debtor, who may subsequently acquire rights in the collateral. Perfection is normally accomplished by an act of publicity such as recording the lien or taking possession of the collateral.

Petition. The pleading filed to initiate a bankruptcy case.

Plenary jurisdiction. Full jurisdiction over the subject matter of the case and the parties, as distinguished from the more limited "summary" jurisdiction of the bankruptcy court. These terms were used in connection with bankruptcy jurisdiction prior to 1978, but have become outmoded under the Code and the current jurisdictional provisions of Title 28.

Pluries writ. A writ of execution issued after the second ("alias") writ. *See* Alias writ.

Preference. An advantage given by the debtor to a creditor through payment or some other transfer that results in the creditor receiving preferential treatment over other similarly situated creditors. Although such preferential treatment is not normally avoidable outside of bankruptcy, the trustee has the power under §547 to avoid a preferential transfer in the prepetition period if the requirements of §547 are satisfied.

Prejudgment remedy or process. Provisional and ancillary relief available to the plaintiff during the pendency of a civil case to prevent loss or harm before the case is finally resolved. Most prejudgment remedies aim at the preservation of property that is claimed in the suit or may ultimately be sold in execution to satisfy the judgment.

Prenegotiated or Prepackaged plan. A prenegotiated plan is one that is negotiated by the Ch. 11 debtor and key creditors prior to the debtor filing a Ch. 11 petition. By agreeing with key creditors on the crucial aspects of the plan before filing the petition, the debtor increases the prospects of creditors voting in favor of the plan after it has been filed. A prepackaged plan is one that has been wholly or substantially settled by the debtor and key creditors before the Ch. 11 petition is filed. The debtor makes all necessary disclosures prepetition, and the requisite number and type of creditor classes have voted to approve the plan of reorganization. The approved plan and a certification of creditor votes is invariably filed along with the bankruptcy petition.

Prepetition planning. The debtor's reordering of his or her affairs prior to filing a bankruptcy petition to maximize the benefits of bankruptcy. A common form of prepetition planning is the realization of nonexempt property and the use of proceeds to acquire exempt property. *See also* Conversion of exempt property.

Present value. *See* Best interests test.

Priming lien. A lien granted to secure postpetition credit under §364(d) with priority over an existing lien in the property.

Priority. The ranking of liens and other interests in the same property.

Priority claim. An unsecured claim (or that portion of it) that qualifies for inclusion in one of the categories entitled to precedence in payment under §507.

Proceedings in aid of execution. *See* Supplementary proceedings.

Proceeds. Any property or money received in exchange for an asset.

Proof of claim. A creditor's formal submission of a claim against the estate under §501.

Provisional remedy or process. *See* Prejudgment remedy or process.

Purchase. The acquisition of rights in property by voluntary act. "Purchase" is not simply a synonym for "buy," but includes also the consensual acquisition of other rights, such as a security interest (§§101(43) and 101(54)).

Purchase-money security interest (PMSI). A security interest in property, to the extent that it secures a loan or credit given to the debtor for the express purpose of acquiring the property and actually used by the debtor for that purpose.

Reach-back period. The period immediately before the filing of a bankruptcy petition, within which transfers are vulnerable to avoidance.

Reaffirmation. The debtor's contractual undertaking, executed in compliance with §524 during the period between the petition and the discharge, to pay an otherwise dischargeable debt.

Receivable. *See* Account.

Receivership. A proceeding, originating in equity, under which a person (receiver) is appointed to take control of property, and to preserve and administer it as the court directs.

Reclamation. A seller's limited right to reclaim goods when the buyer was insolvent upon receipt of the goods and the seller was unaware of the insolvency. Reclamation is governed by UCC §2.702 and is given qualified recognition in bankruptcy by §546(c).

Redelivery bond. A bond posted by the debtor for the purpose of regaining possession of attached property pending final determination of the suit. In the bond, the debtor undertakes to redeliver the property or its value if the creditor ultimately obtains judgment. *Compare* Discharging/dissolution bond. Unlike a discharging bond, a redelivery bond does not release the attachment lien.

Redemption. The debtor's right to buy back property that has been foreclosed upon or otherwise subjected to realization for the satisfaction of debt. Redemption is available only where recognized by principles of equity or by statute (e.g., execution statutes or §722). In some cases, creditors junior to the foreclosing party are also given redemption rights. *See also* Equity of redemption.

Referee. The original name for a bankruptcy judge under the Bankruptcy Act of 1898.

Rehabilitation. In a general sense, resolution of the debtor's financial difficulties through bankruptcy, so that the debtor's fiscal viability is restored. More specifically, bankruptcy relief by means of a plan under Ch. 11 or Ch. 13 as distinct from liquidation.

Rejection of a contract. The estate's repudiation of a prepetition executory contract of the debtor, so that the estate acquires no performance rights and obligations under the contract, and the other party has a general unsecured claim for damages. *Compare* Assumption.

Related proceedings. Litigation concerning a matter of nonbankruptcy law, the outcome of which affects the rights, liabilities, or administration of the estate. Because the controversy has an impact on the estate, it falls within the nonexclusive jurisdiction of the district court. In the absence of consent by the parties, related proceedings cannot be finally determined by the bankruptcy court but must be returned to the district court for final judgment. *Contrast* Core proceeding.

Relation-back. *See* Backdating.

Remand. The bankruptcy court's return of a matter to the court from which it was removed.

Removal. The transfer of related proceedings from another court to the bankruptcy court.

Reorganization. The rehabilitation of a debtor under Ch. 11. Sometimes this word is used in a more general sense to mean rehabilitation under other chapters of the Code as well.

Replevin. A possessory action for the recovery of specific tangible personal property that has been wrongfully taken or retained. As a prejudgment remedy, replevin enables a plaintiff to obtain provisional seizure and possession of property that is the subject matter of the underlying suit. (Replevin is called "claim and delivery" in some states.)

Return. The report submitted by the sheriff that states the action taken on a writ or other process.

Revival of judgment. The renewal of a judgment that has become dormant because it has not been executed upon during its period of enforceability.

Ride-through. An arrangement between the debtor and a secured claimant under which the debtor is permitted to retain the collateral in return for a commitment to maintain payments on the debt as originally contracted. The "ride-through" is an alternative in Ch. 7 cases to the more formal reaffirmation. However, some courts have held that it is no longer available to a debtor because of amendments to various Code provisions by BAPCPA.

Roll-up. An agreement between the debtor and a prepetition lender, under which the lender agrees to make a postpetition loan to the debtor on condition that the proceeds of the postpetition financing will be used first to repay the prepetition debt in full.

Safe harbor. A provision in a statute that shields a person from liability for breach of a statutory duty on condition that the person meets minimum standards of good faith compliance (e.g., under §1125, a person who solicits acceptance or rejection of a plan in compliance with the Code is protected from liability for any violation of securities laws).

Secured debt/claim. A debt is secured to the extent that the debtor's personal obligation to pay is reinforced by a lien on property of the debtor, so that if the debtor defaults, the secured creditor may have recourse to the property to satisfy the debt. In bankruptcy, provided that the secured debt is allowed as a claim, it is treated as secured to the extent of the value of the collateral (§506).

Security agreement. A contract under which a security interest is created (§101(50) and (51)).

Security interest. Although this term is sometimes used to denote a lien of any kind, it is usually confined to mean a consensual lien (§101(51)).

Self-help. The pursuit of a remedy without court proceedings, such as a lienholder's seizure of collateral upon default without court authority. Self-help seizure and foreclosure are permitted only in connection with certain liens and are subject to restrictions even when allowed.

Sequestration. An equitable remedy, similar to attachment, under which the plaintiff may remove property from the defendant's control pending the final resolution of a case. Sequestration is usually available only when the defendant's property interest is equitable in nature and cannot be reached by attachment.

Setoff. When two persons are mutually indebted, the two debts may be treated as canceling each other out so that neither need be paid. If one of the debts is smaller than the other, setoff operates to the extent of the smaller debt.

Spendthrift trust. A trust with restrictions on alienation designed to protect the fund from dissipation by the beneficiary or seizure by the beneficiary's creditors.

Standing trustee. A person appointed by the U.S. Trustee to serve as trustee for all Ch. 13 cases filed in a region. (More than one standing trustee may be appointed if the volume of cases is large.)

Statutory lien. A lien arising by virtue of a statutory provision that confers lien rights on otherwise unsecured creditors in particular types of transactions, under specified circumstances. Statutory liens owe their existence to the rights conferred by statute and are not created by contract or judicial process (§101(53)).

Stay. *See* Automatic stay.

Straight bankruptcy. Liquidation under Ch. 7.

Strict foreclosure. A method of foreclosure under which the lienholder acquires ownership of the collateral in full satisfaction of the debt and is not required to conduct a foreclosure sale. The lienholder is therefore not accountable to the debtor for any value in the collateral in excess of the debt, and may not claim any deficiency from the debtor if the collateral is worth less than the debt. Strict foreclosure is available only in connection with some liens, and is subject to restrictions, even where permitted.

Strip down and strip off. *See* Lien stripping.

Strong-arm clause. The traditional name given to the trustee's avoidance powers under §544(a) and its predecessor in the Bankruptcy Act.

Subordination. The demotion of a claim, either by consent of the claimant (consensual subordination) or under principles of equity (equitable subordination). Equitable subordination is appropriate where fairness so requires, typically when the claimant has behaved in a dishonest or inequitable manner to the prejudice of a more junior party or of creditors in general (§510).

Substantial abuse. The term used in §707(b) prior to its amendment by BAPCPA as a ground for dismissal. Section 707(b) no longer requires a showing of "substantial" abuse, but provides for dismissal of "abuse."

Summary jurisdiction. *See* Plenary jurisdiction.

Superpriority. Special priority classifications given to two types of claim: (1) Priority at the top of the administrative expense category, granted by §507(b) to a claimant, where adequate protection was attempted but proved to be insufficient to fully protect its interest; (2) an even more elevated priority position, senior to all administrative expenses (including superpriority claims under §507(b)), granted to a post-petition financer under §364(c) as consideration for the extension of credit to the estate.

Supplementary proceedings. Statutory proceedings in aid of execution, under which a judgment creditor may seek discovery of executable assets or take other steps to subject the debtor's executable property to the satisfaction of the judgment.

Surplus. The amount in excess of the debt after collateral or property seized in execution has been realized. *See also* Deficiency; Equity cushion.

Title 11. The Bankruptcy Code (11 U.S.C. §§101-1523).

Transfer. Any disposition of property or an interest in property. In the Code, "transfer" is usually used to describe the debtor's transmission of property rights to some other person, resulting in impoverishment of the estate (§101(54)).

Trustee. A private person appointed by the U.S. Trustee (or elected in some Ch. 7 cases) who represents, administers, and distributes the bankruptcy estate (§§321, 322, and 323).

Turnover. The surrender of estate property to the trustee by any person in possession of it (§§542 and 543).

UFCA/UFTA/UVTA. The Uniform Fraudulent Conveyance Act of 1918 and its successors, the Uniform Fraudulent Transfer Act (1984) and the Uniform Voidable Transfers Act (2014), allow a creditor to avoid a disposition of property by the debtor that has the intent or effect of placing executable property beyond the reach of execution. Most states have adopted one of these uniform model acts.

Undersecured debt. *See* Deficiency.

Unfair discrimination. Unjustified differentiation in a plan between claims of comparable rank that should be treated equally.

Uniform Commercial Code (UCC). A uniform code, adopted in all states except Louisiana, covering sales, negotiable instruments, security interests in personal property, and other commercial transactions.

Unimpaired (class of claims or interests). *See* Impaired (class of claims or interests).

Unliquidated claim. A claim on which the debtor's liability has arisen, but the amount of which is uncertain and cannot be calculated arithmetically from known data.

Unmatured claim. A claim for a debt that has come into existence but whose date of payment has not yet fallen due.

U.S. Trustee. A federal official, appointed under 28 U.S.C. §581, who is responsible for the appointment and supervision of bankruptcy trustees and for the general oversight of bankruptcy cases.

Venue. The appropriate federal district for the conduct of the bankruptcy case or related proceedings.

Voluntary case. A bankruptcy case initiated by the debtor.

Wage earner plan. The name for the plan under the predecessor of Ch. 13 in the Bankruptcy Act. The term is obsolete but is still sometimes used to describe a Ch. 13 plan.

Warrant of attorney. A provision in a contract or instrument of debt, appointing the creditor to act as the debtor's agent in confessing to judgment if the debtor should default. *See also* Confession to judgment.

Wildcard provision. A nickname for §522(d)(5) (or an equivalent provision in a state statute), under which the debtor may apply a general exemption to any property selected, up to a prescribed value.

Workout. A negotiated settlement under which the debtor and creditors resolve the debtor's financial difficulties by agreeing to terms of payment. A workout may occur outside of bankruptcy, resulting in a composition and extension, or it may take place in the process of formulating a plan in a bankruptcy case.

Writ. A written order issued pursuant to court authority, requiring the sheriff or some other official to perform an act, such as the levy of execution.

Table of Cases

References are to book sections (denoted by the symbol §) and to Examples and Explanations, denoted by the letter "E" followed by the chapter number and Example number.

Table of Statutes

References are to book sections (denoted by the symbol §) and to Examples and Explanations, denoted by the letter "E" followed by the chapter number and Example number.

11 U.S.C.

Index

References are to sections. This index does not include references to the Examples and Explanations. However, text sections include references to Examples that deal with topics addressed in the text.